The Epistle to the Ephesians

The Epistle to the Ephesians

BRIGHAM YOUNG UNIVERSITY
NEW TESTAMENT COMMENTARY

S. Kent Brown

BYU Studies
Provo, Utah

This Commentary Series is made possible by a generous gift from John S. and Unita W. Welch.

Published by BYU Studies. To contact any member of the board of editors or BYU Studies, write to 1063 JFSB, Brigham Young University, Provo, Utah, 84602, or visit http://byustudies.byu.edu or http://www.byunewtestamentcommentary.com.

Cover images: Left: Library of Celcus at evening, Ephesus, photo by S. Kent Brown. *Center:* Sophia (Wisdom) in the Celsus Library in Ephesus, © José Luiz Bernardes Ribeiro / CC BY-SA 3.0. *Right:* amphitheater in Ephesus, photo by S. Kent Brown.

First time in print. Substantive corrections, additions, questions, or comments may be sent to byu_studies@byu.edu.

Library of Congress Cataloging-in-Publication Data

Names: Brown, S. Kent, author.
Title: The Epistle to the Ephesians / S. Kent Brown.
Other titles: New Testament commentary (Brigham Young University)
Description: Provo, Utah : BYU Studies, [2023] | Series: Brigham Young University New Testament commentary series | Includes bibliographical references and index. | Summary: "A verse-by-verse commentary on the New Testament Epistle to the Ephesians. Provides a modern English version of the text. Cites scriptures of The Church of Jesus Christ of Latter-day Saints (Mormons). Focuses on Jesus Christ and the unity and steadfastness of believers" -- Provided by publisher.
Identifiers: LCCN 2022031818 | ISBN 9781942161974 (hardcover) | ISBN 9781942161981 (ebook)
Subjects: LCSH: Bible. Ephesians--Commentaries. | Church of Jesus Christ of Latter-day Saints--Doctrines. | Mormon Church--Doctrines.
Classification: LCC BS2695.53 .B76 2023 | DDC 227/.507--dc23/eng/20220909
LC record available at https://lccn.loc.gov/2022031818

Printed in the United States of America
10 9 8 7 6 5 4 3 2 1

About the Brigham Young University New Testament Commentary Series

Welcome to the BYU New Testament Commentary, a project by a group of Latter-day Saint specialists offering to readers a careful, new look at the biblical records that witness the life and ministry of Jesus Christ and the first generation of his church. The commentary series seeks to make the New Testament more accessible to Latter-day Saint general readers and scholars by employing much of current biblical scholarship while reflecting important LDS insights. At the same time, this effort may also be helpful to interested readers of other faiths who want to learn how a group of Latter-day Saint scholars understands the Bible. A fundamental article of faith for Latter-day Saints (Mormons) affirms the Bible "to be the word of God" while adding, understandably, that it needs to be "translated correctly" in order for it to be accurately comprehendible to modern language speakers.

These objectives have helped shape the purposes and parameters of this commentary series. Serious LDS readers of the Bible search the scriptures, looking for depth and breadth in passages whose meanings and mandates may ultimately be plain but not shallow. Such readers and interpreters are served by treatments that unite faith and research, reason and revelation, in prayerfully confronting profound and difficult issues that arise in the texts and affect one's path of progression. The New Testament has served as an influential guide to western civilization for centuries. As such, its records have long been studied by lay people and scholars alike, resulting in a rich reservoir of information that illuminates the New Testament era culturally, historically, and linguistically. Selectively, the BYUNTC builds upon this vast body of knowledge, resting on the Greek texts of the New Testament and connecting helpful elements of linguistic, literary, historical, and cultural research and traditional scholarship together with LDS scriptures and doctrinal perspectives. The combination of all these features distinguishes the BYUNTC from other commentaries, which are readily available elsewhere and which readers may also want to consult for more encyclopedic or specialized discussions.

The tone of the BYUNTC aims to be informative rather than hortatory, and suggestive rather than definitive in its interpretation. The opinions expressed in this series are the views of its contributors and should not necessarily be attributed to The Church of Jesus Christ of Latter-day Saints; Brigham Young University, where many of those involved here are headquartered; or anyone else, though these works have benefitted from input and guidance from a number of colleagues, advisors, editors, and peer reviewers.

Each volume in this series sets in two parallel columns the King James Version (KJV) and a new working translation of the New Testament. Calling this a new "rendition" clarifies that it does not seek to replace the authorized KJV adopted by the LDS Church as its official English text. Rather, it aims to enhance readers' understanding conceptually and spiritually by rendering the Greek texts into modern English with LDS sensitivities in mind. Comparing and explaining the New Rendition in light of the KJV then serves as one important purpose for each volume's notes, comments, analyses, and summaries. This effort responds in modest ways to the desire President J. Reuben Clark Jr. expressed in his diary in 1956 that someday "qualified scholars [would provide] . . . a translation of the New Testament that will give us an accurate translation that shall be pregnant with the great principles of the Restored Gospel."

Depending on their personal skills and interests, the authors of these volumes approach their scholarly sources and LDS materials differently but always with careful exposition and engaging perspectives. In several ways, they employ various interpretive tools, including semantic considerations of Greek vocabulary; cultural, historical, critical, literary, and structural analyses; and intertextual comparisons with other biblical passages, the Book of Mormon, and other scriptural works including the Joseph Smith Translation of the Bible. Observations are also proffered about the doctrinal and spiritual reception of New Testament teachings and practices in the broad LDS religious tradition.

The format also varies moderately from volume to volume regarding introductory materials and the style of commentary. Throughout, Greek and Hebrew terms appear in transliterated form in conformity with standards adopted by the Society of Biblical Literature. In some cases, a volume reproduces the Greek New Testament text based on the Greek text published by the Society of Biblical Literature (2010) or draws upon the twenty-eighth edition of the Nestle-Aland text in *Novum Testamentum Graece* (2012).

Contents

Abbreviations

For ancient works, the footnotes follow the style of Patrick H. Alexander and others, *The SBL Handbook of Style for Ancient Near Eastern Biblical and Early Christian Studies* (Peabody, Mass.: Hendrickson Publishers, 1999).

ANF   Roberts, Alexander, James Donaldson, and A. Cleveland Coxe, eds. *The Ante-Nicene Fathers: Translations of the Writings of the Fathers down to A.D. 325.* 10 vols. Reprint. Grand Rapids, Mich.: Eerdmans, 1950.

ABD   Freedman, David Noel, and others, eds. *The Anchor Bible Dictionary.* 6 vols. New York: Doubleday, 1992.

BDAG   Bauer, Walter. *A Greek-English Lexicon of the New Testament and Other Early Christian Literature.* Ed. Frederick W. Danker. 3d English ed. Chicago: University of Chicago Press, 2000.

BDB   Brown, Francis, S. R. Driver, and Charles A. Briggs. *A Hebrew and English Lexicon of the Old Testament.* Corrected ed. Oxford: Oxford University Press, 1953.

EM   Ludlow, Daniel H., ed. *Encyclopedia of Mormonism.* 4 vols. New York: Macmillan, 1992.

KJV   King James Version of the Bible.

LSJ   Liddel, Henry George, and Robert Scott. *A Greek-English Lexicon.* Rev. ed. Henry Stuart Jones. Oxford: Oxford University Press, 1968.

NEB   The New English Bible.

NIV   New International Version, copyright 1984. In *The NIV Study Bible.* Ed. Kenneth L. Barker and others. Grand Rapids, Mich.: Zondervan Publishing House, 1995.

NR   New Rendition.

OCD2   Hammond, N. G. L., and H. H. Scullard, eds. *The Oxford Classical Dictionary.* 2nd ed. Oxford: Oxford University Press, 1970.

RSV   Revised Standard Version of the Bible.

TDNT   Kittel, Gerhard, and Gerhard Friedrich, eds. *Theological Dictionary of the New Testament.* Trans. Geoffrey W. Bromiley, 10 vols. Grand Rapids, Mich.: Eerdmans, 1964–76.

TDOT   Botterweck, G. Johannes, and Helmer Ringgren. *Theological Dictionary of the Old Testament.* Trans. John T. Willis. 15 vols. Grand Rapids, Mich.: Eerdmans, 1976–2004.

TLNT   Spicq, Ceslas. *Theological Lexicon of the New Testament.* 3 vols. Trans. James D. Ernest. Peabody, Mass.: Hendrickson Publishers, 1994.

TLOT   Jenni, Ernst, and Claus Westermann. *Theological Lexicon of the Old Testament.* 3 vols. Trans. Mark E. Biddle. Peabody, Mass.: Hendrickson Publishers, 1997.

Preface

Six years ago, when I began to think about which New Testament document I would like to work on after my effort on Luke's gospel, my mind went first to the Epistle to the Ephesians. Why? Because at the time my wife, Gayle, and I were serving as a church service couple in Izmir, Turkey. The giant archaeological site of Ephesus was a mere hour and a quarter's drive away. By that time, I had visited the site at least fifteen times, a dozen of them during our twenty-one month residence in Izmir. I thought to myself, What better text than Ephesians? After all, I was well acquainted with the exposed remains of ancient Ephesus that included its two massive market places, the huge theater in the lower city, and the outlines of the impressive city hall in the upper city. Between them sat the monument that the emperor Domitian had built to himself, the same person who exiled John the Revelator to the isle of Patmos. Besides, the reconstructed ruins of the Library of Celsus in the lower city stood as the iconic structure that conferred its beauty and grace on all the myriad other archaeological sites in Turkey. Ephesians seemed the natural choice. Little did I suspect.

At the end of my work on this letter, I have spent little more than a couple of solid paragraphs describing Ephesus and its cultural and structural features, reducing my initial thinking to a mere speck (see the Analysis of 1:15–23 and appendix 1). On a personal level, I now see that my initial attraction to Ephesians and Ephesus was misguided, even tainted by a bit of *hybris*. I approached the letter with the thought that the ancient city, the jewel of the eastern Aegean Sea, would inform my writing with insight after insight. It was not to be.

Like all who devote a lot of time and effort to study the New Testament, I was aware that Ephesians presents problems to serious students. The biggest problem is whether Paul wrote the letter or whether an admiring imitator did so a few decades after the Apostle's death. The next biggest problem centers on whether the letter was really addressed to church members in Ephesus or was aimed at another, broader audience. As I plunged into chapter 1, these questions became acute in the first verse, where we read, "Paul, an apostle of Jesus Christ . . . to the saints which are at Ephesus." Before I could even begin, I had to satisfy both myself and potential readers of the commentary on these two issues. I decided to read Roman history that could possibly offer a plausible setting for the Epistle, which others before me had called a "quiet" letter. That is, we find no bumps and bruises caused by the dominant Roman society and we come across no heretics or heretical teachings inside the church. Such problems, it turns out, became issues for early Christians later in the first century AD and particularly during the second century. The most natural setting for Ephesians lay in the middle of the first century when Paul was alive and active. Any other era simply does not match what we can tease out of Ephesians about the historical setting in which it was written.

Like the Gospel of Luke, Ephesians has offered a rolling tutorial to me. Its language has drawn me into a bright world that not only glows with the presence of God the Father and is graced by the gifts of his Son but also rings with the voices of "holy apostles and prophets" and forges together its readers as "an holy temple in the Lord" (3:5; 2:21). At times I have found its language to be not only inspiring but also unspeakable, beyond words. Among other things, the letter discloses what Christians needed to learn in the face of a looming apostasy that was already reaching its tentacles into congregations in Asia (see 4:14; 5:3–7). Paul's directives at the end of his epistle prove the point—"Put on the whole armor of God," he wrote, and "Stand therefore, having your loins girt" (6:11, 14). But that is not the whole story.

Paul invited readers to soar with him above the clouds to the place where the Father had set Christ "at his own right hand in the heavenly places," where the Son had "ascended up far above all heavens" (1:20; 4:10). This same Son, in an ineffable act, carried to believers "redemption through his blood, the forgiveness of sins" (1:7), at the same time spreading out cushions and soft seats where devotees will one day "sit together in heavenly places in Christ Jesus" (2:6). As if these gifts were not enough, when Christ dwells "in your hearts by faith," church members will "be able to comprehend . . . what is the breadth, and length, and depth, and height [of] . . . the love of Christ, which passeth knowledge" (3:17–19). The Father and the Son have set a long table with a smorgasbord of divine delectable delicacies that, when eaten, whisk diners across galactic distances beyond where the human imagination can travel. At the end of this breathless journey reposes the invitation to "become therefore imitators of God" (5:1 NR). Indeed!

With my work on Ephesians at a close, I owe a big debt of gratitude to many. I first salute my colleagues who have committed themselves to producing the volumes in the commentary series. Our meetings every six weeks or so brought encouragement to me in spoken and unspoken ways. Philip Abbott, while a graduate student at Yale, produced a draft of the New Rendition of the letter, complete with extensive notes on his reasons for translating certain passages the way he did. My colleagues, Christopher Meldrum and Dave LeFevre, willingly and capably reviewed pieces of the commentary, as did my friend Dr. D. Corydon Hammond, and made cogent, helpful observations. My thanks also go to neighbors and friends who read one chapter or another while still in draft form. Naturally, my biggest expression of appreciation goes to Gayle, my wife and soulmate for more than fifty-six years, whom I came to admire initially in the University Ward in Berkeley, California, while I was still an undergraduate. She has quietly supported me by her affectionate circumspection when I have been at my writing task.

Introduction

Glorified and exalted, Christ sits enthroned above all. According to the Epistle to the Ephesians, that is where the Father has placed him—seating Christ at his right hand where he presides over the body of the church, which is his own body,[1] and where he controls the activities of "principalities and powers in heavenly places."[2] From this position, and under the tutelage of his Father, Christ lifts believers to where he is, both Jew and especially Gentile.[3] From here, and under the direction of his Father, Christ scatters the warm grace of his Atonement into the hearts and lives of his followers, ever filling them with hope for a better life beyond mortality.[4] Likewise, under the guidance of his Father, Christ carries out the plan set in motion by his Father "before the foundation of the world" that will bring salvation to those who seek it.[5] More than this, with the aid of his Father, Christ reveals a grand mystery kept hidden from the beginning, to wit, that Gentiles will be fully welcomed and embraced among the saved.[6] From his exalted place, and with the blessing of his Father, mortals receive the startling invitation to become "imitators of God," a possibility made available by Christ the exemplar. For in imitating the Father, humans are to "walk in love, just as Christ loved us and gave himself up for us as a fragrant offering and sacrifice to God."[7] Such actions gild the entry into a universe filled with unfading light and everlasting aromas. The reality of these supernal gifts from Christ and his Father was to be impressed on Paul's main audience, his Gentile readers, thus disclosing the letter's purpose.

---

1. Eph. 1:22–23; 4:8–10, 15–16; also Col. 1:18.
2. Eph. 3:10; also 1:21; 6:12.
3. Eph. 2:1–7, 11–22; 3:5–9.
4. Eph. 2:1–7, 11–22; 3:5–9.
5. Eph. 1:4.
6. Eph. 2:1–7, 11–22; 3:5–9.
7. Eph. 5:1–2, New Rendition (NR).

I. HISTORICAL SITUATION

Now we arrive at a two-part question. What brought about this letter, and why does it matter? Conspicuously absent are any hints of persecution and heresy or apostasy.[8] And, as we shall soon see, such items were very much a part of certain early Christian correspondence and teaching. In the first instance, no looming threats to Christians from Roman or civic officials appear on the horizon. Not one in Ephesians. In the second, church teachings are not under threat, except possibly by some who wanted their own way.[9] In my view, omission of such menaces would be unthinkable if in fact church members in Asia were being pressed by these kinds of perils from without and within. Although this observation and any others that a person might make about the character of the Epistle cannot be considered decisive when solving the issues of authorship and dating because we are dealing with probabilities rather than certainties,[10] it takes us in a very important direction.

Except for the occasional drunkard or irreverent or promiscuous person (see 4:25–32; 5:3–5, 18), church leaders evidently were managing their congregations without serious, inner, existential challenges over what the church should be like.[11] In this rather serene situation, Christian believers were to dress themselves in "the whole armour of God, that [they] may be able to stand against the wiles of the devil" rather than "against [the] flesh and blood" of this world. The real struggle, in the words of the letter, was "against spiritual wickedness in high [heavenly] places" (6:11–12).[12]

---

8. Andrew T. Lincoln, *Ephesians,* vol. 42 of the Word Biblical Commentary (Dallas: Word Books, Publisher, 1990), xxxix, lxxx; Ernest Best, *A Critical and Exegetical Commentary on Ephesians* (Edinburgh: T&T Clark, 1998), 2, 504. Best mentions this situation only in passing, making little of it. Also Stephen E. Fowl, *Ephesians: A Commentary* (Louisville, Ky.: Westminster/John Knox Press, 2012), 127.

9. Not all agree that 5:6–8 and 5:11, which address deception, were addressed to church members. Those who hold that these verses were aimed at outsiders include Lincoln, *Ephesians,* 325, and Fowl, *Ephesians,* 168–69; among those who argued for insiders are Best, *Ephesians,* 484, and Markus Barth, *Ephesians: Introduction, Translation, and Commentary,* 2 vols., vol. 34 of the Anchor Bible (New York: Doubleday, 1981), 2:564. The fact that Ephesians devoted so little space so late in the letter to the matter of deception indicates that it was not yet a bonfire, only a smoldering set of coals. See the Notes on 5:6–8, 11.

10. Lincoln, *Ephesians,* lxii; Fowl, *Ephesians,* 16–18.

11. Pheme Perkins in her *Ephesians,* Abingdon New Testament Commentaries (Nashville: Abingdon Press, 1997), 17, wrote, "Ephesians never refers to false teachers whose doctrines must be avoided."

12. As noted in n. 9, the language of 5:11–12, although suggestive of possible conflict with pagan society, is not totally conclusive. Scholars have seen "the unfruitful works

Such observations bring us face-to-face with the question of when this epistle was penned—within Paul's lifetime or afterward when grinding persecution became a regular and frightful reality? The answer, in my view, makes all the difference. If we accept the argument that the letter was written by a close associate of Paul after the Apostle's death, then we find ourselves consenting to the "canonical" Paul whose letter, because it is already in the New Testament and has been included because of its "inspiration," is therefore acceptable and normative for worship and doctrine.[13] If, on the other hand, we embrace the point of view that Paul was the author or even that the Epistle was written under his direction, the letter then carries the weight of an Apostle commissioned by Jesus Christ himself. The gap between the "canonical" Paul and the Apostle Paul is more than minimal. It is enormous.[14] To wit, if the letter came from a later disciple of Paul, then, where it diverges from the teachings of Paul in his other letters, it is open to the criticism that it is adjusting doctrine and church practice. If the letter is from Paul, then his apostolic authority stands behind any reported differences, and they will be seen as refinements of the teachings in his earlier communiqués.

Early on, Christians had been caught in the deadly net of the emperor Nero (AD 54–68). Although the fire that broke out in Rome on 19 July AD 64 and consumed an estimated half of the city led to the diminishing of Nero's popularity because of rampant rumors that he had started the conflagration, he quickly tried to deflect blame onto the Christians, with some success. For thereafter they lived as a despised religious group in the eyes of most citizens of the empire: "loathed for their vices," as Tacitus records; "a new and mischievous superstition," in the words of Suetonius.[15] Whether Jewish residents of Rome helped to stoke the emperor's enmity against the Christians as well as the negative opinion that penetrated the public remains an open possibility. In the end, Christians around the empire stood

---

of darkness . . . which are done of them in secret" (5:11–12) as pointing to shameful acts within the Christian community. Best, *Ephesians,* 491–95; Thomas M. Winger, *Ephesians,* Concordia Commentary (St. Louis: Concordia Publishing House, 2015), 563–65. In contrast, these actions might refer to the behavior of nonbelievers in whose eyes believers can live in such a way that they present an attractive, alternative lifestyle to these nonmember neighbors. Fowl, *Ephesians,* 170–71; Lincoln, *Ephesians,* 329–30; see also 1 Pet. 2:12.

13. The expression "'canonical' Paul" comes from Lincoln, *Ephesians,* lxxiii.

14. Hugh Nibley, *Apostles and Bishops in Early Christianity,* vol. 15 of Collected Works of Hugh Nibley, ed. John F. Hall and John W. Welch (Salt Lake City: Deseret Book; Provo, Utah: Foundation for Ancient Research and Mormon Studies, 2005), 7–13; for a different view, see Fowl, *Ephesians,* 9–11.

15. Tacitus, *Annals* 15.44; Suetonius, *Nero* 6.16.2.

exposed on unstable ground vis-à-vis government and political officials as they took to heart the news that reached their ears of Nero's horrible punishments of their fellow Saints, including attacks by dogs in the emperor's arena and public crucifixions with some victims burned at night to provide light in and around the city. What may have come as equally unsettling news was the execution of the Apostles Peter and Paul in Rome. From the book of Acts, we read that only a couple of years before Paul found himself in Rome, in AD 57 or 58, he and other believers came to know that he faced death (see Acts 20:22–24; 21:11, 13). Although we cannot be certain that Peter and Paul died in the wave of Nero's punishments, they were both taken off the mortal stage in this era by execution.[16]

Second, in succeeding decades, rough times were apparently the norm in western, central, and northern Asia, including the region where Ephesus sat. For it was to church members in "Pontus, Galatia, Cappadocia, Asia, and Bithynia" that the First Epistle of Peter was addressed (1 Pet. 1:1).[17] In that letter, we come upon references to early trials and troubles at the hands of Gentiles. A selection of passages might include "the Gentiles . . . speak against you as evildoers" (1 Pet. 2:12); Christ "when he was reviled, reviled not again; when he suffered, he threatened not" (1 Pet. 2:23); "if ye suffer for righteousness' sake, happy are ye: and be not afraid of their terror" (1 Pet. 3:14); and "rejoice, inasmuch as ye are partakers of Christ's sufferings" (1 Pet. 4:13).[18] Hence, we can reasonably conclude that threats of persecution, if not actual acts of persecution, hung over the heads of Christians throughout this large territory of Asia.[19]

Then, Christian works that were authored late in the first century AD, especially those that reflect conditions in western Asia where Ephesus

---

16. *First Clement* 5.2–7, in *The Ante-Nicene Fathers: Translations of the Writings of the Fathers down to A.D. 325,* ed. Alexander Roberts, James Donaldson, and A. Cleveland Coxe, 10 vols., reprint (Grand Rapids, Mich.: Eerdmans, 1950), 1:6 (hereafter cited as *ANF*); William H. C. Frend, *The Rise of Christianity* (Philadelphia: Fortress Press, 1984), 109–10.

17. Yohanan Aharoni, Michael Avi-Yonah, Anson F. Rainey, and Ze'ev Safrai, *The Carta Bible Atlas,* 4th ed. (Jerusalem: Carta, 2002), §§243, 271.

18. See also "the trial of your faith . . . though it be tried by fire" (1 Pet. 1:7); "Christ also suffered for us, leaving us an example" (2:21); "whereas they speak evil of you, as of evildoers, they may be ashamed that falsely accuse your good conversation in Christ" (3:16); "think it not strange concerning the fiery trial which is to try you" (4:12); "If ye be reproached for the name of Christ, happy are ye" (4:14).

19. Adrian Nicholas Sherwin-White, *The Letters of Pliny: A Historical and Social Commentary,* corrected ed. (Oxford: Oxford University Press, 1985), 694: "It is apparent [from Pliny's letter 10.96] that . . . there had been previous trials in Pontus."

is located, such as the book of Revelation (see Rev. 1:4), mirror the dire consequences of ongoing persecution. As we have seen above, this circumstance was not new. In the earlier years of the emperor Domitian's reign (AD 81–96), Christians were caught by the iron-fisted requirement to offer sacrifice to the deified Roman emperor. Penalties for noncompliance included death and exile. We learn of a man named Antipas from Pergamum in western Asia who paid the ultimate penalty of death for his faith (see Rev. 2:13; see also Rev. 2:10). Moreover, to underscore the reality of persecution, the book of Revelation was written by John on the isle of Patmos after he had been exiled there by Roman authorities because of his faith (see Rev. 1:9). Hence, specifically within western Asia, persecution pressure ratcheted up near the end of the first century.

Third, such pressure erupted again less than twenty years later in the northern parts of Asia, this time in the Roman province of Bithynia-Pontus (*Bithynia et Pontus*)—a region stretching eastward from the Sea of Marmara almost to the territory of Armenia along the Black Sea's south coast.[20] This formed the northern part of the region to which Peter's first letter had been addressed decades earlier. In AD 109, a man named Pliny, known as "the Younger," arrived in Nicomedia, the capital of Bithynia-Pontus.[21] He came as the legate of the emperor Trajan (*Legatus Augusti*). Significantly, Pliny was a literary man who had already published nine volumes of his correspondence that consisted of 248 letters from his prior service to the empire.[22] In Asia, he served for approximately two years until his death in AD 111 during which time he wrote numerous letters to Trajan that are preserved. One of these letters, number 96 in the collection, offers the clearest sketch of Christians and their practices from a Roman author that we possess anywhere. Not surprisingly, he met his first Christians in Asia, not in Rome; they made up a substantial part of the Asian population.

Throughout a series of hearings during the last third of AD 110[23] that involved Christians who refused to offer "incense and wine" to the statue of the emperor, Pliny came to the decision that "those who remained obdurate ... [were] to be executed," a strong indicator that this action was not novel.

---

20. For the extent of the Bithynia-Pontus Province, see Timothy Cornell and John Matthews, *Atlas of the Roman World* (Oxford: Equinox [Oxford], 1982), 150–51; also Carl G. Rasmussen, *Zondervan NIV Atlas of the Bible* (Grand Rapids, Mich.: Regency Reference Library, 1989), 181–82, 185–86; Aharoni and others, *Carta Bible Atlas*, §271.

21. Sherwin-White, *Letters of Pliny*, 80–81.

22. Sherwin-White, *Letters of Pliny*, 9.

23. Sherwin-White, *Letters of Pliny*, 693–94.

To be sure, even though he wrote to the emperor that he was "unaware what [action by a Christian] is usually punished or investigated, and to what extent," his tough response indicates that execution was the established norm used by a Roman official who confronted a religious person's resistance, whether Christian or some other "debased and boundless superstition."[24] Under Roman law at the time, it was possible for "a provincial governor" to try, sentence, and execute people "for capital offences." Executions included even Roman citizens "without any suggestion that such action [by the Roman official] was contrary to the law," even though citizens had the right to appeal to the emperor.[25] And those whom Pliny executed must have included at least a few Roman citizens. Further, in the set of scenes pictured in Pliny's letter, strong hints exist that Roman legislation, whose record has not survived, already "outlawed the religion" and therefore required some sort of action against believers.[26]

We do not know how many believers lost their lives as a result of Pliny's decisions, but the number cannot have been tiny. He did indicate that a number "had abandoned their allegiance" to Christ, thus saving their lives.[27] Even though in his reply to Pliny's letter the emperor Trajan directed that "Christians are not to be sought out" and are to "be punished" only when "brought before you and found guilty,"[28] one has to respect the complaints of Tertullian, an early Christian writer (c. AD 160–225) who circa AD 197 pointed to a large number of deaths at Pliny's hand for the presumed guilt of just being Christian.[29] To be sure, under the emperors Trajan and Hadrian (AD 98–117 and 117–38 respectively), Christians who were Roman citizens had the right to appeal judgments against them and to cross-examine their accusers. Hence, the pressure on Christian citizens specifically may have eased briefly.[30] Nevertheless, by the mid-second century, Christians had become the objects of mob violence that authorities either could not or would not control.

---

24. Pliny, *Letters* 10.96.1, 3, 5, 8, in Patrick Gerard Walsh, *Pliny the Younger: Complete Letters* (Oxford: Oxford University Press, 2006), 278–79.

25. Adrian Nicholas Sherwin-White, *Roman Society and Roman Law in the New Testament*, the Sarum Lectures 1960–1961 (Oxford: Clarendon Press, 1963), 60–61, 72.

26. Mary Beard, *SPQR: A History of Ancient Rome* (New York: Liveright Publishing, 2015), 518.

27. Pliny, *Letters* 10.96.6, in Walsh, *Pliny the Younger,* 278.

28. Pliny, *Letters* 10.97.1–2, in Walsh, *Pliny the Younger,* 279.

29. Tertullian, *Apology* 2, in *ANF,* 3:18. See also Johannes Quasten, *Patrology,* 3 vols. (Utrecht: Spectrum Publishers, 1966), 2:255–60.

30. Frend, *Rise of Christianity,* 150, 181.

Fourth, one of the most famous martyrdoms of antiquity occurred in western Asia in AD 165, that of Polycarp, bishop of Smyrna, who refused to worship the emperor when dragged into the city from his farm after a throng in the amphitheater bayed for his blood. Why did the crowd cry for his death? Because he was a prominent Christian. The sentiment in Smyrna's society was decidedly anti-Christian and had been growing since about AD 150. Such events were not confined to Asia. For their refusal to worship the emperor in AD 177, some church members in Lyon were executed; others were imprisoned where they perished; still others were forced into the arena where they faced certain death by wild beasts.[31] Even though virtually all Christians went to their deaths willingly, even gladly, their loss was a major blow to their families and congregations. In this connection, as Robin Lane Fox reminds us when reviewing the character of Christian martyrs, "the most excellent Christians in the early Church were neither the virgins nor the visionaries [whom we hear about]. They were the Christians whom pagans put to death."[32]

From our review, Roman and Christian sources suggest that persecutions were localized; that is, they were not empire-wide. Further, they did not persist for long periods of time. They came and they went. That said, it is also apparent that word got around so that we see warnings to believers about how to deal with civic officials in such writings as the First Epistle of Peter. From the persecution launched against Christians in Rome by Nero in AD 64 and for the next century, peaceful times were not the lot of believers. To be sure, ten or twenty years might pass between deadly outbursts against church members in one place or another. But Christians never lived with an inner assurance that they were completely safe and secure. Frighteningly, things seemed to change for the worse about AD 150, including a hardening of negative public opinion and official crackdowns on believers.

Fifth, in the Epistle to the Ephesians, by utter contrast to all of this, the only imprisonment and suffering that we hear about is that of Paul himself (see 3:1, 13; 4:1; 6:20). Paul's concerns for his recipients have to do with being "strengthened . . . in the inner man" (3:16) and walking "worthy of the vocation wherewith ye are called" (4:1) while seeking "to keep the unity of the spirit in the bond of peace" (4:3) and avoiding "every wind of doctrine" or deceit that might pass through a congregation (4:14; 5:6). In

---

31. Frend, *Rise of Christianity,* 164–67, 180–84; Polycarp, *Epistle to the Philippians* 9; Eusebius, *Ecclesiastical History* 4.15.1–46; 5.1.1–63.

32. Robin Lane Fox, *Pagans and Christians* (New York: Alfred A. Knopf, 1986), 419.

sum, we are looking at a letter that Markus Barth calls in the context of Jewish and Gentile relations "the peaceful epistle to the Ephesians."[33]

II. HERESY, APOSTASY, AND QUESTIONS OF UNITY

Further, the book of Revelation, with a focus on Asia where Ephesus sits and with a specific message to believers there (see Rev. 2:1–7), exposes the inner turmoil of apostasy among congregations in the region in the days of its composition,[34] an element that is barely hinted at in Ephesians[35] if we are to date it to the latter part of the first century or even to the early second century.[36] In Revelation we read about "them which say they are apostles, and are not" and "the Nicolaitans, which I [the Lord] also hate" (Rev. 2:2, 6, 15) as well as the Lord's complaints about "them that hold the doctrine of Balaam" (Rev. 2:14). If we join to these the worrisome characteristics underlined in the Epistles of John, also written late in the first century or early in the second and mirroring the Christian situation in Asia, we learn about "many antichrists" (1 John 2:18), "many false prophets" (1 John 4:1), "many deceivers . . . who confess not that Jesus Christ is come in the flesh" (2 John 1:7; see also 1 John 4:3), and church leaders who even refuse to receive apostolic representatives (see 3 John 1:9–10).[37] Such vexing observations appear nowhere in Ephesians.

---

33. Barth, *Ephesians*, 1:43; see also Fowl, *Ephesians*, 8, where he observes that the "internal and external threats Paul anticipates in Acts 20" are not "found in the epistle [to the Ephesians]." Further, Richard L. Anderson, *Understanding Paul* (Salt Lake City: Deseret Book, 1983), 261, noted, "His letter addressed no crisis."

34. Frend, *Rise of Christianity,* 128, 137–38.

35. Karl Ludwig Schmidt, in *Theological Dictionary of the New Testament,* ed. Gerhard Kittel and Gerhard Friedrich, trans. Geoffrey W. Bromiley, 10 vols. (Grand Rapids, Mich.: Eerdmans, 1964–76), 3:510–12 (hereafter cited as *TDNT*), argued that when Paul called the church "the body of Christ" in Ephesians (4:12; etc.), he borrowed from Gnostic ideas that had invaded the church and, by framing them differently, structured an opposition to Gnostic teachings that Schmidt perceived to be pressing against the correct understanding of Christ and the church. But it is just as possible that Paul simply borrowed Gnostic strands of thought to frame his own teaching about the nature of Christ and the church.

36. For a possible exception, see the Notes on 5:6–8, 11.

37. Walter Bauer, *Orthodoxy and Heresy in Earliest Christianity,* ed. Robert Kraft and Gerhard Krodel (Philadelphia: Fortress Press, 1971), 91–94, holds that the Epistles of John mirror a struggle between "orthodox" and "heretical" Christians for control of the congregations in Asia with, in some cases, the "orthodox" withdrawing from the so-called heretics because the latter formed the majority of the various congregations.

Any approach to dating Ephesians by appealing to the matter of heresy and apostasy needs to turn to Paul's Epistle to the Galatians, a letter written circa AD 48 whose origins are not in dispute. In a response to Christians residing in central Asia who had turned away from his message of peace and grace to one of laws and strictures, he flared, "I marvel that ye are so soon removed from him that called you into the grace of Christ unto another gospel." Bringing his topic to a boil, he seethed that "there be some that trouble you, and would pervert the gospel of Christ." Next, he thundered, "Though we, or an angel from heaven, preach any other gospel unto you than that which we have preached unto you, let him be accursed." Then, scalding the consciences of his readers more fiercely, he virtually repeated his earlier words: "If any man preach any other gospel unto you than that which ye have received, let him be accursed" (Gal. 1:6–9). The plain, bright lesson? Galatians, written before AD 50, sets before us a painting filled with dark, clashing colors when it comes to church members turning away from principles and doctrines that Paul had taught them, leading him to wonder whether he had "bestowed upon [them] labour in vain" and to ask who "did hinder [them] that [they] should not obey the truth" (Gal. 4:11; 5:7).[38] All of this leads us to wonder in our turn whether Asia was a place of conflicting theological currents, beginning in the middle of the first century AD. Almost nothing of this jangling over principles and doctrines appears in the letter destined for Ephesus, which lies far to the west of the region of Galatia.[39] Hardly a whisper. And what does appear occurs late in the letter, leaving readers with the feeling that such troubles were modest at worst (see 5:6–8, 11).

In fact, the letter to the Galatians does not stand in cool isolation in reflecting back to us situations in Asia of roiling troubles in the churches of the mid-first century. Already in 1 Corinthians, written very possibly while Paul was still in Ephesus in AD 55,[40] we find the Apostle writing about tarrying "at Ephesus until Pentecost" and then, curiously, about facing "many adversaries" (1 Cor. 16:8–9). Soon afterward, he followed this notice with a frightening reference to "our trouble which came to us in Asia, . . . insomuch that we despaired even of life" (2 Cor. 1:8). It was not many months later that, from a ship taking him toward Jerusalem, Paul

---

38. Jerome Murphy-O'Connor, *Paul: A Critical Life* (Oxford: Oxford University Press, 1996), 199.

39. Cornell and Matthews, *Atlas of the Roman World*, 150–51.

40. Frederick Fyvie Bruce, *Paul: Apostle of the Heart Set Free* (Grand Rapids, Mich.: Eerdmans, 1996), 273, 475.

disembarked at Miletus and requested that "the elders of the church" in Ephesus join him there, though he was at least three days' journey from the city (Acts 20:15–17). After the church leaders and others finally reached him, Paul gave a farewell speech, essentially a review of his missionary work in western Asia and specifically in Ephesus. On that occasion and in a perfectly normal tone, he urged those present to "take heed therefore unto yourselves, and to all the flock." He next surprised his Ephesian friends by prophesying "that after my departing shall grievous wolves enter in among you, not sparing the flock." Worse than these assailing outsiders, he warned that "of your own selves shall men arise, speaking perverse things, to draw away disciples after them" (Acts 20:28–30). When Luke recorded these prophetic lines in about AD 80, lines that predicted troubles from without and from within the church, their fulfillment must have already been underway.[41] How do we know? Because other sources, nowadays usually dated to the late first century, point to such troubles.

It is not our purpose here to debate the dating and provenance of the Pastoral Epistles—that is, the two Timothy letters and the one to Titus. Whether they came from Paul late in the AD 60s or whether they were written by a disciple of Paul two or three decades after his death is not essential to resolve here. Key is how these letters, likely composed during the latter part of the first century, portray the situation in Asia where Ephesus lies, a situation that agrees largely with that described in Paul's correspondence to the Galatians and the Corinthians, as we have seen. In fact, "already during the lifetime of the apostle, certain people had appeared there [in Ephesus] whose teaching caused offense and threatened divisions in the community."[42] No wonder that Paul warned his fellow laborers of threats from without and within the congregation (see Acts 20:29–30). What becomes apparent is that Paul, the main founder of the church in Ephesus, was soon forgotten after he left town (see Acts 20:1), so much so that "he and his influence fade[d] rapidly [in Ephesus] in the second century."[43] Evidently, persons outside of the Apostle's circle of close associates and converts must have been responsible for replacing Paul's teachings with their own. "Even *Ephesus* cannot be considered as a center of orthodoxy, but is rather a particularly instructive example

---

41. Bauer, *Orthodoxy and Heresy,* 82–83.
42. Bauer, *Orthodoxy and Heresy,* 82.
43. Bauer, *Orthodoxy and Heresy,* 84.

of how . . . an ancient Christian community, even one of apostolic origin, could erode when caught in the turbulent crosscurrents of orthodoxy and heresy."[44]

In a stunning surprise, we find a complaint attributed to Paul "that all they which are in Asia be turned away from me" (2 Tim. 1:15; see also 2 Cor. 1:8). What is behind such an action? We come upon a hint in the expression "other doctrine" in the first letter to Timothy. In a denigrating caricature, the letter called such teaching "fables and endless genealogies, which minister questions, rather than godly edifying." Then, turning to the Christian virtue of "charity out of a pure heart"[45] that all should strive for, the author groaned that "some having swerved [from charity] have turned aside to vain jangling; desiring to be teachers of the law; understanding neither what they say, nor whereof they affirm" (1 Tim. 1:3–7). In this light, it is possible that the Apostle's further protestation at the end of 1 Timothy ties to this caricature of false teaching. There he called it "godless chatter and the opposing ideas of what is falsely called knowledge, which some have professed and in so doing have departed from the faith" (1 Tim. 6:20–21 NIV). This situation is mirrored in language from the book of Revelation that speaks to the state of affairs in Ephesus at the end of the first century— namely, "You [church members] have forsaken the love you had at first" (Rev. 2:4 NIV). That is, "The controversies which had raged in Ephesus had apparently led to censoriousness, factiousness, and divisions."[46] Even though scholars debate what sort of religious movement had reached western Asia in the late first century,[47] it is plain that what Paul taught had been pushed aside by a very different set of teachings. Nothing of this kind of acute anxiety appears in the Epistle to the Ephesians. Nothing.

One potential source of tension may have arisen from the Jewish Christians who relocated from Palestine following the devastating war between Jewish partisans and Roman legions (AD 66–70). But such tension is hard

---

44. Bauer, *Orthodoxy and Heresy,* 82, emphasis in the original; see also 85.

45. Frend, *Rise of Christianity,* 138, observes, "Erroneous views about Christ's ministry were associated, by orthodox spokesmen, with lack of Christian charity."

46. Robert Henry Charles, *A Critical and Exegetical Commentary on the Revelation of St. John,* The International Critical Commentary, 2 vols. (Edinburgh: T. & T. Clark, 1971), 1:51; see also Richard D. Draper and Michael D. Rhodes, *The Revelation of John the Apostle,* Brigham Young University New Testament Commentary (Provo, Utah: BYU Studies, 2016), 125.

47. Frend, *Rise of Christianity,* 138–39.

to measure. Simply stated, these people evidently "no longer felt safe" in their homeland.[48] Two exemplars of this movement to Asia stand forth. One was Philip the Evangelist, who was the father of four spirit-filled daughters and had moved from Jerusalem to Caesarea on the Mediterranean coast because of persecution in the Holy City (see Acts 6:5; 8:5, 26–40; 21:8–9). Both Papias, who became the bishop of Hierapolis in the early second century during Trajan's reign (AD 98–117),[49] and Polycrates, bishop of Ephesus late in the second century, knew that, in the latter part of the first century, Philip and his daughters had relocated to Hierapolis, which lies about 100 miles or 160 kilometers east of Ephesus.[50] The second prominent person, who probably felt safer in Ephesus, was the Apostle John. Christians like Philip, John, and Philip's daughters, who had all relocated to Asia from the Holy Land, presumably brought a different flavor of the faith when compared to the understanding of the Gentile Christians spread throughout the region.[51] However, whether and how much that different flavor came to assist or, worse, engender strife between native-born Gentile Christians in Asia and emigrants from Palestine remains an unsolved question.

Within a few decades, perhaps within a few years of the composition of the Pastorals depending on when they were written, our focus is jerked back again to debilitating troubles inside the church, this time stretching from eastern to western Asia. From the early second century, we come upon letters written by Ignatius, the bishop of Antioch in the southeast. Even a quick read of this correspondence shows congregations that are breeding grounds of competing factions that have riven the unity of the church. During the reign of the emperor Trajan (AD 98–117), Ignatius was serving as the bishop of the church in Antioch, where he was arrested and condemned to be set upon by wild beasts in Rome. At a point between AD 100 and 118, he was taken to Rome.[52] The exact date remains unknown.

---

48. Bauer, *Orthodoxy and Heresy*, 86.

49. William R. Schoedel, *The Apostolic Fathers: A New Translation and Commentary*, ed. Robert M. Grant, vol. 5, *Polycarp, Martyrdom of Polycarp, Fragments of Papias* (Camden, N.J.: Thomas Nelson and Sons, 1967), 91–92.

50. Eusebius, *Ecclesiastical History* 3.39.9; 3.31.3; 5.24.2–3; see Cornell and Matthews, *Atlas of the Roman World*, 150–51.

51. Bauer, *Orthodoxy and Heresy*, 85–87.

52. William R. Schoedel, *Ignatius of Antioch: A Commentary on the Letters of Ignatius of Antioch*, ed. Helmut Koester, Hermeneia: A Critical and Historical Commentary on the Bible (Philadelphia: Fortress Press, 1985), 1, 5, 10–11.

The first part of the trip was apparently by ship and then overland through western Asia by a military escort of ten soldiers, whom he called "ten leopards."[53] When he reached the west coast, he wrote seven letters that survive. He first spent time in Smyrna, modern Izmir, Turkey, where he wrote three letters to Christian congregations that had sent representatives to greet him and encourage him on his journey. These congregations were located in Ephesus, Magnesia, and Tralles, generally south and southwest of Smyrna. In a famous passage from his fourth letter, which was also composed in Smyrna and was addressed to church members in Rome, he begged that no one intercede on his behalf because "I am the wheat of God, and I must be ground by the teeth of wild beasts, that I may become the pure bread of Christ."[54] At Troas, where he was put on a ship, he wrote three more letters. These were addressed to fellow believers in Smyrna and Philadelphia, a city that lies east of Smyrna, and to Polycarp, the man serving as bishop of Smyrna at the time.[55]

Two of the common themes in Ignatius's letters have to do with a hoped-for unity behind the local bishop and an aggressive concern about an invading heresy. Clearly, something was driving both his insistent appeals for believers to unite behind their bishops, who, for him, stood next to God,[56] and his warning of a cancerous heresy that had invaded churches in Asia and beyond. Philadelphia serves as an example of other congregations in western Asia where Ignatius knew of the presence of what he called "many specious wolves."[57] In William Schoedel's judgment, "a threat to Ignatius' authority by some Antiochene Christians evidently played a significant role in determining what Ignatius was to do and to

---

53. Ignatius, *Letter to the Romans* 5:1; also quoted in Eusebius, *Ecclesiastical History* 3.36.7.

54. Ignatius, *Letter to the Romans* 4:1.

55. Eusebius, *Ecclesiastical History* 3.36.10; Quasten, *Patrology,* 1:64.

56. Quasten, *Patrology,* 1:66–67; Bauer, *Orthodoxy and Heresy,* 61, notes that for Ignatius, "the bishop . . . is like God or Christ in whose place he stands." Frend, *Rise of Christianity,* 139, observes that Ignatius "insisted on the mystical connection between the Christian bishop and the heavenly high priest in which the bishop was the essential link between the Christian community and the Lord." Schoedel, *Ignatius of Antioch,* 22, argues for a moderated view "that in Ignatius the bishop does not occupy the place of God or Christ and that we are still close to NT models." Also see especially Nibley, *Apostles and Bishops,* 61–74.

57. Ignatius, *Letter to the Philadelphians* 2:2.

say."[58] Furthermore, Schoedel mentions Ignatius's "loss of control of the church in Antioch and the emergence of a group opposed to his authority."[59] This group may have been made up of "Judaizers," who pressed the observance of the Mosaic law, because Ignatius "seems to have been more or less prepared with arguments" against such groups in Magnesia and Philadelphia.[60] Moreover, the grinding difficulties between Ignatius and his Christian opponents in Antioch seem to have been driven in part by personal animosities.[61] Overpowering personalities evidently got in the way of unity among those church members. No hint of any of this sort of trouble appears in Paul's Epistle to the Ephesians.

To be sure, Paul raised the matter of unity in the letter to the Ephesians. But its tenor and character were vastly different from Ignatius's entreaties. Writing one of the terms for unity that Ignatius would later employ in his pleas for unity (ἑνότης, *henotēs*),[62] Paul appealed to his readers "to keep the unity of the Spirit" and to look forward to the time when "we all come in the unity of the faith" (4:3, 13). In Ephesians, notably, it was living apostles and prophets who brought about "the perfecting of the saints" and "the unity of the faith" (4:11–13) rather than the local bishop. Moreover, when Paul wrote about deception in his letter, he framed it not in terms of heresy or apostasy but in terms of "the sleight of men, and cunning craftiness" as well as "vain words" (4:14; 5:6). Such deception was to be met by donning "the whole armour of God, that ye may be able to stand against the wiles of the devil," placing the field of combat in the unseen world (6:11).

One of the most compelling reasons to see gnosticizing elements as a big part of the troubles in Asia rests in a man named Marcion. He was a native of Sinope, a city on the south coast of the Black Sea in Pontus, who took his beliefs to Rome about AD 140 and caused an uproar. For his beliefs, he was excommunicated a few years later. But his organizing abilities led to the establishment of Marcionite congregations all over the Roman world that continued for a hundred years after his death (c. AD 160). Among other

---

58. Schoedel, *Ignatius of Antioch*, 11.

59. Schoedel, *Ignatius of Antioch*, 10.

60. Schoedel, *Ignatius of Antioch*, 11 n. 62.

61. Schoedel, *Ignatius of Antioch*, 10–11 and n. 62.

62. Schoedel, *Igantius of Antioch*, 21; Walter Bauer, *A Greek-English Lexicon of the New Testament and Other Early Christian Literature*, ed. Frederick W. Danker, 3rd English ed. (Chicago: University of Chicago Press, 2000), 338 (hereafter cited as BDAG).

things, he was the first to assemble a collection of documents that preceded our New Testament and included an edited copy of Luke's Gospel and ten of Paul's letters. In assembling these texts, he was guided in large measure by his openly anti–Old Testament bias. He believed that the God of the Old Testament was a capricious deity who punished people randomly and was exposed by the loving God whom Jesus preached. In his view, the Apostle Paul was the one apostle who understood this loving God. We ask the question: Did Marcion, who was born about AD 100, generate his ideas in a theological vacuum? Likely not. His views grew out of a contest of teachings that, to one degree or another, were swirling through Christian churches in Asia in the early second century.[63]

Besides these observations, one of the most important pieces to consider for dating the letter appears in the epistle itself and features a very small word—"now." In its Greek form, this temporal adverb is also small (νῦν, *nun*). Of its four occurrences in the letter, one is key. We read, "In other ages [God's mystery] was not made known unto the sons of men, as it is *now* revealed unto his holy apostles and prophets by the Spirit" (3:5, emphasis added; see also 3:10). The question arises whether any apostles were still alive and active at the time the letter was written. If so, then we are talking about the middle of the first century, not its end; that is, we are focused on the era of Paul's greatest activity. Paul had already mentioned "apostles and prophets" in the letter at 2:20 as "the foundation" of the church. He would feature them again at 4:11–12 as those who directed "the work of the ministry." Hence, it is natural that Paul introduced them at 3:5 as the current recipients of God's mystery. Incidentally, it does not do to insist that, in this passage, the term "holy" as applied to "apostles and prophets" points to a bygone era because Christians would not talk about contemporary apostles in this way. Such an insistence boils down to a mere guess (see the Note on 3:5). Rather, the adverb "now" subtly but firmly underscores that apostles, men commissioned by Jesus Christ himself,[64] and other authorized officers of the church were still active, an observation that would support the judgment that Ephesians was composed in the mid-first century.

---

63. Bauer, *Orthodoxy and Heresy,* 91; John J. Clabeaux, "Marcion," in *The Anchor Bible Dictionary,* ed. David Noel Freedman and others, 6 vols. (New York: Doubleday, 1992), 4:514–16 (hereafter cited as *ABD*).

64. Nibley, *Apostles and Bishops,* 1–23.

III. JEWISH AND CHRISTIAN RELATIONS

Paul spent a good deal of space treating Jewish and Gentile matters, even repeating the common Jewish term for Gentiles, "Uncircumcision" (2:11). A person might ask, What light might the interest in Jewish-Gentile relations shed on the question of Paul's authorship of Ephesians? The answer is, quite a lot. We notice that, with regard to synagogue worship, we run into engrossing lines, such as the Gentiles "being aliens from the commonwealth of Israel, and strangers from the covenants of promise" (2:12). But this is only part of the story. Another part has to do with Christ building a bridge between the two societies, breaking "down the middle wall of partition between [them]" (2:14). A further part credits Christ with abolishing "in his flesh the enmity" between the two groups so that they became "one new man, so making peace" (2:15). It is the mention of enmity and peace that catches one's attention. Both are strong words, and both point to historical realities of conflict, particularly the word for enmity (ἔχθρα, *echthra*).

After the days of Jesus' mortal life, two serious conflicts broke out between Gentiles and Jews in the eastern Mediterranean basin. The first exploded in the Egyptian city of Alexandria, beginning in A D 38 and finally winding down in A D 41.[65] The second raged in the city of Caesarea during A D 59–60, with a brief, deadly surge in A D 66.[66] Each of these, which led to the deaths of hundreds, even thousands, was well known throughout the Roman world. In fact, Paul and his associates may have witnessed some of the goings-on in Caesarea while the Apostle was under house arrest there for two years (see Acts 24:27). And the references both in 2:15 and 2:16 to *echthra,* "the enmity," draws up the high likelihood that these events were hovering in the background of Paul's choice of words. He knew, of course, that only Christ could offer peace to the two antagonistic groups, reconciling "both unto God in one body by the cross," thus offering peace to them, both external and internal (2:16). The question is this: How do these observations relate to Paul's authorship of the Ephesians letter? The answer is that because Paul, like everyone else in the Roman world, was surely aware of these two major flare-ups between Gentiles and Jews in

---

65. Emil Schürer, *The History of the Jewish People in the Age of Jesus Christ,* ed. Geza Vermes, Fergus Millar, and Matthew Black, rev. ed., 3 vols. (Edinburgh: T. and T. Clark, 1973–87), 1:389–91, 398; 3:127–29, 132, 150–51, 153.

66. Schürer, *History of the Jewish People,* 1:465–67; 2:117, 183.

Alexandria and Caesarea, they offered him an opportunity to write about the solution that Christ offered through his Atonement. And his plain reference to these occurrences situates the writing of the letter at some time soon after AD 59–60 while the memory of them was still somewhat fresh. It would make no sense for a fabricator to refer to events four or five decades later after memories had faded, including in the imitator's mind (see the Notes on 2:15–16).

IV. The Theological Questions

On his way to favoring the view that the Apostle Paul wrote the letter to the Ephesians, Markus Barth complained that no objective standards can be applied to the question of authorship. We are left, he declared, with "insufficient linguistic and historical arguments."[67] The observations set out above, however, stand as firm historical arguments that push the dating of the epistle into the mid-first century when Paul was still alive and involved.

The nonobjective standards tie to what Barth calls "the prejudicial character of the theological reasons exhibited against Ephesians," largely growing out of a Protestant viewpoint. That viewpoint holds that Paul's gospel "could never have been adulterated by the place attributed in Ephesians to the church, the powers, and social realities."[68] I touch on these items in the paragraphs that follow.

One of the drags on Paul's authorship of Ephesians has to do with the ponderous question about certain terms that appear to be in unusual dress in Ephesians, differing from how they are adorned elsewhere in his other letters. Such terms as "mystery," "head," "fulness," and "dispensation" enjoy membership in this list. Concerning the last term, "dispensation" (οἰκονομία, *oikonomia*), elsewhere it bears the meaning of a divine commission or stewardship given to Paul by God (see 1 Cor. 9:17, "I am entrusted with a commission," RSV; Col. 1:25, "the commission God gave me," NIV). Concerning "mystery" (μυστήριον, *mystērion*), in Ephesians it pertains to the revelation that Gentiles were to be welcomed within God's fold (see

---

67. Barth, *Ephesians*, 1:49. George Bradford Caird, *Paul's Letters from Prison (Ephesians, Philippians, Colossians, Philemon)* (Oxford: Oxford University Press, 1976), 12, notes, "These arguments are neither so trivial that they can be disregarded nor so conclusive as to command general assent."

68. Barth, *Ephesians*, 1:49, 46.

3:3–6). In another passage outside the letter, we find it applied to the Resurrection, a quite different thought: "We shall not all sleep, but we shall all be changed" (1 Cor. 15:51). But to jump on this variance and claim that the authors of the two passages could not possibly be the same individual seems to be an overreaction.[69] If, as is reasonable to assume, Paul wrote Ephesians four or more years after composing 1 Corinthians,[70] who can demonstrate that his understanding about God's mystery did not grow and expand during the interval?

The fact is that the amount of written material preserved in the four certifiably authentic letters of Paul (Rom., 1 and 2 Cor., and Gal.) is simply not enough to draw far-reaching conclusions about authorship. One sample will suffice. The Greek noun for "unity" (ἑνότης, *henotēs*) appears in the New Testament twice, both in Ephesians (see 4:3, 13). The question is this: Does that reduce the possibility that Paul wrote this letter because the author inserted a term found nowhere else in the other letters? Hardly. The noun that bears the opposite meaning is "diversity" (διαίρεσις, *diairesis*), and it occurs in the New Testament only three times, all in its plural form within three verses of 1 Corinthians (see 1 Cor. 12:4–6). No one would ever suggest that this unusual triple occurrence raises questions about the authenticity of 1 Corinthians.[71] And so it goes. Now, let us turn to examine briefly the most important questions that center on the Apostle's imprisonment and then the church and its nature as portrayed in the letter (on Paul as author, see the Notes on 3:8; 4:3, 21; 6:3, 21; and the Analysis of 3:1–13 and 6:1–9).

V. Paul's Imprisonment

One matter that impacts the question of authorship connects to the imprisonment of Paul noted three times in Ephesians (see 3:1; 4:1; 6:20). Why? Because it is important to determine whether the imprisonment mentioned in our letter matches any of the known instances of the Apostle's jail time and whether this experience links to his other references to spending time in "bonds" (see Philip. 1:7, 13–14, 16; Col. 4:3, 18; Philem. 1:1, 10). Although Paul maintained that he had spent far more time in jail

---

69. Caird, *Letters*, 14–15.

70. Bruce, *Paul: Apostle of the Heart Set Free*, 475.

71. John Muddiman, *The Epistle to the Ephesians*, Black's New Testament Commentaries (London: Continuum, 2001), 180–81.

than his Corinthian critics (see 2 Cor. 11:23), we are able to consider only three documented occasions as possible matches: in Ephesus, in Caesarea, and in Rome.

Let us look at Ephesus first, the city where Paul stayed longer—up to three years (see Acts 20:31)—than anywhere else after he began his missionary journeys. Although the book of Acts hints at no imprisonment in Ephesus, which surely would have been known to Luke, small details from Paul's letters may suggest that he underwent this kind of experience. At the end of his first letter to Corinth, the Apostle wrote, "I have fought with beasts at Ephesus," as if he had been a prisoner forced to go into the arena to struggle for his life against wild animals. If he had, he would not have survived. This line, it seems, was a metaphor for his hard labors in a city whose citizens were devotees to the Roman goddess Diana and her spectacular temple that lay nearby. After all, intense resistance to Paul led to a riot in the theater and forced him to leave the city (see Acts 19:23–20:1). Later, in his second letter to Corinth, he did not go into detail but mentioned "our trouble which came to us in Asia, that we were pressed out of measure, above strength, insomuch that we despaired even of life" (2 Cor. 1:8). In this latter case, the pronoun "we" puts other believers into the picture of a shared anxiety whose cause remains unknown. These tiny hints are intriguing. But they are blunted by one observation that arises from Paul's letter to his friend Philemon, who resided in Colossae, which lay a little more than a hundred miles east of Ephesus. While he was a prisoner, the Apostle had met Philemon's runaway slave, Onesimus. Of Onesimus, Paul wrote that he was the one "whom I have begotten in my bonds" (Philem. 1:10). The question is why would Onesimus travel only as far as Ephesus, well within reach of his owner, Philemon? It stands to reason that he would try to get as far away as possible. In light of Paul's known imprisonments, where might Onesimus have landed so that he and the Apostle would meet? What were Onesimus's options for flight? The answer: either Caesarea on the coast of ancient Palestine or Rome, where a mass of people of all classes resided.[72]

Paul underwent two years of restraint in Caesarea. Its exact nature comes to us in small clues (see Acts 24:27). He appears to have enjoyed a rather relaxed containment, at first "in Herod's judgment hall," a section of the seaside palace built by Herod (Acts 23:35). At least his friend Luke, who was in the city and documented important moments, had access to the Apostle so that he learned what had happened during Paul's appearances

---

72. Caird, *Letters*, 2–5.

before the governor and other authorities and later recorded them in the book of Acts. According to Philippians 1:20–24, during his imprisonment, Paul faced a possible death sentence and was even thinking that it might be carried out.[73] If he was in Caesarea when he met Onesimus, we possess no corroborating record that his life was in danger. Instead, the book of Acts presents the issue that drove Paul to appeal to Caesar on different grounds: whether Paul was willing to return to Jerusalem to face a Jewish court. Because he knew that certain Jews would try to kill him once he was out of Caesarea, he appealed his case to the emperor in Rome, exercising his right as a Roman citizen (see Acts 25:3, 9–12).[74]

In Rome, Paul spent two years in house confinement, where he received visitors and freely preached the gospel message (see Acts 28:30–31). His main restraint was the chain that bound his wrist to a soldier's wrist, the soldier being changed every four hours (see Acts 28:16). The question of Onesimus's location when he met the Apostle is more easily answered if he fled to Rome by traveling along the excellent roads that connected the Roman empire. After all, the mention of "the palace" and "Caesar's household" fit most naturally in Rome (see Philip. 1:13; 4:22).[75] Rome was a city of considerable size, and Onesimus could easily fit in with and disappear among the masses (see the Notes on 3:1; 4:1; 6:20).

VI. Character of the Church: External Evidences

The copious references to the church and its character in Ephesians have led some scholars to deny that Paul was the author. Why? Because, in their view, during Paul's service as an apostle, the church consisted of little more than modest-sized, scattered congregations that, first, were awaiting the return of the Lord and, second, possessed little organization, including no quorum of apostles nor a strong centralized organization at Jerusalem. Third, the church was made up of believers who met together weekly, usually in someone's home, to read a few scriptures together, to remind each other of Jesus' words, and to encourage one another. Only because Jesus did not return did these modest assemblies adopt more formal procedures

73. Caird, *Letters*, 5.
74. Contra Winger, *Ephesians*, 122–30.
75. Bruce, *Paul: Apostle of the Heart Set Free*, 389–90, 396–99; contra Caird, *Letters*, 3–4.

and ceremonies, except baptism, which had been with them from the beginning. These more formal approaches to worship came to characterize the growing church of the second century because such operations were not needed earlier, given the rather small, infant sizes of individual congregations.[76] After all, in his other letters, Paul had spent precious little space on the church and its makeup, appealing to his rather standard way of viewing the church as Christ's "body" and writing little about church officers and teachers (see Rom. 12:4–8 and 1 Cor. 12:12–31).

Against such a view must be set the fact that, within Paul's ministry (c. AD 33–65), substantial congregations had grown up in the cities of Jerusalem, Rome, Ephesus, and Antioch, to name but four. Turning to Jerusalem, the fact that Paul described his first trip back to the city so that he could communicate what he had been preaching "among the Gentiles"—that his trip was driven by God and that he had felt compelled to visit "them which were of reputation, lest by any means I . . . had run in vain" (Gal. 2:2)—illustrates the bedrock importance of the Jerusalem leadership at the time he wrote Galatians (c. AD 48). Moreover, the presence of those whom he called "pillars" in Jerusalem, consisting of James, Peter, and John (Gal. 2:9), again fortifies the significance of the Jerusalem leaders for the whole church. Next, turning to Rome, when Paul penned his letter to the believers in that city, he knew that a substantial congregation gathered there on Sundays. For he wrote that already their "faith is spoken of throughout the whole [Roman] world." In fact, so numerous and prominent were they "that without ceasing I make mention of you always in my prayers" (Rom. 1:8–9; see also Rom. 16:19).[77]

Concerning Ephesus, the church had been established in the city long before Paul arrived for his extended stay circa AD 55. Although some scholars might dispute the historicity of some of the stories and details in Acts 19, the chapter that selectively chronicles Paul's years in the city, no one doubts his deep connection to and nourishment of church members there. The riot of the silversmiths in the Ephesus theater over the loss of revenue because of the impact of Christian teachings on potential customers is one of those events that stands beyond the pale of legend or embellished story. For the incident forced Paul to leave town and head north for Macedonia (Acts 19:23–20:1). It was on the latter part of this extended journey, with

---

76. Rudolf Bultmann, *Theology of the New Testament,* 2 vols. in one, trans. Kendrick Grobel (New York: Charles Scribner's Sons, 1951, 1955), 1:53–62; 2:95–111; Helmut Koester, *Introduction to the New Testament,* 2 vols. (Berlin: Walter de Gruyter, 1982), 2:86–94.

77. For the approximate dates, I rely on Bruce, *Paul: Apostle of the Heart Set Free,* 475.

Paul traveling to Jerusalem for the last time, that Luke, the author of Acts, joined Paul's traveling party, as shown by the occurrences of the pronouns "we" and "us" (Acts 20:5–6; etc.). Concerning Antioch, if a person returns to Paul's letter to the Galatians, one sees that the Apostle was part of a large congregation that met at Antioch, his home base for much of his ministry. For in narrating the dustup between Peter and himself, Paul also inadvertently unveiled a church group there that embraced a large number of both Jews and Gentiles (Gal. 2:11–14). Hence, within the duration of Paul's ministry, the church had taken deep root in prominent cities near the eastern and northern shores of the Mediterranean Sea.

When looking for hints of a formally organized church leadership in these places, we touch again upon Paul's talk about "them which were of reputation" and the "pillars" in Jerusalem (Gal. 2:2, 9). Such "pillars" included Peter along with John, son of Zebedee and brother of James, as well as James the Lord's brother. It seems obvious that Paul himself was acknowledging these three men as a presiding group or quorum.[78] For the church in Rome, unfortunately, we possess only scraps about its ecclesiastical officers and their duties from Paul's letter to its members. But these scraps hint strongly at a current organization. For instance, in one passage we run across the term translated "office" (πρᾶξις, *praxis*), a word that means function or responsibility.[79] Following this term, we meet Paul's brief discussion about "gifts," "ministering," "teaching," and "exhortation" in the "body" of the church (Rom. 12:4–8).

At Ephesus the portrait is different and exhibits a richer texture. In Paul's last meeting with Ephesian church leaders, which occurred at Miletus, Luke recorded that Paul sent for "the elders (πρεσβύτεροι, *presbyteroi*) of the church," a plain reference to those who presided (Acts 20:17).[80] This notation does not stand within Paul's final speech to these people, a speech whose makeup could be challenged as Luke's composition even though he was present and heard Paul's words.[81] One important term that sits inside the

---

78. Karl Ludwig Schmidt, *TDNT,* 3:508.

79. Johannes P. Louw and Eugene A. Nida, *Greek-English Lexicon of the New Testament Based on Semantic Domains,* 2 vols., 2nd ed. (New York: United Bible Societies, 1989), §42.5, 8 (hereafter cited as Louw-Nida).

80. BDAG, 862–63; Louw-Nida, §53.77; Frederick Fyvie Bruce, *The Acts of the Apostles: The Greek Text with Introduction and Commentary,* 9th printing (Grand Rapids, Mich.: Eerdmans, 1979), 286; Joseph A. Fitzmyer, *The Acts of the Apostles: A New Translation with Introduction and Commentary,* vol. 31 of the Anchor Bible (New York: Doubleday, 1997), 482–83.

81. For example, Fitzmyer, *Acts of the Apostles,* 674–76.

speech is a mention of "overseers" (ἐπίσκοποι, *episkopoi*, Acts 20:28), a noun that comes to mean "bishop" in later literature (see 1 Tim. 3:2 and Titus 1:7; compare Philip. 1:1, "the bishops [*episkopoi*] and deacons"; and 1 Pet. 2:25). But in the passage that records Paul's meeting with the Ephesians elders, this word seemingly does not yet bear this more specialized, ecclesiastical meaning.[82] Thus, readers encounter language that unfolds to view a burgeoning group of church officers whose titles were not yet settled.

Now, turning our search toward Antioch, we are rewarded by discovering that "at Antioch [resided] certain prophets and teachers," the only officers noted there (Acts 13:1; see 1 Cor. 12:28–29 for an expanded list). We do not know whether any of these "prophets" were among those who had earlier come from Jerusalem, but it is probable that they were (see Acts 11:27). In the light of these passages, it becomes plain that, at a very young age in the church, both small and large congregations enjoyed a leadership structure, even if rather simple in their early histories (see the Notes on 1:22, 23; 5:27).

VII. Character of the Church: Internal Evidences

When we encounter the Ephesians epistle itself, we find ourselves looking at a more robust view of the church than in other letters, except for Colossians. The question remains, Does this observation support the notion of a letter written by someone other than Paul? The short answer is no. The longer answer requires a brief review. The first item has to do with the notion that the church is the "body" of Christ. Readers first encounter the term in the words of chapter one, "the church, which is [Christ's] body" (1:22–23). As he approached the end of the letter, the Apostle affirmed that "we are members of [Christ's] body" (5:30; see also 2:16; 4:4, 12, 16 [twice]; 5:23). Not surprisingly, Paul had touched on this idea in earlier letters, more particularly in 1 Corinthians (see Rom. 12:4–5 and 1 Cor. 12:12–27). But in Ephesians he raised the idea to the heavens where the Father had "put all things under [Christ's] feet, and gave him to be the head over all things to the church, which is his body" (1:22–23). As Gerhard Delling has reminded us, in this epistle readers come upon "an obvious development of the thought of the body" as it is set out in 1 Corinthians 12.[83] The

---

82. BDAG, 379–80; Louw-Nida, §§35.43; 53.71; Bruce, *Acts of the Apostles,* 380; Fitzmyer, *Acts of the Apostles,* 678–79.

83. Gerhard Delling, *TDNT,* 6:304.

doctrine of Christ's body in Ephesians sits on the same ground that it rests on when pointed to in Paul's other letters.

The second feature centers on church officers and how they were to aid the church. We notice initially that it was God who "gave some to be apostles, some to be prophets," and so forth (4:11 NIV). In the light of Ephesians, God was in charge of church organization. And what was its purpose? The answer: "For the perfecting of the saints, for the work of the ministry, for the edifying of the body of Christ." And what was the objective of edifying the body of Christ, the church? It was to assure that "we all come in the unity of the faith, and of the knowledge of the Son of God, unto a perfect man [and woman]." Here, the church serves as the agent for bringing church members "unto the measure of the stature of the fulness of Christ" (4:13). In this brief review, nothing stands outside the trajectory of Paul's words wherein he wrote elsewhere that "God hath set some in the church, first apostles, secondarily prophets, thirdly teachers, after that miracles, then gifts of healings, helps, governments, diversities of tongues" (1 Cor. 12:28). Karl Ludwig Schmidt, unable to decide whether Ephesians was written by the Apostle or one of his close followers, nevertheless wrote that the letter "is wholly Pauline in substance, whether written by Paul himself or one of his disciples"[84] (see the Notes on 1:23; 5:27).

VIII. Purpose and Occasion of the Letter

Trying to set out the reasons for writing Ephesians has sent commentators in a variety of directions. The simplest approach to solving the matter of why Paul wrote this letter is to stand back and see what sits in the emphatic positions. In a few words, what arises at the beginning and end of the epistle frames the emphases. At the letter's opening, a reader encounters the dazzling view of the heavens and what has occurred and will occur therein. It was there that God the Father set out his intentions "before the foundation of the world" that would open "the adoption of children by Jesus Christ unto himself" and grant to Christ's followers "redemption through his blood, the forgiveness of sins" (1:4–5, 7). More than this, at the end-time, "in the dispensation of the fulness of times," the Father will "gather together in one all things in Christ," offering to the faithful "an inheritance" in the celestial realms after being "sealed with that holy Spirit of promise"

---

84. Schmidt, *TDNT,* 3:511.

(1:10–11, 13). In this light, the Apostle plainly presented the grandeur of unfolding, celestially driven events. It was his purpose to remind his readers about unspeakable events that had swirled around them since their premortal existences and were continuing to enrich them in their earthly lives. Why? Because times were about to get rough.

Significantly, Paul did not draw readers' attention to conflict with government authorities as a source of future troubles. Instead, he anticipated that unsavory matters would arise inside the church and were apparently already beginning (see 5:3–7). Internal troubles, of course, could weaken, even cripple, congregations where church members gathered. Seeking to slow evil's penetrating power, he took up the topics that we meet in chapters five and six. This observation sends us to the next point of stress.

At the end of the letter, the second place of emphasis, Paul landed hard on the looming apostasy, whose tentacles were already reaching into the church in the form of lechery and deception (see 5:3–7). To hold this hard-charging, sable mass at bay, he appealed for strong marriages and families, not even excluding slaves who served inside the home (see 5:22–6:9). This emphasis on families brings home an important message. And how might Paul's readers meet the challenge? By becoming "imitators of God" (5:1 NR). Furthermore, they were to "put on the whole armour of God" and "stand" (6:11). Theirs would not be an easy task because it would take inspiration arising from holding to "the word of God"—that is, by embracing the scriptures and "praying always with all prayer and supplication in the Spirit" (6:17–18). In a word, church members stood on the edge of a precipice that overlooked the vast darkness of "spiritual wickedness in high places" (6:12) where their enemies would like to push them. Yes, it would become the worst of times. But the Apostle was trying to rally his associates for a spiritual combat like no other with the real possibility that they would be able to bring others to salvation before the lights went out (see the introduction to chapter 5 and the Notes on 5:5–6, 11, 12; 6:11–13).

In the heart of Ephesians sits the grand purpose of showing to Paul's Gentile readers that they belong to God's "workmanship, created in Christ Jesus unto good works" (2:10), that they are heirs of "the covenants of promise" (2:12), that they are reconciled "unto God" and therefore stand "in one body [with Jewish Christians] by the cross" (2:16), and that they enjoy equal "access by one Spirit unto the Father [and] . . . are no more strangers and foreigners, but fellowcitizens with the saints, and of the household of God" (2:18–19). All of this was brought about by the revelation of "the mystery" both to Paul and to God's "holy apostles and prophets in the Spirit . . . that the Gentiles are fellow heirs" (3:3, 5–6 NR). The church was to welcome

Gentiles into its midst to sit beside Jewish members.[85] Here we meet the Epistle's purpose—to assure Gentile converts that they have "a place and a name" within God's "house" and his "walls" (Isa. 56:5).

IX. Relationship of Ephesians and Colossians

Among the intriguing questions that arise when dealing with similar texts in the New Testament is the issue of why Ephesians and Colossians are so alike. This kind of topic comes up for discussion, for example, when treating the relationship among the synoptic Gospels (Matthew, Mark, and Luke) and between 2 Peter and Jude. Because of their parallels, including long word-for-word passages, the matter of the connection between Colossians and Ephesians pushes itself forward, demanding answers.[86]

We notice initially that the two letters exhibit elements that others of Paul's epistles do not. For example, we detect that the two letters share the trait of very long sentences that hang together because of a series of participles, a feature not seen in other epistles (see 1:3–14, 15–23; Col. 1:9–20). In them we miss both the staccato of the short sentences in Galatians when Paul was so upset and the expansive view of salvation that he painted in broad strokes in Romans. That said, the similarities point to an obvious connection between Ephesians and Colossians. In a few passages, the wording is exactly the same, including thirty-two words in the same order that are shared between Ephesians 6:21–22 and Colossians 4:7–8.[87] The question presses for an answer: Was Ephesians written first and then Colossians came about as a digest of the longer letter, or was Colossians the earlier text from which Ephesians drew material in a freely expanding manner? Most scholars hold to the latter view that Ephesians drew much of its language from Colossians. The efforts to suggest otherwise have met with little success.[88]

---

85. Caird, *Letters*, 11.

86. Helpful charts that display similarities and dissimilarities appear in Lincoln, *Ephesians*, xlix, and Winger, *Ephesians*, 131–34.

87. There are two minor exceptions. The expression "how I do" (τί πράσσω, *ti prassō*) in Eph. 6:21 does not appear in Colossians, and the words "and fellowservant" (καὶ σύνδουλος, *kai syndoulos*) in Col. 4:7 do not occur in Ephesians.

88. I. Howard Marshall, "Ephesians," in *Eerdman's Commentary on the Bible*, ed. James D. G. Dunn and John Rogerson (Grand Rapids, Mich.: Eerdmans, 2003), 1386; Morna D. Hooker, "Colossians," in *Eerdmans Commentary on the Bible*, 1404.

This state of affairs has led modern students of the New Testament to the inevitable question, Why would Paul copy from himself? The opposite question is just as relevant: Why not? If Paul was indeed the author of both Colossians and Ephesians, what is the possibility that he wrote the same or similar things? If, in fact, he wrote these two letters along with the Philemon epistle within the span of, say, a couple of weeks while imprisoned, would it not be odd for him to try to make Ephesians and Colossians as different as possible? Such a scenario of composing the letters at the same time allows readers to escape the imagined Pauline school, whose existence is unproven and whose members supposedly crafted the two epistles as statements to honor the memory of their now-deceased mentor, Paul. To be sure, substantial sections of the two compositions stand independent of the other. In a first example, the hymn to "the firstborn"—that is, the cosmic Christ in Colossians—sits as a unique piece (see Col. 1:15–20). Only a few phrases from this song have found their way into Ephesians, and not in any particular order. In a second instance, only in Colossians do we spot Paul's overt effort to turn his readers from false teachings (see Col. 2:1–3:4), whereas in Ephesians the issue is more subtle, as if evil has not yet taken up its place fully among church members (see Eph. 5:3–7). Third, the Apostle's appeal for unity in Ephesians is not matched in Colossians (see Eph. 4:3–6). A fourth example presents the most striking difference: the appeal to "put on the whole armour of God" that appears only in Ephesians and is absent from Colossians (see Eph. 6:11–17). In this brief review, it seems apparent that the messages from the Apostle for his different audiences meant tailoring his words to their needs, a feature of all his other letters (see the Note on 6:21).[89]

X. THE JOSEPH SMITH TRANSLATION (JST)

Joseph Smith's work on his translation of the New Testament impacted the letter to the Ephesians but little. Only four passages rate mention. At 3:3, we read, "How that by revelation he [God] made known unto me the mystery." The Joseph Smith Translation presents the following: "*As ye have heard* that by revelation he [God] made known unto me the mystery *of Christ*" (emphasis added). By these adjustments, Joseph Smith drew

---

89. Muddiman, *Ephesians*, 283, 296–98.

attention to Paul's calling, an event that his readers had surely heard about, and changed the focus onto "the mystery" as being about Christ, harmonizing with verse 3:4. Importantly, by this alteration some of the emphasis on the mystery as pointing to "the Gentiles," who were now "fellowheirs," is diminished, placing a stronger stress on Christ as the key in revealing the mystery of welcoming the Gentiles into God's earthly and heavenly realms.

In a second verse, 4:10, the Apostle referred to Christ's descent and ascension in these words: "He that descended is the same also that ascended up far above all heavens." The JST splashes celestial color onto the Father by rendering this verse as follows: "He who descended is the same also who ascended up *into heaven, to glorify him who reigneth over all heavens*" (emphasis added). This change folds itself into the dominant theme of this letter that elucidates and celebrates the grand role of God the Father in the unfolding of salvation to his children.

The third instance arises in 4:21 where we find the difficult line "if so be that ye have heard him [Christ]." It is as if some among Paul's readers had personally heard Jesus teach. The JST aids the reader by adjusting the verb "heard" to "learned" when we read "if so be that ye have *learned* [of] him" (emphasis added). Even though the preposition "of" has to be supplied to aid the sense of the line, the JST holds to the thought that people in Paul's audience had not heard Jesus' voice.

The fourth and final example introduces readers to one of the most puzzling statements found in scripture. It occurs at 4:26 and says, "Be ye angry, and sin not." Joseph Smith rendered this line as a question: "Can ye be angry, and not sin?" The alteration makes all the difference in how a person understands this verse (see the Notes on 3:3; 4:10, 21, 26).[90]

XI. CEREMONY AND RITUAL

A set of verbs gives life to sacred ceremonies that lie mostly out of sight in Ephesians. Those verbs are six in number: "to walk," "to sit," "to stand," "to put on," "to take up [weapons]," and "to take" or "to receive." Yes, the verb

---

90. It is important for me, Kent Brown, the author of this volume, to affirm that in the New Testament the JST does not represent a lost, original text. Instead, it clarifies and elucidates the text, occasionally supplying the backdrop of a saying or miracle of Jesus in the Gospels. Never in all my years of teaching and lecturing have I suggested that the JST restores the ancient reading of a New Testament passage.

"to walk" in our letter regularly touches on the manner of a person's walk through life—that is, how one behaves. But standing nearby is the sense of a person moving from one holy place to another during a ritual celebration. The verb "to put on" has to do with a person donning God's armor, therefore one's clothing, an act that bears sacred overtones and fits within a holy rite. And so it goes (see more in the Notes on 2:10; 4:13, 20, 22, 24; 5:2, 8, 14, 20; 6:11, 13–14, 16–17; the Analysis of 6:10–20; and appendix 1).

A person has a right to challenge this view of such verbs. After all, in Paul's other letters precious few ceremonial hints appear outside of baptism and partaking of the Eucharist or sacrament. Did not the Apostle write, "I determined not to know any thing among you, save Jesus Christ, and him crucified" (1 Cor. 2:2)? This declaration sends readers to a rather simple set of ordinances, does it not? The answer is yes and no. If we embrace the idea that this statement represents all of what Paul was about in his preaching, then we have to admit that his world of worship was very uncluttered. But indications arise particularly in his correspondence written to his converts in Thessalonica, perhaps only three weeks after he was forced to flee the city for his safety (see Acts 17:1, 10), that point unmistakably to a broad set of teachings and sacred actions. Such indicators are not to be swept aside (see appendix 1).

XII. Modern Sources

Readers of this volume will soon discover from the footnotes that citations particularly from the *Theological Dictionary of the New Testament* (*TDNT*) and less frequently from the *Theological Dictionary of the Old Testament* (*TDOT*) appear more often than references to the works of modern commentators. Without trying to put too fine a point on the matter, I can say that these two multivolume works have offered the clearest insights into the text of Ephesians. Because of their nature, the dictionaries present word studies that examine the history of words from their earliest appearances in their respective languages, Greek and Hebrew, down to their appearances in the biblical record. Within their pages, I came across a multitude of enlightening observations that enriched my own understanding and presentation in the pages that follow, observations that, I judged, belonged in this commentary. The most notable related to the enabling power of the Atonement, the spirit world, and vicarious work for the dead. Modern commentators passed over these topics in almost complete silence.

Concerning the first, what we might call the enabling power of the Atonement, modern scripture is rich in its clarity (see the Note on 1:9 and note 85 in chapter 1). Significantly, authors in the two dictionaries teased out this important concept from the Bible and led me to see its place in Paul's letters. I paired those references to a couple of modern Latter-day Saint treatments and thereby significantly augmented what I could say about certain verses in Ephesians (see the Notes on 1:9, 16, 21; 2:7, 16; 3:16; 4:30).[91]

The second topic that was treated by no fewer than fourteen authors in the *TDNT* bears on departed spirits and Christ's ministry to them. For in their world Christ reigned supreme. Once again, recent authors mentioned this topic almost not at all. This subject was raised mainly in connection with the notice of Christ's descent into the underworld in 4:9–10. What was he doing there? His purpose in visiting the spirits of the dead is set out most clearly in 1 Peter, where we read that Christ was "put to death in the flesh, but quickened by the Spirit: by which also he went and preached unto the spirits in prison" (1 Pet. 3:18–19). Why? It was so these individuals "might be judged according to men in the flesh, but live according to God in the spirit" (1 Pet. 4:6; compare Rom. 14:9 and Rev. 11:18). Of this scene, Albrecht Oepke wrote, "That a journey to the lowest regions [the spirit prison] preceded that to the upper is seldom emphasized in the NT but everywhere presupposed" (see the Notes on 3:10; 4:4–5, 9–10; 5:8; 6:1, 9).[92]

Third, the matter of vicarious work for the dead arises in Paul's famous pair of questions: "What shall they do which are baptized for the dead, if the dead rise not at all? why are they then baptized for the dead?" (1 Cor. 15:29). Again, silence reigns supreme among modern commentators on Ephesians. The exception comes in the person of Harald Riesenfeld, an author in *TDNT*. Of Paul's questions in 1 Corinthians, he observed that the attempts to sidestep the conclusion that church members were being

91. David A. Bednar, "In the Strength of the Lord," in *Brigham Young University 2001–2002 Speeches* (Provo, Utah; Brigham Young University, 2002), 121–28; Carolyn J. Rasmus, "The Enabling Power of the Atonement," *Ensign* 43, no. 3 (March 2013): 18–21; Hermann Eising, *TDOT*, 4:349, 353–55; Walter Grundmann, *TDNT*, 2:313–16; Albrecht Oepke, *TDNT*, 2:542–43; Gerhard Friedrich, *TDNT*, 2:730; Herbert Braun, *TDNT*, 6:464.

92. Albrecht Oepke, *TDNT*, 2:424; also see Joachim Jeremias, *TDNT*, 1:148–49; Gerhard Delling, *TDNT*, 1:488–89; Gerhard Friedrich, *TDNT*, 2:718–19; Albrecht Oepke, *TDNT*, 3:213; Walter Grundmann, *TDNT*, 3:399–401; Friedrich Büchsel, *TDNT*, 3:641–42; Gerhard Friedrich, *TDNT*, 3:707–8; Joachim Jeremias, *TDNT*, 3:746–47; Johannes Schneider, *TDNT*, 4:597–98; Günther Bornkamm, *TDNT*, 4:821–22; Helmut Traub, *TDNT*, 5:525–26, 533; Friedrich Hauck and Siegfried Schulz, *TDNT*, 6:577–78; and Eduard Schweizer and Friedrich Baumgärtel, *TDNT*, 7:1078–79.

baptized for the dead have failed. Rather, with good reason, a person "may suppose the candidate was baptised for himself as well as with respect to someone who had died unbaptised" (see the Notes on 3:8, 10, 19; 4:5, 9; 5:8; 6:10; and the Analysis of 3:1–13; 4:1–16).[93]

XIII. FORMAT

A brief note about format is in order. The current way to write a commentary features very long paragraphs that discuss an entire verse, with the verse number bolded as the only clue about the content of the paragraph. A reader sees a mass of undifferentiated print on a page and has to hunt through the paragraph for the few lines devoted to the word or expression of interest. The effort is mildly frustrating to the casual student because nothing inside the paragraph signals visually the topic under discussion. In the BYU New Testament Commentary, my colleagues and I have set out road maps for ease of finding the issue that a reader seeks. And what are these maps? Simply stated, we have set out the item under discussion in bold letters so that a student can quickly locate the word or line that holds interest. No hunting license is required.

---

93. Harald Riesenfeld, *TDNT,* 8:512–13; the quotation is from 8:513. See also Albrecht Oepke, *TDNT,* 1:542.

Chapter 1

INTRODUCTION

The Apostle Paul lifts our gaze into the highest heavens, toward events that took place there "before the foundation of the world" (1:4), and trains our eyes on two key results of a council meeting that took place in that far-off era. The first, as we might expect, has to do with the saving powers graciously set in motion through the Lord Jesus Christ: "redemption through his blood" (1:7) by his suffering, death, and Resurrection. The second has to do with joining Gentiles to "the commonwealth of Israel, and . . . the covenants of promise" (2:12). Israelites, who had enjoyed a long relationship with God, stood with him in earlier eras. Now Gentiles have been invited inside the covenant tent, becoming "fellow heirs" (3:6 NR; see also 4:17). These results, the Apostle assures us, were part of a master plan, "the good pleasure of [the Father's] will" (1:5), as Paul wrote it. This latter result, the invitation to Gentiles, was made possible only through Christ, by whom "we have [all] obtained an inheritance" (1:11), both Jews and Gentiles.[1]

This grand plan, especially as it affects Gentiles, is called a "mystery" throughout the letter (see 1:9; 3:3–4, 9; 6:19). This mystery, "which from the beginning of the world hath been hid in God" (3:9), has become "known unto us," and most certainly to Paul (see 3:3–4), by "the spirit of wisdom and revelation in the knowledge of [Christ]" (1:17), which is now available to all through Christ's gracious act. Importantly, that saving act, called the Atonement in modern terms, arises from "the riches of [Christ's] grace" (1:7); this grace flows from that act alone, as the oft-repeated word for grace illustrates (see 1:2, 6–7; 2:5, 7–8; 3:2, 7–8; 4:7, 29; 6:24). No person, no matter how many good works he or she may undertake, can take credit for the unspeakable free gift from Jesus Christ that has opened the celestial doors to salvation (see 2:8).

---

1. Caird, *Letters,* 32.

Further, in this chapter we are pulled high into the clouds and beyond to the celestial landscape inhabited by the Father and his Son. There we learn that we have been with them since the beginning when they chose the believing and faithful to share eternal life with them. Hence, the emphasis here rests on the majesty and power of Christ, an obvious attempt to elevate the sight of readers to the glories that the Son has made available to us and will yet offer to other believers.

Those glories arise within a heavenly inheritance (see 1:14, 18; 5:5). The idea of inheritance is at home in all ancient societies, including Israelite. What is truly distinctive in the New Testament is the insistence on adoption in preference to natural, physical descent, particularly from Abraham. The concept of adoption of a foreigner as an heir was at home in certain ancient law codes, although not in the Old Testament laws on inheritance.[2] Reading Jesus' teachings, we learn that "many shall come from the east and west, and shall sit down with Abraham, and Isaac, and Jacob, in the kingdom of heaven. But the children of the kingdom shall be cast out into outer darkness" (Matt. 8:11–12; see also Luke 13:28–29). This prospect is darkly dreary for those who claim Abraham as their founding ancestor.[3] What is more, John the Baptist had sent up a vivid warning flare earlier when he declared to his hearers, "Think not to say within yourselves, We have Abraham to our father: for I say unto you, that God is able of these stones to raise up children unto Abraham" (Matt. 3:9).

To be sure, in the Old Testament we encounter instances in which God called Israel his child. But this is not the same as adoption into a celestial inheritance. For instance, as early as the Exodus saga, Moses was commanded to say to Pharaoh, "Thus saith the Lord, Israel is my son, even my firstborn" (Ex. 4:22). Hosea later penned the lines, "When Israel was a child, then I loved him, and called my son out of Egypt" (Hosea 11:1). More than a century after Hosea, from Jeremiah's record we hear the Lord utter the words "I am a father to Israel, and Ephraim is my firstborn" (Jer. 31:9).[4]

At this juncture, we hasten to add that, according to Paul, even the children of Abraham became sons and daughters by adoption through faith, just as Abraham became God's chosen one because of his faith: "He believed in the Lord; and he counted it to him for righteousness" (Gen. 15:6). When we read Paul's majestic letter to the Romans, we run into these

---

2. Edouard Lipiński, *TDOT,* 9:323.

3. Foerster, *TDNT,* 3:782.

4. Lipiński, *TDOT,* 9:328.

words: "If the Spirit of him that raised up Jesus from the dead dwell in you, he that raised up Christ from the dead shall also quicken your mortal bodies by his Spirit." And what will be the result? As Paul declared, "As many as are led by the Spirit of God, they are the sons [and daughters] of God." Indeed, "ye have received the Spirit of adoption, whereby we cry, Abba, Father" (Rom. 8:11, 14–16). And what does this adoption consist of? It consists of "the redemption of our body" (Rom. 8:23). But this is not the whole story. For "if [we are] children, then [we are] heirs, heirs of God, and *joint heirs* with Christ" (Rom. 8:17, emphasis added).

This is exactly the picture that we meet in Ephesians, continuing and preserving the New Testament teaching of an inheritance with Christ. For we run across "the adoption of children by Jesus Christ to himself." Specifically, it is from him that "we have obtained an inheritance." This is no earthly inheritance because not our parents but the "holy Spirit of promise . . . is the earnest [guarantee] of our inheritance" (1:5, 11, 13–14). In this secure state, God "hath raised us up together, and made us sit together in heavenly places in Christ Jesus" (2:6; see appendix 2).

On a more pedestrian level, the chapter naturally falls into three parts. The first is Paul's greeting (1:1–2). The second consists of a hymn, written as one long sentence, that celebrates the premortal council and its intended effects in this world (1:3–14). The third sets out Paul's hymn-like prayer for the recipients of his letter (1:15–23). In a grammatical sense, however, we find a different arrangement. The greeting still holds as a unit. But the object of the next few verses has to do with "us" who have been the beneficiaries of Christ's gracious gifts (1:3–12). Then, at this point, Paul swivels his gaze to the recipients of his letter, "you" Gentiles (1:13–18). In a fourth section, he draws together both Gentiles and Jews to whom God's tremendous power, which is manifested in Jesus' Resurrection and subsequent exaltation, has been demonstrated (1:19–23).

"PAUL, AN APOSTLE OF JESUS CHRIST" (1:1–2)

These words of greeting mirror the language of others of Paul's letters, as we shall see below. Hence, it is natural for a person to conclude, almost unthinkingly, that the epistle comes from the Apostle. But, as we have discovered in the introduction sections I–VII, things are not so simple. The element in the greeting that especially turns scholars sideways is the question whether the words "at Ephesus" were written as part of the original greeting (1:1). The answer to this question is, Possibly not. How so? Because this phrase does not appear in the earliest and most important of the preserved manuscripts of this letter.

How shall we characterize this letter if "at Ephesus" was not originally part of the epistle? All of the ancient manuscripts, including those that omit this phrase, carry the added second-century title "To the Ephesians" for this letter. Hence, at least from the second century, Christians understood this epistle as destined for Ephesus. Nevertheless, because of the absence of this phrase in important early copies of the letter, we must still ask this question: Do we think of it as a circular letter from Paul, as others do, to be read in a number of congregations in western Asia Minor, including at Ephesus? Possibly. This view may be as accurate as any other we could propose.[5] As a further indicator that it may have been a circular letter, the epistle does not possess the feeling that Paul is writing to friends and acquaintances in a city where he spent upwards of three years (see Acts 20:31; compare Acts 19:10).

King James Translation

1 Paul, an apostle of Jesus Christ by the will of God, to the saints which are at Ephesus, and to the faithful in Christ Jesus: 2 Grace be to you, and peace, from God our Father, and from the Lord Jesus Christ.

New Rendition

1 Paul, an apostle of Christ Jesus through the will of God, to the saints who are in Ephesus and to the faithful in Christ Jesus: 2 Grace to you and peace from God our Father and our Lord Jesus Christ.

Notes on 1:1–2

1:1 *Paul, an apostle:* The placement of this name and this calling as the first words of the letter should be considered odd if, in fact, the author is someone other than Paul himself (compare 2 Cor. 1:1; Gal. 1:1; and Col. 1:1). Why? Because Paul was already well known among Christian congregations in both Asia Minor and Greece. To attempt to write in his name at a date, say, after his death at Rome in the late 60s of the first century and to pass this letter off as one written by him would be most difficult to carry out. As F. F. Bruce observed, if a disciple of Paul authored this letter, "one may add a note of surprise that such a disciple has left no other trace, with

---

5. Frederick Fyvie Bruce, *The Epistle to the Ephesians: A Verse-by-Verse Exposition* (Basingstoke, Eng.: Pickering Paperbacks, 1983), 13; Caird, *Letters,* 10, 12.

the observation that Paul's Roman imprisonment provides the most plausible *dramatic* life-setting for the letter."[6]

apostle: The term (ἀπόστολος, *apostolos*) ties to the verb ἀποστέλλω (*apostellō*), which means "to send forth" or "to send out [a representative]." Hence, the title bears the sense of an ambassador sent on an assignment, a point that Paul, in his case, makes clear in 3:1–3. Furthermore, in none of his epistles did Paul claim to be a member of the founding Twelve of the church. However, in this letter he places himself among the "apostles and prophets" to whom the special revelation about including Gentiles has come (3:5–7). Moreover, he is among the "apostles and prophets" on whom the foundation of the church rests (2:19–22). In addition, he stands within this remarkable group of men who carry on "the perfecting of the saints" and "the work of the ministry" in order to bring church members "unto the measure of the stature of the fulness of Christ" (4:11–13). Not incidentally, in modern scripture, the Lord calls him "mine apostle" (D&C 18:9), underlining the reality and significance of Paul's claim. In its Christian sense, a person becomes an apostle only through the initiative of Jesus Christ, not of other believers. Importantly, Paul always insisted that his appointment originated through Christ and no one else. His was not a calling originating through human agency (see the Notes on 2:20; 3:5; 4:11).[7]

Jesus Christ: A number of important early manuscripts preserve this reading. But others, including the earliest ($\mathfrak{P}^{46}$), preserve "Christ Jesus," perhaps the preferred reading in light of this order at the end of the verse. If so, then in this position, Christ is likely a title rather than a personal name—the equivalent of saying the Messiah Jesus.[8]

by the will of God: The point, of course, is that the will of God had manifested itself in the vision that burst onto Paul on his way to Damascus. No human agent came to him; his contact was with the divine Jesus (see 3:2; Acts 9:1–9; 22:3–11; 26:12–18; and Gal. 1:11–17). Moreover, this line

---

6. Bruce, *Paul: Apostle of the Heart Set Free,* 424, emphasis in original. Barth, *Ephesians,* 1:50, makes a similar point.

7. Karl Heinrich Rengstorf, *TDNT,* 1:398–404, 422–43; BDAG, 120–22; Louw-Nida, §§33.194, 53.74; Best, *Critical and Exegetical Commentary on Ephesians,* 96–97; Fowl, *Ephesians,* 32–33; Nibley, *Apostles and Bishops,* 1–23.

8. Barth, *Ephesians,* 1:66; William J. Larkin, *Ephesians: A Handbook on the Greek Text* (Waco, Tex.: Baylor University Press, 2009), 1; Best, *Ephesians,* 97. Friedrich Blass and Albert Debrunner, *A Greek Grammar of the New Testament and Other Early Christian Literature,* trans. Robert W. Funk (Chicago: University of Chicago Press, 1961), §260(1), hold a different view, calling the expression "a proper name."

"expresses with striking brevity and force the complete subjection of his ministry to his [divine] commission" (see the Notes on 1:5; 2:3; 5:17; 6:6).[9]

saints: This term, which bears the meaning "holy ones" (ἅγιοι, *hagioi*), always appears in the plural and carries the sense of those "called" by God for his special purposes (see 1 Cor. 1:2). It ultimately derives from the Old Testament concept of a people who are set apart by a covenant with God (see Ex. 19:6; Deut. 7:6; 33:3; Ps. 31:23; etc.). Because the letter is addressed to Gentiles, by writing "saints," Paul brings these people fully within the circle of the people of God (see the Notes on 1:18; 2:19; 5:26).[10]

the saints which are: The expression is strange if it stands alone without the phrase "at Ephesus" completing its meaning (see Philip. 1:1, "the saints . . . which are at Philippi"). If we omit the phrase "at Ephesus" (see the Note below), then the sense may be something like "those who really are saints," perhaps capturing the elevated sense of "saints" in 1 Corinthians, "sanctified in Christ Jesus, called to be saints" (1 Cor. 1:2;[11] see the Note on 1:13). But further on in the letter, the main distinction between groups of church members lies between Gentiles and Jews, not the more faithful and the less, thus weakening the earlier point (see 2:11–16). Among the surviving texts of this letter, two readings vie for the original reading. One reading, called the A text, says, "To the saints who are in Ephesus and faithful." The B text reads, "To those who are saints and faithful." On grammatical grounds, neither is satisfactory. The expression that causes trouble in both is the dative form of "who are" (τοῖς οὖσιν, *tois ousin*). All manuscripts preserve these two words and have given commentators much to talk about, with no fully satisfactory explanation.[12]

at Ephesus: As noted earlier, this phrase is omitted in some of the earliest manuscripts of this epistle, including 𝔓[46], ℵ*, B*, Origen, and presumably Marcion. As late as the fourth century, Basil of Caesarea in Asia Minor, known as Basil the Great (c. AD 330–79), reported that none of the early manuscripts he had seen bore this phrase.[13] If we also reckon the rather

---

9. Rengstorf, *TDNT*, 1:438; Gottlob Schrenk, *TDNT*, 3:59; the quotation is from the latter source.

10. Caird, *Letters*, 31; Barth, *Ephesians*, 1:66; Fowl, *Ephesians*, 33; BDAG, 10–11; Louw-Nida, §11.27.

11. Richard D. Draper and Michael D. Rhodes, *Paul's First Epistle to the Corinthians,* Brigham Young University New Testament Commentary (Provo, Utah: BYU Studies, 2017), 65–66.

12. Blass and Debrunner, *Greek Grammar,* §413(3); Best, *Ephesians,* 98–99; Lincoln, *Ephesians,* 2–4.

13. Quasten, *Patrology*, 3:209–10; Bruce M. Metzger, *A Textual Commentary on the Greek New Testament, Second Edition: A Companion Volume to the United Bible Societies' Greek New*

impersonal nature of the letter, possibly not sent to people whom Paul had brought into the church and therefore had known well during his years in Ephesus (see 1:15; 3:2; 4:21; and Acts 20:31), it may be reasonable to conclude that the Epistle was not written to church members whom he knew in that city.[14] This said, however, we notice that all ancient manuscripts of this letter bear the second-century title "To the Ephesians," inviting another explanation. If we omit the phrase "in Ephesus," we create "a grammatical anomaly." For we see that the Greek participle οὖσιν (*ousin*) lacks a predicate, a situation that "goes against Paul's normal practice, particularly in his letter openings (Rom 1:7; Phil[ip] 1:1; cf. 1 Cor 1:2; 2 Cor 1:1)."[15] On this basis, perhaps we need to hold onto the phrase "in Ephesus" rather than discard it.

faithful: When the Greek adjective πιστός (*pistos*) means "believing," it is usually followed by an object—believing something. Here, the term stands absolute, without an object.[16] Concerning its application to Paul's audience, being "saints" or holy ones as well as faithful people arises directly from their relationship to Jesus Christ.[17] Moreover, the translation "and to the faithful" in the KJV and New Rendition fits with the view that this letter was a circular message to church members in Asia Minor rather than one sent only to believers in Ephesus. If a person holds the opinion that the epistle was not addressed to the Ephesian Saints, then the translation "to the saints who are also faithful" is preferred.

in Christ Jesus: The basis of the enduring, eternal fellowship of the Saints and the faithful lies in their commitment to the Savior. For Christians, this lasting link to one another does not arise from family or clan or nationality but from the covenant made at baptism.[18]

1:2 *Grace . . . and peace:* These two terms, χάρις . . . καὶ εἰρήνη (*charis . . . kai eirēnē*), are the elements of a "two-membered oriental formula of greeting" that predates Paul and his fellow Christians.[19]

from God . . . and from the Lord: Although to a casual reader these expressions may seem to be words of a common greeting (see 1 Cor. 1:3; 2 Cor. 1:2; Gal. 1:3; etc.), they appear to be more. For they strongly hint at

Testament (Fourth Revised Edition) (Stuttgart: Deutsche Bibelgesellschaft, 2016), 532. See Basil, *Adversus Eunomium*, 2:19.

14. Caird, *Letters*, 9–10; Lincoln, *Ephesians*, 1–2.

15. Larkin, *Handbook*, 2; see also Benjamin L. Merkle, *Exegetical Guide to the Greek New Testament: Ephesians* (Nashville, Tenn.: B&H Academic, 2016), 5–6.

16. Rudolf Bultmann, *TDNT*, 6:204, 214; BDAG, 820–21.

17. BDAG, 820–21; Fowl, *Ephesians*, 34.

18. Hans Freiherr von Soden, *TDNT*, 1:144 n. 1; Albrecht Oepke, 2:541–42.

19. Hans Conzelmann and Walther Zimmerli, *TDNT*, 9:394.

a personal acquaintance with the Father and the Son that transcends mere verbal acknowledgments, much like Nephi intermittently quoting words that he has heard from the Father and the Son as he treats the texture of the doctrine of Christ (see 2 Ne. 31:2, 10–12, 14–15, 20).

"BEFORE THE FOUNDATION OF THE WORLD" (1:3–14)

The exalted language of this next section points to events that unfolded during the premortal council as well as to events that have followed in the mortal sphere, especially to those tied to the ministry of Jesus Christ.[20] For, as this section illustrates, he stands at the center of all. In a celebratory manner, likely quoting a hymn-like formula of early Christian origin[21] that forms one long sentence, Paul enlightens our understanding of how the Savior (a title that does not appear here) fulfills the Father's plan—"the precosmic plan of God" in G. B. Caird's words[22]—and opens the gates of heaven to all, including to Gentiles. It is the teaching of these people, the Gentiles, that remained the special charge of Paul (see 3:1–9; Acts 9:15–16; and Gal. 1:15–16; 2:1–2, 9).

The keys to grasping that this section focuses on the premortal council lie in the Greek verbs and nouns that begin with a προ- (*pro-*) prefix, a prefix that in the New Testament mainly has to do with "before" in the temporal sense but occasionally means "in front of" in the spatial sense.[23] Among the verbs, we find προορίζω (*proorizō*) in 1:5 and 1:11 ("to foreordain"), προτίθημι (*protithēmi*) in 1:9 ("to set before"), and προελπίζω (*proelpizō*) in 1:12 ("to be the first to hope"). Two nouns also come up for notice: the first, πρὸ καταβολῆς (*pro katabolēs*), in a prepositional phrase in 1:4 ("before the foundation") and the second, πρόθεσις (*prothesis*), in 1:11 ("purpose" or "plan"). All of these terms hold up to our view an event, or series of events, in the premortal sphere that led to the atoning ministry of Jesus Christ.

---

20. Rodney Turner, "Grace, Mysteries, and Exaltation," in *Studies in Scripture, Volume Six: Acts to Revelation*, ed. Robert L. Millet (Salt Lake City: Deseret Book, 1987), 108–9, points to "those councils of heaven," holding that Christ's church was organized in the premortal realm and individuals were "given" to Christ there. See Anderson, *Understanding Paul*, 264–65.

21. Herbert Preisker, *TDNT*, 2:588; Walter Grundmann, Franz Hesse, Marinus de Jonge, and Adam Simon van der Woude, *TDNT*, 9:559. Barth, *Ephesians*, 1:97, calls these verses a "benediction" in the Jewish sense of the term.

22. Caird, *Letters*, 40; see also Gerhard Delling, *TDNT*, 9:592–93.

23. Blass and Debrunner, *Greek Grammar*, §213.

King James Translation

3 Blessed be the God and Father of our Lord Jesus Christ, who hath blessed us with all spiritual blessings in heavenly places in Christ: 4 According as he hath chosen us in him before the foundation of the world, that we should be holy and without blame before him in love: 5 Having predestinated us unto the adoption of children by Jesus Christ to himself, according to the good pleasure of his will, 6 To the praise of the glory of his grace, wherein he hath made us accepted in the beloved. 7 In whom we have redemption through his blood, the forgiveness of sins, according to the riches of his grace; 8 Wherein he hath abounded toward us in all wisdom and prudence; 9 Having made known unto us the mystery of his will, according to his good pleasure which he hath purposed in himself: 10 That in the dispensation of the fulness of times he might gather together in one all things in Christ, both which are in heaven, and which are on earth; even in him: 11 In whom also we have obtained an inheritance, being predestinated according to the purpose of him who worketh all things after the counsel of his own will: 12 That we should be to the praise of his glory, who first trusted in Christ. 13 In whom ye also trusted, after that ye heard the word of truth, the gospel of your salvation: in whom also after that ye believed, ye were sealed with that holy Spirit of promise, 14 Which is the earnest of our inheritance until the redemption of the purchased possession, unto the praise of his glory.

New Rendition

3 Blessed is the God and Father of our Lord Jesus Christ, who blessed us with every spiritual blessing in the heavenly realms in the presence of Christ 4 when he chose us in him before the foundation of the universe to be holy and unblemished before him in love, 5 having preordained us for adoption as children unto himself through Jesus Christ, according to the benevolence of his will. 6 For the praise of his glorious grace which he showered upon us by his Beloved!

7 In him we have redemption through his blood—the dismissal of transgressions—according to the riches of his grace 8 which he has lavished upon us. In all wisdom and prudence, 9 he made known to us the mystery of his will, according to his benevolence which he appointed beforehand in Christ 10 for the administration of the fullness of times, to sum up all things in Christ—things in the heavenly realms and things on the earth in him. 11 In him also we were appointed a heritage, having been preordained according to the plan of the one enacting all things according to the design of his will: 12 that we, who have already hoped in Christ, might be for the praise of his glory.

13 In him—after you heard the word of truth (the gospel of your salvation) and believed—you were sealed by the Holy Spirit of Promise, 14 which is a guarantee of our inheritance, confirming the redemption of his possession. To the praise of his glory!

Notes on 1:3–14

1:3 *Blessed be the God and Father:* With this verse, Paul comes to his message of celestial reassurance—that is to say, that the divine world connects directly to our world. What happens in that heavenly place affects us in wonderfully powerful ways, graciously conferring on us "all spiritual blessings" through an "adoption . . . by Jesus Christ to himself" and by the "redemption through his blood," which consists of the stunning gift of "the forgiveness of sins" and leads to "an inheritance" with God (1:5, 7, 11, 14). Paul also establishes the main actor in salvation history: God the Father (see 1:17–22). He is its author, he is its director, he is its inspiration (see John 7:16–17; 8:15–19, 25–29, 38–42; Moses 1:6, 32–33; 2:1; etc.).

The opening of this verse mirrors exactly 2 Corinthians 1:3 as well as 1 Peter 1:3. Such a line bears liturgical meaning because similar expressions appear in the Old Testament in worship settings. Hence, we find ourselves pulled along by rhythmic patterns, such as "according to his good pleasure" (1:5, 9) and "to the praise of his glory" (1:6, 12, 14).[24] Further, "the God and Father" are the same person, not to be separated as if two persons, as we see in "One God and Father of all" (4:6; see the Notes on 4:5–6).

of our Lord Jesus Christ: Although the phrase may be understood as formulaic and thus little more than convention, in fact it underlines the real relationship of Jesus Christ to God: Son and Father, mirroring other New Testament passages (see Matt. 3:17; 17:5; Mark 1:11; 9:7; Luke 3:22; 9:35; John 17:1–5; Rom. 1:1–4; 1 Cor. 1:3–4; etc.).

who hath blessed us: The question arises, When did God bless us in a special way "with all spiritual blessings in heavenly places"? On earth? Possibly, but not likely. The most natural answer is in heaven. If so, what was the occasion? Again, the most natural answer is at or near the time of the premortal council where "he chose us" and "preordained us" (1:4, 5 NR; see also the Note on 3:9; Jer. 1:5; Gal. 1:15; Moses 4:1–3; and Abr. 3:21–28; compare Isa. 49:1, 5; 1 Cor. 2:7; and 1 Pet. 1:1–2; 2:8).[25]

all spiritual blessings: The text reads "every spiritual blessing," the singular εὐλογία (*eulogia*) for "blessing," and could carry the sense of "a willing gift" (see 2 Cor. 9:5 RSV; compare "a generous gift" NIV).[26] We are to

---

24. Caird, *Letters,* 32–33. For a sampling of similar expressions beginning with "Blessed," see Gen. 9:26; 24:27; Ex. 18:10; Mark 11:9–10; Luke 1:68; 19:38; Alma 7:4; etc.

25. John L. Lund, "Council in Heaven," in *Encyclopedia of Mormonism,* ed. Daniel H. Ludlow, 4 vols. (New York: Macmillan, 1992), 1:328–29 (hereafter cited as *EM*).

26. BDAG, 408–9; Louw-Nida, §57.105.

reckon among such blessings receiving "redemption through [Jesus'] blood, the forgiveness of sins" (1:7), being "sealed with that holy Spirit of promise" (1:13), obtaining "an [exalted] inheritance" (1:11, 14), receiving "access by one Spirit unto the Father" (2:18), and being "raised . . . up together, [to] . . . sit together in heavenly places" where Christ is seated (2:6).

in heavenly places: A better sense may be "in heavenly realms" because of the context. The Greek plural expression ἐν τοῖς ἐπουρανίοις (*en tois epouraniois*) means literally "in the heavenlies." (The phrase occurs also in 1:20; 2:6; 3:10; 6:12.) On the one hand, we are dealing with the celestial regions both where action took place in a premortal setting and where bold action occurs that not only assists us in our present personal struggles but also will settle important issues at the end-time (see 6:12). The future triumphs of Jesus in all realms—in heaven, on the earth, and under the earth—will make it possible for us to take our places with him (see 2:6–7; 4:7–10; and Philip. 2:10; 3:20–21).[27] On the other hand, the expression in Ephesians always has to do with a place, a locale. That is, it is the place of Christ's throne (1:20), the location of the thrones of those raised to be with Christ (2:6), the locale of "the principalities and powers" in the unseen world (3:10), and possibly the place of "powers" hostile to the Saints (6:11–13).[28] Hence, one gets the sense that, except possibly an abode that houses inimical forces, Paul is here pointing to a celestial locale prepared for the faithful, elsewhere called "mansions" in the house of the Father (see John 14:2; D&C 59:2; 72:4; etc.; the Notes on 1:20; 2:6; 3:10; 6:12; and the Analysis of 1:15–23).

in Christ: This phrase stands as the grand key to understanding all else in the epistle.[29] For Paul, in the living center of creation stands the Christ, the Messiah, who makes all else possible by his ineffable gifts to mortals. The repeated phrase "in whom" that we meet later (see 1:7, 11) ties back to this expression, "in Christ" (see the Notes on 1:7, 11, 13).[30] Taking the title Christ (Χριστῷ, *Christō*) as a dative of place, we come to the meanings "in the presence of Christ" or "in fellowship with Christ," each of which offers an intriguing possibility for seeing a premortal event.[31]

---

27. Helmut Traub and Gerhard von Rad, *TDNT,* 5:538–42; BDAG, 388.
28. Barth, *Ephesians,* 1:78–79.
29. Caird, *Letters,* 34.
30. Larkin, *Handbook,* 6–7, 9, 13, 15.
31. Joseph H. Thayer, *Thayer's Greek-English Lexicon of the New Testament,* rpt. of 4th ed. (Peabody, Mass.: Hendrickson's Publishers, 2017), 211.

1:4 *chosen:* Being chosen puts a person among the elect, as it were, joining the Savior, who stands as the Elect One.[32] In this instance, the chosen ones are linked to God's choice of Jesus because both actions of choosing occurred in the premortal realm, both for him (see Moses 4:1–4 and Abr. 3:27–28) and for those chosen. The potential blessings opened to those thus identified are "that we should be holy and without blame" (1:4), that we receive "the adoption of children [through] Jesus Christ" (1:5), that "we have redemption through his blood" (1:7), and that we obtain "the mystery of his will" (1:9). Among the responsibilities of those chosen—and responsibilities do come with being selected—is to "bring forth fruit" for Christ (John 15:16). In an enlightening passage from modern scripture that underscores this observation, as it applies specifically to Abraham in a premortal setting, we read that "I [God] came down in the beginning in the midst of all the intelligences . . . and among all these there were many of the noble and great ones. And God saw these souls that they were good, . . . and he said: These I will make my rulers; . . . and he said unto me: Abraham, thou art one of them; thou wast chosen before thou wast born" (Abr. 3:21–23; see also Jer. 1:4–5 and the Notes on 1:3, 6).

chosen us: The responsibilities of election, which underlie this expression, were first carried by the Savior, who bore "the whole burden of the world's sin, shame, and sorrow."[33] He has now chosen others to join him. In one sense, as the Elect One he stands on the other side of the divide between the divine and the human because he did for us in the Atonement what we could not do for ourselves—bringing us to the Father and to salvation. In another sense, he stands with us on our turf. How so? Because as he lifted and aided those around him, so we are to lift and aid those around us. And he assists us in that effort.

before the foundation of the world: This notation frames the beginning point in time for these poetic lines, long before the Creation (see 3:9).[34] This expression, in the first instance, applies particularly to Jesus, who, as the Chosen One in premortal life, received the nourishing love of the Father (see John 17:24) and "was foreordained before the foundation

---

32. S. Kent Brown, *The Testimony of Luke,* Brigham Young University New Testament Commentary (Provo, Utah: BYU Studies, 2015), 478, 811–12, and 1079, on Luke 9:35; 18:7; and 23:35.

33. Caird, *Letters,* 35.

34. Albert Debrunner, Hermann Kleinknecht, Otto Procksch, Gerhard Kittel, Gottfried Quell, and Gottlob Schrenk, *TDNT,* 4:175. For other examples of this line, see John 17:24; 1 Pet. 1:20; D&C 124:33, 41; 127:2; 128:5; 132:5, 63; Moses 5:57; see also Abr. 1:3.

of the world" (1 Pet. 1:20; see also Moses 5:57). Second, celestial laws that would bring blessings to people in the terrestrial sphere were "appointed" before the Creation (D&C 132:5, 63; see also Abr. 1:3). Third, things hidden and revealed only in a later era, including essential ordinances, such as baptism for the dead, were "instituted from before the foundation of the world" (D&C 124:33, 41; 128:5). Fourth, during this long-ago, premortal era, people like the prophets Jeremiah, Paul, and Joseph Smith were foreordained to their work (see Jer. 1:5; Gal. 1:15–16; and D&C 127:2; see also Isa. 49:1, 5; 1 Cor. 2:7; 1 Pet. 1:1–2; 2:8; Abr. 3:21–23; and the Note on 2:10).[35] According to Jewish literature, certain elements that appear in this world were created before the world was. They include the Torah or law of Moses, God's throne of glory, the patriarchs, Israel, the temple, and the name of the Messiah.[36] The idea behind these instances is that the world, including the universe, was created for these elements because of their unparalleled importance for the human race, an evidence of God's continuous concern for our welfare.

holy and without blame: Unlike a common view that, for a believer, this state of holiness and blamelessness is the result of "undeserved forgiveness" through free grace,[37] this condition clearly implies the believer's earlier genuine repentance. To be sure, we receive "forgiveness of sins" through Jesus' Atonement, "through his blood" alone (1:7) and not through any act of our own. Yet, access to his ineffable gift comes about when we repent, as Jesus himself reminds us (see Mark 1:14–15). To return to our expression, the same two terms (ἅγιος and ἄμωμος, *hagios* and *amōmos*) appear at 5:27 in connection with the cleansed and perfected church because of the people in it, "not having spot, or wrinkle" (see the Note on 5:27). Hence, these terms make us think of links to what the church offers to its members, whether the ongoing rhythms of redeeming ritual or the soul-feeding fellowship therein (see Col. 1:21–23 and the Analysis of 1:3–14).[38]

without blame: The first sense of the Greek term ἄμωμος (*amōmos*) is "without blemish" (Hebrew תמימים *temimim*), as in the case of a sacrificial animal (see LXX Ex. 29:1; LXX Lev. 1:3, 10; 3:1; LXX Num. 19:2; etc.). Thus,

---

35. Hermann Sasse, *TDNT,* 3:885; compare Anderson, *Understanding Paul,* 264–65.

36. Jacob Neusner, *Genesis Rabbah: The Judaic Commentary to the Book of Genesis, a New American Translation,* 3 vols. (Atlanta, Ga.: Scholars Press. 1985), 1:10–12, cited in Debrunner, Kleinknecht, Procksch, Kittel, Quell, and Schrenk, *TDNT,* 4:175 n. 112; Caird, *Letters,* 35.

37. Caird, *Letters,* 35.

38. Best, *Ephesians,* 121–22.

even though the context here has mainly to do with blamelessness in a moral sense, a sturdy strand ties this term to sacred rituals and celebrations, bringing temple links into Paul's message (see the Notes on 1:20; 2:6, 21). Elsewhere, as we might expect, the word characterizes Jesus, whose "precious blood," spilled in temple-like sacrifice, has "redeemed" us "as of a lamb without blemish" (1 Pet. 1:18–19; see also Heb. 9:14).[39]

before him: The general sense of this improper preposition (κατενώπιον, *katenōpion*) is "in the presence of," meaning in the presence of God. Here, the term likely bears a spatial sense of a person either before a temple altar, which represents the presence of God, or before the veil of the temple, which both hides and discloses the presence of God (see LXX Lev. 4:17 and LXX Dan. 5:22; compare Luke 1:75 and Col. 1:22).[40]

in love: This phrase may go with this verse or with the next. The love seems to be God's love for us rather than our love for him. If so, then the import is "because of his love for us" or "through his love for us." The other passages wherein the phrase "in love" brings a conclusion to a concept or ends a sentence occur at 3:17, 4:2, 4:15, and 4:16. In these cases, it is the love that believers share with others, except at 3:17, where the love appears to be two-way: from God and Christ to us and from us to them[41] (see the Note on 3:17).

1:5 *predestinated:* The meaning of the Greek verb προορίζω (*proorizō*), here an active participle, is "to foreordain" (see Rom. 8:28–30; the Notes on 1:11; 2:10),[42] a doctrine that receives clarity and reinforcement in the book of Jeremiah, where the Lord says to the prophet, "Before I formed thee in the belly I knew thee; and before thou camest forth out of the womb I . . . ordained thee a prophet unto the nations" (Jer. 1:5).[43] In addition, we find a similar concept in the book of Abraham, an ancient scriptural text translated in the modern era. There we read that Abraham and

---

39. BDAG, 56; B. Kedar-Kopfstein, *TDOT,* 15:699–711; Klaus Koch, *TLOT,* 3:1424–28.

40. BDAG, 531; Blass and Debrunner, *Greek Grammar,* §214(5); see also Barth, *Ephesians,* 1:80.

41. Barth, *Ephesians,* 1:371.

42. Gottlob Schrenk, *TDNT,* 1:635; Karl Ludwig Schmidt, *TDNT,* 5:456; Barth, *Ephesians,* 1:105–7; Best, *Ephesians,* 123–24. In contrast, on p. 146, Best suggests that the term "probably . . . does not refer to 'ordination' within the time between creation and prior to the coming of Christ."

43. The verb translated "ordained" in Jer. 1:5 is a past-tense form of the Hebrew verb נתן (*natan*), which means at base "to extend the hand." In its ritual sense, it has to do with consecration or setting apart; see Edouard Lipiński and Heinz-Josef Fabry, *TDOT,* 10:90–91, 102–7.

other "noble and great ones" were "chosen before [they were] born" to be God's leaders in mortality (Abr. 3:22–23; see also Gal. 1:15–16; compare Isa. 49:1, 5; 1 Cor. 2:7; and 1 Pet. 1:1–2; 2:8). The concept that God determines a person's eternal fate in advance of being born, known as predestination—that embraces the notion that a person's eternal destiny arises from "the result of some sort of a divine roll of the dice"[44]—is contrary to the scriptural teaching that free agency is a gift that comes from Jesus Christ (see John 8:36 and 2 Ne. 2:27). Starting with the premortal council, Jesus stood against Satan's plan that proposed to "redeem all mankind, that [by compulsion] one soul shall not be lost" (Moses 4:1). Moreover, it becomes clear that free agency was a characteristic of premortal life because fully a third of the spirits chose to follow Satan, engaging first in conflict and thereafter being forced to depart from God's presence (see Rev. 12:7–9; Moses 4:3–4; Abr. 3:28; and D&C 29:36). Further, we learn from the prophet Lehi, as he muses on the grand acts of creation, that because "the Messiah" will "redeem the children of men from the fall . . . they have become free forever, knowing good from evil; to act for themselves" (2 Ne. 2:26; see also 2 Ne. 10:23; Mosiah 5:7–8; Alma 58:40–41; Hel. 14:30; D&C 29:39; 93:31–32; etc.). Hence, Jesus is the source and guarantor of freedom to decide and to act. He impels no one to heaven. Or to hell.[45]

unto the adoption of children: This phrase in Greek (εἰς υἱοθεσίαν, *eis huiothesian*) bears the simple meaning "for adoption." At play here is the concept that Paul has spelled out elsewhere that we are "joint-heirs with Christ" (Rom. 8:17). There Paul set out the principle that, in Christ, we are adopted and thereby become "the children of God" (Rom. 8:15–16; see also Gal. 4:1–9) and therefore heirs of celestial glory. Said another way, we are to receive a celestial "inheritance" (1:11); that is, after repenting and making covenants with him, we become "the children of Christ, his sons and his daughters" (Mosiah 5:7). Through this adoption process, which is not metaphorical but real,[46] we shall come to where Christ is, enjoying "all that [the] Father hath" (D&C 84:38; see also the Note on 1:11).

In a different but related vein, in the wider Roman world, poor people could adopt children, often by picking them up from rubbish heaps and keeping them alive. They needed no formal ceremony. Within the empire,

---

44. Fowl, *Ephesians,* 49.

45. C. Terry Warner, "Agency," in *EM,* 1:26–27; David E. Bohn, "Freedom," in *EM,* 2:525–27.

46. Barth, *Ephesians,* 1:80–81.

adoption was "a strategy for binding clans to one another, as well as for making good genetic defects"[47]—that is, for ridding genetic defects from the next generation of an afflicted family. Most notably, beginning with Julius Caesar, emperors adopted sons as a means of identifying the persons whom those emperors wanted as successors.[48] Obviously, the doctrine as taught by Paul carved a different furrow than did Roman practices, literally bringing the person into the family of Jesus himself. But, as in Roman law, it was as if the person went through a new birth, with all previous debts forgiven, thus entering a new life.[49]

by Jesus Christ to himself: The adoption process ultimately leads a believer to Jesus through his Father, as Paul wrote to other church members: "Ye have received the Spirit of adoption, . . . that we are the children of God: And if children, then heirs; heirs of God, and joint-heirs with Christ" (Rom. 8:15–17). Importantly, this adoption applies to Gentiles who, like a wild olive tree, are grafted into the main Israelite olive tree and thereby become part of the people of God (see Rom. 11:13–25).

good pleasure: Both the Greek noun (εὐδοκία, *eudokia*) and the Hebrew noun (רצון, *ratson*) bear the sense of goodwill or favor. Not incidentally, the related Greek verb (εὐδοκέω, *eudokeō*) appears in the baptismal and Transfiguration accounts with the sense "well pleased" (Matt. 3:17; 17:5; Mark 1:11; Luke 3:22). Within the Old Testament, through the Hebrew term, one encounters regular ties to the temple and its ceremonies wherein the sacrificial animals are to be without blemish so that God receives them as acceptable and favorable and so that worshipers find favor in God's sight (see Lev. 19:5–8; Ps. 51:17–18; Micah 6:7; and Mal. 1:10). Furthermore, this favorable sense is to extend even to the flesh of the animal that the worshipers will eat so that it is appropriate for them to partake as they establish covenants with God (see Lev. 22:26–33). Thus, through the equivalent term in Hebrew, we discover a further link to temple interests.[50] We see another temple connection in LXX Haggai 1:8, wherein the Lord will "take

---

47. Anthony Everitt, *Augustus: The Life of Rome's First Emperor* (New York: Random House, 2006), 50.

48. Adolf Berger and Barry Nicholas, "Adoptio," in *The Oxford Classical Dictionary,* ed. N. G. L. Hammond and H. H. Scullard, 2nd ed. (Oxford: Oxford University Press, 1970), 8–9 (hereafter cited as *OCD2*).

49. David J. Williams, *Paul's Metaphors: Their Context and Character* (Peabody, Mass.: Hendrickson Publishers, 1999), 64–66.

50. Gottlob Schrenk, *TDNT,* 2:745–47; Hans M. Barstad, *TDOT,* 13:626–27; Gillis Gerleman, *TLOT,* 3:1260–61.

pleasure" (εὐδοκέω) when his house, which has lain in ruins, is properly constructed.

the good pleasure of his will: This formulation has to do with God's will as it was framed "before the foundation of the world" (1:4) in the pre-mortal council, wherein many counseled together and adopted a plan for the salvation of the human race (see the Notes on 1:4, 11; Moses 4:1–3; Abr. 3:27–28; and D&C 29:36–37). This observation is made plain in Paul's later expression "[God] worketh all things after the counsel of his own will" (1:11). Moreover, the implication is clear that God derives joy in warmly offering to his children the blessings that Paul identified here.[51]

will: Precisely, God's will is to make "children" out of us through the spiritual process of "adoption." That process, of course, makes us "accepted in the beloved" and offers "redemption through his blood" (1:6–7). Adding these together, we come very close to the declaration found in Moses 1:39, though in different words, that "this is my [God's] work and my glory—to bring to pass the immortality and eternal life of man" (see the Notes on 1:1; 2:3; 5:17; 6:6).

1:6 *To the praise of the glory:* Almost identical expressions appear in 1:12 and 1:14, "to the praise of his glory." These word clusters close off the three sections of the prayer, one devoted to the Father (see 1:3–6), one to the Son (see 1:7–12), and the last to the Holy Spirit (see 1:13–14).[52]

praise: In this context, the singing of praise embraces, first, our fore-ordination to be adopted as "children by Jesus Christ" in the premortal life (1:5) and, second, the moment that we "first trusted in Christ" as new converts (1:12). Further, praise celebrates events of the end-time when God himself will offer praise to those who have lived their lives as he has asked and we shout praise at the final redemption (see Rom. 2:29; 1 Cor. 4:5; 1 Pet. 1:7; and D&C 75:5; and the Notes on 1:12, 14). The appearance of this term (ἔπαινος, *epainos*), particularly in its connection with the word for glory (δόξα, *doxa*), further solidifies the liturgical or hymnic character of this passage. For praise forms the most common occasion for singing the psalms and other hymns (see Ps. 22:3, 25; 35:27; and D&C 136:28). In addition, these two characteristics, praise and glory, are said to surround God's presence, his throne (see 1 Chr. 16:27; Ezek. 1:28; and Rev. 4:9).[53]

51. Schrenk, *TDNT,* 2:744; Barth, *Ephesians,* 1:81.
52. Winger, *Ephesians,* 192–93.
53. Preisker, *TDNT,* 2:587–88.

glory: The concept of glory (δόξα, *doxa*) is multifaceted. Its sense as a heavenly radiance is a late meaning that arises only in the New Testament era.[54] Initially, in its Hebrew form, either as a verb or a noun (כבד and כבוד, *kaved* and *kavod*), glory has to do with weightiness, whether referring to a person's honor that he or she has won among other mortals or whether touching on God's weightiness because of who he is. One of its senses is the "being of God." This notion opens up an interesting possibility that is little discussed. In Isaiah 17:3–4, we see the "glory of the children of Israel" and "the glory of Jacob" as their flesh, their bodies (see also Isa. 10:16, 18). It is a short but intriguing step to suggest that God's glory, at least in part, also has to do with his embodiment, with his physical weight and presence (see Ex. 29:43; 40:34–35; Lev. 9:23; etc.).[55] This idea is not as far-fetched as it may appear initially, for, as we have seen, the Hebrew verb and its associated noun carry the meaning of physical heaviness.[56] Perhaps germane and perhaps not, in some Old Testament passages God's glory is revealed in the power of thunderstorms, which unveil his control of nature (see Ex. 19:16 and Ps. 29:3–8; 97:1–5; compare Ex. 24:15–17 and Judg. 5:4).[57] In this connection, we notice the intriguing language from modern scripture: "How oft have I called upon you . . . by the voice of thunderings, and by the voice of lightnings, and by the voice of tempests, . . . and great hailstorms" (D&C 43:25; see also Ps. 29:3, "the God of glory thundereth"; and D&C 87:6; 88:90; 133:21–22).[58]

Knowing that Paul's language background included Aramaic, a Semitic tongue, even though he wrote in Greek and spoke the language fluently, lends color to certain words and phrases. In this case, the Old Testament expression כבוד אדוני (*kavod Adonai*), usually translated "glory of the Lord," not only denotes "the [physical, weighty] presence of the Lord" (see Ex. 16:10; 24:15–18; 40:34–35; and Ps. 8:4–6)[59] but also represents a human form and is at home in the temple (see Ezek. 1:26, 28; 43:1–9).[60] The plain

---

54. Gerhard von Rad and Gerhard Kittel, *TDNT*, 2:237.

55. Francis Brown, S. R. Driver, and Charles A. Briggs, *A Hebrew and English Lexicon of the Old Testament,* corrected ed. (Oxford: Oxford University Press, 1953), 457–59 (hereafter cited as BDB); von Rad and Kittel, *TDNT*, 2:238–39.

56. BDB, 457–59; Christoph Dohmen and P. Stenmans, *TDOT*, 7:13, 17; Moshe Weinfeld, *TDOT*, 7:23, 25, 27.

57. Von Rad and Kittel, *TDNT*, 2:239.

58. Walter Grundmann, *TDNT*, 2:292–93.

59. Alexander T. Strecker, "Kovod Adonai" (PhD diss., Hebrew University of Jerusalem, 1972).

60. Von Rad and Kittel, *TDNT*, 2:241.

implication is that God could be seen. When he visited the former Hebrew slaves in the wilderness, in almost all instances he was hidden by a cloud (see Ex. 13:21–22; 16:10; 19:9; 24:15–18; 40:34; etc.). But twice he showed himself. The first occurred on the holy mount during the covenant ratification ceremony when Moses, Aaron and his sons, "and seventy of the elders of Israel . . . saw the God of Israel" (Ex. 24:9–11). The second happened much later, on the initial Day of Atonement. On that occasion, God was seen by "all the people" (Lev. 9:23; see also Lev. 9:6). In these last two Leviticus passages, English translations render the verb "to be seen" as "appeared," as if a subtle spiritual experience like a vision had occurred. But both the Hebrew text and the Septuagint translation of these passages render the verb in the passive, "was seen." The point is that these people saw God in his physical glory, directly and clearly.[61]

Significantly, the passages in Exodus 24 and 40, plus Leviticus 9, all tie in one way or another to concrete historical events at Mount Sinai—the reception of the law and the making of the covenant with God. Such a sense connects to Paul's appeal to God's glory here: that such glory links to real historical events that led to Jesus' Atonement (see Luke 9:29); that such glory displays itself at this moment in the loving, lasting "redemption through his blood, the forgiveness of sins" (1:7); that such glory promises an everlasting, celestial "inheritance" in Christ (1:11).

Another meaning points to royalty and the temple; the idea is that glory is represented by a crown. In Job's words about his misfortunes at the hand of God, he lamented, "He hath stripped me of my glory, and taken the crown from my head" (Job 19:9). In a positive vein, the Psalmist asks the Lord, "What is man, that thou art mindful of him?" In response, we hear pleasant words: God "hast made him a little lower than the angels, and hast crowned him with glory and honor" (Ps. 8:4–5).[62] In a third instance that exhibits ties to a sacred place and holy occasion, the Lord took Israel as his bride, anointing her "with oil" and clothing her "with fine linen and . . . with silk" before placing "a beautiful crown upon [her] head" (Ezek. 16:9–12). According to modern scripture, the faithful whom Christ gathers will "be crowned with celestial glory" (D&C 101:65). In slightly different terms, "I, the Lord, have promised unto you a crown of glory at my right hand" (D&C 104:7). Back to

---

61. The *nifal* (passive) form of the Hebrew verb ראה (*r'h*), "to see," stands in Lev. 9:6, 23. The Greek translation mirrors this form with the passive of ὁράω (*horaō*), "to see." See BDB, 908; Weinfeld, *TDOT,* 7:23–25, 31; Wilhelm Michaelis, *TDNT,* 5:317, 324, 342, 356.
62. Weinfeld, *TDOT,* 7:27.

Ephesians, after Jesus completed his Atonement, he was seated "at [God's] own right hand in the heavenly places," doubtless receiving a crown of glory (1:20). For believers, coming to Christ means receiving a crown of glory in a holy place as "heirs of God, and joint-heirs with Christ" (Rom. 8:17; see also 1 Pet. 4:12–14). In light of these observations, the words "the glory of his grace" invite an expanded meaning, something like "the physical, enthroning effects of his grace [on believers]" (see the Notes on 1:12, 14, 18; 3:13, 16; especially 4:1).

he hath made us accepted: The Greek verb χαριτόω (*charitoō*), with the meaning "to bestow favor upon," is related to the noun translated "grace."[63] This verb occurs only twice in the New Testament, here and at Luke 1:28 in the scene where the angel Gabriel approached the youthful Mary and where the participle is translated in the King James text as "highly favored." The literal thought is "he graced upon us." This reading is accurate but awkward. Perhaps a better English rendition is "he has showered [grace] upon us." The "he," of course, is God.[64]

the beloved: We find a related term (ἀγαπητός, *agapētos*), an adjective meaning "beloved," in the baptism and Transfiguration scenes (see Matt. 3:17; 17:5; Mark 1:11; 9:7; and Luke 3:22). Here, Paul has written the word ἠγαπημένῳ (*ēgapēmenō*), a perfect passive participle from the same root. Certainly, in all these passages the idea is the same: "the beloved [Son]."[65] In Colossians 3:12, we see that this participle is paired with the term "chosen" and applied to Christians, who are to wear these characteristics as garments (see the Note on 1:4).[66]

1:7 *In whom:* The antecedent of the relative pronoun "whom" is "the beloved" in 1:6 and points even farther back to Christ, who is mentioned in 1:3, as well as to the next occurrences of the phrase "in whom" (1:11, 13; see also the Notes on 1:3, 11, 13). Each of the other occurrences of this phrase points to the same person;[67] he is the one who gives us "an inheritance" (1:11) and the one who has become the object of our faith (see 1:13).

redemption . . . forgiveness of sins: The noun for redemption (ἀπολύτρωσις, *apolytrōsis*), with the basic meaning of "setting free for a ransom," has lost some of its attachment to the Israelite Exodus and now links more

---

63. BDAG, 1081.

64. This is how Best understands the pronoun (*Ephesians*, 127).

65. Gottfried Quell and Ethelbert Stauffer, *TDNT*, 1:49–52; BDAG, 5–7; Winger, *Ephesians*, 194–95.

66. Winger, *Ephesians*, 194–95.

67. Winger, *Ephesians*, 195.

closely to the Atonement and thus forgiveness of sins (see Col. 1:14). Notably, this word is linked to events of the end-time in 1:14 and 4:30[68] in the expressions "the earnest of our inheritance until the redemption of the purchased possession" and "ye are sealed unto the day of redemption." Hence, redemption is both immediate with the forgiveness of sins at baptism and future in its reference to the day wherein faithful believers are to receive their promised inheritance. In this light, in 1:7 "the concept of redemption is fully parallel to that of atonement."[69] Concerning "the forgiveness of sins," the mortal Jesus offered this gift on the spot to many who sought his aid. His forgiveness gave to them the unspeakable gift of freedom from entangling sin as well as a spiritual wholeness (see Luke 5:20, 24; 7:47–48; see also Hel. 5:9–10).[70] Of course, the reason he could forgive sins is because he paid for them through his suffering (see Acts 5:31; 13:38; 1 John 1:9; 3:5; Mosiah 4:2; and Alma 7:13). Such a notion exhibits a link back to the Servant Song of Isaiah 53, wherein we read, "He was wounded for our transgressions, he was bruised for our iniquities: . . . and with his stripes we are healed" (Isa. 53:5; see also Isa. 53:8, 11; and the Notes on 1:14; especially 4:30 on "redemption" and 5:2 on "given himself for us").

through his blood: The image of blood stirs memories of sacrifices at the Jerusalem temple as well as at pagan temples around the Roman world. The envisioned sacrifice, of course, took place in Jerusalem, and Jesus was its victim (see 5:2, "hath given himself for us an offering and a sacrifice to God"). Unlike sacrifices under the Mosaic law, particularly the one on the Day of Atonement, which atoned for worshipers' sins for the past year (see Ex. 30:10 and Lev. 16:3–22, 30, 33–34) and thus had to be repeated,[71] Jesus' sacrifice "through [the shedding of] his blood" became the permanent redemption or deliverance from debilitating sin (1:7; see also Heb. 9:12–15, 22; and the Note on 2:13).

forgiveness: Paul writes the Greek word ἄφεσις (*aphesis*), whose verb, ἀφίημι (*aphiēmi*), means "to let go" or "to release." When these terms have to do with the forgiveness of sins or trespasses, it is usually God who forgives, who grants release (see Matt. 6:14–15; 18:21; Mark 11:25; Luke 5:21, 24; etc.).[72] Forgiveness, of course, is tied to Jesus' blood (see Rom. 3:25),

---

68. Otto Procksch and Friedrich Büchsel, *TDNT,* 4:352.

69. Procksch and Büchsel, *TDNT,* 4:354.

70. Brown, *Testimony of Luke,* 291–94, 385–86.

71. Jacob Milgrom, *Leviticus 1–16,* vol. 3 of the Anchor Bible (New York: Doubleday, 1991), 1033–34, 1059.

72. Rudolf Bultmann, *TDNT,* 1:509–12; BDAG, 155–57.

something that Jesus himself linked to the wine of the sacrament that he shared at the Last Supper (see Matt. 26:27–28; Mark 14:23–24; and Luke 22:20). Among ordinances, it connects to baptism; the promise of such forgiveness goes all the way back to John the Baptist, who preached "the baptism of repentance for the remission [*aphesis*] of sins" (Mark 1:4; Luke 3:3;[73] see the Note on 4:5).

sins: Paul's noun παράπτωμα (*paraptōma*), which normally bears the sense of "transgression" or "trespass," differs from the usual New Testament word for sin (ἁμαρτία, *hamartia*).[74] In 2:1, the two terms are combined, and in Colossians 1:14 we find Christ's "forgiveness of sins" (ἁμαρτία, *hamartia*; see the Notes on 2:1, 5).

riches: These riches (πλοῦτος, *ploutos*) do not mirror those of the world. Instead, they represent what comes to a person who follows Jesus and, like him, grasps that true riches—our real "inheritance" (1:18; see also 2:7; 3:16)—are derived from loving others in a way that does not seek personal benefit but only the benefit of the one loved. In this way, with Paul we can speak of God being "rich in mercy" and of "the unsearchable riches of Christ" (2:4; 3:8; see also the Notes on 1:18; 2:4, 7; 3:16; for the possibility that Paul was setting God's riches against those of the temple of Diana at Ephesus, see the Note on 3:8).[75]

1:8 *he hath abounded:* The general sense of the Greek verb περισσεύω (*perisseuō*) points to overflowing abundance, first in material things and second in spiritual gifts from God. In this instance, the verb is transitive with the idea of providing "the riches of his grace" in abundance.[76] It is at the end-time that the fulness of God's gifts will become a reality. Although this life might be fraught with want or poverty, the next life will offer to faithful believers an outpouring of blessings and possessions, such as a "miraculous fruitfulness" from food-bearing plants and a "wealth of children."[77] We are reminded of promises residing in other sources to the effect that, during the coming days of the Messiah, the earth will yield in her abundance: "The earth will also yield fruits ten thousandfold" (2 Bar. 29:5;[78] see also *1 En.* 10:19 and Isa. 5:10). In this life, of course, believers

---

73. Winger, *Ephesians*, 196.
74. BDAG, 770, 50–51.
75. Friedrich Hauck and Wilhelm Kasch, *TDNT*, 6:328–29; BDAG, 832.
76. Louw-Nida, §59.54; BDAG, 805.
77. Friedrich Hauck, *TDNT*, 6:58–61, quotation on 6:59; BDAG, 805.
78. Also Irenaeus, *Against Heresies* 5.33.3, in *ANF*, 1:563.

receive from God the gifts of "wisdom and prudence" (see 1 Cor. 12:4–8; Moro. 10:8–9; and D&C 46:8–12, 17).

in all wisdom and prudence: In the Epistle to the Colossians, this pair is adjusted to "wisdom and spiritual understanding" (Col. 1:9). The meaning is basically the same. In Ephesians 1:8, the two nouns (σοφία, *sophia,* and φρόνησις, *phronēsis*) illumine the abundant gifts that faithful believers receive from God (see 1:17; 3:10; and Col. 1:26–27; 2:3). It is in Colossians that we learn that wisdom has to do with knowing God's will and walking "worthy of the Lord" until we are "perfect in Christ Jesus" (Col. 1:9–10, 28). Further, by "the spirit of wisdom and revelation," we come to "the knowledge of [God]" (1:17). This latter statement opens the possibility that church members not only knew that God exists but also enjoyed an understanding of his true character and attributes.[79] Importantly, the wisdom that comes from God is not available without a search, for it is hidden and comes to us only through sincere efforts to find it, as we are reminded in the Hymn to Wisdom (Prov. 8:22–36): "Blessed is the man that heareth me [wisdom]. . . . For whoso findeth me findeth life" (Prov. 8:34–35). In addition, "Happy is the man that findeth wisdom. . . . For the merchandise of it is better than . . . fine gold" (Prov. 3:13–15; see also Job 28:12–28).[80]

The Hymn to Wisdom in Proverbs 8 especially celebrates wisdom as a personality who was with God in the beginning and, in the light of modern scripture, is the blazer and keeper of the paths that mortals should walk in during their lives (see Prov. 8:32, where the plural "ways" is the common term for roads or paths [דֶּרֶךְ, *derech*];[81] also compare Mosiah 2:36, "wisdom's paths"; 8:20; and Hel. 12:5). Further, she acts as an agent of God in accomplishing his will (see 2 Ne. 20:13, quoting Isa. 10:13). Concerning the term *phronēsis,* it appears in only one other passage in the New Testament, and there the end-time is the focus. After the angel quoted a line from Malachi 4:6 to Zacharias the priest, he then said that Zacharias's new son would turn "the disobedient to the wisdom of the just," where the King James translators chose to render this term (*phronēsis*) as "wisdom" (Luke 1:17). The noun *phronēsis* bears the sense of "understanding" or "way of thinking," thus standing close to wisdom (*sophia*) in its meaning. The line

---

79. *Lectures on Faith,* lecture 3, §4 and question 6, in *The Lectures on Faith in Historical Perspective,* ed. Larry E. Dahl and Charles D. Tate Jr. (Provo, Utah: BYU Religious Studies Center, 1990), 65, 70.

80. Ulrich Wilckens and Georg Fohrer, *TDNT,* 7:498.

81. BDB, 202–3.

in Luke could be translated "the disobedient to the understanding of the righteous" or, more fully in one modern translation, "people who now disobey God will begin to think as they ought to" (Contemporary English Version; see the Notes on 1:17; 3:10; 5:15).[82]

1:9 ***Having made known unto us:*** It is revelation, direct and pure, that rests behind this statement. This revelation has been entrusted "unto us," meaning both the broader Christian community, including Gentile converts, and, more narrowly, the group of believers in Ephesus. The persons to whom it came for the whole church must have been "the holy apostles and prophets by the spirit" (3:5). In advance of this revelation, God called Paul "to bear [the Lord's] name before the Gentiles" (Acts 9:15). Thus, Paul writes in Ephesians that this knowledge came "unto me" quite independent of others (3:3; see the Note below and the Notes on 1:17; 3:3, 5, 10; 4:20; 6:19).

the mystery of his will: One element of this mystery, which has obviously been revealed by prophecy "unto us," has to do with the gathering "together in one all things in Christ" during "the dispensation of the fulness of times" (1:10), an event still in the future. Another part is that the mystery is Christ, who revealed himself to Paul (see 3:3–4). A third piece is Christ's relationship to the church of which he is now the head (see 1:22; 5:23, 32; and Col. 1:18). A fourth aspect, related to this one, holds that "Gentiles should be fellowheirs, and of the same body," which is Christ's body, or the church, with their fellow Jewish members of the church (3:6). This last mystery has "been hid in God," as Paul wrote, "from the beginning of the world" (3:9; see also Rom. 16:25 and 1 Cor. 2:7), and has only recently been revealed "unto us" (1:9), "unto me" (3:3), and "unto the holy apostles and prophets by the spirit" (3:5; see the Note above and the Notes on 1:17; 3:4, 9; 5:32; 6:19).

This revelatory character of what is hidden in God connects back to the Old Testament, wherein the Persian loan word רז (*raz*), rendered "secret" in the KJV, has to do with disclosing what is known only to God (see Dan. 2:18–19, 29, 47; 4:6 [4:9 in the English translation]). It also links to the Hebrew noun סוד (*sod*), which points to what is decided in Jehovah's council and then revealed through a prophet (see Isa. 6; Jer. 23:18, 22; Amos 3:7; and Job 15:8; compare Ps. 89:7, where *sod* points to God's "assembly" with "the saints").[83] In Ephesians, when the mystery embraces the relationship

---

82. Wilckens and Fohrer, *TDNT,* 7:523–24; Georg Bertram, *TDNT,* 9:233–34; BDAG, 934–35, 1066; Louw-Nida, §§26.15; 32.30, 37; Brown, *Testimony of Luke,* 100–1.

83. BDB, 691, 1112; William Gesenius, *Complete Hebrew-Chaldee Lexicon to the Old Testament,* trans. Samuel P. Tregelles (Grand Rapids, Mich.: Eerdmans, 1980), 580, 763;

between "Christ and the church" wherein Christ "nourisheth and cherisheth" the church (5:29, 32), we witness a relationship that Clinton E. Arnold calls "the provision of power and enablement to believers."[84] This notion is known among Latter-day Saints as the enabling power of the Atonement, a power that flows from the Savior's atoning act and enables believers both to deal with the vicissitudes of life and to accomplish tasks beyond their natural abilities (see the Notes on 1:16, 21; 2:7, 16; 3:16; 4:30).[85]

hath purposed: The basic sense of the verb (προτίθημι, *protithēmi*) has to do with planning beforehand or, perhaps preferred, concerns the act of setting something before a god or before the public. That is, we here come upon a divine plan that is set before a public, whether a celestial or a terrestrial public. The phrase points both to the premortal divine council meeting, where God's plan was set before his children and accepted, and to the announcement of God's plan to a mortal public by his emissaries (see Rom. 3:25; 8:28–30;[86] Moses 4:1–3; Abr. 3:27–28; D&C 29:36–37; and the Notes on 1:5, 10–11; 3:11). In its temple connection, the verb has to do with the weekly setting out of the twelve loaves of the bread of the presence, or shewbread, in the moveable tabernacle and, thereafter, in the temple (see LXX Ex. 29:23; 40:4, 23; and Lev. 24:8).[87] In Old Testament literature, the notion of God's plan (עצה, *'ētsah*) is very old. It arises both in wisdom literature (see Prov. 19:21) and in the prophetic books (see Isa. 11:2 and 44:26,

---

Heinz-Josef Fabry, *TDOT,* 10:171–76; Clinton E. Arnold, *Ephesians: Power and Magic* (Cambridge: Cambridge University Press, 1989), 127; Francis I. Andersen and David Noel Freedman, *Amos: A New Translation with Introduction and Commentary,* vol. 24A of the Anchor Bible (New York: Doubleday, 1989), 399.

84. Arnold, *Ephesians,* 127; compare Alma 7:12, "That he may know according to the flesh how to succor his people according to their infirmities."

85. "Bible Dictionary," in the LDS Edition of the King James Version of the Bible (1979), s.v. "Grace." Also consult Bednar, "In the Strength of the Lord," 121–28; Rasmus, "Enabling Power of the Atonement," 18–21; see Moses 6:32, "Go forth and do as I [the Lord] have commanded thee. . . . Open thy mouth, and it shall be filled, and I will give thee utterance"; Mosiah 9:17, "In the strength of the Lord did we go forth to battle . . . for I [Zeniff] and my people did cry mightily to the Lord that he would deliver us"; Alma 7:12, "He [Jesus] will take upon him their infirmities, . . . that he may know according to the flesh how to succor his people"; Alma 20:4, "Lamoni said unto Ammon: I know, in the strength of the Lord thou canst do all things"; Alma 26:12, "I [Ammon] will boast of my God, for in his strength I can do all things." See also Eising, *TDOT,* 4:349, 353–55; Grundmann, *TDNT,* 2:313–16; Oepke, *TDNT,* 2:542–43; Friedrich, *TDNT,* 2:730; Braun, *TDNT,* 6:464.

86. Christian Maurer, *TDNT,* 8:164–67; BDAG, 889; Larkin, *Handbook,* 11; see also Delling, *TDNT,* 9:592–93.

87. Maurer, *TDNT,* 8:165.

where we encounter the translation "counsel" in the sense of prediction or plan). Here and elsewhere, God's planning, a result of deliberation whose decisions are announced by his prophets, is intended to be implemented in the mortal sphere (see Isa. 14:26; 19:17; Jer. 18:18; 49:20; 50:45; and Ezek. 7:26).[88]

1:10 *dispensation:* The general meaning of this noun is "direction" or "(household) administration" (οἰκονομία, *oikonomia*). In this passage, it can also mean "plan of salvation."[89] The noun also appears in 3:2 and 3:9 (also Col. 1:25; etc.); in 3:9, it is translated "fellowship" (see the Notes on 1:5, 9, 11; 3:2, 9).

dispensation of the fulness of times: In its meanings "administration" and "plan of salvation," the noun rendered "dispensation" (οἰκονομία, *oikonomia*) sketches a scene of a divinely managed gathering of believers. In this case, the gathering occurred during the ministries of Jesus, Paul, and the other apostles. These believers have joined one another in a distinctive and identifiable household or congregation. This congregation helps its assembled faithful members—Jew and Gentile—to negotiate a path to salvation according to God's plan that was set in motion "before the foundation of the world" (1:4). This picture agrees in the main with the Latter-day Saint view that a "dispensation" is an era, occasionally following a period of apostasy, wherein the gospel message is established on the earth through a prophetic figure who gathers receptive people into an extended group of believers, basically into an assembly or church, who together can assist in offering the blessings of heaven to those who will join them.[90] Specifically, in Latter-day Saint doctrine "the dispensation of the fulness of times" points to our day, which is called "the final dispensation of the Gospel."[91] Intriguingly, Joseph Smith added that "Adam holds the keys of the dispensation of the fulness of times, i.e. the dispensation of all the times, [which]

---

88. Gesenius, *Hebrew-Chaldee Lexicon,* 647; BDB, 420; L. Ruppert, *TDOT,* 6:156–60, 164, 166–69, 171–81.

89. Otto Michel, *TDNT,* 5:151–53; the quote is from 152; BDAG, 697–98; Louw-Nida, §§30.68; 46.1.

90. Robert L. Millet, "Dispensation of the Fulness of Times," in *Encyclopedia of Latter-day Saint History,* ed. Arnold K. Garr, Donald Q. Cannon, and Richard O. Cowan (Salt Lake City: Deseret Book, 2000), 297; Stephen E. Robinson and H. Dean Garrett, *A Commentary on the Doctrine and Covenants,* 4 vols. (Salt Lake City: Deseret Book, 2000–2005), 4:91–92.

91. Anderson, *Understanding Paul,* 268–69; Joseph Fielding McConkie and Craig J. Ostler, *Revelations of the Restoration: A Commentary on the Doctrine and Covenants and Other Modern Revelations* (Salt Lake City: Deseret Book, 2000), 203.

have been and will be revealed through him from the beginning to Christ and from Christ to the end of all the dispensations that are to be revealed."[92] In evocative language from modern scripture, we learn, "I [the Lord] deign to reveal unto my church things which have been kept hid from before the foundation of the world, things that pertain to the dispensation of the fulness of times" (D&C 124:41; see also D&C 112:30; 128:18, 20–21).

fulness: The idea of fulness is a bit challenging to wrap into a simple package, especially because of the multiple contexts that this letter presents. For example, we find such expressions as "his [Jesus'] body, the fulness of him that filleth all in all" (1:23; see also Col. 1:18–19; 2:9–12); "to know the love of Christ . . . that ye might be filled with all the fulness of God" (3:19); and "the measure of the stature of the fulness of Christ" (4:13). The first has to do with the church, Jesus' "body"; the second with a set of sacred experiences that brings us to a godlike life and Christ-like love (see 3:16–19); and the third with a spiritually mature, Christ-like ability to resist being "carried about with every wind of doctrine . . . and cunning craftiness" by those who "lie in wait to deceive" (4:14). In its earliest occurrences, the Greek noun "fulness" (πλήρωμα, *plēroma*) ties to a fulness of contents; in other words, it signifies that which fills a vessel or container. This idea carries over into the New Testament, wherein the contents are regularly spiritual in character. In sum, we observe that "fulness" usually expresses the brimming love of Christ, manifested during his mortal ministry, that can come to reside in the heart of a believer, a love that the believer can then share with others.[93]

For Latter-day Saints, the word bears similar meanings, as illustrated in the following prayer: "May God grant, in his great fulness, that men might be brought unto repentance and good works, that they might be restored unto grace for grace, according to their works" (Hel. 12:24). In addition, in many passages in modern scripture, the principle of fulness is linked to glory, usually Jesus' glory (see D&C 76:20, 56, 71, 76–77; 84:24; 88:29; 93:6; 132:6; see also D&C 76:94). Further, in Latter-day Saint parlance, the expression "the dispensation of the fulness of times" has to do with the last days and points to this era as the one wherein an endowment of all the powers, knowledge, and blessings that God has ever given to his children in prior ages of

---

92. "History, 1838–1856, Volume C-1 [2 November 1838–31 July 1842]," October 5, 1840, 16 [addenda], Joseph Smith Papers, https://www.josephsmithpapers.org/paper-summary/history-1838-1856-volume-c-1-2-november-1838-31-july-1842/551.

93. Gerhard Delling, *TDNT,* 6:302–5.

human history will occur (see D&C 27:13). Within this grand endowment, the love of Christ, from him to us, will stand as its centerpiece (see the Notes on 1:23; 3:19; 4:13).[94]

times: In many of its occurrences in the New Testament, this noun (singular καιρός, *kairos*) denotes a critical moment, usually a time of decision.[95] But in the expression "the dispensation of the fulness of times," it takes the sense of a "historical epoch" with possible pointers toward the end-time, much like we find in Luke 21:8: "Many shall come in my name, saying, I am Christ; and *the* [last] *time* draweth near" (emphasis added).[96] In a challenging passage to translate, 6:18 presents a different sense for *kairos* in Paul's plea for prayers "for all saints" and "for me" (6:19). Here, the King James Version translates the phrase ἐν παντὶ καιρῷ (*en panti kairō*, literally "in every time") with the adverb "always." In contrast, the New Rendition presents it as "at all times," where *kairos* "acquires the greatly weakened sense of a mere term for time."[97] That said, in 6:18 the word ties to the critical need for believers always to engage in prayer (see the Notes on 5:16; 6:18).[98]

gather together: Paul's words have been building to this action. Now we learn what God intends as a climactic ending to his work. The rare but rich verb here (ἀνακεφαλαιόω, *anakephalaioō*) is related to the noun "head" (κεφαλή, *kephalē*), found often in Ephesians (see 1:22; 4:15; 5:23). The verb bears the meaning "to sum up." In this instance, a fertile set of meanings run together in this verb, including "to summarize (a speech)," "to repeat (an original action)," and "to gather things together." In this context, we are to think of the grand summation "in Christ" at the end-time, pulling together "all things . . . in heaven, and . . . on earth,"[99] not the least part of which are Gentiles marching into the kingdom (see 2:11–18 and 1 Cor. 15:24).

in one: The sense is not unity but rather a whole or a totality. In a passage characterized as prophetic, the high priest Caiaphas was reported to say that, in Jesus' dying, "he should gather together in one the children of God that were scattered abroad" (John 11:51–52). According to Ephesians, such a gathering is to occur "in the dispensation of the fulness of times," not before.

---

94. Robinson and Garrett, *Commentary on the Doctrine and Covenants,* 4:92; McConkie and Ostler, *Revelations of the Restoration,* 203–4.

95. Gerhard Delling, *TDNT,* 3:455.

96. Delling, *TDNT,* 3:461; Best, *Ephesians,* 139; Larkin, *Handbook,* 12.

97. Delling, *TDNT,* 3:457.

98. Delling, *TDNT,* 3:461.

99. Heinrich Schlier, *TDNT,* 3:682; BDAG, 65; Larkin, *Handbook,* 12.

in heaven, and . . . on earth: The combination of these terms, heaven and earth, often points to the totality of creation (see Deut. 3:24; 1 Chr. 29:11; Ps. 135:6; and Col. 1:16). "'Everything in heaven and on earth' is the body of which Christ is the Head." Said another way, "Everything that exists in the heavens . . . and on earth is integrated as a body whose head is Christ" (see 1:22 and Col. 1:20).[100]

in heaven: This Greek phrase appears in the plural (ἐπὶ τοῖς οὐρανοῖς, *epi tois ouranois*) and features the preposition which answers the question "Where?" This preposition (ἐπί, *epi*) carries the meaning of "on" or "above." Hence, the meaning is "above the heavens" or "in the heavens."[101] It is impossible to know whether Paul was thinking of multiple heavens or was writing in the common plural, which often means simply "heaven" (see 4:10, "far above all heavens" [ὑπεράνω πάντων τῶν οὐρανῶν, *hyperanō pantōn tōn ouranōn*], and the Note thereon).[102] Perhaps importantly, the plural form "the heavens" occurs eight times in Ephesians and Colossians, whereas the plural occurs only three times in Paul's other letters, excluding Hebrews.[103] One question is whether this observation leads away from the notion that Paul is the author of this epistle (see the Notes on 3:15; 6:9).

on earth: The relationship between heaven and earth is crucial for grasping how events of the end-time will play out. In one sense, actions in heaven will be mirrored on the earth, bringing a unity to the results of God's plan. That is, the earth will be the scene of crucial events that introduce the end-time into the human experience (see Luke 18:8; 21:23, 25; and Rev. 21:1). Some of these events that are connected to the grand summing up, of course, will occur in heaven. But not exclusively. Notably, the notion of Jesus' body, which embraces institutions located in heaven— giving meaning to the words "all things in Christ" (see 4:3–6; 5:23; see also 3:10)—ties visibly to the earthly church (see 1:22–23; 2:16; 3:6; 4:12, 16; see also Col. 1:18), thus imparting a divine unity to all that will happen (see also Matt. 16:19; 18:18; and the Notes on 4:9; 6:3).[104]

1:11 *In whom:* This phrase repeats what we find in 1:7 and 1:13 (twice). It ties back to the phrase "in Christ" at the end of 1:3. Taken together, the two phrases impart a unity to the whole of these early verses in the letter. But

---

100. Traub and von Rad, *TDNT,* 5:517–18.
101. BDAG, 363.
102. Traub and von Rad, *TDNT,* 5:510–11, 513; BDAG, 738.
103. Traub and von Rad, *TDNT,* 5:513.
104. Hermann Sasse, *TDNT,* 1:678–80; Traub and von Rad, *TDNT,* 5:517–18.

far more than that, they underscore the wondrous gifts that come to believers from the now-exalted Christ (see the Notes on 1:3, 7, 13).

also: One question is whether the word "also" (καί, *kai*) attaches to the subject ("we too have obtained an inheritance") or to the verb ("we have also obtained an inheritance"). Possibly it attaches to neither. Why? Because it resumes the series introduced by the phrase "in Christ" (1:3) and continued by "in whom also" in 1:7 and 1:13 (see the Note on 1:3).[105] But this is not the whole story. By introducing the word "also," Paul adds more to the major point that he made in the prior verse. Furthermore, throughout the prior verses, everything has been building toward "the dispensation of the fulness of times" and the special events that are to occur in that future "historical epoch" (see the Note on 1:10). Those important events, among other things, will entail receiving "an inheritance" of which we have already obtained "the earnest" in this life (1:14), "the guarantee of [a believer's] future possession of salvation."[106]

we: The reference shifts. No longer is "we" to be understood as all Christians, as in 1:3–9. Here, "we" refers to believing Jews, usually called Jewish Christians.[107]

we have obtained an inheritance: The entire expression derives from the aorist passive of the verb κληρόω (*klēroō*), meaning "to be appointed by lot."[108] This verb occurs only here in the entire New Testament. Its meaning is something like "we have been given a lot [by divine means], an inheritance."[109] Importantly, no sense of randomness attaches to this action, as if a person were playing a game of chance. All is guided by God's hand (see Acts 1:23–26; 1 Pet. 1:4; and D&C 85:7).[110]

inheritance: Although the noun for "inheritance" (κληρονομία, *klērono-mia*) does not appear here, it does so at 1:18 and 5:5. The concept is very much a part of the verb κληρόω (*klēroō*; see above). The notion of inheritance is old and rich and goes back to the Old Testament, where it bears the sense of "lot" or a possession received by lot, usually an allotment of land (נחלה and גורל, *nahalah* and *goral*).[111] Receiving an inheritance of land

---

105. Larkin, *Handbook,* 6–7, 9, 13, 15.

106. Johannes Behm, *TDNT,* 1:475; see also BDAG, 134.

107. Caird, *Letters,* 40; Winger, *Ephesians,* 203. Best, *Ephesians,* 144–45, argues that the audience does not change here.

108. Johannes Hermann and Werner Foerster, *TDNT,* 3:764–65; BDAG, 548–49.

109. Larkin, *Handbook,* 13.

110. Horst Seebass, Jan Bergman, and Helmer Ringgren, *TDOT,* 2:76; Winger, *Ephesians,* 202.

111. BDB, 174, 635; Lipiński, *TDOT,* 9:319–24.

was a major change for the Israelites, who had never owned land. In a famous case of Joshua deciding whether daughters could inherit land if they had no brothers, we read that "according to the commandment of the Lord [Joshua] gave them an inheritance among the brethren of their father" (Josh. 17:4; see also Num. 27:1–8). Such a heritage came from the Lord alone—not Joshua—and, early on, was considered a permanent, nontransferrable possession of the clan and family, though that changed over time (see Lev. 25:23; Isa. 5:8; Ezek. 46:18; and Micah 2:2).[112] In Old Testament times, moreover, as an extension of the original law, a widow could not inherit her husband's estate.[113]

In a major shift, New Testament authors wrote about inheritance as eternal, as something that a person shares with fellow Saints, as "an inheritance incorruptible, and undefiled, and that fadeth not away, reserved in heaven for you" (1 Pet. 1:4; see also Acts 20:32; Col. 3:24; and Heb. 9:15). This remarkable refocus links to Jesus as God's heir, a concept spelled out in Jesus' parable of the wicked husbandmen, wherein "the heir is the Son, and the inheritance is God's kingdom" (see Matt. 21:33–46; Mark 12:1–12; and Luke 20:9–19).[114] Like in the Old Testament, the sonship of Jesus is here established as the basis for inheritance. But believers' status as heirs, or "joint-heirs with Christ," as we find in Romans 8:17, does not depend on physical descent but on "adoption . . . by Jesus Christ to himself" (Eph. 1:5; see also Mosiah 5:7). For "many [non-Jews] shall come from the east and the west, and shall sit down with Abraham, and Isaac, and Jacob, in the kingdom of heaven" (Matt. 8:11; see also Luke 13:29; appendix 2; and the Notes on 1:5, 18; 2:3; 5:5).[115]

predestinated: The verb is the same as at 1:5 (προορίζω, *proorizō*), but here it is a passive participle. The active meaning is the same: "to foreordain" (see the Note on 1:5). It is important to grasp that foreordination and election, or being chosen, belong together as related principles, both arising out of God's love for us. In effect, we stand as his beloved (see Rom. 11:28; 1 Thes. 1:4; and 2 Thes. 2:13).[116] But God's love for us and, implicitly, his trust in us are not the sole drivers for choosing individuals for celestial blessings, whether in this life or the next. His choice to foreordain a person

---

112. Ze'ev W. Falk, *Hebrew Law in Biblical Times,* 2nd ed. (Provo, Utah: BYU Press; Winona Lake, Ind.: Eisenbrauns, 2001), 84–85.

113. Lipiński, *TDOT,* 9:325; Falk, *Hebrew Law,* 153–55.

114. Hermann and Foerster, *TDNT,* 3:781–83, quotation on 3:781.

115. Hermann and Foerster, *TDNT,* 3:781–83; V. Ben Bloxham, "Law of Adoption," in *EM,* 2:810; Brown, *Testimony of Luke,* 674–77.

116. Quell and Stauffer, *TDNT,* 1:49.

also may center on the needs of the many, on the needs of his congregation of all believers. That is to say, God is concerned with giving leadership to his earthly children, with providing "rulers" who will assist all those desiring to come to him (Abr. 3:23; see also Deut. 14:1–2), and with bringing regularity to his kingdom (see Deut. 18:5; 1 Sam. 2:27–28; 10:24; etc.; and the Note on 4:12).[117]

the purpose: We have already met the verb of this noun (πρόθεσις, *prothesis*) in 1:9 (see the Note thereon and on 3:11). In its basic sense, it has to do with a designed presentation or plan—in this case, a plan unveiled in the premortal world.[118]

worketh: Of the four occurrences of this verb in Ephesians, three have to do with God's actions on our behalf, including this one (see 1:11; 3:20), and one concerns Satan's efforts (see 2:2). Throughout the New Testament, this verb (ἐνεργέω, *energeō*) sets out the active involvement of either God or the devil in the workaday world, often through miracles or acts of power (see Rom. 7:5; 1 Cor. 12:11; 2 Cor. 4:12; Gal. 2:8; 2 Thes. 2:7; etc.). Twice, "mighty works" are ascribed to the supposedly resurrected John the Baptist (Matt. 14:2; Mark 6:14). Only once does the verb apply to the actions of humans (see Philip. 2:13, "to do"). Hence, almost uniformly, the verb spells out influences or deeds that come from the unseen world[119] (see the Notes on 1:11; 2:2; 3:7, 20).

the counsel: Because of the context, resting within this noun (βουλή, *boulē*) lies the unexpressed notion of a divine council that, after deliberation, arrives at a plan (see Ps. 82; Jer. 23:18, 22; Amos 3:7; Job 15:8;[120] Moses 4:1–4; Abr. 3:27–28; and the Notes on 1:4–5, 9–10; compare D&C 29:36–39). Through Joseph Smith, Latter-day Saints have come to understand that the title "Man of Counsel" refers to deity, an appellative that ties directly to

---

117. Seebass, Bergman, and Ringgren, *TDOT*, 2:76–79, 82–86; Debrunner, Kleinknecht, Procksch, Kittel, Quell, and Schrenk, *TDNT*, 4:152–64, 174–75, 186–87.

118. Maurer, *TDNT*, 8:164–67; Delling, *TDNT*, 9:592–93; BDAG, 869; Winger, *Ephesians*, 203.

119. Georg Bertram, *TDNT*, 2:652–53.

120. Henry George Liddell and Robert Scott, *A Greek-English Lexicon*, rev. ed., revised by Henry Stuart Jones (Oxford: Oxford University Press, 1968), 325 (hereafter cited as LSJ); Gottlob Schrenk, *TDNT*, 1:633–37; BDAG, 181–82; Fabry, *TDOT*, 10:174–75; Andersen and Freedman, *Amos*, 399; John L. Lund, "Council in Heaven," in *EM*, 1:328–29; E. Theodore Mullen Jr., "Divine Assembly," in *ABD*, 2:214–17; further, Brent L. Top, "War in Heaven," in *EM*, 4:1546–47; see also Joseph Smith, "Letter to Emma Smith, 21 March 1839," [2], Joseph Smith Papers, https://www.josephsmithpapers.org/paper-summary/letter-to-emma-smith-21-march-1839/2, where we come across "the council of his own will."

God as a counselor, whether in the premortal council, in ongoing heavenly councils, or in human situations (see Moses 7:35 and Isa. 6:8; 25:1; see also Job 38:2; 42:3; Ps. 33:11; 73:24; Prov. 19:21; Isa. 5:19; 14:26; 46:10; Jer. 49:20; Micah 4:12; and Acts 20:27; compare Isa. 9:6; 44:26; 46:11). Additionally, it is important to note here that the noun *boulē* does not appear elsewhere in Paul's letters.[121]

1:12 *praise:* The occurrence of this word (ἔπαινος, *epainos*) underscores the liturgical or hymnic quality of the entire passage (see the Notes on 1:6, 14). At base, it bears the meaning of approval, especially of God's approval of the soul at the time of judgment. Thus, a person's often sought-for approval from fellow humans is diminished in favor of God's acceptance. From the human perspective, it has to do with the praise that we offer to God in worship and on other occasions.[122]

the praise of his glory: This expression also appears in 1:14 and, with minor differences, in 1:6. These words in 1:12 mark the end of the section of the prayer that focuses on the Son. From an ancient, lost text that has come to light only in modern times, we read, "This is my work and my glory—to bring to pass the immortality and eternal life of man" (Moses 1:39). This declaration fits comfortably with Paul's words that point to believers who have already "obtained an inheritance" with God, thus becoming a part of his glory (1:11; for the term "glory," see also 1:14, 17–18; 3:13, 16, 21; and the Notes on 1:6, 14, 18; 3:13, 16).

we . . . who first trusted: Does this reference have to do with the first believers in Jesus' message, those from Galilee and elsewhere in ancient Palestine? Possibly. That is how early Christian commentators understood the expression. As a Jew, certainly Paul included himself in this number, distinguishing himself from Gentiles who "trusted, after that [they] heard the word of truth" (1:13). Perhaps importantly, the reference to the "dispensation of the fulness of times" (1:10) may broaden the scope of Paul's words to include all who will come to believe before the end-time.[123] In a different vein, the "we" here shifts specifically to Jewish believers. To this point in the letter, Paul has included in "we" both Jews and Gentiles. This detail is made certain by the appearance of the second person plural "ye" in the next verse (ὑμεῖς, *hymeis,* the plural "you").[124]

---

121. Schrenk, *TDNT,* 1:633–36.
122. Preisker, *TDNT,* 2:586–88; BDAG, 357.
123. Rudolf Bultmann and Karl Heinrich Rengstorf, *TDNT,* 2:534–35; BDAG, 868.
124. For a different view, see Larkin, *Handbook,* 15.

who first trusted in Christ: The sense is "who first hoped in Christ" and can mean either the Jewish hope in a Messiah or the hope of the first Christians, who were Jewish by birth, in Jesus as the Messiah after he had come (see the Note on 1:13).[125] The object of hope, of course, frequently centers on expected events of the end-time, such as resurrection, judgment, and rewards (see Job 6:11; Ps. 16:9–10; Prov. 11:7; 14:32; Acts 2:26–27; 23:6; 1 Cor. 15:19; Col. 1:5; Alma 22:14; 25:16; 27:28; etc.; and the Notes on 1:18; 2:12; 4:1, 4).

1:13 ***In whom:*** This phrase and its twin farther on in this verse frame much of the unity that extends from 1:3 to the end of the next verse, assisting to glue this long sentence into a single unit (1:3–14). It picks up with "in Christ" (1:3) and sticks together a catalog of divine gifts that stretch eternally backward and forward, subtly underlining a person's progression through time. Looking far back in time, the sequence opens with the declaration that "he hath chosen us in him before the foundation of the world" (1:3–4). The next adhesive, which exhibits a temporal attachment to Jesus' atoning ministry, turns our minds to the ineffable "redemption through [Christ's] blood" and the accompanying "forgiveness of sins" (1:7). Then, we encounter "an inheritance" in both this life and the next that has graciously adhered to us through Christ (1:11). The final element in this exalted series has to do with a bonding—that is, our being "sealed with that holy Spirit of promise," which is "the earnest of our [unfading] inheritance" (1:13–14; see also the Notes on 1:3, 7, 11).

In whom ye also trusted: The italics for "trusted," as we know, mean this word was supplied by the KJV translators. In light of the note on the prior verse, a better sense is "in whom ye also had hope." Paul's focus here rests on the distant future beyond this life—that is, on "our inheritance until the redemption of the purchased possession" (1:14; see also the Note on 1:12).

after that ye heard: Paul knew from his own experience that hearing the gospel message came from someone preaching it. In Ephesus, he was one of the first to preach in the city (see Acts 18:19–21; 19:1, 10). As he wrote elsewhere, "How shall they believe in him of whom they have not heard? and how shall they hear without a preacher?" (Rom. 10:14). More than this, "true hearing of preaching involves more than listening; it is also obedience."[126] We find this principle strongly implied in Jesus' oft-repeated refrain "He that hath ears to hear, let him hear" (Matt. 11:15; Luke 8:8; 14:35).

---

125. Caird, *Letters*, 40–41.
126. Gerhard Friedrich, *TDNT*, 3:712.

the word of truth: The gospel message, the content of missionaries' preaching, traveled under different titles in this era (see James 1:18 for the same expression). Among more than a dozen labels, we notice "the gospel" (1:13; Matt. 4:23; Mark 1:1; etc.), "the message" (1 John 3:11),[127] "glad tidings" or "good tidings" (Luke 1:19; 2:10; 8:1; Acts 13:32; Rom. 10:15),[128] "word" (Mark 2:2; Luke 1:2; John 8:31; Acts 6:4; 1 Thes. 1:6; 2 Tim. 4:2; etc.), "word of God" (Luke 8:21; 11:28; Acts 4:31; 8:14; etc.), and "word of the Lord" (Acts 8:25; 13:48; 1 Thes. 1:8; 2 Thes. 3:1; etc.).[129]

the gospel of your salvation: Paul unpacks the prior expression "the word of truth" and, by adding these words, tells us what he meant. Remarkably, almost beyond words to express, the simple words of the gospel or good news can lead a person not only to salvation or preservation in this life but more significantly to salvation in the next.

salvation: The Greek term σωτηρία (*sōtēria*) carries meaning for this life and the next. It can have to do with human well-being that arises from deliverance or preservation from enemies or afflictions (see LXX Gen. 28:21; LXX Ex. 14:13; LXX Judg. 15:18; LXX 1 Kgs. 11:9, 13 [1 Sam. 11:9, 13 KJV]; and Luke 1:71; etc.). In the spiritual or heavenly sphere, the word points to the privilege of being associated with God (see LXX Isa. 49:6; 52:7; LXX Jer. 3:23; LXX Obad. 1:17; Luke 1:77; Acts 4:12; Rom. 1:16; 11:11; Philip. 2:12; Heb. 5:9; etc.).[130] Impacting and enriching the term's metaphorical meaning is the fact that the name Jesus itself derives from the Hebrew root יש׳ (*yashaʿ*) which has to do with salvation. A host of similar names in the Old Testament come from the same root, including Hoshea, Joshua, Hosea, Isaiah, and Elisha (see the Note on 6:17).[131]

after that ye believed: These words are the translation of the past participle of πιστεύω (*pisteuō*), whose sense is "having believed" and whose meaning ties to the following main verb, "you were sealed." The sense may well be both temporal ("after" or "when") and instrumental ("because"). Hence, we might understand the participle to mean "after you believed" or "because

---

127. This passage contains the only occurrence of ἀγγελία (*angelia*) in the New Testament.

128. The middle form of the verb εὐαγγελίζω (*euangelizō*) stands at the base of the expression "to bring good news" or "to proclaim good tidings." BDAG, 402.

129. One compares "a good profession" (1 Tim. 6:12), "profession" (Heb. 3:1; 4:14; 10:23), "doctrine" (1 Tim. 4:13, 16; 6:1; Titus 2:10), "word of life" (Philip. 2:16), "word of Christ" (Col. 3:16), and "word of this salvation" (Acts 13:26).

130. BDAG, 985–86.

131. John F. Sawyer and Heinz-Josef Fabry, *TDOT*, 6:441–46, 448–49.

you believed" or both. A person's belief, of course, arises from the firm acceptance of the gospel message, which, after baptism, opens up the lofty, beck-
oning invitation to be "sealed with that holy Spirit of promise" (1:13).

sealed: The practice of stamping with seals enjoys a very long history,
beginning circa 3,000 BC in Mesopotamia. Over time, seal marks made in
clay by stamps, small cylinders, or signet rings came to certify the authenticity of items as diverse as royal correspondence, shipments of goods,
personal property, and the manufacturers of certain articles. By the New
Testament era, the act of sealing had acquired religious senses, taking on
the import of not only God making something or someone his own but also
God transferring his authority to a human representative, with himself as
the guarantor of the representative's actions (see John 6:27). When we turn
to the Apostle Paul, two concepts present themselves. First, circumcision
as a seal is a sign that ratifies a person's relationship to God as an heir (see
4:30); second, God's endowment of believers with his Spirit serves as a seal
(see Rom. 4:11 and 2 Cor. 1:22).[132] In our passage here, the verb σφραγίζω
(*sphragizō*) also carries an eschatological meaning that points to the end-
time when being sealed will bear eternal outcomes (see LXX Job 14:17;
LXX Isa. 29:11; LXX Ezek. 9:3–11; LXX Dan. 12:4, 9; and the Note on 4:30).[133]

The question has arisen whether being sealed in this verse really points
to baptism and not to a separate, later event. Because baptism is received
after a believer's faith, according to the book of Acts, and because baptism is noted only once in this letter (see 4:5) and is frequently alluded to
(see 4:22–24; 5:8–11, 14, 26), some scholars have argued that the sealing
is really the baptism ceremony. On the other side stands the language of
4:30: "Grieve not the holy Spirit of God, whereby ye are sealed unto the day
of redemption." In this passage, it becomes clear that being sealed comes
from the Holy Spirit, not from the ordinance of baptism, as is also plain
from another relevant statement from Paul: "[God] hath also sealed us, and
given the earnest of the Spirit in our hearts" (2 Cor. 1:22).[134]

sealed with that holy Spirit: If Paul had meant that this event took place
at the moment of baptism, he surely could have said so.[135] This simple omission, it seems evident, points not to a confirmation ceremony in which
a person receives the Holy Ghost soon after baptism but to some other

---

132. Gottfried Fitzer, *TDNT*, 7:939–50.
133. BDAG, 980.
134. Barth, *Ephesians*, 1:135–43, summarizes the arguments from both viewpoints.
135. Caird, *Letters*, 41–42.

occurrence that came later in a believer's ongoing experience in the church. Not incidentally, the passive voice here points to God as the one who has performed the sealing.[136]

holy Spirit of promise: The advanced spiritual status of some of Paul's audience appears here, for the Holy Spirit of Promise does not come except to the truly faithful (see the Note on 1:1). In 4:30, we read about "the holy Spirit of God, whereby ye are sealed," evidently another reference to the coming of this Spirit to individuals. This event "is the earnest of our [celestial] inheritance" (1:14), which essentially guarantees eternal life to a person, as other references to this Spirit clarify in modern scripture. For example, they "who overcome by faith, and are sealed by the Holy Spirit of promise . . . are they into whose hands the Father has given all things. . . . Wherefore, as it is written, they are gods,[137] even the Sons [and Daughters] of God" (D&C 76:53, 55, 58; see also D&C 88:3–5; 124:124; 132:7, 18–19, 26; and the Notes on 2:18; 4:30; 5:18).

1:14 *earnest:* The definite article "the" is not present in the text. The term ἀρραβών (*arrabōn*) derives from ancient Semitic forms attested in texts as early as the second millennium BC. The words—verbs and nouns— almost uniformly have to do with a creditor's pledges that guarantee payment either through the pledge of property or through a family member who becomes the servant of the lender until the loan is repaid.[138] In the New Testament, only the writings of Paul repeat the word. In the main, this term has to do with a "first installment," yet a full guarantee, against which the Holy Spirit will make further payments (see 2 Cor. 1:22; 5:5).[139]

our inheritance: Paul writes as if the inheritance was already in hand. And it was insofar as the "earnest" payment had been made. In the New Testament, the Greek term κληρονομία (*klēronomia*) points to an inheritance (see Mark 12:7; Luke 12:13; Acts 7:5; etc.), and very often to one that comes from God (see Gal. 3:18 and Col. 3:24).[140] In this latter sense, it is characterized as "an eternal inheritance" (Heb. 9:15), which is "incorruptible, and undefiled, and that fadeth not away, reserved in heaven for you" (1 Pet. 1:4).

---

136. Larkin, *Handbook*, 16.

137. The quotation rests probably on Ps. 82:6, "Ye are gods," a passage Jesus quoted in John 10:34.

138. Edouard Lipiński, *TDOT*, 11:326–30. The Hebrew derivatives of these terms in the Old Testament appear in Gen. 38:17–18, 20; Lev. 25:39, 47; Deut. 15:2, 12; 1 Sam. 17:18; Neh. 5:2–3, 5–7; Job 17:3; Ps. 119:121–22; and Prov. 6:1; 17:18; 20:16.

139. Johannes Behm, *TDNT*, 1:475; BDAG, 134; Best, *Ephesians*, 151–52.

140. BDAG, 547–48; Louw-Nida, §57.140.

According to Paul, the inheritance in this verse becomes ours when "the redemption of the purchased possession" is paid, apparently not before (see also the Notes on 1:11, 18; 5:5; and appendix 2).

the redemption of the purchased possession: This event obviously is not the Atonement, the notice of which arises in 1:7, but something that occurs at a later time. Paul's words elsewhere illuminate this concept: "He which hath begun a good work in you will perform it until the day of Jesus Christ" (Philip. 1:6). That is to say, God's work that began with a person's reception of the Holy Spirit will be completed at the Second Coming of the Savior.[141] In one sense, Paul repeats what he has written in 1:10; at the end-time, "in the dispensation of the fulness of times," God will "gather together in one all things in Christ." Said another way, "in the ages to come [God will] . . . shew the exceeding riches of his grace in his kindness toward us through Jesus Christ" (2:7).

redemption: As we have seen at 1:7, in its original sense, the noun *apolytrōsis* means "setting [a person] free for a ransom [paid]." In the New Testament, the noun is always associated with Jesus' Atonement (see Rom. 3:24 and Col. 1:14) and leads us to the end-time when "the day of redemption" will occur (4:30;[142] see the Notes on 1:7 and especially 4:30).

the purchased possession: The pair of English words "purchased possession" comes from one Greek noun, περιποίησις (*peripoiēsis*). In its earliest attestations, this term bore the ideas of preserving and acquiring.[143] These meanings have passed into the New Testament. The first of these concepts appears in the words "we are . . . of them that believe to the saving [preserving] of the soul" (Heb. 10:39). The second sense, that of acquiring, shows up in Paul's letters to the Thessalonian Saints. There we learn that "God has not destined us to the terrors of judgment, but to the full attainment [acquisition] of salvation through our Lord Jesus Christ" (1 Thes. 5:9 NEB). Further, God "called you by our gospel, to the obtaining of the glory of our Lord Jesus Christ" (2 Thes. 2:14). In Ephesians, the word takes on the additional meaning of possessing.[144] It is not our possession but God's. For the concept is that believers are God's special possession, his "peculiar people" as we read in 1 Peter 2:9, with the sense of God's "treasured people," drawing its meaning from the Hebrew word סגלה (*segullah*; see Ex. 19:5;

---

141. Fowl, *Ephesians*, 50–51.
142. Procksch and Büchsel, *TDNT,* 4:352, 354; BDAG, 117.
143. LSJ, 1384.
144. BDAG, 804.

Deut. 7:6; 14:2; 26:18; and Ps. 135:4; in Mal. 3:17, this Hebrew word is translated "jewels"; and in LXX Mal. 3:17, *peripoiēsis* appears as its translation).[145]
In this connection, this Greek term firmly brings forward "language that
ties the Ephesian believers to the people of Israel" (see the Note on 2:12).[146]

the praise of his glory: Mirroring language in 1:12 and closely mirroring
that in 1:6, this expression rounds off a series of saving actions attributed to
the Father (see 1:3–6), to the Son (see 1:7–12), and to the Holy Spirit (see
1:13–14 and the Note on 1:6).

praise: In this context, the praise that we offer to God grows out of the
events of the end-time that make up our final, full "redemption" after being
"sealed with that holy Spirit of promise" (1:13). The earlier praise, which
exhibits a time stamp, was in celebration of the Father's willingness to facil-
itate our "adoption" as "children by Jesus Christ to himself," an act that
was set in motion long ago by our foreordination in the premortal sphere
(1:5–6). In a second act of praising, which also carries a time tie, we offered
praise after we "first trusted in Christ" in this life (1:12). Hence, we give
our praise to God for what he has done in a premortal setting, in our initial
acceptance of his Son during this life, and at the end-time when we have
received our everlasting "redemption," joining those who are God's "purchased possession[s]" or "treasures" (see the Notes on 1:6, 12). In this last
instance, God himself will offer praise to those who have lived their lives as
he has asked.[147]

his glory: The hymn that Paul is quoting here ascribes this glory to the
Father, much as we read elsewhere when Jesus talks of his relationship to
the Father: "He that speaketh of himself seeketh his own glory: but he that
seeketh [the Father's] glory that sent him, the same is true, and no unrighteousness is in him" (John 7:18). Further, a proper measure of honor or
glory (δόξα, *doxa*) will eventually come from the Father to us: "How can ye
believe, which receive honor one of another, and seek not the honor [*doxa*]
that cometh from God only?" (John 5:44; see also 1 Pet. 4:12–14; D&C
6:30; 29:12; 58:3–4; etc.). This latter glory from God, which exhibited a
fiery splendor in one of its earliest manifestations (see Ex. 24:16–17; see also
Luke 2:9; 9:31–32; 2 Pet. 1:17; etc.), comes to an individual not in the form
of anticipated glory in this life but in the form of a full reception of glory in
the next. As Paul wrote elsewhere, "We all . . . are changed into the same

---

145. Edouard Lipiński, *TDOT,* 10:144–48, esp. 147–48; Winger, *Ephesians,* 209.

146. Fowl, *Ephesians,* 51.

147. Preisker, *TDNT,* 2:587.

image from glory [in mortality] to glory [in the next life]" so that, as "heirs of God, and joint-heirs with Christ . . . we may be also glorified together" with Christ (2 Cor. 3:18; Rom. 8:17; see also Col. 3:4 and Philip. 3:21).[148]

The celestial radiance associated with glory is linked in the Old Testament to the concept of weight or weightiness, which is then transferred metaphorically to the concept of importance. Such ideas can characterize goods as well as individuals. It is Ezekiel who ascribes fully these notions of weight and importance to the person of God (see Ezek. 1:26–28 and the Notes on 1:12, 18; 3:13, 16; especially the Note on 1:6).[149]

Analysis of 1:3–14

These verses, 1:3–14, present to our view the grand sweep of salvation history, opening vivid vistas onto the premortal council, then onto the unspeakable gift of Christ's Atonement, and finally onto the windup scene wherein all promised blessings will be realized. Two gateways lead into a valley bathed with a warm and bright sun that illumines these events in celestial colors. The first is revelation, plain and simple. Speaking of the Father's gracious actions toward us, Paul wrote that he had "made known unto us the mystery of his will" (1:9). He has repeated this theme throughout the letter, effectively pausing to allow readers to take in the supernal view that presents itself through revelation. In his prayer for the Ephesian Saints, he intoned, "May [God] give unto you the spirit of wisdom and revelation in the knowledge of him" (1:17), effectively saying that God and his purposes are knowable. Paul did not stop here. Now that the "eyes of your understanding [are] opened," never to be closed, believers can come to "know what is the hope of [God's] calling, and what [are] the riches of the glory of his inheritance" that he offers to "the saints" (1:18). In a word, the view of what lies in store for the faithful is truly glorious, all made available to us through revelation (see 2:4–7 and the Notes on 1:9; 3:3, 5).

The second gateway is framed by ordinances, those divinely authorized acts that carry force both in this life and the next. The first, of course, was foreordination (see the Notes on 1:5, 11). This action did not consist only of God's premortal choosing or designation of certain "noble and great" spirits to be his "rulers" or leaders in mortality (Abr. 3:22–23). As in the case

---

148. Von Rad and Kittel, *TDNT*, 2:247–51.
149. Von Rad and Kittel, *TDNT*, 2:236–41.

of Jesus being set apart for his role as the Redeemer,[150] so humans experienced a setting apart, a foreordination in the premortal world for roles in this life, exactly as the passage in the book of Abraham tells us. But this is not the only illustration. Jeremiah was "ordained" before he came "out of the womb" (Jer. 1:5); in one of the Servant Songs of Isaiah, the prophet wrote about the coming Servant in these words: "The Lord hath called me from the womb; from the bowels of my mother hath he made mention of my name" (Isa. 49:1); and Paul wrote that God "separated me from my mother's womb" in what was evidently a premortal act (Gal. 1:15; see also Isa. 49:5; 1 Cor. 2:7; and 1 Pet. 1:1–2; 2:8).

The complementing ordinance was baptism. To be sure, Paul does not mention this ordinance directly in Ephesians except in a rather fixed way (see 4:5). Importantly, other language points unmistakably to baptism. Such an act surely lies behind the words "holy and without blemish." In a first instance, this pair of adjectives has to do with individuals; in another, the adjectives concern the church itself, which is made up of individuals (see 1:4; 5:27). Moreover, the ordinances hinted at in this expression cover more ground than just baptism, nodding also in the direction of temple ceremonies (see the Note on 1:4). In this connection, the scrubbing of the church "with the washing of water by the word" surely leads our thoughts to baptism as the purifying agent (5:26). More than this, "the forgiveness

---

150. Perhaps the most direct statements lie in John 3:35 and 13:3, which declare that the Father had "given all things into [Jesus'] hands," drawing up the image of consecrating priests in the Old Testament, who had their hands filled when receiving priesthood power in a ceremony that consisted of several parts: a washing with water, a receipt of sacred garments, an acceptance of a diadem or crown, and an anointing on the head. See Ex. 29:4–9; see also Ex. 28:41; 32:29; Lev. 8:33; etc.; see also BDB, 570; Lambertus Arie Snijders and Heinz-Josef Fabry, *TDOT,* 8:301–6. Further, Matt. 11:27, Luke 10:22, and D&C 93:4 all hold that Jesus received his authorization directly from his Father. See also Friedrich Büchsel, *TDNT,* 2:171; Ethelbert Stauffer, *TDNT,* 2:348; Hermann Kleinknecht, Gottfried Quell, Ethelbert Stauffer, and Karl Georg Kuhn, *TDNT,* 3:103–4; Schmidt, *TDNT,* 5:452–53; Bo Reicke and Georg Bertram, *TDNT,* 5:895; James E. Talmage, *Jesus the Christ,* 35th ed. (Salt Lake City: Deseret Book, 1963), 9; Joseph Fielding Smith, *Answers to Gospel Questions,* 5 vols. (Salt Lake City: Deseret Book, 1957–1966), 2:132–33; Andrew F. Ehat and Lyndon W. Cook, comp., *The Words of Joseph Smith: The Contemporary Accounts of the Nauvoo Discourses of the Prophet Joseph* (Provo, Utah: BYU Religious Studies Center, 1980), 246 ("receiving the fulness of preisthood [*sic*]"); JST Luke 9:25 ("whom God hath ordained"); Luke 22:22; John 17:2, 7, 18; Acts 2:23; 10:42; 17:31; Rom. 1:4; Heb. 1:2, 9 (quoting Ps. 45:7); 3:2; 5:10 (compare 7:21; 8:3); 1 Pet. 1:2, 20; Ether 3:14; D&C 93:17; *Pseudo-Clementine Recognitions* 1.45.5; compare also 1 Cor. 2:6–7.

of sins" (1:7), or "remission of sins" as translated elsewhere,[151] comes to a person for the first time in baptism, an observation at home elsewhere in the New Testament (see Mark 1:4; Luke 3:3; and Acts 2:38).[152]

Among the dominant themes in these verses are grace and glory. The term "grace," of course, points to the ineffable gift from Jesus to believers. And Paul lifts up this word to our gaze again and again, introducing it in almost every chapter (see 1:6–7; 2:5, 7–8; 3:2, 7–8; 4:7, 29; 6:24). In the prime place stands the grace that flows to believers from Jesus' Atonement, bringing forgiveness of sins and ultimately salvation (see 1:6–7; 2:5, 8). Another dimension appears, first in the rescue of Paul from his former life as a persecutor of church members and then in the divine assignment to him to preach the gospel to the Gentiles (see 3:2, 7–8). Last but not least is the enabling power of the Atonement that assists all of us in meeting challenges and opportunities with more than natural abilities (see Notes on 1:9, 21).[153] Paul called such a dimension "the exceeding riches of [God's] grace" (2:7). Among its aspects is the power to give to "every one of us . . . grace according to the measure of the gift of Christ" (4:7). Said another way and applied to a concrete situation, what "proceed[s] out of your mouth" carries the power to "minister grace unto [your] hearers" (4:29; see also the Note on 4:7).

The meanings of the word "glory" are among the richest not only in the New Testament but also in this epistle, as the number of occurrences attests (see 1:6, 12, 14, 17, 18; 3:13, 16, 21). As the scriptural saying goes, "This is my work and *my glory*—to bring to pass the immortality and eternal life of man" (Moses 1:39, emphasis added). Glory has to do with God. At its base rests the concept of weightiness. On one level, this weight represents the honor that one has qualified for, or, in the case of God, the honor that is due to him. On another level, it hints at God's embodiment. God's glory has manifested itself in various ways, including the brightness of his presence, pictured early on in the pillar of fire that stood over the Israelite tabernacle (see Ex. 40:38 and Num. 9:15–16). This link to the tabernacle brings forward temple connections that appear in the special, bright

---

151. The Greek term translated "forgiveness" and "remission" is ἄφεσις (*aphesis*). BDAG, 155.

152. These instances, and others, are gathered in Winger, *Ephesians*, 222 n. 186.

153. Bednar, "In the Strength of the Lord," 121–28; Rasmus, "Enabling Power of the Atonement," 18–21; see also Eising, *TDOT*, 4:349, 353–55; Grundmann, *TDNT*, 2:313–16; Oepke, *TDNT*, 2:542–43; Braun, *TDNT*, 6:464. See W of M 1:14; Mosiah 9:17; 10:10; Alma 20:4; etc.

clothing that participants wore in sacred settings (see Ezek. 16:9–12). In this connection, whatever modest honor we may enjoy in God's sight in this life will be realized fully in the celestial kingdom, including wearing "a crown of glory at [his] right hand" (D&C 104:7; see also D&C 101:65 and the Notes on 1:6, 14).

These observations lead us to one of the structural elements in these verses. Almost identical expressions appear in 1:12 and 1:14, "to the praise of his glory," and with a minor difference in 1:6, "to the praise of the glory of his grace." These word clusters mark off the three sections of the hymn—one devoted to the Father (see 1:3–6), one to the Son (see 1:7–12), and the last to the Holy Spirit (see 1:13–14). The remarkable harmony that these parts exhibit illustrates not only the cadences and balance of this hymnic piece but also the knowledge that Paul had come to in understanding the roles of the members of the Godhead. To wit, it was the Father who initiated the seminal events of the grand council "before the foundation of the world" (1:4). The Son offered unfathomable "redemption" and "forgiveness" as well as a future punctuated by "an inheritance" (1:7, 11). In time, as a fitting capstone to the believers' mortal experience, the Holy Spirit is to perform a sealing that "is the earnest" or down payment for "our [heavenly] inheritance" (1:13–14).

"MAKING MENTION OF YOU IN MY PRAYERS" (1:15–23)

Paul's focus now turns from a hymn to a prayer. With a spirit of rejoicing at the Ephesians' acceptance of the gospel message, his letter gathers together warmth and a spirit of instruction. As in other letters, he affirms that, after learning of their conversions, he has ceased "not to give thanks for you, making mention of you in my prayers" (1:16; see also 3:14–19; Philip. 1:8–11; Col. 1:3, 9; and 2 Thes. 1:11). Now that the "eyes of your understanding [are] enlightened," Paul prays for three blessings to come to these people—"to know what is the hope of [God's] calling" to them; to grasp "the riches of the glory of his inheritance" that God has now offered to them; and to understand "the exceeding greatness of [God's] power to us-ward who believe," a power that was unveiled "when he raised [Christ] from the dead" (1:18–20). There is more.

In a prayer that exhibits hymn-like qualities, Paul has sought to uncover the majesty of the Risen Christ. His exalted stature within the universe is underlined by the fact that the Father, in a formal act, "set him at his own right hand in the heavenly places." In this lofty spot, the Resurrected Savior resides "far above all principality, and power, and might, and dominion," whether earthly or heavenly. Besides all this, Christ's name has eclipsed "every name that is named, not only in this world, but also in that which is to come." That is to say, no name, whether royal or military or religious, is to be compared to that of the Son of God. All dim in dignity and power. To emphasize the impoverished nature of heavenly and earthly powers when viewed from a divine perspective, Paul next wrote that God "hath put all things under [Christ's] feet, and gave him to be the head over all things to the church." The church, it turns out, now "is his body," Christ's special domain and responsibility (1:20–23).

In this section especially, we expect a direct mention of acquaintances, something that is missing both from Paul's introduction to this letter and from his final greetings (see 1:1–2; 6:21–24). This lack in a letter written to a congregation in Ephesus where Paul spent up to three full years (see Acts 20:31) has led some scholars to conclude that not Paul but another person penned this epistle. But this need not be so (see the Note on 6:21 and the Analysis of 6:21–24).

King James Translation

15 Wherefore I also, after I heard of your faith in the Lord Jesus, and love unto all the saints, 16 Cease not to give thanks for you, making mention of you in my prayers; 17 That the God of our Lord Jesus Christ, the Father of glory, may give unto you the spirit of wisdom and revelation in the knowledge of him: 18 The eyes of your understanding being enlightened; that ye may know what is the hope of his calling, and what the riches of the glory of his inheritance in the saints, 19 And what is the exceeding greatness of his power to us-ward who believe, according to the working of his mighty power, 20 Which he wrought in Christ, when he raised him from the dead, and set him at his own right hand in the heavenly places, 21 Far above all principality, and power, and might,

New Rendition

15 For this reason, I especially, having heard about the faith in the Lord Jesus among you and your love for all the saints, 16 do not stop giving thanks for you, remembering you in my prayers. 17 I pray that the God of our Lord Jesus Christ, the Father of glory, may give to you the spirit of wisdom and revelation in knowing him. 18 I pray that, with the eyes of your heart enlightened, you may know what is the hope of his calling, what is the wealth of his glorious inheritance among the saints, 19 and what is the surpassing greatness of his power toward us, the ones who believe according to the action of his mighty strength, 20 which he enacted in Christ when he raised him from the dead and seated him at his right hand in the heavenly realms, 21 far above all

and dominion, and every name that is named, not only in this world, but also in that which is to come: 22 And hath put all things under his feet, and gave him to be the head over all things to the church, 23 Which is his body, the fulness of him that filleth all in all.

rule, authority, power, dominion, and every name that is named, not only in this age, but also in the one to come. 22 And he placed all things under his feet, and gave him as head over all things in the church, 23 which is his body—the fullness of the one filling all things in every way.

Notes on 1:15–23

1:15 *I also:* The words consist of a crasis or joining of two Greek words, καί and ἐγώ (*kai* and *egō*), a conjunction and personal pronoun. The force of the expression accentuates not only Paul as the author and sender of the letter, as in 3:1 and 4:1, but also his apostolic authority. How so? "It is typical of Paul to interrupt more general descriptions of God's relation to the church and the world with references to himself. These references . . . express a high apostolic self-consciousness which has its root in the function entrusted to the apostle by God."[154]

I heard of your faith: Plainly, other missionaries have been at work among the Gentiles in Ephesus and Asia Minor, people whom Paul elsewhere called "fellowlaborers" (see Philip. 4:3; 1 Thes. 3:2; and Philem. 1:1, 24). In Ephesians, Paul has named no one who had engaged in missionary labors in this city. That said, might he have authorized such people to continue his work even as he hastened to leave Ephesus after the outbreak of public opposition in the theater (see Acts 20:1)? Or more preferably, might we view the account of his last meeting with the "elders" and "overseers" from Ephesus as his commission to them to continue the work he had begun in the city (Acts 20:17, 28)? For he asked them "to feed the church of God," a line that can be rendered more expressively as "to shepherd the church of God" (Acts 20:28). In this passage in Acts, the verb ποιμαίνω (*poimainō*) has to do with shepherding or caring for others; the plural of the noun ποιμήν (*poimēn*) appears in Ephesians 4:11 with the translated meaning "pastors" (see the Note on 4:11).[155]

---

154. Barth, *Ephesians,* 1:145; see also Lincoln, *Ephesians,* 54; Larkin, *Handbook,* 18. Some of Paul's references to himself appear in Rom. 7:24–25; 15:15–21; 2 Cor. 3:1–3; Gal. 1:10–2:21; Eph. 3:3–4.

155. BDAG, 842.

heard: The issue centers on whether the author of the letter has only heard of the faith and love of the Ephesian Saints, therefore being unacquainted with them, or whether, knowing some of these people from earlier experiences, he has received an update from a traveler, someone like Tychicus (6:21; Col. 4:7). If the former, then the author cannot be Paul, who had spent a long time in the city of Ephesus among church members. If the latter, and several years had passed since Paul was in Ephesus, then the author was almost assuredly the Apostle.[156]

faith: Some scholars have argued that because the word "love" is likely not original with this letter, the term πίστις (*pistis*) should be rendered "faithful," as in 1:1.[157] But reasons exist for seeing "love" as the primal reading (see the Note below).

love: This term and its definite article (τὴν ἀγάπην, *tēn agapēn*) are missing from the earliest and best manuscripts, including 𝔓[46], raising a question about its authenticity. Three observations are worth noticing. First, Colossians 1:4 repeats the full expression that we find here, "the love unto all the saints" (τὴν ἀγάπην τὴν εἰς πάντας τοὺς ἁγίους, *tēn agapēn tēn eis pantas tous hagious*), making perfect sense in both passages. Next, if "love" is omitted, the second definite article (τήν, *tēn*) has no natural referent; it modifies nothing. Last, because the two definite articles are close together (*tēn . . . tēn*), it is very likely that the eye of an early copyist fell on the second one and mistakenly omitted the term for love.[158] If "love" were to be omitted, the line would read, "after I heard of your faithfulness toward the Lord Jesus and toward all the saints."

As is apparent to those who go through a true conversion experience, genuine love follows the onset of faith, as implied here (see Gal. 5:22; 1 Tim. 1:5; 1 Pet. 1:5–7; and D&C 4:6; see also the Note on 3:17). In addition, Paul regularly paired both faith and love (or charity) with hope, a word that appears in 1:18 (see Rom. 5:1–5; 1 Cor. 13:13; Gal. 5:5–6; and 1 Thes. 5:8).

1:16 *Cease not to give thanks:* If the author of the epistle is not the Apostle but instead is writing in his name, the falsity deepens and becomes more grating with the claim of contact with God through prayer (see Rom. 1:8–10; Col. 1:3; 1 Thes. 1:2–3; and Philem. 1:4).

---

156. Barth, *Ephesians,* 1:10–11; Fowl, *Ephesians,* 55; Winger, *Ephesians,* 235.

157. Lincoln, *Ephesians,* 6, 54–55; Best, *Ephesians,* 160.

158. Metzger, *Textual Commentary,* 533; Caird, *Letters,* 43–44; Barth, *Ephesians,* 1:146–47; Larkin, *Handbook,* 18; Merkle, *Guide,* 40.

prayers: Just out of sight but fully present is Paul's unexpressed confidence that his prayers will make a difference in believers' lives. From his own experience, he understood the principle enunciated by James that the "fervent prayer of a righteous man [or woman] availeth much" (James 5:16). From the Old Testament, one of the most significant examples comes from Jeremiah. Because the prophet's prayers were impacting heaven, the Lord asked Jeremiah not to pray, a stunning request. The Lord knew that the citizens of Jerusalem deserved punishment for a long list of willful missteps. Yet the prophet was pleading for them, with clear effect. We read, "Pray not thou for this people, neither lift up cry nor prayer for them, neither make intercession to me: for I will not hear thee" (Jer. 7:16). The Lord had made up his mind: "I [the Lord] will not hear them in the time that they cry unto me for their trouble" (Jer. 11:14; see also Jer. 14:11). Remarkably, both before and after the sack of Jerusalem, some citizens at last grasped the effectiveness of Jeremiah's prayers and came to the prophet, asking that he pray for them (see Jer. 37:3; 42:2, 20).

In other scripture, we see that prayer unwraps a divine power that can be made available to humans, what some have called "the enabling power of the Atonement."[159] A short set of selections makes the point, all from modern scripture. We find the following language: "In the strength of the Lord did we go forth to battle ... for I [Zeniff] and my people did cry mightily to the Lord that he would deliver us" (Mosiah 9:17); "he [Jesus] will take upon him their infirmities, ... that he may know according to the flesh how to succor his people" (Alma 7:12); "Lamoni said unto Ammon: I know, in the strength of the Lord thou canst do all things" (Alma 20:4); "I [Ammon] will boast of my God, for in his strength I can do all things" (Alma 26:12; see also W of M 1:14; Mosiah 10:10; etc.; the Notes on 1:9, 21; 2:7, 16; 3:16; 4:30; and the Analysis of 1:3–14).

1:17 *That:* In this instance, the Greek conjunction ἵνα (*hina*), usually with the meaning "in order that," marks the beginning of the content of Paul's prayer,[160] a regular occurrence elsewhere in his correspondence (see 3:16; Rom. 1:11; 15:31–32; 2 Cor. 1:11; Col. 1:9; etc.).

---

159. Bednar, "In the Strength of the Lord," 121–28; Rasmus, "Enabling Power of the Atonement," 18–21; see also Eising, *TDOT,* 4:349, 353–55; Grundmann, *TDNT,* 2:313–16; Oepke, *TDNT,* 2:542–43; Braun, *TDNT,* 6:464.

160. BDAG, 475–77; Best, *Ephesians,* 161; Larkin, *Handbook,* 19; Merkle, *Guide,* 41.

the God of our Lord Jesus Christ: God is the subject of the rest of this chapter. For instance, it is he who has enlightened "your understanding," has disclosed "the hope [that rests in] his calling" of believers into his kingdom, and has "put all things under [Christ's] feet" (1:18, 22). Moreover, Paul sets out our relationship to the Father because this title, "God of our Lord Jesus Christ," both "emphasizes the humanity of Jesus" and establishes "the pattern for his relationship with other men," thus leading believers to his Father.[161] Further, by this language Paul affirms the relationship between God and Jesus,[162] two members of the divine Godhead. One is God, "the Father of glory," and the other is the Son, "our Lord Jesus Christ" (see the Note on 1:6; especially 4:1).

the Father of glory: In its context, this expression links most directly to the enlightening of "the eyes of your understanding" (1:18; see also 2 Cor. 4:4, 6).[163] That is, God's glory carries revelatory power. Said another way, this glory comes to believers as divine "light that quickeneth your understandings," aiding them in grasping eternal realities (D&C 88:11). From the records of Jesus' post-Resurrection ministry, this power was first manifested when the eyes of the two travelers to Emmaus "were opened, and they knew him" (Luke 24:31). Paul has written of this celestial phenomenon in other letters. In its form as light, he wrote that "God, who commanded the light to shine out of darkness, hath shined in our hearts, to give the light of the knowledge of the glory of God in the face of Jesus Christ" (2 Cor. 4:6; see also 2 Cor. 4:4). As in this epistle (see 1:20), Paul featured this power in the Resurrection of Jesus and in our lives: "As Christ was raised up from the dead by the glory of the Father, even so we also should walk in newness of life" (Rom. 6:4; see also 1 Cor. 6:14; and the Notes on 1:6, 12, 14; 2:18; 4:6).

may give: Although the manuscripts differ on the proper reading of this verb, whether a subjunctive or optative of δίδωμι (*didōmi*),[164] the force is not to be missed. Paul plainly reminded readers that all which follows in his prayer for them is to come as a gift from God. Nothing will or can be earned.

the spirit of wisdom and revelation: Even though the definite article "the" is missing before the term for "spirit" and, therefore, is not part of

---

161. Caird, *Letters,* 44.
162. Lincoln, *Ephesians,* 56; Best, *Ephesians,* 161.
163. Lincoln, *Ephesians,* 56: "the power to illuminate [the mind]."
164. Larkin, *Handbook,* 20.

the text, its presence is plainly implied.[165] Hence, Paul was pointing to that Holy Spirit that comes to a person following baptism, as the Gospels make clear (see 1:13; Matt. 3:11; Mark 1:8; Luke 3:16; and John 3:5), and which serves as a revelatory agent (see 3:3, 5; 1 Cor. 12:3–4, 8–11; Moro. 10:8–17; and D&C 46:10–28), bearing "record of the Father and the Son" (3 Ne. 11:32 and Moses 1:24; 5:9; 7:11). A rough equivalent of "wisdom and revelation" is framed by "wisdom and prudence" (1:8). But revelation (ἀποκάλυψις, *apokalypsis*) is richer from the divine side, for it implies an open conduit between God and believer (see the Note on 1:8).

wisdom: Paul's plea that believers receive this gift touches on the spiritual gifts that we find listed in other contexts (see 1 Cor. 12:4–11; Moro. 10:8–18; and D&C 46:8–27). Twice, the first gift noted is "the word of wisdom," indicating that the possessor is to teach what has been divinely granted to him or her (1 Cor. 12:8; Moro. 10:9). Only in D&C 46 is this gift preceded by the mention of other gifts (see D&C 46:17). Perhaps significantly, in all the lists "the word of wisdom" is followed by "the word of knowledge," again with the implied or specified imperative that the possessor teach others (1 Cor. 12:8; Moro. 10:10; D&C 46:18; see also Rom. 11:33 and the Notes on 1:8; 3:10; 5:15).

revelation: In one sense, we must look to the Old Testament to get our bearings about revelation (ἀποκάλυψις, *apokalypsis*). From the Old Testament, we learn that Jehovah revealed himself to the ancient Israelites, instructing them about how he wanted them to worship him and to treat one another. But he was not the God of that group of people alone. He also declared himself to be "the Creator and Lord of the world." As such, all peoples are to "share [in] the revelation of salvation."[166] For Paul, that moment had now come through revelations both "unto me" and "unto his [God's] holy apostles and prophets by the Spirit" (3:3, 5). That fact is apparent in the way that Paul has addressed his Gentile readers in this letter, calling them former "aliens from the commonwealth of Israel, and strangers from the covenants of promise, having no hope, and without God in the world" (2:12). But after Jesus' Atonement, Gentiles "who sometimes were far off are made nigh by the blood of Christ" (2:13). In addition, "through [Christ] we both [Jews and Gentiles] have access by one Spirit unto the Father." As a result, Gentiles "are no more strangers and

---

165. Winger, *Ephesians,* 239.
166. Albrecht Oepke, *TDNT,* 3:574.

foreigners, but fellowcitizens with the saints, and of the household of God" (2:18–19), a wonderful ending to the Gentiles' general inability to access salvation. In another sense, as already noticed above, revelation is the means by which God has disclosed himself and his will to the ancients and the means by which he will continue to reveal himself and his will to followers in the future (see the Notes on 1:9; 3:3; 4:20).

knowledge of him: Paul, writing a noun with an objective genitive,[167] points to the ultimate treasure that comes from receiving divine wisdom and revelation—coming to know God. Even though we are mortal and reside in an imperfect world, this knowledge will graciously come to us from a celestial plane, as the context indicates. What is more, it is possible to "be filled with the knowledge of [God's] will in all wisdom and spiritual understanding," with the practical consequence that we "walk worthy of the Lord . . . being fruitful in every good work." For those who pursue this path, it means "increasing in the knowledge of God" (Col. 1:9–10), even enjoying an "intimate companionship with God."[168] This special relationship with God, arriving as it does through revelation, is not restricted to Paul and the other apostles. It is available to all believers (see the Notes on 3:18–19; 4:13, 17; 5:5).[169]

1:18 *The eyes of your understanding:* In the language of scripture, the light from God and specifically from his Son, which is called in one place both "the light of truth" and "the light of Christ," has ignited physical light in the universe, including the light from the sun and the stars. This light allows us to see (D&C 88:6–11). But that is only part of the story. This divine light "is the same light that quickeneth your understandings" (D&C 88:11). Hence, such light possesses both physical and spiritual qualities. It is the spiritual nature of light that touches "the eyes of your understanding." The term translated "understanding" here is the term for "heart" (καρδία, *kardia*). In this setting, it has to do with "inner awareness" (see 1 Cor. 4:6 and 2 Pet. 1:19).[170] For the opposite, that of spiritual obtuseness, see Isaiah 6:9–10 and the passages that roughly quote or cite this pair of verses (see Matt. 13:15; John 12:40; Acts 28:26–27; and Rom. 11:8; see also Jer. 5:21; Ezek. 12:2; and the Notes on 4:6, 18).

---

167. Herbert Weir Smyth, *Greek Grammar,* rev. Gordon M. Messing (Cambridge, Mass.: Harvard University Press, 1956), §§1331–34; Larkin, *Handbook,* 20; Merkle, *Guide,* 42.

168. Franz-Josef Helfmeyer, *TDOT,* 3:395.

169. Lincoln, *Ephesians,* 57.

170. BDAG, 508; see also Friedrich Baumgärtel and Johannes Behm, *TDNT,* 3:611–13.

being enlightened: The passive verb, here the perfect participle of φωτίζω (*phōtizō*), "to illuminate, enlighten," points to God as the agent who illumines this light.[171] This verb also appears in 3:9. The Resurrected Jesus, in an act of spiritual enlightenment, opened the eyes of the two travelers to Emmaus so that "they knew him." Within a few hours, the Risen Savior showed himself to "the eleven [apostles] and . . . them that were with them." Throughout that night, the Resurrected Lord "opened . . . their understanding, that they might understand the scriptures" (Luke 24:31, 33, 45).[172] These examples are among several recorded in scripture. Later in this epistle, for instance, Paul begged his readers to "walk as children of light" because "Christ shall give thee [spiritual] light" (5:8, 14). Further, by eating the forbidden fruit in the Garden of Eden, the eyes of Adam and Eve "were opened," and thereby they came to understand their condition (Gen. 3:5–7; Moses 4:11–13). Finally, as the prophet Alma taught among a people known as Zoramites, he promised his hearers that, if they planted the word of God in their hearts and nourished it, then "your understanding [would] begin to be enlightened, and your mind [would] begin to expand" (Alma 32:34; see also the Notes on 3:9; 4:17; 5:8, 14).

know: In this case, a believer will come to know three prospects that Jesus' Atonement presents, prospects unrivaled in other religions. These promises now follow, tied together by the repetition of the word "what."

what: The rolling cadence produced by the threefold repetition of the Greek indefinite pronouns for "what" in this and the next verse (τίς, τίς, τί, *tis, tis, ti*)[173] not only aids a reader's memory but also deftly summarizes what has come and will yet come to the person who has embraced the gospel message.

the hope of his calling: This hope (ἐλπίς, *elpis*), the first of three promises voiced in Paul's prayer, comes from God alone and has an immediate impact. Most often, a person's hope centers in the distant future, the end-time (see Acts 2:26–27; 23:6; 1 Cor. 15:19; Col. 1:5; etc.; and the Notes on 1:12; 2:12; 4:4).[174] In this verse, however, hope also brings to the initiate an unlooked-for welcome within the celestial family of God. For the believer, this experience becomes, in effect, "an act of creation and election; through this act [a convert's] non-being becomes being, [a] non-beloved [stranger] becomes

---

171. BDAG, 1074; Larkin, *Handbook,* 20–21.
172. Brown, *Testimony of Luke,* 1124–26, 1135.
173. BDAG, 1006–7.
174. Bultmann and Rengstorf, *TDNT,* 2:530–33.

beloved," effectively wrapping believers "in the power of God"[175] (see 2:12; 4:1; Rom. 5:1–5; and Col. 1:27).[176] About the calling, in the New Testament the Greek term κλῆσις (*klēsis*) generally points to a call or invitation from God, whether direct (see 2 Thes. 1:11; Philip. 3:14; 2 Tim. 1:9; and Heb. 3:1) or, less often, through an authorized human agent (see Heb. 5:4).[177] Such a calling has to do with both God's invitation to the initiate to come inside the kingdom and a specific calling to serve within the church (see Matt. 11:28–30; D&C 58:26–28; 107:99;[178] and the Notes on 4:1, 4).

the riches of the glory of his inheritance: Beginning with the word "riches" (πλοῦτος, *ploutos*), we behold a tripling of nouns that underline in bright colors the abundance of God's gifts. In the next verse, 1:19, a similar grouping of nouns appears, thereby underscoring God's power and majesty. In the King James translation, we read, "the working of his mighty power," wherein three nouns are joined: ἐνέργεια (*energeia*, "action"), κράτος (*kratos*, "might"), and ἰσχύς (*ischys*, "strength"). This type of conjoining is not accidental but emphatic, as Romans 11:33 and Colossians 1:11 demonstrate.[179]

riches: Called elsewhere "the unsearchable riches of Christ" and "the riches of his goodness and . . . longsuffering" (3:8; Rom. 2:4), this wealth (*ploutos*)[180] has almost nothing to do with this life, except when God prospers people for his own aims (see Gen. 12:2–3; 22:16–18; 2 Sam. 12:7–14; 1 Ne. 2:20; 15:18; Mosiah 25:24; and 4 Ne. 1:7). These riches lie in the custody of God and Christ, a characteristic that Paul calls "the depth . . . of the wisdom and knowledge of God" (Rom. 11:33; see also Rom. 9:23; 10:12; and 2 Cor. 8:9),[181] and have much to do with the next life when "he that receiveth me [Jesus Christ] receiveth my Father; and he that receiveth my Father receiveth my Father's kingdom; therefore all that my Father hath shall be given unto him" (D&C 84:37–38; see also the Notes on 1:7; 2:4, 7; 3:8, 16).

glory: A person can argue that we should understand this noun, "glory" (δόξα, *doxa*), to be an attributive genitive to the word for "riches" (*ploutos*), with the meaning "rich glory."[182] However, for our purposes, we

175. Barth, *Ephesians*, 1:151.
176. BDAG, 320.
177. Schmidt, *TDNT*, 3:491–92; BDAG, 549.
178. Brian L. Pitcher, "Callings," in *EM*, 1:248–50.
179. Walter Grundmann, *TDNT*, 3:402.
180. BDAG, 832.
181. Hauck and Kasch, *TDNT*, 6:328–29.
182. Larkin, *Handbook*, 21–22, citing Best, *Critical and Exegetical Commentary on Ephesians*, and Daniel B. Wallace, *Greek Grammar Beyond the Basics: An Exegetical Syntax of the New Testament* (Grand Rapids, Mich.: Zondervan, 1996).

observe that "glory" in this context stands next to the following noun, "inheritance" (κληρονομία, *klēronomia*), resulting in the KJV sense "the glory of [God's] inheritance." This glory will belong to believers but lies in the future (see the Note on 1:14). And it has everything to do with the kind of inheritance that will assuredly come from God, bringing with it a glory that will rest on the faithful in the next life. As the Risen Christ inspiringly reminds us, "If ye are faithful ye shall be ... crowned with honor, and glory, and immortality, and eternal life" (D&C 75:5; see also Rom. 9:23–24; D&C 88:107; and the Notes on 1:12, 14; 3:13, 16; especially the Note on 1:6).

his inheritance: Ultimately, any inheritance belongs to God, whether earthly or heavenly. The persisting question concerns whether we will share this inheritance with God in the future life. The answer is that it depends largely on us, as Paul reminded readers later in this epistle: "No whoremonger, nor unclean person, nor covetous man ... hath any inheritance in the kingdom of Christ and of God" (5:5). As we have observed above, the faithful person "that receiveth [Christ] ... receiveth [his] Father's kingdom [and] ... all that [his] Father hath" (D&C 84:37–38). That is to say, for "those who fear me [God], and delight to honor those who serve me in righteousness, ... great shall be their reward and eternal shall be their glory" (D&C 76:5–6; see also the Notes on 1:14; 5:5; and appendix 2).

in the saints: A better translation is "among the saints" (NR). In this instance, the common Greek preposition usually translated "in" (ἐν, *en*) points to a place or location—that is, "among" or "within" a certain group of people.[183] The term "saints" here has nothing to do with current fellow members of the church but connects directly with the "saints" whom believers will meet in the next world, people who have truly become holy, as is implied in the Greek noun ἅγιοι (*hagioi*), which means "holy ones" (see the Notes on 1:1; 2:19; 5:26).[184]

1:19 what: This interrogative pronoun, τί (*ti*), introduces the third and final prospect that Paul's prayer seeks for Gentile converts (see the Note on 1:18). Here, he introduces his readers to God's immense powers (see Matt. 17:20; Mark 11:23; Luke 17:6; Acts 16:25–26; Ether 12:13, 30; etc.).[185] In this

---

183. BDAG, 326–27.

184. Otto Procksch and Karl Georg Kuhn, *TDNT*, 1:107 n. 61: "Eph. 1:18, then, can hardly be interpreted in any other way, so that we have to think of the saints in heaven"; see also BDAG, 10–11.

185. Brown, *Testimony of Luke,* 784.

case, they were manifested in what the Father did through Christ after the Crucifixion, beginning with the teaching of the departed spirits and then engineering the Resurrection (see 1 Pet. 3:18–20; 4:6; see also Rom. 14:9 and Rev. 11:18).

the exceeding greatness of his power: Prior to writing the set of three nouns at the end of this verse, Paul writes a pair of nouns that anticipate the three. The pair of nouns, μέγεθος (*megethos,* "greatness")[186] and δύναμις (*dynamis,* "power"), are often treated as if in an attributive relationship, producing the meaning "surpassingly great power."[187] Nevertheless, the doubling of nouns adds to the importance of what follows with the triple nouns.[188]

to us-ward who believe: The prepositional phrase εἰς ἡμᾶς (*eis hēmas*) signals a direction toward something, with the meaning "toward us."[189] When Paul writes "who believe," he scoops up into his gospel vessel those who have embraced both Christ and the saving message linked to him. And when we arrive at 2:5–7, we shall meet extraordinary blessings released to believers through God's power.

the working of his mighty power: The first concept to establish is that the three nouns in this expression come hard one after another, producing a thunderclap effect that snaps the reader's attention toward God's breathtaking powers (see 6:10 and Isa. 40:26).[190] Hence, it is worth noticing the fuller lexicographical, structural, and grammatical picture of this line in order to capture the blistering force of what Paul has written, underscoring God's matchless power. The first noun, ἐνέργεια (*energeia*), bears the meaning "action" or "working" and has to do with "realized power"—that is, with divine power that is already at work among believers. We have identified this aspect as "the enabling power of the Atonement" (see the Notes on 1:9, 16, 21; 3:7, 20; 4:16 and the Analysis of 1:3–14). The second noun, κράτος (*kratos*), carries the sense of "might" or "strength" and constitutes "resident power"—that is, the compressed, packed intensity of might or power. The third noun, ἰσχύς (*ischys*), pushes forward the notion of "strength" or "power" that is inherent in God's capacity to operate without restraint or external resistance.[191] The combined intensity of these terms, of course, is manifest most plainly in what God has done for his Son,

---

186. This noun appears in the New Testament only at Eph. 1:19.
187. Larkin, *Handbook,* 22; Merkle, *Guide,* 44.
188. Grundmann, *TDNT,* 3:402.
189. BDAG, 289; Larkin, *Handbook,* 22; Merkle, *Guide,* 44.
190. Grundmann, *TDNT,* 3:402.
191. BDAG, 335, 484, 565.1; Larkin, *Handbook,* 22–23.

raising "him from the dead" and seating "him at his own right hand" while putting "all things under his feet" and establishing "him to be the head over all things to the church" (1:20, 22). In the mortal world, such power is made available to believers. For within a few lines, the Apostle will affirm that, with his matchless power, God "hath raised us up together [with Christ], and made us sit together in heavenly places in Christ Jesus" (2:6). Additionally, we recall the dazzling power (*dynamis*) that not only strengthens "the inner man" but also blesses us "exceeding abundantly above all that we ask" from God (3:16, 20; see also the Notes on 1:21; 3:7, 16, 20).

Structurally and grammatically, we are looking at a series of genitives whose relationship to one another is usually expressed in English by the preposition "of." Thus, "the working of the might of his power" frames an understandable translation of these words. But most translators treat the second and third nouns as standing in an attributive relationship where the latter noun acts as an adjective. That is to say, they carry a meaning something like "his mighty power" rather than "the might of his power."[192] For English readers, as a person quickly detects, this means the full force of Paul's potent Greek nouns becomes somewhat diminished in translation.

Some of this power, especially that which was displayed in Jesus' visit to the spirit world (see 1 Pet. 3:18–20; 4:6) and in his Resurrection (see Rom. 14:9), presses forcefully forward to defeat Satan. For later in this epistle, Paul begged his readers to "be strong in the Lord, and in the power of his might" by donning "the whole armour of God, that ye may be able to stand against the wiles of the devil" (6:10–11). Much of this effort will have to take place in the home that is sited on a firm foundation.[193]

The synoptic Gospels, Luke's especially, paint a picture of Satan's attempts to undercut the home as a bastion of tranquility and goodness. There Jesus sketched scenes of "a house divided against itself"; "a strong man [who] keepeth his palace [house]" but is "overcome" by "a stronger than he"; and "the unclean spirit" that is pushed out of its human host or house and forced to travel "through dry places" until it returns with "seven other spirits more wicked than himself" (Luke 11:17, 21–22, 24, 26). The common denominator in these short stories is the house or home, the place where a family dwells together. Taken as a cluster, these stories warn Jesus' listeners about the potential for losing ground in their families to evil influences. But the good news is that the "stronger" person is the Savior,

---

192. Smyth, *Greek Grammar*, §986; Larkin, *Handbook*, 22–23.
193. Brown, *Testimony of Luke*, 345–47.

and, with his power, he can and will displace and "overcome" the evil "strong man" (Luke 11:21–22; see also Mark 3:27 and the Note on 6:10).[194]

1:20 Which: The feminine relative pronoun links back to the feminine noun that is translated "working" (ἐνέργεια, *energeia*) in 1:19, setting up a wordplay on the following verb (ἐνήργησεν, *enērgēsen*, "to be working").[195] Not incidentally, although the relative pronoun reaches back to the prior verse, it also signals the end of Paul's prayer and the beginning of a hymn-like praise of God's "mighty power" that runs to the end of the chapter.[196]

wrought: This verb, here the past or aorist tense of ἐνήργησεν (*enērgēsen*; see the Notes on 1:11; 2:2; 3:20), ties to the noun translated "working" in 1:19.[197] One notices the rhythmic repetition of similar sounding words, including the Greek word translated "raised" (ἐγείρας, *egeiras*), adding to the memorable character of the passage. What God has done rolls out in four statements articulated both in this verse and in 1:22, roughly matching what God has done for both Jewish and Gentile believers in 2:5–6 (see the Notes on 2:5–6).

in Christ: This prepositional phrase holds within it a title, for the term "Christ" is preceded by the definite article, making the phrase "in the Christ" (ἐν τῷ χριστῷ, *en tō christō*).[198] Further, the fact that the manifestations of power that Paul will rehearse next have all occurred "in Christ" (see 1:3) brings the reader face-to-face with God's power exercised for good. Nothing here hints at a deity's "destructive or terrifying" powers unleashed on unsuspecting humans as one might find in pagan religions.

raised him from the dead: These words form the first of four declarations of God's acts in exalting his Son, spelled out in this verse and 1:22.[199] Paul's appeal to God's power in 1:19 finds its most striking illustration in the reuniting of Jesus' body and spirit in his Resurrection.[200] What is more, Jesus' Resurrection, long before it occurred, served as the anchor for his authority in no less an undertaking than cleansing the Jerusalem temple: "The Jews [asked], . . . What sign shewest thou unto us, seeing that thou doest these things? Jesus answered and said unto them, Destroy this temple,

---

194. Gerhard von Rad and Werner Foerster, *TDNT*, 2:79–80; Grundmann, *TDNT*, 3:400–1; Brown, *Testimony of Luke*, 564–75.

195. BDAG, 335; Larkin, *Handbook*, 23; Merkle, *Guide*, 44.

196. Winger, *Ephesians*, 252, 261.

197. BDAG, 335.

198. Larkin, *Handbook*, 23.

199. Winger, *Ephesians*, 244.

200. Grundmann, *TDNT*, 2:315–16.

and in three days I will raise it up" (John 2:18–19). In another important vein, Jesus' Resurrection impacts believers in the here and now. How so? His Resurrection spills into our inner lives. As Paul wrote in another place, "If the Spirit of [God] that raised up Jesus from the dead dwell in you, he that raised up Christ from the dead shall also quicken your mortal bodies by his Spirit that dwelleth in you" (Rom. 8:11). The verb translated "quicken" (ζωοποιέω, *zōopoieō*) possesses the meaning "to enliven, make alive."[201] It is in this sense that we read later in the letter to the Ephesians, "Even when we were dead in sins, [God] *hath quickened* us together with Christ, ... and hath raised us up together" (2:5–6, emphasis added; see also 1 Cor. 6:14; Philip. 3:21;[202] and the Notes on 2:1, 5; 5:14). Such statements make clear that the faithful will enjoy what Jesus enjoys, being "heirs of God, and joint-heirs with Christ" (Rom. 8:17; see also the Notes on 1:18; 2:6).

raised: The active participle of ἐγείρω (*egeirō*)—ἐγείρας (*egeiras*) in this case—adds to the similar sounding ἐνέργεια and ἐνήργησεν (*energeia* and *enērgēsen*) that we have just met. Thus, by placing together similar sounding words, Paul has artfully emphasized that God's "working" has been aimed at the eventual raising of Jesus from the dead. In its active voice, the verb *egeirō* has to do with lifting or raising, meanings that migrate into the spiritual realm and attach themselves to the Resurrection of Jesus (see Matt. 14:2; 27:52; 28:6–7; Mark 16:6; Luke 24:6, 34; etc.).[203] Although the verb ἀνίστημι (*anistēmi*) also denotes the Resurrection, it occurs much less frequently in the New Testament (see 5:14 and the Note thereon; Acts 2:24, 32; 10:40; 1 Thes. 4:14; etc.).[204] The verb *egeirō* also connects to ordinances in Paul's thinking, specifically to baptism. For we read in Romans 6:4, "We are buried with [Christ] by baptism into death; that like as Christ *was raised up* [passive of *egeirō*] from the dead . . . even so we also should walk in newness of life" (emphasis added). The passive, of course, alludes to God as the one who raised Christ from death. And "newness of life" does not characterize only those living on earth but also those residing in the spirit world.

---

201. BDAG, 431–32; Louw-Nida, §23.92.

202. The verb in 2:5 is συζωοποιέω (*suzōopoieō*), an expanded form of ζωοποιέω (*zōopoieō*), which we run across in 1:20 and which has added the preposition συν (*sun,* "with") as a prefix, whose meaning is "to make alive together with someone." BDAG, 954–55.

203. Albrecht Oepke, *TDNT,* 2:334–37; BDAG, 271–72.

204. Albrecht Oepke, *TDNT,* 1:368–72; BDAG, 83.

set him at his own right hand: This expression unfolds the second of the four divine actions that God undertook to exalt Jesus. Jesus did not seat himself at his Father's right hand. Far from it. Heaven exhibits more formality than that, including its seating arrangements. It is God who seated Jesus in such a place of honor, as anticipated in Psalm 110:1 ("Sit thou at my right hand"), a passage that has helped to shape passages like this one (see Acts 2:34–35; 5:31; Heb. 1:13; Rev. 4:2–11; etc.). Texts that speak of Jesus seating himself at his Father's side seem to be written from an after-the-fact viewpoint (see Col. 3:1; Heb. 1:3; Rev. 4:2, 9; 5:13; D&C 20:24; 76:20; etc.). On a different track, because God's act of exalting Christ took place "in the heavenly places," it thereby eternally and concretely united actions on earth, which on one level began with the Resurrection of Christ, with those that occur in heaven. This grand binding fulfilled the expected unity of heaven and earth found elsewhere in scripture (see Matt. 6:10; 16:19; 18:18–19; 28:18; compare Luke 15:18, 21; and 1 Cor. 8:5–6).[205]

set: This verb, here the active participle of καθίζω (*kathizō*), bears the sense "to cause to sit down" and underlines the Father's role in the exaltation of Jesus to a place at his right hand.[206] Although Jesus regularly sat in places out-of-doors during his mortal life, thus disclosing his love of nature, here he is welcomed to a throne, fulfilling the expected enthroning of the Messiah King (see Ps. 47:8; Isa. 6:1; 52:13; Rev. 3:21; etc.).[207] Besides this, when applied to human believers, the act of being seated in a holy place (see 2:6) openly points to sacred acts in a sacred place (see the Notes on 2:10; 4:1, 13, 20, 22, 24; 5:2, 8, 14; 6:11, 13–14; the introduction section IX; and appendix 1).

at his own right hand: From this point, Paul's thoughts through the end of the chapter are spatial in character and no longer chronological: "at his own right hand" followed by "in the heavenly places," "far above," and so forth.[208] The right hand, of course, is the hand of blessedness and honor (see Ps. 80:17; Jer. 22:24; Matt. 25:32–33; and Rom. 8:34). It was purposely on the right side of the altar of incense that the angel Gabriel appeared to Zacharias, the priest, and brought the good news of a son to be born to Zacharias and his wife, Elisabeth (see Luke 1:11).[209] Besides this, God's right hand symbolizes

---

205. Traub and von Rad, *TDNT*, 5:517–20.
206. BDAG, 491–92.
207. Carl Schneider, *TDNT*, 3:440–43.
208. Fowl, *Ephesians*, 60.
209. Brown, *Testimony of Luke*, 98.

his power (see Ps. 20:6; 118:15) and his right to govern (see Deut. 33:2). As examples, with his right hand, he created the earth, and, in a gracious act, he rescued the Hebrew slaves from Egypt, fixing his claim to rule over them (see Ex. 15:6, 12; Isa. 48:13; etc.).[210]

in the heavenly places: This phrase appears earlier in 1:3 at the beginning of Paul's hymn. In the prior passage, the phrase linked to premortal events. Here, it sketches the scene wherein the exaltation of Christ occurred. As in 1:3, the Greek expression ἐν τοῖς ἐπουρανίοις (*en tois epouraniois*) means literally "in the heavenly" or "in the heavenlies." A translator has to supply a noun that helps to clarify the sense of the phrase, something like "realms," because the term "heavenly" is an adjective.[211] Naturally, supplying another word adds an interpretative layer, as one quickly grasps when introducing words like "places" or "kingdoms" or "glories." For implicit in such terms is the interpreter's view of the heavenly world, whether it is peopled by God and Christ alone or, in their company, by the souls of good people or by other personalities (see the Notes on 1:3; 2:6; 3:10; 6:12).

1:21 *Far above:* The action that is recounted in the prior verse and this one has taken place far from this world, in an elevated sphere. As a prelude to these events, the Risen Christ "ascended up far above all heavens" (4:10; see also the Note thereon; Dan. 7:13–14, 27; and 2 Cor. 12:2).

all principality, and power, and might, and dominion: Because the first two entities are mentioned twice more in this letter, one time in a positive setting (see 3:10) and another time in a negative context (see 6:12), it is important to grasp what these terms mean. In the end, we learn that, whether they represent forces for good or evil, all exist under the oversight of God and are allowed to function with his permission (see Job 2:1–7; 2 Thes. 2:7–10; D&C 19:2–3; 121:4; 122:9; and the Notes on 3:10; 6:12).

principality: This English word translates the Greek term ἀρχή (*archē*), which can mean either "power" or "beginning." At base, it presents the idea of "primacy," either of rank or of time.[212] In this verse, we are dealing with an entity that holds and exercises significant influence, though in what form is not fully clear. Each of the following entities, "power, and might, and dominion," are to be seen in the same light. In Ephesians, we see remarks about

---

210. Walter Grundmann, *TDNT,* 2:37–40; Jan Alberto Soggin and Heinz-Josef Fabry, *TDOT,* 6:99–104; Winger, *Ephesians,* 244–45.

211. A. Van Roon, *The Authenticity of Ephesians,* vol. 39 of *Supplements to Novum Testamentum* (Leiden: E. J. Brill, 1974), 213–15; BDAG, 737.

212. Gerhard Delling, *TDNT,* 1:479; BDAG, 137–38; Louw-Nida, §§67.65; 68.1; 89.16.

"spiritual wickedness in high [heavenly] places," serving notice that we may not be concerned here with benevolent powers (6:12; see also 2:2; and John 12:31; 16:11).[213] As an example, during his mortal ministry, Jesus found himself in a struggle with powers from the unseen world, most readily chronicled in the many exorcisms of devils that he performed. We discover a hint that, as early as Jesus' descent into this world, powers of darkness set upon him: "The light [Christ] shineth in darkness; and the darkness comprehended it not" (John 1:5). The verb here translated "to comprehend" (καταλαμβάνω, *katalambanō*) means in its first sense to seize physically, usually in a hostile way, and secondly to grasp mentally (see John 12:35, "lest darkness come upon you"; and 1 Thes. 5:4, "that that day should [not] overtake you as a thief").[214] That is only part of the story.

We also meet language about unseen, undetected darkness: "We wrestle . . . against the rulers of the darkness of this world" (6:12).[215] Jesus knew this darkness. At the time of his arrest, he declared to the arresting party, "This is your hour, and the power of darkness" (Luke 22:53). To be sure, the night of his arrest was dark, but it was also illumined by the Passover full moon. Hence, Jesus' reference was to something more menacing than the lack of sunlight. To his audience during his earlier Sermon on the Mount, he ominously intoned, "If thine eye be evil, thy whole body shall be full of darkness." He then warned, "If therefore the light that is in thee be darkness, how great is that darkness" (Matt. 6:23; see also Luke 11:34–36 and John 3:19; compare Col. 1:13 and 1 Pet. 2:9). There is more.

In the New Testament, as we have noticed, the term ἀρχή (*archē*) points to power or authority. In its plural form in Ephesians, the word is translated in the King James Version as "principalities" (3:10; 6:12). As noted above, Paul wrote that "we wrestle not against flesh and blood, but against principalities [ἀρχή, *archē*], against powers, against the rulers of the darkness of this world" (6:12). In almost all cases in the New Testament, this term represents impersonal power, not a person (see Luke 20:20, translated "power"; Rom. 8:38, "principalities"; 1 Cor. 15:24, "rule"; Col. 1:16, "principalities"; 2:10, "principality"; 2:15, "principalities"; and Titus 3:1, "principalities"). However, in one passage, ἀρχή (*archē*) points to human authorities, there translated "magistrates": "When they bring you unto the synagogues, and unto [Roman] magistrates, . . . take no thought how or what thing ye shall answer" (Luke 12:11).

---

213. Delling, *TDNT*, 1:481, 488–89; Louw-Nida, §12.44.
214. Gerhard Delling, *TDNT*, 4:9–10; BDAG, 519–20.
215. Delling, *TDNT*, 1:483–84.

A related term, ἄρχων (*archōn*), unambiguously refers to a person who possesses such power. Paul wrote the expression "the princes [plural of *archōn*] of this world," drawing reference to current government or religious officials (1 Cor. 2:6, 8). These persons, therefore, are a part of the human sphere (see Matt. 9:18, 23; Luke 12:58; 18:18; etc.). But the matter goes deeper. In the unseen world, personalities exist that are also called ἄρχων (*archōn*). In the Septuagint, an angel attached the label *archōn* ("prince") to Michael, who, from the heavens, helped God to control the Persians and to assist the Jews (see LXX Dan. 10:13, 20–21; 12:1). In sharp contrast, some heavenly persons, usually categorized as demons or devils, have stood against God and have sought to undermine his purposes. As we might expect, such individuals have a leader, called in this letter "the prince [*archōn*] of the power of the air" (2:2). This character, who is surely Satan, bears another title, "the prince [*archōn*] of this world" (John 12:31; 14:30; 16:11).[216]

The important news is that Jesus has overcome all such inimical forces. Luke preserved a prophecy about this future occurrence. When Jesus was accused of casting out "devils through Beelzebub, the chief of the devils," he responded by telling a short story: "When a strong man armed keepeth his palace, his goods are in peace. But when a stronger than he shall come upon him, and overcome him, he taketh from him all his armour wherein he trusted, and divideth his spoils" (Luke 11:15, 21–22; compare Dan. 7:13–14, 27). All commentators agree that the "strong man" in this story is the devil and the "stronger" person is Jesus. Hence, until Jesus came into the world, the devil's palace or house[217] was largely undisturbed. But when Jesus stepped onto the mortal stage, he began to strip the devil of his possessions, including the souls of men and women, whether alive or residing in the world of departed spirits.[218] Though the demons and their leader are not yet controlled, they surely will be and are no match for God's power, as demonstrated in the Resurrection of Jesus (see D&C 21:6, "the Lord God will disperse the powers of darkness from before you"; and the Notes on 1:10, 19; 2:2; 3:10; 4:8, 10; 6:12).[219]

power: This term (ἐξουσία, *exousia*) occurs no fewer than 101 times in the New Testament, virtually always with the meanings "power" or "authority." In the Gospels especially, this word is regularly translated "authority"

---

216. Delling, *TDNT*, 1:488–89; Traub and von Rad, *TDNT*, 5:525–26, 533.

217. The term translated "palace" is αὐλή (*aulē*), which denotes a courtyard around which a house, even a palace, is constructed. BDAG, 150.

218. Grundmann, *TDNT*, 3:399–401; Brown, *Testimony of Luke*, 568–70, 573–75.

219. Delling, *TDNT*, 1:483–84; von Rad and Foerster, *TDNT*, 2:79–80; Fowl, *Ephesians*, 59.

in the King James Version (see Matt. 7:29; 8:9; Mark 1:22; 11:28; Luke 4:36; 19:17; John 5:27; etc.), as well as "power." With one exception, we find that ἀρχή (*archē*), discussed above, is always paired with *exousia* when *archē* has the meaning of "power" or "principality." (In Jude 1:6, *archē* is translated "first estate" in the KJV and "dominion" in the NEB.)[220] Incidentally, *exousia* appears much more frequently in the New Testament than does *archē*. In the impersonal sense of *exousia* as "authority" or "power," we read, "They watched him [Jesus] . . . so they might deliver him unto the power [*archē*] and authority [*exousia*] of the governor" (Luke 20:20). In its personal meaning, in Luke's Gospel we discover the plural of *exousia* in its sense of "powers" or "authorities." The germane section reads, "When they bring you unto the synagogues, and unto magistrates [*archē*], and powers [*exousia*], take ye no thought how or what thing ye shall answer" (Luke 12:11). It is with this threatening, personal meaning that we meet *exousia* at the end of Ephesians. There we find the declaration that "we wrestle not against flesh and blood, but against principalities [*archē*], against powers [*exousia*], . . . against spiritual wickedness in high places" (6:12).

This ambiguity between impersonal and personal meanings leaves us with a dilemma about how to understand the occurrence of *exousia* in 1:21. To gain a clearer sense, we begin by noticing that all authority or power on earth ultimately goes back to God and will be subject to him at the end. As an example of the arc of God's power to the end-time, Jesus warned hearers to "fear him, which after he hath killed hath power [*exousia*] to cast into hell" (Luke 12:5). Further, at the time of his ascension, Jesus responded to his disciples' question about the end-time by declaring that "it is not for you to know the times or the seasons, which the Father hath put in his own power [*exousia*]" (Acts 1:7; see also Rom. 9:21). In this connection, Jesus derives his own power and authority from his Father (see note 150 in this chapter). For instance, in his last instructions to his disciples, Jesus said, "All power [*exousia*] is given unto me in heaven and in earth" (Matt. 28:18). In this passage, the passive verb "is given" points to God as the giver. As a further reference, when praying to his Father, Jesus remarked in reference to himself, "As thou hast given [to the Son of man] power [*exousia*] over all flesh, that he should give eternal life to as many as thou hast given him" (John 17:2; see also John 5:27; 10:18).

The church, the community of believers, also derives its authority and power from God through Christ. For example, we discover that "as many

---

220. Delling, *TDNT,* 1:482–83.

as received him [Christ], to them gave he power [*exousia*] to become the sons of God" (John 1:12). In another instance, Paul wrote to Corinthian church members, "I should boast somewhat more of our authority [*exousia*], which the Lord hath given us for edification [of the church]" (2 Cor. 10:8; see also Acts 8:13 and 2 Cor. 13:10).[221]

Perhaps surprisingly, or not surprisingly, Satan receives his power by God's allowance. For when he came to the famished Jesus to tempt him, Satan announced that "all this power [*exousia*] . . . is delivered unto me; and to whomsoever I will I give it" (Luke 4:6). Again, the passive verb "is delivered" signals God as the one who has passed on the power to Satan that allows him to act. For, as the Risen Jesus explained to Paul as the latter was on his notable journey to Damascus, when individuals seek "to turn . . . from darkness to light, and from the power [*exousia*] of Satan unto God," they are able to do so, receiving in the process "forgiveness of sins, and [an] inheritance among them which are sanctified" (Acts 26:18; see also Col. 1:12–13). In this connection, the allies of Satan, such as the antichrist and the destructive beasts that appeared in the Revelation of John, work with derivative power from God through Satan (see 2 Thes. 2:7–10 and Rev. 13:2, 4–7).[222]

Such divine empowerment extends also to earthly governments. As Paul wrote to church members in Rome, signifying the positive functions of "the higher powers [*exousia*]," whether governmental or even ecclesiastical, "Let every soul be subject unto the higher powers [*exousia*]. For there is no power [*exousia*] but of God: the powers that be are ordained of God. Whosoever therefore resisteth the power [*exousia*], resisteth the ordinance of God" (Rom. 13:1–2; see also Rom. 13:3). An example of derived civil power is that exercised by Pilate at the trial of Jesus. We read, "Then saith Pilate unto [Jesus], . . . knowest thou not that I have power [*exousia*] to crucify thee, and have power [*exousia*] to release thee? Jesus answered, Thou couldest have no power [*exousia*] at all against me, except it were given thee from above" (John 19:10–11; see also Luke 20:20).[223]

In the bright light of the above, it becomes clear that all power, exercised for good or ill, comes from God. Said another way, it is allowed to function because of him.[224] Hence, whether we interpret the power in 1:21 as

---

221. Werner Foerster, *TDNT*, 2:565, 568–69.

222. Foerster, *TDNT*, 2:567–68; Bertram, *TDNT*, 2:653; BDAG, 352–53.

223. Foerster, *TDNT*, 2:565.

224. M. Sæbø, *TDOT*, 15:85, 87; Foerster, *TDNT*, 2:566.

personal or impersonal, whether as supportive of or inimical to Christians, all such are subject to divine, overruling influences. In its singular form here, it appears to indicate a powerful influence that God has harnessed in the heavens in the process of exalting his Son. This entity, however, links somehow to "the prince of the power [*exousia*] of the air," who is up to no good because this personality, "the prince," is "the spirit that now worketh in the children of disobedience" (2:2). But one more element is in play. It has to do with context. We have now determined the context for *exousia* and *archē* in this passage. But the contexts for their other occurrences in this letter exhibit their own characteristics. In 3:10, the setting is clearly positive because the church is in the mix, now an instrument in making "known . . . the manifold wisdom of God" to these personalities. In 6:12, the context is plainly negative because they are paired with "the rulers of the darkness of this world." (The plural form for *exousia* appears in 3:10; 6:12; and Col. 1:13; see also D&C 21:6 and the Notes on 2:2; 3:10; 6:12.)

might: Like the earlier two nouns, this one (δύναμις, *dynamis*), often a term for miracles (see Matt. 11:20–21, 23; Mark 6:2; 9:39; Luke 5:17; Acts 2:22; 2 Cor. 12:12; 1 Thes. 1:5; etc.),[225] offers a broad set of meanings, thus enriching what Paul has presented to his readers.[226] It is this word that stands beneath the expression "the power of the Spirit" and similar sayings, capturing the important connection between God's Spirit and his power (see Luke 1:17; 4:14; and Rom. 15:13; compare Luke 24:48–49; Acts 1:8; and 1 Cor. 2:4–5).[227] Additionally, in its personal sense that occurs in the Septuagint, the plural of this noun sits in the expression "the hosts of heaven" (see LXX 4 Kgs. 17:16; 21:3, 5; 23:4–5 [2 Kgs. 17:16; 21:3, 5; 23:4–5 KJV]). Furthermore, we notice that this term occurs in four other passages in Ephesians, all tied to God's work and purposes (see 1:19; 3:7, 16, 20). Importantly, the related Greek verb δύναμαι (*dynamai*), with the meaning "to be able,"[228] occurs five times in this epistle, all on the good side of the ledger and all associated in one way or another with the enabling power of God (see 3:4, 20; 6:11, 13, 16; see also 1 Pet. 1:3–5 and the Notes on 1:9, 16, 19; 2:7, 16; 3:16, 20; 4:30; see also 1 Chr. 29:10–12; Ps. 68:32–35; Rom. 15:19; 1 John 3:9; and the Analysis of 1:3–14).[229]

---

225. Grundmann, *TDNT,* 2:301–5; Louw-Nida, §76.7.
226. BDAG, 262–63.
227. Grundmann, *TDNT,* 2:310–12.
228. BDAG, 261–62.
229. Eising, *TDOT,* 4:349, 353–55; Grundmann, *TDNT,* 2:313–16; Oepke, *TDNT,* 2:542–43; Braun, *TDNT,* 6:464; Bednar, "In the Strength of the Lord," 121–28; Rasmus, "Enabling Power of the Atonement," 18–21.

dominion: We find this word (κυριότης, *kyriotēs*) only three other times in the New Testament (see Col. 1:16; 2 Pet. 2:10; and Jude 1:8). In mild contrast, it appears rather regularly in apocryphal literature in connection with other terms that point to heavenly entities. These entities are usually assigned to one of a list of seven heavens. Always appearing in the plural, these entities in this literature, including "dominions," are frequently joined with the first two items translated in this verse as "power" (ἀρχή, *archē*) and "might" (ἐξουσία, *exousia*). In its occurrences, *kyriotēs* can represent either the "majestic power" of the Lord (κύριος, *kyrios*) or a "class" of celestial beings. The meaning largely depends on whether the word occurs in its singular ("power") or plural ("beings") form. In Ephesians, the referent is singular, thus pointing to a dominion or power, in this case belonging to God.[230] At this juncture, therefore, we find another clue that Paul in this verse is talking about realities that are under God's control and, after the exaltation of the Risen Jesus, occupy a position far below the Resurrected Christ, whether hostile or not (see 1 Pet. 3:21–22).[231]

every name that is named: Knowing the destination of this letter, to Asia Minor in general and to Ephesus in particular, the sense of this expression becomes clear. Why? Because people in that region were known in antiquity for their promotion of pagan religions, which, of course, featured many deities. Especially in the world of magic, the act of calling on the names of deities, demons, and potent forces was the one essential step to unlocking and controlling their frightful powers for the benefit of the initiate.[232] Notably, it was in Ephesus that the one attempt at magic recorded in the New Testament backfired on some Jewish "exorcists" who pronounced the name of Jesus in a misguided attempt to rid a person of evil spirits (see Acts 19:13–17). Further, in another act tied to Ephesus, virtually in the shadow of the world-famous Temple of Artemis, converts to Christianity demonstrated their newly found faith by bringing their books of "curious arts"—that is, their magic books—to a place in the city where they "burned them" (Acts 19:19). This event sent shudders through the community that relied on tourist traffic to the pagan temple and soon led to the noisy

---

230. Foerster, *TDNT*, 2:571; Gottfried Quell and Werner Foerster, *TDNT*, 3:1096–97; BDAG, 579. Lincoln, *Ephesians*, 62, calls this entity one of four "defeated cosmic powers," and Best, *Ephesians*, 173, terms all of these entities as "hostile powers." But that seems not to be the case.

231. Lincoln, *Ephesians*, 63–64.

232. Arnold, *Ephesians*, 123–25.

protest of silversmiths in the giant theater at Ephesus, which permanently forced Paul out of the city (see Acts 19:23–20:1).

According to the New Testament, God has given to his Son "a name which is above every name" (Philip. 2:9; see also Heb. 1:4), and it is through this name that salvation comes to individuals (see Acts 2:21 and Rom. 10:13; see also 2 Ne. 25:20; 31:21; Mosiah 3:17; etc.). In Ephesians 1:21, it appears that, with a final flourish, Paul has written his affirmation that no deity or mysterious force, known or unknown, earthly or heavenly, will escape the supernal power of God (see the Note on 3:15).[233]

this world . . . also . . . that which is to come: Paul here has set out "the wide expanse of eternity" (D&C 38:1), at least from this moment on. By doing so, he has declared that in all times, in all seasons, God's power that had exalted Christ never sleeps, never weakens, never withdraws.

this world: The noun αἰών (*aiōn*) here carries the meaning of the present age—that is to say, the age which will come to an end at the Second Coming of Christ. This confined era is contrasted with "that [age] which is to come," offering the only occurrence in the New Testament of the so-called "doctrine of the two aeons," wherein the present and future eras are differentiated[234] (see the Notes on 2:2, 7; 3:9, 11, 21).

1:22 put: This verb (ὑποτάσσω, *hypotassō*) stands in third place in the Greek sentence, following the words translated "and" and "all things." Its basic meaning is "to subject, to subordinate"[235] (see the Note on 5:22).

all things: The Greek word here is πάντα (*panta*), the accusative form of πᾶς (*pās*), and it stands in the emphatic first place in this expression, coming after the conjunction "and" and possessing the force "and *all things* he has put under his feet" (emphasis added). In another setting, when drawing on the language of Psalms 8:6 and 110:1, Paul lays stress on Christ putting down "all enemies," including "the last enemy . . . death." With a hint of humor, Paul wrote that the Father "is excepted" when stating that "all things" will be put "under [Christ's] feet" (1 Cor. 15:25–27; see also Heb. 2:8). Elsewhere, we read about "all things [being] created by [Christ], and for him" (Col. 1:16); then about the "one Lord Jesus Christ, by whom are all things, and we by him" (1 Cor. 8:6); and finally about the eventual gathering into "one all things in Christ" (Eph. 1:10). Significantly, the aggregate

233. Arnold, *Ephesians*, 54–56; Lincoln, *Ephesians*, 65; Winger, *Ephesians*, 247–48.
234. Hermann Sasse, *TDNT*, 1:205–6.
235. BDAG, 1042; Thayer, *Lexicon*, 645.

of these events takes place on a plane that unites what is done in heaven to what happens on earth, brightly underscoring God's dominion (see Matt. 6:10; 16:19; 18:18–19; Luke 15:18, 21; and Col. 1:20).[236]

In the world of language, Paul's evident appeal to Psalm 8:6 ("thou hast put all things under his feet") for some of the expressions in this verse continues his mining of the Psalms as a source that enriches what we can elucidate about the Christ (see Ps. 110:1, "Sit thou at my right hand, until I make thine enemies thy footstool";[237] and the Notes on 1:20; 4:8). In addition, by writing the term *pās* four times in the last two verses of this chapter,[238] Paul hammers home the notion that God's elevation of Jesus to his position in the heavens left nothing to chance, left nothing out, took account of everything.

under his feet: Initially, the image of Christ as victor leaps to mind. And this concept is not incorrect. For the notion of subduing under one's feet is as old as the creation story (see Gen. 1:28). The Bible exhibits pointers to subduing others (see Num. 32:22), including making slaves of such persons (see 2 Chr. 28:10; Neh. 5:5; and Jer. 34:11). But this is not the end of the story. According to Micah 7:18–19, a passage that overflows with God's compassion, we come across these lines: "[God] retaineth not his anger for ever, because he delighteth in mercy. He will turn again, he will have compassion upon us; he will subdue our iniquities." Further, in light of Genesis 1:28, where we pick up God's language that Adam and Eve are to "subdue" the earth and "have dominion" over it, we encounter the sense that humans, created in God's image and therefore standing as co-rulers over the earth (see Gen. 1:26; see also Moses 2:26 and Abr. 4:26), are to subdue the earth as God subdues it, with responsible, caring action.[239] On this view, the idea is not to put one's foot on an enemy's neck in a hostile act but to take care of the earth as God takes care of what he walks on (see Deut. 11:24; Josh. 1:3; 14:9; etc.). Such "dominion" is to be understood "as a blessing," not a conquest (see Ps. 8:4–6;[240] D&C 59:16–20; and the Note on 2:10).

---

236. Traub and von Rad, *TDNT,* 5:517–18.

237. Werner Foerster, *TDNT,* 2:813–14; Gerhard Delling, *TDNT,* 8:41–42.

238. Larkin, *Handbook,* 25.

239. Siegfried Wagner, *TDOT,* 7:54.

240. H.-J. Zobel, *TDOT,* 13:335–36; see also Hugh Nibley, "Subduing the Earth," in *Nibley on the Timely and the Timeless: Classic Essays of Hugh W. Nibley,* vol. 1 of Religious Studies Monograph Series (Provo, Utah: BYU Religious Studies Center, 1978), 85–99.

With this in mind, the image is of the earth and "all things" sitting beneath Christ's feet, picturing them almost as his footstool. Again, this representation does not necessarily offer a portrait of hostility, as some would suggest,[241] especially if the powers listed in 1:21 are not thought to be uniformly inimical. As we observe in the Analysis below, these powers likely include those in God's service. Hence, Christ's position can also be seen as one of generosity and blessing. To be sure, feet can symbolize power over one's enemy (see Josh. 10:24 and D&C 76:106). But they also have to do with God's majesty (see Ex. 24:10; Matt. 3:11; Mark 1:7; etc.) and with sacred worship at God's feet (see 1 Chr. 28:2 and Rev. 7:11; 11:16; compare Matt. 17:6; 1 Cor. 14:25; etc.; compare 1 Ne. 19:7 for the exact opposite of worship).[242]

gave: In this passage, the Father "gave" (δίδωμι, *didōmi*) the Risen Christ to preside over the church, "which is his body" (1:23). We notice initially that divine giving, when associated with Jesus, is a sacred action. At some point before his ministry, during the holy commissioning, "the Father . . . [had] given all things into [Jesus'] hands" (John 3:35).[243] Then, in pursuing his ministry, Jesus' works were a gift from the Father: "The works which the Father hath given me to finish . . . bear witness of me, that the Father hath sent me" (John 5:36). Next, in the greatest of Jesus' works, he came "to give his life a ransom for many" (Matt. 20:28; Mark 10:45;[244] see the Note on 4:12). In a related sense, within the realm of sacred acts, we find an echo of covenant making in the verb "to give." In early stories from the Old Testament, the distinctive language is that God "gives" a covenant: "And God said, This is the token of the covenant which I make [נָתַן, *natan,* "give"] between me and you" (Gen. 9:12). Again, we read, "I [God] will make [נָתַן, *natan,* "give"] my covenant between me and thee" (Gen. 17:2; see also Mosiah 19:15, 22, "granted"). In the New Testament, one clear case appears in the Epistle to the Galatians. The passage reads, "They gave to me and Barnabas the right hands of fellowship; that we should go unto the heathen" (Gal. 2:9). This scene is more than glad-handing, more than welcoming Paul and Barnabas into the Christian leadership club. To give the right hand means to make an agreement, to make a covenant. And

---

241. Caird, *Letters,* 46–47; Arnold, *Ephesians,* 51; Fowl, *Ephesians,* 61–62; Winger, *Ephesians,* 249.

242. Konrad Weiss, *TDNT,* 6:624–31.

243. See note 150 in this chapter for references to Jesus' commissioning by the Father.

244. Büchsel, *TDNT,* 2:166.

Paul's words "that we should go unto the heathen" spell out the agreement between him, Barnabas, and the three "pillars" of the Jerusalem church with whom they were meeting (Gal. 2:9;[245] see the Notes on 4:7–8, 11).

the head: Encountering this noun (κεφαλή, *kephalē*), we find ourselves in a room with many mirrors, each reflecting back a slightly different image. How is this possible? Because Paul pairs the term "head" with a range of other observations about Christ. First of all, in this verse Jesus is titled "the head over all things for the church" (RSV),[246] essentially saying that the church operates under his supervision, a circumstance that is revealed by Jesus' Resurrection and God's placing him "at his own right hand in the heavenly places" (1:20; see also Col. 1:18). Second, at 5:23, we learn that "Christ is the head of the church" in a similar way that "the husband is the head of the wife" (see the Notes on 5:22–23). This observation, then, brings Paul to write that Christ "is the saviour of the body [of the church]" (5:23), understanding the body to consist of church members. Perhaps importantly, the image may be one of a sacred marriage wherein Christ is the exemplar of permanence and kindness, and the church, metaphorically, is his bride (see 1 Cor. 11:3).[247] Third, if we now back up a few verses, we run across another image. With a connection to "all things" (see the Note above) and a closer tie to the human sensitivities among believers, Paul pictures that we "grow up into him in all things, which is the head, even Christ" (4:15). Possibly we gain a slightly clearer view in the New Rendition: "We are to grow in every way unto him who is the head, Christ." The content and context of this line leads readers to the concept of spiritual maturity, both as a church and as individuals. For we hear, "He [Christ] gave some, apostles; and some, prophets ... till we all come in the unity of the faith, ... unto a perfect man, unto the measure of the stature of the fulness of Christ" (4:11–13). This last line presents in clear fashion the spiritual maturity that results from our efforts to mirror our head, the Christ.

Christ as the "head" appears elsewhere in the New Testament. First, in the structure of the kingdom, Jesus is the "head of the corner"—that is to say, the precut stone over the doorway that is laid last in the construction

---

245. BDB, 678; Lipiński and Fabry, *TDOT,* 10:90 91, 102; BDAG, 217; Louw-Nida, §34.42; Michael L. Barré, "Treaties in the ANE," in *ABD,* 6:654.

246. The phrase "to the church" or "for the church" (τῇ ἐκκλησίᾳ, *tē ekklēsia*) is a dative of advantage, "for the advantage of" or "for the benefit of." See Smyth, *Greek Grammar,* §1481; Blass and Debrunner, *Greek Grammar,* §188. For Christ as the head to whom all power is given, see Foerster, *TDNT,* 2:566, 568–69.

247. Schmidt, *TDNT,* 3:509–11, argues that the marriage imagery comes from Gnostic influences; see also Best, *Ephesians,* 632–33.

of a building, bringing it to completion and effectively measuring whether it was built to specifications (see Matt. 21:42; Mark 12:10; Luke 20:17; Acts 4:11; 1 Pet. 2:7; and the Note on 2:20).[248] In Colossians, we encounter two further images. The first ties Christ to authorities or powers that may or may not reside in the heavens: "[Christ] is the head of all principality [ἀρχή, *archē*] and power [ἐξουσία, *exousia*]" (Col. 2:10). We have already discussed these nouns of authority and power. In this passage, Christ is explicitly called "the head" of these entities, as though he now stands in a formal relationship to them, whereas in Ephesians 1:21 he is said to sit spatially "far above" them. This implied formality goes beyond what Ephesians has described about Christ and these powers (see the Note on 1:21). Only a few lines later, we come across a very different image of Christ as the head. We read about Christ "the Head, from which all the body by joints and bands having nourishment ministered, and knit together, increaseth with the increase of God" (Col. 2:19). Here, we meet Paul's conception of the church as the body of Christ that, in its parts, fits together like a human body and receives "nourishment . . . with the increase [of] God." Notably, a few lines above, we meet the expression "the body [of the church] is of Christ" (Col. 2:17). This conception of the church as the body of Christ generally matches the term that we discover in Ephesians: "his body" (1:23; see also 4:12, 16; 5:23, 30). Such an image largely mirrors what Paul has written elsewhere that "the body [of the church] is not one member but many" and consists of "the body of Christ" (1 Cor. 12:14, 27; see also 1 Cor. 12:12–27; D&C 84:109–10; the next Note; and the Note on 5:23).

the church: As it appears here, this term, ἐκκλησία (*ekklēsia*), points to the church as a whole, taking all the scattered congregations as a unit. Elsewhere in Paul's writings, it can bear the meaning of a single assembly or branch (see Rom. 16:5; 1 Cor. 1:2; 11:18; 14:28; 16:19; 2 Cor. 1:1; etc.). The idea of people gathering together to worship under God's direction is extremely old. The idea even includes the efforts of Adam and Eve to call "upon the name of the Lord" while situating themselves on the path that ran "toward the Garden of Eden," perhaps the earliest indication of a "sacred way" that led to a temple-like enclosure, which came to characterize ancient worship patterns (Moses 5:4; see also the Notes on 2:2, 6, 10; 4:1; 5:2, 8, 15; 6:11, 13).[249] In its earliest occurrences in the Greek language, *ekklēsia* bore a sociopolitical meaning, nodding toward the city council or

---

248. Joachim Jeremias, *TDNT*, 1:792; Brown, *Testimony of Luke*, 907–8.

249. Richard D. Draper, S. Kent Brown, and Michael D. Rhodes, *The Pearl of Great Price: A Verse-by-Verse Commentary* (Salt Lake City: Deseret Book, 2005), 57–58.

assembly. Only in New Testament times did the word acquire the meaning of "church" both in its collective sense as a term for all church members and in its narrower sense as the name for individual congregations (see the Notes on 3:10, 21; 4:12; 5:27).[250]

1:23 *his body:* The expression wraps itself around "the church" (1:22). To this point in the letter, we have learned that Christ is both "the head" of the church and its body, presenting a view that certainly goes beyond what we find Paul presenting about the body of Christ in the epistles to the Romans and the Corinthians. In the shorter of the two treatments, Paul wrote that "we have many members in one body" and that this body is "in Christ." Hence, one underlying connection has to do with unity among believers. For "we, being many," respond to our brothers and sisters as "members one of another" (Rom. 12:4–5). Then we come to 1 Corinthians, where we encounter a similar image, but it is vastly expanded. We glimpse that "the body is one, and hath many members, . . . so also is Christ. . . . That there should be no schism in the body; but that the members should have the same care one for another" (1 Cor. 12:12, 25). So far, we find agreement with Romans 12:4–5.

But that is not the whole story. Paul then drops into a discussion of the parts of the body and how church members fit into this fresh portrait. He first makes the point that "whether we be Jews or Gentiles," we are "all baptized into one body" (1 Cor. 12:13), an organism that is "the body of Christ" (1 Cor. 12:27). But we don't all fit into that "one body" in the same way. Someone stands as "the foot," another is "the hand," still another forms "the ear," and someone else serves as "the eye" (1 Cor. 12:15–16). And so forth. But none of these body parts stand independent of the others, for "the eye cannot say unto the hand, I have no need of thee: nor again the head to the feet, I have no need of you." Moreover, when it comes to the least among believers, "those members of the body, which seem to be more feeble, are necessary." Even those members whom "we think to be less honorable, upon these we bestow more abundant honor" (1 Cor. 12:21–23). Thus, the unity of the body of the church becomes the launchpad for embracing all equally, for nourishing all evenly, for loving all unconditionally.

Even though Karl Ludwig Schmidt holds that the "complicated notion" of Christ's body presented in Ephesians "can hardly have been developed from the statements of Paul" in Romans 12 and 1 Corinthians 12, in my opinion—and I am not alone—the view of the church presented in Ephesians lies

---

250. Schmidt, *TDNT*, 3:502–5; BDAG, 303–4; Louw-Nida, §11.32–33, 78.

on a simple trajectory from what we see especially in 1 Corinthians 12.[251] For there we glimpse Paul's link between the body of the church and some of its officers. For after mentioning "the body of Christ," he then declares that "God hath set some in the church, first apostles, secondarily prophets, thirdly teachers" (1 Cor. 12:28). Such a listing virtually matches what we come across in Ephesians: "the foundation of the apostles and prophets" (2:20) as well as other officers, such as "evangelists," "pastors," and "teachers," whose ministries are "for the edifying of the body of Christ" (4:11–12; see also the introduction section VII; and the Notes on 2:16; 3:8; 4:3–4, 12, 16; 5:23, 27).

the fulness of him: We have already met the term translated "fulness" (πλήρωμα, *plērōma*; see 1:10) and will meet it twice more in this letter (see 3:19; 4:13). Attempts to see Gnostic influences in this word and therefore to push the composition of Ephesians into the second century—effectively questioning whether Paul was the author of the letter—fail upon close examination. Such attempts remain unconvincing.[252] Structurally, this line stands in apposition to the term "his body" and thus explains and enlarges its meaning. The question is whether to understand *plērōma* in its active sense, "filling" (i.e., the church fills Christ), or, better, in its passive meaning, "filled" or "full" (i.e., the church is filled by Christ).[253] Christ's possession of the fulness of power, glory, and love has resulted not only from his transcendent ministry but also from his Resurrection (see 1:20–22; Col. 1:18–19; 2:9; and D&C 93:6, 16).[254] One clear message is that God has filled him with these attributes and now Christ can fill his body, the church, with these same traits. Another message is that he did not always possess such fulness. He received it only as he "continued from grace to grace" during his mortal ministry (D&C 93:12–14; see also John 1:16 and the Notes on 1:10; 3:19; 4:13).

filleth: The verb is a participle of the middle form of πληρόω (*plēroō*), "to fill," and thus pictures an act that Christ does for himself: "Christ is filling for himself all things in every way."[255] To get a clearer grasp of the meaning of this line, we turn to modern scripture which teaches us that

---

251. Schmidt, *TDNT,* 3:510, 512. See the discussion in Draper and Rhodes, *Paul's First Epistle to the Corinthians,* 599–613, and a contrary view to that of Schmidt in Caird, *Letters,* 48, and Delling, *TDNT,* 6:304.

252. Barth, *Ephesians,* 1:158–59, 200–3; Lincoln, *Ephesians,* 68–70; Best, *Ephesians,* 186.

253. Barth, *Ephesians,* 1:158–59; Fowl, *Ephesians,* 63–64; Larkin, *Handbook,* 26; Winger, *Ephesians,* 250–52.

254. Delling, *TDNT,* 6:302–5.

255. Larkin, *Handbook,* 26.

Jesus brought the attributes of "life," "light," "grace," and "truth" into the world and into his mortal ministry (D&C 93:9, 11). Then, after his Atonement, the Father was the one who filled Christ with further traits: "[Christ] received a fulness of the glory of the Father; and he received all power, both in heaven and in earth, and the glory of the Father was with him" (D&C 93:16–17). Now exalted and filled with the fulness of God's power and glory, Christ is in a position to fill "all things in every way" as he judges fit (1:23 NR). That is not to say that he makes decisions and takes action independent of, or even contrary to, his Father. Rather, Christ's unity with the Father remains a bedrock staple of their relationship, and a number of · passages underscore this fact. For example, literally on the eve of his death, Jesus prayed for his disciples that "they all may be one; as thou, Father, art in me, and I in thee, . . . that they may be one, even as we are one . . . that they may be made perfect in one" (John 17:21–23). Months later, the Resurrected Christ declared the following memorable words to hearers in the New World: "The Father, and the Son, and the Holy Ghost are one; and I am in the Father, and the Father in me, and the Father and I are one" (3 Ne. 11:27; see also the Notes on 3:19; 4:10; 5:18).

all in all: Above, we have tried to pry open the meaning of this verse and the prior one, an effort that has presented difficulties for generations of commentators.[256] This last expression is no easier. Two characteristics become immediately apparent. First of all, the last two of the four occurrences of πᾶς (*pās*) appear in this line (see the Note on 1:22). Second, we encounter a series of terms that begin with the "p" sound, underscoring the alliterative, oral character of the hymn-like lines that Paul is apparently quoting at this point—πλήρωμα (*plērōma*), πάντα (*panta*), πᾶσιν (*pāsin*), and the participle of πληρόω (*plēroō*).[257] When we turn toward the meaning of this line, we perceive that it could bear the sense "in every way." But this meaning, frankly, forms a vapid ending to the long poetic prayer. The power of the preceding verses almost demands a more substantive significance. And those prior verses help to fill out the content of "all in all." For the ever-encompassing "all" derives from God's "mighty power" (1:19). Hence, Christ has been seated "far above all" after being "raised . . . from the dead" in advance of all others and has been "set . . . at [God's] own right hand" to preside over all (1:20–21). As a result, all "hath [been] put . . . under his feet," and he has been given the right "to be the head over *all*

---

256. Barth, *Ephesians*, 1:156; Best, *Ephesians*, 183; Fowl, *Ephesians*, 63.
257. Lincoln, *Ephesians*, 72; Winger, *Ephesians*, 250.

things to the church" (1:22, emphasis added). This role of presiding over all, including the church, enfolds within his rulership "all the forces which have become subject to him,"[258] including the spirits of the departed dead (see Rom. 14:9; 1 Pet. 3:18–20; 4:6; and Rev. 11:18). Further, in a fitting climax at the end, "all things" will be gathered "together in one . . . in Christ, both . . . in heaven, and . . . on earth" (1:10).

Analysis of 1:15–23

At the heart of this long run-on sentence (1:15–23), which forms a carefully compacted prayer of praise, rests the "mighty power" of God (1:19), which spends itself to lift believers into the church where they can receive incomparable blessings from Christ, his Son. For those who resided in and around Ephesus, the power of paganism was forcefully present at every turn:[259] statues depicting Roman gods, temples celebrating emperors, tombs memorializing important officials, processions every two weeks through the city featuring priests from the nearby Temple of Artemis,[260] Hellenistic schools offering the education and training of youth, coins bearing images of pagan deities and the emperor, a huge stadium hosting athletic contests and gladiatorial competitions, a massive theater showing performances based in part on the capricious activities of pagan gods and goddesses, shops selling magic books and silver images of the huge yet exquisite Temple of Artemis, and the ever-present government officials presiding officiously in the upper city and at the sea docks. Paul's words, rolling out in an impressively crafted cadence, encouraged his readers to understand that God's "mighty power" had already begun to overgrow all other powers, whether "in heaven" or "on earth," whether "in this world" or "in that which is to come" (1:10, 19, 21). Members should go forward in "faith," "love," and "hope," not looking back (1:15, 18).

In Paul's prayer, he openly begged God to furnish two things to his readers: first, that God would give to them "the spirit of wisdom and revelation" so that they would come to "the knowledge of [God]" and, second, that "the eyes of [their] understanding" would be "enlightened" (1:17–18). With such an unprecedented understanding, they could withstand the withering

---

258. Delling, *TDNT*, 6:292.

259. Peter S. Williamson, *Ephesians,* Catholic Commentary on Sacred Scripture (Grand Rapids, Mich.: Baker Academic, 2009), 51–52.

260. Lilian Portefaix, "Ancient Ephesus: Processions as Media of Religious and Secular Propaganda," *Scripta Instituti Donneriani Aboensis* 15 (January 1993): 199.

influence of any "principality, and power, and might, and dominion" that might beset them (1:21). For God and his Christ had surmounted them all, including "every name that is named . . . in this world," even admitting the names of emperors and heathen gods and overweening government officials. Besides such individuals, as we have seen, God's power also controls all powers and denizens of "that [world] which is to come" (1:21). This set of observations means that "already" and "not yet" characteristics are at play. That is to say, Christ now stands victorious above all powers, terrestrial and celestial, meaning that believers can rely on his aid to negotiate the dispiriting difficulties of this life. It also means that, because "at present we do not see everything subject to him," as will be the case at the end-time (Heb. 2:8 NIV), Christ has yet to suppress all evil powers in a final subjugation (see 1 Cor. 15:24; Rev. 20:10;[261] 2 Ne. 9:16; and D&C 88:112–14).

That said, the chief beneficiaries of Christ's new status, "far above all," were to be church members. Of these, Christ has now become "the head." There is more. He is specifically "over all things for [the benefit of] the church" (1:22).[262] As an added measure, in a seemingly complicating formula, the church "is his body" as well. However, the obvious unity that is implicit in Christ being both "head" and "body" of the church should have been reassuring to Paul's audience. How so? Church members now glimpsed the clear pointer to the unity that they would share with Christ himself because they too made up his body. In memorable words, "ye [believers] are complete in him" (Col. 2:10). In fact, "we are members of his body, of his flesh, and of his bones" (Eph. 5:30). It is in this sense that Paul wrote about "the head, even Christ: from whom the whole body fitly joined together and compacted by that which every joint supplieth [is united] . . . unto the edifying of itself in love" (4:15–16; see also D&C 84:109–10).

Although the citing of "all principality, and power, and might, and dominion" may have to do with earthly entities, it may lead to heavenly realities as well (1:21). Standing in front of this outlook, we readily see that we know little about the populations in the heavens. Of those who constantly seek to undo God's purposes, we encounter the devil and those who followed him out of heaven (see Rev. 12:3–4; Moses 4:1–4; Abr. 3:27–28; and D&C 29:36–37). Whether other powers are to be added to this

---

261. Williamson, *Ephesians*, 54; see also Winger, *Ephesians*, 268.

262. See Wagner, *TDOT*, 7:54, 56; and Zobel, *TDOT*, 13:335–36, for the blessed aspects of God's dominion; see also Nibley, "Subduing the Earth," 85–99.

immense group is impossible to say.[263] On the other side, in God's service, we encounter angels and archangels,[264] Cherubim (see Gen. 3:24; Moses 4:31; etc.) and Seraphim (see Isa. 6:2, 6), and even those whom scripture calls "gods" and "children of the most High" (Ps. 82:6). Beyond these, we possess little information. To be sure, Paul's experience of ascending into the "third heaven" gives us a small peek. But he does not disclose very much, only that he "heard unspeakable words," which is characteristic of those who have been enfolded into such visions (2 Cor. 12:2, 4).[265] To the modern church, Joseph Smith was recorded as saying at the funeral of James Adams, "Could you gaze in[to] heaven 5 minute[s,] you would know more than you would by read[ing] all that ever was writt[e]n on the subject."[266] Evidently, we lack even a modest understanding of the heavens.

---

263. Arnold, *Ephesians,* 51–52, holds that these powers were "demonic" and that in 1:21 we come upon "a substantial list of the 'enemies' subjected to Christ"; Draper and Rhodes, *Paul's First Epistle to the Corinthians,* 765, term these as "powers that oppose the sovereignty of the Father and the Son" and are to be annihilated at the end. Barth takes the broad view that these powers are "angelic or demonic beings that reside in the heavens." Barth, *Ephesians,* 1:154. Fowl possesses a kinder view. For him, at the end all such powers listed in 1:21 "will be restored to their proper place in God." Fowl, *Ephesians,* 62. We remind ourselves that Paul, in another place, wrote that Christ "must reign, till he hath put all enemies under his feet" (1 Cor. 15:25).

264. 1 Thes. 4:16; Jude 1:9; D&C 29:26; 88:112; 107:54; 128:21.

265. See also 2 Ne. 27:22; Ether 4:1–2, 5; compare 2 Ne. 27:7, 11, 21; 3 Ne. 17:17; 19:34; 26:1, 3–5.

266. "Journal, December 1842–June 1844; Book 3, 15 July 1843–29 February 1844," October 9, 1843, [121], Joseph Smith Papers, https://www.josephsmithpapers.org/paper-summary/journal-december-1842-june-1844-book-3-15-july-1843-29-february-1844/127. The quotation has been edited slightly for spelling. See also D&C 107:19, "to have the heavens opened unto them, . . . and to enjoy the communion and presence of God the Father, and Jesus the mediator of the new covenant."

Chapter 2

INTRODUCTION

Front and center in this chapter stands the principle or doctrine of *theosis*—that is, making believers divine. It comes about in the following way. As God "raised [Christ] from the dead and set him at his own right hand in the heavenly places," so God "hath raised us up together [with Christ],[1] and made us sit together in heavenly places in Christ Jesus" (1:20; 2:6). Here, Paul shares the expansive, bright understanding of what it means to share in "the life of God" (4:18) and to become "heirs of God, and joint-heirs with Christ" (Rom. 8:17). To be sure, Paul does not write that the faithful will be seated "at [God's] own right hand" in those "heavenly places," a seat designated for Christ alone. But believers will be there, close at hand.[2] One of the main avenues for such human exaltation passes through Jesus' birth, which introduced him into mortality, wherein he came to share our flesh and its attendant experiences. For "as the children [of this world] are partakers of flesh and blood, [Christ] also himself likewise took part of the same" so that he could "deliver them" from "death" and "the devil" (Heb. 2:14–15). But Jesus' Atonement offers more than deliverance; it also offers exaltation, becoming like God.[3] In the same vein, the second-century church writer Irenaeus wrote, "Our Lord Jesus Christ, who did, through His transcendent love, become what we are, that He might bring us to be even what He is Himself."[4]

---

1. Col. 2:12, "Buried with [Christ] in baptism, wherein also ye are risen with him"; 3:1, "If ye then be risen with Christ."

2. K. Codell Carter, "Godhood," in *EM*, 2:553–55.

3. Winger, *Ephesians*, 303–4, looks at the inviting vista of the "divinization" of humans in Paul's words in Ephesians and then pulls back from this possibility.

4. Irenaeus, *Against Heresies*, preface to book 5, in *ANF*, 1:526.

As chapter 2 unfolds, we initially discover the everlasting benefits for believers from God the Father's acts of power that elevated his Son to "his own right hand in the heavenly places" (1:20). The opening half of this chapter, 2:1–10, gives voice to the merciful works of God the Father that, as we encountered above, have "quickened us together with Christ" and "raised us up together" to sit "in heavenly places" with him, all through his matchless "grace, . . . *the gift* of God" (2:5, 6, 8, emphasis added). The listing of such blessings follows naturally from Paul's acknowledgment of God's stupendous power in chapter 1 when raising Jesus from the dead and exalting him above "all things," including "every name that is named, not only in this world but also in that which is to come" (1:20–22). This power has rescued believers from the spiritual death that had captured them because of their "trespasses and sins," a death that let them rot "in the lusts of our flesh" and led them directly into the path of God's oncoming, fearsome "wrath" (2:1, 3).

When we turn our gaze onto the second part of the chapter, 2:11–22, we run across a switch in Paul's audience from the all-embracing "we" and "us" to "ye . . . Gentiles" (2:3–5, 11). From this point on (2:11), Gentiles make up the Apostle's main focus. Within this tightened circle, the actions of the Son have made Gentiles "nigh" to himself through his "blood," thus reconciling Gentile and Jew "in one body, by [Christ's] cross, having slain the enmity thereby" (2:13, 16). As a result, through Jesus' atoning act, both Gentile and Jew wondrously "have access by one Spirit unto the Father" (2:18). What is more, Gentile members "are no more strangers and foreigners, but fellowcitizens with the saints, and of the household of God" (2:19). Perhaps most notably, "together" with their fellow Jews, Gentiles will become "an habitation of God through the Spirit," effectively offering to God and his Son a temple-like dwelling on earth (2:22; see also John 14:23, "we will . . . make our abode with [them]").

Significantly, Paul's insistence that Gentiles can and have come to Christ, and are thus partakers of salvation (2:11–19), stood against the prevailing notion among Jews that salvation was chiefly for them: "All Israelites have a share in the world to come" except those who say "there is no resurrection of the dead" or "the Law is not from heaven" or who are "an Epicurean."[5] The Joseph Smith Translation fleshes out this view even more sharply in

---

5. *Mishnah Sanhedrin* 10:1, in Herbert Danby, trans., *The Mishnah: Translated from the Hebrew with Introduction and Brief Explanatory Notes* (Oxford: Oxford University Press, 1933), 397.

a statement on the lips of John the Baptist, who imputes it to some of his hearers: "We have kept the commandments of God, and none can inherit the promises but the children of Abraham" (JST Luke 3:8). From a mid-point in his ministry, it is evident that Jesus intended the Gentiles to be gathered into the gospel net, as the calling of the Seventy illustrates when he suspended Jewish food laws for their mission (see Luke 10:1, 7).[6]

"HATH RAISED US UP TOGETHER" (2:1–10)

The chasm that divides the person trapped "in trespasses and sins" through the machinations of "the prince of the power of the air" (2:1–2) from the person "created in Christ Jesus unto good works" (2:10) is too wide to bridge without Christ's merciful aid. Of course, a high level of self-discipline can raise a person from physical and moral doldrums to a place of mastery over oneself. But such an effort does not bring one inside the spiritual nurture of God. The latter comes about through the gift of "grace," which offers salvation to the one who turns toward God with a will. At that moment, all heavenly gates swing open, and the spirit of healing and lifting of the soul pours down on the individual, exhibiting God's "kindness toward us through Christ Jesus" (2:7). More than this, after a time believers find themselves "quickened . . . together with Christ [and] . . . raised . . . up together [with him and seated] . . . in heavenly places in Christ Jesus" (2:5–6). The whole experience is almost beyond description. Let us see how the pieces fit together.

King James Translation

1 And you hath he quickened, who were dead in trespasses and sins; 2 Wherein in time past ye walked according to the course of this world, according to the prince of the power of the air, the spirit that now worketh in the children of disobedience: 3 Among whom also we all had our conversation in times past

New Rendition

1 And you were dead through your trespasses and sins, 2 in which you once walked in accordance with this present world, in accordance with the ruler of the dominion of the sky, the spirit who is now impacting those who are disobedient. 3 Among them, too, all of us once lived in the desires of our flesh, doing

---

6. Wilhelm Michaelis, *TDNT*, 5:68–69; Joachim Jeremias, *The Parables of Jesus*, rev. ed. (New York: Charles Scribner's Sons, 1963), 64–65; Brown, *Testimony of Luke*, 508, 512, 514–16, 670, 701, 704, commenting on Luke 10:1, 7–8; 13:23; 14:15, 23.

in the lusts of our flesh, fulfilling the desires of the flesh and of the mind; and were by nature the children of wrath, even as others. 4 But God, who is rich in mercy, for his great love wherewith he loved us, 5 Even when we were dead in sins, hath quickened us together with Christ, (by grace ye are saved;) 6 And hath raised us up together, and made us sit together in heavenly places in Christ Jesus: 7 That in the ages to come he might shew the exceeding riches of his grace in his kindness toward us through Christ Jesus. 8 For by grace are ye saved through faith; and that not of yourselves: it is the gift of God: 9 Not of works, lest any man should boast. 10 For we are his workmanship, created in Christ Jesus unto good works, which God hath before ordained that we should walk in them.

the will of the flesh and of its thoughts. And we were by nature children of wrath, even like the others. 4 But God— being rich in mercy because of his great love for us, 5 and we being dead through trespasses—made us alive with Christ (by grace are you saved!) 6 and raised us up and seated us together in the heavenly realms in the presence of Christ Jesus, 7 so that in the coming ages he might show the matchless wealth of his generous grace towards us in Christ Jesus. 8 For by grace you have been saved through faith, and this is not from you; it is the gift of God. 9 It is not from works, so that no one can boast. 10 For we are his handiwork, brought into being through Christ Jesus to do good deeds, which God prepared in advance in order that we might walk in them.

Notes on 2:1–10

2:1 *you:* At this important juncture, Paul unfolds the ethnic origin of those whom he is addressing—Gentiles "who were [once] dead in trespasses and sins" and "who are called Uncircumcision" (2:11). To these people, who represent the vast majority of the Roman Empire and the dominant majority in Ephesus,[7] Paul points out the freshly opened path to salvation.

hath he quickened: The main verbs of Paul's first sentence in chapter 2 appear in 2:5–6 ("hath quickened us together . . . hath raised us up together . . . made us sit together"). This expression, in italics in the KJV and borrowed from 2:5, was added here by the translators to allow the English reader to make quicker sense of the chapter's opening.

dead: Noting the literal senses of the word νεκρός (*nekros*), which can mean "a corpse" (noun) or "lifeless" (adjective), we observe its appearance in 1:20 and 5:14. In this verse, 2:1, we encounter the earliest of several possible metaphorical messages.[8] First, people are "dead" because of sin. This is the

---

7. From Acts 19:8–9, we learn of a synagogue in Ephesus, though its remains have not yet been discovered or identified.

8. Rudolf Bultmann, *TDNT,* 4:893–94; BDAG, 667–68; Louw-Nida, §§23.121, 65.39, 74.28.

situation in this verse, though, as we shall discover, this denotation does not exhaust the term. It is from this kind of death, a spiritual death, that Jesus has rescued us. Second, we glimpse the opposite posture of a godly life, one lived in the flesh but not one that "belongs to God." In the ancient Christian view, a person "is dead before baptism" (see 2:5; Col. 2:13).[9] Third, with a slightly different bent, we grasp that life without Christ is robbed of its vitality, "of its true quality," and is essentially dead. For life "in Christ" is lived "for" someone or "for" a divine cause. If these characteristics are missing, we experience a lack of life—that is, death.[10] Fourth, Jesus was the "firstborn" of those in the realm of the dead, thus offering them resurrection. The word "firstborn" is πρωτότοκος (*prōtotokos*) and appears in Colossians 1:18 and Revelation 1:5 with this meaning.[11] At base rests the thought that the redeemed dead enjoy an "adoption" which lifts them out of the world of departed spirits and pushes them to the front of the line for resurrection (1:5; Rom. 8:23; compare Acts 26:23; Rom. 8:29; and 1 Cor. 15:20).[12] This adoption may well mirror and be an extension of God's adoption of the early Hebrew tribes, whom he had redeemed from slavery: "Thus saith the Lord, Israel is my son, even my first-born" (Ex. 4:22; see also Jer. 31:8–9[13] and the Notes on 1:20; 2:5; 5:14).

trespasses and sins: The difference in meaning between the two terms (singular παράπτωμα and ἁμαρτία, *paraptōma* and *hamartia*) is difficult to draw because here the two nouns are effectively synonyms, the one reinforcing the other. In their plural form, the two nouns bring readers to "actual sins as distinct from a sinful condition."[14] Fundamentally, in Paul's writings, *paraptōma* can refer to Adam's transgression (see Rom. 5:15, 17–18, 20, "offence") and, additionally, to acts that disrupt a person's "relation to God through his [or her own] fault"[15] (see Rom. 4:25, "for our offences [*paraptōma*]"; 2 Cor. 5:19, "their trespasses [*paraptōma*]"; and Col. 2:13). The noun *hamartia,* in mild contrast, has to do with sin that has invaded the world (see Rom. 5:12), perhaps entangling a person even before birth (see Ps. 51:4–5 and Moses 6:55).[16] It exhibits its power in our flesh (see Rom. 6:19; 7:5, 11; James 1:15; etc.) and can bring us

---

9. Gerhard von Rad, Georg Bertram, and Rudolf Bultmann, *TDNT,* 2:863 and n. 267; Bultmann, *TDNT,* 4:893.

10. Rudolf Bultmann, *TDNT,* 3:17–18 and n. 76.

11. Bultmann, *TDNT,* 4:893.

12. Wilhelm Michaelis, *TDNT,* 6:877.

13. Matitiahu Tsevat, *TDOT,* 2:127.

14. Best, *Ephesians,* 200.

15. Wilhelm Michaelis, *TDNT,* 6:172; BDAG, 770.

16. Klaus Koch, *TDOT,* 4:314.

to spiritual death (see 1 John 5:16).[17] In its fundamental sense, sin puts a person crosswise with God and, anciently, had to be atoned for vicariously in the sanctuary by the sacrifice of an animal,[18] anticipating Jesus' vicarious sacrifice for our sins (see Isa. 53:12; Heb. 9:11–15, 24–28; 1 John 3:4; and Moses 5:5–7). Jesus, of course, could offer that sacrifice because, like an unblemished animal, "in him [was] no sin," no blemish (1 John 3:5; see also John 8:46).[19] Incidentally, even though the noun *hamartia* occurs much more frequently than *paraptōma* throughout the New Testament, this is the only occurrence of *hamartia* in Ephesians (see the Notes on 1:7; 2:5).

2:2 *in time past:* This bygone time centers on the believer's lifetime before receiving and accepting the message, the preaching, about Jesus Christ.

walked: The verb περιπατέω (*peripateō*) at base presents the idea of walking around, of walking from one place to another (see Matt. 4:18; John 1:36; etc.). In this verse, we come upon the metaphorical meaning that revolves around how a person conducts his or her life. For example, "They [Zacharias and Elisabeth] were both righteous before God, *walking* in all the commandments and ordinances of the Lord blameless" (Luke 1:6, emphasis added; see also Rom. 6:4; 8:4; 1 John 1:6–7; etc.).[20] This idea of walking in the "way" or path of God is distinctive of Christian thought and is divorced from the Hellenistic world.[21] This meaning for the verb *peripateō,* which shows up in seven verses in this letter, stands against any effort to make Ephesians into a second-century production influenced by Hellenistic thought. The concept of walking in the path of God, and even in his company, goes back to both the Old Testament and Hebrew thought[22] (see Gen. 5:22, 24; 6:9; etc.; and the Notes on 2:10; 4:1, 17; 5:2, 8, 15).

Andrew Lincoln perceptively singled out the verbs "to walk," "to sit," and "to stand" as threads that bind Ephesians together. For him, they sum up believers' deep commitment to Christ, with the sense that they walk, sit, and stand with him, resisting the evil powers and joining Christ in his victory over them.[23] But does this exhaust the matter? Each of these verbs picture

---

17. Gottfried Quell, Georg Bertram, Gustav Stählin, and Walter Grundmann, *TDNT,* 1:296, 311; BDAG, 50–51.

18. Koch, *TDOT,* 4:313, 317.

19. Quell, Bertram, Stählin, and Grundmann, *TDNT,* 1:304, 306.

20. BDAG, 803; Louw-Nida, §§15.227; 41.11.

21. Heinrich Seeseman and Georg Bertram, *TDNT,* 5:940–41, 944; Barth, *Ephesians,* 1:213–14.

22. Franz-Josef Helfmeyer, *TDOT,* 3:388–96.

23. Lincoln, *Ephesians,* 460; Philip Abbott drew my attention to Lincoln's observation.

actions at home in ceremonial settings. As early as Adam and Eve, according to modern scripture, a path led into the east side of the Garden of Eden where a gate evidently stood. It was at that entry point "that God placed cherubim and a flaming sword on the east of the garden of Eden, lest our first parents should enter and partake of the fruit of the tree of life" (Alma 12:21; see also Alma 42:2). In another place, this path is called "the way" in the expression "the way of the tree of life" (Moses 4:31). It was on this path, which led into the garden, that Adam and Eve would walk to call "upon the name of the lord," and where, in response, "they heard the voice of the Lord from the way [that led] toward the Garden of Eden, speaking to them." When Adam and Eve stood or sat on that "way" or "path," God "gave unto them commandments" (Moses 5:4–5). Hence, walking on that path toward the garden, likely standing or sitting at a predetermined spot, became a sacred act for Adam and Eve and enhanced their reception of God's "commandments." It is a simple step to see this worshipful activity as the beginning of ancient processions wherein devotees would walk on a processional path toward and into a sanctuary in order to make contact with a deity (see the Notes on 1:22; 2:6, 10; 4:1, 13; 5:2, 8, 15; 6:11, 13; the introduction section XI; and appendix 1).

according to the course of this world: At first glance, this expression seemingly bears the usual sense, shaded negatively, of how this world and its citizens coexist, complete with dirt, sickness, poverty, corruption, wealth, greed, and death. But because these words are followed by a further refinement of subject matter—"according to the prince of the power of the air," a reference to the devil—the meaning of the first expression, "according to the course of this world," now takes on an unseen, unearthly import, swelling its sinister fibers.

course: We have met the Greek term αἰών (*aiōn*) in 1:21, where it is translated as "world." A noun that occurs 126 times in the New Testament and 7 times in Ephesians, it is regularly translated "world" or "ever," as in "forever," depending on the context and the idiom. In its earliest appearances in classical literature, it bore the denotations of "vital force," "lifetime," "era," or even "eternity."[24] In its occurrence in Ephesians, the word bears the sense of the limited, temporal existence of this sinful world that will not last beyond the end-time or the Second Coming of the Savior.[25] Because of the following personal noun, "the prince," a pointer to Satan,

---

24. LSJ, 45; Sasse, *TDNT*, 1:197–98.
25. Sasse, *TDNT*, 1:205–6.

the term αἰών (*aiōn*) also comes to bear almost a personal meaning, as if it is a living entity that opposes God (see the Notes on 1:21; 2:7; 3:9, 11, 21).[26]

this world: This second occurrence of the noun κόσμος (*kosmos*) links to the term's first appearance, "from the foundation of the world" (1:4), wherein the world is first alluded to as transitory and impermanent because it has a beginning and therefore an end. In the earlier passage, the world appears in positive dress. But here it wears the frightful, fetid clothing of "the prince of the power of the air."[27] Hence, the temporal and temporary world is not to be equated with the earth, which will remain eternally, though in a changed state (see Isa. 65:17–25; 66:22; 2 Pet. 3:13; Rev. 21:1; 2 Ne. 30:10–18; D&C 88:14–26; 101:23–32; and the Notes on 1:4; 2:12).[28]

the prince of the power of the air: As Paul's readers would have known, he was directing their attention to Satan, who "worketh in the children of disobedience." Unlike "all principality, and power, and might, and dominion," whose identities remain unclear (see the Note on 1:21), in this verse we face the devil himself.

prince: In most cases where this noun (ἄρχων, *archōn*) appears in the New Testament, the King James translators render it "ruler" or, in its plural form, "rulers" (see Matt. 9:18; Luke 8:41; 18:18; John 3:1; Acts 3:17; etc.). In a few instances, this term is translated "prince" (see Matt. 9:34; John 14:30; 1 Cor. 2:6; etc.). As this sampling of verses will show, the term *archōn* regularly denotes a person possessing earthly authority—that is, a Roman or Jewish official. But in certain passages, it also is about those who bear authority over unseen, ungodly forces. For instance, according to Gospel accounts, demonic powers are released through "the prince of devils," known popularly as Beelzebub (see Matt. 12:24 and Mark 3:22; see also Luke 11:15). But for Christians, the power of this personality is already broken (see John 12:31; 14:30; 16:11), though he continues to be master of "the children of disobedience" and "the children of [God's eventual] wrath" (2:3; see the Notes on 1:21; 2:2; 3:10; 4:27; 6:11–12).[29]

power: As in 1:21, the Greek noun translated "power" is ἐξουσία (*exousia*). Here, the sense is different. How so? Because, unlike in 1:21, where the term refers to a person (see the Note on 1:21),[30] in this passage it has to do with

---

26. Sasse, *TDNT,* 1:207–8.
27. Sasse, *TDNT,* 3:885, 892–93.
28. Hermann Sasse, *TDNT,* 1:678–79.
29. Delling, *TDNT,* 1:488–89; von Rad and Foerster, *TDNT,* 2:79–80; Traub and von Rad, *TDNT,* 5:533.
30. Louw-Nida, §12.44.

the territory or dominion in which Satan acts, essentially his kingdom (see Col. 1:13).[31] The idea of Satan's kingdom is widespread; he thus holds power in a kingdom-like setting: "how shall then his [Satan's] kingdom stand?" (Matt. 12:26); "the dragon [Satan] gave him [the beast] his power, . . . and great authority [ἐξουσία, *exousia*]" (Rev. 13:2); "the dragon . . . gave power [ἐξουσία, *exousia*] unto the beast" (Rev. 13:4); "and power [ἐξουσία, *exousia*] was given him [the beast] over all kindreds, and tongues, and nations" (Rev. 13:7). The notice that Satan dominates a sphere of influence persists into modern scripture. For instance, Joseph Smith wrote in an account of his First Vision, "I was destined to prove a disturber and an annoyer of his [Satan's] kingdom" (JS–H 1:20). Further, we read of "his [Satan's] own dominion" (D&C 1:35); "they . . . build up the kingdom of the devil" (D&C 10:56); "the enemy, even Satan, sitteth to reign" (D&C 86:3; see also 2 Ne. 2:29); and "the prince of this world cometh" (D&C 127:11). Importantly, this dominion of evil, this kingdom of the devil, exists only under the control of God and is allowed to function only for a limited era (see Col. 1:16;[32] D&C 29:47; and the Notes on 1:21; 3:10; 6:12).

air: The Apostle now described where Satan makes his home and has his power base—in the air or, perhaps better, the sky (ἀήρ, *aēr*).[33] He is confined to this region so that he does not interfere with the ongoing work of Christ, who is now "far above . . . this world" (1:21) and whose "fulness . . . filleth all in all" (1:23).[34] Nor can he influence the Saints, who, after death, are freed from the atmosphere of this world where the devil operates. Moreover, one glimpses a connection here between "the air" and the following explanatory expression, "the spirit that now worketh in the children of disobedience." In English, the connection between "air" and "spirit" is not immediately apparent. But in both Hebrew and Greek, the same noun serves for blowing wind, for a person's breath, and for spirit, whether belonging to a person or to God, thus presenting an intriguing tie between the two nouns, "air" and "spirit."[35]

---

31. Foerster, *TDNT*, 2:567–68; Edmond Kidley Simpson and Frederick Fyvie Bruce, *Commentary on the Epistles to the Ephesians and the Colossians,* The New International Commentary on the New Testament (Grand Rapids, Mich.: Wm. B. Eerdmans, 1965), 48; Best, *Ephesians,* 204–5; Winger, *Ephesians,* 283; Louw-Nida, §37.36.

32. Foerster, *TDNT*, 2:565, 567–68; Bertram, *TDNT*, 2:653.

33. Werner Foerster, *TDNT*, 1:165–66; BDAG, 23; Louw-Nida, §§1.6–7.

34. Friedrich Büchsel, *TDNT*, 3:642 n. 13.

35. Caird, *Letters,* 51; BDB, 924–25; S. Tengström and Heinz-Josef Fabry, *TDOT,* 13:368, 379–90; BDAG, 832–36; Louw-Nida, §§12.33; 14.4; 23.186; 26.9.

In the Old Testament, the air was the space between the earth and the dome of heaven or "the firmament." It was inhabited by "the host of heaven" (Gen. 1:6–20; Ps. 19:1; 1 Kgs. 22:19; 2 Kgs. 17:16; 21:3; etc.)[36] and was pictured as the place of fowls (see Gen. 1:26, 28, 30; Deut. 4:17; D&C 49:19; etc.). In Judaism, devotees saw the air as peopled by "angels and demons, and found in the air the abode of the latter."[37] But this space is to belong to such foul individuals only for a restricted time. For at the Second Coming, "we which are alive and remain shall be caught up together . . . to meet the Lord in the air" (1 Thes. 4:17). From that moment, the air will belong to Christ.

We know from other scriptural references that Satan and his minions were "cast down" from heaven. On this view, heaven is not considered an extension of the air but stands above it. The earliest text that relates to the fall of Satan occurs in the book of Moses: "I [God] caused that he [Satan] should be cast down; . . . he became Satan, . . . the father of all lies, to deceive and to blind men" (Moses 4:3–4). In Isaiah's book, we come across these words, which link Satan to the earth and to Sheol below it: "How art thou fallen from heaven, O Lucifer, son of the morning! how art thou cut down to the ground, . . . thou shalt be brought down to hell [Sheol], to the sides of the pit" (Isa. 14:12, 15). This view is mirrored in part by John's vision of the great dragon: "His tail drew the third part of the stars of heaven, and did cast them to the earth" (Rev. 12:4). Modern scripture implies, but does not say directly, that Satan, who was thrust down from heaven, came to the earth. We glimpse this in the following: "A third part of the hosts of heaven [the forces of Satan] turned he away from [God]. . . . They were thrust down, and thus came the devil and his angels" (D&C 29:36–37), and "an angel of God who was in authority . . . was thrust down from the presence of God and the Son" (D&C 76:25; see also 2 Ne. 2:17–18).

spirit: In this passage, the term translated "spirit" (πνεῦμα, *pneuma*) does not fit within the usual idea of a helpful influence, such as the Spirit of God (see 1:17; 2:18, 22; 3:5, 16; etc.). Rather, the noun πνεῦμα (*pneuma*) identifies Satan as a spirit personage like the "lying spirit" of 1 Kings 22:23 or "the evil [one]" of John 17:15 (see Luke 7:21; 8:2; Acts 19:15–16; Mosiah 3:6; etc.). This spirit, who is Satan, "is at work in the lost."[38] One problem with the identification of this spirit with Satan is the fact that the words

---

36. G. Bartelmus, *TDOT*, 15:209–10.

37. Foerster, *TDNT*, 1:165; see BDAG, 23.

38. Hermann Kleinknecht, Friedrich Baumgärtel, Werner Biedner, Erik Sjöberg, and Eduard Schweizer, *TDNT*, 6:445; see also Louw-Nida, §§12.37–39.

translated "the spirit" do not appear in the same Greek grammatical case as those translated "the prince," the one in the accusative and the other in the genitive. But such incongruities are not rare, and the sense of the passage requires that "the prince" and "the spirit" be identified as the same (see the Notes on 2:18, 22; 3:16; 4:4; 5:9).[39]

worketh: This is one of two occurrences of this verb (ἐνεργέω, *energeō*) in connection with the powers of evil (see 2 Thes. 2:7, "the mystery of iniquity doth already work"). Even though "the prince of the power of the air" possesses the ability to influence people for wicked purposes and will exhibit "all power and signs and lying wonders" (2 Thes. 2:9), his power is limited by God. For God, "who now restrains it [the evil power] will do so until he [Satan] is out of the way" (2 Thes. 2:7 RSV; see also D&C 29:47 and the Notes on 1:11, 20; 3:20).[40]

the children of disobedience: This Hebraic expression[41] brims with significance. The English word "disobedience" is the proper translation of ἀπειθεία (*apeitheia*; see 5:6 and Col. 3:6). Widening this thought, the noun *apeitheia* can also carry a sense of disbelief (see Rom. 11:30, 32; and Heb. 4:6, 11).[42] Beyond this, we ask ourselves how an evil power can influence one's life. The first part of an answer is to recognize that, according to scripture, the evil one is able to exert a real influence in people's lives. For instance, as the plots against Jesus thickened during the last days of his life, we read that "Satan [entered] into Judas [who] . . . communed with the chief priests and captains, how he might betray [Jesus] unto them" (Luke 22:3–4). In a second example, on the last night of his mortal life, Jesus prayed that his Father would "protect [the disciples] from the evil one" (John 17:15 NIV). A third example derives from the Book of Mormon. In an enthralling scene, the Lord instructed a missionary named Ammon to lead his Lamanite converts away from their homeland because of threats: "Get this people out of this land," said the Lord, "that they perish not; for Satan has great hold on the hearts of the Amalekites, . . . against their brethren to slay them; therefore get thee out of this land" (Alma 27:12). Because of these observations, this question now pushes itself toward us even more urgently—How does Satan come to influence people?

---

39. Blass and Debrunner, *Greek Grammar,* §137(3); Best, *Ephesians,* 205; Larkin, *Handbook,* 28; Winger, *Ephesians,* 283; contra Lincoln, *Ephesians,* 96.

40. Bertram, *TDNT,* 2:652–53.

41. Blass and Debrunner, *Greek Grammar,* §165; Larkin, *Handbook,* 29.

42. BDAG, 99.

A person's first step in coming under the influence of the devil, evidently, is to yield to temptation, as Adam did (see D&C 29:40). If thereafter one persists in a pattern of succumbing to temptation, that person begins to bring "forth evil works" and to hearken "unto [the devil's] voice." If these actions remain uncorrected, the result is that one becomes "a child of the devil." Why? Because that person chose to "follow him" (Alma 5:41). For those who have entered this path, "the devil did enter into them, and take possession of their house," their soul (Alma 40:13; see also Luke 11:24–26 and 2 Ne. 9:46, "the devil hath obtained me"). Scripture elucidates two classic examples. The first involves Judas, as noted above. As becomes apparent from John's Gospel, Judas was tempted to turn Jesus over to Jewish religious authorities: "The devil . . . put into the heart of Judas Iscariot, Simon's son, to betray [Jesus]" (John 13:2). Though John does not specify that Judas yielded to the temptation and thereafter met with those authorities, the rest of the story makes these occurrences apparent (see Luke 22:4–6). Then, at the Last Supper, "Satan entered into [Judas]." Now captured by the devil, Judas left the meal to rendezvous with the chief priests and others to lead them to Jesus (John 13:27, 30).

The second case has to do with the fate of the lost Book of Mormon manuscript of 116 pages. The story begins with the temptation that came over those who were in possession of it: "Satan hath put it into their hearts to alter the words" of the text, said the Lord (D&C 10:10, 15). They yielded to this temptation and made changes to the manuscript so that, if Joseph Smith tried again to translate that part of the Book of Mormon, the two versions would "not agree, and [the possessors would] say that [Joseph Smith] has lied in his words" (D&C 10:18). For those individuals, the cataclysmic result of such an action, guided by Satan, was that "Satan [had] great hold upon their hearts; . . . their hearts are [now] corrupt, and full of wickedness and abominations; and they love darkness rather than light, because their deeds are evil" (D&C 10:20–21). Their journey was now complete; they had "become subjected to the spirit of the devil, . . . and the devil hath all power over [them]" (Alma 34:35; see also the Note on 5:6).

2:3 *we all*: After writing exclusively to Gentiles, beginning with 1:13, Paul now brings Jews back into his audience, as he did in 1:3–11. Paul has strengthened this language of inclusion by inserting "also" and the following "all."[43] Of course, Paul himself is Jewish. He will tie everyone, Jew and Gentile, who is unredeemed to "the lusts of our flesh" and "the desires of the flesh, and of our mind."

---

43. Lincoln, *Ephesians,* 97.

had our conversation: The verb ἀναστρέφω (*anastrephō*) finds its noun counterpart in 4:22 (ἀναστροφή, *anastrophē*). At base, the verb bears the sense "to walk (in one's life), to behave." This meaning of moral conduct for the verb *anastrephō* appears in other epistles (see 2 Cor. 1:12; 1 Tim. 3:15; Heb. 13:18; etc.). In contrast, in John 2:15, the verb has to do with Jesus overturning the tables of the moneychangers; in Acts 5:22, it pertains to officers returning to the religious council (see also Acts 15:16, which loosely quotes LXX Amos 9:11; and the Notes on 4:17, 22).[44]

lusts: This noun (singular ἐπιθυμία, *epithymia*) bears two major senses, both having to do with strong desires. In one, it expresses a potent desire to do or possess something. For example, "With desire [*epithymia*] I have desired to eat this Passover with you" (Luke 22:15; see also Mark 4:19; Luke 17:22; and Heb. 6:11). In the other, it has to do with an intense desire to do something wrong or to possess something belonging to another. For instance, "Abstain from fleshly lusts [plural of *epithymia*], which war against the soul" (1 Pet. 2:11; see also John 8:44; Rom. 1:24; Gal. 5:16; 1 John 2:16; 2 Ne. 10:24; etc.). According to Galatians 5:24, with Christ's aid it is possible to crucify our unruly "flesh with its passions and desires [plural of ἐπιθυμία, *epithymia*]" (RSV; see the Note on 4:22).[45]

flesh: In this first of ten appearances of this noun in Ephesians (σάρξ, *sarx*), we notice initially that it is a favorite word of Paul, as shown by its dense presence in other letters—eighty-nine times, including Hebrews. In both occurrences in this verse, the term strikes a decidedly negative tone. However, although the flesh is the home of our "lusts," we are to consider the flesh as a dominant element of human nature in general rather than thinking of our flesh as a pointer to a baser nature.[46] To be sure, in its two manifestations in this verse, it is possible to see "how σάρξ [*sarx*] can take on an increasingly personal demonic character."[47] But that is not the case with its other appearances in Ephesians (see the Notes on 2:11, 15; 5:29, 30; 31; 6:5, 12). After saying this and noticing that Paul broadened his audience to include Jews, we grasp that the Apostle was preparing both Jews and Gentiles "for the same solution in Christ."[48]

fulfilling the desires of the flesh and of the mind: This expression pads the prior clause, both sharpening and extending the implications of what

44. Georg Bertram, *TDNT*, 7:715–17; BDAG, 72–73; Louw-Nida, §41.3.

45. Louw-Nida, §25.12, 20.

46. Louw-Nida, §§26.7; 58.10.

47. Eduard Schweizer, Friedrich Baumgärtel, and Rudolf Meyer, *TDNT*, 7:137; see also Lincoln, *Ephesians*, 97–98.

48. Winger, *Ephesians*, 284.

it means to be caught "in times past in the lusts of our flesh." Those "lusts," those "desires," have enjoyed more or less free reign in both the carnal self and the mental self, effectively consuming the whole person.

fulfilling: The participle of ποιέω (*poieō*) takes on a broader import than merely "fulfulling." The verb's fundamental meaning is "to do." From such a basic definition, one senses the ongoing, self-imbibing actions of an individual that accord with "the desires of the flesh," the person offering no resistance to inner impulses. Thus, he or she acts in harmony with "prince of the power of the air" (2:2; see also the Notes on 6:6, 8).[49]

desires: We have already met this noun four times in this letter, where it is translated "will" (θέλημα, *thelēma*; see 1:1, 5, 9, 11). We shall run into it again, twice (see 5:17; 6:6). Only in this verse does it carry a pejorative meaning, escorting us into the world of evil. Usually appearing as a singular noun, it occurs elsewhere only twice in the plural, with the meaning of God's will (see Mark 3:35 [in two manuscripts only, including the important Vaticanus] and Acts 13:22). In two passages, John 1:13 ("the will of the flesh . . . the will of man") and 1 Corinthians 7:37 ("hath power over his own will"), we encounter the term linked to the "sexual impulse," though under control. Only once in the New Testament do we meet this noun describing the devil's power over people (see 2 Tim. 2:26). In our verse, it appears synonymously with "the lusts of our flesh," casting these desires as uncontrolled, unbounded impulses toward a licentious lifestyle (see the Notes on 1:1, 5; 5:17; 6:6).[50]

the mind: Outside the New Testament and in the Septuagint and Greek philosophical works, the noun διάνοια (*dianoia*) often points not only to the mind and its thought patterns but also to a person's moral or ethical consciousness. In this verse and in 4:18, we find the meaning "thought" or "impulse of will." Elsewhere in the New Testament, especially in passages that quote the Septuagint or are influenced by it, the key notion is "understanding" or "mind." For example, in fulfilling "the first commandment," believers are to "love the Lord thy God with all thy heart, and with all thy soul, and with all thy mind [διάνοια, *dianoia*], and with all thy strength" (Mark 12:30, quoting LXX Deut. 6:5). In addition, "I [the Lord] will put my laws into their mind [διάνοια, *dianoia*], and write them in their hearts" (Heb. 8:10, quoting LXX Jer. 38:33 [31:33 KJV]; see also Heb. 10:16). It is in such passages that we discover the close connection between "heart" and "mind" (see the Note on 4:18).[51]

---

49. Herbert Braun, *TDNT,* 6:479.

50. Schrenk, *TDNT,* 3:54, 61, quotation on 61; see also BDAG, 447.

51. Johannes Behm and Ernst Würthwein, *TDNT,* 4:963–67; see also BDAG, 234.

nature: This noun (φύσις, *physis*) enjoyed a long history as a significant term in philosophical and scientific discussions, as is shown by the size of the entry for φύσις (*physis*) in the large standard Greek-English lexicon.[52] It is possible to glimpse touches of the common views of this noun in such places as Romans 11:24 ("the olive tree which is wild by nature") and Galatians 2:15 ("we who are Jews by nature"; see also Rom. 2:27; 11:21; 1 Cor. 11:14; and James 3:7). In our verse, the word shades into theological meaning where, ominously, unbelieving Jews, like Gentiles, stand squarely in the path of God's wrath. Unlike his Jewish contemporaries, Paul believed that Jews had no special claim on God's saving acts. In notable contrast, many of his contemporaries held that most Jews would be saved and only some Gentiles (see the Note on 1:11; introduction to this chapter).[53]

children of wrath: This expression has to do typically with those who have breached God's laws and therefore will reap God's anger, such as "the children of disobedience" (2:2; 5:6) and, in apocryphal literature, Cain, who is called a "child of wrath" in the *Apocalypse of Moses* 3.[54] Standing opposite these persons, we observe those called "children of light" (τέκνα φωτός, *tekna phōtos*; 5:8; see also Luke 16:8, "the sons of light," RSV) and "children of God" (τέκνα θεοῦ, *tekna theou*; John 1:12; Rom. 8:16; Philip. 2:15; 1 John 3:1–2, 10; 5:2; see also the Notes on 4:31; 5:6).[55]

2:4 ***But God:*** For the soul that has been trapped "in the lusts of our flesh" and "the desires of the flesh, and of the mind" (2:3), these words ring an ever-melodious bell of hope. God himself has stepped forward with his full-flowered mercy in an effort not only to rescue believers from their actions "in times past" (2:2–3) but especially to elevate them with his Son. Not incidentally, "God" is the delayed subject of the long sentence that begins with 2:1 and ends in 2:7.[56]

rich in mercy: Paul here begins to unfold the generous gifts that God will give to those who believe (2:4–7), gifts that match what he has offered to Christ in elevating him into the "heavenly places" (1:20; 2:6). The

---

52. LSJ, 1964–65.

53. Helmut Köster, *TDNT,* 9:274–75.

54. Constantinus Tischendorf, *Apocalypses apocryphae Mosis, Esdrae, Pauli, Johannis, item Mariae Dormitio: additis Evangeliorum et actuum Apocryphorum supplementis* (Leipzig: Herm. Mendelssohn, 1866), 2, https://archive.org/details/apocalypsesapocooperkgoog/page/n79/mode/2up, cited by Hermann Kleinknecht, Oskar Grether, Otto Procksch, Johannes Fichtner, Erik Sjoeberg, and Gustav Stählin, *TDNT,* 5:415 n. 232.

55. Kleinknecht, Grether, Procksch, Fichtner, Sjoeberg and Stählin, *TDNT,* 5:415 n. 231, 435, 438.

56. Winger, *Ephesians,* 286.

significance is to say that steadfast believers will receive what Christ has already received and will join him in his exalted, divine state. Among other things, the contrast between God's mercy (ἔλεος, *eleos*) and his "wrath" (2:3) now comes into trimmed focus.[57] Onto the believer and out of his infinite riches, God will pour his mercy (see Rom. 9:23; 11:30–32; 1 Pet. 1:3;[58] and the Notes on 1:7, 18; 2:7; 3:8, 16).

his great love: According to Paul, this love (ἀγάπη, *agapē*) points at two events that church members have already undergone in the broad sweep of their lives, a "pre-temporal ordination and temporal [earthly] calling" into Christ's gospel (see Rom. 11:28 and 1 Thes. 1:4).[59] This two-step process of election, coming about initially in the premortal world and then in the mortal sphere, stands as proof of God's loving, determined, and unending "work" to bring us to "immortality and eternal life" (Moses 1:39; see also the Notes on 3:19; 5:2).

he loved us: God's most gracious sentiment is loving us, his wayward children who exhibit on occasion a willingness and ability to follow him and to love him for his unstinting generosity toward us. Some form of this verb (ἀγαπάω, *agapaō*) occurs ten times in this letter, disclosing one of Paul's most enduring themes. But only in 5:2 does the verb take on the same character, the loving from a divine personality: "Christ also hath loved us."[60] In this latter passage, we can grasp the depth and breadth of this love when we run across these words: "[Christ] hath given himself for us an offering and a sacrifice to God" (5:2). Hence, the most majestic manifestation of this love was Christ's willingness to suffer to bring about his Atonement (see Rom. 5:8[61] and the Note on 5:2).

2:5 *dead:* This death characterized believers' lives before they came to faith. Why? Because they were "dead in [their] sins and the uncircumcision of [their] flesh" (Col. 2:13). It is in a similar spiritual sense that the prodigal son "was dead, and is alive again" (Luke 15:24, 32). In the physical meaning of the word "dead" (νεκρός, *nekros*), Jesus was "the firstborn from the dead" or "the first begotten of the dead," emerging from death's rock-hard, limiting bands (Col. 1:18; Rev. 1:5). These two thoughts, death as both a spiritual and a physical experience,[62] unite in the doctrine that Jesus is the

---

57. Lincoln, *Ephesians,* 100; Best, *Ephesians,* 213; Fowl, *Ephesians,* 72.
58. Rudolf Bultmann, *TDNT,* 2:483–84; Hauck and Kasch, *TDNT,* 6:328–29.
59. Quell and Stauffer, *TDNT,* 1:49 and n. 139.
60. BDAG, 5; see also Quell and Stauffer, *TDNT,* 1:23, 27.
61. Barth, *Ephesians,* 1:219; Lincoln, *Ephesians,* 100.
62. BDAG, 667–68; Louw-Nida, §§23.121; 74.28.

judge of "the quick [the living] and the dead" (Acts 10:42; 2 Tim. 4:1; 1 Pet. 4:5). For in his capacity as judge of all, because he holds the keys of both life and the underworld (see Rev. 1:18 and Moses 7:38–39), he will interact not only with those from the world of departed spirits (see Rom. 14:9; 1 Pet. 3:18–20; 4:6; and D&C 138:16, 18), whom he has freed from "death and hell" (see Rev. 20:13[63] and 2 Ne. 9:26), but also with those who are living at the time of his return (see Isa. 40:5; 63:1–4; Dan. 7:9–14; Mal. 3:1; D&C 43:29, 32; 63:50–51; 101:22–29; 133:41–52; and the Notes on 1:20; 2:1; 5:14).

sins: Paul refers to the sins (plural of παράπτωμα, *paraptōma*) that render a person dead, a strong spiritual metaphor. By such, a person is totally debilitated not only in this life but in the next because Satan will be master of individuals there, at least until Christ rescues them from his grasp. For, as Jesus reminded a somewhat hostile crowd who had challenged how he managed to free people from evil spirits, "when a stronger [Jesus] than [the devil] shall come upon him, and overcome him, he taketh from [the devil] all his armour . . . and divideth his spoils," the spoils (σκῦλον, *skylon*) being the souls whom the devil has captured and now holds both in this life and the next (Luke 11:22; see also Isa. 49:24–25; 53:12; Mark 3:27; Rev. 20:13; and 2 Ne. 2:29).[64]

But this is not the end of the story. The sins (*paraptōma*) that hold a person in the clutches of death predate the giving of the Mosaic law. That is to say, this noun envelops all sin. For instance, in Romans 5:15, 17–18, Paul wrote this noun to specify Adam's transgression. But its significance is wider than this event. For it carries the meaning of "offences against God" and, secondarily, against fellowmen in Matthew 6:14–15 and Mark 11:25 ("trespasses"). In addition, in the case of offenses committed against other persons, such actions are tantamount to offending God because they are perpetrated against his children. Moreover, when we combine Romans 5:13 and 5:20, it becomes clear that "until the law [of Moses] sin [ἁμαρτία, *hamartia*] was in the world" and that "the law [of Moses] entered" with the result that "the offence [*paraptōma*] might abound." In a word, noting that *hamartia* and *paraptōma* are equivalents, as in Ephesians 2:1, the coming of

---

63. Bultmann, *TDNT*, 4:893; S. Kent Brown, "Peter's Keys," in *The Ministry of Peter, the Chief Apostle*, ed. Frank F. Judd Jr., Eric D. Huntsman, and Shon D. Hopkin, 43rd Annual Brigham Young University Sidney B. Sperry Symposium (Provo, Utah: BYU Religious Studies Center; Salt Lake City: Deseret Book, 2004), 93–96.

64. Von Rad and Foerster, *TDNT*, 2:79–80; Grundmann, *TDNT*, 3:399–401; Albrecht Oepke and Karl Georg Kuhn, *TDNT*, 5:300–2; BDAG, 770, 933; Brown, *Testimony of Luke*, 568–70, 573–74.

the Mosaic law had the effect of intensifying the seriousness of all offenses (see the Notes on 1:7, "sins"; and 2:1, "trespasses").[65]

quickened . . . together: This verb (συζωοποιέω, *syzōopoieō*) is the first of three successive verbs that bear the prefix συν- (*syn-*), which is a preposition. In this case, the preposition's final letter has been absorbed into the first letter of the verb's root.[66] The preposition carries the meaning "with" or "in the company of," making the verb say "to make alive together with someone." The other two verbs occur in quick succession in 2:6 (συνεγείρω, *synegeirō,* and συγκαθίζω, *synkathizō*); respectively, they mean "to cause to rise with" and "to cause to sit down with."[67] By employing this quick repetition of sounds (all begin with *syn-*)—the letter was to be read aloud in congregations (see Col. 4:16; compare Rev. 1:3)—Paul forcefully and audibly underscores his point that, in the end-time, and even in the present, believers will enjoy what Jesus enjoys and will share what he possesses (see Rom. 8:17; Philip. 3:20; D&C 84:37–38; and the Notes on 1:20; 2:21; 3:6).

quickened us together with Christ: As we have discovered above, the force of the verb *syzōopoieō,* which appears again in the New Testament only at Colossians 2:13, is "to make alive together with someone."[68] One all-important element is that this verb, and the two verbs that follow in 2:6, links believers to Christ in the unfolding events of the end-time. In contrast, the verb in 2:22 that also exhibits a σύν- (*syn-*) prefix (συνοικοδομέω, *synoikodomeō*) revolves around events of this world where followers "are *builded together* for an habitation of God through the Spirit" (emphasis added). We must then conclude that the four verbs with *syn-* prefixes in 2:5, 6, and 22 frame a unity that undergirds all of chapter 2. As a person might conclude, the meaning of *syzōopoieō* splits between the image of resurrection, wherein we are made alive through God's actions, and the notion that, by believing in Christ, we are made alive spiritually in this life (see Moses 6:65, "quickened in the inner man"). In this passage, the latter sense carries the most weight, as Colossians 2:13 illustrates: "quickened together with him, [he] having forgiven you all [your] trespasses." But because of the verbs in 2:6, we must not lose sight of the firm link to the Resurrection. Furthermore, in the Colossians verse, we encounter an allusion to baptism when, in a sacred moment, a person's sins are forgiven, whether Jew or Gentile.[69]

---

65. Michaelis, *TDNT,* 6:170–72; see also BDAG, 770.

66. Smyth, *Greek Grammar,* §101.a.

67. Walter Grundmann, *TDNT,* 7:770, 786–87, 793; BDAG, 951, 954–55, 967.

68. BDAG, 954–55; Lincoln, *Ephesians,* 101–2; Larkin, *Handbook,* 31.

69. Lincoln, *Ephesians,* 102; Winger, *Ephesians,* 287–88 and n. 33; for a contrary view, see Best, *Ephesians,* 215–16.

In addition, when comparing the fourfold acts of God laid out in 1:20 and 1:22 ("raised . . . set . . . put . . . gave") with the three spread out between this verse and 2:6 ("quickened . . . raised . . . made us sit together"), this quickening is the only action that does not mirror what we read in chapter 1. Paul thus emphasizes that our spiritual life is "with Christ" and with no other. Modern scripture buttresses this observation: "We are made alive in Christ because of our faith" (2 Ne. 25:25). Noticing a different tack that features the Holy Spirit as the quickening agent, we come across "the Comforter . . . which quickeneth all things, which maketh alive all things" (Moses 6:61; see also the Note on 1:20).

by grace ye are saved: Besides the abrupt subject change from "us" to "you," which has led some to view this expression as a part of a Christian celebration,[70] the words seem more likely to be a "joyful interjection" that happily honors what God has done for those who believe, as Paul has just outlined in prior verses.[71]

grace: The important noun "grace" (χάρις, *charis*) appears twelve times in Ephesians[72] and specifies the most vital path to salvation in two places in this epistle, here and in 2:8. The Greek expression in each passage is identical, save for the addition of the definite article "the" in 2:8 (χάριτί ἐστε σεσῳσμένοι, *chariti este sesōsmenoi,* "by grace are ye saved"). In the long history of the term *charis* and its Hebrew counterpart (חן, *hēn*), *charis* sketches out a reciprocal relationship, usually between a person in a position of authority and another person in a more humble state. In essence, a freely given gift (*charis*) from the more powerful person to the other, whether the lesser person had sought for it or not, was to be reciprocated by a gift of equal value, whether in the form of material goods or acts of loyalty. The reciprocal gift from the humbler person, of course, rarely equaled the initial gift from the stronger. In ancient literature, including the Old Testament, these gifts also characterized the relationship between God and his people, maturing into a covenantal bond.[73] This relationship, we must always keep in mind, grew out of God's love for humans, not the other way around.[74]

70. Barth, *Ephesians,* 1:221; Winger, *Ephesians,* 288.

71. Fowl, *Ephesians,* 74; see also Best, *Ephesians,* 216–17.

72. Eph. 1:2, 6, 7; 2:5, 7, 8; 3:2, 7, 8; 4:7, 29; 6:24.

73. Conzelmann and Zimmerli, *TDNT,* 9:373–74, 376, 378; see also David Noel Freedman, Jack R. Lundbom, and Heinz-Josef Fabry, *TDOT,* 5:22–24, 27–28; Ceslas Spicq, *TLNT,* 3:501–6; H. J. Stoebe, *TLOT,* 1:439–47; Brent J. Schmidt, *Relational Grace: The Reciprocal and Binding Covenant of* Charis (Provo, Utah: BYU Studies, 2015), 15–18, 22–23; and Draper and Rhodes, *Paul's First Epistle to the Corinthians,* 67–68, especially 74–100.

74. Draper and Rhodes, *Paul's First Epistle to the Corinthians,* 76–85.

After a long review of the rich meaning of *charis* in ancient sources, Hans Conzelmann and Walther Zimmerli arrive at the New Testament era and conclude that, in Paul's letters, *charis* meant "free unmerited grace," adding that "we are saved by grace alone," effectively trending toward so-called "easy grace" and discoloring their own earlier observations about reciprocal relationships formed by God's granting of *charis* and the needed human responses to his free gift, such as baptism, humility, and efforts to remain on the path of God (see Matt. 7:13–14; 28:19–20; Luke 13:24–29; 18:13–14; John 3:5; Philip. 2:12; and 2 Ne. 31:17–21).[75]

To be sure, Conzelmann and Zimmerli identified a passage, Psalm 102:13–14, as illustrating God's willingness to give a free gift, requiring nothing in return.[76] But this view has been disputed: "One can no more say that *hēn* [in the Old Testament] signifies a spontaneous demonstration of grace."[77] Rather, because the Hebrew *hēn* and Greek *charis* have denoted reciprocal relationships, especially between God and the upright, the connections of these terms to sacred acts, to essential "works," are predictably many. If we begin with the fourth Gospel's observation, "the Word was ... full of grace and truth" (John 1:14), we encounter Jesus and his Father as the possessors of all essential grace, as the dispensers of every celestial gift, and as the guarantors of spiritually nourishing relationships. Examples are many: from our generous God have come the gifts of life's necessities, including deliverance from enemies and want (see Ps. 18; 30; 32; 54; 66:16–20; etc.);[78] from the gracious Christ came the gift of Paul's apostolic office (see Rom. 1:5; 12:3; 15:15; and 1 Cor. 3:10); from the suffering Savior came the gifts of "redemption" and "forgiveness of sins" through baptism (1:7; see also Col. 1:14, 20; and the Note on 1:7); and from the giving Father came Jesus' dignity as Lord (see Matt. 11:27; Luke 10:22; John 3:35; 13:3; D&C 93:4; etc.).[79] Notably the Father's gift to Jesus came as "a reward given *for His obedience*" rather than deriving from God's conjectured freely awarded grace (emphasis added).[80] There is more to the story.

---

75. Conzelmann and Zimmerli, *TDNT*, 9:394–95, quotations on 394. Following Rudolf Bultmann, they hold that "grace ... negates all human preparation" (934 n. 180). Also Lincoln, *Ephesians*, 104, wrote about "God's sovereign *freedom from obligation* in saving them" (emphasis added).

76. Conzelmann and Zimmerli, *TDNT*, 9:377.

77. Stoebe, *TLOT*, 1:442.

78. Freedman, Lundbom, and Fabry, *TDOT*, 5:24, 30–31.

79. See chap. 1 n. 150 herein.

80. Conzelmann and Zimmerli, *TDNT*, 9:396–97; the quotation, which stands firmly against the notion of *charis* as "free unmerited grace," is from 9:396; see also Freedman, Lundbom, and Fabry, *TDOT*, 5:24, 30, 32, 34.

In Paul's writings, this passage and 2:8 highlight a concept found twice elsewhere. In 1 Thessalonians 5:9, we read that "God hath not appointed us to wrath, but to obtain salvation [σωτηρία, *sōtēria*] by our Lord Jesus Christ." In 2 Thessalonians 2:13, we learn that "God hath from the beginning chosen you to salvation." Each of these passages affirms God's free gift of salvation. Salvation's character as a gift, as an act of "grace" or divine giving, has never been in dispute because it has come from the Father through Christ without believers being able to offer any helps. In fact, however, a close review leads to the conclusion that believers have contributed substantially, but in a negative manner. Specifically, it was our sins and misdeeds that intensified Jesus' suffering almost "unto death" in Gethsemane (Mark 14:34; see D&C 19:18–19).

That said, in a positive vein, other dimensions come into play. First, we notice that, for Paul, salvation is linked to faith or belief: "The gospel of Christ ... is the power of God unto salvation [*sōtēria*] to every one that believeth" (Rom. 1:16). This is precisely the essence of 2:8: "For by grace are ye saved *through faith*" (emphasis added). Furthermore, salvation is connected with repentance: "Godly sorrow brings repentance that leads to salvation [*sōtēria*]" (2 Cor. 7:10 NIV). Moreover, salvation can be aided by prayer: "This [preaching] shall turn to my salvation [*sōtēria*] through your prayer," Paul recounted (Philip. 1:19). In addition, salvation is tied to enduring to the end in the presence of "adversaries," who see their acts of persecution as a "token" of loss when such acts are actually an indicator "of salvation, and that of God" because believers are "to suffer for [Christ's] sake" (Philip. 1:27–29; see also Acts 14:22). It is apparent, therefore, that salvation does not consist of a smooth, enlarged tube through which, after one has received God's "grace," one fluidly slides into heaven with no bumps or required tasks.

We are still not at the end of the rope, so to speak. Through Paul, the notion of converts' reciprocal actions in response to God's gifts stands forth in visible strength. To say it another way, Paul stood in a client-patron relationship to God and, correspondingly, held a patron-client relationship to his converts (see 1 Cor. 9:1–2).[81] How do these situations manifest themselves? In the letter to the Ephesians sit two notices of Paul's imprisonment. In one, he called himself "the prisoner of Jesus Christ for you Gentiles"; in the other, he spoke of himself simply as "the prisoner of the Lord" (3:1; 4:1; compare 2 Cor. 1:6 and Philip. 1:7, 13–14). With this kind of language, he underscored "his dependence on God as [his] guardian in

---

81. Schmidt, *Relational Grace*, 88, 94–96.

a patron-client relationship informed by charis"—that is, by divine gifts.[82] That relationship of dependence came about through God's unexpected, unmerited calling of Paul to the ministry, which then led to God's care of him in very adverse circumstances. Such circumstances included, but were not limited to, receiving "stripes above measure" and "in prisons," being "beaten with rods" and "stoned," and being thrown into the sea in a "shipwreck" (2 Cor. 11:23, 25). Paul responded to God's loving gifts by his relentlessly active pursuit of Gentile converts, as he was initially directed (see Acts 9:15; 20:18–20; 22:14–15; 26:15–18; and Gal. 1:11–12). God's calling of the Apostle and then watching over him were mirrored in Paul's loving care in calling people around the Mediterranean Sea into the divine gospel and then, as their spiritual guardian, exercising a watchful eye over them. Toward Paul, they responded with prayers and acts of loving kindness, including accompanying him when traveling (see Acts 20:4, 14; and Philip. 1:7, 9, 19) and making contributions to the poor believers in Jerusalem as a reciprocal gift for Jerusalem's centrality as the source of spiritual aids that flowed out into other Christian congregations (see Acts 24:17; 1 Cor. 16:1–4; 2 Cor. 8–9; and Gal. 2:10).[83] Paul, as a matter of fact, wrote that his continuing gifts to his converts were still needed. For example, his remaining "in the flesh is more needful for you," he wrote, than his leaving mortality (Philip. 1:24).

In light of the above observations, the conclusion is warranted that "grace," as the primary ingredient in a person's salvation, is a free gift, plain and simple. However, it does not stand proudly isolated and independent from believers' implied obligations. Such obligations, especially those toward God for his inestimable gifts, have characterized the patron-client relationship between him and devotees for as long as records that feature *hēn* and *charis* and related terms have been kept. As Paul will affirm a few lines later in this epistle, "we are [God's] workmanship, created in Christ Jesus unto good works" (2:10). Exactly. Otherwise, God's inexpressible gift will have been wasted on us (see the Notes on 2:8, 10; 4:1, 7, 29).

saved: The form of this verb, which means "to save," is the perfect passive participle of σῴζω (*sōzō*). The perfect tense refers to a past occurrence whose influence is still felt. Among Paul's letters, only in 2:8 does this participle appear again, effectively saying that our salvation was a past event,

---

82. Schmidt, *Relational Grace,* 94.

83. Stephan Joubert, *Paul as Benefactor: Reciprocity, Strategy and Theological Reflection in Paul's Collection* (Tübingen: Mohr Siebeck, 2000), 88–115, 155–203.

not a future one. In only one other passage did Paul write about salvation as a past occurrence: "In this hope we were saved" (Rom. 8:24 NIV). Because elsewhere Paul held salvation to be a future event (see Rom. 5:8–9; 9:27; and 1 Cor. 3:13–15), some have jumped to the conclusion that Paul could not be the author of Ephesians.[84] Admittedly, the notion of salvation as a past occurrence is unusual in Paul's letters. But it seems to be merely "a different use" of the verb "with no basic distinction of content."[85] What is unusual is making salvation a matter that comes "by grace" or by "faith" (2:8). Customarily, Paul wrote about a person *being justified* by "grace" or by "faith" rather than being saved (emphasis added; see Rom. 3:24, 28; 5:1; Gal. 2:16; 3:11, 24; and Titus 3:7; see also D&C 20:30 and the Note on 2:8).[86] The difference in meaning is straightforward. To be justified has to do with God offering a freewill gift, usually following repentance, and generously making a person upright in his divine sight.[87] This circumstance, embraced within a covenant relationship, applies both to this life and to the next (see Matt. 12:36–37; Luke 18:13–14; Rom. 3:23–24; Gal. 2:16–20; etc.).[88] To be saved, of course, characterizes one's status in the next life, though it is possible for a person to come to know in this life that his or her salvation is assured (see 2 Pet. 1:10 and D&C 132:19–20).

2:6 *raised us up together*: Paul has already ascribed this kind of action to the Father when touching on Jesus' Resurrection "from the dead" (1:20). The verb here (συνεγείρω, *synegeirō*) derives from the same root as that in 1:20 ("raised," ἐγείρω, *egeirō*), with the added prepositional prefix σύν- (*syn-*), whose sense is "with" or "together with."[89] Surely, the import of "raised us up together" bears a spiritual sense rather than physical because Paul's readers were not yet resurrected. In this verse, we encounter "a realized eschatology" of sorts; that is, what is yet to occur at the end-time is already influencing the present.[90] We find a similar idea in Philippians 3:10: "That I may know him, and the power of his resurrection, and the fellowship of his sufferings."

84. Lincoln, *Ephesians*, 104; Best, *Ephesians*, 217; James Leslie Houlden, *Paul's Letters from Prison: Philippians, Colossians, Philemon, and Ephesians* (Philadelphia: Westminster Press, 1977), 283–84.

85. Werner Foerster and Georg Fohrer, *TDNT*, 7:994; see also Caird, *Letters*, 53; Barth, *Ephesians*, 1:221; and Fowl, *Ephesians*, 74.

86. Lincoln, *Ephesians*, 104; Fowl, *Ephesians*, 74.

87. Draper and Rhodes, *Paul's First Epistle to the Corinthians*, 83–84.

88. Gottfried Quell and Gottlob Schrenk, *TDNT*, 2:214–19; Louw-Nida, §34.46.

89. BDAG, 271–72, 967.

90. Grundmann, *TDNT*, 7:793; Louw-Nida, §23.95.

Likewise, we read, "Therefore, if you have been raised with Christ, keep seeking the things above" (Col. 3:1 NR). In a similar vein, we learn that the Atonement of Christ was in force hundreds of years before Jesus' mortal life from the words of the prophet Nephi: "We preach of Christ, we prophesy of Christ, and we write . . . that our children may know to what source they may look for a remission of their sins" (2 Ne. 25:26). Coming back to Paul, we also notice that the thought is "raised together with Christ" rather than "raised with one another." Finally, we meet a connection to ordinances, specifically baptism. Taking up the same verb (*synegeirō*), Paul wrote about being "buried with him [Christ] in baptism, wherein also ye *are risen with* him through the faith" (Col. 2:12, emphasis added; see also Rom. 6:4–5; and the Note on 1:20).

together: The term "together" does not appear in the text but is implicit in the prefix σύν- (*syn-*) and is completed by the phrase "with Christ" (2:5). Thus, anticipating the Resurrection, Paul wrote that God has effectively raised readers "with Christ" at that moment, placing them promisingly in his lofty company at the end-time (see the Notes on 1:20; 2:5; 3:6).

made us sit together: The causal form of this verb (συγκαθίζω, *synkathizō*) appears here in the sense "to cause to sit down with."[91] Like the prior verb, the phrase "with Christ" (2:6) completes the thought. At base, the substance has to do with exaltation, with sitting on thrones as Christ sits on his throne (see 1:20, "[God] set him at his own right hand"). The following promise comes to faithful believers: "To him that overcometh will I [Christ] grant to sit with me in my throne, even as I . . . am set down with my Father in his throne" (Rev. 3:21). This notion goes back to the Old Testament notations that kings, queens, and rulers sat on thrones, much like God does, even sitting in God's presence (see Ps. 110:1 and 1 Chr. 17:16; see also Ex. 11:5; 1 Kgs. 1:17–20; 3:6; etc.). Such enthronements prefigure the exalted occupancy of thrones by the faithful (see the Notes on 1:20; 2:5).[92] Although some resist the thought that the faithful will enjoy the same exalted status as Christ, drawing attention to the distinctively unique position of Christ "at [God's] own right hand" (1:20),[93] plainly the path is open to that exaltation for those who diligently seek it (see Rom. 8:16–17, "joint-heirs with Christ"; and D&C 84:36–38, "all that my Father hath shall be given unto him"; see also Mosiah 5:7–8).

Sitting is a common posture. In a culture that lacked a lot of chairs and that saw people reclining or sitting on mats or pillows on the floor to eat,

---

91. BDAG, 951; Louw-Nida, §17.17.
92. Carl Schneider, *TDNT,* 3:442.
93. Best, *Ephesians,* 219; Lincoln, *Ephesians,* 107; Winger, *Ephesians,* 289.

a chair with a back and arms was usually reserved for honored guests in one's home.[94] In public places, such as synagogues, most people sat on wide masonry benches that were built out from the walls.[95] Even here, how-ever, special seats were reserved for honored individuals, such as scribes and Pharisees (see Matt. 23:6; Mark 12:39; and Luke 11:43).[96] Hence, the thought of sitting draws up images of honored people, who often wore special robes to distinguish themselves from others in their society (see Matt. 23:5; Mark 12:38; and Luke 20:46).[97] At the pinnacle reposed "Moses' seat," which was occupied by the scribes and Pharisees, those who were entrusted with the divine truths communicated to Moses and were tasked with teaching them (Matt. 23:2).[98] Jesus himself demonstrated that sitting was the posture of the honored teacher,[99] who often sat to teach (see Matt. 5:1; 13:1–2; 15:29; Mark 4:1; 9:35; Luke 5:3; John 6:3; 8:2; etc.).[100] What is the upshot of these observations? Simply stated, we find ourselves in a world of sacred, revealed knowledge first disclosed to Moses. This knowl-edge was not for everyone, and its tenets were kept secret, to be shared only with the worthy (see Luke 11:52).[101] To be sure, the custodians of this revelation often behaved badly, seeking the best places at feasts and syna-gogue services as if such honors sat squarely and rightly on their shoulders. But Jesus evidently did not fault their roles as teachers nor the content of their teaching. He faulted them because they taught one thing and did another (see Matt. 23:3, 13, 23).[102] In sum, in one real sense, the act of sit-ting links to the world of sacred teaching and learning. It therefore joins walking and standing as indicators of holy rituals that rest just behind the language of this letter (see the Notes on 2:10; 4:13, 20, 22, 24; 5:2, 8, 14; 6:11, 13–14; introduction section XI; and appendix 1).

---

94. Wilhelm Michaelis, *TDNT,* 6:870 n. 3.

95. Lee I. Levine, *The Ancient Synagogue: The First Thousand Years,* 2nd ed. (New Haven, Conn.: Yale University Press, 2005), 185, 337–40.

96. Michaelis, *TDNT,* 6:871 n. 3; Levine, *Ancient Synagogue,* 339–40.

97. Ulrich Wilckens, *TDNT,* 7:690–91.

98. Wolfgang Schrage, *TDNT,* 7:822 n. 143; Rudolf Meyer and Konrad Weiss, *TDNT,* 9:43, 48.

99. Michaelis, *TDNT,* 6:871 and n. 3.

100. Schneider, *TDNT,* 3:443. According to Mark 13:2, Jesus sat to give his sermon on the Mount of Olives; the resurrected Christ in modern scripture corrected this notation, quoting him as saying, "I stood before [my disciples] in the flesh" (D&C 45:16).

101. Joachim Jeremias, *TDNT,* 1:741; Joachim Jeremias, *Jerusalem in the Time of Jesus* (Philadelphia: Fortress Press, 1969), 253.

102. Günther Bornkamm, *TDNT,* 6:662.

in heavenly places: Many want to understand this expression as both pointing to the location where believers will join Christ and to heaven as that locale. They see the plural "heavenlies" (ἐπουράνιοι, *epouranioi*), or "heavenly places," as a rendition of the Hebrew plural שׁמים (*shamayim*), which generally means "heaven" or "heavens."[103] If that is so, then they also have to explain how Paul could write about wrestling "against principalities, against powers, against the rulers of the darkness of this world, against spiritual wickedness in *high places* [*epouranioi*]" (6:12, emphasis added). In this light, heaven appears to be home to more than benevolent entities, something that requires explanation (see the Notes on 1:3, 20; 3:10; 6:12; and Analysis of 1:15–23).

2:7 *the ages to come:* The expression could be rendered "the coming ages" or "the coming eras." The noun αἰών (*aiōn*) is usually thought of as splitting its meanings between the world in which we now live and the one that will usher in eternity. Perhaps significantly, in the entire New Testament, this split is best spelled out in 1:21: "Not only in this world, but also in that which is to come." Such a view of two ages, called "the biblical doctrine of time and eternity,"[104] differs from that of Latter-day Saints, who hold to the notion of "dispensations" or virtually self-contained eras of salvation history during the course of human history, which themselves were preceded by other vast eras before the appearance of Adam and Eve on the earth (see Abr. 5:13, "after the Lord's time, . . . for as yet the Gods had not appointed unto Adam his reckoning [of time] "; D&C 130:4–5; Abr. 3:3–10;[105] and the Notes on 1:21; 2:2; 3:9, 11, 21).

the exceeding riches of his grace: In the Gospels, especially Luke, rich persons are often singled out for criticism, not the riches themselves. As presented in Luke's narrative, these individuals are not good candidates for membership in the kingdom of God (see Luke 1:53; 6:24; 8:14; 16:22–23; 18:25; 21:1–4; etc.). The Apostle Paul, on the other hand, focuses on riches or wealth but not on earthly riches. Instead, he transfers the concept to those which God and Christ possess and can offer to their people. Naturally, these riches are chiefly bound up with the *eschaton,* the end-time, when

---

103. BDB, 1029–30; Traub and von Rad, *TDNT,* 5:539; Bartelmus, *TDOT,* 15:205; Jan Alberto Soggin, *TLOT,* 3:1369; Larkin, *Handbook,* 6, 32.

104. Sasse, *TDNT,* 1:205.

105. Hugh Nibley, "Before Adam," *Old Testament and Related Studies,* ed. John W. Welch, Gary P. Gillum, and Don E. Norton, vol. 1 of the Collected Works of Hugh Nibley (Salt Lake City: Deseret Book; Provo, Utah: Foundation for Ancient Research and Mormon Studies, 1986), 70–71, 73–77.

God will parcel out heavenly riches to the faithful at the Judgment (see Rom. 9:23; 10:12; 11:33; and 2 Cor. 8:9).[106] But that is not the end of the story. God is "rich in mercy" in the here and now (2:4). Not only does this endowment of mercy manifest itself in "redemption through [Christ's] blood" and in "the forgiveness of sins" (1:7), but it also pushes itself into the believer's personal life and confers more than normal strength when facing challenges (see 1 Chr. 29:10–12; Ps. 68:32–35; 1 Pet. 1:3–5; Alma 7:12; 20:4; 26:12; the Notes on 1:7, 9, 16, 18, 21; 2:16; 3:7–8, 16; 4:30; and the Analysis of 1:3–14).[107]

exceeding: The verb ὑπερβάλλω (*hyperballō*), appears in its dress as a present participle (ὑπερβάλλον, *hyperballon*) that acts as an adjective. In this form, the participle bears the meanings supreme, extraordinary, boundless, and the like.[108] Because the description is applied to God, a good rendition might be "matchless," with the sense that nothing in creation can match the "riches of his grace [directed] . . . toward us through Christ Jesus."

in his kindness: The noun χρηστότης (*chrēstotēs*), appears only in the writings ascribed to the Apostle Paul, usually with the meaning of God's "goodness" or "kindness."[109] This kindness or generosity, of course, emanates to us "through Christ Jesus." In the New Rendition, the noun and its preposition are translated as the adjective "generous" for ease of reading.

through Christ Jesus: This Greek phrase, literally "in Christ Jesus" (ἐν Χριστῷ 'Ιησοῦ, *en Christō Iēsou*), is "not found prior to Paul and [is] rare outside the Pauline corpus. [Such phrases] are largely peculiar to Paul, and he is perhaps their author."[110] That said, little difference in substance appears whether the phrase is translated "in Christ Jesus" or "through Christ Jesus" unless the preposition "in" is thought to feature an imagined mystical union between the believer and the Savior, which it does not. Rather, the unity that reposes "in" Christ centers on a unity of will and a sanctifying purpose (see 2:19–22; John 17:17–23; 2 Cor. 12:2; Philip. 3:8–9; 4:7; 1 Thes. 4:16; 3 Ne. 11:27–30; etc.).[111]

---

106. Hauck and Kasch, *TDNT,* 6:328–29.

107. Eising, *TDOT,* 4:349, 353–55; Grundmann, *TDNT,* 2:313–16; Oepke, *TDNT,* 2:542–43; Braun, *TDNT,* 6:464; Bednar, "In the Strength of the Lord," 121–28; Rasmus, "Enabling Power of the Atonement," 18–21.

108. Gerhard Delling, *TDNT,* 8:520–22; BDAG, 1032; Louw-Nida, §78.33; Larkin, *Handbook,* 32.

109. See Rom. 2:4; 3:12; 11:22 (three times); 2 Cor. 6:6; Gal. 5:22; Col. 3:12; Titus 3:4; BDAG, 1090; Thayer, *Lexicon,* 672.

110. Oepke, *TDNT,* 2:541.

111. Oepke, *TDNT,* 2:541–42.

2:8 ***For by grace are ye saved:*** The second occurrence of this expression within a short space of the letter acts as an emphatic hammer (see 2:5, χάριτί ἐστε σεσῳσμένοι, *chariti este sesōsmenoi*). In our passage, Paul has added the definite article "the" to point back to the grace which he has held up in 2:5 and 2:7.[112] Its strong character is driven home by the addition of the clarifying phrase "through faith" (διὰ πίστεως, *dia pisteōs*), a common phrase that we run across elsewhere in Paul's letters (see 3:12, 17; Rom. 3:22, 25, 31; 2 Cor. 5:7; Gal. 2:16; 3:14, 26; etc.). The connective "for" (γάρ, *gar*) introduces the explanation for what Paul meant by writing "the exceeding riches of his grace" (2:7).[113]

grace: For Latter-day Saints, the doctrine of "grace" has been fraught with possible misunderstanding. As a sample of this difficulty, we consult 2 Nephi 25:23: "It is by grace that we are saved, after all we can do." At first glance, it appears that believers are to do as many good works as they can in their lives, and then the Lord makes up the rest from his reservoir of grace.[114] No less than the Apostle Paul wrote that we are to "work out [our] own salvation with fear and trembling" (Philip. 2:12). James held "that faith without works is dead" (James 2:20). The cumulative weight of these and other passages rests on "works" as the main driver of salvation. Case closed? Not by a long shot. These passages are offset by a sheaf of other scriptural passages that invitingly emphasize something quite different and escort us to a different observation point on the matter (see the Notes on 2:5; 4:30 on "redemption").

As background, Latter-day Saints are concerned about the so-called "easy grace" that emanates from certain Christian teachers, a grace that is either predestined to wash over and save a person, whether the person seeks it or not, or comes readily and fully to a person who simply confesses that Jesus is Lord and Savior. Latter-day Saints worry that within these teachings lurks a salvation that requires nothing more than an individual's belief.[115] The helpful remark that "salvation requires *both* grace and works [and] is a revealed yet commonsense reconciliation of these contradictory positions" does press home a sensible approach between grace and works,

---

112. Lincoln, *Ephesians*, 111; Best, *Ephesians*, 225.

113. Lincoln, *Ephesians*, 111.

114. Robert L. Millet, *Grace Works* (Salt Lake City: Deseret, 2003), 65–83, 135–45; Draper and Rhodes, *Paul's First Epistle to the Corinthians*, 86.

115. Stephen E. Robinson, *Believing Christ: The Parable of the Bicycle and Other Good News* (Salt Lake City: Deseret Book, 1992), 13–17, 23, 27–28; Millet, *Grace Works*, 6–7, 42–43; Draper and Rhodes, *Paul's First Epistle to the Corinthians*, 85–86.

respectively, as the chief paths to salvation.[116] But we may not be able to tie up the horse just yet.

In an echo of Paul's insight in his Epistle to the Ephesians, "by grace are ye saved" (2:5, 8), a prophet named Abinadi, speaking to a hostile group of royal advisers more than a century before Jesus' birth, intoned that "were it not for the atonement, which God himself shall make for the sins and iniquities of his people, . . . they must unavoidably perish" (Mosiah 13:28). In a word, Christ's Atonement bridges the gulf that gapes open precipitously between humans' imperfect state and God's offer of salvation. Nothing else creates this bridge. Nothing. There is more.

The unalloyed, unconditional benefits of Christ's gracious Atonement bring two groups to salvation without any intervening requirement: those who have died without law and children, who are innocent in God's eyes. As a first example, we hear the words of Jacob: "Where there is no law given there is no punishment . . . and where there is no condemnation the mercies of the Holy One of Israel have claim upon them, because of the atonement" (2 Ne. 9:25). Next, the words of Mormon: "All little children are alive in Christ, and also all they that are without the law. For the power of redemption cometh on all them that have no law" (Moro. 8:22; see also D&C 45:54). Third, from a record of Adam, we discover that "the Son of God hath atoned for original guilt, wherein the sins of the parents cannot be answered upon the heads of the children, for they are whole from the foundation of the world" (Moses 6:54). From these last words, it becomes evident that Latter-day Saints do not believe that children are born into sin but rather into a state of innocence, a state of wholeness (see Moses 6:54, "children . . . are whole from the foundation of the world"; Moro. 8:8, "little children are whole, for they are not capable of committing sin").

This doctrine is one of the most densely attested in modern scripture. Children's state of innocence has been guaranteed by Jesus' Atonement, as Mormon quoted the Savior: "I came into the world not to call the righteous but sinners to repentance; . . . wherefore, little children are whole, for they are not capable of committing sin; wherefore the curse of Adam is taken from them in me, that it hath no power over them" (Moro. 8:8). Again from Mormon, we encounter the principle that "little children cannot repent . . . for they are all alive in him because of his mercy" (Moro. 8:19). From the Resurrected Christ, we come across the strong affirmation that "little children are redeemed from the foundation of the world" (D&C 29:46; see also

---

116. Bruce C. Hafen, "Grace," in *EM*, 2:560, emphasis in the original.

D&C 93:38). Furthermore, "they cannot sin, for power is not given unto Satan to tempt little children" (D&C 29:47). This is not all.

An additional notice of universal grace directs us to the Resurrection alone. All humans will be resurrected, regaining their mortal bodies and escaping the effects of an endless death. A few samples will suffice. From Jacob, son of Lehi, we learn that "[Christ] suffereth this ['the pains of every living creature'] that the resurrection might pass upon all men" (2 Ne. 9:21–22). From the prophet Abinadi we hear, "The grave hath no victory, and the sting of death is swallowed up in Christ" (Mosiah 16:8). From Moroni, son of Mormon, we find out that "all men are redeemed, because the death of Christ bringeth to pass the resurrection" (Morm. 9:13). From Christ himself, we discover that "Michael, mine archangel, shall sound his trump, and then shall all the dead awake, for their graves shall be opened . . . yea, even all" (D&C 29:26; see also Mosiah 15:20 and Alma 11:42; 12:8; 40:4).

From the days of Adam and Eve, humankind has enjoyed agency—that is, the ability and freedom to make choices and, importantly, to be accountable for such choices.[117] How so? Because God gave them power to choose, as we glimpse in God's words to Adam and Eve: "Of the tree of the knowledge of good and evil, thou shalt not eat of it, nevertheless, *thou mayest choose* for thyself, for it is given unto thee" (Moses 3:17, emphasis added). As scripture attests, their choice to partake of the fruit led to their expulsion from the Garden of Eden and the imposition of mortality onto the human race: "By reason of [Adam's] transgression cometh the fall, which fall bringeth death" (Moses 6:59). Significantly, Jesus' Atonement has erased the transgression of Adam and Eve when they chose this option: "I have forgiven [Adam and Eve their] transgression in the Garden of Eden," and "the Son of God hath atoned for original guilt" (Moses 6:53–54). Perhaps more crucially, their choice led to the power to become parents, to beget children, as we are reminded: "Adam fell that men might be" (2 Ne. 2:25), and "because that Adam fell, we are" (Moses 6:48). As we have just seen, those children were not born with sin adhering to them, as we discover in other passages: "Little children are alive in Christ, even from the foundation of the world" (Moro. 8:12), and "God having redeemed man from the fall, men became again, in their infant state, innocent before God" (D&C 93:38).

Returning to the ability to choose, we meet one of God's most important gifts, that of freedom. In its earliest manifestation, this freedom was granted to Adam and Eve: "In the Garden of Eden, gave I unto man his

---

117. C. Terry Warner, "Accountability" and "Agency," in *EM*, 1:13, 26–27.

agency" (Moses 7:32). Therefore, because God "gave unto [Adam] that he should be an agent unto himself" (D&C 29:35), Adam and Eve and their descendants "are agents unto themselves," capable of making choices (Moses 6:56). Naturally, people across the world experience different levels of personal freedom depending on their circumstances. Yet, in the matter of private consciences, scripture holds that people "are free to choose liberty and eternal life, through the great Mediator of all men, or to choose captivity and death, according to the captivity and power of the devil" (2 Ne. 2:27; see also 2 Ne. 10:23; Alma 61:15; and D&C 58:27–28; 88:86).[118]

We now come to the devil's place in God's plans in the following: "The devil should tempt the children of men, or they could not be agents unto themselves; for if they never should have bitter they could not know the sweet" (D&C 29:39; see also Moses 6:55, "they taste the bitter, that they may know to prize the good"). The serious consequences of yielding to the devil's temptations emerge from the Savior's words: "Adam ... partook of the forbidden fruit and transgressed the commandment, wherein he became subject to the will of the devil, because he yielded unto temptation" (D&C 29:40). At this point, repentance enters.

Amidst a series of quoted lines from the Father and the Son, Nephi summarized that "the gate by which ye should enter is repentance and baptism by water; and then cometh a remission of your sins by fire and by the Holy Ghost" (2 Ne. 31:17). Repentance, followed by baptism, marks the inescapable path that a person must follow, no matter the grace showered on that individual (see Mark 1:15; John 3:5; Acts 2:38; 2 Ne. 31:11–13; and Moro. 8:25). This is exactly what we concluded when examining the expressions "redemption through his blood" and "the forgiveness of sins" (1:7; see the Note thereon; see also Col. 1:14). These actions—repenting, being baptized, and entering the divine gate (see Matt. 7:13–14; Luke 13:24; and 2 Ne. 31:8–9)— are all works "which God hath before ordained that we should walk in them" (2:10). First came grace, mediated to us by the Father and the Son; then came the necessary, celestially ordained "works" that allow us to approach God and his kingdom.

But our works, no matter how nicely placed and timely done, will never catch us up to God's gracious gifts to us. Especially relevant are words from King Benjamin in his final public address to his people at the temple of Zarahemla. He first reminded his attentive audience that "if you should render all the thanks and praise [to God] which your whole soul has power

---

118. David E. Bohn, "Freedom," *EM*, 2:525–27.

to possess, . . . yet ye would be unprofitable servants." For, in acts of grace, God "hath created you, and granted unto you your lives, for which ye are indebted unto him." This is only part of the story. God "doth require that ye should do as he hath commanded you." If a person does as God commands, "he doth immediately bless you; and therefore he hath paid you. And ye are still indebted unto him." Indeed, we "will be [indebted to God], forever and ever" (Mosiah 2:20–21, 23–24).

At this point, we circle back to the passage with which we began: "We know that it is by grace that we are saved, after all we can do" (2 Ne. 25:23). We ask, Does the meaning have to be that we first do all in our power and then God makes up the difference? This understanding is certainly one possibility. But another stands close by. It holds that, because God has already made grace available to us through granting our lives to us and providing a Savior to rescue us from sin and death, we are therefore under the necessity of doing all we can, including accepting his gifts of redemption and forgiveness and acting to acquire them through repentance and baptism. That is, God acts first, and we then respond as best we can (see the Notes on 2:5, 10; 4:7, 29).[119]

saved: The same passive participle of the verb σῴζω (*sōzō*) that we find in 2:5 occurs in this verse, pointing to salvation as a past event. This notion causes trouble for some, though in the end it seems to make little difference (see the Note on 2:5). The Gospels, where the verb *sōzō* is often translated "to make whole" (see Matt. 9:22; Mark 5:28, 34; 10:52; and Luke 7:50; 8:48; 17:19; 18:42), report that divine blessings, including healings, are accessed through faith. In one instance, that of the cleansing of ten lepers, a genuine expression of gratitude led to the release of Jesus' saving powers, a remarkable outcome. For, in response to Jesus healing them of their leprosy, nine of the lepers obediently went away to find a priest, who could declare them clean. But one turned back to Jesus, "giving him thanks." The translators of the KJV then quote Jesus as saying, "Thy faith hath made thee whole." But we uncover the deeper sense if we translate this line "thy faith *hath saved* thee" (Luke 17:12–19, emphasis added).[120]

through faith: Paul often employs a variant expression for "through faith" or "by faith" that differs from this one. Elsewhere, we encounter ἐκ πίστεως (*ek pisteōs*)[121] as frequently as we do διὰ πίστεως (*dia pisteōs*),

---

119. Robinson, *Believing Christ,* 90–93; Millet, *Grace Works,* 132.

120. Brown, *Testimony of Luke,* 788–90.

121. See Rom. 1:17; 3:30; 5:1; 9:30, 32; 10:6; Gal. 3:8, 11, 12, 22; 5:5.

like here.[122] Depending on the contexts, the meanings of the phrases are essentially the same. In the case before us, "faith" directs us to the faith of the believer in Christ, not to either Christ's faithfulness or his trust in us.[123] Faith, of course, grants the believer access to God's saving grace, activating it. Paul contrasts faith with works of the law of Moses but never with personal efforts or works that improve oneself or serve others (see Rom. 3:28; 4:2; Gal. 2:16; etc.). This faith, which has responded to the preaching of the gospel and has welcomed specifically the message of Christ's death and Resurrection, leads a person to "righteousness," a state of being justified before God (see Rom. 3:20–22; 4:5–6, 24; 9:30–32; 10:3–9; 1 Cor. 15:11; Gal. 3:6–12; Philip. 3:9; Col. 2:12; etc.).[124] This faith, like that of Abraham, which was "counted . . . to him for righteousness" (Gen. 15:6; see also Rom. 4:3), "is completely certain of the full agreement between God's promise and his power, which can call into being things which are not," such as giving "Abraham a posterity" (see the Notes on 3:12, 17).[125]

not of yourselves: As Paul has reminded his readers here, any human effort to provide a bridge to God and his world is simply impossible to undertake. Only Jesus' redeeming sacrifice can link us to the heavens, something that is effectively going on for believers: "Even when we were dead in sins, [God] hath quickened us together with Christ, . . . And hath raised us up together, and made us sit together in heavenly places in Christ Jesus" (2:5–6; see also Rom. 6:4–5; Col. 2:12–13; and Moses 6:61, 65).

gift of God: The term for "gift" (δῶρον, *dōron*) regularly links to gifts that a worshiper brings to the temple altar (see Matt. 5:23–24; 8:4; 23:18–19; and Heb. 5:1; 8:3–4; 9:9; 11:4). Hence, the aroma of sacred ceremony hovers nearby, raising to view covenants made and renewed in a holy setting. In such light, we come to witness both God's free gift of salvation through his Son and an implied expectation that we shall reciprocate by "good works, which God hath before ordained that we should walk in them" (2:10; see also 2 Ne. 26:27; and the Note on 2:5).

2:9 *Not of works:* Consistently and regularly in Paul's letters, readers run across his concern with "works of the [Mosaic] law" (ἔργα νόμου, *erga nomou*; see Rom. 3:20, 28; 9:32; Gal. 2:16; 3:2, 5, 10) in contrast to the

---

122. See Rom. 3:22, 25, 31; 2 Cor. 5:7; Gal. 2:16; 3:14, 26; Philip. 3:9; 1 Thes. 3:7.

123. Best, *Ephesians,* 226; Fowl, *Ephesians,* 78.

124. Quell and Schrenk, *TDNT,* 2:206–7; Bultmann and Weiser, *TDNT,* 6:208–10, 214, 217, 219–20.

125. Delling, *TDNT,* 6:310.

"work of God" (see Rom. 14:20 and Philip. 2:30, "work of Christ"). For Jews, of course, such works of the law of Moses sped a person toward God and his kingdom. For Paul, however, no one is justified before God through the works of the law (see Gal. 5:1–6). That happens only through God and his declarations and gifts to believers (see Luke 18:14, "I tell you"; Rom. 3:20–25, 28; 4:5; 5:1–2, 9; 8:30; 1 Cor. 6:11; and Gal. 2:16; 3:11, 24; 5:4–6). The whole point is that works of the law lead to death; no celestial life is in them (see Heb. 6:1; 9:14; and the Notes on 2:10; 4:1; 5:2).[126]

boast: The verb "to boast" (καυχάομαι, *kauchaomai*) and its related nouns often carry the senses "glorying" and "rejoicing." In Paul's hands, the verb and its nouns mirror the earlier positive and negative meanings from the Septuagint and Judaism—namely, a person glorying in God's blessings and a person glorying in his or her own accomplishments. The prophet Jeremiah captured both senses in his words "Thus saith the Lord, Let not the wise man glory in his wisdom, neither let the mighty man glory in his might, let not the rich man glory in his riches: but let him that glorieth glory in this, that he understandeth and knoweth me, that I am the Lord" (Jer. 9:23–24 [9:22–23, Hebrew text]; see also Prov. 27:2). In the Septuagint, the Greek verb *kauchaomai* is the regular translation of the Hebrew התהלל (*hithallel*), which denotes praise of oneself.[127] Paul carried through the substance of the verb *kauchaomai* from Judaism, holding that trust in God rather than self-promotion is key to one's relationship with the divine (see 2 Cor. 3:4 and Philip. 3:3–4), that God is the source of all good things rather than ourselves (see 1 Cor. 3:21–23; 4:7), that God's use of the small things of the earth to overcome the mighty renders boasting irrelevant (see 1 Cor. 1:25–29), and that, in an ironic twist, a person's boasting is to center on one's sufferings and persecution because they prove that God has granted to that person his or her life in Christ (see Rom. 5:3; 2 Cor. 4:7–11; and Philip. 3:7–12).[128]

2:10 *workmanship:* After Paul's insistence that we have been saved "by grace ... and ... not of yourselves" and that we must discount our good "works, lest any man should boast" (2:8–9), he hastened to add that "good works" somehow rest in our souls, in the essence of our beings. How so? Because "we are [God's]

---

126. Bertram, *TDNT,* 2:651–52; Turner, "Grace, Mysteries, and Exaltation," 110–11.

127. Helmer Ringgren, *TDOT,* 3:409–10; the nine occurrences are found in LXX 3 Kgs. 21:11; LXX Ps. 48:7 (49:7 Hebrew Bible); LXX Prov. 25:14; 27:1; LXX Jer. 9:23–24 (9:22–23 Hebrew Bible; five occurrences of the verb).

128. Rudolf Bultmann, *TDNT,* 3:646–50.

workmanship," and, as such, we have been "created in Christ Jesus unto good works," not for some other purpose. To make his point all the more clear, Paul insisted that, in the premortal era, "God hath before ordained that we should walk in [good works]" (2:10), very probably a reference "to all that was decided upon by God before the foundation of the world (1:4–10)" (see the Notes on 2:5, 8; 3:20; 5:5).[129]

Let us switch focus. On one level, humans are God's "workmanship" (ποίημα, *poiēma*) because they are his creation, his doing (see LXX Gen. 1:27 and Acts 17:26). On another level, unlike other creatures, humans are brought into a direct relationship to God because, first and most remarkably, they are "in [his] image, after [his] likeness" (Gen. 1:26; Moses 2:26; Abr. 4:26), and, second, he has granted to them his powers of stewardship over the earth to bless it (see Gen. 1:28; Moses 2:28; Abr. 4:28; and the Note on 1:22).[130] Yet they, in their best efforts to come to him, fail without Christ's intervention on their behalf (see Acts 4:12; Rom. 10:13; and Mosiah 3:17; 5:8; etc.).

created in Christ: The phrase "in Christ Jesus" (ἐν Χριστῷ Ἰησοῦ, *en Christō Iēsou*) and similar wording found in Paul's letters "are largely peculiar to Paul, and he is perhaps their author."[131] This distinctive phrase—coupled with the passive of the verb, which means we are "created [by God]" (κτίζω, *ktizō*)—pushes our attention back to the earliest verses of the Old Testament wherein "God said, Let us make man in our image, after our likeness" (Gen. 1:26). In light of the plural pronoun "our" in Genesis, we ask, To whom was God speaking? One answer is that he was addressing Wisdom, the female governess whom God created before all else (see Prov. 8:22–30). A better answer, hinted at in Paul's words here, is that God was talking to the premortal Savior. As we learn elsewhere, "I, God, said unto mine Only Begotten, which was with me from the beginning: Let us make man in our image, after our likeness" (Moses 2:26; see also John 1:1–3).

The expression "created in Christ" also directs our thoughts to the contrast between the natural world made by God and the spiritual realm that becomes available to us through Christ. We must grasp that, in the view of scripture, the natural world is full of life, not just the organic parts but also the inorganic parts: "All that God has created is life; even so-called

---

129. Barth, *Ephesians*, 1:227.
130. Gerhard Kittel, Gerhard von Rad, and Hermann Kleinknecht, *TDNT*, 2:390; Braun, *TDNT*, 6:464; Zobel, *TDOT*, 13:335–36.
131. Oepke, *TDNT*, 2:541.

inorganic nature is full of life."[132] These include thunder and lightning and the earth itself, all of which possess voices and powers.[133] We live within this creation; it is home to all God's creatures.

Side by side with God's natural creation sits his creation of a new spiritual life in Christ. Why is this spiritual life needed? Because of the Fall of Adam and Eve and because the natural world lies under the power of Satan. Therefore, this world is filled with temptation, which pulls us away from God, its creator, thus enslaving us. But we as humans are called to glory, called to celestial possibilities. Here enters Jesus Christ.[134] Through him, we "put off [our] old self" and are "made new in the attitude of [our] minds" so that we can "put on the new self, created to be like God" (4:22–24 NIV). Said another way, we "have discarded the old nature with its deeds and have put on the new nature, which is being constantly renewed in the image of its Creator and brought to know God" (Col. 3:9–10 NEB). Thus, becoming a new creature is the goal of the spiritual life.[135] And baptism is the ordinance that opens the door to that new life.[136] Not incidentally, the mention of "image" and "Creator" brings us full circle back to Genesis 1:26: "in [God's] image, after [God's] likeness." Through Christ, we enjoy the unique relationship with God that was initiated when God created us in his image (see the Notes on 2:12–13, 15).

good works, which God hath before ordained: A person is justified in asking, What are these "good works" that God had prepared earlier for us to do? Are we talking about good works generally or good deeds performed inside the community of the committed? Are we talking about ordinances or acts of devotion that we do to honor God? Are we talking about doing the deeds of Christ because we were "created in Christ Jesus" for such deeds? In response, at a minimum, we are talking about "a changed lifestyle" (see 4:1–2; 5:1–5; and the Notes on 1:5, 11; 2:9; 4:1, 12; 5:2, 11).[137]

good works: These works are the works of Christ, celestially guided in their character, as the context demands (see Philip. 1:6). These actions

---

132. Werner Foerster, *TDNT,* 3:1031; also see Siegfried Wagner, *TDOT,* 1:342, where creation praised God, though in unintelligible speech.

133. See Isa. 48:13; Jer. 6:19; 22:29; Luke 19:40; Rev. 4:5; 16:9; 1 Ne. 19:11–12; 2 Ne. 27:2; D&C 43:21–22, 25; 87:6; 88:90; 128:23; Moses 7:48, 56.

134. Foerster, *TDNT,* 3:1031–34.

135. Lincoln, *Ephesians,* 114; Best, *Ephesians,* 230; Fowl, *Ephesians,* 80.

136. Heinrich Seeseman and Georg Bertram, *TDNT,* 5:944–45; Winger, *Ephesians,* 295.

137. Lincoln, *Ephesians,* 116; see also Seeseman and Bertram, *TDNT,* 5:944.

are to be distinguished from the "works" in 2:9—that is, works of the law of Moses (see the Note on 2:9). How so? Because believers "are [God's] workmanship" and were "created ... unto good works" through the aid of "Christ Jesus"; moreover, "God [himself] hath before ordained that we [believers] should walk in them" (2:10). Hence, we sense that our "good works" are for the benefit of fellow believers, the aggregate of the faithful. But it does not stop there. Even our employment and related activities by which we keep ourselves and our families in good stead are reckoned among such works (see 4:28; Rom. 13:13; and 1 Thes. 4:2–12). Then the actions and ordinances that draw us closer to God's kingdom, such as repentance and baptism, come into play.

All such acts, whether taken collectively or considered individually, come to rest in divine love blossoming from faith, whether the love that descends onto us from above or the love that we feel for one another. A few scriptural passages will illustrate. To the Roman Saints, Paul wrote that God "will render to every man [and woman] according to [their] deeds" (Rom. 2:6). But these deeds, to make a marked difference both for the actor and for the recipient, are to show selflessness, doing something for "him that needeth" (4:28); they are to demonstrate the "work of faith, and labor of love, and patience of hope" (1 Thes. 1:3);[138] they are to step past "circumcision" and "uncircumcision" and to manifest, rather, "faith which worketh by love" (Gal. 5:6; see also 1 Thes. 5:15); they are to "do works meet for repentance" (Acts 26:20); and they are to exhibit that "he that doeth truth cometh to the light, that his deeds may be made manifest, that they are wrought in God" (John 3:21). The first payoff is "that all things work together for good to them that love God, to them who are the called according to his purpose" (Rom. 8:28). The second consists in "being fruitful in every good work, and increasing in the knowledge of God" (Col. 1:10).[139]

before ordained: In the New Testament, this Greek verb (προετοιμάζω, *proetoimazō*, "to prepare in advance or beforehand")[140] occurs only here and at Romans 9:23. It has to do with the "good works" that believers are to undertake. Importantly, the προ- (*pro-*) prefix ("before," "prior") sends us to an era long before Paul penned this verb. One asks the question, When were such "good works" framed and assigned to believers? The most natural

---

138. This passage combines faith (*pistis*), love (*agapē*), and hope (*elpis*).

139. Walter Grundmann, *TDNT*, 1:16–17; Bertram, *TDNT*, 2:649–50; see also Turner, "Grace, Mysteries, and Exaltation," 112–13.

140. BDAG, 869; Louw-Nida, §77.4.

answer is not at the time of one's birth or conversion to Christianity but, rather, during premortality,[141] in the premortal council, or perhaps even before. Modern scripture offers help. In one place, we read that "there is a law, irrevocably decreed in heaven before the foundations of this world, upon which all blessings are predicated." In this light, the law for "all blessings" was fixed in the preexistence, and, because of its divine origin, it remains irrevocable, immovable. There is more: "When we obtain any blessing from God," affirms the Lord, "it is by obedience to that law" (D&C 130:20–21; see also D&C 132:5, 63; and Abr. 1:3). In addition, essential ordinances for salvation have been revealed, such as baptism by water and by the Holy Ghost (see Acts 19:4–6 and Moses 6:52, 59–60, 64–65) and baptism for the dead, which were "instituted from before the foundation of the world" (D&C 124:33, 41; 128:5; see also the Note on 1:4).

From that era, we possess few clues. But enough hints exist to grasp some of what went on. At an important premortal gathering, one of the contestants to come to earth as Redeemer proposed that he would "redeem all mankind, that one soul shall not be lost" (Moses 4:1). Surely, this path would have involved enforced, compulsory good works for salvation. Then came the proposal from the "Beloved Son," who offered free agency instead of compulsion. On that occasion, he is quoted as saying, "Father, thy will be done" (Moses 4:2). And how do these words fit with "good works"? In a partial answer, we learn in another place that the earth was created "to see if [humans] will do all things whatsoever the Lord their God shall command them" (Abr. 3:25). In a later setting, Adam became "an agent unto himself," free to choose his path. As guides, as we might expect, he received commandments from God. But, as God has reminded modern-day readers, "no temporal commandment gave I unto [Adam], for my commandments are spiritual." In fact, all God's "commandments are spiritual" (D&C 29:35).

Perhaps notably, Jewish savants created lists of things that God created at the end of the sixth day of creation, just before the seventh. But none are works. Included were "the mouth of the earth [see Num. 16:32 and Moses 7:48], the mouth of the well,[142] the mouth of the she-ass, the rainbow, and the manna and the rod and the Shamir,[143] the letters and the writing and the

---

141. Barth, *Ephesians*, 1:227; Lincoln, *Ephesians*, 115–16.

142. See Num. 21:16–18 about the well that gave water to the Hebrews; compare Ex. 15:23–25; 17:1–6; Num. 20:2–11.

143. According to the rabbis, this small, hard stone was used to inscribe the tribal names into the shoulder stones that were attached to the ephod that the high priest wore about his neck (see Ex. 28:9–12). It also cut the stones for the temple that Solomon built. See *Mishnah Sotah* 9:12, in Danby, *Mishnah*, 305 n. 10.

Tables [of stone]."[144] As we might surmise, other lists exist which name different significant items in the Israelites' history.[145]

walk: The verb is the same as at 2:2 (περιπατέω, *peripateō*), marking off these verses as a unit.[146] The idea is that a person walks on an elevated path after being rescued from walking "in trespasses and sins" (2:1; see also 1 Cor. 7:17 and Col. 2:6). That is to say, he or she becomes a new creature (see 4:24; 2 Cor. 5:17; and Gal. 6:15) and effectively walks with God.[147] The notion that we move through our lives with a purpose that leads us into a nourishing communion with God is extremely old. In the Old Testament, a common expression is "to walk with God," with the extended implication of not only conducting oneself in a manner pleasing to God but, more notably, enjoying an "'intimate companionship' with God."[148]

Among the earliest individuals said to "walk with God" (הלך, *halakh*, "to go," "to walk") were Enoch and Noah. Within the four verses devoted to Enoch in Genesis 5, twice we read that "Enoch walked with God" (Gen. 5:22, 24). In a greatly expanded account, we read that God told Enoch, "Go forth and do as I have commanded thee." In faithful response, "Enoch went forth in the land . . . and cried with a loud voice" the message that God had entrusted to him (Moses 6:32, 37). At a later date, after Enoch had established a city whose citizens "were of one heart and one mind, and dwelt in righteousness," we learn that "Enoch and all his people walked with God" (Moses 7:18, 69). Similarly, God commanded Noah "that he should go forth and declare his Gospel unto the children of men" (Moses 8:19). Because he did so, Genesis recorded that "Noah walked with God" (Gen. 6:9; see also Moses 8:27).[149] In a passage that draws together the main threads of our walk in this life, Isaiah almost sings, "Come ye, and let us walk in the light of the Lord" (Isa. 2:5). Remarkably, this light points to the next life, life with God, as we discover: God "hast delivered my soul from death . . . that I may walk before God in the light of the living [ones]" (Ps. 56:13; see also Matt. 22:32; Mark 12:27; Luke 20:38; John 6:57, 69; Rom. 9:26; 14:9; etc.; and the Notes on 2:2; 4:1, 17; 5:2, 8, 15).

Walking with a divine purpose, of course, sends us to sacred ceremony, to sacred actions. This subject does not appear more or less out of thin air.

---

144. *Mishnah Aboth* 5.6, in Danby, *Mishnah,* 456.

145. Walter Grundmann, *TDNT,* 2:705–6; the notation about other lists appears on 2:706.

146. Winger, *Ephesians,* 296.

147. Caird, *Letters,* 54.

148. Helfmeyer, *TDOT,* 3:394.

149. Helfmeyer, *TDOT,* 3:393–94.

No, when paired with other hints in the text of Ephesians, we discover firm and inviting connections to the world of holy ritual (see the Notes on 2:6; 4:13, 20, 22, 24; 5:2, 8, 14; 6:11, 13–14; the introduction section XI, "Ceremony and Ritual"; and appendix 1).

Analysis of 2:1–10

For the spiritually conscious person, the old life, lived "in time past," was besotted "in the lusts of the flesh," specifically in "fulfilling the desires of the flesh and of the mind" (2:3). Such a person, captured by spiritual depravity, Jesus said, was his to deliver and "set at liberty" (Luke 4:18; see also Isa. 61:1 and D&C 138:18, 30–31). In Paul's experience, that is exactly what was happening. Through Christ, believers had become God's spiritual "workmanship" and had been spiritually "created in Christ Jesus unto good works" (2:10). But before those good works could visibly manifest God's blessings, shining out from believers to others, his grace arrived, free-flowing and generously bestowed.

Though the noun "grace" (χάρις, *charis*) appears twelve times in Ephesians,[150] the two that carry the most vital significance for us occur in the expression "By grace are ye saved" (2:5, 8). The latter passage adds the phrase "through faith" so that it reads, "By grace are ye saved through faith." One monumentally important point follows: "Not of yourselves: it is the gift of God" (2:8). Nothing can be clearer—salvation that flows from Jesus' atoning act, accessed "through faith," "is the greatest of all the gifts of God; for there is no gift greater than the gift of salvation" (D&C 6:13; see also Rom. 5:14–17; 6:23; and D&C 14:7).

Were strings attached? Of course, and they took the form of the "good works" then expected from believers (2:10), framed like the patron-client arrangements of earlier eras. Such an agreement consisted of a reciprocal relationship formed between God and his children that was grounded in a covenant.[151] For, after converts had welcomed into their hearts the ineffable gift of the Atonement, their subsequent baptisms meant that these new believers were "buried with [Christ] by baptism into death ... so [they] should walk in newness of life" (Rom. 6:4; see also Rom. 6:11). Notably, these baptisms brought "redemption through [Christ's] blood, [and] the

---

150. Eph. 1:2, 6, 7; 2:5, 7, 8; 3:2, 7, 8; 4:7, 29; 6:24.

151. Conzelmann and Zimmerli, *TDNT*, 9:373–74, 376, 378; see also Freedman, Lundbom, and Fabry, *TDOT*, 5:22–24, 27–28; Spicq, *TLNT*, 3:501–6; Stoebe, *TLOT*, 1:439–46; and Schmidt, *Relational Grace*, 87–114.

forgiveness of sins" (1:7). But the story does not end here. Paul pled with church members to "walk honestly, . . . not in rioting and drunkenness, . . . not in strife and envying" (Rom. 13:13). More briefly, Paul said, "As you have therefore received Christ Jesus the Lord, so walk ye in him" (Col. 2:6; see also 1 Cor. 7:17). Hence, converts were expected to make earnest, permanent adjustments in their lives.

One of the longest lists of expected good works lies in Paul's first letter to the Thessalonians. These are joined by clear instructions in Ephesians. Directing his readers to the "commandments we gave you by the Lord Jesus," he wrote that "this is the will of God . . . that ye should abstain from fornication." Furthermore, no one was to "defraud his brother in any matter, because . . . the Lord is the avenger of all such." Indeed, "God hath not called us unto uncleanness, but unto holiness." Then, turning the believers' gazes toward each other, he drove home the old commandment that "ye yourselves are taught of God to love one another." In this connection, Paul himself had instructed these Christians "to do your own business and to work with your own hands, as we commanded you; that ye may walk honestly toward them that are without," here underscoring his concern for the ever-present poor (1 Thes. 4:2–12; see also Gal. 6:2–10; and the Note on 4:28).[152]

In our letter, Paul directed his readers' focus first inward and then toward each another, begging that they "should walk worthy of the vocation wherewith ye are called," proceeding "with all lowliness and meekness, with long suffering, forbearing one another in love." This love would be made firm by "endeavoring to keep the unity of the Spirit [among believers] in the bond of peace" (4:1–3). How do we know that this "unity of the Spirit" had to do with other believers—that is, with the church? Because Paul immediately thereafter mentioned "one body, and one Spirit" (4:4), the body pointing to the church of which Christ is the head (see 1:22–23; 4:15–16). In a later passage, he instructed believers that they "put on the new man [or woman], which after God is created in righteousness and true holiness," which meant "putting away lying" and instead speaking "every man truth with his neighbor." Additionally, they should not let "the sun go down on [their] wrath." Further, "let him that stole steal no more: but rather let him labor, working with his hands . . . that he may have to give to him that needeth." Besides this recurring interest in the poor, Paul

---

152. Seeseman and Bertram, *TDNT,* 5:944–45; Freedman, Lundbom, and Fabry, *TDOT,* 5:24, 28.

required that "no corrupt communication proceed out of [their] mouth, but that which is good." He appealed that "all bitterness, and wrath, and anger, . . . and evil speaking, be put away from you, [along] with all malice." This would lead to being "kind to one another, tenderhearted, forgiving one another, even as God for Christ's sake [at baptism] hath forgiven you" (4:24–26, 28–29, 31–32; see also 5:1–5).

A final and significant touch is required. Inside these verses, readers meet the verbs "to walk" (2:2) and "to sit" (2:6). As the Notes disclose, these verbs lead believers into the world of sacred actions, sacred ceremonies. Within worship activities, walking leads a person along a path that runs to the holy presence of God; sitting settles a devotee at a place near a teacher of eternal truths. More than this, sitting places worshipers "together in heavenly places [with] Christ Jesus" (2:6). For individuals, just getting to such a locale involves not only passing "by the angels . . . which are set there, to their exaltation" (D&C 132:19) but also passing through the Judgment. All of these pieces are miniaturized and compressed in sacred rites, escorting devotees ritually to an exalted place in God's presence (see the Notes on 2:2, 6, 10; 4:13, 20, 22, 24; 5:2, 8, 14; 6:11, 13–14; the introduction section XI; and appendix 1).

"YE ARE NO MORE STRANGERS" (2:11–22)

King James Translation

11 Wherefore remember, that ye being in time past Gentiles in the flesh, who are called Uncircumcision by that which is called the Circumcision in the flesh made by hands; 12 That at that time ye were without Christ, being aliens from the commonwealth of Israel, and strangers from the covenants of promise, having no hope, and without God in the world: 13 But now in Christ Jesus ye who sometimes were far off are made nigh by the blood of Christ. 14 For he is our peace, who hath made both one, and hath broken down the middle wall of partition between us; 15 Having abolished in his flesh the enmity, even

New Rendition

11 So then, remember that at one time you, the Gentiles in the flesh, those called "uncircumcised" by the so-called "circumcision" (which is done in the flesh by human hands), 12 remember that in that time you were without Christ— excluded from the citizenship of Israel and strangers to the covenants of the promise, having no hope and without God in the world. 13 But now you are in Christ Jesus; you who once were far away have become near in the blood of Christ.

14 For he himself is our peace, who has made both groups into one and has broken down the dividing wall, the hostility, having negated by his flesh 15 the

the law of commandments contained in ordinances; for to make in himself of twain one new man, so making peace; 16 And that he might reconcile both unto God in one body by the cross, having slain the enmity thereby: 17 And came and preached peace to you which were afar off, and to them that were nigh. 18 For through him we both have access by one Spirit unto the Father. 19 Now therefore ye are no more strangers and foreigners, but fellowcitizens with the saints, and of the household of God; 20 And are built upon the foundation of the apostles and prophets, Jesus Christ himself being the chief corner stone; 21 In whom all the building fitly framed together groweth unto an holy temple in the Lord: 22 In whom ye also are builded together for an habitation of God through the Spirit.

law of commandments based in regulations, in order that he might create through himself the two into one new human, thus making peace, 16 and might reconcile them both in one body to God through the cross, having put hostility to death in himself.

17 And he came and brought the message of peace to you who were far away and peace to you who were near. 18 For through him we both have access in one spirit to the Father. 19 So then you are no longer foreigners and strangers, but you are fellow citizens with the saints and members of God's family, 20 because you have been built on the foundation of the apostles and prophets, with Christ Jesus himself as the cornerstone. 21 In him the whole building being joined together grows into a holy temple in the Lord; 22 and in him you also are built together into a dwelling place of God in the Spirit.

Notes on 2:11–22

2:11 *remember:* Because this verb (μνημονεύω, *mnēmoneuō*) is a present imperative, the emphasis descends onto the Gentile Christians among Paul's readers remembering what God has done and is now doing in their lives.[153] This notion exhibits ties to the Old Testament, wherein God remembered his covenant made of old and tied himself anew to his promises (see Gen. 9:15–16; Ex. 2:24; 6:5; Ps. 105:8–10; etc.). In turn, his people were to remember him and his gracious blessings (see Num. 15:39–40 and Deut. 8:2, 18), maintaining "the purity of faith."[154] Although most commentators sidestep mentioning any ceremonial links with this verb, such connections cannot be avoided. For this remembering includes the memory of both Paul's initial teaching when readers were investigators and his continuing teaching after their baptisms.[155] Moreover, the remembering

---

153. Best, *Ephesians,* 237; BDAG, 655; Larkin, *Handbook,* 36.
154. Otto Michel, *TDNT,* 4:675.
155. Winger, *Ephesians,* 309–10.

surely embraced their baptism and, over time, the repeated renewal of the baptismal covenant when partaking of the Eucharist or sacrament.[156]

ye being ... Gentiles in the flesh: This passage points plainly to Paul's audience (see also 3:1, 6–8; 4:17). On one level, the expression "Gentiles [ἔθνη, *ethnē*] in the flesh" sends us to all peoples who are not Jewish, a distinction opened up in the Old Testament with the noun ‏גוי‎ (*goy*), meaning a Gentile nation or a non-Israelite people, though in one place we find a hope that the Israelites themselves will become "one nation [*goy*]" (Ezek. 37:22). On another level, the words pertain to the uncircumcised in the flesh in contrast to Jews who have received circumcision. In a third sense, the passage directs us to nonmembers of the Christian church as distinguished from members.[157] In this verse, the second concept seems to fit better.

in the flesh: This phrase points to the mortal condition. Here, it is tied not to everyone, only to Gentiles. The thought is that being a Gentile "in the flesh" no longer defined who a person was, even if seen that way by Jews, but whether one was "in Christ" (2:13).[158]

flesh: In its basic sense, the noun translated "flesh" (σάρξ, *sarx*) "denotes earthly life in its totality." Significantly, *sarx* is not in and of itself "hostile to God, but simply [is] limited and provisional [in mortality]."[159] Yet, when set against spiritual matters, the "flesh" wars against the spirit, pulling down the person who seeks spiritual blessings and growth (see Gal. 5:16–24). But discussing this matter is not Paul's interest in Ephesians. Rather, he is saying that the difference between Jew and Gentile, the circumcised and uncircumcised, is merely temporary and is subject to the bridging, healing influence of Christ.[160] Moreover, as an assurance to all believers, "the soul of every living thing, and the breath of all mankind" is in God's "hand" (Job 12:10; see also Mosiah 2:21, "lending you breath, that ye may live and move"; D&C 61:6, "all flesh is in mine hands"; 101:16, "all flesh is in mine hands; be still and know that I am God"; Moses 6:32; and the Notes on 2:3, 15; 5:29–31; 6:5, 12).[161]

Uncircumcision: Only Jews would call other people "Uncircumcision" (ἀκροβυστία, *akrobystia*, literally "foreskin").[162] The noun possessed almost no meaning outside Jewish circles in Paul's day. Hence, he was writing from

---

156. Michel, *TDNT,* 4:682.

157. Georg Bertram and Karl Ludwig Schmidt, *TDNT,* 2:365, 369–71; Ronald E. Clements and G. Johannes Botterweck, *TDOT,* 2:426, 428–31.

158. Winger, *Ephesians,* 311.

159. Schweizer, Baumgärtel, and Meyer, *TDNT,* 7:126.

160. Schweizer, Baumgärtel, and Meyer, *TDNT,* 7:137.

161. N. Panagiotis Bratsiotis, *TDOT,* 2:328, 330–31.

162. BDAG, 39; Louw-Nida, §11.52.

the viewpoint of his own Jewishness. In addition, the term took on its mainly spiritual meaning in connection with the word "circumcision" (see Rom. 2:25–29; 4:9–12; 1 Cor. 7:18–19; Gal. 5:6; 6:15; and Col. 3:11; compare Acts 7:51).[163]

Circumcision: The presence of circumcision (περιτομή, *peritomē*) in the males of the wider public was not an issue in the days of Jesus and John the Baptist, for virtually everyone they met was Jewish ("Jews by nature" [Gal. 2:15]). But as soon as missionaries like Paul began an earnest, systematic effort to reach out to Gentiles, it became an ever-present core of contention.[164] For most believers, the resulting conflict was settled at the Jerusalem Council recorded in Acts 15:1–29 and Galatians 2:1–10. Later, Paul learned about Jewish believers who had been touring the branches of Galatia in Asia Minor and had tried, with some success, to convince church members to adopt the trappings of a Jewish life (see Gal. 1:6–12). We do not know, however, whether the appeal of these Jewish church members included the requirement of circumcision, a major commitment for an adult male. But it is possible (see Acts 15:1). On an occasion that also followed the Jerusalem Council, in Antioch, a major city near the northwest corner of the Mediterranean Sea, a group of believers from Jerusalem who claimed authority "from James" influenced Peter to withdraw from table fellowship with Gentile church members, surprisingly refusing to break bread with them, for which he received an earful from Paul (see Gal. 2:11–17).

Some have pointed to this confrontation to claim that henceforth the church was split into two parts, the one following Peter and the other following Paul. But that was surely not the case.[165] To be sure, because of events in Galatia and Antioch, Paul could not let down his guard. Yet in some ways, it was a losing battle. For, on one occasion, he complained, "trouble . . . came to us in Asia, [so] that we were pressed out of measure, above [our] strength, insomuch that we despaired even of life" (2 Cor. 1:8). In a much later correspondence, we read, "All they which are in Asia be turned away from me" (2 Tim. 1:15).

In Paul's deft grasp, the practice of "circumcision" became a means of expressing spiritual truths—namely, that true circumcision was of the heart and meant entering a life of following Christ with real intent. He thus broke

163. Karl Ludwig Schmidt, *TDNT,* 1:225–26.
164. Rudolf Meyer, *TDNT,* 6:81–82.
165. S. Kent Brown, "James the Just and the Question of Peter's Leadership in the Light of New Sources," in *Sidney B. Sperry Symposium Papers* (Provo, Utah: BYU Press, 1973), 10–16.

with his Jewish learning that "only physical circumcision mediates salvation both in this world and the next."[166] To make his point, Paul wrote bluntly that "in Jesus Christ neither circumcision availeth any thing, nor uncircumcision; but faith which worketh by love" (Gal. 5:6). He was not finished: "Circumcision is nothing, and uncircumcision is nothing, but the keeping of the commandments of God" (1 Cor. 7:19; see also Gal. 6:15, "a new creature"). Furthermore, "He is not a Jew, which is one outwardly; neither is that circumcision, which is outward in the flesh: But he is a Jew, which is one inwardly; and circumcision is that of the heart" (Rom. 2:28–29; see also Col. 3:11). His biggest step was to declare that those whose hearts were circumcised were effectively the new Israel—that is, the Christians whose inner parts were circumcised rather than their outward parts: "For we [believers] are the circumcision, which worship God in the spirit, and rejoice in Christ Jesus, and have no confidence in the flesh" (Philip. 3:3).[167]

made by hands: This adjective (χειροποίητος, *cheiropoiētos*) always has to do with things made in this world.[168] Its opposite, "made without hands" (ἀχειροποίητος, *acheiropoiētos*), bears on things made in the heavenly world. Most frequently, we find the two terms applied to temples, one to the earthly temple, where sacred ceremonies take place, and one to the transcendent temple.[169] Therefore, temple associations of these two terms are rich and deep, particularly those of *cheiropoiētos,* whose five other occurrences in the New Testament all have to do with the earthly temple or tabernacle (see Mark 14:58; Acts 7:48; 17:24; Heb. 9:11, 24). But there is more to the story. Baptism forges another bright ceremonial link that occurs outside the temple; as Paul wrote, "Ye are complete in [Christ], . . . in whom also ye are circumcised with the circumcision *made without hands,* in putting off the body of the sins of the flesh by [being] . . . *buried with [Christ] in baptism*" (Col. 2:10–12, emphasis added).[170] Additionally, Paul connects *acheiropoiētos* ("not made with hands") to our resurrected, celestialized bodies. In the context of a discussion of the "outward man" and "inward man" and "things which are seen" and "things which are not seen" (2 Cor. 4:16, 18), he wrote that "we know that if our earthly house of this tabernacle [of our body] were dissolved, we have a building of God, an

---

166. Meyer, *TDNT,* 6:82.
167. Meyer, *TDNT,* 6:82–83.
168. Foerster, *TDNT,* 3:1031.
169. Eduard Lohse, *TDNT,* 9:436; BDAG, 159–60, 1083.
170. Lohse, *TDNT,* 9:436.

house not made with hands, eternal in the heavens." He continued, "For in this [body] we groan, earnestly desiring to be clothed upon with our house which is from heaven" (2 Cor. 5:1–2).[171]

2:12 *That:* This conjunction (ὅτι, *hoti*) marks the second thing that readers are to "remember," resuming the *hoti* ("that") in 2:11.[172]

· ***at that time:*** The dative of time, which appears here, specifies the time at which an event took place, whether a short period or a long. In this case, Paul refers to the period before his Gentile readers accepted the gospel message. Now things have changed remarkably.[173]

without Christ: Sung in Paul's voice, this phrase emits a forlorn tone. For him, this state mournfully and hopelessly characterized the lowest, deepest abyss. This condition resulted in people being "aliens" and "strangers" and, worse, "dead," existing miserably as captives of "the prince of the power of the air" (2:1–2, 12; see also 2 Ne. 2:27). But help had arrived, help that could lift a believer to heaven to dwell with God. For, astonishingly, God had "raised [Christ] from the dead" and placed him "at his own right hand in the heavenly places" as preliminary acts before raising us "together [with Christ]" and seating us "in heavenly places in Christ Jesus" (1:20; 2:6). For the relief and support of church members, God had "put all things under [Christ's] feet" and made him to be "the head over all things to the church" (1:22), meaning the entire church, not limited to certain individual congregations.[174]

being aliens: The sense of the passive participle of ἀπαλλοτριόομαι (*apallotrioomai*), in its secular meaning, is to be estranged from others or even from one's own property.[175] In the three passages where this verb occurs in the New Testament, including this one, the alienation of Gentiles is spiritual (see 4:18 and Col. 1:21) and, of course, carries consequences (see 2 Pet. 2:20–21). For God does not hold guiltless those who, "in the vanity of their mind" and "blindness of their heart" (4:17–18), have turned away from his invitation to come to Christ.[176] In an interesting connection, we notice that Jesus was to be delivered up to Gentiles, "the very last people to whom the Messiah of the people of God should be handed over" (see Matt. 20:19; Mark 10:33; and Luke 18:32).[177]

---

171. Michel, *TDNT*, 5:146–47; see also Hermann Hanse, *TDNT*, 2:825.
172. Larkin, *Handbook*, 37; Merkle, *Guide*, 68.
173. Smyth, *Greek Grammar*, §§1539–40; Gustav Stählin, *TDNT*, 4:1115 and n. 59, 1117.
174. Rengstorf, *TDNT*, 1:423.
175. LSJ, 176.
176. Friedrich Büchsel, *TDNT*, 1:265–66.
177. Bertram and Schmidt, *TDNT*, 2:370.

In the New Testament, Titus 3:3 characterizes rather fully the exclusion from God[178] that Gentiles suffered before conversion: "We ourselves also were sometimes foolish, disobedient, deceived, serving divers lusts and pleasures, living in malice and envy, hateful, and hating one another." But these unwanted, nasty traits were not limited to unbelieving Gentiles. They could also creep into congregations of believing members, as James warned his readers. For, pointing an accusing finger toward fellow Christians, he raised a hue and cry against "wars and fightings among you"; against asking God "amiss, that ye may consume it upon your lusts"; against becoming "adulterers and adulteresses"; and against pursuing "the friendship of the world [which] is enmity with God." To those besmirched by such actions, he pled that they "draw nigh to God" with the promise that "he will draw nigh to you" and, thankfully, "shall lift you up" (James 4:1, 3–4, 8, 10; see also Col. 1:21 and the Note on 4:18).[179]

commonwealth of Israel: The noun translated "commonwealth" ("citizenship" NR) is πολιτεία (*politeia*), which often bears the meaning of an "established people" or "organized body."[180] In Acts 22:28, its sense is "civil rights," though the KJV translates it "freedom." An issue arises whether the expression "commonwealth of Israel" points to the continued existence of the Jewish state before its fall to the Romans in AD 70. Though Best and Fowl discount the possibility that Jerusalem and its temple still stood, evidence one way or the other from this Ephesians letter is lacking, notwithstanding the claim that believers then constituted "an holy temple in the Lord" (2:21), as if they were a replacement for the presumedly fallen temple in Jerusalem (see the Note on 2:21).[181] In our passage, "commonwealth of Israel" carries a figurative sense. It does not refer to a political organization or social network of naturally born Israelites. Rather, it points to Gentile persons who can now receive the "promise" allotted earlier to ancient Israel by her God.[182] The "established people," of course, is made up of all believers, and their citizenship lies in the church. However, their ultimate "homeland" is "in heaven,"[183] in "a city . . . whose builder and maker is God," "the heavenly Jerusalem" (Heb. 11:10; 12:22; see also Heb. 11:16). For "here [on earth] we have no continuing city, but we seek one to

178. Barth, *Ephesians,* 1:257.
179. Gustav Stählin, *TDNT,* 2:925.
180. BDAG, 845; Louw-Nida, §§11.67, 70.
181. Best, *Ephesians,* 244; Fowl, *Ephesians,* 87.
182. Hermann Strathmann, *TDNT,* 6:534–35; Winger, *Ephesians,* 313.
183. Strathmann, *TDNT,* 6:535.

come" (Heb. 13:14). In notable fashion, for these Gentiles and other believers, their "citizenship is in heaven" (Philip. 3:20 NIV); they have effectively received "civil rights in heaven" (see the Note on 2:19).[184]

Israel: For Paul, being an Israelite is a high distinction: "I also am an Israelite, of the seed of Abraham, of the tribe of Benjamin." Furthermore, despite what some Gentiles may have thought, "God [has not] cast away his people" (Rom. 11:1). As a matter of fact, Israelites form "the root and the fatness of the olive tree" into which the Gentiles, like "a wild olive tree, . . . [are] grafted in among them." The Israelite branches "because of unbelief . . . were broken off," whereas the Gentiles enter the people of God not by conversion to Judaism but "by faith" (Rom. 11:17, 20; see also Gal. 6:15–16).[185]

strangers: Prior to their conversion, Gentiles generally were "strangers" (plural of ξένος, *xenos*) to the heritage that God had granted to the ancient Hebrews, knowing nothing of it. The exceptions were the "proselytes," who were Gentiles who had embraced the synagogue and its lifestyle (see Acts 2:10; 6:5; 13:43, 48). Naturally, as soon as a Gentile became converted to the gospel message, he or she then became a stranger within the larger society, often subject to alienation and persecution, living as a "sheep in the midst of wolves" (Matt. 10:16; see also John 15:19; 17:14, 16; 1 Pet. 4:4, 12–14; 1 John 4:4–6; and the Note on 2:19).[186]

the covenants of promise: In one important passage wherein Paul illustrated the concept of "covenant" (διαθήκη, *diathēkē*), he drew his example from "ordinary life," holding that "when a man's will and testament [*diathēkē*] has been duly executed, no one else can set it aside or add a codicil," or adjustment (Gal. 3:15 NEB). In a word, a person's written "will" is unchangeable. So it is with God's covenants. At base, they are inviolable and unalterable. The former covenant of the Old Testament was designed to lead God's people to himself. But because the Jews faltered in their efforts to reach God through the Mosaic law, he instituted a new covenant through his Son, "not [written] in tables of stone, but in fleshy tables of the heart . . . not of the [written] letter, but of the spirit: for the letter killeth, but the spirit giveth life" (2 Cor. 3:3, 6). Such words demonstrate that the prophecy of Jeremiah the prophet had been fulfilled that "the days come,

---

184. Gustav Stählin, *TDNT,* 5:29. Also see Diether Kellermann, *TDOT,* 2:449. According to Rev. 20:7–9, the scene of the final battle that will break the power of Satan is to occur in "the beloved city." Strathmann, *TDNT,* 6:531.

185. Gerhard von Rad, Karl Georg Kuhn, and Walter Gutbrod, *TDNT,* 3:386–87.

186. Stählin, *TDNT,* 5:29–30.

saith the Lord, that I will make a new covenant with the house of Israel . . . not according to the covenant that I made with their fathers. . . . I will put my law in their inward parts, and write it in their hearts" (Jer. 31:31, 33). For Gentiles, this meant they and their Jewish Christian friends were "all the children of God by faith in Christ Jesus" (Gal. 3:26; see the Note on 3:6).[187]

promise: This noun (ἐπαγγελία, *epangelia*) often appears in the plural, sending us to "promises" that come from God (see Rom. 9:4; 15:8; 2 Cor. 1:20; 7:1; and Gal. 3:16). According to Paul, they included promises of "inheritance" (see Rom. 4:13 and Gal. 3:18, 29), "life" (see Rom. 4:17, "quickeneth the dead" [see the Note on 2:5]; and Gal. 3:21), "righteousness" (see 4:24; 5:9; 2 Cor. 5:21; and Gal. 3:21; 5:5), "spirit" (see 1:13 and Gal. 3:14), and "adoption" (see Rom. 9:8; Gal. 4:22–31; and the Note on 1:5).[188]

In the Old Testament, a covenant was often "confirmed by an oath" (see Gen. 21:22–24; Deut. 29:9–15; Josh. 9:15–20; 2 Kgs. 11:4; etc.; see also D&C 84:33–41), as well as with a sacred meal to secure the mutual promises (see Gen. 26:26–31 and Ex. 24:3–11).[189] Moreover, God's covenants with Abraham and with David, whose promises Paul often and correctly drew on (see Rom. 4:1–3, 6–16; 9:6–8; and Gal. 3:5–18, 29; 4:21–24), were of "the promissory type." That is to say, "God swears to Abraham to give the land to his descendants, and similarly promises to David to establish his dynasty without imposing any obligations on them" (see Lev. 26:44 for Abraham and 2 Sam. 7:13–15 for David). In contrast, the Mosaic covenant and its promises came with obligations of loyalty and obedience (see the Notes on 3:6; 6:2).[190]

having no hope: This expression ties to the phrase "in the world" at the end of the verse in contrast to "in Christ Jesus" (2:13). Hope in this sense centers on the end-time following the Judgment, when believers will arrive at their hoped-for celestial destinations (see Job 6:11; Ps. 16:9–10; Prov. 11:7; 14:32; Acts 2:26–27; 23:6; 1 Cor. 15:19; Col. 1:5; Alma 22:14; 25:16; 27:28; etc.). To be sure, pagans held out some sort of hope for the next life, though whatever it was fell woefully short of what Christians had been hoping for through Christ's redemption (see 1:7; 2:18; 3:12; and Col. 1:14). But Paul

---

187. Gottfried Quell and Johannes Behm, *TDNT,* 2:129–30; Julius Schniewind and Gerhard Friedrich, *TDNT,* 2:582–84.

188. Schniewind and Friedrich, *TDNT,* 2:583–84.

189. Moshe Weinfeld, *TDOT,* 2:256, 263.

190. Weinfeld, *TDOT,* 2:270–72, quotation on 2:270; see also Wagner, *TDOT,* 1:329, 331–32, 337–38; Werner H. Schmidt, Jan Bergman, and H. Lutzmann, *TDOT,* 3:100–102, 104 (on 1 Kgs. 2:4), 116–17.

discounted such Gentile hopes, holding that, in the ultimate end, they amounted to "no hope" (1 Thes. 4:13; see also the Notes on 1:12, 18; 4:4).[191]

without God: The Greek word ἄθεος (*atheos*) is made negative by the alpha-privative, as it is called. That is, the prefixing letter alpha renders certain Greek adjectives negative in meaning.[192] The same thing happens with English adjectives such as "amoral," "amorphous," or "apathetic." The term *atheos,* which appears only here in the New Testament, can pertain to atheism, a common charge against Christians who openly rejected the imperial cult with its worship centered on the current Roman emperor.[193] But Paul's repetition of the word *atheos* sounds a more mournful note, sadly playing a dirge to the effect that pagans know not the true God nor how to worship him.[194]

world: The world (κόσμος, *kosmos*) stands opposed to God. The world, transitory when compared to the permanence of the earth, is home to a wisdom that pales next to God's wisdom because God's wisdom, though despised by the wise people of this world, presents accurate standards for assessing life on earth (see 1 Cor. 1:20–21, 26–30; 2:6–8, 12; 3:19); the sorrow of the world leads to more sorrow and ultimately to death, whereas "godly sorrow brings repentance that leads to salvation and leaves no regret" (2 Cor. 7:10 NIV); the guilt and resulting condemnation of the world arises from sin and is reconciled only through Christ (see Rom. 5:12 and 2 Cor. 5:19); and the makeup of this world will eventually be replaced by a new heaven and new earth (see Isa. 65:17; 2 Pet. 3:13; and Rev. 21:1; see also the Notes on 1:4; 2:2).[195]

2:13 *But now:* With these words, Paul turned from the Gentiles' frightful state of being "without Christ" and "without God" (2:12) to being "in Christ Jesus." This happy, dramatic shift in people's lives came about not because of some psychological or emotional turnaround but because of the historical intervention released by Jesus' atoning sacrifice begun in Gethsemane and finished on the cross. After that event, which took place in this world, in a real locale, Christ had visited the world of departed spirits and delivered them (see Rom. 14:9 and 1 Pet. 3:18–20; 4:6), had been resurrected

---

191. Bultmann and Rengstorf, *TDNT,* 2:532; Hanse, *TDNT,* 2:824–25; Lincoln, *Ephesians,* 138; Winger, *Ephesians,* 314–15.

192. Smyth, *Greek Grammar,* §§1428, 2071a; Blass and Debrunner, *Greek Grammar,* §§117(1), 120(2).

193. Kleinknecht, Quell, Stauffer, and Kuhn, *TDNT,* 3:120–21; BDAG, 24.

194. Gustav Stählin, *TDNT,* 2:925, cites a number of equivalent terms and phrases that match *atheos* in the New Testament.

195. Sasse, *TDNT,* 1:678; Sasse, *TDNT,* 3:892–93.

from the dead and exalted to the "right hand" of God (1:20), had been appointed as "the head" of the church (1:22; 4:15–16; 5:23), and had taken his place as the healer of both the estrangement between God and his children (see 2:14–16 and Rom. 5:10) and the divisions and differences among those inside and outside the circle of believers (see 2:19–22 and Isa. 57:19).[196]

in Christ Jesus: Unlike the similar expression "in Christ" in 2:10, which has to do with the Creation, in this instance we find ourselves dealing with the Redemption, with the power of "the blood of Christ" to bring believers "nigh" to God (see the Notes on 2:10, 13).

far off: Often, the adverb μακράν (*makran*) conveys the sense of distance, "far away"; in other instances, it concerns a time far in the future.[197] In our case, the meaning is figurative and carries spiritual overtones. Those who were once at a long distance from God's healing blessings have now been brought near to him. We find this idea in Jesus' response to a certain scribe: "Thou art not far from the kingdom of God" (Mark 12:34). It also occurs in his telling of the parable of the prodigal son, wherein the father, still anxious about his younger son after a long interval, saw his son "a great way off . . . and ran" to him, closing both the spatial and spiritual distance between the two (Luke 15:20; see the Note on 2:17).[198]

made nigh: The thought generated by the combination of this verb and adverb (γίνομαι εγγύς, *ginomai engus*) is "to make a change of location," as in John 6:19: "They see Jesus . . . drawing nigh unto the ship."[199] The metaphorical idea is the same, "to draw near,"[200] a notion perhaps borrowed from the language of a person becoming a proselyte to Judaism.[201] The passive of the verb *ginomai* means that someone or something has brought people near God—namely, "the blood of Christ."[202] Additionally, in Paul's words, the expression also bears a connection to the end-time because a person's ultimate destiny in eternity ties clenchingly to drawing near to God (see the Note on 2:17).[203]

---

196. Gerard von Rad and Werner Foerster, *TDNT,* 2:415–16; Grundmann, Hesse, de Jonge, and van der Woude, *TDNT,* 9:556–57.

197. BDAG, 612.

198. Herbert Preisker, *TDNT,* 4:373–74.

199. Larkin, *Handbook,* 39.

200. BDAG, 199.6.g.

201. Lincoln, *Ephesians,* 139; Best, *Ephesians,* 245.

202. Fowl, *Ephesians,* 89, and Best, *Ephesians,* 245, against Larkin, *Handbook,* 39, who holds that the verb is in the middle voice.

203. Herbert Preisker, *TDNT,* 2:331–32.

the blood of Christ: These words carry a special, precise meaning; they are about Jesus' blood "shed" during his suffering, both in Gethsemane and on the cross. This blood was spilt for our "redemption," for "the forgiveness of sins" (1:7). To be sure, twice the Book of Mormon directs us to the blood that coursed through the veins of the mortal Jesus during his youth and adulthood, underscoring his mortality (see Mosiah 7:27 and Ether 3:9). But that interest is not at play here. Instead, the expression "the blood of Christ" centers principally on the Eucharist, the sacrament wherein believers partake of the emblems of Jesus' death, celebrating them because they have come to offer life both here and hereafter.[204] Of the accounts of Jesus instituting the blessing on the wine at the Last Supper (see Matt. 26:28 and Mark 14:24; compare John 6:53–56), all were written decades after the event, with only two agreeing word for word (see Luke 22:20 and 1 Cor. 11:25). The eyewitness record reports that the Resurrected Christ referred to "my blood," with the same significance (see 3 Ne. 18:11; 20:8). Not incidentally, a number of New Testament passages that refer to Christ's blood may also have to do with baptism, not just the Eucharist or sacrament (see 1:7; 1 Pet. 1:2, 18–19; 1 John 1:7; Rev. 1:5; 7:14;[205] and the Note on 1:7).

Christ: Christ's blood, of course, had admitted Paul's readers to a place "with the saints" through baptism (2:19). Therewith, they gained access to his "grace," his "peace," and his "light" (2:5, 8, 14–15; 5:13–14), which are available in the church of which he is "the head" (1:22). Thus, Christ became both the source of these life-sweetening gifts that had washed over believers, adding a divine fragrance to their lives, and the goal of people's ascent to heavenly spheres, reaching "unto the measure of the stature of the fulness of Christ" (4:13; see the Notes on 2:10, 12).[206]

2:14 *our peace:* This terminology does not just lead us to a Christian teaching about peace in the world, nor to an early doctrine about divine peace (εἰρήνη, *eirēnē*). In Paul's conception, Christ is the embodiment of peace, the personification of peace. He has become peace[207] (see Isa. 9:6; 52:7), much like God has made Christ to be "wisdom, and righteousness, and sanctification, and redemption" (1 Cor. 1:30; see also Rom. 5:1; 8:6; 15:13; 1 Cor. 7:15; Gal. 5:22; and 2 Thes. 3:16). With Christ as "our peace," believers can experience

---

204. Johannes Behm, *TDNT,* 1:174–75.

205. Claus-Hunno Hunzinger, *TDNT,* 6:984 n. 44.

206. Grundmann, Hesse, de Jonge, and van der Woude, *TDNT,* 9:557–59.

207. Stählin, *TDNT,* 2:922; Debrunner, Kleinknecht, Procksch, Kittel, Quell, and Schrenk, *TDNT,* 4:126; Grundmann, Hesse, de Jonge, and van der Woude, *TDNT,* 9:557–58; Lincoln, *Ephesians,* 140.

"the healing of all relationships."[208] But that is not the whole story. Christ has brought about a peace that has led to "the cessation of hostilities and the resulting situation of unity."[209] Such a peace implies serious bouts of "enmity" between Gentiles and Jews (see the Notes on 2:15, 17; 4:3; 6:15).

made both one: The "both" (ἀμφότεροι, *amphoteroi,* a plural)[210] directs us to Gentiles (2:11) and to Jews, the latter being "the commonwealth of Israel" (2:12). This is made secure because *amphoteroi* appears in the neuter, thus relating to an entity rather than to individuals, bringing us to Gentiles as a group and Jews as a group.[211] Because Christ had surmounted one of the most prickly of divisions in the ancient world, that between Gentile and Jew, the two groups "are no longer what they previously were."[212] They are more, enjoying a peace "which passeth all understanding" (Philip. 4:7).

hath broken down: The verb λύω (*luō*) exhibits a wide range of meanings, including "to undo," "to set free," and "to destroy."[213] It is in the last sense, and perhaps the first, that a person understands the message of the verb here (see John 2:19; 5:18; 10:35; and 1 John 3:8).[214]

middle wall: One possibility that has drawn attention is that this barrier (μεσότοιχον, *mesotoichon*), noted only here in the New Testament, pointed to the boundary wall that stood between Gentiles and the Court of Women at the Jerusalem temple.[215] Indeed, we find temple allusions throughout the letter (see the Notes on 1:4–5, 9; 2:8, 11, 21–22). Another suggestion has focused on the fallen walls of Jerusalem after their destruction in AD 70.[216] But neither of these interpretations holds much credence. For, one can ask, What do Gentile believers in western Asia Minor know about the architecture of the temple in Jerusalem? Or how would they know about the state of the surrounding walls of the city after the Roman capture of the place? To be sure, Jewish Christian leaders such as Philip the Evangelist and John the Apostle took up residence in Asia Minor after AD 70.[217] But two questions arise: first,

---

208. Von Rad and Foerster, *TDNT,* 2:415.

209. Lincoln, *Ephesians,* 140.

210. BDAG, 55.

211. Lincoln, *Ephesians,* 140–41; Larkin, *Handbook,* 40.

212. Lincoln, *Ephesians,* 141.

213. BDAG, 606–7.

214. Procksch and Büchsel, *TDNT,* 4:336.

215. Raymond E. Brown, *An Introduction to the New Testament,* Anchor Bible Reference Library (New York: Doubleday, 1997), 634 n. 35.

216. Barth, *Ephesians,* 1:283–87, and Best, *Ephesians,* 253–56, have set out the possible interpretations.

217. Bauer, *Orthodoxy and Heresy,* 86–87.

how much did these two Jewish leaders, fresh from Palestine, interact with Gentile Christians, and, second and more crucial, was the letter to the Ephesians written after the fall of Jerusalem? As I argue in the introduction, it was written earlier, during Paul's lifetime (see the introduction sections I–VII). Instead, the context, which talks of "enmity," "the law," "ordinances" (2:15), reconciliation of Jews and Gentiles "in one body" (2:16), and joint "access [to God] by one Spirit" (2:18), pertains to a spiritual removal of barriers, chiefly the law of Moses, effected by Christ.[218]

partition: This term (φραγμός, *phragmos*) simply completes and reinforces the idea of a dividing wall, referring to a "fence" or other kind of barrier, such as a "hedge."[219]

2:15 Because of the word order and the overall sense of the passage, editions of the Greek text almost uniformly place the expression "in his flesh the enmity" into verse 2:14. (In Greek, the word order of this line is reversed: "the enmity, in his flesh" (τὴν ἔχθραν ἐν τῇ σαρκὶ αὐτοῦ, *tēn echthran en tē sarki autou*). Thus, 2:15 opens, "Having abolished . . . the law of commandments." Below, the versification of the KJV is maintained, but the New Rendition matches modern editions of the text of 2:14–15.

Having abolished: Of the twenty-seven occurrences of this verb in the New Testament, here written in the past participle, twenty-six appear in works associated with Paul. The verb (καταργέω, *katargeō*) bears meanings as diverse as "to render ineffective," "to invalidate," and "to abolish."[220] In this verse, the sense "to put out of use" seems best because Paul was writing about both "the enmity" and "the law" that Christ had surmounted and repaired for a higher purpose: "to make in himself . . . one new man, so making peace." For Christ had not abolished the law, or at least parts of it, as the words of the mortal Jesus and Paul affirmed (see 6:2; Luke 16:16–17; 18:20; Rom. 3:31; 13:8–10; and the Note below on "the law").[221]

his flesh: In all instances that deal with salvation, as our case here, the flesh (σάρξ, *sarx*) belonged to Christ, and the noun specifically directed readers to his flesh that had died, broken and torn, as a result of his Atonement.[222]

---

218. Carl Schneider, *TDNT*, 4:625; Georg Bertram, *TDNT*, 8:614; Lincoln, *Ephesians*, 141–43; Best, *Ephesians*, 256–63; Fowl, *Ephesians*, 91.

219. BDAG, 1064.

220. BDAG, 525–26. Louw-Nida, §76.26, holds to the meaning "to abolish."

221. Gerhard Delling, *TDNT*, 1:452; Fowl, *Ephesians*, 91–92; Brown, *Testimony of Luke*, 758–60, 762, 827–28.

222. Exceptions in the New Testament are few and have to do with Jesus' mortality; see 1 John 4:2–3; 2 John 1:7.

Language that John preserves about those who partake of the Eucharist or the sacrament presses home the observation that those who "eat the flesh of the Son of man, and drink his blood [have] ... eternal life; and ... dwelleth in me" (John 6:53–54, 56). That said, Christ still possesses his flesh as a resurrected person, though now in an immortal state. In this connection, we read the Risen Jesus' own words to his gathered followers: "Handle me, and see; for a spirit hath not flesh and bones, as ye see me have" (Luke 24:39; see also 5:30; Acts 2:31; and 3 Ne. 11:13–15).[223] Paul's statement "that flesh and blood cannot inherit the kingdom of God" does not contradict Jesus' words because blood combined with flesh characterizes mortal life,[224] not immortal life (1 Cor. 15:50). To be sure, both flesh and blood are subject to "corruption" (see Acts 13:33–37; 1 Cor. 15:42; and Gal. 6:8). But the life of the mortal flesh lies in the blood and belongs to God (see Gen. 9:4; Lev. 17:11, 13–14; Deut. 12:23–24).[225]

In the Old Testament, "flesh" (בשר, *basar*) has generally to do with human life,[226] and the term "all flesh" often centers on all living creatures, human and otherwise.[227] In the case of humans, their flesh becomes susceptible to temptations, whether willingly received or not.[228] But all is not lost. God offers forgiveness and, in his mercy, has promised that "a new heart also will I give you, and a new spirit will I put within you: and I will take away the stony heart out of your flesh" (Ezek. 36:26). From Ezekiel's earlier contemporary Jeremiah come these words: "Behold, the days come, saith the Lord, that I will make a new covenant with the house of Israel, and with the house of Judah. . . . I will put my law in their inward parts, and write it in their hearts; and will be their God, and they shall be my people . . . for I will forgive their iniquity, and I will remember their sin no more" (Jer. 31:31, 33–34).[229] In the case of sacrifices, the flesh of the sacrificial animal is considered holy (see Lev. 7:19; Jer. 11:15; and Hag. 2:12), and if it is eaten, rules apply to whether the

---

223. For a contrary view, see Schweizer, Baumgärtel, and Meyer, *TDNT,* 7:124.

224. Bratsiotis, *TDOT,* 2:318, 327–28; Benjamin Kedar-Kopfstein and Jan Bergman, *TDOT,* 3:239–40.

225. Bratsiotis, *TDOT,* 2:320, 327–28.

226. See Gen. 2:21, 23–24; Job 33:21; 34:14–15; Ps. 78:38–39; Prov. 5:11; Lam. 3:4; Moses 3:21, 23–24; and Mosiah 23:7.

227. See Gen. 6:12–13; 9:11, 15–17; Ps. 136:25; 145:21; Isa. 40:5–8; 1 Cor. 15:39; Moses 8:17, 29–30; and Bratsiotis, *TDOT,* 2:319, 325–28, 331.

228. See Gen. 6:3, 12–13; Deut. 5:26; 2 Chr. 32:8; Ps. 56:4–7; 78:37–42; Eccl. 2:3; 5:5–6; Jer. 17:5; Zech. 2:13; see also 2:3, 11; Rom. 6:19; 7:5, 18; 2 Cor. 10:2; Gal. 4:14; 5:17; etc.; and Bratsiotis, *TDOT,* 2:327, 329–31.

229. Bratsiotis, *TDOT,* 2:329, 332.

flesh is to be consumed by priests or worshipers.[230] Moreover, worshipers were to be in a state of holiness and inner purity because they were renewing a binding covenant with God (see the Notes on 2:3, 11; 5:29–31; 6:5).[231]

enmity: This concept (ἔχθρα, *echthra*) holds at least two meanings. First, it concerns the enmity or hostility in a person's soul toward God (see Rom. 8:7 and James 4:4). Second, the noun centers on the enmity between people, such as that which bedeviled Gentiles and Jews (see Luke 23:12 and Gal. 5:20).[232] Both ideas are present in the repeated noun in 2:16. The horrific examples of clashes between these people were the riots and killing sprees that broke out in such population centers as Alexandria in Egypt[233] and the coastal city of Caesarea in Palestine,[234] respectively in AD 38–40, 59–60, and 66. At one base of such incidents, whether deriving from spiritual or social and political animosity, stood the law of Moses, a tension that Jesus resolved (see the Notes below and on 2:14, 16).[235]

the law: As Paul made clear, for him "the law" stood on the same level as "the enmity." In some way, the Mosaic law was linked to hostility both between humans and God as well as between Gentiles and Jews. In the first case, as a quick sampling will show, Christ had rendered the law null and void for believers. For if people are made "heirs" of God by "the law," then "faith [in Christ] is made void" (Rom. 4:14). Further, those who escape the effects of "sin . . . are not under the law, but under [divine] grace" (Rom. 6:14). Above all, "Christ hath redeemed us from the curse of the law, being made a curse for us" by being hanged "on a tree" (Gal. 3:13; see also Rom. 7:4). On the other hand, in believers' efforts to stand upright before God, "now we are delivered from the law . . . that we should serve in newness of spirit" (Rom. 7:6). In this light, "love is the fulfilling of the law" (Rom. 13:10; see also Rom. 13:8). In all, "the law was our schoolmaster to bring us unto Christ [but] . . . we are no longer under a schoolmaster" (Gal. 3:24–25). For the individual, "I through the law am dead to the law, that I might live unto

---

230. See Ex. 12:8–12; 29:31–32; Lev. 6:24–30; 7:11–18; 8:31; Num. 18:15–19; Deut. 12:27; 1 Sam. 2:13–14; Bratsiotis, *TDOT*, 2:322; and Milgrom, *Leviticus 1–16*, 402, 407, 418–19, 423, 534–35.

231. See Ex. 19:5–6; Lev. 14:2–9; 16:2–4, 24, 26–28; 17:15–16; 22:2–7; Num. 19:7–8; Deut. 14:1–2; 26:16–19; Bratsiotis, *TDOT*, 2:322–24; and Milgrom, *Leviticus 1–16*, 830, 1015–18, 1033–34, 1048–53.

232. Werner Foerster, *TDNT*, 2:815; BDAG, 419; Louw-Nida, §39.10.

233. Schürer, *History of the Jewish People*, 1:389–91, 398; 3:127–29, 132, 150–51, 153.

234. Schürer, *History of the Jewish People*, 1:465–67; 2:117, 183.

235. Von Rad and Foerster, *TDNT*, 2:415.

God" (Gal. 2:19). Plainly, in Jesus' coming, the law of Moses was set aside as a stone-free path back to God.

In another vein, hostilities between Jews and Gentiles were numerous and well-documented. It does not take much imagination to grasp the social and political reasons for such enmity.[236] For their part, Jews who observed the law in the larger Roman society drew scorn from Gentiles for their beliefs and customs, as the banishment of Jews from Rome in AD 49 by the emperor Claudius illustrates (see Acts 18:2). Suetonius, a Roman biographer (born c. AD 69) and our main source outside of Luke's notation, wrote that because "the Jews constantly made disturbances at the instigation of Chrestus, [Claudius] expelled them from Rome."[237] The general consensus among scholars holds that the name "Chrestus" was the Greek title "Christos"—that is, Christ. If this was indeed the case, then Jewish Christian believers had reached Rome a few years earlier and had engaged fellow Jews in gospel conversations with Christ at the center, as the conversion of Aquila and Priscilla demonstrated (see Acts 18:2, 26; Rom. 16:3–5; and 1 Cor. 16:19).[238] The resulting noisy rancor over Jesus' role as the Jewish Messiah, documented in alarming detail through Paul's preaching to Jews in Asia Minor and Greece (see Acts 13:50; 14:2–5, 19; 16:19–24; 17:5, 13), had reached such a pitch in Rome that government officials, including the emperor, felt the need to expel Jews from the capital city.

ordinances: Except in Colossians 2:20, where the verb δογματίζω (*dogmatizō*) clearly concerns physical or tactile experiences, its noun, δόγμα (*dogma*), revolves around written decrees (see Luke 2:1; Acts 16:4; 17:7; and Col. 2:14).[239] Hence, the term "ordinances" here does not have to do with sacred acts, such as making a covenant, consecrating an item to God, or laying on of hands for an ordination. Instead, it reinforces the fact that the law was written down. It is this written law that Christ had fulfilled and brought to an end as an avenue into God's kingdom (see Matt. 5:17–18; Luke 16:16; 24:44; Rom. 10:4; Heb. 8:13; Alma 34:13; and 3 Ne. 15:3–5, 8).[240]

---

236. Lincoln, *Ephesians*, 142.

237. Suetonius, *The Deified Claudius* 5.25.4.

238. Schürer, *History of the Jewish People*, 3:77–78; Fitzmyer, *Acts of the Apostles*, 619–20, 639; Peter Lampe, "Aquila," in *ABD*, 1:319–20; Murphy-O'Connor, *Paul: A Critical Life*, 171–72, 263; Draper and Rhodes, *Paul's First Epistle to the Corinthians*, 854.

239. Gerhard Kittel, *TDNT*, 2:230–31; BDAG, 254.

240. Kittel, *TDNT*, 2:231.

to make: The verb is κτίζω (*ktizō*), which conveys the sense "to create,"[241] a meaning that the New Rendition repeats. Christ's creation, of course, is "one new man" out of Gentile and Jew who, together with all fellow believers, can enjoy God's "great love wherewith he loved us" (2:4) as well as "access by one Spirit unto the Father" (2:18; see also the Notes on 2:10; 4:24).[242]

one new man: The joining of Jew and Gentile into "one new man" is, through the "cross," the same as Christ "reconciling both [groups] unto God in one body" (2:16). This new creation has lifted the recipients away from their old lives as creatures who "walked according to the course of this world [and] . . . in the lusts of [their] flesh" (2:2–3). Now, the individuals so rescued are "hid with Christ in God" (Col. 3:3), ready to take their rightful place in Christ's kingdom when he comes again.[243]

making peace: This expression can be viewed as pointing to a spiritual peace between a person's soul and God, which are often separated by the individual's sins (see Rom. 3:23, "all have sinned"). But the reconciliation noted in 2:16 centers on two kinds of persons becoming "one body" so that they are "no more strangers and foreigners, but fellowcitizens with the saints" (2:19). Thus, we are escorted back to the well-known, fierce troubles that had erupted between Gentiles and their Jewish neighbors in places like Alexandria (AD 38–40) and Caesarea (AD 59–60, 66), as well as the nasty confrontations between Paul's Jewish and Gentile detractors on the one side and Paul and his companions on the other (see Acts 13:50; 14:2–5, 19; 16:19–24; 17:5, 13). One question naturally arises, inviting us to ask whether these observations lead us to Paul as the author of the letter to the Ephesians. As argued in the introduction section III, this verse has a lot to say about the answer (compare Col. 1:21, "you, that were . . . enemies . . . by wicked works"). For such events took place during Paul's lifetime, and, as is certain, the first brouhaha in Caesarea occurred during his two-year house arrest in that city, making the incident all the more memorable and personal.[244] And, buttressed by the double occurrence of the term "the enmity" within a few

---

241. Foester, *TDNT,* 3:1028–29; BDAG, 572.

242. Foester, *TDNT,* 3:1034.

243. Foester, *TDNT,* 3:1034; Eduard Schweizer and Friedrich Baumgärtel, *TDNT,* 7:1077–78.

244. Schürer, *History of the Jewish People,* 1:465–67; 2:117. See Acts 23:23–24:27 for an all too brief summary of Paul's experiences during his two years with the Roman governor Felix in Caesarea.

lines (2:15–16), we conclude that Paul's language here leads us directly back to the angry, hateful clashes between Gentiles and Jews (see the Notes on 2:14, 17; 4:3; 6:15).

2:16 *might reconcile*: Paul did not write here that the two sides had already been reconciled. He would do so only at Colossians 1:22 (Greek text: "he reconciled," past tense of ἀποκαταλλάσσω, *apokatallassō*).[245] Of course, one of Christ's intents in going to the "cross" was "to reconcile all things unto himself . . . whether they be things in earth, or things in heaven" (Col. 1:20). Such a reconciliation, which, according to Colossians 1:20, included a rapprochement of even those who are not part of this world, "does not refer merely to [a person's] guilt before God."[246] It is bigger than that and embraces "the enmity" that has separated the two groups, Gentiles and Jews. This judgment is illustrated in cases of reconciliation between individuals who have experienced conflict with one other, with one party then seeking to reestablish peaceful relations, such as the worshipper at the altar (see Matt. 5:23–24) or the marriage partner who faces estrangement (see 1 Cor. 7:10–11).[247]

in one body: The question is, Which body? Is it Christ's crucified body, his body that a person spiritually partakes of in the Eucharist or sacrament, or the body of the church? The noun σῶμα (*sōma*) occurs nine times in this letter, presenting all three meanings.[248] In this verse, the close proximity of the phrase "by the cross" tugs us first toward the understanding that this "one body" is Christ's crucified body.[249] That said, we next must notice that Christians have celebrated his crucified body in the Eucharist, thus underlining the intimate connection between crucifixion and the sacrament: "Take, eat: this is my body, which is broken for you: this do in remembrance of me" (1 Cor. 11:24).[250] Third, we cannot rule out that "the one body" represented the church into which both Gentile and Jew entered and found reconciliation "unto God" in their newly minted fellowship one with another, an occurrence that would happen nowhere else. In this engaging fellowship within Christ's body, church members now

---

245. BDAG, 112.

246. Friedrich Büchsel, *TDNT,* 1:259.

247. Büchsel, *TDNT,* 1:255. The verb in these two passages is καταλλάσσω (*katalassō*), which bears a similar meaning. BDAG, 521.

248. See 1:23; 2:16; 4:4, 12, 16 (twice); 5:23, 28, 30.

249. Johannes Schneider, *TDNT,* 7:577 n. 40; Schweizer and Baumgärtel, *TDNT,* 7:1077–78.

250. Schweizer and Baumgärtel, *TDNT,* 7:1067.

enjoyed the ability and help to fend off the evil one (see the Notes on 1:23; 4:4, 12, 16; 5:23, 28, 30).[251]

having slain: Christ is the subject of this action (the verb is ἀποκτείνω, *apokteinō*).[252] As Paul presented the matter, Christ not only was slain on "the cross" but, at the same time, slew "the enmity," thus "making peace" (2:15). In a figurative but genuine sense, Christ "does away with the hatred" that has bedeviled human relationships.[253] Hence, Jesus underwent the Atonement both to be slain for our sins and misdeeds and to slay "the enmity" both between God and humans and between one person and another. To be sure, his suffering released an "all-embracing expiatory power."[254] But it was more than that. He also set in motion an "enabling power" that offers strength and intelligence beyond a person's own (see 1 Chr. 29:10–12; Ps. 68:32–35; 1 Pet. 1:3–5;[255] Alma 7:12; 20:4; 26:12; the Notes on 1:7, 9, 16, 18, 21; 2:7; 3:7–8, 16; 4:30; and the Analysis of 1:3–14). He did all of this "in his flesh" by, first, abolishing the law (2:15; see also Rom. 7:4).[256]

the enmity: In one of its senses, this term (ἔχθρα, *echthra*) pertains to enmity toward God (see Rom. 8:7 and James 4:4). Otherwise, it revolves around the rancor between humans.[257] Because Paul has repeated this term from the prior verse, one concludes that, beyond the usual and rather regular jostling between Gentiles and Jews when they resided close to one another, he had in mind known conflicts between Jews and their neighbors in the Roman world, such as at Alexandria and Caesarea. In the main, their differences arose from spiritual and social causes and led to few serious consequences. But in notable cases, those differences exploded into physical acrimony and tension between Gentiles and their Jewish neighbors (see the Notes on 2:14–15).

2:17 came and preached peace unto you: The fundamental concept here pictures Jesus at his mortal coming, bringing the good news to all who would listen, including "unto you"—that is, to both Jews and Gentiles. His preaching among Jews was, of course, well-known among believers.

---

251. Schweizer and Baumgärtel, *TDNT,* 7:1078–79.

252. BDAG, 114; Louw-Nida, §20.61.

253. Louw-Nida, §13.44.

254. Schneider, *TDNT,* 7:576.

255. Eising, *TDOT,* 4:349, 353–55; Grundmann, *TDNT,* 2:313–16; Oepke, *TDNT,* 2:542–43; Braun, *TDNT,* 6:464; Bednar, "In the Strength of the Lord," 121–28; Rasmus, "Enabling Power of the Atonement," 18–21.

256. Schneider, *TDNT,* 7:577.

257. Foerster, *TDNT,* 2:815.

His interactions with Gentiles were many fewer. Only a few reports were preserved in tradition, some making their way into the Gospels,[258] these stories presumably being known to Paul and others who taught Gentile investigators (see Matt. 15:21–28; Mark 7:24–30; and John 12:20–21). Additionally, Paul was likely aware of the mission of the Seventy disciples, who traveled among Gentiles. We know about the Seventy's all-embracing mission because, at their departure, Jesus suspended Jewish food laws (see Luke 10:7–8).[259] That said, it is highly doubtful that anyone in Ephesus or, more broadly, in Asia Minor knew any of the Gentiles whom Jesus or one of the Seventy disciples had met. In this light, the thought must be that Christ's good news had reached the ears of Paul's audience through Christ's authorized agents. In effect, "the coming of Jesus to earth, His life and death, were the great message of peace, the great proclamation of peace" (see the Notes on 2:14–15; 4:3; 6:15).[260]

This verse derives its shape and character from two passages in Isaiah, both from their Septuagint renditions. One reads, "Peace upon peace to them that are far off, and to them that are nigh" (LXX Isa. 57:19). In the other, the Lord says, "I am present, as a season of beauty upon the mountains, as the feet of one preaching glad tidings of peace" (LXX Isa. 52:6–7).[261] The expression "preaching glad tidings of peace" rests beneath Paul's language here. By focusing his remarks on these passages, Paul has now drawn his readers from a vista where they saw the death of Christ and its consequent blessings of serenity (see 2:13–16) to a place where they could witness him as the embodiment of the glad tidings of peace (see 2:14; Luke 1:79; 2:14; John 14:27; Acts 10:36; Rom. 5:1; and 2 Thes. 3:16).[262] From here, believers could undergo the experience "that Christ may dwell in your hearts by faith" so that they are "able to comprehend . . . the love of Christ, which passeth knowledge, that ye might be filled with all the fulness of God" (3:17–19; see also the Notes on 3:17–18; 6:15).

preached: This verb is not the verb that describes the simple act of preaching in the New Testament (κηρύσσω, *kēryssō*) but one that conveys the richer, more engaging sense of "bringing good news" (εὐαγγελίζομαι, *euangelizomai*; see Luke 1:19; 2:10; 4:18; Rom. 1:15; 10:15; 1 Thes. 3:6; etc.;

---

258. Winger, *Ephesians*, 326.
259. Brown, *Testimony of Luke*, 505, 512, 515.
260. Gerhard Friedrich, *TDNT*, 2:718.
261. Von Rad and Foerster, *TDNT*, 2:415.
262. Barth, *Ephesians*, 1:266–67.

and the Note on 3:8).[263] The two verbs occur together at Luke 8:1, offering "a comprehensive picture of the whole activity of Jesus,"[264] who was "preaching and shewing the glad tidings of the kingdom of God." It is the latter verb that Paul picked up from LXX Isaiah 52:7: "preaching glad tidings [*euangelizomai*] of peace."

peace: Of the seven occurrences of this noun (εἰρήνη, *eirēnē*) in Ephesians (see 1:2; 2:14, 15, 17; 4:3; 6:15, 23), it appears twice in this verse, though the KJV reproduces it only once. The New Rendition correctly repeats it: "Peace to you who were far away and peace to you who were near." In the initial reading of this line, one perceives that this peace is "vertical"; that is, it bears on the relationship of a person, or even of an entire people, with God. How so? Because in this verse "peace" is linked first to "you" Gentiles, the "afar off," and then very specifically to Jews, "them that were nigh." Such language does not direct us to a "peace" that now ties the two groups together but rather to a divinely driven circumstance that grants that "both have access by one Spirit unto the Father" (2:18),[265] allowing them to surmount "tribulation [in] . . . the world" (John 16:33; see also the Notes on 2:14–15; 4:3).[266]

afar off: At this point, Paul addresses his main audience, Gentiles, "you which were afar off." In earlier verses, he called them "children of disobedience," "Uncircumcision," "aliens from the commonwealth of Israel," "strangers from the covenants of promise," those "without God in the world," and those "who sometimes were far off" (2:2, 11–13). Almost inexplicably, through Christ, Gentiles and Jews have been joined together, linked not only spiritually in their quest for salvation but also physically in their congregations, to become "the new people of God," replacing the old (see the Note on 2:13).[267]

nigh: Earlier in this letter, Paul had characterized fellow Jewish Christians as "the Circumcision," "the commonwealth of Israel," and those burdened by "the law of commandments" (2:11–12, 15). Of course, "them that were nigh" were Jews. And Paul wanted his readers to grasp this fact. Beyond this, these were the people who, throughout their long history, had drawn nigh to or stood near holy places or sanctuaries, keeping fresh

---

263. BDAG, 402, 543–44.
264. Friedrich, *TDNT*, 2:718.
265. Lincoln, *Ephesians*, 147–48.
266. Von Rad and Foerster, *TDNT*, 2:413.
267. Preisker, *TDNT*, 4:374.

their relationship to God (see Gen. 18:22–23; 19:27; Ex. 3:5; 24:9–11; Lev. 3:1, 7; 9:5; 1 Sam. 2:21; 14:36; James 4:8; etc.). Hence, they could be named "them that were nigh." Further, the essence of being near to the divine also introduces the idea of eventual salvation at the end-time (see Ps. 69:18; 107:18–19; and Heb. 7:19; compare Judg. 18:6; see also the Note on 2:13).[268] It may be of interest to notice that, at this point, the better manuscripts add a second "peace" (εἰρήνη, *eirēnē*) so that the expression reads, "and peace to those who were near" (NIV), adding "significantly to the force of the writer's statement."[269]

2:18 *we both have access:* Almost singing, Paul celebrated the common, shared avenue that leads both Jew and Gentile "unto the Father." With a joyous outcome, "through" Christ, all will enjoy access to "all that my Father hath" (D&C 84:38).

access: This noun (προσαγωγή, *prosagōgē*) occurs in only two other passages in the New Testament (see 3:12 and Rom. 5:2). Its general sense is "a way of approach, access,"[270] which may well rest on scenes of temple sacrifice. In this connection, it is the verb προσάγω (*prosagō*) that initiates intrigue, especially in its transitive form, "to bring into someone's presence."[271] In the first place, key sacrificial passages in the Septuagint repeat this verb. For example, we read, "If any man of you shall bring gifts to the Lord, ye shall bring your gifts of the cattle and of the oxen and of the sheep" (LXX Lev. 1:2). Again, "he shall bring it a male without blemish" (LXX Lev. 1:10; see also LXX Lev. 3:1, 3, 7, 12; 4:14; 5:8; etc.).[272] Moreover, the verb lays out the preliminary sacred acts before the consecration of priests: "*Do thou take* to thyself both Aaron thy brother, and his sons, . . . so that . . . [they] may minister to me" (LXX Ex. 28:1, emphasis added). Such acts include washing, anointing, clothing, and offering sacrifice for the priests (see LXX Ex. 29:4, 8, 10; 40:12 [40:13 KJV]; LXX Lev. 7:25; 8:13–14; etc.).[273] Hence, we come upon important temple linkage and language.

Second, one of the verb's four appearances in the New Testament (see Luke 9:41; Acts 16:20; 27:27; and 1 Pet. 3:18) leads us to a passage frequently quoted by Latter-day Saints: "For Christ also hath once suffered for sins, . . . that he might *bring us to* God, being put to death in the flesh, but quickened

---

268. Preisker, *TDNT*, 2:331.
269. Metzger, *Textual Commentary*, 534.
270. BDAG, 876.
271. BDAG, 875–76.
272. Merkle, *Guide*, 76.
273. Karl Ludwig Schmidt, *TDNT*, 1:131–32.

by the Spirit: by which also he went and preached unto the spirits in prison" (1 Pet. 3:18–19, emphasis added; see also D&C 138:7–8). In this light, the notion of Christ escorting a person to God's presence plays a familiar tune both to mortal believers and to those who come to believe in the next life. Therefore, the "access" offered to followers is not limited to this life but retains its relevance and potency among departed spirits. In fact, it is God who has brought people to himself: "I took you up as on eagles' wings, and I *brought you near* to myself" (LXX Ex. 19:4, emphasis added). In a last touch, the verb also has to do with the act of a servant who, brought to the doorpost of the temple, willingly and permanently submits to the master (see LXX Ex. 21:5–6).[274] Such a scene, in a holy place, evokes covenants that believers willingly make with God, their eternal master (see the Note on 3:12).

one Spirit: The KJV translators were correct to translate the word "Spirit" (πνεῦμα, *pneuma*) with a capital letter. In Paul's presentation of this Spirit, elsewhere called the Holy Ghost (πνεῦμα ἅγιον, *pneuma hagion*), he marked off several functions or roles. Perhaps the best known focuses on the Spirit as the giver of spiritual gifts.[275] In the three lists that we possess, we discover a level of uniformity, which suggests a common revelatory source, but not a written source. In this order, we come across the gifts of wisdom, knowledge, exceptional faith, healing, working of miracles, prophecy, and tongues (see 1 Cor. 12:4–11; Moro. 10:8–18; and D&C 46:10–29). Above these rides the gift of discernment, which resides with the presiding officer, "lest there shall be any among you professing and yet be not of God" (D&C 46:27). Moreover and notably, we are reminded "that every good gift cometh of Christ" (Moro. 10:18). Said another way, "all these gifts come from God," specifically "for the benefit of the children of God," not generally for unbelievers (D&C 46:26; see also Rom. 1:11 and 1 Cor. 14:12, 22–24).

After baptism, believers receive the gift of the Holy Ghost (see Acts 19:4–6). In this ordinance, two things happen. First, the Spirit acts as a cleansing agent, as we read in the words of John the Baptist: "I indeed baptize you with water: but one mightier than I cometh, . . . he shall baptize you with the Holy Ghost and with fire" (Luke 3:16; see also Matt. 3:11; 2 Ne. 31:13–14, 17; 3 Ne. 9:20; 11:35; 12:1–2; 27:20; Morm. 7:10; Moro. 6:4; and D&C 19:31; 20:41; 33:11; 39:6; compare Ether 12:14). Second, the Spirit enfolds the person into the body of Christ, into the church (see 1:14, "the earnest of our inheritance"; 4:30, "sealed unto the day of redemption"; Gal. 5:5, "the hope

---

274. Schmidt, *TDNT,* 1:132.
275. Kleinknecht, Baumgärtel, Bieder, Sjöberg, and Schweizer, *TDNT,* 6:437.

of [future] righteousness"; see also Acts 2:38; 1 Cor. 12:12–14, 27; and D&C 20:41; 35:6). In this manner, the Spirit creates a new member, "one new man [or woman]" (2:15), and, thereafter, keeps the person on the right path leading to eternal life (see John 14:26 and D&C 121:46). A person's reception of the Spirit is not simply "an initial event" that soon passes away but rather establishes an enduring relationship[276]—"that they may *always* have his Spirit to be with them" (Moro. 4:3; D&C 20:77, emphasis added).

Closely linked to the Spirit's power to usher a person into the church is his power to grant the knowledge "that Jesus is the Lord." This understanding comes only "by the Holy Ghost" (1 Cor. 12:3; see also Luke 12:12 and John 14:26). We find this view buttressed elsewhere: "Hereby know ye the Spirit of God: Every spirit that confesseth that Jesus Christ is come in the flesh is of God" (1 John 4:2). This role of the Spirit, as we learn from modern scripture, arises because "the Holy Ghost . . . beareth record of the Father and the Son" (Moses 1:24; see also Moses 5:9; 7:11; 2 Ne. 31:18; 3 Ne. 28:11; Ether 12:41; and D&C 20:27). This specific knowledge, of course, is part of the Spirit's broader powers as a revelator, a revealer (see 3:3, 5, "revealed . . . by the Spirit"; 1 Cor. 2:10, 12, 14; see also John 16:13; 2 Ne. 32:5; Moro. 10:5; and D&C 39:6).[277] Some examples arise from Jesus' ministry. For instance, after his baptism, Jesus "was led by the Spirit into the wilderness" for forty days of fasting and temptation (Luke 4:1). Following his test at the hands of the devil, "Jesus returned [home] in the power of the Spirit into Galilee" (Luke 4:14). In a different vein, Jesus promised believers who would be under threat that "the Holy Ghost shall teach you in the same hour what ye ought to say" (Luke 12:12; see also Matt. 10:19–20; Mark 13:11; Luke 21:14–15; 1 Cor. 2:4, 12–13; and the Notes on 1:13; 2:2, 22; 3:16; 4:3–4, 30; 5:9, 18).[278]

unto the Father: Paul has already set out where the "access" leads—to that sacred path strewn with the flowering aromas of "adoption . . . by Jesus Christ" (1:5) and "forgiveness of sins" (1:7), a path which all, both Circumcision and Uncircumcision, step onto "through faith" when "quickened . . . together with Christ" (2:8, 5). Our approach to the Father is graced by a relationship to him as child to father. "For ye have not received

---

276. Kleinknecht, Baumgärtel, Bieder, Sjöberg, and Schweizer, *TDNT*, 6:426–27, quotation on 6:426.

277. Kleinknecht, Baumgärtel, Bieder, Sjöberg, and Schweizer, *TDNT*, 6:425.

278. Modern scripture brings forward other roles of the Holy Ghost. Two important tasks are to serve as the source of scripture (see 2 Pet. 1:19–21; D&C 68:4) and to grant to the faithful the power to speak with "a new tongue," "the tongue of angels" (2 Ne. 31:13–14; 32:2–3; see 33:1).

the spirit of bondage again to fear; but ye have received the Spirit of adoption, whereby we cry, Abba, Father. The Spirit itself beareth witness with our spirit, that we are the children of God" (Rom. 8:15–16). Moreover, "because ye are sons [and daughters], God hath sent forth the Spirit of his Son into your hearts, crying, Abba, Father" (Gal. 4:6).[279] Said another way, "Because of the covenant ye have made ye shall be called the children of Christ, his sons, and his daughters; for behold, this day he hath spiritually begotten you" (Mosiah 5:7; see also Deut. 32:6; Isa. 63:16; and D&C 25:1). But this is only part of the story.

Significantly, the language of these letters clearly discloses the Father and the Son to be separate persons, as a quick perusal will demonstrate. At Ephesians' opening, we read, "Blessed be the God and Father of our Lord Jesus Christ" (1:3). Farther in chapter 1, we encounter "the God of our Lord Jesus Christ, [who is] the Father of glory" (1:17). We meet a similar sense of two distinct persons deeper into Ephesians: "For this cause I bow my knees unto the Father of our Lord Jesus Christ" (3:14). In his final greeting, Paul wrote about "peace" and "love" that have come "from God the Father and the Lord Jesus Christ" (6:23). This thought continues in Colossians. There we find that "the Father . . . hath delivered us from the power of darkness, and hath translated us into the kingdom of his dear Son" (Col. 1:12–13). In a reference to prayer and thanksgiving, we run across an even clearer image of the distinction between the two divine persons: "Whatsoever ye do in word or deed, do all in the name of the Lord Jesus, giving thanks to God and the Father by him" (Col. 3:17; see also the Notes on 3:14–15; 4:5–6; 6:2; especially 4:1 on "Lord").

We notice that the title "the Father" (ὁ πατήρ, *ho patēr*), with the definite article, occurs in Paul's letters only in Ephesians and Colossians,[280] with six of those in Ephesians and three in Colossians, excluding references to earthly fathers. These references and others emphasize God the Father as the architect of both creation and redemption (see the Notes on 2:10; 4:24, 30). For it is he who "hath chosen us in him before the foundation of the world" (1:4). It is he who controls "all principality, and power, and might, and dominion, and every name that is named" (1:21). It is he who sent Christ to offer "redemption through his blood, the forgiveness of sins" (1:7). It is he who "raised [Christ] from the dead, and set him at his

---

279. Gottlob Schrenk and Gottfried Quell, *TDNT*, 5:965–66; Lincoln, *Ephesians*, 149–50.
280. Schrenk and Quell, *TDNT*, 5:1008. See Eph. 1:3, 17; 2:18; 3:14; 5:20; 6:23; Col. 1:3, 12; 3:17.

own right hand in the heavenly places" (1:20). It is he "of whom the whole family in heaven and earth is named" (3:15). It is he "who is above all, and through all, and in you all" (4:6).[281] In more intimate and personal tones, "the Lord's portion is his people," who are "unto him a people of [his eternal] inheritance, as ye are this day" (Deut. 32:9; 4:20). Hallelujah!

2:19 *ye:* Since 2:11, Paul has been addressing Gentiles; here, he turns attention to both audiences, Gentiles and Jews, welcoming them as "the household of God."

strangers and foreigners: Paul may have been following convention in writing two nouns (ξένοι καὶ πάροικοι, *xenoi kai paroikoi*). How so? Because in the Old Testament, a person finds an expression like "stranger and sojourner" in the KJV translation to describe those not native to the indigenous people (see Gen. 23:4; Lev. 25:23, 35, 47; Num. 35:15; 1 Chr. 29:15; and Ps. 39:12 [39:13 Hebrew text]). In light of such passages, Paul's double noun is not surprising. One issue naturally arises: With the two nouns, did he mean to distinguish between Gentiles and Jews, applying one noun to one group and one to the other? Probably not. The two terms are virtual synonyms and bear little difference in meaning, as their appearance in the Septuagint demonstrates.[282]

In contrast, the Hebrew Bible does distinguish between groups of outsiders. The three terms are נכרי, גר, and תושב (*nokhri, ger,* and *toshav*). The second of these, *ger,* points to a foreigner who has come to reside among Israelites and, because he or she embraces the Hebrew faith, becomes a proselyte and enjoys the same protections and worship privileges that other Israelites enjoy.[283] Such people included Ruth, the Moabite daughter-in-law of Naomi who became a great-grandmother of King David, and those who fled Samaria and settled in Jerusalem after the obliteration of the northern kingdom of Israel by the Assyrians in 722 BC.[284] Those refugees doubtless included the ancestors of Lehi, who counted himself of the northern tribe of Manasseh (see Alma 10:3). As a matter of fact, God called the Israelites themselves "sojourners"—that is, resident aliens on land that belonged to him and to no one else.[285] The noun *toshav,* "stranger," almost always

---

281. Schrenk and Quell, *TDNT,* 5:1018–19.

282. Stählin, *TDNT,* 5:8; BDAG, 684, 779; Lincoln, *Ephesians,* 150. Barth tries to make a distinction, but his arguments are not convincing. Barth, *Ephesians,* 1:268–69.

283. Kellermann, *TDOT,* 2:443, 446–48.

284. Kellermann, *TDOT,* 2:443, 445.

285. Jacob Milgrom, *Leviticus 23–27,* vol. 3B of the Anchor Bible (New York: Doubleday, 2001), 2187–88.

occurs with the term *ger*. The two terms differ. *Toshav*, a "stranger," is one "taken in by a fully enfranchised Israelite citizen" and is "a nonproselyte."[286] The word *nokhri* directs us to a "foreigner" or a person of "another" family or nation. Like the *toshav*, a *nokhri* generally lived without legal or social protections and remained unassimilated.[287] None of these refinements are present in Paul's expression "strangers and foreigners," for all were invited inside God's household. Of course, some of this bridging between peoples had already been pioneered when Jews of Paul's era invited interested Gentiles into their synagogues (see Acts 13:42–43; 14:1; 17:1–4; 18:4, 7; and the Note on 2:12).

fellowcitizens: This noun (συμπολίτης, *sympolitēs*) appears nowhere else in the New Testament. In its context, it has nothing to do with citizenship in the wider Roman world, though that is its usual connection, as Paul's appeal to a related term (πολίτης, *politēs*) illustrates: "I am a Jew, from Tarsus in Cilicia, a *citizen* of no ordinary city" (Acts 21:39 NIV, emphasis added). Instead, *sympolitēs* pertains to a spiritual citizenship, one "with the saints," literally "with the holy ones" (ἅγιοι, *hagioi*). Significantly, such citizenship extends beyond the society of fellow believers in this world, beyond membership in the church. It makes church members "people of God's country," citizens of his heavenly city (see Philip. 3:20; Heb. 11:10, 16; 12:22; 13:14; and the Note on 2:12).[288]

saints: In early Christian circles, this plural noun (ἅγιοι, *hagioi*), which occurs nine times in Ephesians (1:1, 15, 18; 2:19; 3:8, 18; 4:12; 5:3; 6:18), had come to signify church members, as a number of Paul's greetings disclose (see Rom. 1:7; 16:2, 15; 1 Cor. 1:2; 16:15; 2 Cor. 1:1; 13:13; Philip. 1:1; etc.). As Paul presented his case, to be a "saint" meant far more than being a member of "the commonwealth of Israel" and a recipient of "the covenants of promise" (2:12). Everyone, Gentile and Jew, had been "made nigh by the blood of Christ"; all had been created a new people of God, as if "one new man" (2:13, 15). Such eternally powerful acts had brought all believers within God's kingdom, both in its earthly manifestation and within its heavenly realm, promising a life with God (see 1 Cor. 15:23–26; Col. 1:12–13; 1 Thes. 2:12; Heb. 12:28; and the Notes on 1:1, 18; 3:18; 4:12; 5:3, 26).[289]

---

286. Kellermann, *TDOT*, 2:448; compare BDB, 444.

287. Bernard Lang and Helmer Ringgren, *TDOT*, 9:424–27; see also BDB, 648–49.

288. Louw-Nida, §11.72; see also Kellermann, *TDOT*, 2:449; Strathmann, *TDNT*, 6:534–35; BDAG, 959.

289. Procksch and Kuhn, *TDNT*, 1:106–7.

household of God: We face the concept of household in this noun (the plural οἰκεῖοι (*oikeioi*) signifying "members of a household"; see also Gal. 6:10).[290] Its significance runs deeper than welcoming or enfranchising church members who have suddenly become foreigners in the world at the time of their conversion (see John 15:19; 17:14, 16). Because they have come to enjoy "access . . . unto the Father" (2:18), they have entered "the whole family [of God] in heaven and earth" (3:15). Simply said, the image is that of a family,[291] everlasting and celestial in its character. That is to say, these people are no longer as if among former homeless associates. To this point, with the aid of Christ's grace, they have traveled a long way from being "dead in trespasses and sins" and being besotted with "the desires of the flesh and of the mind" (2:1, 3;[292] see the Notes on 1:5; 3:15; 5:23).

2:20 *built upon:* This verb (ἐποικοδομέω, *epoikodomeō*), a passive participle here, occurs eight times in the New Testament with the basic sense "to build upon, to build up."[293] The force of the passive, as in other cases, is to say that God was the builder (see Heb. 11:10, 16; and Rev. 21:2, 10, 23).[294] The language of construction reminds us of the words of John the Baptist about building a smooth, unobstructed road for the approaching Messiah. Quoting Isaiah 40:3–4, he intoned, "Prepare ye the way of the Lord, make his paths straight. Every valley shall be filled, and every mountain and hill shall be brought low; and the crooked shall be made straight, and the rough ways shall be made smooth" (Luke 3:4–5). In the case of *epoikodomeō,* the idea is to build upward from a foundation. Paul metaphorically wrote in another place, "I have laid the foundation, and another buildeth thereon." Then he added a caution that "every man take heed how he buildeth thereupon." Why? Because "other foundation can no man lay than that is laid, which is Jesus Christ" (1 Cor. 3:10–11; see also Rom. 15:20). Paul had laid the foundation of Christ but then left the rearing of the superstructure to other leaders.[295]

Two points are relevant. First, the true foundation that Paul laid in Corinth was "Jesus Christ, and him crucified" (1 Cor. 2:2). But within the next few words in Ephesians, Paul has written about "the foundation of the apostles and prophets" and called "Jesus Christ himself . . . the chief corner stone," not the foundation. Why the shift in imagery? Because, as

290. Merkle, *Guide,* 79–80.
291. BDAG, 694; Louw-Nida, §10.11.
292. Stählin, *TDNT,* 5:29; Best, *Ephesians,* 279; Lincoln, *Ephesians,* 152.
293. BDAG, 387; see Acts 20:32; 1 Cor. 3:10 (twice), 12, 14; Col. 2:7; Jude 1:20.
294. Blass and Debrunner, *Greek Grammar,* §§130(1), 313; Jeremias, *Parables,* 122 n. 31.
295. Michel, *TDNT,* 5:147–48.

Draper and Rhodes point out, the imagery of apostles and prophets as the gospel foundation in our passage would not suit the situation at Corinth, where, sadly, the community's internal "factions boasted of following one Apostle or another."[296] Second, although the foundation may be properly laid, builders can and did erect an unsuitable, mismatched superstructure. For the resulting upper part of the building to equal the foundation, it must match "the quality and . . . excellence of that foundation."[297]

foundation: Across the Old Testament, the concept of foundations was broad and rich. But the metaphorical notion of foundations common in the New Testament (θεμέλιον and θεμέλιος, *themelion* and *themelios*), such as standing under church communities and resting on Christ himself (see Rom. 15:20; 1 Cor. 3:10–11; Col. 1:23; 1 Tim. 6:19; 2 Tim. 2:19; and Heb. 6:1), is largely missing from the Old Testament (but see Isa. 14:32; 54:11–17 on the founding of Zion). In the Old Testament, we usually encounter the literal sense of foundations for houses, sanctuaries, or cities (see Ex. 9:18; 1 Kgs. 7:8–10; Job 4:19; Isa. 16:7; etc.) and the cosmological idea of mountains and the earth and the heavens resting on foundations (see 2 Sam. 22:8; Job 38:4–6; Ps. 18:7; 87:1; 104:1–8; Isa. 48:13; 51:13; Zech. 12:1; etc.).[298]

It is in the verb form (θεμελιόω, *themelioō*) that we find intriguing interrelationships. For instance, in Matthew 7:25, we hear about a house "founded [*themelioō*] upon a rock [πέτρα, *petra*]" that withstood "rain" and "floods" and "winds" (see Luke 6:48). It is apparent that the founding of the house on bedrock came to be synonymous with the erecting of the entire structure, a transfer or sharing of meaning that is termed *metonymy,* a common feature of Old Testament language about foundations.[299] Similarly, in the famous scene near Caesarea Philippi, in response to Peter's confession that Jesus is "the Christ, the Son of the Living God," Jesus replied, "Thou art Peter, and upon this rock [*petra*] I will build my church; and the gates of hell shall not prevail against it" (Matt. 16:16, 18; the verb οἰκοδομέω [*oikodomeō*], translated "to build" here, is a cognate of *themelioō* and envisions the same activity).[300] Thus, the revelation that Jesus spoke about in Matthew 16:17 ("flesh and blood hath not revealed it unto thee [Peter], but my Father

---

296. Draper and Rhodes, *Paul's First Epistle to the Corinthians,* 201 n. 71.

297. Draper and Rhodes, *Paul's First Epistle to the Corinthians,* 196.

298. Magnus Ottosson and Jan Bergman, *TDOT,* 1:394; R. Mosis, *TDOT,* 6:110–20; BDAG, 448–49.

299. Mosis, *TDOT,* 6:112; see, for example, "garments stained," which also represents stained souls before God's judgment bar (Alma 5:22).

300. Karl Ludwig Schmidt, *TDNT,* 3:63–64.

which is in heaven") was to become the foundation stone of the Christian church.[301] That foundation, because it originated with the Father, would be permanent and immovable. And that is exactly the message in the earliest accounts of God's founding acts, including the heaven and the earth.[302]

This foundation stone's connection with the temple and its sanctuary will become immediately visible in 2:21 and 2:22, where Paul wrote about "all the building" of the church growing "into a holy temple in the Lord," which will stand as "a dwelling place of God in the Spirit" (RSV). This concept is at home in the Old Testament where God is portrayed as the builder of the temple and its altar, including laying the cornerstone (see Isa. 28:16; compare Ps. 8:3, 6). According to one passage, God founded (יסד, *yasad*) his heavenly temple upon the earth: he "builds his upper chambers in the heavens, and founds [*yasad*] his vault upon the earth," thus linking heaven and earth (Amos 9:6 RSV). Because of God's involvement, the whole becomes fixed and eternal: "He built his sanctuary like the high heavens, like the earth, which he has founded [*yasad*] for ever" (Ps. 78:69 RSV).[303]

What is more, strong hints exist that God planned all this divine activity long before the foundation of the heavens and earth, in a premortal era beyond the knowledge of humans. For example, God prepared or founded "the place" where "the mountains rose, [and] the valleys sank down" (Ps. 104:8 RSV). Further, because the Psalmist grasped that "all [God's] commandments are true . . . have I [the Psalmist] known from thy testimonies that thou hast founded [*yasad*] them for ever," articulating his laws long before human life appeared upon the earth (Ps. 119:151–52 RSV). According to Proverbs, it was "at the beginning of [God's] work, the first of his acts of old," that "he assigned to the sea its limit [חקה, *huqah*], so that the waters might not transgress his command, when he marked out the foundations of the earth" (Prov. 8:22, 29 RSV).[304] This planning activity all occurred "in that primordial 'age' accessible only to Yahweh and his wisdom, but beyond the ken of human beings" (see the Note on 3:17).[305]

---

301. For the view that Peter was to be the foundation stone, see Oskar Cullmann, *TDNT,* 6:108; see also Ulrich Wilckens, *TDNT,* 7:735.

302. Mosis, *TDOT,* 6:116.

303. Mosis, *TDOT,* 6:111, 113, 116; Schmidt, *TDNT,* 3:63–64.

304. See also Job 38:33, "the ordinances [חקה, *huqah*] of heaven"; Ps. 148:6, "he hath made a decree [חק, *haq*] which shall not pass"; Jer. 5:22, "a perpetual decree [*haq*]"; 31:35, "the fixed order [*huqah*] of the moon and the stars for light by night" (RSV); 33:25, "the ordinances [*huqah*] of heaven and earth" (KJV); see Helmer Ringgren, *TDOT,* 5:141–42.

305. Mosis, *TDOT,* 6:118.

the apostles: The definite article "the" brings us directly to the doorstep of the original Twelve (the plural genitive τῶν ἀποστόλων, *tōn apostolōn*), or at least to the reconstituted Twelve following Judas's death (see Acts 1:15–26 and 1 Cor. 15:5).[306] The definite article also appears at 3:5 and 4:11, again leading us to Jesus' Twelve. Some grammarians have sought to modify this view. Larkin admitted that "the term [here] probably refers to the Twelve," but may well have included "the 120–500 who saw the risen Lord [and] . . . who could have been commissioned by Christ."[307] However, no such broad commissioning has been noted elsewhere in the New Testament or by later Christian authors. With more restraint and without elaboration, Merkle wrote that these apostles "included the twelve, Paul, and possibly a few others."[308] The "others" would permit "prophets" noted elsewhere into the mix (see Acts 11:27; 13:1; 15:32; 21:10; 1 Cor. 12:28–29; etc.). Such individuals, evidently, did not include Old Testament prophets, with the possible exception of John the Baptist, who, it seems, was thought to be part of the old order of prophets (see Matt. 11:7–13; 14:3–5; 21:26; Mark 11:32; Luke 7:24–28; 16:16, "the law and the prophets were until John"; etc.; see also the Note below).[309]

The concept of God or Jesus commissioning and sending representatives links firmly to the call and sending of Isaiah. We find out that, after being introduced into the council of Jehovah as a part of his first vision, Isaiah "heard the voice of the Lord, saying, Whom shall I send, and who will go for us?" Because his lips had just been cleansed by one of the divine seraphs, thus turning him into the mouthpiece of God, Isaiah could hardly keep from replying, "Here am I; send me" (Isa. 6:6–8). The commissioner and sender was God, the divine person who launched Isaiah as his messenger (see also Gen. 45:5, 7–8; Ex. 3:12–15; 4:28; Jer. 1:7; etc.).[310]

It seems certain that Jesus did not call himself an apostle (*apostolos*). As an aside, *apostolos* is a Greek term that means "one sent." The verb ἀποστέλλω (*apostellō,* "to send forth") forms the verbal counterpart to the noun *apostolos.* We do possess a plethora of sayings that apply to Jesus that bring us close to the idea of "one sent." For example, Luke recorded Jesus' affirmation, "Therefore I am sent" by God to "preach the kingdom" (Luke 4:43; see also Matt. 10:40;

306. Rengstorf, *TDNT,* 1:422.
307. Larkin, *Handbook,* 45.
308. Merkle, *Guide,* 81.
309. Brown, *Testimony of Luke,* 759, 762.
310. Rengstorf, *TDNT,* 1:400–401.

15:24; Mark 9:37; John 3:17; 5:36; Heb. 3:1; etc.). That said, we can be sure that the title "apostle" originated with Jesus himself, although in its Aramaic form (שליחה, *shlicha*).[311] Jesus gave this title to the twelve men whom he called early in his ministry (see Matt. 10:1–4; Mark 3:13–19; and Luke 6:13–16). However, it appears that the expression "twelve apostles" did not originate with him (see Matt. 10:2 and Rev. 21:14; Luke 22:14 has a textual problem: the earliest manuscript, $\mathfrak{P}^{45}$, omits "apostles," as do other early texts). Significantly, after his Resurrection, Jesus renewed their commission to carry his message "unto the uttermost part of the earth" (Acts 1:8; see also Matt. 28:16–20 and Luke 24:48–49).[312]

Concerning Paul, we of course possess his own words, both oral and written, about his call and commission by Christ during his now-famous journey to Damascus from Jerusalem (see 3:2–3; Acts 9:3–6; 22:6–15; 26:12–18; 1 Cor. 9:1; and Gal. 1:15–17), an event that he connected to God's will (see 1:1; 1 Cor. 1:1; 2 Cor. 1:1; and Col. 1:1). In this, he was the first apostle of record "to trace back the apostolate to God Himself."[313]

Now we are ready to ask, Why were others outside the Twelve, including Paul, referred to as apostles? For example, Paul himself has directed our attention to others whom he called "apostles," including two early converts, "Andronicus and Junia, my kinsmen, and my fellowprisoners, who are of note among the apostles, who also were in Christ before me" (Rom. 16:7). In another place, and perhaps not unexpectedly, he centered "James the Lord's brother" among "the apostles" (Gal. 1:19), though we possess no record of James's call to the apostleship. Moreover, in the book of Acts, Luke labeled Barnabas as an "apostle" in his ministering efforts with Paul (see Acts 14:4, 14). Perhaps, as in the case of Timothy, it would have been better to call these people "brothers" (see 2 Cor. 1:1; Col. 1:1; and Philem. 1:1). But initially we have to accept what the New Testament authors have presented to us. Perhaps, in these cases, we are looking at "a comprehensive term for 'bearers of the [New Testament] message.'"[314] But there is more to the story. Among Jews until the fourth century AD, annual temple dues were carried to the Jerusalem authorities by representatives known as *apostoli,* a title that, as in the New Testament, designated an authorized agent (see the Notes on 1:1; 3:5; 4:11).[315]

---

311. Rengstorf, *TDNT,* 1:428; Nibley, *Apostles and Bishops,* 10–11.
312. Rengstorf, *TDNT,* 1:430.
313. Rengstorf, *TDNT,* 1:438; see also 1:422; and Fowl, *Ephesians,* 32–33.
314. Rengstorf, *TDNT,* 1:422–23, quotation on 1:422; see also Best, *Ephesians,* 96–97.
315. Schürer, *History of the Jewish People,* 3:124–25.

prophets: The question arises whether Paul had Old Testament prophets in mind or contemporary church members who possessed the divine gift of prophecy. It could be both, but the weight goes onto Christian prophets. To be certain, the prophecies and teachings of the earlier prophets served as a foundation for what came about in the New Testament era. All that preparation was necessary before the coming of the Messiah.[316] In this sense, the Old Testament prophets must have been in plain view. The New Testament, however, is filled with references to contemporary prophets who, graced with the spirit of prophecy, were members of local congregations and served as inspired guides to fellow church members.[317]

We begin with John the Baptist. It was Jesus who first labeled John as a prophet. Although he gained a reputation as a baptizer, especially as the one who baptized Jesus (see Matt. 3:1–6, 13–17; Mark 1:4–5, 9–11; Luke 3:2–3, 21–22; John 1:24–34; and Acts 1:21–22), John was elevated by Jesus' words as not only "a prophet" but "more than a prophet" (Matt. 11:9 and Luke 7:26). Furthermore, Jesus declared that of "them that are born of women there hath not risen a greater than John the Baptist" (Matt. 11:11; see also Luke 7:28, where, in a spirit of caution, we find a textual problem). On one level, notably, Jesus viewed John as a representative of the earlier Old Testament age: "The law and the prophets were until John: since that time the kingdom of God is preached" (Luke 16:16).[318] Besides all this, Josephus portrayed John in a most interesting light, picturing him as a person who had God's eye as well as the respect of the public. For he wrote that "the destruction of Herod's [Antipas's] army seemed to be divine vengeance . . . for his treatment of John, surnamed the Baptist." Why? Because "Herod had put him to death, though he was a good man and had exhorted the Jews to lead righteous lives." It was because "Herod became alarmed" after John's hearers "were aroused to the highest degree by his sermons [since] . . . it looked as if they would be guided by John in everything that they did." After the execution of John, "the destruction visited upon Herod's army was a vindication of John, since God saw fit to inflict such a blow on Herod" (see Matt. 21:26; Mark 11:32; Luke 20:6; and Acts 13:25).[319]

---

316. S. Kent Brown and Richard Neitzel Holzapfel, *The Lost 500 Years: What Happened between the Old and New Testaments* (Salt Lake City: Deseret Book, 2006), 7–27, 111–41.

317. Helmut Krämer, Rolf Rendtorff, Rudolf Meyer, and Gerhard Friedrich, *TDNT,* 6:849–50; Best, *Ephesians,* 282–83.

318. Brown, *Testimony of Luke,* 759.

319. Josephus, *The Antiquities of the Jews,* 18.5.2 (§§116–19).

Next, we take up Jesus. Indeed, certain New Testament texts portray him as the fulfillment of Moses' prophecy in Deuteronomy 18, a passage known in both the Old World and the New. In Deuteronomy, we read Moses' words to the effect that "the Lord thy God will raise up . . . a Prophet from the midst of thee, of thy brethren, like unto me [Moses]; unto him ye shall hearken" (Deut. 18:15). The prophecy goes on, with an emphasis now resting on Jehovah's words: "I will raise them up a Prophet from among their brethren, like unto thee [Moses], and will put my words in his mouth [and] . . . whosoever will not hearken unto my words which he shall speak in my name, I will require it of him" (Deut. 18:18–19). It was while preaching a short sermon on the Jerusalem temple grounds, following the healing of a lame man at the gate called Beautiful, that Peter said of Christ, "For Moses truly said unto the fathers, A prophet shall the Lord your God raise up . . . like unto me; him shall ye hear in all things" (Acts 3:22). In a second sermon of record, this one from Stephen in defense of his faith before the Jerusalem Sanhedrin, Stephen cited the same prophecy, applying it to Christ: "This is that Moses, which said unto the children of Israel, A prophet shall the Lord your God raise up unto you of your brethren, like unto me; him shall ye hear" (Acts 7:37). There is more.

During Jesus' mortal ministry, after feeding the five thousand and asking his disciples to gather "the fragments that remain, that nothing be lost," the disciples counted "twelve baskets" of leftovers. These men, sensing the grandeur of what they had just witnessed, said to one another, "This is of a truth that prophet that should come into the world" (John 6:12–14). Jesus himself hinted in this direction when, referring to his approaching suffering and death, he said, "I must walk to day, and tomorrow, and the day following: for it cannot be that a prophet perish out of Jerusalem" (Luke 13:33). As a capstone, in a New World setting following his Resurrection, Jesus declared openly, "Behold, I am he of whom Moses spake, saying: A prophet shall the Lord your God raise up unto you of your brethren, like unto me; him shall ye hear in all things." Then, mirroring and intensifying the words in the second part of Moses' prophecy, the Risen Jesus warned "that every soul who will not hear that prophet shall be cut off from among the people" (3 Ne. 20:23; compare Matt. 21:11, 46; Mark 6:15; 8:28; Luke 7:16; and John 1:45; 5:46).

Concerning "certain prophets and teachers" noted in the New Testament (Acts 13:1), we discover a surprising number among the earliest churches. Under ideal circumstances and in conformity with the words of Joel the prophet, God was to "pour out [his] spirit upon all flesh; and your sons and your daughters shall prophesy, your old men shall dream dreams, your young men shall see visions" (Joel 2:28). On the day of Pentecost, that is exactly what happened in Jerusalem. Those who gathered with the apostles witnessed that these twelve men "were all filled with the Holy Ghost, and began to speak with other tongues, as the Spirit gave them utterance" (Acts 2:4). Out of this unexpected and, to some, confusing scene, Peter made sense by quoting Joel's prophecy and then adding the twenty-ninth verse: "On my servants and on my handmaidens I will pour out in those days of my Spirit." Peter next appended the words "and they shall prophesy" (Acts 2:18). Plainly, believers were to enjoy the spirit of prophecy (see Acts 4:31 and Rom. 12:6). But the story does not end here.

In practice, only a few members of any congregation carried the gift of prophecy. But this does not mean that the gift was for a chosen few nor does it mean that persons with the gift served as presiding officers. No, their roles embraced tasks as diverse as offering "exhortation" when needed, ministering "comfort" to those in trying circumstances (1 Cor. 14:3; see also Acts 15:32), making known God's will "unto the sons of men" (3:5), and receiving "all mysteries, and all knowledge" as helps to others (1 Cor. 13:2). They also spoke of future events. In one case, a man named Agabus prophesied "a great dearth throughout all the world . . . in the days of Claudius Caesar" (Acts 11:28); in another, the same man, by dramatically tying up "his own hands and feet," predicted that Paul would be bound by "Jews at Jerusalem" and delivered "into the hands of the Gentiles" (Acts 21:10–11; see also Acts 20:22–23; 21:4).

In addition, prophets became involved in the work of the Christian ministry. When Paul was first called to missionary work, following his experience with the Resurrected Jesus on the road to Damascus, he and his friend Barnabas were set apart in his home congregation in Antioch by the laying on of hands by three "prophets," who "had fasted and prayed" beforehand (Acts 13:1–3). In his turn, Timothy was set apart to his ministry "by prophecy, [and] with the laying on of the hands" (1 Tim. 4:14; see also 1 Tim. 1:18).[320] Hence, the gift of prophecy was alive and well in that earliest generation of church members. It is its disappearance that would be troubling (see the Notes on 3:5; 4:11).[321]

chief corner stone: This term (ἀκρογωνιαῖος, *akrogōniaios*) most likely points to the capstone or to the cornerstone of a building rather than a

---

320. Krämer, Rendtorff, Meyer, and Friedrich, *TDNT,* 6:848–49, 855.
321. Nibley, *Apostles and Bishops,* 220.

keystone in an arch.[322] According to Isaiah 28:16, it is the Lord God who lays "in Zion for a foundation a stone, a tried stone, a precious corner stone, a sure foundation." This foundation stone, laid deep and with great care, is not to be hidden but rather gives to Zion its "solidity and security" for its future.[323] We are led to a similar image in our passage. It was God who set Jesus Christ as the main foundation stone of the church, imparting immovable consistency to it and its members (see 1 Pet. 2:7; and the Note on 1:22; compare Ps. 118:22; Matt. 21:42; Mark 12:10; Luke 20:17; and Acts 4:11).[324]

2:21 *all the building:* The noun for "building" (οἰκοδομή, *oikodomē*) can, of course, pertain to a physical structure. Generally, the meaning centers either on a building under construction or on a completed edifice. In our case, "all the building" bears a metaphorical or spiritual message relating to an entire building that is growing "without hands" (Mark 14:58; see also 2 Cor. 5:1). This thought includes Paul's audience, who "are builded together for an habitation of God through the Spirit" (2:22; see also 1 Cor. 3:9, "ye are God's building"). Because Paul wrote this letter to church members scattered across western Asia Minor in a number of branches, here the concept of the building is about the larger church, not a single congregation (see the Notes on 4:12, 16, 29).[325]

fitly framed together: This verb (συναρμολογέω, *synarmologeō*), which occurs also at 4:16, does not appear in earlier Greek literature. It was mainly later Christian writers who picked it up. This observation has led commentators to agree that Paul made up the word and later writers borrowed it from him.[326] On a practical level, the verb sends us to the scene of skilled workmen who cut and polished stones, created bronze dowels, drilled holes in the finished stones for these connecting dowels, and then heated and poured molten lead to secure the dowels in a bottom row of stones so that the next line of stones could be secured on top of them.[327] In a completely different vein, the verb is one of several that begin with the prefixing preposition συν- (*syn-*), whose basic sense is "with."[328] When examined, the force of these verbs pushes the reader to visualize Christ as the one to whom we

---

322. BDAG, 39–40; Louw-Nida, §7.44; Lincoln, *Ephesians,* 154–56.
323. Mosis, *TDOT,* 6:113, 119, quotation on 6:119.
324. Jeremias, *TDNT,* 1:792–93; Fowl, *Ephesians,* 98–99.
325. Michel, *TDNT,* 5:145–47; BDAG, 696–97; Barth, *Ephesians,* 1:272; Best, *Ephesians,* 286; Lincoln, *Ephesians,* 156; Winger, *Ephesians,* 336.
326. Barth, *Ephesians,* 1:272–73; Merkle, *Guide,* 82.
327. Barth, *Ephesians,* 1:272; Best, *Ephesians,* 286–87; Winger, *Ephesians,* 336.
328. BDAG, 961–62; Louw-Nida, §§89.105, 107.

are all attached, toward whom we are all directed (see the Notes on 2:5, 22; 3:6; 4:16).[329]

groweth: The intransitive verb αὐξάνω (*auxanō*) appears here with the meaning of growing.[330] Hence, we find an uncommon image that blends organic growth with the inorganic stone of a structure, a joining of planting and building (see 1 Cor. 3:9, "ye are God's husbandry, ye are God's building"). It is akin to the "living stones" of 1 Peter 2:5 (NIV). The present tense of the verb underlines the current, ongoing growth of believers "in the Lord" (see "in whom" at the beginning of 2:21 and 2:22).[331] Such a view contrasts sharply with the early Christian notion that the church would not survive beyond the earliest generation or two, falling headlong into apostasy (see the introduction section III, "Heresy, Apostasy, and Questions of Unity").[332] In such a light, the present tense, a seemingly small detail, brings us face-to-face with an early date for this letter, pushing it into Paul's lifetime (see the Note on 4:15).

an holy temple: This letter is full of allusions to temple matters (see the Notes on 1:4–7; 2:11, 14, 18, 21). Obviously, this temple consists of believers who, resting on the foundation of apostles and prophets and the cornerstone of Christ, manifest a spirit of holiness in their lives and invite a quality of sanctity into their actions. We discover such a concept that bears on assembled church members elsewhere in Paul's writings. For instance, he wrote to the Corinthian Saints "that ye are the temple of God" and that "the temple of God is holy, which temple ye are" (1 Cor. 3:16–17). Again, with an acknowledgment that our bodies are residing places of the Holy Ghost, he wrote, "Know ye not that your body is the temple of the Holy Ghost which is in you, . . . and ye are not your own?" (1 Cor. 6:19). Elsewhere, he presented the same doctrine—namely, that "ye are the temple of the living God." Then, paraphrasing and quoting Leviticus 26:11–12, he wrote that God himself "will dwell in them, and walk in them; and I will be their God, and they shall be my people" (2 Cor. 6:16; see also Jer. 31:33 and Ezek. 37:26–27). All this fits with Paul's teaching that steadfast believers form "an habitation of God through the Spirit" (2:22; see also 1 Pet. 2:5, "built up a spiritual house"), a concept that does not appear in the Old Testament.

---

329. Christian Maurer, *TDNT,* 7:856; Merkle, *Guide,* 82.

330. Blass and Debrunner, *Greek Grammar,* §101; BDAG, 151.

331. Gerhard Delling, *TDNT,* 8:518; Best, *Ephesians,* 287.

332. Hugh Nibley, "The Passing of the Primitive Church: Forty Variations on an Unpopular Theme," in *When the Lights Went Out: Three Studies on the Ancient Apostasy* (Salt Lake City: Deseret Book, 1970), 1–32.

holy: Any holiness that Paul's readers had received arose from being "in the Lord." As a part of this special relationship, they were to grasp that, potentially, "the Spirit of God dwelleth in you" (1 Cor. 3:16). In another place, with temple trimmings affixed, Paul pled with his readers "that ye present your bodies a living sacrifice, holy, acceptable unto God, which is your reasonable service" (Rom. 12:1).[333] This condition of believers could be brought to an end, of course, because "any man [could] defile the temple of God"—that is, defile themselves (1 Cor. 3:17; see also Heb. 2:1–3).

temple: The term is ναός (*naos*), a noun that very often points to the inner sanctuary of the Jerusalem temple rather than to the entire temple complex, which is usually represented by ἱερόν (*hieron*).[334] Hence, we are talking about the true meeting place between God and his children. Nothing in this letter, including the words in this verse, hints that the Jerusalem temple had already fallen (August of AD 70). Paul has simply adopted metaphorical language, as he often did, to make a point about the need for temple-like holiness in the lives of believers (see the Notes just above).

We see this metaphorical dimension in another place where he called "James, Cephas, and John . . . pillars" (Gal. 2:9). There, Paul adopted the term "pillars" (singular στῦλος, *stylos*) that is commonly associated with ancient temples. He applied this noun to three church leaders in Jerusalem[335]—namely, James the Lord's brother; Peter, who was known as Cephas ("rock" in Aramaic); and John the younger brother of James and one of the three leading apostles (see Mark 9:2; 14:33; etc.). We come upon the same image, which suggests a pattern, in the words of the Resurrected Christ when he declared that "him that overcometh will I make a pillar in the temple of my God, and he shall go no more out: and I will write upon him the name of my God" (Rev. 3:12).

In one significant vein, the celestial temple ultimately rests in heaven and is the residence of God. It was to this place that the prophet Isaiah was swept in vision and saw there "the Lord sitting upon a throne, high and lifted up . . . and the house [temple] was filled with [incense] smoke" (Isa. 6:1, 4; see also Ps. 11:4; 18:7 Hebrew Bible [18:6 KJV]). The book of Revelation adds detail to Isaiah's narration. In one passage, we learn that God, who "sitteth on the throne" in his heavenly temple, "shall dwell among" the faithful, an exalted

---

333. Procksch and Kuhn, *TDNT,* 1:106.

334. Gottlob Schrenk, *TDNT,* 3:235; Otto Michel, *TDNT,* 4:882, 885; BDAG, 470, 665–66; Louw-Nida, §§7.15–16.

335. Otto Michel, *TDNT,* 4:887; Wilckens, *TDNT,* 7:734–35.

and exalting promise (Rev. 7:15; see also John 14:23). At the end, we shall all hear "a great voice out of the temple of heaven, from the throne, saying, It is done" (Rev. 16:17; see also Rev. 11:19; 14:15, 17; 15:5-6; 16:1).[336]

One final point. In a measure, the members of the church became God's temple, and his promise was to dwell among them, thus securing believers as a people made holy because of God's presence. On the basis of these observations, scholars have dismissed the importance of the Jerusalem temple in Christian worship, arguing that it had run its course and was replaced by the spiritual temple embodied in the early church.[337] However, it is one thing to say that believers as an aggregate, living the gospel as they should, in effect become God's temple, which is what we have concluded above; it is quite another thing to maintain that the burgeoning church as an entity, complete with church officers and a few houses of worship, had taken the place of the temple, thus becoming the exclusive residence of God's Spirit. If this indeed were the case, then it is difficult to grasp the ongoing, undying Christian yearning for the temple.[338] To be sure, the future New Jerusalem will not possess a temple.[339] But that situation will arise because of God's enduring presence in that city (see Rev. 21:22-23).

2:22 *builded together:* We encounter another verb with a συν- (*syn-*) prefix, in this case συνοικοδομέω (*synoikodomeō*), which occurs only here in the New Testament (see the Notes on 2:5, 21; 4:16).[340] The passive voice leads us to God as the builder, and the present tense indicates that the process was then ongoing. The broad sweep of the *syn-* verbs in this letter ties each faithful believer directly and firmly to Christ: "quickened us together with Christ" (2:5), "raised us up together" (2:6), "made us sit together" (2:6), "framed together" (2:21), and "joined together" (4:16; see the Notes on 2:5-6). The nouns that begin with *syn-* carry much the same sense: "fellowcitizens" (2:19), "fellowheirs" (3:6), "of the same body" (3:6), and "partakers" (3:6; 5:7;[341] see the Note on 3:6).

for: The preposition is εἰς (*eis*), which when attached to the verb *synoiko-domeō* bears the meaning "into." Of course, we are dealing with a verb projecting its metaphorical sense. But we cannot completely strip away its

---

336. Schrenk, *TDNT,* 3:247; BDAG, 666.

337. Schrenk, *TDNT,* 3:246-47; Michel, *TDNT,* 4:887-88; Barth, *Ephesians,* 1:274; Lincoln, *Ephesians,* 159, 162, 165; Winger, *Ephesians,* 338.

338. Hugh Nibley, "Christian Envy of the Temple," in *When the Lights Went Out,* 55-88.

339. Michel, *TDNT,* 4:889.

340. BDAG, 974.

341. Merkle, *Guide,* 82.

literal essence. Truth be told, on one level, we run across workmen in this scene who are building believers "into a dwelling place of God" (2:22 NR), inserting them into the structure itself so that they make up its parts.[342]

habitation: In the New Testament, the only other occurrence of this noun (κατοικητήριον, *katoikētērion*) is found at Revelation 18:2, where it refers to "the habitation of devils" in fallen Babylon, a totally different image from that in our passage.[343] What becomes apparent is that even devils possess residences of some sort. In our text, in contrast, this residence or dwelling place belongs to God and is normally off limits to humans, though here, in a metaphorical manner, "the reference is to the spiritual edification of the whole community."[344] In other passages, the dwelling place is called God's "bosom" (see Moses 7:24, 47, 63, 69; and D&C 38:4; 88:13; compare John 14:23).[345]

The notion that conquered Babylon had become "the habitation of devils" (Rev. 18:2) may well go back to the Septuagint reading of Jeremiah 9:11, where the fallen Jerusalem is called "a dwelling place of serpents" or "a dwelling place of dragons" (κατοικητήριον δρακόντων, *katoikētērion drakontōn*; see also LXX Jer. 10:22 and LXX Nahum 2:12 [Nahum 2:11 KJV]). The Hebrew expression is "a lair of jackals" (Jer. 9:11; 10:22; 51:37 RSV).[346]

The noun *katoikētērion* occurs rather often in the Septuagint and touches also on God's dwelling place.[347] For example, in the song of Moses, God's abode is said to rest in a tabernacle that God himself had prepared: "Bring [thy people] in and plant them in the mountain of their inheritance, in thy prepared habitation, which thou, O Lord, hast prepared; the sanctuary, O Lord, which thine hands have made ready" (LXX Ex. 15:17; see also LXX Ps. 75:3 [76:2 in Hebrew Bible and KJV]). In a blend of the earthly and heavenly habitations of God, we discover that, in King Hezekiah's day, when "the priests [and] the Levites rose up and blessed the people[,] . . . their prayer came into [God's earthly] holy dwelling-place, even into heaven" (LXX 2 Chr. 30:27). Otherwise, God's abode is strictly in heaven. For instance, in Solomon's dedicatory prayer for the Jerusalem temple, he intoned that, when his fellow Israelites are in trouble in foreign lands, they

---

342. Michel, *TDNT*, 5:148; BDAG, 974; Lincoln, *Ephesians*, 158, 160; Winger, *Ephesians*, 338; Merkle, *Guide*, 82.

343. BDAG, 534–35.

344. Michel, *TDNT*, 5:156.

345. Draper, Brown, and Rhodes, *Pearl of Great Price*, 127.

346. Gesenius, *Hebrew-Chaldee Lexicon*, 492, 868; BDB, 733, 1072.

347. Michel, *TDNT*, 5:155; Lincoln, *Ephesians*, 158; Merkle, *Guide*, 82.

can "turn to [God] with all their heart . . . and pray," and God will "hear [them] out of heaven, out of thy prepared dwelling-place . . . and shalt be merciful to thy people" (LXX 2 Chr. 6:38–39; see also LXX 3 Kgs. 8:39, 43, 49 [1 Kgs. 8:39, 43, 49 KJV]; LXX 2 Chr. 6:30, 33; LXX Ps. 32:14 [Ps. 33:14 KJV]; and the Note on 3:17).

through the Spirit: In one sense, this prepositional phrase (ἐν πνεύματι, *en pneumati*), which could be translated "in the Spirit," as in the New Rendition, parallels the phrase "in the Lord" just above (2:21). In another, the ministry of "the Spirit" has now come to Gentiles—the "ye" of this verse. It is not to be a personal ministry of the Resurrected Christ among Gentiles but one that the spiritually attuned will grasp inwardly. This observation leads us directly to the words of the Risen Jesus that he uttered to a New World audience. On that occasion, he referred to his Old World disciples' lack of understanding about how Gentile believers would come to the truth of the gospel, saying, "They understood me not that the Gentiles should not at any time hear my voice—that I should not manifest myself unto them save it were by the Holy Ghost" (3 Ne. 15:23; see also Matt. 15:24 and 1 Pet. 1:12, "preached the gospel unto you with the Holy Ghost sent down from heaven"). In a prophecy uttered about six hundred years before Jesus' earthly ministry, we catch a similar thought: "The Messiah, . . . after he had been slain he should rise from the dead, and should make himself manifest, by the Holy Ghost, unto the Gentiles" (1 Ne. 10:11). Not surprisingly, by that Spirit, the "revelation [of] . . . the mystery of Christ" that has welcomed the Gentiles into the fold has come to the "apostles and prophets" (3:3–5). Moreover, for each individual the "guarantee of our inheritance" has been "sealed by the Holy Spirit of Promise" (1:14, 13 NR; see also the Notes on 1:13; 2:2, 18; 3:5, 16; 4:4; 5:9).[348]

Analysis of 2:11–22

These verses, 2:11–22, frame the high point of the letter and, as one might expect, shine a unified focus on Christ. In addition, they can be separated into three long paragraphs.[349] The first concerns the Gentile believers' former circumstance of "being aliens" and "being far off" from Christ (2:11–13). The second centers Christ's reconciliation of Jews and Gentiles on making the two of them into "one new man" (2:14–18). Within these lines,

---

348. Kleinknecht, Baumgärtel, Bieder, Sjöberg, and Schweizer, *TDNT,* 6:444–45.

349. Barth, *Ephesians,* 1:275–76; Lincoln, *Ephesians,* 159–60; Best, *Ephesians,* 236; Fowl, *Ephesians,* 84; Winger, *Ephesians,* 340.

some have detected a hymn, perhaps revised, about Christ's sweet "peace," which he has effected even in the face of a divisive, fracturing "middle wall" between Gentiles and Jews whose existence has led to serious "enmity." The third element introduces a welcoming notice to Gentile Christians that, along with fellow Jewish Christian believers, their spiritual lives rest on Christ as their foundation stone, each one enjoying a fellowship with all Saints, including "the apostles and prophets" (2:19–22).

In the first section (2:11–13), it appears that Paul's words to his Gentile readers derived entirely from his Jewish viewpoint. How so? Because he specifically called them "aliens from the commonwealth of Israel" before their conversion. Moreover, they had lived as "strangers from the [Old Testament] covenants of promise." These circumstances had left them adrift in their lives. Borrowing the language of scripture,[350] Paul continued to paint a dark picture of Gentiles' lives before they found the gospel, writing that they had "no hope, and [were] without God in the world" (2:12). Even though they were now "in Christ Jesus," they had been "far off" from true spiritual life, which had its beginnings inside "the commonwealth of Israel" (2:12–13). What is more strikingly Jewish, probably offering readers a glimpse into how his fellow Jews and even Paul himself commonly characterized Gentile neighbors, is his comment that they had been "called Uncircumcision" by the Jews, by those "called Circumcision" (2:11). It was almost as though the best way to view Gentiles was through a Jewish lens.[351] But he pulled back, for that was only part of the story.

At the end of this first segment, Paul wrote that now the Gentiles "are made nigh by the blood of Christ," completely repairing everything in their previous lives (2:13). At this moment, Paul plunged into his discussion of reconciliation through Christ that makes up his second part (2:14–18).[352] Fundamentally, Jews and Gentiles stand on the same ground. For "the law of commandments" from Moses did the Jews no lasting service (2:15).[353] To their aid and to the aid of the Gentiles came Christ, a tower of "peace" (see

---

350. Barth, *Ephesians*, 1:276.

351. Lincoln, *Ephesians*, 136, argues that this aspect sends us to "a Jewish Christian disciple of Paul" who was the author of Ephesians, a viewpoint that denies Paul's Jewishness.

352. Best, *Ephesians*, 247–50, reviewed the suggestions that an old hymn underlay 2:14–18 and found the proposals unconvincing. For a view that these verses present a hymn, see Grundmann, Hesse, de Jonge, and van der Woude, *TDNT*, 9:560 n. 433; Barth, *Ephesians*, 1:253, 260–62; and Lincoln, *Ephesians*, 159–60.

353. Lincoln, *Ephesians*, 163–64.

Acts 10:36) who, through his atoning actions, "made both [peoples] one" by knocking "down the middle wall of partition between [them]" (2:14), wholesomely reconciling "both [peoples] unto God" by slaying with "the cross . . . the enmity" that had divided Gentiles and Jews (2:16). The result? Stunningly, it is "through [Christ that] we both have access by one Spirit unto the Father" (2:18). Both groups needed Christ to perch them at a place where the Father was accessible.[354]

In the third part (2:19–22), Paul addressed Gentiles directly. Rather than sitting "far off" (2:13), doing the bidding of "the prince of the power of the air" (2:2), they were now "fellow citizens." But they were not citizens of the Jewish synagogue and certainly not under obligation to follow the Mosaic law. Instead, they were fellow members "with the saints," residing completely within "the household of God." Their lives as "strangers and foreigners" to the gospel message lay in the past (2:19). They could rejoice that they were structural stones in "the building fitly framed together [as the] . . . habitation of God." All this was made possible, of course, "through the Spirit" (2:19, 21–22). Almost beyond belief, within God's dwelling place, they could savor fellowship with "the apostles and prophets" as well as "Jesus Christ himself" (2:20).

Turning to the matter of authorship, the present tense of the verb "to grow" at 2:21 pushes a reader into the era of church growth during the early decades of the first century before the fall of Jerusalem and its temple in AD 70 (see the Note on 2:12). Even bigger are the references to "the enmity" between Gentiles and Jews (2:15–16). On a spiritual level, Christ of course had "abolished in his flesh the enmity" (2:15) because "he is our peace" (2:14). But what did this enmity consist of? Mere hostile glances between Gentiles and Jews in the marketplaces of cities and towns around the Roman world? It is plain that the double reference to "the enmity" hints at real events more than references to Gentiles being spiritually "dead in sins" (2:5), being called "Uncircumcison" (2:11) and "aliens" (2:12), and being "without Christ" and "without God" (2:12). Language like "hath broken down the middle wall" is too strong and points to a long, rough history of hostility and enmity. We compare Colossians 1:21, "You, that were . . . enemies . . . by wicked works."

In this light, we discover allusions to the relative dating of the letter's composition in two interesting expressions that stand almost side by side.

---

354. Lincoln, *Ephesians*, 159–60.

As noted, in his discussion of the inflow of Gentiles into the Christian fellowship, Paul wrote the expression "the enmity" twice. He also wrote about "making peace" (2:15–16). The usual approach to understanding these particulars acknowledges tensions between Jews and Gentiles wherever they lived side by side in the Roman Empire and then turns to an understanding of "enmity" and "making peace" in their scriptural senses—that is, Jesus' Atonement breaking down any enmity and making peace between the two groups.[355] Certainly, these are important observations, and they can fit here. But they do not exhaust all possibilities. As we observed in the Notes on 2:15 and 2:16, two historical events surge into view: deadly clashes between Jews and Gentiles in Alexandria, Egypt,[356] and Caesarea, Palestine,[357] in AD 38–40 and 59–60 respectively.

Perhaps significantly, the troubles in Caesarea broke out while Paul was under house arrest in the city, though Luke does not mention them (see Acts 23:33–35; 24:23).[358] In each case, in the face of discrimination, the minority Jewish population struggled for its civic rights that it had enjoyed for decades and longer. In each case, the majority Gentiles sought to keep these unwanted people in their places. In each case, the clashes led to physical harm, spoiling of property, and even death. In each case, delegations representing the disputing factions went to Rome to appeal to the reigning emperor, first Caligula and later Nero. In each case, the decision favored the Gentiles of the city, to the deep disappointment of the Jewish population.[359] We ask, Might these and other like events stand in the background of Paul's notation about the ending of enmity and the making of peace? Though we cannot be totally certain, the high probability is not to be discounted. As an added note, according to Josephus—likely writing with unrestrained exaggeration—before Vespasian and his troops arrived in Caesarea in AD 66 to lead the Roman military in its response to the Jewish uprising, the Gentile

---

355. For instance, see Barth, *Ephesians,* 1:264–66, 291–98; Fowl, *Ephesians,* 90–96; Winger, *Ephesians,* 322, 324–26.

356. Schürer, *History of the Jewish People,* 1:389–91, 398; 3:127–29, 132, 150–51, 153.

357. Schürer, *History of the Jewish People,* 1:465–67; 2:117, 183.

358. Josephus, *The Jewish War* 2.13.7 (§§266–70); Josephus, *Antiquities* 20.8.7 (§§173–78).

359. For Alexandria, see Philo, *In Flaccum* 4.16–24; 6–7.36–47; 7–8.52–57; 9–10.65–85; 11–12.95–106; Philo, *Legatio ad Gaium* 18.121–22; 19.127–31; 20.132–34, 137; 26–28.166–83; 2.185–88; Josephus, *Antiquities* 18.8.1 (§§257–60). For Caesarea, see Josephus, *Jewish War* 2.13.7 (§§266–70); 2.14.1 (§271); Josephus, *Antiquities* 20.8.7 (§§173–78); 20.8.9 (§§182–84); 20.14.4 (§§284–92).

citizens of Caesarea viciously turned on the Jewish inhabitants of the city and massacred twenty thousand of them "within one hour."[360]

All of these instances show Jews receiving the brunt of persecution at the hands of Gentiles. According to Paul in Ephesians, it was Jews who stood in a position to welcome Gentiles into the fold (see 2:11–13). This observation opens the door to criticism that might say, if severe Gentile persecutions of Jews lay in the background of Paul's letter, would he not have hinted at them when writing about Jews embracing these same Gentiles? In response, he effectively did this in his characterization of Gentile life before they came to Christ (see 2:1–3, 11–12).

In a doctrinal vein, these lines lay out the almost unspeakable truth that "we both have access by one Spirit unto the Father" (2:18). To this point in his letter, all that Paul has written about flows from the Father. As we noticed in the Note on 2:18, we are his children, sharing his heritage. For Paul wrote to the Roman Saints, "The Spirit itself beareth witness with our spirit, that we are the children of God" (Rom. 8:15–16; see also Deut. 32:6; Isa. 63:16; Gal. 4:6; Mosiah 5:7; and D&C 25:1). More than this, we shall be his heirs in the future. For "if [we are his] children, then [we are] heirs, heirs of God, and joint-heirs with Christ" (Rom. 8:17). As if this were not enough, modern scripture adds with notable specificity that "all that [the] Father hath shall be given unto [his faithful children]" (D&C 84:38).

As in the Note on 2:18, the Father is the guiding force behind both creation and redemption.[361] For he "hath chosen us in him before the foundation of the world" (1:4); he controls "all principality, and power, and might, and dominion, and every name that is named" (1:21); he sent Christ to offer "redemption through his blood, the forgiveness of sins" (1:7); he "raised [Christ] from the dead, and set him at his own right hand in the heavenly places" (1:20); he is the one for "whom the whole family in heaven and earth is named" (3:15); he "is above all, and through all, and in you all" (4:6). Hallelujah!

---

360. Josephus, *Jewish War* 2.18.1 (§457); 7.8.7 (§§361–62); Schürer, *History of the Jewish People,* 2:117.

361. Schrenk and Quell, *TDNT,* 5:1018–19.

Chapter 3

INTRODUCTION

Turning to face his Gentile readers in Asia Minor, the Apostle opened two vistas to them. First, he sketched why he, and no one else, had initially carried the gospel message into their midst (see Rom. 11:13). It was a "revelation" that not only set him on his current course but also uncovered for him "the mystery" of the divine plan to sweep Gentiles into God's kingdom, where they were to receive celestial nourishment—"the unsearchable riches of Christ"—from God's "apostles and prophets" (3:2–9). One is immediately taken back to Paul's experience with the Resurrected Jesus on the road to Damascus, where he was called as Christ's representative, later to learn that he was to bear Christ's word to the Gentiles (see Acts 9:1–17; 22:3–15; 26:11–20). The Lord Jesus, on his part, besides seizing Paul's attention and healing him of his temporary blindness through the faithful Ananias, revealed to the Apostle one important fact during the following days and months, as he had to "his holy apostles and prophets." Christ disclosed that the plan to bring Gentiles into the gospel fellowship was now activated and that this plan had not been revealed before that moment (see 3:5–6 and the Note on 3:3).[1]

---

1. For references to things that God has kept hidden "from before the foundation of the world," see Note on 3:5; D&C 76:7, 10, 12; 124:38, 41; 128:18; compare Isa. 48:6 ("I have shewed thee new things from this time, even hidden things"); Matt. 11:25 ("thou hast hid these things from the wise and prudent, and hast revealed them unto babes"); Luke 10:21; Mosiah 8:17 (by [seers] . . . shall secret things be made manifest, and hidden things shall come to light"); Alma 40:3 ("many mysteries which are kept, that no one knoweth . . . save God himself"); D&C 76:7 ("to them will I reveal all mysteries, yea, all the hidden mysteries of my kingdom from days of old"); 77:6 ("the hidden things of [God's] economy concerning this earth"); 89:19 ("great treasures of knowledge, even hidden treasures"); 101:32–33 ("hidden things which no man knew"); 123:13 ("all the hidden things of darkness").

The Apostle enclosed the second vista inside the words of a prayer, framing a sight like no other. Within this panorama, Paul pictured the inexpressible gifts that the believer will come to see and experience. Initially, he prayed that each individual would "be strengthened with power in the inner person through [God's] Spirit" (3:16 NR). Unbidden, this strengthening power would lift a church member in ways that she or he had never experienced, whether in a spiritual, physical, or emotional manner. Next, Christ would arrive "to dwell in your hearts by faith" (3:17), keeping a pledge that he had made to the Eleven the evening before he was crucified: "I will not leave you comfortless: I will come to you." More than this, the Father and the Son "will come unto [the believer], and make [their] abode with [that person]" (John 14:18, 23). At this point, Paul implored God that his readers would "be able to comprehend . . . what is the breadth, and length, and depth, and height . . . [of] the love of Christ, which passeth [human] knowledge." What is the end of all these indescribable blessings? It is "that ye might be filled with all the fulness of God" (3:18–19). And how do these gifts come to believers? They flow unasked for from "him who is able to do immeasurably more than all we ask" (3:20 NIV), which distantly recalls a line from modern scripture that our eternal rewards "without compulsory means . . . shall flow unto [us] forever and ever" (D&C 121:46).

"HE MADE KNOWN UNTO ME THE MYSTERY" (3:1–13)

King James Translation

1 For this cause I Paul, the prisoner of Jesus Christ for you Gentiles, 2 If ye have heard of the dispensation of the grace of God which is given me to you-ward: 3 How that by revelation he made known unto me the mystery; (as I wrote afore in few words, 4 Whereby, when ye read, ye may understand my knowledge in the mystery of Christ) 5 Which in other ages was not made known unto the sons of men, as it is now revealed unto his holy apostles and prophets by the Spirit; 6 That the Gentiles should be fellowheirs, and of the

New Rendition

1 For this reason I, Paul, the prisoner of Christ Jesus for you Gentiles— 2 assuming you have heard about the administration of God's grace that was given to me for you, 3 that by revelation the mystery was made known to me, as I have already written briefly. 4 When you read this, you will be able to perceive my understanding about the mystery of Christ, 5 which was not made known to people in other generations as it has now been revealed to his holy apostles and prophets in the Spirit: 6 the mystery is that the Gentiles are

same body, and partakers of his promise in Christ by the gospel: 7 Whereof I was made a minister, according to the gift of the grace of God given unto me by the effectual working of his power. 8 Unto me, who am less than the least of all saints, is this grace given, that I should preach among the Gentiles the unsearchable riches of Christ; 9 And to make all men see what is the fellowship of the mystery, which from the beginning of the world hath been hid in God, who created all things by Jesus Christ: 10 To the intent that now unto the principalities and powers in heavenly places might be known by the church the manifold wisdom of God, 11 According to the eternal purpose which he purposed in Christ Jesus our Lord: 12 In whom we have boldness and access with confidence by the faith of him. 13 Wherefore I desire that ye faint not at my tribulations for you, which is your glory.

fellow heirs, fellow members of the body, and fellow partakers of the promise in Christ Jesus through the gospel. 7 Of this gospel I have become a servant according to the gift of God's grace that was given to me by the handiwork of his power. 8 To me, the very least of all saints, this grace was given: to preach to the Gentiles the unsearchable wealth of Christ 9 and to illuminate for everyone the administration of the mystery that was hidden from the beginning in God who created all things. 10 This was done so that now, through the church, the manifold wisdom of God might be made known to the rulers and authorities in the heavenly realms, 11 according to the plan of the ages, which he set out in Christ Jesus, our Lord, 12 in whom we have courage and confident access through faith in him. 13 So then, I ask that you not lose heart because of my afflictions for you, which are your glory.

Notes on 3:1–13

3:1 *For this cause:* This phrase appears again in 3:14, where it resumes this opening line of chapter 3. Why? Because verse 3:1, an incomplete sentence, does not really lead into what follows immediately but only into 3:14 and what comes after that verse.[2] Hence, Paul's notation that he is a prisoner is made visual and concrete when we think of him bowing his "knees unto the Father" in his earnest effort to ask God's help for these Gentile church members (3:14). Further, the opening phrase points backward to Paul's comments about the integration of Gentiles into the spiritual temple of God (see 2:11–22, especially 2:19–22).[3]

I: The independent pronoun ἐγώ (*egō*) is emphatic. Here, the Apostle stresses his deeply personal link to the mission to the Gentiles in a way that

---

2. Barth, *Ephesians,* 1:327; Lincoln, *Ephesians,* 167, 172; Merkle, *Guide,* 85–86.
3. Best, *Ephesians,* 294; Larkin, *Handbook,* 48; Merkle, *Guide,* 86.

brings us face-to-face with Paul himself as the author of this letter.[4] Else-where, this pronoun stands as a certification of his authority on a subject (see 2 Cor. 10:1; Gal. 5:2; 1 Thes. 2:18; and Philem. 1:19).[5]

prisoner: Paul's status as a prisoner "for you Gentiles" ties this letter to those sent to the Philippians, to the Colossians, and to his friend Philemon (see Philip. 1:7, 13; Col. 4:3, 18; and Philem. 1:1). It is uncertain whether we are to think of a single imprisonment behind all of these epistles because elsewhere he wrote about being "often imprisoned" (2 Cor. 11:23 NEB). What is more, Paul has called himself a prisoner to underscore "his depen-dence on God as guardian in a patron-client relationship." Thus, he was both a prisoner dependent on a jailer in a stockade and a prisoner or servant dependent on God's grace (see also 4:1, 17–19, 22).[6] What is also important to notice is that, even if Paul sits in prison, "the word of God is not bound" by prison walls (2 Tim. 2:9; see also the Notes on 2:5; 4:1, 3; 6:20).[7]

you Gentiles: In most occurrences of the noun ἔθνος (*ethnos*), "Gentile" in the New Testament, this group of people are perceived to stand outside the people of God (see 2:12; Matt. 6:32; 10:5; Mark 10:33; Acts 14:16; etc.).[8] But here, recalling their position within "the household of God" (2:19), the Apostle places them within "the whole family in heaven and earth" (3:15), within reach of "the love of Christ, which passeth knowledge" (3:19), and within God's "power that worketh in us [believers]" (3:20).

3:2 *If ye have heard:* Generally, scholars take this expression as evidence that Paul did not write these lines because church members in Ephesus would have known Paul from his earlier, long stay in the city (c. AD 52–55;[9] see Acts 19:10; 20:31). But this view assumes, first, that most of Paul's former converts were all still living; second, that recent converts knew the story of his dramatic encounter with the Risen Christ; and, third, that the letter to the Ephesians was not a circular letter but was addressed specifically to members of the Ephesian congregation.[10] It is just as plausible to hold

---

4. As one might expect, this conclusion is disputed. On Paul as author, consult the views of K. L. Schmidt on the conception of the church in Ephesians as likely coming from Paul (*TDNT,* 3:511); Houlden, *Paul's Letters from Prison,* 295; Muddiman, *Ephesians,* 145–47; Merkle, *Guide,* 86.

5. Barth, *Ephesians,* 1:327; Best, *Ephesians,* 295.

6. Williams, *Paul's Metaphors,* 217; Schmidt, *Relational Grace,* 94–96, quotation on 94.

7. Friedrich, *TDNT,* 2:733.

8. Bertram and Schmidt, *TDNT,* 2:370–71.

9. Bruce, *Paul: Apostle of the Heart Set Free,* 475.

10. Houlden, *Paul's Letters from Prison,* 297; Lincoln, *Ephesians,* 173; Best, *Ephesians,* 297.

that, at this point in time, "the mutual acquaintance of the apostle and the Ephesians was based on indirect information."[11] In a notable change, the Joseph Smith Translation moves the entire expression to the beginning of 3:3 and replaces it with "for," which bears the sense "because of" (3:2 JST).

dispensation: In 1:10, the noun οἰκονομία (*oikonomia*) bears the meanings "(household) administration" or "plan of salvation," effectively God's activity of administering a plan or entity. Here, the term carries more of a sense of Paul's actual office as an administrator in the church (see Luke 16:2–4; 1 Cor. 9:17; and Col. 1:25).[12] This sliding from one denotation to another, from the divine realm to the mortal, which is of course under the direction of the divine, should not surprise a reader since such shifts happen in virtually all languages and in Paul's writings (see the Notes on 1:5, 9–11; 3:9).[13]

3:3 *by revelation:* This revelation cannot refer to Paul's experience with the Risen Christ on the road from Jerusalem to Damascus. Why not? Because, as far as our sources inform us, the disclosing of "the mystery" came to him later. Certainly, from the Risen Jesus and from Ananias, Paul learned that he was to go as a missionary to the Gentiles (see Acts 9:15; 22:15; 26:17). But no hint exists that at this time Paul learned that God had kept back the plan to sweep Gentiles into his kingdom (see also the Notes on 1:9, 17; 3:7). In a related vein, within this verse we meet three words that all have to do with revelation: the noun "revelation" (ἀποκάλυψις, *apokalypsis*),[14] the verb "to make known" (γνωρίζω, *gnōrizō*),[15] and the noun "mystery" (μυστήριον, *mystērion*).[16] Bundling these terms together in this manner underlines the divine, revelatory character of Paul's experience in coming to know God's will for himself.[17]

he made known unto me: Earlier, in 1:9, the Apostle had written that God had "made known unto us the mystery of his will," a declaration that embraces all of Paul's readers as recipients of God's revelatory gift. Such a statement was true, to be sure, because Gentile church members knew that God was the instigator of Paul's efforts to bring the gospel message to them. So far, so good. But in this passage, the Apostle signaled that he was a recipient of a

---

11. Barth, *Ephesians,* 1:328.

12. Michel, *TDNT,* 5:151–53; BDAG, 697–98; Louw-Nida, §30.68; Lincoln, *Ephesians,* 173–74.

13. Caird, *Letters,* 13–15, 23–24, 28–29.

14. BDAG, 112.

15. BDAG, 203.

16. BDAG, 661–2.

17. Best, *Ephesians,* 301–2.

particular revelation specifically granted to him that unpacked this "mystery." But he was not the only one. For in his days, this mystery was "now revealed unto [God's other] holy apostles and prophets" (3:5), fulfilling the need for more than one witness and ensuring that all church leaders would be on the same page (see the Notes on 1:9; 3:5; 4:20; 6:19).

the mystery: The Joseph Smith Translation expanded this term to "the mystery of Christ" (3:3 JST). With this adjustment, Joseph Smith placed the focus onto "the mystery" as linking to Christ, harmonizing with verse 3:4, rather than on welcoming "the Gentiles," who were now "fellowheirs" (3:6). Thus, in the JST, the stress falls on Christ as the instigator of welcoming the Gentiles into God's earthly and heavenly realms. Just as importantly, "the mystery of Christ" was revealed to Paul on that remarkable day when he traveled to Damascus (see Acts 9:3–5).

as I wrote afore: The verb προγράφω (*prographō*) is not about a prior correspondence from Paul, now lost, as the KJV translation might lead us to believe.[18] In fact, a number of commentators have suggested passages in a couple of Paul's other letters that this language might refer to, but without convincing results. Instead, Paul has sent us to something that he has written earlier in this letter,[19] likely to 1:9–10 and 2:11–22, where he has taken up both the mystery and the place of Gentiles in God's embrace.[20]

3:4 *Whereby:* The Greek expression πρὸς ὅ (*pros ho*) is unusual in the New Testament and carries the sense "in accordance with," inviting the audience members to make up their own minds about Paul's claim to revelation on the matter of taking the gospel to Gentiles. Importantly, he did not press his apostleship as the authority for what he had said, but rather revelation from God.[21] Further, this kind of invitation would not come from anyone other than the Apostle himself. It was not the sort of thing that would derive from a pseudonymous author.[22]

when ye read: This pointer to reading likely directs us into a public reading either in a church service or another gathering of church members[23]

---

18. Thayer, *Lexicon,* 538.

19. Gottlob Schrenk, *TDNT,* 1:770–72; BDAG, 867.

20. Barth, *Ephesians,* 1:329; Caird, *Letters,* 64; Lincoln, *Ephesians,* 175; Best, *Ephesians,* 302–3.

21. BDAG, 875.3.e.δ; Lincoln, *Ephesians,* 175–76; Winger, *Ephesians,* 357; Merkle, *Guide,* 88.

22. Caird, *Letters,* 64. Others hold to a different view. For instance, see Lincoln, *Ephesians,* 176–77; Best, *Ephesians,* 304.

23. Rudolf Bultmann, *TDNT,* 1:343; Barth, *Ephesians,* 1:330; Best, *Ephesians,* 303; Merkle, *Guide,* 88.

because many of Paul's audience were illiterate (see Col. 4:16; 1 Thes. 5:27; and Rev. 1:3). What Paul expects to become clear "is his insight, his grasp of the significance of the secret which God has disclosed [to him] in Christ."[24]

my knowledge: The Greek term σύνεσις (*synesis*) bears the meaning of understanding or comprehension (see Luke 2:47, where the word applies to Jesus).[25] Here, the concept links to the divinely granted knowledge or understanding that the Lord had handed to Paul on the road to Damascus. Surely, Paul was pulling out his authority for speaking, as he did about God's mystery entrusted to him, but not in a forceful or defensive way, as he did in other situations when his authority was challenged (see 1 Cor. 15:8–10; 2 Cor. 10:1–18; 11:4–6, 22–28; and Gal. 1:6–20; 2:1–10).[26] In a different vein, coming to this sort of comprehension—seeing or understanding as God does—is frequent in the callings of prophets (see Ex. 3:4–12; Isa. 6:1–13; Jer. 1:9–16; Hosea 1:2–9; Moses 6:26–36; Abr. 1:16–19; and JS–H 1:16–20). This sort of knowledge does not refer to the secular grasp of a topic (see 1 Cor. 1:19).[27]

the mystery of Christ: This expression can be thought of as the secret that undergirds the uniting of Jew and Gentile into one heavenly whole. This act of unification, of course, should be seen as a part of the larger effort to "gather together in one all things in Christ, both which are in heaven, and which are on earth" (1:10; see also the Notes on 1:9; 3:9; 5:32; 6:19).[28] Moreover, this mystery's disclosure has come by divine revelation, as the various terms associated with its unwrapping make visible ("revelation," 3:3; Rom. 16:25; "to reveal," 3:5; 1 Cor. 2:10; "to make known," 1:9; 3:3, 5; 6:19; Rom. 16:26; Col. 1:27; "to make manifest," Rom. 16:26; Col. 1:26).[29]

3:5 *was not made known . . . it is now revealed:* As we shall see in 3:9, the scriptural idea that God has kept back important principles and information until a later period of human history is not uncommon. For instance, in Luke 10:21, a passage that bears on the release of divine power through Jesus' disciples, we read that God has "hid these things from the wise and prudent, and hast revealed them unto babes" (see also Matt. 11:25). We can quickly multiply examples (see note 1 in this chapter; Rom. 16:25; 1 Cor. 2:7; Col. 1:26; D&C 124:41; and the Note on 3:9). At issue stands the question whether God has revealed everything from the beginning. The correct

---

24. Lincoln, *Ephesians,* 176.

25. BDAG, 970; Louw-Nida, §32.6.

26. Barth, *Ephesians,* 1:331; Lincoln, *Ephesians,* 176.

27. Best, *Ephesians,* 304.

28. Günther Bornkamm, *TDNT,* 4:820; Best, *Ephesians,* 304.

29. Bornkamm, *TDNT,* 4:821.

answer is no. That said, modern scripture often paints a picture that shows God entrusting to early generations more than is recorded in the Bible. For example, Adam and Eve learned by divine means that a Savior, "the Only Begotten of the Father," was to come and redeem them from their transgression that had led to the Fall (Moses 5:6–11). This event is nowhere recorded or hinted at in the biblical text. Enoch is another example of one who, in an extended vision, also found out about "the Righteous [One]," the Redeemer (Moses 7:45–47, 55–56). Neither the vision nor the information disclosed to Enoch about the coming Savior appears in the Bible (see the Notes on 1:9; 3:3, 10; 6:21).

ages: Though the singular of this noun can mean an "age" or era (γενεά, *genea*; see also Acts 14:16, "times"; 15:21), it usually carries the idea of a "generation" of people who lived at a specific time or who were descended from the same stock of people (see Matt. 1:17; 11:16; Mark 8:12; Luke 1:48, 50; etc.; see also the Notes on 1:21; 2:2, 7; 3:9, 11, 21).[30]

the sons of men: An unusual plural expression in Greek, appearing only here and in Mark 3:28 in the New Testament, it is not atypical in Hebrew or Aramaic, as its appearance in the Hebrew Bible and the Septuagint illustrate (see LXX Gen. 11:5; LXX Ps. 11:2, 9; 44:3; 48:3 [Ps. 12:1, 8; 45:2; 49:2 KJV]; LXX Joel 1:12; etc.).[31] The term translated "men" (ἄνθρωπος, *anthrōpos*) stresses the human character of persons.[32]

as: Though a small word (ὡς, *hōs*), its force in this context is to say that nothing in Old Testament literature could have prepared anyone to see this "new thing"—that is, to anticipate the church as "a new creation that transcends the categories of Jew and Gentile," welcoming both equally.[33]

now: This temporal adverb, νῦν (*nūn*), establishes the time when the "holy apostles and prophets" were functioning in the church—at the time of the writing of this epistle in contrast to "other [prior] generations" noted in this verse (3:5 NR;[34] see the Notes on 3:10; 5:8). It is not a pointer to a supposed earlier, bygone age during which the apostles and prophets were still active.[35]

is now revealed unto his holy apostles and prophets: The passive "is now revealed" leads us to God as the revealer. According to Colossians 1:26, the

30. Friedrich Büchsel, *TDNT*, 1:662–63; BDAG, 191–92; Louw-Nida, §§10.4, 28; 11.4; 67.144; Thayer, *Lexicon*, 112.

31. Herbert Haag, *TDOT*, 2:160–61.

32. BDAG, 79–82; Louw-Nida, §§9.1–2.

33. Lincoln, *Ephesians*, 177; see also Best, *Ephesians*, 305–6.

34. Gustav Stählin, *TDNT*, 4:1118; Hermann W. Beyer, *TDNT*, 2:703; Caird, *Letters*, 65.

35. Lincoln, *Ephesians*, 162; Best, *Ephesians*, 307, 309; Muddiman, *Ephesians*, 154.

"mystery . . . now is made manifest to his saints." Is this Colossian expression saying something different from this verse by saying that believers are recipients of God's revealed mystery? Or are we looking at the Saints as recipients of what the apostles and prophets have come to know and have taught in that current era? Likely the latter (see 3:5, 10; Acts 1:2; 1 Cor. 4:1;[36] D&C 66:2; and the Notes on 1:1; 2:20; 3:3; 4:11). As an added detail, already in the words of the Baptist (see Luke 3:7–8) and in a saying of Jesus (see Matt. 8:11 and Luke 13:29; see also the Note on 1:11), we see the promise that outsiders will be included in the kingdom. Efforts to apply the words "his holy" only to the apostles and not to the prophets in this expression seem to parse the words too finely.[37] The simple questions are whether God would shy away from claiming his own prophets in any age and whether he would consider them not to be holy, especially after inviting them into his councils (see Amos 3:7, where the noun translated "secret" means a council's plan or resolution;[38] see also Isa. 6:8–12; Jer. 23:14–22; and Alma 10:7, 9).

holy: As an adjective, the term ἅγιος (*hagios*) is often linked to the temple (see 2:20–21 and 1 Cor. 3:17; 6:19), thus drawing up not only ties to sacred sacrifice, as embodied in Christ's sacrifice (see 5:2 and 1 Cor. 5:7), but also links to the angels and other personalities who minister in the heavenly temple (see Isa. 6:1–7). This latter point comes clear in the invocation "Rejoice over [Babylon], O heaven! Rejoice, saints [heavenly holy ones] and apostles and prophets" (Rev. 18:20 NIV), where the "saints" or "holy ones" (*hagioi*) stand between heaven and the earthly representatives of God, the "apostles and prophets" (see also Dan. 7:22; Mark 8:38; Luke 9:26; and 1 Thes. 3:13).[39]

prophets: Unlike the apostles, who did not belong to individual congregations but to the church in general, prophets belonged to communities. We learn that occasionally more than one prophet resided in a congregation and were noted for the spirit of prophecy that had settled on them, just as on Old Testament prophets (see 1 Cor. 14:26–31). Moreover, in the end-time, they will be singled out for their special place in the kingdom, particularly those who have suffered martyrs' deaths (see Rev. 11:18; 16:6; 18:24;[40] and the Notes on 2:20; 4:11).

by the Spirit: The Spirit here has become the mediator of divine truths that go beyond the initial revelation of the Christ to investigators (see Acts 1:2).

---

36. Oepke, *TDNT*, 3:583.

37. Lincoln, *Ephesians*, 179–80.

38. Fabry, *TDOT*, 10:176.

39. Procksch and Kuhn, *TDNT*, 1:105, 109.

40. Rengstorf, *TDNT*, 1:423; Günther Bornkamm, *TDNT*, 6:669 n. 111; Krämer, Rendtorff, Meyer, and Friedrich, *TDNT*, 6:849–50, 853.

Such truths, noted in this letter, are made up of the ineffable gift of "the forgiveness of sins, according to the riches of [Christ's] grace" (1:7); "the surpassing strength of his power toward us" (1:19 NR), including the spiritual strengthening that comes to "the inner man" (3:16); "the manifold wisdom of God" made "known by the church" to its members (3:10; see also the Note thereon); the detection of "erroneous words" of apostasy (5:6 NR); and the sacred power residing in "the word of God," the scriptures (6:17).[41]

3:6 *That the Gentiles should be fellowheirs:* A person could argue that, in these words, we have reached the pinnacle of the epistle, the point that Paul has been aiming for all along. To be sure, he had set out this notion before this line, penning that Gentile converts had been "quickened ... together with Christ" (2:5) and were "no more strangers and foreigners, but fellowcitizens with the saints" (2:19). But these are all woven parts of a single fabric. Here, we meet the apex. These believers are now, and in the future, coheirs (συγκληρονόμος,[42] *synklēronomos*), holding a heavenly inheritance that stretches into the eternities (see Rom. 8:17; Heb. 11:9; and the Notes on 1:11, 14, 18; 5:5). But that is not the whole story. According to 1 Peter, this heirship is to be realized not in some state of austere loneliness, but rather with one's spouse, "*being heirs together* of the grace of life" (1 Pet. 3:7, emphasis added).[43] Not incidentally, such a passage hints strongly at standardized steps or ordinances that open this door to coheirship with one's spouse and, by implication, one's family. In addition, a heavenly heirship or inheritance always bears an unspoken promise of ruling and reigning in the hereafter (see Matt. 25:21; Luke 19:17; Rom. 5:17; and Rev. 1:6; 5:10; 20:4; 22:5; compare 1 Cor. 4:8;[44] see also the Notes on 2:10; 3:15; 4:1, 13, 20, 22, 24; 5:8, 14; 6:11, 13–14; and appendix 1).

fellowheirs: The noun συγκληρονόμος (*synklēronomos*),[45] translated "fellow heirs" in the New Rendition, stands as the first of three terms in this verse with the συν- (*syn-*) prefix, recalling the three verbs with the same prefix in 2:5–6, the noun "fellowcitizen" in 2:19, and the two verbs "fitly

---

41. Bornkamm, *TDNT*, 4:821; Kleinknecht, Baumgärtel, Bieder, Sjöberg, and Schweizer, *TDNT*, 6:444.

42. BDAG, 952.

43. Thayer, *Lexicon*, 593.

44. Foerster, *TDNT*, 3:783.

45. BDAG, 952. The συν- (*syn-*) prefix of each of the three terms is spelled differently because the "n" sound changes when it sits before certain other spoken sounds—to an "ng" phoneme before a "k," to an "s" before another "s," and to an "m" prior to another "m" sound.

framed together" and "builded together" in 2:21–22. Evidently, Paul in one vein wanted not only to capture the rolling euphony of words beginning with the same sound but also, in another vein, to envelop his message within lines easily remembered, even creating a new Greek term (see the next Note). Besides this, the earlier passages in chapter 2 were framed with Christianized Jews in mind, those with whom Gentile Christians were "fellowcitizens" and with whom they were together "built upon the foundation of the apostles and prophets" (2:19–20). But here, in a fresh manner, they are "fellowheirs" of Christ and "of the same body"—that is, Christ's body, in this regard standing independent of any others (see the Notes on 2:5–6, 19, 21–22).[46]

the same body: The adjective σύσσωμος (*syssōmos*) is not attested in Greek before Paul. Hence, it seems evident that this term is his invention that appears only in later Christian sources, nowhere else.[47] It is with this word that Paul turns us back to the unification of Gentiles with Jews "in one body"—that is, the crucified body of Christ and, by extension, the body of the church (2:16; 4:4).[48]

partakers: The third in the series of terms beginning with the prefix συν- (*syn-*), the noun συμμέτοχος (*summetochos*)[49] occurs in the New Testament only here and at 5:7. It is translated "fellow partakers" in the New Rendition to take account of the force of the prefix. Without the prefix, the term μέτοχος (*metochos*) means "partner."[50] The word *summetochos* in this verse directs us into the newly forged unity between Gentiles and believing Jews, but not unbelieving Jews. Why not? Because this unity rests "in Christ,"[51] not in the law. Further, Gentile church members are expected, like their Jewish fellow believers, to pursue their fellowship with Christ by "faithful perseverance." We read the following in Hebrews 3:14: "We have become partners [plural of *metochos*] with Christ if we hold tightly to our original confidence in him to the end" (Wayment).[52] The right to be called a "fellow partaker" does not come as a gift with no responsibilities attached (see the Note on 5:7).

---

46. Kleinknecht, Baumgärtel, Bieder, Sjöberg, and Schweizer, *TDNT,* 6:444–45; Lincoln, *Ephesians,* 180–81; for a different view, see Barth, *Ephesians,* 1:337; Best, *Ephesians,* 312; Fowl, *Ephesians,* 110.

47. BDAG, 978; Lincoln, *Ephesians,* 180; Best, *Ephesians,* 311–12.

48. Schweizer and Baumgärtel, *TDNT,* 7:1077–78, 1080; Lincoln, *Ephesians,* 180–81.

49. BDAG, 958; Louw-Nida, §57.8; Thayer, *Lexicon,* 596.

50. BDAG, 643.

51. Best, *Ephesians,* 312.

52. Hanse, *TDNT,* 2:831 n. 5, 832. The words "faithful perseverance" come from 2:832.

his promise: Believing Gentiles now take their places as recipients of the promise made to Abraham, whereas in earlier times, only Israelites did. As we learn from 2:11–22, that former promise has been co-opted by Christ through his "blood" and by his successful effort both to break "down the middle wall" and to eliminate "the enmity" that separated Jew and Gentile in earlier ages. What is more, standing just out of sight is the principle that the promise does not connect to the Mosaic law. Why not? Because, in Paul's view, if this law has become a governing part of God's promise through Christ, disobedience to the law brings the most serious consequences—namely, God's wrath, which, undeterred, will hunt down the lawbreaker. Rather, we access the promise through faith. We read, "If they which are of the law be heirs, faith is made void, and the promise made of none effect: because the law worketh wrath. . . . Therefore [the promise] is of faith . . . which is the faith of Abraham; who is the father of us all, (As it is written, I have made thee a father of many nations)" (Rom. 4:14–17). Expressed more sharply, we find that "if the inheritance be of the law, it is no more of promise: but God gave it to Abraham by promise" (Gal. 3:18).[53] Incidentally, the earliest and best manuscripts, including $\mathfrak{P}^{46}$, read "the promise" (NR) rather than "his promise" (see the Notes on 2:12, 15).

in Christ: The earliest and best manuscripts read differently, "in Christ Jesus" (NR). Paul is likely the originator of this sort of phrase.[54] In this verse, which forms the apex of Paul's remarks on the divine mystery that welcomes Gentiles, he points us to the individual who makes everything work for these children of God—namely, Jesus Christ, the one who offers to all "adoption . . . [as] children" (1:5), "redemption through his blood" (1:7), and full fellowship "with the saints, and of the household of God" (2:19). Because of Christ, none are excluded.

3:7 ***I was made a minister:*** Paul returns to his conversion experience, picking up a thread from 3:2–3, where he first touched on it. The recorded language of commissioning took different forms. When we appeal to a biographical source (that is, one not authored by the Apostle) we turn to Luke's book of Acts. In this book, three accounts go back to Paul, but he did not write them. In Luke's first rehearsal of Paul's experience, we brush but lightly against commissioning language. The Resurrected Lord said to Ananias, who would restore Paul's sight in Damascus, that Paul was "to bear [Jesus'] name before the Gentiles, and kings, and the children of Israel" (Acts 9:15).

---

53. Schniewind and Friedrich, *TDNT,* 2:582–84.
54. Oepke, *TDNT,* 2:541.

In a second scene that occurred on the northern boundary of the Jerusalem temple area, at the bottom of the staircase that led up into the Antonia Fortress, Paul told a Jewish audience about Ananias coming to him while he was blind and saying, "The God of our fathers hath chosen thee, that . . . thou shalt be his witness unto all men" (Acts 22:14–15). In this instance, we learn that Ananias not only knew what God had in mind for Paul but informed Paul of it. On a subsequent occasion, Paul spoke to King Agrippa within a central room in Herod's palace at Caesarea on the Mediterranean Sea coast. There, he quoted the Risen Savior as saying, "I have appeared unto thee . . . to make thee a minister and a witness . . . [to] the Gentiles, unto whom I now send thee" (Acts 26:16–17). We notice initially that, in this last passage, Ananias did not come into play as an intermediary; rather, Paul heard directly from the Savior. We also notice the verb "to send," the same that appears in accounts of the sending of the Twelve and the Seventy (ἀποστέλλω, *apostellō*; see Matt. 10:5; Mark 3:14; 6:7; and Luke 9:2; 10:1). This is a key commissioning term (see LXX Ex. 3:10, 13–15; Isa. 6:8; and Ezek. 2:3).[55]

When we come to Paul's abbreviated autobiographical story, which is encased in his letter to Galatian church members (see the further Note on 3:7), we pick up important language that is not identical to Luke's narrations. In the earliest reference to his experience, written before AD 50,[56] Paul declared that "it pleased God, who . . . called me by his grace, to reveal his Son in me, that I might preach him among the heathen [Gentiles]" (Gal. 1:15–16; compare Rom. 15:15–16; 1 Cor. 15:9–10; and 1 Tim. 1:12–14). This is Paul's clearest statement, and it emphasizes God's grace in calling the Apostle to preach to Gentiles, as does this line written to the Ephesians. A few verses later, when referring to a time following his days in Damascus, he wrote that when church leaders in Jerusalem "saw that the gospel of the uncircumcision was committed unto me" and that "the same [God] was mighty in me toward the Gentiles . . . they gave unto me and Barnabas the right hands of fellowship; that we should go unto the heathen, and they unto the circumcision" (Gal. 2:7–9). This acknowledgment by church leaders of Paul's divinely driven mission to Gentiles served to unify his ministry with that of the other apostles, who were proclaiming the gospel to Jews (see the Note on 3:3).[57]

---

55. Julie M. Smith, *The Gospel according to Mark* (Provo, Utah: BYU Studies, 2018), 222–23; Brown, *Testimony of Luke*, 445.

56. Bruce, *Paul: Apostle of the Heart Set Free*, 475.

57. Friedrich, *TDNT*, 2:733.

minister: Although the noun "minister" (διάκονος, *diakonos*) denotes "deacon" in some New Testament contexts (see Philip. 1:1 and 1 Tim. 3:8, 12), it here pertains to the Apostle. It usually carries the idea of servant or minister. In Paul's case, he often associates the term with God or Christ (see "minister of God" in Rom. 13:4; 2 Cor. 6:4; 1 Thes. 3:2; "minister of Christ" in 2 Cor. 11:23; 1 Tim. 4:6; and the feminine in Rom. 16:1).[58] In one instance, Paul wrote a different word for "minister," ὑπηρέτης (*hypēretēs*), which denotes "a helper" (see 1 Cor. 4:1; see also Acts 26:16, wherein the Risen Christ intends to make Paul a *hypēretēs*).[59] In other places, he preferred the term "servant" for himself (δοῦλος, *doulos*;[60] see Rom. 1:1; 2 Cor. 4:5; Gal. 1:10; Philip. 1:1; and Titus 1:1). Once he designated himself a "minister of Jesus Christ to the Gentiles . . . that the offering up of the Gentiles might be acceptable" (Rom. 15:16). Although the term "minister" (λειτουργός, *leitourgos*) usually has to do with government or temple workers (see Rom. 13:6 and Heb. 8:2),[61] in Romans 13:6 it carries a distinctive temple flavor because of the language of sacrifice.[62] What does all this mean? It seems apparent that Paul preferred always to portray himself as a subordinate serving under God's direction (see the Note on 6:21).

gift of the grace of God: This is not the only occasion when Paul has written the word "grace" (χάρις, *charis*) to frame the unlooked-for gift that God handed to him when he was rescued from the path of persecuting believers, a path that would have led him into the grinding grasp of an offended God (see Heb. 10:31). The earliest recorded instance was in his Epistle to the Galatians. There, he wrote concisely that "it pleased God, who . . . called me by his grace" (Gal. 1:15). Then, writing about his visit to church leaders in Jerusalem, he noted that "when James, Cephas [Peter], and John . . . perceived the grace that was given unto me, they gave to me and Barnabas the right hands of fellowship" (Gal. 2:9). A few years later, Paul wrote these lines to church members in Corinth: "I am the least of the apostles . . . because I persecuted the church of God. But by the grace of God I am what I am" (1 Cor. 15:9–10). Subsequent to that, Paul wrote his majestic letter to church members in Rome. In that epistle, he said that he would dare to instruct

---

58. BDAG, 230–31; Thayer, *Lexicon*, 138; Winger, *Ephesians*, 363–64.

59. Karl Heinrich Rengstorf, *TDNT*, 8:530–33, 542–43; BDAG, 1035; Louw-Nida, §35.20.

60. Karl Heinrich Rengstorf, *TDNT*, 2:261, 271, 276–77; BDAG, 259–60; Louw-Nida, §87.76.

61. BDAG, 591–92; Thayer, *Lexicon*, 376.

62. Hermann Strathmann and Rudolf Meyer, *TDNT*, 4:230.

these people whom he had not met "because of the grace that is given to me of God, that I should be a minister of Jesus Christ to the Gentiles" (Rom. 15:15–16; compare 1 Tim. 1:12–14; see also the Notes on 1:9, 16, 21; 2:7, 16; 3:8; and the Analysis of 1:3–14).[63]

effectual working: In the New Testament, this noun (ἐνέργεια, *energeia*), which signifies "action" and "working,"[64] and its associated verb (ἐνεργέω, *energeō*) always point to "the work of divine or demonic powers" (see 1:19; 4:16; Matt. 14:2; Mark 6:14; 1 Cor. 12:6; Philip. 3:21; 2 Thes. 2:9; etc.).[65] On the divine side stand "the word of God" (Heb. 4:12), the divine workings manifested in spiritual gifts (see 1 Cor. 12:6, 11), "the working of miracles" (1 Cor. 12:10; see also Rom. 15:18–19; 2 Cor. 12:12; and Gal. 3:5), the power of God that supports missionary efforts (see 1 Cor. 2:4; Col. 1:28–29; and 1 Thes. 1:5), the power that undergirds apostolic officeholders (see Gal. 2:8 and Col. 1:29), and the act of being brought to "salvation" itself (Philip. 2:12–13). On the negative side, particularly when the verb is in the middle voice, Paul focuses our attention on frightful activities in the world such as "sinful passions" (Rom. 7:5 NIV), mortal "death" (2 Cor. 4:11–12), and "the secret power of lawlessness" (2 Thes. 2:7 NIV; see the Notes on 1:11, 19; 3:20; 4:16).[66]

power: This power (δύναμις, *dynamis*), coming from God and manifested in Christ, once rescued Paul when the Risen Jesus turned him from his ill-conceived path of persecuting Christian believers by blinding him and crackling loudly in his ears, "Saul, Saul, why persecutes thou me?" (Acts 9:4; 22:7; 26:14). From experience, Paul later learned that, astonishingly, the Spirit could bring an inner strength to church members "with might [*dynamis*]," bracing "the inner man" (3:16). This power could also bring a person "to know the love of Christ, which passeth knowledge" (3:19), and to bask in "the peace of God," which transcends "all understanding" (Philip. 4:7). There is more to the story. For even more astonishingly, God "is able to do immeasurably more than all we ask or imagine according to his power [*dynamis*] that is at work within us" (3:20 NIV; see also the Notes on 1:21; 3:16, 20).

3:8 *less than the least:* Paul has written an unusual double comparison (ἐλαχιστότερος, *elachistoteros*) by which he effectively characterizes

63. Bednar, "In the Strength of the Lord," 121–28; Rasmus, "Enabling Power of the Atonement," 18–21; Schmidt, *Relational Grace,* 97.

64. BDAG, 335; Louw-Nida, §42.3.

65. Bertram, *TDNT,* 2:652.

66. Bertram, *TDNT,* 2:653–54.

himself as "the very least."[67] This judgment of himself reminds us of his self-effacement: "I am the least of the apostles, that I am not meet to be called an apostle, because I persecuted the church of God" (1 Cor. 15:9). The bright link between his self-effacing status and his former persecution of church members in both 1 Corinthians and Ephesians forms an obvious affirmation that the author of Ephesians is really Paul, not some later disciple who sought to place the Apostle on such a low platform. It will not do to claim, as some do, that a supposed later writer was interested in portraying the Apostle in the dreary dress of misrepresented modesty and humility.[68] Such an idea collapses because of its own pretension into weightlessness and inaccuracy (see the Notes on 1:23; 3:10, 21; 4:3, 21; 5:27; 6:3, 5; and the Analysis of 3:1–13; 6:1–9).

all saints: Although the early manuscript 𝔓[46] omits the word "saints" (plural of ἅγιος, *hagios*), this term is secure because of the plethora of texts that preserve it.[69] Paul was certainly not saying that he was less than all other people, which would be the case if "saints" is not original. Rather, although in 1 Corinthians 15:9 Paul was comparing himself to the other apostles, here he was contrasting himself to other church members, assuring them of his continuing humility in their service.[70]

this grace given: Paul left no doubt about what he meant by these words. The passive, of course, centers on God as the giver; this grace, he affirmed, allowed him to "preach among the Gentiles the unsearchable riches of Christ." Thus, God's grace had touched Paul in a personal, divine-directing way. It was not only that, unexpectedly, God had forgiven Paul's misguided actions to quash the primitive Christian movement but also that he was permitted to remedy these earlier actions by being sent to Gentiles while bearing the good news of Christ's redeeming gift. More than a century earlier, in a far-off land, another person named Alma, who had also mangled believers' hopes and faith, was offered forgiveness and the opportunity to repair some of the damage that he had done (see Alma 36:24–26). Such generous, sweet gifts say much to us about God's kind willingness to

---

67. Blass and Debrunner, *Greek Grammar*, §§60(2); 61(2); BDAG, 314; Thayer, *Lexicon*, 202.

68. Bruce, *Ephesians*, 12; Merkle, *Guide*, 94; Muddiman, *Ephesians*, 157. See Lincoln, *Ephesians*, 182–83; and Houlden, *Paul's Letters from Prison*, 300, for the view that an anonymous author created a fake humility here.

69. Best, *Ephesians*, 317.

70. Barth, *Ephesians*, 1:340.

save our souls and to undo our mistakes, those done both wittingly and unwittingly.

Not incidentally, the effort to say that the grace bestowed upon the Apostle in 1 Corinthians 15:9–10 "was the grace which saved Paul," whereas that noted in 3:8 was "the grace equipping him for his mission,"[71] is a viewpoint that hunts for reasons to discount Ephesians as the Apostle's letter. In fact, it runs aground on Paul's words to the Corinthian Saints that, because of "the grace of God . . . I labored more abundantly," bringing "the grace of God which was with me" to full fruition, an obvious reference to the Apostle's mission (1 Cor. 15:10). Speaking of Paul's mission of preaching the gospel, the mention of grace has subtly introduced the baptismal teaching that a person received before embracing the new faith. For that teaching included the twin doctrines that through Christ "we have redemption through his blood, [and] the forgiveness of sins, according to the riches of his grace" (1:7; see also Col. 1:14, 20; and the Note on 3:7).[72]

preach: As in 2:17, the verb εὐαγγελίζομαι (*euangelizomai*) hands to readers a richer sense than the customary verb "to preach" (κηρύσσω, *kēryssō*; see the Note on 2:17). A better translation would be "preach the gospel" (Rom. 1:15) or "bring glad tidings" (see Luke 2:10).[73] Besides the obvious meaning of declaring the good news "among the Gentiles," another stands close at hand—namely, the preaching of the gospel to the dead. Although this activity is not often touched on directly in the New Testament, it is "everywhere presupposed" (see 4:8–10; Matt. 12:40; Luke 4:18; Acts 2:27, 31; Rom. 10:7; Jude 1:6; and Rev. 1:18; see also Ps. 146:7 and Isa. 49:25; 53:12; 61:1).[74]

The two verbs *euangelizomai* and *kēryssō* undergird the two scriptural passages that come up for review in any discussion of Jesus' visit to the realm of departed spirits. We read, "For this cause was the gospel preached [passive of *euangelizomai*] also to them that are dead, that they might be judged according to men in the flesh" (1 Pet. 4:6). An earlier statement in the same epistle reads, "Christ also hath once suffered for sins, . . . being put to death in the flesh, but quickened by the Spirit: by which also he went and preached [*kēryssō*] unto the spirits in prison" (1 Pet. 3:18–19). One ancient source, the *Gospel of Nicodemus* 18.2–19.1, claims that Jesus

---

71. Best, *Ephesians*, 317.
72. Conzelmann and Zimmerli, *TDNT*, 9:397.
73. BDAG, 402, 543–44.
74. Oepke, *TDNT*, 2:424.

was joined by John the Baptist in his preaching efforts.[75] Such interest in departed spirits has to do with Jesus' determination to free those held captive by the devil, whether in this life or in the next. This divine determination set up a contest for the souls of men and women that has lasted since the days of Adam and Eve and has continued into the realm of the dead (see Luke 10:18–19; 11:21–22).[76]

According to modern scripture, "an innumerable company of the spirits of the just" who were "rejoicing together because the day of their deliverance was at hand" (D&C 138:12, 15) greeted Jesus' arrival in the place of dead spirits. While among them, Jesus "preached the everlasting gospel" and then "organized his forces . . . [to] carry the light of the gospel to them that were in darkness, . . . and thus was the gospel preached to the dead" (D&C 138:19, 30; see also D&C 138:36–37, 57). The earliest notice of a "prison" prepared for departed spirits occurs in Moses 7:38–39: "A prison have I [God] prepared for them" (see also D&C 29:38, "there is a place prepared for them from the beginning, which place is hell"). In the verses from Moses, we discover that God's "Chosen" had "pled before [his] face" for the souls of those who "shall perish in the floods." He was to suffer "for their sins" even though they were to remain in captivity. What was worse than imprisonment was the fact that "until that day [of the Atonement] they shall be in torment" (Moses 7:38–39). In an affirmation of the reality of this torment, we read elsewhere that "the Holy One of Israel . . . delivereth his saints from . . . that lake of fire and brimstone, which is endless torment" (2 Ne. 9:19; see also 2 Ne. 9:26). In a similar vein, "by the power of the resurrection of the Holy One of Israel," the inimical forces "death and hell must deliver up their dead, and hell must deliver up its captive spirits," a happy prospect (2 Ne. 9:12; see also D&C 21:6;[77] the Notes on 3:10, 19; 4:5, 9; 5:8; 6:10, 18; and the Analysis of 3:1–13; 4:1–16).

---

75. Edgar Hennecke and Wilhelm Schneemelcher, eds., *New Testament Apocrypha*, trans. R. McL. Wilson and others, 2 vols. (Philadelphia: Westminster Press, 1963, 1965), 1:471–72.

76. Joachim Jeremias, *TDNT*, 1:148–49; Delling, *TDNT*, 1:488–89; Friedrich, *TDNT*, 2:718–19; Albrecht Oepke, *TDNT*, 3:213; Grundmann, *TDNT*, 3:399–401; Büchsel, *TDNT*, 3:641–42; Friedrich, *TDNT*, 3:707–8; Joachim Jeremias, *TDNT*, 3:746–47; Johannes Schneider, *TDNT*, 4:597–98; Bornkamm, *TDNT*, 4:821–22; Traub and von Rad, *TDNT*, 5:525–26, 533; Friedrich Hauck and Siegfried Schulz, *TDNT*, 6:577–78; Schweizer and Baumgärtel, *TDNT*, 7:1078–79.

77. Brown, *Testimony of Luke*, 274, 568–70, 573–74; see 244–45 for a list of early Christian authors who took up the topic of Jesus' visit to the spirits in prison while his body lay in the tomb.

unsearchable: Appearing only twice in the New Testament, this term (ἀνεξιχνίαστος, *anexichniastos*) may go back to a liturgical or worship setting, as hinted by the rhetorically balanced nature of the Romans passage: "How unsearchable are his judgments, and how incomprehensible [*anexichniastos*] his ways" (Rom. 11:33, Wayment).[78] At base, the adjective bears the sense of "incomprehensible" or "fathomless."[79] The idea is that no imaginable limit can be assigned to God's gracious bounty.[80] Even though one may argue that, based on our verse, God's works and certainly God himself are beyond our comprehension,[81] we discover an intriguing statement in modern scripture which declares that "the day shall come when you shall comprehend even God, being quickened in him and by him" (D&C 88:49).

riches: The unfathomable "riches [plural of πλοῦτος, *ploutos*] of Christ," of course, ultimately come from the Father (see 2:4, 7; 3:14–16). In Paul's measure, worldly wealth does not come into play at all. For him, the only riches that count are those from God, who offers them to us through Christ. Perhaps oddly, such divine riches appear to be folly in the view of the world (see 1 Cor. 1:18, 23; 3:18). That condition is because those in the world lack the true "wisdom and knowledge of God" (Rom. 11:33; see also 1 Cor. 1:20, 24, 30; 12:8; and Col. 2:3). Christ came into possession of these heavenly riches by following an unusual path. For "though he was rich [in his premortal life], yet for your sakes he became poor [in mortality], that ye through his poverty might be rich [in eternity]" (2 Cor. 8:9; see also Philip. 2:7–9).[82] Notably for believers—that is, those of the terrestrial world—Paul prayed "that the God of our Lord Jesus Christ . . . may give to you the spirit of wisdom and revelation in knowing him . . . [that] you may know . . . the wealth of his glorious inheritance among the saints" (1:17–18 NR). Although God's riches are incomprehensible, they surely can be known and identified through the spirit of revelation and wisdom.

Another element may have been stirring in Paul's mind when he chose to highlight God's riches. During his extended residence in Ephesus (see Acts 19:10; 20:31), he surely had visited, perhaps multiple times, the magnificent temple built to Artemis or, as she is called in Roman sources, Diana. This stunning structure, standing a mere mile and a half from the commercial center

---

78. Erik Peterson, *TDNT,* 1:358.
79. BDAG, 77; Louw-Nida, §32.23.
80. Lincoln, *Ephesians,* 183.
81. Barth, *Ephesians,* 1:341.
82. Hauck and Kasch, *TDNT,* 6:328–29.

of Ephesus, was one of the seven wonders of the ancient world and drew pilgrims from all over the Mediterranean basin and far beyond. The temple covered an area twice the size of the Parthenon in Athens, and its 127 decorated marble columns soared sixty feet into the air. Its opulence, maintained largely by the donations of visitors, was well-known.[83] In contrast to the wealth on public display at this temple stood God's wealth, undisturbed by time and everlasting in its nature (see the Notes on 1:7, 18; 2:4, 7; 3:16).

3:9 to make all men see: The verb φωτίζω (*phōtizō*), "to illuminate, enlighten,"[84] has already appeared in 1:18, where it treats the enlightenment that has allowed Gentiles, with celestial aid, to grasp what are to others the incomprehensible workings of God—to understand "what is the surpassing greatness of [God's] power toward us" (1:19 NR). In time, church members could ask with Paul, "What communion hath light with darkness?" (2 Cor. 6:14). Now they knew the difference. The associations of the verb *phōtizō* in other sources is illuminating. For instance, we notice "the true Light, which lighteth [*phōtizō*] every man that cometh into the world" (John 1:9; see also D&C 84:45–47; 88:6–13; 93:2), a private and spiritual manifestation that comes unbidden to each person born into this world and that is often called "the light of Christ."[85] In Paul's frame of reference, when God lightens our souls, "with the eyes of your heart enlightened" (1:18 NR), we thereafter follow a different course in our lives, designing a new existence, a new beginning (see Rom. 13:12 and 1 Thes. 5:5).[86]

In a very different vein, tucked into descriptions of heavenly glory at the end-time instead of the enlightenment that accompanies birth and beginnings, we encounter this: "The [heavenly Jerusalem] had no need of the sun, . . . for the glory of God did lighten [*phōtizō*] it, and the Lamb of God is the light thereof" (Rev. 21:23). Buttressing this claim, further on we read, "There shall be no night there; . . . for the Lord God giveth them light [*phōtizō*]: and they shall reign for ever and ever" (Rev. 22:5; see also Isa. 60:19, "the sun shall be no more thy light by day; neither for brightness shall the moon give light unto thee: but the Lord shall be unto thee an everlasting light").[87] Thus, the enlightenment from God comes both at the beginning of mortal life and throughout eternal life (see the Notes on 1:18; 5:8, 14).

---

83. Pliny, *Natural History* 36.21; Williams, *Paul's Metaphors*, 185.
84. BDAG, 1074; Louw-Nida, §28.36; Thayer, *Lexicon*, 663.
85. Robinson and Garrett, *Commentary on the Doctrine and Covenants*, 3:50, 102–3; McConkie and Ostler, *Revelations of the Restoration*, 606–7, 628–29, 667.
86. Hans Conzelmann, *TDNT*, 9:347–48.
87. Draper and Rhodes, *Revelation of John the Apostle*, 818.

fellowship: Translated "dispensation" at 1:10 and 3:2, a better meaning here for οἰκονομία (*oikonomia*) would be "administration" (NR) or "premortal plan" because of its connection to "the beginning of the world."[88] It is God who has quietly held aside this secret plan to make "the Gentiles . . . fellowheirs, and of the same body" with Jews (3:6), creating by this means a genuine fellowship that abolished "the enmity" that had bedeviled relationships and gave "both . . . access by one Spirit unto the Father" (2:15–16, 18; see also the Notes on 1:5, 9–11; 3:2).

mystery: As affirmed here, this mystery (μυστήριον, *mystērion*) "hath been hid in God." It consisted of a hidden plan to introduce the Gentiles into God's kingdom, both here and hereafter, making them "fellow citizens with the saints and members of God's [eternal] family" (2:19 NR). In another place, Paul declared that "the mystery, which was kept secret since the world began, . . . now is made manifest, and by the scriptures [writings] of the prophets . . . [is] made known to all nations" (Rom. 16:25–26).[89] Where might we hear that prophetic voice? The earliest hint sits not in the prophetic books but in the book of Genesis. For in the catalog of the ancestors of the nations of the earth—that is, the Gentile nations—a person counts seventy ancestral names in the Hebrew Bible (see Gen. 10:2–29). To be sure, the Septuagint adds two names so that its total is seventy-two.[90] And the ambiguity between seventy and seventy-two persists among the manuscripts of Luke 10:1 and 10:17, which recount Jesus' call of other disciples besides the Twelve. But seventy is the original number, not seventy-two.[91]

Why is this significant? Because as we have noticed, seventy represents the number of Gentile nations descended from the sons of Noah (see Gen. 10:32). Hence, the number's appearances elsewhere direct us to Gentiles, specifically in the books of Exodus, Numbers, and Ezekiel. Even though the following incidents have nothing to do directly with Gentiles, the number seventy itself stands as a reminder of God's interest in these outside people. In the first, the Lord commanded Moses to lead Aaron, his two sons, "and seventy of the elders of Israel" onto the sacred mountain where "they saw the God of Israel . . . and did eat and drink" in an act of covenant

---

88. Michel, *TDNT*, 5:151–52; BDAG, 697–98, 2(b); Louw-Nida, §30.68.

89. Conzelmann, *TDNT*, 9:348 n. 309.

90. The additional names appear in LXX Gen. 10:2 (Elisha following Jovan) and 10:22 (Cainan following Aram).

91. S. Kent Brown, "The Seventy in Scripture," in *By Study and Also By Faith: Essays in Honor of Hugh W. Nibley,* ed. John M. Lundquist and Stephen D. Ricks, 2 vols. (Salt Lake City: Deseret Book; Provo, Utah: FARMS, 1990), 1:25–45.

ratification (Ex. 24:1, 10–11). In a second, the Lord directed Moses to gather seventy of the Hebrew elders to the tabernacle where God's spirit came to rest on them to such a pitch that they began to prophesy and did not stop, a sign that henceforth these men would assist Moses in his continuing duties (see Num. 11:16, 24–25). The third arises in Ezekiel's book and indirectly has to do with Gentile influences, most likely from Egypt. In a vision of the Jerusalem temple, Ezekiel, whose residence was in far-off Babylon, was shown an inner chamber wherein "seventy elders of the house of Israel" had gathered and, in an act of misguided devotion, were worshiping in front of paintings that pictured "all kinds of crawling things and detestable animals and all the idols of the house of Israel" (Ezek. 8:10–11 NIV). But the story does not end on this negative note.

The Old Testament features an outreach well beyond the Israelite nation. For instance, foreigners were allowed to join Sabbath worship (see Lev. 25:6) and to pray "in this house [the temple]" so that, in a public information move, "all people of the earth may know [God's] name, and fear [him]" (2 Chr. 6:32–33; see also 1 Kgs. 8:41–43). Beyond this, it is among Isaiah's prophecies that we hear the prophetic voice and begin to grasp how God intends to reach out to "strangers." In the Lord's words to Isaiah, we come upon this directive: "Let not the foreigner who has joined himself to the Lord say, 'The Lord will surely separate me from his people'" (Isa. 56:3 RSV). As hinted here, there is more. To make matters perfectly clear that he will not push strangers away, the Lord invitingly intones, "The foreigners who join themselves to the Lord, . . . to love the name of the Lord, and to be his servants, everyone who keeps the sabbath, . . . and holds fast my covenant—these will I bring to my holy mountain, and make them joyful in my house of prayer [the temple]; for my house shall be called a house of prayer for all peoples" (Isa. 56:6–7 RSV). Clearly, everyone is welcome within God's kingdom, for, as a remarkable saying affirms, "all are alike unto God" (2 Ne. 26:33; see also the Notes on 1:9; 3:4–5; 5:32; 6:19).

from the beginning of the world: The issue has to do with how αἰών (*aiōn*) in the plural is to be understood. Translated here as "the beginning of the world," does it center on past "ages" of the world (see 3:21), or does it take on the meaning of "eternal" (3:11), or does it refer to divine "beings" from the unseen world as we might find in writings from an author like Plato?[92] To suggest that Paul, the prized product of Jewish schools, here

---

92. BDAG, 32–33; Louw-Nida, §§12.44; 67.133. Barth, *Ephesians*, 1:343–44, holds that the mystery was hidden from both earthbound humans and heavenly personalities.

points to "beings" in the unseen world, the last option, ascribes to him an understanding of Greco-Roman philosophy which he has brought forward only in this passage and nowhere else in his writings. Two connections now need discussion.

First, it is true that this letter sends readers to the unseen world, which is populated not only by Satan, "the prince of the power of the air" (2:2), but also by "principalities, . . . powers, . . . [and] rulers of the darkness of this world" (6:12; see also 1:21). Hence, in this Epistle, Paul is thinking about spaces beyond this earth. Second, in Colossians 1:26, we discover the following: "the mystery which hath been hid from ages [*aiōn*] and from generations [*genea*]," making these two terms—"ages" and "generations"—virtually the same. When we come to Ephesians, we discover that several written lines stand between God's hiding of the mystery of Gentile inclusion from the "people in other generations [*genea*]" (3:5 NR) and his secretive activity "from the beginning [*aiōn*]" that, in his own time, he would reveal to all creatures (3:9 NR). The separation of these nouns in Paul's text opens the possibility that God's mystery was hidden not only from generations of earthly people (*genea*) but also from those "beings" (*aiōn*) who inhabit the unseen world, if we adjust the translation of *aiōn* to this sense. However, for the reason already noted about Paul's Jewish education, it would be utterly sensational if in fact he was producing here a meaning for *aiōn* that was at home in the Platonic schools of thought.

Rather, it seems the better part of wisdom to let what Paul has written elsewhere be our guide. Notably, in Paul's First Epistle to the Corinthians, we discover the following about earlier epochs and the current one: "We impart a secret and hidden wisdom of God, which God decreed before the ages [*aiōn*] for our glorification. None of the rulers of this age [*aiōn*] understood this" (1 Cor. 2:7–8 RSV; see also the Notes on 1:21; 2:2, 7; 3:5, 11, 21).

created all things: Although we have heard the peals of praise for God creating a spiritually new person, usually called a new man (see 2:10, 15; 4:24; and Col. 3:10), here the joyous line celebrates God's earliest creation of "all things" (see Col. 1:16; Rev. 4:11; 10:6; and the Notes on 2:10, 15; 4:24).[93]

by Jesus Christ: This phrase is present only in late manuscripts and is unattested in the earlier texts, especially 𝔓[46]. Even though the words were added by a later copyist and are doctrinally correct, they were not part of Paul's letter.[94]

---

93. Lincoln, *Ephesians*, 185.
94. Metzger, *Textual Commentary*, 535; Merkle, *Guide*, 95.

3:10 *To the intent:* The particle ἵνα (*hina*) here introduces a purpose clause, "in order that," which is followed by a subjunctive form of the passive verb "to be known." It draws in the force of the prior two infinitives, "to preach" (3:8) and "to make known" (3:9), in order that we may grasp the strength or role of the church in making known "the manifold wisdom of God" to "the principalities and powers in heavenly places" (3:10).[95]

now: The appearance of this temporal adverb, νῦν (*nūn*), fixes the time as the current moment, the same as when the mystery was "revealed unto his holy apostles and prophets" (3:5; see also the Notes on 3:5; 5:8).

principalities and powers: As noted in the discussion on 1:21, the plural of the noun ἀρχή (*archē*), rendered here as "principalities," always directs us to impersonal powers in the New Testament except in one instance outside Ephesians. At Luke 12:11, we meet it translated in the KJV as "magistrates" of Roman courts. In the case of the term translated "powers" (ἐξουσία, *exousia*), we have already established that these entities or personalities operate with God's permission. Furthermore, according to Paul, such powers in the earthly sphere operate in governments with God's leave. We come upon what Paul wrote to church members in Rome when he noted the positive functions of "the higher powers [*exousia*]." There, he held that "every soul [should] be subject unto the higher powers [*exousia*]." Why? "[Because] there is no power [*exousia*] but of God: the powers that be are ordained of God. Whosoever therefore resisteth the power [*exousia*], resisteth the ordinance of God" (Rom. 13:1–2; see also Rom. 13:3). Thus, we are to subject ourselves to these powers because God stands behind them, making them a beneficent influence in our lives. Our verse here, 3:10, steps beyond this passage, Romans 13:1–2, and provides a fogless lens for seeing the personalities of these "principalities and powers" as possessing good qualities, at least in this case.[96] How so? Simply stated, according to this verse, they reside "in heavenly places" and are the beneficiaries of the work of "the church," which discloses to them "the manifold wisdom of God" (see the Note on 1:21).

As in the other appearances of these persons (that is, the "principalities and powers" of 1:21 and 6:12) such individuals are citizens of the unseen world. Moreover, and perhaps oddly, in 3:10 they enjoy a link to the earthly

---

95. Lincoln, *Ephesians*, 185.

96. Bornkamm, *TDNT*, 4:821–22. Others hold that these individuals are inimical to God's purposes. For instance, see Lincoln, *Ephesians*, 187; Best, *Ephesians*, 322–23, 327; Winger, *Ephesians*, 369.

church, as we have noticed. What could that link possibly consist of? Was Paul writing about angels? Certainly not. Elsewhere in his writings, when he deals with angels, he does so without any varnish: "I am sure that neither death, nor life, nor angels, nor principalities [plural of *archē*], nor things present, nor things to come, nor powers [plural of *dynamis*], ... will be able to separate us from the love of God in Christ Jesus our Lord" (Rom. 8:38–39 RSV; see also 1 Cor. 4:9; 13:1; 2 Thes. 1:7; and Titus 3:1).[97]

We now have to ask whether these persons are known in scripture as inhabitants of the heavenly world, such as cherubim or seraphim. Likely not. In the Hebrew Bible, the mention of cherubim, a masculine plural noun in Hebrew, leads us first to the divine garden where sacred plants grew. Here, they were involved in protecting the pathway into God's garden according to Genesis 3:24 and Moses 4:31 ("[God] placed at the east [entrance] of the garden of Eden cherubims and a flaming sword ... to keep the way of the tree of life"). The term also brings us to winged creatures that are involved in transporting God. It is Ezekiel's initial vision that portrays most clearly the role of winged cherubim in taking God from one place to another on his chariot-throne. We read, "When they went, they went in any of their four directions without turning as they went. ... And when they went, I heard the sound of their wings like the sound of many waters, like the thunder of the Almighty, ... when they stood still, they let down their wings" (Ezek. 1:17, 24 RSV; see also Deut. 33:26; Isa. 19:1; and Ps. 68:4, 33; 104:3).[98]

Seraphim, a masculine plural noun too, presents a different picture. But the result is the same—no connection to our passage. In the view of some, these creatures were like serpents or Uraeus figures that, poised above a deity, offered protection. That might explain how the seraphim in Isaiah's call-vision were allowed to perch above the Lord's throne where a human-like creature would not normally stand. Certainly, in the iconography of the Ancient Near East, no human-like persons are ever pictured as sitting or standing above a god. Yet the seraphim of Isaiah 6 exhibit human characteristics, including faces, feet, and singing voices. Their distinctive traits arise from their six wings and, when authorized, their atoning acts, one of which cleansed Isaiah of his sins. For the seraphic creature that flew to

97. The KJV follows manuscripts that preserve a different order in this verse and are later than the earliest texts, exhibiting a copyist's influence that resulted in a changed order of Paul's list; see Metzger, *Textual Commentary*, 458–59.

98. David Noel Freedman and Michael Patrick O'Connor, *TDOT*, 7:310–13.

Isaiah holding a hot coal with tongs said to him, "Thine iniquity is taken away, and thy sin purged" (Isa. 6:6).[99] But because such creatures dwell in the presence of God, there is nothing that the earthly church can teach or offer them.

We are now left to ask this question: Do "the principalities and powers," these persons of the unseen world, reside in the spirit prison?[100] Asked another way, Does the church's efforts to carry on the redeeming work of Jesus for the departed dead affect those in the unseen world? This matter comes to the fore when we observe that in 3:10 the church is involved in making known God's wisdom to these "principalities and powers," presumably by preaching. To be sure, we saw earlier that the same two Greek nouns appear in three passages in the letter. But the context of each differs. Clearly, in 1:21, they are part of the realm surmounted by the now-exalted Jesus. Here in 3:10, we detect no judgment about their sinful or righteous state. In 6:12, by contrast, the nouns are to be understood as linked to "the darkness of this world" and "spiritual wickedness in high places." Even so, might we think of these personalities, *archē* and *exousia,* as redeemable from their earlier misspent sojourns on the earth? That such redemption might come through the aid of the church is not beyond our comprehension nor beyond New Testament evidence.[101] After all, in the church of Paul's day, people were "baptizing for the dead" in acts of compassion and salvation (1 Cor. 15:29; see the Notes on 1:21; 2:2; 6:12).[102] This is not all.

In chapter 4, we spot a brief discussion of Jesus' descent "into the lower parts of the earth" (4:9). This event is not his burial but his descent into the world of departed spirits, carrying with him the power to allow them to "come to God's life in the Spirit" (1 Pet. 4:6, Jerusalem Bible). Significantly, this short introduction to Christ's descent and ascent (see 4:8–10) stands directly in front of, and thus is tied closely to, the notice of church organization and its purpose—"apostles ... prophets ... evangelists ... pastors and teachers" (4:11). Why? "For the perfecting of the saints, for the work of the ministry, for the edifying of the body of Christ" (4:11–12). Unless

---

99. Udo Rütersworden, *TDOT,* 14:223–28.

100. Best, *Ephesians,* 325, also opens this possibility.

101. Jeremias, *TDNT,* 1:148–49; Delling, *TDNT,* 1:488–89; Friedrich, *TDNT,* 2:718–19; Oepke, *TDNT,* 3:213; Grundmann, *TDNT,* 3:399–401; Büchsel, *TDNT,* 3:641–42; Friedrich, *TDNT,* 3:707–8; Jeremias, *TDNT,* 3:746–47; Schneider, *TDNT,* 4:597–98; Bornkamm, *TDNT,* 4:821–22; Traub and von Rad, *TDNT,* 5:525–26, 533; Hauck and Schulz, *TDNT,* 6:577–78; Schweizer and Baumgärtel, *TDNT,* 7:1078–79.

102. Harald Riesenfeld, *TDNT,* 8:512–13.

we insist on holding to the notion that the now-edified church, the "body of Christ," consisted only of mortal church members and did not include those whom he had rescued from the spirit prison, we must insist that Jesus' descent was an act that came up short. How so? Because his effort to carry the gospel to those in the spirit prison had no effect and did not rescue them from their sinful pasts or include them within the larger congregation of believers. But that is not what scripture says (see Rom. 14:9; 1 Pet. 3:18–20; 4:6; and note 101 in this chapter). Hence, placing Jesus' descent and the church's organization side by side is a compelling observation that the church has had much to do with redeeming the dead (see the Notes on 3:8, 19; 4:5, 8–10; 5:8; 6:10, 18; and the Analysis of 3:1–13; 4:1–16).

heavenly places: A better translation is "heavenly realms" for the phrase ἐν τοῖς ἐπουρανίοις (*en tois epouraniois*). The plural is curious. It could bear on the places or "mansions" promised to the faithful (see John 14:2 and D&C 59:2; 72:4) or on the notion that the unseen world is made up of separate regions populated by good personalities and bad (see the Notes on 1:3, 20; 2:6; 6:12; and the Analysis of 1:15–23).

known: The process is revelatory. That is to say, the church is the agency for disclosing the secret of "the manifold wisdom of God" to "the principalities and powers" whom Paul had in mind. To be sure, this mystery, this elevating revelation resides "in Christ" (3:11).[103] But here the church takes its rightful place as the dispenser of celestial truth (see the Notes on 1:9; 3:3, 5; 6:21).

by the church: As Christ's "body," the church takes its directions from him, executes his will, and serves as the agent that dispenses his truth. Because all revelation comes from God, its dissemination through any instrument, including the church, is by his inspiration and consent. Thus, ideally the church is to stand above human decision-making and the sharp-elbow jockeying that often invades earthly institutions, including governments. Moreover, its authorized leaders, specifically apostles, carry the power to bind and loose "on earth," acts which bear consequences "in heaven" (Matt. 16:19; 18:18).[104] Such power points to the redemptive work for the dead (see Rom. 14:9; 1 Cor. 15:29; 1 Pet. 3:18–19; 4:6; see also Rev. 11:18; and D&C 127:7; 128:8). In a different vein, the phrase διὰ τῆς ἐκκλησίας (*dia tēs ekklēsias*), which occurs only here in the New Testament, could be

---

103. Bornkamm, *TDNT,* 4:821–22.
104. Houlden, *Paul's Letters from Prison,* 301.

translated "through the church" (NR) with the same effect (see the Notes on 1:22; 3:21; 4:11–12; 5:27).

manifold: This appearance of the adjective πολυποίκιλος (*polypoikilos*) is the only one in the New Testament. It bears the basic sense of "many and diverse" or "many-sided," underlining that God's wisdom does not run in one track but in innumerable paths.[105] More than that, true wisdom always comes from God and from no other source (see Job 28).

wisdom: Often portrayed as a female person (see Prov. 8:22–36; Mosiah 2:36; 8:20; and Hel. 12:5), here wisdom exhibits her practical side, wherein the purposes of God are made known. In one sense, wisdom is the equivalent of "mystery" in this letter (see the Notes on 1:8, 17; 5:15).[106]

3:11 *the eternal purpose:* The freshly disclosed role of the church in making known the wisdom of God to citizens of the unseen world (see 3:10) stands in accord with God's purpose, his eternal purpose. In its earlier occurrence at 1:11, the term πρόθεσις (*prothesis*) bears the sense of God's eternal "purpose" or plan that was set out in the premortal world.[107] In our current context, it is apparent that the role of the church in manifesting God's wisdom was framed in that premortal setting (see the Notes on 1:9, 11).

If we understand the plural of αἰών (*aiōn*) here to pertain to what has happened in the very distant past, we arrive at the idea of an "eternal" plan or purpose. Literally, we are to think of "the plan of the [distant] ages" (NR). Grammatically, the noun and its definite article, "the ages," are interpreted as an adjective, which is a feature of Hebrew style that has crept into the expression "eternal purpose,"[108] infusing the plan with an everlasting grandeur, with a majestic origin in premortality (see the Notes on 1:21; 2:2, 7; 3:9, 21).

purposed: The verb is unusual in this kind of setting: ποιέω (*poieō*) at base signifies "to do" or "to make." Among its meanings, it can bear two senses that link directly to the notion of a divine, premortal plan. It can point to the act of making or creating (see Luke 14:12); it can also direct us to the execution or carrying out of such a plan (see John 6:38).[109]

---

105. BDAG, 847; Louw-Nida, §58.46.

106. Lincoln, *Ephesians*, 56–57, 187.

107. Mauer, *TDNT*, 8:164–67; Delling, *TDNT*, 9:592–93; BDAG, 869; Winger, *Ephesians*, 203.

108. Blass and Debrunner, *Greek Grammar*, §165.

109. Barth, *Ephesians*, 1:346–47; BDAG, 839–42; Thayer, *Lexicon*, 524–27; Winger, *Ephesians*, 371.

Christ Jesus our Lord: This titling is similar to but not identical with what we find elsewhere in this letter. In those other passages, the emphasis falls on "Lord" in the expression "Lord Jesus Christ" (see 1:2, 3, 17; 5:20; 6:23, 24). Here it lands on "Christ." And we find a twist—the definite article before the title Christ—that binds this emphasis ever more securely to the appellation Christ, so that we sense something like "the Messiah Jesus, our Lord," putting the expression into its original Semitic or Hebrew dress rather than into the somewhat awkward English "the Christ Jesus, our Lord."[110] That a Semitic blanket lies over this passage is evident in the expression translated "eternal purpose" (see the Note above and on 4:1).

3:12 *boldness and access with confidence:* The passage that leaps to mind derives from modern scripture and appends a plea that unlocks "confidence" in God's presence: "Let virtue garnish thy thoughts unceasingly." Then comes the payoff for virtue—that "thy confidence [shall] wax strong in the presence of God" (D&C 121:45; see also 1 John 3:21). Clearly, this sort of confidence does not arise early in a person's relationship with God. For Jesus reminds us in his story about the publican and the Pharisee that one must first approach God in humility. We read that "the publican," not wanting to offend God by coming into his holy house, stood "far off [from the sanctuary, and] would not lift up so much as his eyes unto heaven, . . . saying, God be merciful to me a sinner" (Luke 18:13).

boldness: The noun παρρησία (*parrēsia*) bears the meanings "boldness" and "confidence" in what are often threatening situations.[111] Regularly, this term concerns boldness in the presence of other persons (see 6:19; Acts 2:29; 4:13, 29, 31; 1 Thes. 2:2; and Philem. 1:8). But *parrēsia* more frequently has to do with boldness in God's presence or in the act of representing him (see 1 Tim. 3:13; Heb. 3:6; 4:16; 10:19, 35; 1 John 2:28; 3:21; 4:17; 5:14;[112] and the Notes on 6:19–20).

access: This term, προσαγωγή (*prosagōgē*), in Greek sends us to a rich set of sacred actions in the Old Testament. Specifically, the noun in the Septuagint and its associated verb in its transitive sense, προσάγω (*prosagō*), point to a long series of approaches to the divine, often to bringing a sacrifice or to offering a gift to God. They may be undertaken by authorized priesthood holders, such as priests or prophets (see LXX 1 Kgs. 1:25 [1 Sam. 1:25 KJV]; LXX 3 Kgs. 18:30–32 [1 Kgs. 18:30–32 KJV];

---

110. Muddiman, *Ephesians,* 162.

111. Louw-Nida, §25.158.

112. Heinrich Schlier, *TDNT,* 5:883; BDAG, 781.3.b.

LXX Ezek. 44:15; and LXX Mal. 3:3), brought by priests or prophets on behalf of worshipers (see LXX Num. 28:3, 9, 11, 19, 27; 29:36; LXX 1 Kgs. 10:20–21; 23:9 [1 Sam. 10:20–21; 23:9 KJV]; etc.), brought by individuals (see LXX Josh. 4:5; LXX 1 Kgs. 14:34 [1 Sam. 14:34 KJV]; LXX 4 Kgs. 16:14 [2 Kgs. 16:14 KJV]; LXX 2 Chr. 29:31; LXX Isa. 34:1; 48:16; and LXX Mal. 1:7–8), or initiated by the Lord himself (see LXX Ezek. 37:7 and LXX Dan. 7:13 [in certain Septuagint texts of Daniel, the Son of Man is "brought to" the Ancient of Days]).

In the New Testament, we meet the same message of bringing something to God, with a bit of a twist. The one who brings is Christ, and the one to whom a person is brought is God himself: "Christ also hath once suffered for sins, . . . that he might bring us to God" (1 Pet. 3:18). Even when we turn to the intransitive sense of the term, with the meaning of a person drawing near or approaching, Christ stands in the picture. We read, "By [Christ] also we have access [*prosagōgē*] by faith into this grace wherein we stand" (Rom. 5:2). Without him, without faith in him, access to God is impossible (see 2 Cor. 3:4 and the Note on 2:18).[113]

with confidence: This prepositional phrase (ἐν πεποιθήσει, *en pepoithēsei*) bears the meaning of an adjective when paired with the prior noun, "access," with the idea of "confident access" (NR). On one level, "boldness" and "confident access" are synonyms and have to do with a believer's relationship to the Father through his Son.[114] Church members may enter the doors to God's presence through prayer, assured "that they will receive an audience."[115]

by the faith of him: The KJV rendition of this phrase is awkward and exhibits a slavish literalism. It makes more sense to read the pronoun translated "of him" as an objective genitive—that is, as the object of one's faith. In this light, the expression should read "by faith in him" or "through faith in him" (NR) rather than through Christ's faith (see the Notes on 2:8; 3:17).[116]

3:13 Wherefore: The force of this conjunction (διό, *dio*) is to sum up what Paul has said in the previous twelve verses. It carries the basic meaning "therefore" or "so then" (NR).[117]

---

113. Schmidt, *TDNT,* 1:131–34; Grundmann, Hesse, de Jonge, and van der Woude, *TDNT,* 9:557; BDAG, 875–76.

114. Rudolf Bultmann, *TDNT,* 6:8.

115. Best, *Ephesians,* 329.

116. Best, *Ephesians,* 330, sees both possibilities.

117. BDAG, 250; Louw-Nida, §89.47.

I desire that ye faint not: The Greek text is rather ambiguous. The sentence could mean something like "I pray that I not lose heart," with Paul as the subject of the whole, or it could convey the sense "I beg you not to lose heart." We notice that nowhere in Paul's letters, including this one, do we come upon him admitting despondency. Hence, the first alternative seems very distant. The second meaning fits better with the rest of the verse.[118]

my tribulations: Paul's view that his sufferings, including imprisonment (see 3:1), are a gain for him because he is suffering with Christ is well established (see Rom. 8:17 and Philip. 1:29; 3:7–8). In one sense, he has expressed this notion to encourage believers to face current and expected difficulties with a cheery heart and dogged determination, knowing that such suffering in a way mirrors Jesus' own elevating suffering and will bring church members closer to the Savior (see Rom. 5:3–5; 2 Cor. 1:5–7; 4:11–12; and Col. 1:23–24).

for you: Of all the statements in this letter about Paul's relationship to his readers, this one is the most puzzling. How are we to understand it? The prepositional phrase is plain (ὑπὲρ ὑμῶν, *hyper hymōn*). It means "for you" or "on your behalf." Was he writing about himself as a representative sufferer? That is to say, Did he view himself as one whose tribulations elevated and adorned other Christians with eternal life? The answer is no. To be sure, fellow Jews saw Abraham as possessing excess merit that he could share with his descendants, guaranteeing them a place next to God in the next life.[119] Such a view underlay the notion that Jesus' Atonement, undertaken for others, had the power to lift believers into the heavens. But nothing in Paul's teachings suggests that he held this kind of view about himself.[120] Rather, it makes more sense to understand this short phrase as revolving around the idea that, in our discipleship of Christ, of which Paul is a supreme example to us, we Christians willingly accept "suffering and death" as possible outcomes. These results, we trust, will be to "the advantage of fellow Christians," offering suitable examples to guide and encourage other believers experiencing afflictions (see 3:1 and Rom. 1:11, "to the end ye may be established").[121] On his part, Paul wished for the power

---

118. Best, *Ephesians,* 330–31.

119. Joachim Jeremias, *TDNT,* 6:927, "Abraham is called the rock . . . for he carries all creation." Also Schrenk and Quell, *TDNT,* 5:977 and nn. 192–93. See Isa. 51:1–2; see also Josephus, *Antiquities of the Jews* 8.9.2 (§278), for the merit of Solomon making intercession for later generations.

120. Contra Barth, *Ephesians,* 1:349; Winger, *Ephesians,* 374.

121. Harald Riesenfeld, *TDNT,* 8:511; see also Heinrich Schlier, *TDNT,* 3:147.

to suffer for his fellow Jews, but he did not possess it: "I could wish that myself were accursed from Christ for my [Jewish] brethren" (Rom. 9:3).

your glory: This terminology (δόξα, *doxa*) potentially pulls us into a difficult discussion. Why? Because the noun can center on a number of possible connections, such as radiance, gleaming (see Matt. 4:8 and Luke 4:6), honor (see Luke 14:10, "then shalt thou have worship [*doxa*]"; 1 Cor. 11:15; 1 Thes. 2:6, 20; and Philip. 3:19), or the repute and glory of royalty (see Rev. 21:24, 26).[122] Somehow Paul's afflictions, which he has suffered as God's representative, assist in unfolding to his readers, perhaps especially his converts, a measure of eschatological glory. That is, his tribulations in the work have unbarred doors—nothing more—for believers to enjoy a glorious association with Jesus Christ in the next life. This association will blossom into an enhanced royal status for each person, bringing them to rule and reign with God (see Matt. 25:21; Luke 19:17; Rom. 5:17; and Rev. 1:6; 5:10; 20:4; 22:5; compare 1 Cor. 4:8; see also the Notes on 1:6, 14, 17–18; 3:6, 16, 21).[123]

Analysis of 3:1–13

These verses (3:1–13) frame the most personal part of the letter. Within these lines, Paul leads us to his unexpected calling not only to minister in Jesus' name but to pursue potential believers among the Gentiles, all to be done through Christ's unforeseen grace (see 3:3, 7). Just as verses 2:11–22 have set out how Gentiles gained access to the gospel through God's grace offered through Christ, so 3:1–13 elucidate how God's grace generously reached out to Paul and made him an instrument in God's design to bring those Gentiles within the divine fold. To establish this point, Paul appealed to his past when Christ first appeared to him and granted to him "the dispensation of the grace of God which is given me . . . by revelation" (3:2–3). Yes, everything rested on revelation, specifically that revelation of God's Son as Paul traveled from Jerusalem across the Jordan Valley and up to Damascus.

Grammatically, verse 3:1 ties to 3:14. They begin with identical phrases, "For this cause" (τούτου χάριν, *toutou charin*), suggesting that Paul began with one set of ideas in mind and, caught by another, wrote what we now possess in 3:2–13. Thereafter, he returned to his original thought now

---

122. Von Rad and Kittel, *TDNT*, 2:237.
123. Hermann and Foerster, *TDNT*, 3:783.

expressed in 3:14, a prayer for the celestial strengthening of his Gentile readers. The invading memory, which brought back the enduring impact of God's unlooked-for grace on him, beginning on that fateful day when Christ appeared to him, must have always been with him. So he decided to say something about how God had blessed him in an unexpected way. Hence, we now possess his mature reflections and feelings in 3:2–13, schooled by decades of missionary service. At center stage stood "the mystery" recently revealed "unto me [Paul]" and "unto his holy apostles and prophets" to the effect that the Gentiles were to take their places in God's eternal spaces as "fellowheirs, and of the same body" (3:3, 5–6). His task, handed to him not only by the Resurrected Jesus but also in a priesthood blessing under the hands of the faithful Ananias, was to "preach among the Gentiles the unsearchable riches of Christ" (3:8; see also Acts 9:15; 22:15; 26:16–18).

It has become common to hold the view that verses 3:2–23 depend directly on Colossians 1:23–28 and, in fact, fill in the picture of what we read in the Colossians passage. This notion rests on the unproven assumption that Ephesians depends on Colossians. Some have even created tables of correspondences between the two passages.[124] That the two letters would correspond should not surprise us if we believe that the two letters came from the same author. After all, the same person might enjoy similar thoughts from time to time. But if we step into the world of pseudonymous authors, postulating that Ephesians and Colossians were not written by Paul, all becomes soupy and without boundary markers. For who is to say that these two letters were not written by different authors? How does one prove or disprove that proposition, seeing that we possess such small samples of writing in these two epistles? It is better to adopt Muddiman's cautionary observations—namely, that "on closer inspection, [the suggested similarities between the Colossians and Ephesians passages] become not only inconclusive but . . . inexplicable on the theory of the direct dependence of Ephesians on Colossians."[125]

One of the surprises in this section has to do with the distinct possibility that in 3:10 Paul was alluding to work for the dead undertaken by the church. As we discovered, the context for mentioning "principalities and powers" is openly positive, unlike the mention of these personalities in 6:12, where they are tied to "the rulers of the darkness of this world, [and] . . .

---

124. Lincoln, *Ephesians,* 169; Winger, *Ephesians,* 379; Perkins, *Ephesians,* 79–80.
125. Muddiman, *Ephesians,* 147.

spiritual wickedness in high places." In stark contrast, in 3:10 "the manifest wisdom of God" becomes "known" to "the principalities and powers . . . by the church." Somehow the church is involved in bringing God's stunning wisdom to the knowledge of these persons who now dwell "in heavenly places." Such an observation directs us into the world of vicarious ordinances or actions performed on behalf of the departed dead, just as Paul's featuring of baptism for the dead does (see 1 Cor. 15:29).[126]

What remains puzzling is the effort by most scholars not only to deny that these lines were penned or dictated by the Apostle but also to suggest that an unknown person, decades after his death, feared not to speak in Paul's name, writing brazenly that "I was made a minster, according to the gift of the grace of God given unto me by . . . his power" (3:7). Thereafter, this person, in the spirit of 1 Corinthians 15:9 ("I am the least of the apostles"), wrote as if in the Apostle's voice that he was "less than the least of all saints" (3:8), a subtle diminishing of Paul by comparing him to ordinary church members rather than to the Twelve. We listen to one scholar who takes the pen out of the Apostle's hand: "By speaking in the name of Paul and having Paul reflect on the significance of his ministry, the [unidentified] writer can develop his own understanding of the mystery of the Christ event and, at the same time, back his insights with the apostle's authority."[127] Is that what this is, a letter written by an unknown author that grabs at Paul's name and authority to establish this person's legitimacy? Such a view is blunted by Muddiman's observation that "second only perhaps to the final postscript, 6:21–22, chapter 3 of Ephesians has the strongest claim to be from Paul's own hand."[128] Another scholar called the supposed unknown author, who wrote as if he were Paul, "one particular human being,"[129] a description that falls into the lap of F. F. Bruce's trenchant observation, "Of such a second Paul early Christian history has no knowledge" (see the Notes on 1:23; 3:8; 4:3, 21; 5:27; 6:3, 5).[130]

---

126. Riesenfeld, *TDNT,* 8:512–13.

127. Lincoln, *Ephesians,* 193.

128. Muddiman, *Ephesians,* 147; see the observations of K. L. Schmidt on the conception of the church in Ephesians as likely being from Paul (*TDNT,* 3:511).

129. Best, *Ephesians,* 293; see also Muddiman's response (*Ephesians,* 146).

130. Bruce, *Ephesians,* 12.

"I Bow My Knees" (3:14–21)

King James Translation

14 For this cause I bow my knees unto the Father of our Lord Jesus Christ, 15 Of whom the whole family in heaven and earth is named, 16 That he would grant you, according to the riches of his glory, to be strengthened with might by his Spirit in the inner man; 17 That Christ may dwell in your hearts by faith; that ye, being rooted and grounded in love, 18 May be able to comprehend with all saints what is the breadth, and length, and depth, and height; 19 And to know the love of Christ, which passeth knowledge, that ye might be filled with all the fulness of God. 20 Now unto him that is able to do exceeding abundantly above all that we ask or think, according to the power that worketh in us, 21 Unto him be glory in the church by Christ Jesus throughout all ages, world without end. Amen.

New Rendition

14 For this reason, I kneel before the Father 15 (from whom every family in the heavenly realms and on earth derives its name) 16 so that according to the wealth of his glory he may grant that you be strengthened with power in the inner person through his Spirit. 17 I pray that Christ may dwell in your hearts through faith, you being rooted and grounded in love, 18 so that you may be able to grasp with all the saints what is the breadth and length and height and depth, 19 and to know the love of Christ that surpasses knowledge, so that you may be filled with all the fullness of God.

20 Now to the one who is able, above all, to do more abundantly whatever we ask or consider thoughtfully, according to the power acting in us—21 to him be the glory in the church and in Christ Jesus throughout all generations of time and forevermore, Amen.

Notes on 3:14–21

3:14 *For this cause:* This phrase connects back to the same phrase in 3:1 (τούτου χάριν, *toutou charin*). It is evident that Paul began to write one thing, and then, when his thoughts were interrupted by the memory of his vision of Jesus, he digressed for a few lines before resuming his original train of thought.[131]

I bow my knees: This action forms the ultimate gesture of submission. In this case, Paul submits himself in prayer to God on behalf of his readers. In the Septuagint, the verb κάμπω (*kampō*), "to bow," always joined to the term "knee," refers to the act of praying or petitioning for a blessing

---

131. Larkin, *Handbook,* 60; Merkle, *Guide,* 103.

(see LXX 4 Kgs. 1:13 [2 Kgs. 1:13 KJV]; LXX 1 Chr. 29:20; and LXX 2 Chr. 6:13; 29:29). The only exception appears in LXX Isaiah 45:23–24, where we read God's words: "By myself I swear . . . that to me every knee shall bend, and every tongue shall swear by God."[132] In this case, God utters an oath that, at the end-time, the peoples of the earth will acknowledge him as their Lord and King. We find a similar sentiment in the New Testament at Romans 14:11 and Philippians 2:10–11, wherein Jesus Christ is to be the object of veneration. In a different vein, one observes that kneeling in worship occurs infrequently in the Old Testament and therefore may point to this kind of action as a rarity in ancient worship rather than the rule. Even in Jesus' story about the Pharisee and the publican, both stood as they prayed (see Luke 18:11, 13; see also Mark 11:25 and Rom. 5:2).[133]

With one exception (see Heb. 12:12, "the feeble knees"), throughout the New Testament, the noun for "knee" (γόνυ, gonu) appears only in instances of kneeling down or prostrating oneself. Such an act may occur when praying (see Luke 22:41 and Acts 7:60), when seeking a blessing (see Matt. 17:14 and Mark 1:40; 10:17), or when paying homage, whether sincere or not (see Matt. 27:29; Rom. 14:10–11; and Philip. 2:10).[134]

the Father: According to 2:18, steadfast believers, both Jew and Gentile, enjoy "access by one Spirit unto the Father." This unspeakable opportunity to approach the God of the universe, to make of him one's counselor and guide, paints a most inviting picture for mere humans. Now, in 3:14–15, readers learn that the fatherhood of God reaches far beyond the earth, embracing what is called "the whole family in heaven and earth" (better, "every family"). Furthermore, it is worth noting that Paul does not identify "the Father" with "the Lord," a title reserved for Jesus (κύριος, *kyrios*). Nor is God called anyone's "master" (δεσπότης, *despotēs*).[135]

The textual evidence leaves the words "the Father" isolated, omitting the later-added phrase "of the Lord Jesus Christ" and preparing for the line that he is the one for "whom the whole family in heaven and earth is named" (3:15). As already noted, the phrase "of the Lord Jesus Christ" appears to be a later scribal addition (see the Note below) and limits the fatherhood of God to just Jesus Christ, effectively diminishing his relationship to humankind

---

132. Heinrich Schlier, *TDNT,* 3:594–95; BDAG, 507.
133. Barth, *Ephesians,* 1:377–79; Best, *Ephesians,* 336–37; Fowl, *Ephesians,* 118–19.
134. Heinrich Schlier, *TDNT,* 1:738; BDAG, 205.
135. Schrenk and Quell, *TDNT,* 5:1009.

and those who inhabit heaven.[136] Not incidentally, the title "Father" (πατήρ, *patēr*) prepares us to meet the noun "family" in 3:15, which is spelled similarly and sounds much the same (πατριά, *patria*).

Thus, this passage and 2:18 set "the Father" by himself. Elsewhere in the epistle, we find this title tied to the term for God (θεός, *theos*; see 1:2; 4:6; 5:20; 6:23) or to the "Lord Jesus Christ" (1:3). In its isolated state, as here, it relates to two personality traits that emerge in the New Testament. First, we notice that it has to do with his absolute sovereignty, his lordship, a characteristic that is often emphasized by pairing the titles God and the Father. As our sovereign, he demands our obedience, which, generously, leads to our sanctification (see 2 Cor. 7:1; Heb. 12:9–10; and 1 Pet. 1:2) and, of course, brings celestial rewards in the next life (see 1 Thes. 3:13). Christ is the one who has introduced us to his Father, the Ruling One, "the Father of glory" (1:17), and will, in that distant day, yield up all things into the hands of the Father (see 1 Cor. 15:24–28). Second, it is from the Father that saving grace rolls forth into our lives. This gift is joined most often with other gifts, such as mercy, comfort, hope, and love (see 2 Cor. 1:3–4; 2 Thes. 2:16–17; 1 Pet. 1:3; and Jude 1:1–2). Direct "access . . . unto the Father" is one of those gifts (2:18; see also Rom. 5:2). Moreover, the Holy Spirit is always the one who leads us to him, whether we come as individuals or as a broader community, marking us as God's children (see Rom. 8:14;[137] the Notes on 2:18; 3:6; 5:1; 6:2; and the Analysis of 3:14–21).

of our Lord Jesus Christ: The manuscript evidence is split, though not evenly, on whether this expression was original; it is missing from a lot of important texts, including the earliest, 𝔓[46] (c. AD 200). It appears to be a gloss by a scribe who thought that, in the rhythm of the passage's language, this worshipful line should be added. One point is that purposely omitting this line would make no sense if it was really a part of the text. Hence, the texts that do not preserve this phrase are original.[138]

3:15 *Of whom:* This prepositional phrase bears on the origin or source of the naming, not on the action of giving a name. That is to say, we are not talking about the Father as the giver of the names whereby he effectively confers a reality or existence on those in heaven and on earth, as did Adam

---

136. Best, *Ephesians*, 337.

137. Schrenk and Quell, *TDNT*, 5:1010–11.

138. Barth, *Ephesians*, 1:367; Lincoln, *Ephesians*, 196; Best, *Ephesians*, 337; Metzger, *Textual Commentary*, 535.

when he gave names to the animals (see Gen. 2:19–20 and Moses 3:19–20). Rather, we take our names from him as from an easily accessible source and without compulsory means.[139] He is our father, after all, and we derive our existence and meaning from him.

the whole family: A better translation is "every family" (NR). The expression "the whole family" would require the definite article in the Greek text, which is not present.[140] Hence, "every family" or "each family" are better renditions.[141] This seemingly small distinction impacts how we see family life in heaven.

family: All commentators notice the obvious connection between the term for "father" (πατήρ, *patēr*) and "family" (πατριά, *patria*). This similarity, both in sound and spelling, surely emphasizes the inner link between the Father and families. On a very connected level, he is intimately bound to the existence of and the enduring, sacred qualities of families. That has been the case since the days of Adam and Eve and will continue to be so, as Jesus himself declared. For him, the first marriage pointed decisively to the eternal continuation of marriage and, by extension, to everlasting family relationships. We hear his words spoken to the Pharisees in response to their question about divorce. The matter reposed in the Father's involvement in the creation of Adam and Eve, followed by their marriage under his hand. To the Pharisees, Jesus declared, "He which made [Adam and Eve] at the beginning made them male and female . . . and they twain shall be one flesh. . . . What therefore God hath joined together, let not man put asunder" (Matt. 19:4–6; see also Mark 10:6–9).

On the other side of this relationship, families themselves owe their character of holiness to the special ceremonies that inaugurate family units in marriages. This sanctified sense started when God performed the first marriage, that of Adam and Eve, as we have just established (see Gen. 2:18, 21–24; Moses 3:18, 21–24;[142] and the Notes on 2:18–19). In this case, the family is not the church or the body of Christ. Rather, Paul envisions a real family with everlasting family ties. And all is made possible through Christ. For, as we were taught earlier in this letter, God will "gather together in one all things in Christ, both which are in heaven, and which are on earth" (1:10; see also

---

139. Best, *Ephesians,* 338; Merkle, *Guide,* 104; contra Fowl, *Ephesians,* 119.

140. Lincoln, *Ephesians,* 202; Best, *Ephesians,* 338.

141. Schrenk and Quell, *TDNT,* 5:1018.

142. The First Presidency and Council of the Twelve Apostles of The Church of Jesus Christ of Latter-day Saints, "The Family: A Proclamation to the World." *Ensign* 25, no. 11 (November 1995): 102.

Rom. 8:14, "as many as are led by the Spirit of God, they are the sons of God"; and the Note on 5:1).[143]

in heaven: Do we detect more than a whiff of eternal family relationships? Part of that relationship, of course, rests in the kinship of all humankind with the Father. But this verse invites readers, including Paul's readers, to think of family ties that persist into heaven, especially in light of the preceding words, "every family." This possibility has sent commentators scrambling to find reasons to deny such bonds. It is almost comical to see them bobbing and weaving and running for cover behind Jesus' words quoted in Mark 12:25: "They neither marry, nor are given in marriage, but are as the angels . . . in heaven" (see also Matt. 22:30 and Luke 20:35). For example, Helmut Traub confidently assures us that "the families in heaven are angels."[144] In a straining attempt to claim that family units cannot exist in heaven, G. B. Caird writes, "There can be no families in heaven, where they neither marry nor are given in marriage (Mark 12:25)."[145] Traub and Caird are not alone.

Andrew Lincoln writes tepidly of "family groupings" but quickly qualified these words with "classes of angels" and "spirit powers."[146] Ernest Best spreads out a number of possible meanings for "family in heaven," including a sort of "(social) grouping" and "angels . . . in groups with leaders." He rejects "groups in heaven . . . of dead believers."[147] Pheme Perkins only admits to "the one clan" as the meaning of this verse, without further elaboration.[148] Yet the plain sense of Paul's language is that "every family" in some way bears God's divine name "in heaven" as well as on the earth. What is simpler than the notion of eternal families? Obviously, these scholars do not understand that marriage is an earthly ordinance that does not occur in heaven. Further, they have little sense about the eternal character of families, which is hinted at strongly in this phrase.

Let us examine two New Testament passages that buttress this teaching. The first is simpler and more direct. In the First Epistle of Peter, we find a discussion of husbands and wives. Among other items, Peter wrote that couples will be "heirs together of the grace of life" (1 Pet. 3:7). The

---

143. Traub and von Rad, *TDNT,* 5:517–18 and n. 158; Schrenk and Quell, *TDNT,* 5:1017–19; Best, *Ephesians,* 633.

144. Traub and von Rad, *TDNT,* 5:518 n. 159.

145. Caird, *Letters,* 68.

146. Lincoln, *Ephesians,* 202.

147. Best, *Ephesians,* 338–39.

148. Perkins, *Ephesians,* 89.

noun "life" in this context, and in almost all contexts in the New Testament, revolves around eternal life, God's life.[149] Hence, this line is about husbands and wives, indeed "families," becoming "heirs together" in the eternities. We come upon the second passage in John's Gospel in the scene of Jesus interacting with the Samaritan woman at Jacob's well. Near the middle of their conversation, Jesus offered to the woman "living water." When the woman responded, "Sir, give me this water, that I thirst not," Jesus said, "Go, call thy husband." We all know her answer: "I have no husband." To this Jesus said, "Thou has had five husbands; and he whom thou now hast is not thy husband." Most commentators focus on Jesus setting the woman up for his unexpected reply about her five husbands and her paramour, all of which led her perceptively to say, "Thou art a prophet" (John 4:10–19). But the key element is Jesus' directive, "Go, call thy husband." Plainly stated, the water of life that Jesus was offering to her is not available except in a married state, a status that will continue into the next life. Why? Because it was Jesus, the eternal Lord, who was offering an enduring gift to her (see the Notes on 1:10; 3:6; 4:10; 5:1, 22; 6:9).

is named: The passive verb of ὀνομάζω (*onomazō*) centers on God's action. The force of the phrase "of whom" tilts away from God's role as the one who granted names and instead onto him as the source of names (see Isa. 40:26).[150] In other words, our identity derives from him,[151] a fact that subtly frames our relationship with him in the premortal world as well as in this world and especially the next. Thus, the entire, everlasting span of our lives, from premortality to immortality, spreads out an affirmation of his fatherhood and our childhood. That relationship is not confined to a one-time naming event but forms an eternal and intimate bond between father and child (see Jer. 31:1, 9; and the Notes on 1:21; 5:3).

3:16 *the riches of his glory:* This expression almost repeats the language of 1:18, "the riches of the glory of his inheritance." Though the language is similar, the meanings of the two expressions differ notably. In the earlier passage, the emphasis falls on the *eschaton,* the end-time, wherein a believer is to receive an everlasting inheritance. In our case, the expression "the riches of his [the Father's] glory" centers on the here and now because it points to strengthening "the new person" (4:24 NR), "the inner person" (3:16 NR; see also Rom. 9:23). This empowering of the individual "by his

---

149. Hermann Hanse, *TDNT,* 2:825.
150. Schrenk and Quell, *TDNT,* 5:1017; Best, *Ephesians,* 337–38.
151. Winger, *Ephesians,* 391.

Spirit" stands close to the notion of the enabling power of the Atonement (see the Notes on 1:9, 16, 21; 2:7, 16; 4:30).[152] Elsewhere in this letter, we read of "the riches of [God's] grace" (1:7; 2:7). The two concepts sit close together. Grace, of course, emphasizes the surpassingly generous gift that is conferred on us by Jesus' Atonement, opening the door into the sunlit expanse of eternal life. Glory has to do both with God's very nature and with the opportunity that he warmly extends to us to share in his life in the eternities, though in a way his glory is already with us, "for the spirit of glory and of God [now] resteth upon you" (1 Pet. 4:14; see also 2 Cor. 4:6).[153]

Whereas the Gospels portray Jesus shunning wealth because of its debilitating effects, as we see, for instance, in the parable of the sower (see Matt. 13:22; Mark 4:19; and Luke 8:14), Paul attributes real riches to God and Christ. In Romans 2:4, he wrote about "the riches of [God's] goodness" and, in Romans 11:33, about "the riches of the wisdom and knowledge of God." The Son, too, is a possessor and distributor of celestial wealth in the mortal world. Paul could declare that "the same Lord [Jesus Christ] . . . is rich unto all that call on his name" (Rom. 10:12). Moreover, in an intriguing statement, Paul wrote that "our Lord Jesus Christ . . . was rich, yet for your sakes he became poor [in mortality], that ye through his poverty might be [eternally] rich" (2 Cor. 8:9;[154] for "riches," see the Notes on 1:7, 18; 2:4, 7; 3:8; for "glory," see the Notes on 1:6, 14, 17–18; 3:13, 21).

to be strengthened with might: The passive, as elsewhere, points to an agent or a person who performs the action. In this case, it is God's Spirit. Such power or might (δύναμις, *dynamis*) stands on a continuum with the power released in Jesus' Resurrection, which was brought about by God's strong act (see 1:19–20) and will be the energizing element in our resistance against "the wiles of the devil" (6:10–11). This power, mediated to humans by God's Spirit, is a means of revelation, illuminating "the inner person" (3:16 NR) by leading an individual where a human "eye hath not seen, nor ear heard, neither have entered into the heart of man, the things which God hath prepared." It is this Spirit, infused into believers, which by revelation's power "searcheth all things, yea, the deep things of God" (1 Cor. 2:9–10). It is this strengthening influence that empowers us by

---

152. Bednar, "In the Strength of the Lord," 121–28; Rasmus, "Enabling Power of the Atonement," 18–21; see also Eising, *TDOT*, 4:349, 353–55; Grundmann, *TDNT*, 2:313–16; Oepke, *TDNT*, 2:542–43; Braun, *TDNT*, 6:464, who discussed Elisabeth and Mary (see also Luke 1:25, 49).

153. Von Rad and Kittel, *TDNT*, 2:250–51.

154. Hauck and Kasch, *TDNT*, 6:327–29.

revelatory means to "be able to comprehend with all saints [in all ages] what is the breadth, and length, and depth, and height . . . [of] the love of Christ, which passeth knowledge" (3:18–19). The reception of that love is simply not available to just any observer. It comes to one only by revelation (see D&C 76:116–18, "they are only to be seen and understood by the power of the Holy Spirit"; 121:26, "God shall give unto you knowledge by his Holy Spirit"; Moro. 10:4–5, 7; and the Notes on 1:19, 21; 3:7, 20).[155]

his Spirit: As we have seen, in this verse God's Spirit is the agent of revelation. That is one of his functions. An aspect of this assignment, if we can call it thus, is to bear record of the Father and the Son (see Moses 1:24; 5:9; 7:11). According to Ephesians, the interaction of the Spirit and believers is rich and enduring. In 2:18, we learn that the Spirit is an influence for unity. Its manifestation resides in the unimpeded access to God for both Jews and Gentiles. The sense is similar in 2:22, where we discover that both Gentiles and Jews have become members of the earthly "habitation of God through the Spirit," a habitation that will continue into the eternities. Unity frames Paul's remark that "there is one body [of the church], and one Spirit" that ties all together "in the bond of peace" (4:3–4). According to 5:9, "the Spirit" bears within a person's soul the extraordinary "fruit . . . [of] goodness and righteousness and truth." As we might expect, a dark spirit also operates in the human sphere, trying to contravene the Spirit of God. Paul calls this spirit "the prince of the power of the air, the spirit that now worketh in the children of disobedience" (2:2; see also 1 Cor. 2:9–16 and the Notes on 2:2, 18, 22; 4:4; 5:9).[156]

the inner man: This expression (τὸν ἔσω ἄνθρωπον, *ton esō anthrōpon*) pulls our focus onto the part of a person that rests at each individual's core, "the hidden man of the heart" (1 Pet. 3:4), the one part of ourselves that we can willingly surrender to God for his purposes.[157] In baptism, the old person "is crucified with [Christ], . . . that henceforth we should not serve sin" (Rom. 6:6). Elsewhere, we find this ordinance serving as the gate to the inner person, "the washing of regeneration" (Titus 3:5). But the expression "the inner man" does not feature strictly the contrast between the old person of sin (see 4:22) and the new one who is regenerated (see 2:15;

---

155. Kleinknecht, Baumgärtel, Bieder, Sjöberg, and Schweizer, *TDNT,* 6:444.

156. Kleinknecht, Baumgärtel, Bieder, Sjöberg, and Schweizer, *TDNT,* 6:444–45, discuss these passages with a different emphasis.

157. Johannes Behm, *TDNT,* 2:699; Neal A. Maxwell, "Becoming a Disciple," *Ensign* 26, no. 6 (June 1996): 12–19; see also Mosiah 15:7, "the will of the Son being swallowed up in the will of the Father."

4:24; and Rom. 12:1–2).[158] The strengthening which touches "the inner man" by the granting of divine power to that person comes as a further step beyond baptism, one activated by the Holy Spirit on a constant basis rather than a onetime event like baptism (see 2 Cor. 4:16). This empowerment or endowment brings a person into contact with "the powers of the world to come" (Heb. 6:5); though they remain invisible to one's sight, they are nevertheless real.[159] From modern scripture come the words "sanctified by the Spirit unto the renewing of their bodies" (D&C 84:33), relating to a spiritual elevation that has an impact on a person's physical self (see the Notes on 2:15; 4:22, 24).

3:17 *That Christ may dwell in your hearts:* Grammatically, this expression stands in a parallel relationship to the words above, "to be strengthened with might by his Spirit" (3:16), and therefore expands and clarifies that line, meaning God's Spirit—that is, the Holy Ghost—and Christ. Hence, the larger sense of Paul's prayer invites aid from two members of the Godhead.[160] What is the advantage of Christ dwelling in our hearts? At a minimum, it has to do with being "able to comprehend . . . what is the breadth, and length, and depth, and height" of "the love of Christ" (3:18–19; see also the Notes on 2:17; 3:18; 6:15).

Christ: The title appears here with a definite article, bearing the meaning "the Messiah" or "the Christ." Within this title, of course, sits the atoning essence of his being, which Paul will elucidate in almost psalmic language later in the letter while addressing the believer: "Awake, O sleeper, rise from the dead, and Christ will shine upon you" (5:14 NR; see also Rom. 13:11; 1 Cor. 15:34;[161] Col. 3:1; and the Notes on 3:19; 5:14).

dwell: The indwelling of Christ was already anticipated by Jesus' words spoken during his mortal ministry. For he pledged to the Eleven, "I will come to you" (John 14:18). In an expansion of this promise, he gave his word to any person who "will keep my words . . . [that] my Father [and I] . . . will come unto him, and make our abode with him" (John 14:23). Even more to the point, "at that day ye shall know that I am in my Father, and ye in me, *and I in you*" (John 14:20, emphasis added). In another passage, it was Paul who wrote that "the life I now live is not my life, but the life which Christ

---

158. Joachim Jeremias, *TDNT,* 1:365–66.

159. Michaelis, *TDNT,* 5:349–50.

160. Barth, *Ephesians,* 1:369–70; Lincoln, *Ephesians,* 206; Best, *Ephesians,* 341; Winger, *Ephesians,* 394–95.

161. Grundmann, Hesse, de Jonge, and van der Woude, *TDNT,* 9:560.

lives in me" (Gal. 2:20 NEB; see also Rom. 8:9–11). But this is not the whole story. The verb κατοικέω (*katoikeō*) has to do with residing permanently in a place, not with a transitory residence.[162] The associated noun κατοικητήριον (*katoikētērion*) occurs at 2:22, where it is linked to God's habitation and, for our passage here, raises to view the steadfast believer's eternal, permanent dwelling in Christ (see the Note on 2:22).

by faith: The status of Christ in us does not mean that he absorbs us in some unknown way, wrapping our personalities within his and engulfing our minds in his, thus freeing us of individual responsibility for our actions and thoughts. If so, we would need neither faith nor trust in him. The point is that, with Christ dwelling in our hearts, we as individuals are to go forward in faith, with full trust that he will do as he has promised to his faithful followers (see the Notes on 2:8; 3:12).[163]

rooted: The form that underlies this term is the perfect passive participle of ῥιζόω (*rhizoō*).[164] Paul has drawn the imagery from the world of farming. Such ideas are at home in the Old Testament, where we find metaphorical language like that here in Ephesians.[165] There, after God has lifted his people with heavenly gifts, they will "be called [by God] trees of righteousness, the planting of the Lord." In such a state, they become God's glory, effectively mirroring who he is (Isa. 61:3). But more than glorifying God, the faithful follower "shall be like a tree planted by the rivers of water, that bringeth forth his fruit in season." In this blessed circumstance, "his leaf"—a sign of the person's ongoing, everlasting life—"also shall not wither; and whatsoever he doeth shall prosper [eternally]" (Ps. 1:3; see also Col. 2:7 and 2 Thes. 1:3).

grounded: This form too is a perfect passive participle, this time of the verb θεμελιόω (*themelioō*). This verb, which carries the literal meaning "to found" and the metaphorical sense "to establish,"[166] appears frequently in the Septuagint with the meaning "to lay the foundation" of a city or temple (see LXX Josh. 6:26; LXX Ps. 47:9 [Ps. 48:8 KJV]; LXX Isa. 44:28; LXX Hag. 2:18; LXX Zech. 4:9; 8:9; etc.) or, in the realm of God's acts, to set the foundation of the earth itself (see LXX Ps. 8:4; 23:2 [Ps. 8:3; 24:2 KJV]; LXX Isa. 48:13; 51:13, 16; LXX Zech. 12:1; etc.). In its metaphorical and

---

162. Barth, *Ephesians*, 1:370; Louw-Nida, §85.69.

163. Lincoln, *Ephesians*, 207.

164. Barth, *Ephesians*, 1:371; Larkin, *Handbook*, 62–63.

165. Williams, *Paul's Metaphors*, 38.

166. Schmidt, *TDNT*, 3:63–64; BDAG, 449; Louw-Nida, §§7.42; 31.94; Thayer, *Lexicon*, 287.

spiritual dress, we read that it is God who "builds his ascent up to the sky, and establishes [*themelioō*] his promise on the earth," thereby promoting the connection of his people to the heavens (LXX Amos 9:6). Moreover, in a more targeted manner, "the Lord has founded [*themelioō*] Zion" for the sake of the poor so that "by him the poor of the people shall be saved" (LXX Isa. 14:32; see also LXX Ps. 8:4; 23:2; 47:9 [Ps. 8:2; 24:2; 48:8 KJV]).

Thus, the verb already bears much significance when it crosses the historical divide into the New Testament, particularly when it has to do with God's actions. As one might expect, the literal sense migrated into a couple of passages, including the "founding" of the house on a rock, both of which withstood the fierce winds and raging water (see Matt. 7:25 and Luke 6:48). Not surprisingly, the verb implicitly rests under the passage wherein Jesus promised that the Father would found his church upon the rock of revelation (see Matt. 16:18). Furthermore, as in numerous Septuagint passages, we discover that "thou, Lord, in the beginning hast laid the foundation [*themelioō*] of the earth; and the heavens are the works of thine hands" (Heb. 1:10). In the case of individuals, we meet Peter's prayer: "[May] the God of all grace, . . . after that ye have suffered a while, make you perfect, stablish [*themelioō*], strengthen, settle you" (1 Pet. 5:10; for the noun, see the Note on 2:20).

in love: In the Greek text, this prepositional phrase precedes the two participles "rooted and grounded." Hence, because the participles are in the perfect tense and therefore have to do with an already attained status, Paul was evidently writing in a mixed metaphor about a state that the believer had already gained, which, like a living plant, was "rooted" in the soil of love and, like a building, was "grounded" on the firm foundation of love or charity (ἀγάπη, *agapē*).[167]

Without being comprehensive, this noun, as most know, bears a noble set of meanings, including "envieth not [and] . . . vaunteth not itself [and] . . . thinketh no evil" (1 Cor. 13:4–5). Of the six Greek terms that express one or another dimension of love, *agapē* arrived in the Christian era with fewer meanings attached to it than the others. Thus, Christians were able to fill this noun, as it were, with a set of meanings that persist to this day. For example, "charity [*agapē*] suffereth long, and is kind; . . . is not puffed up. Doth not behave itself unseemly, seeketh not her own, is not easily provoked, . . . rejoiceth in the truth" (1 Cor. 13:4–6). We understand that Paul was not the only person to speak of this love. Jesus himself demanded

---

167. Barth, *Ephesians*, 1:371–72.

that we love our enemies, something that no one in his society had publicly taught (see Matt. 5:44 and Luke 6:27–28). He also articulated the public heights to which love can lift his followers: "All men [shall] know that ye are my disciples, if ye have love [*agapē*] one to another" (John 13:35).

The verb form of *agapē* shows up in Jesus' famous saying about what is to follow the act of truly loving him: "If ye love me, keep my commandments" (John 14:15). That this love is an integral part of the celestial world can be seen in Jesus' saying, "As the Father hath loved me, so have I loved you: continue ye in my love [*agapē*]" (John 15:9). But that is only part of the story. John cemented this notion by writing, "Let us love one another: for love is of God" (1 John 4:7). Further, "whoso keepeth his word, in him verily is the love of God perfected: hereby know we that we are in him" (1 John 2:5). The notion of being perfected has to do with being complete or being made whole (passive of τελειόω, *teleioō*).[168] From what John has declared here, it is apparent that keeping God's word leads to the perfecting of God's love in us.[169] For the record, the noun "love" (*agapē*) occurs ten times in Ephesians, at 1:4, 15; 2:4; 3:17, 19; 4:2, 15–16; 5:2; and 6:23 (see the Notes on 1:15; 5:25, 28).

3:18 be able: The verb ἐξισχύω (*exischuō*) occurs only here in the New Testament. Its prefix (ἐξ-, *ex*-) intensifies the action, impelling the basic meaning of the root from "to be able" to "to be fully able."[170] Plainly implicit is the sense that believers have received an endowment of power, an enriching empowerment that allows those persons "to comprehend" celestial matters in the fullest manner possible for humans (see the Note on 3:20).

to comprehend: The middle form of the infinitive of καταλαμβάνω (*katalambanō*), which stands in parallel to the infinitive "to know" in 3:19, draws up the sense "to understand" or "to grasp," often with the sense of surprise (see Acts 4:13, "perceived"; 10:34, "perceive"; 25:25, "found").[171] The understanding that comes to a person does not consist of some vague divine mystery, unless one wants to classify Jesus' death on the cross, his visit to the spirits in prison, and his subsequent Resurrection as such a mystery, as Paul does elsewhere (see 1 Cor. 2:7). Rather, in an unlooked-for, spiritually discerning way, a believer, with the aid of God's Spirit, comes to

---

168. BDAG, 996; Thayer, *Lexicon,* 618–19.

169. Quell and Stauffer, *TDNT,* 1:37, 44–52; Draper and Rhodes, "Excursus on Love/ Charity," in *Paul's First Epistle to the Corinthians,* 655–65.

170. BDAG, 350, 484; Louw-Nida, §74.10; Thayer, *Lexicon,* 224; Merkle, *Guide,* 107.

171. Delling, *TDNT,* 4:10; BDAG, 520.

grasp clearly the nature of Jesus' Atonement. Prefacing his remarks in 1 Corinthians 2, Paul wrote that "I determined not to know any thing among you, save Jesus Christ, and him crucified" (1 Cor. 2:2). Then he plunged into what for him are "the deep things of God" that are not discerned by "the natural man [who] receiveth not the things of the Spirit of God." Why not? Because "they are foolishness unto him." Worse, "neither can he know them" (1 Cor. 2:10, 14). That is, a person's natural ability and natural intelligence cannot grasp the grandeur, the infinite compass of Jesus' death and Resurrection. These truths simply remain out of that person's reach.

The comprehension that the Spirit activates in the inquiring, faithful believer is not simply the initial spiritual experience that that person undergoes when an investigator. This event, as a New World prophet reminded his readers, involves "the power of the Holy Ghost." But God has promised much more through his Spirit. For "by the power of the Holy Ghost [we] may know the truth of all things," a dazzling prospect (Moro. 10:4–5). So too Paul—for him, "the deep things of God," which are also called "the things of God," are available only through revelation "by [God's] Spirit" (1 Cor. 2:10–11). Said another way, "the depth of the riches both of the wisdom and knowledge of God [are] ... unsearchable ... and his ways past finding out" (Rom. 11:33; see also 2 Cor. 5:5). Only by the power of the Spirit are such divine delicacies made known (see the Notes on 1:17; 3:19; 4:13; 5:5).

with all the saints: This phrase is essentially a statement of fellowship with other church members. We find this fellowship embraced in the broad, inclusive "we" of "we have received, not the spirit of the world, but the spirit which is of God." And what is the result of our reception of God's Spirit? It is "that we might know the things that are freely given to us of God" (1 Cor. 2:12). Only believers can come to grasp the panorama and the drama of the Atonement.[172] It is not available to those who possess merely "the spirit of the world" (see the Notes on 2:19; 4:12; 5:3).

breadth, and length, and depth, and height: This series of terms frames the dominion of God as the ancients conceived it. This dominion consisted of a cube with length and depth and, interchangeably, height or depth. The interchangeable character of the last two words, "height and depth" (NR), is manifest in the differences between manuscripts. In some, including the earliest, $\mathfrak{P}^{46}$, the terms "depth" and "height" are reversed. But it makes little difference here. We also see the divine cubic stamp on the heavenly Jerusalem

---

172. Kleinknecht, Baumgärtel, Bieder, Sjöberg, Schweizer, *TDNT*, 6:426 and n. 617.

when we read that "the length and the breadth and the height of [the city] are equal," extending almost 1,400 miles in each direction (Rev. 21:16).[173]

3:19 *to know:* Grammatically, this infinitive of γινώσκω (*ginōskō*) stands in tandem with "to comprehend" in 3:18, complementing and thereby strengthening it, as the conjunction "and" (the Greek postpositive conjunction τε, *te*) demonstrates.[174] This two-fisted insistence on an individual's need to grasp or understand pushes itself forward because of the enthralling object of one's understanding—the inexpressible "love of Christ" (see the Notes on 1:17; 3:18; 4:13; 5:5).

the love of Christ: In his prayer for his readers, Paul has brought them to the pinnacle of Christian life—namely, to experience Christ's love for them and, just as important, to comprehend it. Behind these sits the greatest and deepest manifestation of that love, the Atonement. And what is the guide to this deep understanding? It is the Spirit, as Paul has reminded us in another place: "The fruit of the Spirit is love" along with other flavorful blessings, such as "joy, peace, . . . [and] gentleness" (Gal. 5:22; see also Rom. 5:5; 2 Cor. 5:14 RSV, "the love of Christ controls us"; Alma 7:11–13; and the Notes on 2:4; 5:2, 25).

Christ: In a teaching conversation with two of his followers, the Resurrected Jesus applied this title to himself for the first time on the road to Emmaus, but only after his Resurrection (see Luke 24:26).[175] The Greek text adds the definite article "the" both in the Luke passage and here so that it reads, "the Christ." When approaching Emmaus on the day of his Resurrection, Jesus effectively announced that he was now the bearer of God's love among both the living and the dead. Perhaps not surprisingly, song celebrates the moment that he arrived at the gates of the spirit prison and freed those held within. We sing lines that hint at this notable event in "Glory to God on High," written by James Allen: "Tell what his arm has done, / What spoils from death he won."[176] In lyrics written by Charles Wesley, we sing with more detail about that event: "The keys of death and hell / To Christ the Lord are giv'n."[177] Bringing further clarity and

---

173. For the length of a furlong or *stadion,* see Marvin A. Powell, "Weights and Measures," in *ABD,* 6:901.

174. Blass and Debrunner, *Greek Grammar,* §443; Merkle, *Guide,* 108.

175. Brown, *Testimony of Luke,* 1122.

176. "Glory to God on High," in *Hymns of the Church of Jesus Christ of Latter-day Saints* (Salt Lake City: The Church of Jesus Christ of Latter-day Saints, 1985), hymn no. 67, verse 2.

177. "Rejoice, the Lord Is King," in *Hymns of the Church of Jesus Christ,* hymn no. 66, verse 3.

casting the event in more descriptive language, we intone Richard All-dridge's lines in "We'll Sing All Hail to Jesus' Name": "He seized the keys of death and hell / And bruised the serpent's head; / He bid the prison doors unfold, / The grave yield up her dead."[178] This "gift of Christ" (4:7), framed here as a rescue of departed spirits under the control of death and hell, is brought about "by His descent to [the depths of the] earth and ascent to heaven" (see 4:8–10).[179] In sum, the Christ has acted in a way that humans cannot, making it possible, in the words of John Nicholson, "That man might not remain a slave / Of death, of hell, or of the grave" (see D&C 88:6, "he that ascended up on high, as also he descended below all things, in that he comprehended all things, that he might be . . . the light of truth"; the Notes on 3:8, 10, 17; 4:5, 9; 5:8; 6:10, 18; and the Analysis of 3:1–13; 4:1–16).[180]

passeth: The picture that the participle displays for readers (from the verb ὑπερβάλλω, *hyperballo*) portrays more than the basic thought "to pass." Rather, it means "to far surpass," lifting or bringing something to a high degree.[181] When compared to the old order of the Old Testament, "the new [order] is all surpassing" (see Philip. 4:7).[182]

filled: Rather like the earlier occurrence of the verb πληρόω (*pleroo*), wherein Christ and the church are the ones who fill and possess fulness (see 1:22–23 and Col. 1:19; 2:9), in our passage it is individual church members who are to be filled, one by one, with a more potent content, "the fullness of God [himself]." Furthermore, this process of filling is ongoing and will last into the eternities.[183] In addition, we are to recall the sacred filling of a priest's hands for a holy purpose at the temple, always in an act of consecration (see Ex. 28:41; 29:9, 29; etc.). The difference from the Old Testament era to that of the New Testament is that, rather than consecrat-ing or filling the hands of priests only, each believer enjoys access to the divine actions that make one holy, filling that person with "the fulness of

---

178. "We'll Sing All Hail to Jesus' Name," in *Hymns of the Church of Jesus Christ*, hymn no. 182, verse 3.

179. Grundmann, Hesse, de Jonge, and van der Woude, *TDNT*, 9:558.

180. "While of These Emblems We Partake," in *Hymns of the Church of Jesus Christ*, hymn no. 173, verse 3.

181. Louw-Nida, §78.33.

182. Delling, *TDNT*, 8:521.

183. Bruce, *Ephesians*, 69.

God."[184] This filling includes the unbounded gifts of God, especially "the knowledge of the love of Christ" (see the Notes on 1:23; 4:10; 5:18).[185]

knowledge: Our initial impression leads us to human knowledge (γνῶσις, *gnōsis*), which cannot grasp eternal truths and, indeed, cannot "know the love of Christ." That is to say, this kind of knowledge, unsparked by divine help, cannot understand "the mysteries of the kingdom of heaven" that Jesus helped his disciples to comprehend (Matt. 13:11; see also Mark 4:11 and Luke 8:10). On the other side of the coin, scripture almost always dresses up common terms in heavenly clothing. So it is here. Yes, knowledge unaided by celestial means remains earthly, worldly. But when it is attached to revelation (see 1:17), to an otherworldly anchor, it leads us to "the Son of God" and to "the measure of the stature of the fulness of Christ" (4:13). By following the lit path of divine knowing, believers come to "know thee the only true God, and Jesus Christ, whom thou hast sent" (John 17:3; see also Col. 3:10 and the Notes on 3:18; 4:13).

fulness: The condition of fulness (πλήρωμα, *plērōma*) results from a gift or endowment. That gift comes from Christ to each person, essentially resulting in deification.[186] How so? Because "in [Christ] dwells all the fulness of deity in bodily form" (Col. 2:9, Wayment). He is able to give such a gift not only because of his mortal life but also because of his postmortal experiences of descending "into the lower parts of the earth" and ascending "far above all heavens" (4:9–10). But it was not always so. According to modern scripture, the Son did not enjoy the fulness of God at first. Instead, it came to him in a special act of his Father, who "gave me [Christ] of his fulness." In fact, "he received not of the fulness [of God] at the first, but continued from grace to grace, until he received a fulness." As a result, "he was called the Son of God, because he received not of the fulness at the first." Further, when he received the endowment from his Father, Christ "received a fulness of the glory of the Father" as well as "all power, both in heaven and on earth" (D&C 93:4, 13–14, 16–17). These gifts of glory and power form aspects of God's fulness, which he offers to his children: "For if you keep my commandments," Christ told believers, "you shall receive of [God's] fulness, and be glorified in me as I am in the Father." There is more. As Christ "received a fulness of truth," so will we. Moreover, in the Resurrection, the faithful will "receive a fulness of joy" (D&C 93:20, 26,

---

184. Barth, *Ephesians,* 1:373–74.

185. Delling, *TDNT,* 6:292, 302, quotation on 6:302; Fowl, *Ephesians,* 122–23.

186. Winger, *Ephesians,* 400.

33–34). Thus, fulness embraces a kaleidoscope of heavenly endowments, all coming from the Father to the Son and then to us (see the Notes on 1:10, 23; 4:13).

3:20 *unto him:* This construction opens a doxology that offers praise to God for what he can and will do for his children, promising them in a real sense that he will bless them beyond anything that they can "ask or think." Such efforts to praise God appear elsewhere in the New Testament, usually in connection with the term "glory" (δόξα, *doxa*; see Rom. 11:36; 16:25–27; Gal. 1:5; Philip. 4:20; and Jude 1:24–25; etc.).[187]

is able: It goes without saying that God is able, that he has the power to bring about his purposes. The verb is δύναμαι (*dynamai*), which is linked to the noun translated as "power" (δύναμις, *dynamis*) later in this verse. Such divine ability is tied to the release of majestic powers in the Creation (see Gen. 1:3; Moses 2:3) and in the exercise of faith (see Matt. 17:20; Mark 11:23; Luke 17:6; 1 Cor. 13:2; and Ether 12:30). These powers, these abilities, are effective because God possesses them. They are his. What is more, he can transmit them to us as we exercise faith. Just as importantly, he can give them to us when such a transfer suits his purposes. These occasions allow us to possess and exercise his powers on behalf of others, such as raising the sick from their afflictions (see James 5:14–15). In addition, church members have or possess other notable gifts from God. For example, they have hope (see 2:12; Acts 24:15), an advocate (see 1 John 2:1), a good conscience (see Acts 24:16 and 1 Pet. 3:16), access to God (see 2:18; 3:12), and access to redemption (see 1:7; Col. 1:14;[188] and the Notes on 1:19, 21; 3:7; 4:30 on "redemption"; 6:11, 13, 16).

exceeding abundantly above all: This piling up of words serves to underscore the massive abilities or powers that God possesses. There is no limit. The beneficiaries, of course, are "we [who] ask or consider thoughtfully" (NR), exercising faith that God will do for us what we cannot do for ourselves. In the order of the Greek text, "above all" (ὑπὲρ πάντα, *hyper panta*) comes first, stressing that God's powers surge far above those available to us from any other source. Later comes the adverb translated "more abundantly" (NR; ὑπερεκπερισσοῦ, *hyperekperissou*), which emphasizes an extreme degree (see 1 Thes. 3:10, "we pray *most earnestly*," NIV, emphasis added).[189]

---

187. Best, *Ephesians*, 348–49.
188. Hanse, *TDNT*, 2:824–26 and n. 58.
189. BDAG, 1033; Louw-Nida, §78.34.

think: The verb νοέω (*noeō*) bears a richer sense than just "to think." It stands within the concepts "to consider thoughtfully" (NR) or "to think over" (see 3:4, "perceive," NR; and 2 Tim. 2:7, "think over what I have said," Jerusalem Bible; see also Mark 13:14).[190] The message centers on the fact that God will bless us far beyond our ability to think of things to ask him for and beyond what we may request in our petitions to him.[191] Said another way, and with a different emphasis, we read about "the surpassing greatness of his power toward us, the ones who believe according to the action of his mighty strength" (1:19 NR).

the power that worketh in us: The power noted here does not touch on miracles (for those performed by apostles, see Acts 15:12; 19:11; Rom. 15:18–19; 2 Cor. 12:12; Gal. 3:5; and 1 Thes. 1:5). Rather, we encounter the force that undergirds our inner strength, that is "the inner man" (3:16) or "the new man" (4:24), and that results from our lives of faith. This empowerment or endowment came dynamically to Jesus when God "raised him from the dead, and set him at his own right hand in the heavenly places" (1:20). Thereafter, God "put all things under his feet, and gave him to be the head over all things to the church" (1:22). Then, in an act of divine graciousness, as Paul reminded his readers, God "quickened us together with Christ [and] . . . raised us up together, and made us sit together [with him] in heavenly places" (2:5–6). Such actions make believers "heirs of God, and joint-heirs with Christ," with the proviso that we willingly "suffer with him, that we may be also glorified together" (Rom. 8:17).

Because Christ possesses this power, he is in the position to distribute it to us as we need it or as he sees fit. According to one ancient source composed before Jesus' birth, "he will take upon him [his people's] infirmities, . . . that he may know according to the flesh how to succor his people according to their infirmities" (Alma 7:12). It was Jesus' mortal experiences that put him in a position to understand our mortal needs, as we find in another place: "Because he himself has suffered and been tempted [tried], he is able to help those who are tempted [tried]" (Heb. 2:18 RSV; see also Heb. 5:8).[192] Hence, when he exercises power on our behalf, he can direct that power in a precise, informed manner so that he solves our problems completely or in the way that he deems best for us. As we have learned, this

---

190. Louw-Nida, §30.3; see also BDAG, 674–75.

191. Lincoln, *Ephesians*, 216; Winger, *Ephesians*, 401.

192. The verb translated "tempted" or "tried" (πειράζω, *peirazō*) is the same as that which describes Jesus' temptations or trials in the wilderness (see Matt. 4:1; Mark 1:13; Luke 4:2). See BDAG, 792–93; Louw-Nida, §§27.31, 46; 88.308; Thayer, *Lexicon*, 498.

power, when he exercises it on behalf of believers, has been fittingly called "the enabling power of the Atonement."[193] Not least is the victory of the Resurrection, when he brings us forcefully out of the grasp of death and of demonic powers, which hold sway in the unseen world (see the Notes on 1:9, 21; 2:7, 16; 3:7, 16, 18; 4:30).[194]

worketh: We come upon the same verb (ἐνεργέω, *energeō*) that we met in 1:20, which, in that passage, explained God's "mighty power" (1:19) that was unleashed on behalf of his Son. That power of God "was wrought [*energeō*] in Christ when he raised him from the dead, and set him at his own right hand in the heavenly places." Now, that same working, that same exertion, "worketh in us," exalting us to unimagined heights. But the story does not end here. In 4:16, where Paul wrote the noun form ενέργεια (*energeia*), he held that this remarkable energy or force would work through individuals to strengthen the body of the church, Christ being its head (see 1:22–23). This would happen "according to the effectual working [*energeia*] in the measure of every part ... unto the edifying of itself in love" (4:16). Hence, such power is not reserved for individuals only but is intended to bless the community of believers, the church.[195] And God is the source of that unifying strength. Though "apostles" and "prophets" are essential to "the work of the ministry" (4:11–12), it is ultimately "God that giveth the increase" (1 Cor. 3:7; see also Rom. 12:4–8; 1 Cor. 12:12–28; James 5:16, "availeth much"; and the Notes on 1:11, 20; 2:2, 10; 4:16).[196]

3:21 *Unto him:* The case of this pronoun (αὐτῷ, *autō*), the dative, which mirrors that of the prior verse, both closes Paul's prayer, which begins in 3:14, and ties off the first three chapters of the letter, hinting strongly at the liturgical or worshipful character of this long first part of the epistle.[197]

glory: This term (δόξα, *doxa*) is almost always a part of doxologies, coming at the end of prayers or expressions of praise. Those who sing or recite such paeans aim their thanksgiving and praise toward God. His glory, of course, is one of his most distinguishing features. This kind of glory is said to be manifested in some form of visible intensity; that is, it can be

---

193. Bednar, "In the Strength of the Lord," 121–28; Rasmus, "Enabling Power of the Atonement," 18–21; see also Eising, *TDOT*, 4:349, 353–55; Grundmann, *TDNT*, 2:313–16; Oepke, *TDNT*, 2:542–43; Braun, *TDNT*, 6:464, who treats Elisabeth and Mary (see also Luke 1:25, 49).

194. Grundmann, *TDNT*, 2:314–16.

195. Braun, *TDNT*, 6:464; Lincoln, *Ephesians*, 261–62; Winger, *Ephesians*, 473–74.

196. Best, *Ephesians*, 412–13.

197. Lincoln, *Ephesians*, 197–201; Best, *Ephesians*, 348.

seen, such as in the account of the angel's appearance to the shepherds of Bethlehem (see Luke 2:9), in the story of Jesus' Transfiguration (see Luke 9:31–32), or in the narrative of Paul's experience on the way to Damascus (see Acts 22:11). In doxologies, the intoning of *doxa* is not simply an acknowledgment of God's wondrous attribute but an "extolling of what [actually] is" (see Luke 2:14; 19:38; Rom. 11:36; 16:27; Philip. 4:20; D&C 20:4; etc.; and the Notes on 1:6, 14, 17–18; 3:13, 16).[198]

in the church by Christ Jesus: Here, we meet a textual problem that is reasonably easy to solve. The earliest texts from the fourth and fifth centuries insert the Greek conjunction "and" (καί, *kai*) between the two phrases so that together they read, "in the church and in Christ Jesus." The King James translators had access to a later version of the text that had apparently been adjusted by scribes who thought that mentioning the church before Christ was disrespectful and needed to be fixed. It was as if the church and Christ, its head, were being equated in some fashion. A few other texts inverted Christ and the church so that Christ stood first. But the earliest reading "in the church and in Christ Jesus" is intrinsically suitable. For it is as if the Apostle is ending his prayer in the name of Christ Jesus. Further, in Ephesians the church and Christ are intimately connected. For example, Christ is the head of the church and its fulness dwells in him (see 1:22–23; 4:15–16); Christ is its cornerstone (see 2:20); Christ is the Savior of the church (see 5:23); finally, Christ is to present the church to his Father as "holy and without blemish" (5:27; see the Notes on 1:23; 3:8, 10; 4:12; 5:27).[199]

throughout all ages, world without end: This line, coming at the end of Paul's prayer, could readily be translated "through all generations of time, and throughout all eternity." Commentators agree that the first part of the expression has to do with historic time and the second element stretches off into eternity.[200] The term translated "generations" (γενεά, *genea*) spreads a wide and rich set of meanings before a reader, everything from those of the current generation to those who descended from a notable ancestor to those who are of the same ethnic stock to generations far in the future.[201] In all, the senses tie either to past, present, or future time

198. Von Rad and Kittel, *TDNT*, 2:247–48, quotation on 248. See also Best, *Ephesians,* 350.
199. Schmidt, *TDNT,* 3:509; Barth, *Ephesians,* 1:375–76; Lincoln, *Ephesians,* 217; Best, *Ephesians,* 350–51; Winger, *Ephesians,* 402–3.
200. Schrenk and Quell, *TDNT,* 5:1018; Lincoln, *Ephesians,* 218; Merkle, *Guide,* 110.
201. Büchsel, *TDNT,* 1:662–63; Louw-Nida, §§10.4, 28; 11.4; 67.144.

and to this earth (see D&C 20:4, "both now and forever"; and the Notes on 1:21; 2:2, 7; 3:5, 9, 11).

Amen: One of two occurrences of this term in Ephesians (see 6:24), it comes at the end of a doxology or an expression of praise, hence functioning as Paul's hope that God will not only accept his offering of praise but will also make it secure as an expression of truth. In effect, Paul is saying, "Let it be so." In other words, true "glory belongs to God in the Church and in Christ Jesus in history and on into eternity [and] is to be confirmed by the readers with their 'Amen.'"[202]

The term "amen" (Hebrew אָמֵן, *amēn*; Greek ἀμήν, *amēn*) enjoyed a long history before Paul's day. What we lack is a firm time frame for its earliest use and development. The evidence from the Old Testament, our main source, is not completely reliable. For instance, in its earliest occurrence during a public gathering on the occasion of King David's celebration of the arrival of the ark of the covenant in Jerusalem, "all the people said, Amen, and praised the Lord" (1 Chr. 16:36). But we cannot determine whether this scene is the creation of a later scribe because it is missing in the parallel passage in the usually more reliable book of 2 Samuel (see 2 Sam. 6:17–18). On the other hand, the recitation of "amen" in a much later scene—on the occasion of Ezra reading the law of Moses in a public setting—is most likely genuine (see Neh. 8:6). But it is impossible to tell whether the crowd's response, "Amen, Amen," is an already established custom for a sacred occasion, the more likely scenario, or is recorded as a first-time event. As an individual, Jeremiah uttered, "Amen: the Lord do so: the Lord perform thy words which thou has prophesied," as a response to Hananiah's misguided prophecy that Babylon's yoke would be broken within two years (Jer. 28:6). In this case, the meaning of "amen" is as above, "Let it be so" (see 1 Kgs. 1:36 for an earlier example).[203]

So it is in the New Testament. "Amen" repeated at the end of prayers or sayings of praise bears the sense of surety, of validity, with the speakers affirming their own firm links to God and his work. For hearers, intoning "amen" at the end of a prayer or doxology signals agreement with what has been said (see Rom. 1:25; 9:5; 11:36; 1 Cor. 14:16; Gal. 1:5; Philip. 4:20; 1 Tim. 1:17; etc.). To the side but in lockstep with these avowals ride Jesus' frequent intonations of "amen" or "amen, amen" to underscore the reliability of his sayings. We see these in the King James translation of the

---

202. Lincoln, *Ephesians*, 218.
203. Alfred Jepsen, *TDOT*, 1:320–21.

Gospels as "Verily" or "Verily, verily" (see Matt. 5:18, 26; Mark 3:28; Luke 4:24; John 1:51; etc.).[204]

Perhaps not surprisingly, the word "amen" also serves as a name for Jehovah and Christ. In Isaiah's book, we read that "he who invokes a blessing on himself in the land shall do so by the God whose name is Amen, and he who utters an oath in the land shall do so by the God of Amen" (Isa. 65:16 NEB). Besides underscoring the enduring connection between a person's sacred utterances and the holy character of God's land, whereon the person speaks those words, this passage introduces one of Jehovah's names—Amen, the trusted, steady One. In what must be an intentional tie to this passage, the Risen Christ dictated the following words to John the Revelator: "To the angel of the church in Laodicea write: 'The words of the Amen, the faithful and true witness, the beginning of God's creation'" (Rev. 3:14 RSV).[205] This title, with its meaning spelled out in the expression "the faithful and true witness," signifies "that he is exactly true to his word, never misrepresenting himself either by exaggeration or suppression."[206]

Analysis of 3:14–21

These last eight verses of chapter 3 (3:14–21) frame a second prayer in Ephesians, this time a plea that readers "be strengthened with might by [God's] Spirit in the inner man" and "that Christ may dwell in your hearts by faith" (3:16–17). And what is the chief object or main goal of Christ's indwelling? The answer is knowledge, but a special knowledge. It is that they "may be able to comprehend ... what is the breadth, and length, and depth, and height ... [of] the love of Christ, which passeth knowledge" (3:18–19). Similarly, the Apostle's first prayer in this letter begged God to "give to you [readers] the spirit of wisdom and revelation in knowing him ... with the eyes of your heart enlightened." Once again, the goal is knowledge. But the nature of the knowledge is different—to "know what is the hope of his calling, [and] what is the wealth of his glorious inheritance among the saints" (1:17–18 NR). That is to say, believers were to come to grasp whom they were worshiping and what he was offering to them. A further objective beckons. For Paul's readers, it rests in being "filled with all the fulness of God" (3:18–19). Let us parse some of these concepts.

---

204. The occurrences of "Verily" or "Verily, verily" number thirty in Matthew, thirteen in Mark, seven in Luke, and twenty-five in John.

205. Heinrich Schlier, *TDNT*, 1:335–38; Jepsen, *TDOT*, 1:322.

206. Draper and Rhodes, *Revelation of John the Apostle*, 185.

In his prologue (see 3:14–15), the Apostle has spiritually turned his gaze to "the Father" (3:14; as we have seen above, the phrase "of our Lord Jesus Christ" is not original). With this seemingly simple title, "the Father," Paul has both drawn our attention to and undraped the one person in the universe to whom all believers turn and, like him, bow in prayer and adoration. By scratching this ordinary term, his pen has joyously transported us all the way to the heavenly throne and to the One who sits upon it. No one stands between us and him; no sin turns us aside from the corridors where he dwells; no agent blocks our path into his holy chamber; no blemish, physical or mental or emotional, holds us back from placing our petitions at his holy feet. There is more.

Paul next pulls our eyes to the most meaningful relationship in the cosmos, that of parent and child, which gains its celestial nourishment from a family kinship with God himself. The plain sense of "every family in the heavenly realms, and on earth" (3:15 NR) being "named" by the Father—that is, being given their identities[207]—lays before us God's eternal fatherhood from our premortal days to our earthly lives and on into the expanses of eternity. But these words hint at far more than our divine childhood status in the family of the Father. The expression "every family" or "each family" points us directly at distinct, eternal family units that persist beyond the boundaries of our mortal lives. Distinguished commentators have clearly seen this possibility in Paul's words and have made every effort to say that this eventual outcome could not be, twisting the idea of an eternal "family" into everything from "angels" to "spirit powers" to social "groupings" to even a vague clustering of "clans."[208] But the plain sense of Paul's words about the Father giving "every family" an everlasting status by granting names to them plays better on the Broadway of eternal family units that persist "in heaven" than that of "angels" who hover in the ether (3:15; see the Note thereon).

Moving through the Apostle's words we come upon the Spirit. One of "the riches of [God's] glory" (3:16 KJV) is to "be strengthened with power in the inner person through his Spirit" (3:16 NR). Thus, the Spirit serves as a conveyor of God's power, his might. For example, by the Spirit, we "have access . . . unto the Father" (2:18). Latter-day Saints are familiar with the prophet Moroni's words that "by the *power* of the Holy Ghost [we] may

---

207. Winger, *Ephesians*, 391.

208. Traub and von Rad, *TDNT*, 5:518 n. 159; Caird, *Letters*, 68; Lincoln, *Ephesians*, 202; Best, *Ephesians*, 338–39; Perkins, *Ephesians*, 89.

know the truth of all things" (Moro. 10:5, emphasis added). Likewise, on his part, Paul is not talking about the Spirit influencing believers in a gentle, almost imperceptible manner. No, he has raw power in mind, the kind that the Father wielded when he "created all things" and, later, "raised [Christ] from the dead, and set him at his own right hand" (3:9; 1:20). "The great passage in Eph. 3:14ff.," writes Walter Grundmann, "is highly significant in this regard [of the operating power of the Holy Spirit]."[209] Moreover, we must add, the Spirit is a revelator as hinted in Moroni's words. It is he who makes it possible that the "eyes of your understanding [are] enlightened" (1:18). It is he who "revealed unto his holy apostles and prophets" the "mystery" of the heavenly door that is open to the Gentiles (3:4–6). It is he who assists us "to comprehend . . . what is the breadth, and length, and depth, and height; and to know the love of Christ" (3:18–19). This is no soft or vague apprehension of truth. The Spirit is the agent for believers coming to know firmly and to grasp robustly God's truths (see 1 Cor. 2:6–10).[210]

Besides the Spirit serving as a medium of power and revelation, with his aid "Christ [shall] dwell in your hearts by faith" (3:17). On the human side, faith is the active ingredient that makes possible this welcome indwelling of Christ in people's lives. But faith does not stand solitary by itself. In fact, it is joined by the elevating influence of love (*agapē*). For in another place, Paul has repeated in elegant detail the virtues of this love, including the sobering declaration that "though I have all faith, . . . and have not charity [*agapē*], I am nothing" (1 Cor. 13:2; see also Moro. 7:46). Hence, love is the constituent that threads itself through our lives such that we are "rooted and grounded in [that] love" (3:17). In this state, the Apostle avers, believers are "able to comprehend . . . and to know the love [*agapē*] of Christ" (3:18–19). But more than a lofty love coming to church members from Christ or the love that believers feel toward him, this Christlike love resides inside the true disciple (see 1 Thes. 3:12, "[may] the Lord make you to increase and abound in love"). For we can "be filled with this love, which [God] hath bestowed upon all who are true followers of his Son" (Moro. 7:48). Clearly implied in Jesus' words to the Eleven at the Last Supper is the notion that his disciples already possessed a measure of this love: "This is my commandment, that ye love one another, as I [Jesus] have loved you" (John 15:12, taking up the verb form of *agapē*; see also 1 John 3:17; 4:12).

---

209. Grundmann, *TDNT*, 2:314.
210. Kleinknecht, Baumgärtel, Bieder, Sjöberg, Schweizer, *TDNT*, 6:425, 444.

The breathtaking news is that love does not fill up the volume in the container of God's gifts. Love will be joined with God's fulness—his majesty and grandeur—which he will infuse into believers, filling them "with all the fulness of God" (3:19). This eventuality will involve leading them from "grace to grace" as he did for his Son (D&C 93:13). It was in this way that Christ "received all power, both in heaven and on earth." As a result, "the glory of the Father was with him" in full measure (D&C 93:17). Expressed another way, following Christ's Resurrection, the Father "placed all things under his feet, and gave him ... the fullness of the one filling all things in every way" (1:22–23 NR). According to the testimony of John the Baptist, believers can begin to enjoy God's fulness in this life. As he declared, "As many as received [Christ], to them gave he power to become the sons of God," for "of his fulness have all we received, grace for grace" (John 1:12, 16). With more clarity, and referencing a lost record written by the Baptist, Christ stated that those who "come unto the Father in my name ... [will] in due time receive of his fulness" (D&C 93:19). The key expression is "in due time." Then comes this crescendo: "If you keep my commandments you shall receive of [God's] fulness, and be glorified in me as I am in the Father" (D&C 93:20). In addition to being bathed in God's glory, a person who "keepeth his commandments receiveth truth and light, until he is glorified in truth and knoweth all things" (D&C 93:28). Indeed!

One added coloration: throughout chapter 3, where we are initially greeted with a reminiscence of Paul's first experience with the Resurrected Jesus and his thoughtful analysis of it (see 3:2–9), the Apostle refrains from making reference to his status as a commissioned apostle or to highlighting some other familiar expressions that characterize him, features that we see in other letters.[211] If this letter is not from the hand of Paul but from someone else, this restraint is puzzling. Why? Because a fabricator would surely want readers to believe that they were looking at a genuine missive from Paul's hand; and this chapter is the perfect place to make this point, especially the way it begins. But such language is conspicuously absent. The natural conclusion? The silence points to Paul as the epistle's author.[212]

---

211. Rom. 11:13, "I am the apostle of the Gentiles"; 1 Cor. 9:1–2, "Am I not an apostle?"; 15:9, "I am the least of the apostles"; see also 2 Cor. 11:5; 12:11.

212. Muddiman, *Ephesians,* 146–47.

Chapter 4

INTRODUCTION

Paul now pivots. He seamlessly moves from doctrinal matters to hortatory; that is, from teaching his readers about their place in God's grand plan[1] to offering direction about their proper behavior. But his pivot is not total. From time to time, he turns to doctrinal teachings such as his words on unity (see 4:4–6) and on Jesus' descent into the world of departed spirits (see 4:8–10). For the rest, it is almost as if Paul is barking out orders. His directives naturally raise questions about the all-encompassing grace that some argue for, setting works completely aside and shoving them onto the edges of the path to salvation (see 2:8–9, "For by grace are ye saved . . . not of works").[2] The issue arises noticeably in 4:7, where we read about the grace "given unto every one of us . . . according to the measure of the gift of Christ." This sounds as if the measurements of grace given to each are different, apparently according to an individual's needs. And, if different, then perhaps the differing measures of grace are in need of supplemental action when God brings a person all the way from the weaknesses of mortality to the perfections of salvation. On this view, works may well be required to make up certain deficits at least in modest ways (see the Note on 4:7).

Chapter 4 breaks out into two distinct parts. The underpinning element in the first portion, 4:1–16, has to do with the church and its organization, though not in a lot of detail. The thoroughgoing theme of the second segment, 4:17–32, centers on "the conduct and motivation of each single saint."[3] The basic characteristic of the church's organization as described in 4:1–16 is unity—"to keep the unity of the Spirit . . . one body, and one Spirit,

---

1. Perhaps oddly, Barth, *Ephesians,* 2:426, calls chapters 1–3 "doxological," mainly an extended praise.

2. Fowl, *Ephesians,* 125–27.

3. Barth, *Ephesians,* 2:451, 525, quotation on 525.

... One Lord, one faith, one baptism, One God and Father of all" (4:3–6). A reader cannot miss the force and direction of Paul's language. Besides all these features, God "gave the apostles, the prophets, the evangelists, the shepherds and teachers, to equip the Saints for the work of ministering, for the building up of the body of Christ" (4:11–12 NR). And what will be the results of unity and church organization? The results will be witnessed in each individual member, who will certainly be impacted. How so? Because the grand purposes pertain to "the perfecting of the [individual] saints [and] ... the edifying of [the members of] the body of Christ." But this is not the end of the story. For as a body, astonishingly, "we [shall] all come in the unity of the faith ... unto the measure of the stature of the fulness of Christ" (4:12–13). In fact, in the church, in the body of Christ, "the whole body [will be] fitly joined together and compacted ... according the effectual working ... of every part"—that is, according to the efforts of every individual (4:16).

In the opening lines of 4:17–32, the latter part of the chapter, Paul appeals to readers to turn away totally from their past lives, lives that were bedeviled by walking "in the vanity of their mind" and "being alienated from the life of God [and] ... being past feeling" (4:17–19). That path through life brought them to a "darkened" understanding, a "blindness of their heart," and to behavior given "over unto lasciviousness" (4:18–19). As if to hammer these bleak, bottom-feeding dangers into submission and to lift readers' eyes to grander possibilities, Paul wrote "that [this] is not the way you learned Christ [and] ... the truth is in Jesus" (4:20–21 NR).

According to the second section (see 4:22–24), these formerly benighted patterns of converts' lives, of course, were to be replaced. But the replacement was not to be of modest character. Their best efforts were "to put off ... the old man, which is corrupt." In its place was to be a heaven-sent renewal "in the spirit of your mind" so that believers could "put on the new man" (4:22–24) as though putting on a new garment, as we find in the language of the sacramental prayer, "to take upon them the name of thy Son" (Moro. 4:3; see also Gal. 3:27, "have put on Christ"). Such a new person, unspeakably, is "after [the pattern of] God ... created in righteousness and true holiness" (4:24; see also 2 Cor. 5:1–4).

In the final and longest segment of the second half of the chapter (see 4:25–32), the Apostle comes to the heart of what it means to turn away from one's past and, with heaven's help, become a new person. It means good works, plain and simple. And our good actions are to arise within our relationships with other people, because "we are members one of another"

(4:25). Such works gain their foothold from our words, from what we say. For "every man" is to speak "truth with his neighbor" and is to allow "no corrupt communication [to] proceed out of your mouth," avoiding "evil speaking" (4:25, 29, 31). But, as we might expect, more is involved than our utterances. At the top of a person's actions is perched the imperative not to "give place to the devil" and to "grieve not the holy spirit of God" (4:27, 30). We do that by being "kind one to another, . . . forgiving one another, even as God for Christ's sake hath forgiven you" (4:32). At times, pursuing good works means giving up old practices and replacing them with new actions. For example, the person "that stole [should] steal no more." In the place of stealing to support oneself and one's family, the individual—likely a slave— is to "labor, working with his hands . . . that he may have to give to him that needeth" (4:28). As Paul promises, honest efforts will lead to enough abundance to meet the needs not only of ourselves but also of those who are without means to support themselves. In a word, our works impact others, bringing blessings into their lives as well as our own.

"FOR THE PERFECTING OF THE SAINTS" (4:1–16)

King James Translation

1 I therefore, the prisoner of the Lord, beseech you that ye walk worthy of the vocation wherewith ye are called, 2 With all lowliness and meekness, with longsuffering, forbearing one another in love; 3 Endeavouring to keep the unity of the Spirit in the bond of peace. 4 There is one body, and one Spirit, even as ye are called in one hope of your calling; 5 One Lord, one faith, one baptism, 6 One God and Father of all, who is above all, and through all, and in you all. 7 But unto every one of us is given grace according to the measure of the gift of Christ. 8 Wherefore he saith, When he ascended up on high, he led captivity captive, and gave gifts unto men. 9 (Now that he ascended, what is it but that he also descended first into the lower parts

New Rendition

1 I, therefore, the prisoner in the Lord, urge you to walk worthy of the calling to which you were called, 2 with all humility and gentleness, with patience, accepting one another in love, 3 striving to maintain the unity of the spirit through the bond of peace. 4 There is one body and one Spirit (just as you have been called in one hope of your calling), 5 one Lord, one faith, one baptism, 6 one God and Father of all, who is over all and through all and in all. 7 Now to each one of us grace was given according to the measure of Christ's gift. 8 This is why it says, "When he ascended on high, he captured a host of captives and gave gifts to humans." 9 Now, the expression "he ascended," what does it mean except that he also

of the earth? 10 He that descended is the same also that ascended up far above all heavens, that he might fill all things.) 11 And he gave some, apostles; and some, prophets; and some, evangelists; and some, pastors and teachers; 12 For the perfecting of the saints, for the work of the ministry, for the edifying of the body of Christ: 13 Till we all come in the unity of the faith, and of the knowledge of the Son of God, unto a perfect man, unto the measure of the stature of the fulness of Christ: 14 That we henceforth be no more children, tossed to and fro, and carried about with every wind of doctrine, by the sleight of men, and cunning craftiness, whereby they lie in wait to deceive; 15 But speaking the truth in love, may grow up into him in all things, which is the head, even Christ: 16 From whom the whole body fitly joined together and compacted by that which every joint supplieth, according to the effectual working in the measure of every part, maketh increase of the body unto the edifying of itself in love.

descended to the lower regions of the earth? 10 He who descended is the very one who also ascended far above all the heavenly realms in order that he might fill all things. 11 And it was he who gave the apostles, the prophets, the evangelists, the shepherds and teachers, 12 to equip the saints for the work of ministering, for the building up of the body of Christ, 13 until we may all attain to the unity of the faith and of the knowledge of the son of God, the perfect man, and attain to the measure of the stature of the fullness of Christ, 14 that we may no longer be children, tossed about by the waves and carried about by every wind of teaching, by human trickery, by cunning, in the scheming of deception. 15 But speaking the truth in love, we are to grow in every way unto him who is the head, Christ, 16 from whom the whole body, joined and held together by every joint providing support, generates bodily growth, according to the activity of each individual part, for the purpose of building itself up in love.

Notes on 4:1–16

4:1 *I:* The pronoun ἐγώ (*egō*) is emphatic. Paul does not seem to be saying, "Woe is me, I am a prisoner in a jail." Instead, he appears to be affirming that he is as his readers are—that is to say, prisoners of Christ, a label in which the noun "prisoner" (δέσμιος, *desmios*) is an essential part. Why? Because to be another's prisoner in the ancient world meant that the jailer held all the powers over the prisoner (see 3:1; Philip. 1:13; and Philem. 1:9, 13).[4] But there is a difference. In the New Testament, prisoners and slaves are never spoken of in the "contemptuous fashion [that is] common in the Greek and

---

4. Gerhard Kittel, *TDNT,* 2:43; BDAG, 219.

Hellenestic world."[5] Rather, they are valued as brothers and sisters and fellow travelers on this earth (see the Notes on 3:1; 6:20).[6]

therefore: The conjunction οὖν (*oun*), translated "therefore," essentially brings to an end the first three chapters, preparing the reader for the inferences to be drawn from the previous doctrinal teachings.[7] But those inferences do not unpack and rephrase those teachings. Instead, they direct us to the kind of behavior that grows out of those doctrines. This type of reasoning appears in other passages from Paul, all introduced by the same conjunction (see Rom. 12:1, "therefore"; Col. 3:1, "then"; and 1 Thes. 4:1, "then").

the prisoner of the Lord: Although Paul is a prisoner somewhere, it is not so much that he is drawing attention to himself as a prisoner, but rather that his experience, unpredictable whether he will enjoy good times or ill, serves as an example to all believers (see 2 Cor. 6:4–10). For they are captives or slaves of Christ as he is and do not have the option of choosing what they may be asked to undergo for the Lord.[8] It is essential to stress that this situation involves a covenant between a person and God as well as the exercise of grace or graciousness on God's side of the relationship (see the Notes on 2:5, 8; 4:3).[9]

prisoner: Paul is surely imprisoned in some location, as he also indicates in 3:1 and 6:20, either inside a jail cell or, more probably, under house arrest. Other letters refer to an imprisonment, possibly tying all of them to the same experience (see Philip. 1:7, 13; Col. 4:3, 18; and Philem. 1:1). As the introduction to this volume makes clear, Ephesians and these companion Epistles were likely not written during Paul's two-year stretch under house arrest in Caesarea (see Acts 23–26, especially 24:27). Rather, it is more probable that he wrote these missives later, while under guard in Rome (see the introduction section V and the Notes on 3:1; 6:20).[10]

Lord: In this simple title (κύριος, *kyrios*), we find the underpinnings of the directives and imperatives that follow in this letter—all is to be undertaken in the name of the Lord. Although supplied by translators, the omission of the definite article in the Greek text brings us closer to the divine

5. Rengstorf, *TDNT,* 2:271.

6. Kittel, *TDNT,* 2:43; Rengstorf, *TDNT,* 2:278.

7. Barth, *Ephesians,* 2:426; Larkin, *Handbook,* 68; Merkle, *Guide,* 111–12.

8. Kittel, *TDNT,* 2:43; Winger, *Ephesians,* 353, 427.

9. Schmidt, *Relational Grace,* 94–96.

10. Bruce, *Paul: Apostle of the Heart Set Free,* 411–12; Caird, *Letters,* 2–5; contra Winger, *Ephesians,* 122–30.

name יהוה (Hebrew "Yahweh" or "Jehovah").[11] The Greek expression "the Lord" (ὁ κύριος, *ho kyrios*) is a title, not a name.[12] Throughout the prior three chapters, we have consistently met the expression "the Lord Jesus Christ" or its equivalent (see 1:2, 3, 15, 17; etc.), with one exception (see 2:21, "the Lord"). From 4:1 on, almost uniformly we encounter "the Lord," which appears in eighteen spots (see 4:5, 17; 5:8, 10; 6:1, 4; etc.), with a mere three exceptions (see 5:20; 6:23–24). It may be that the phrase "in the Lord" (4:1, 17 NR; ἐν κυρίῳ, *en kyriō*), of which the Apostle is the apparent inventor, exhibits Paul's preference "in contexts of moral exhortation like this," rather than using the phrase "in Christ."[13] But more may be going on than meets the eye.

The Apostle employed varying expressions in other contexts to introduce "moral exhortation." For example, his exhortations came to readers "in Christ" (Philip. 2:1), "by the mercies of God" (Rom. 12:1), "for the Lord Jesus Christ's sake, and for the love of the Spirit" (Rom. 15:30), "by the name of our Lord Jesus Christ" (1 Cor. 1:10), "by the meekness and gentleness of Christ" (2 Cor. 10:1), and "by the Lord Jesus" (1 Thes. 4:1). In this light, the phrase "in the Lord" in Ephesians is not the norm elsewhere and invites us to explore some of its important meanings. That said, all of the appeals to good behavior in the following verses tie to the verb "beseech" in this letter (παρακαλέω, *parakaleō*; see the Notes on 4:17; 6:22).[14]

A shift in titles for Deity often directs us to a joining of two sources. For example, we evidently encounter a second source that has been grafted onto a prior source in the change from "God" to "Lord God" at Genesis 2:4. The title "Lord God" thereafter joins strategically with the ten appearances of the expression "these are the generations of . . ." in the book of Genesis, suggesting the welding of two or more sources at Genesis 2:4 (see also Moses 3:4; 6:8).[15] No evidence exists, however, that Paul has put two extended sources together in this letter. His shift to the name-title "Lord" runs smoothly and seamlessly. Something else is at work. The most ready

---

11. David Noel Freedman, Michael Patrick O'Connor, and Helmer Ringgren, *TDOT*, 5:512.

12. Quell and Foerster, *TDNT*, 3:1059.

13. Muddiman, *Ephesians*, 178. Oepke, *TDNT*, 2:541, holds that Paul is the evident inventor of both expressions, "in Christ" and "in the Lord."

14. Otto Schmitz and Gustav Stählin, *TDNT*, 5:795.

15. Roland Kenneth Harrison, *An Introduction to the Old Testament* (Grand Rapids, Mich.: Eerdmans, 1969), 543–51. The passages that repeat the Hebrew expression אלה תולדות (*eleh toldot*), "these are the generations of . . . ," occur in Gen. 2:4; 6:9; 10:1; 11:10, 27; 25:12, 19; 36:1, 9; 37:2; compare the similar expression at Gen. 5:1, "the book of the generations."

resource for him is the Old Testament and its characterization of the One called "the Lord." Naturally, we cannot dive deeply into this topic because the number of occurrences runs into the thousands. But a few elements rise quickly to our view that allow us to make a few observations about what lies behind Paul's switch in titles.

At the foundation of the appearance of *kyrios* rests "a concept of relationship" with the Lord on which all believers depend for "their very being as Christians." In other words, blossoming out of this dependent relationship with him come "all things" that make believers who they are and who they can become.[16] The first attribute of *kyrios* that we turn to centers on the fact that he is the dispenser of justice and mercy, the two essential qualities that eventually balance good and evil.[17] On the side of justice, in a quotation that includes Isaiah 42:1 and 42:3, Matthew wrote that Jesus fulfilled the prophecy that "my servant whom I have chosen . . . will proclaim justice to the nations . . . till he leads justice to victory" (Matt. 12:18, 20 NIV). In another setting, Jesus once proclaimed in a harsh, accusatory voice, "Woe unto you . . . Pharisees, you hypocrites . . . you have neglected the more important matters of the law—justice, mercy, and faithfulness" (Matt. 23:23 NIV; see also Luke 11:42). Jesus himself was robbed of justice in this life. For that is how one is to understand the scriptural passage that the Ethiopian eunuch was reading and could not understand until Philip came to his aid. While reading Isaiah's book, the eunuch came upon the passage "In his humiliation he was deprived of justice" (Acts 8:33 NIV, quoting Isa. 53:8).[18] At this point, "Philip opened his mouth . . . and preached unto him [the eunuch] Jesus" (Acts 8:35). But Jesus the Lord will be robbed no more and will be the eternal steward of justice.

On another side is the Lord's mercy. The scriptural texts present a glowing richness. We hear words of desperation from "a woman of Canaan" who begged Jesus, "Have mercy on me, O Lord. . . . My daughter is grievously vexed with a devil" (Matt. 15:22). And what did Jesus do? After a short back and forth about "the lost sheep of the house of Israel," Jesus "said unto her, O woman, great is thy faith: be it unto thee even as thou wilt." From "that very hour" the woman's "daughter was made whole" (Matt. 15:24, 28). From an earlier moment in Jesus' ministry, in a spare, revealing

---

16. Quell and Foerster, *TDNT,* 3:1091.

17. Quell and Foerster, *TDNT,* 3:1084; Freedman, O'Connor, and Ringgren, *TDOT,* 5:518–19.

18. BDAG, 569, s.v. "κρίσις (*krisis*)."

couplet, we listen to Jesus' words that spell out our needs both to be merciful and to receive mercy: "Blessed are the merciful: for they shall obtain mercy" (Matt. 5:7). The Apostle Paul, quoting Exodus 33:19, a passage wherein Moses had requested to see the glory of the Lord, penned the Lord's response: "He saith to Moses, I will have mercy on whom I will have mercy" (Rom. 9:15). This declaration finds its balancing ballast in Jesus' assurance to his hearers that the Father is merciful: "Be ye therefore merciful, as your Father also is merciful" (Luke 6:36). The opposite of mercy will fall upon the person who shows no mercy: "[The final] judgment without mercy will be shown to anyone who has not been merciful" (James 2:13 NIV).[19] But that is not the whole story.

We do not exhaust the Lord's influence in our lives through his justice and mercy. For example, his continuing influence in believers' lives is something they recognize when they acknowledge his exalted authority over their futures and their actions. James brought this to our attention when he wrote that, understanding this authority, we should "say, If the Lord will, we shall live, and do this, or that" (James 4:15). Paul also picked up this thread, expressing it multiple times when he wrote about his hopes to visit church members in Corinth: "I will come to you shortly, if the Lord will" (1 Cor. 4:19). Then, in similar language, he wrote that "I trust to tarry a while with you, if the Lord permit" (1 Cor. 16:7). The Lord's authority can also flow from his inspired representatives. Such was the case when the Apostle pointed out to his readers that "a prophet, or spiritual [person will] . . . acknowledge that what I am writing to you is a command of the Lord," thus highlighting the divine influence that permeates the lives of believers who accept and live according to such commandments (1 Cor. 14:37 RSV).[20]

To continue, the Risen Lord impacts the lives of all. This circumstance jumps out in the matter of titles. For instance, Paul called Christ "the Lord of glory." We read the Apostle's words about the gruesome act carried out by "the princes of this world" who knew not that they were crucifying "the Lord of glory," impacting us all (1 Cor. 2:8).[21] Whether these "princes" will eventually receive forgiveness remains unknown. From the Joseph

---

19. Louw-Nida, §§88.75–77, 80–82.

20. Quell and Foerster, *TDNT*, 3:1090; see also Draper and Rhodes, *Paul's First Epistle to the Corinthians*, 726, on 1 Cor. 14:37. The earliest manuscript, $\mathfrak{P}^{46}$, and others preserve the reading "command" or "commandment" rather than the plural noun "commandments." See Barbara Aland and others, eds., *Novum Testamentum Graece*, 28th ed. (Stuttgart: Deutsche Bibelgesellschaft, 2012), 466.

21. Quell and Foerster, *TDNT*, 3:1086.

Smith Translation, it becomes clear that, in the moment when Jesus prayed, "Father, forgive them," he was not praying for the authorities who had engineered his execution. Rather, those who "know not what they do [were] . . . the soldiers who crucified him" (JST Luke 23:34). Hence, it was for those soldiers that Jesus begged the Father's forgiveness, not the officials.[22] In another place, we discover the title "the Lord of peace," which points to the Lord's authority and power to grant peace, including peace to an individual. In a strong wish for his friends in Thessalonica, Paul expressed his deep desire that "the Lord of peace himself give you peace always [and] . . . be with you all" (2 Thes. 3:16).[23]

In our service to others, we are to perform it to the Lord, and not in a way that draws the praise and admiration of others to ourselves, but invites his notice alone. Saying this much reminds us of Jesus' memorable words about giving alms, offering prayers, and fasting in ways that only the Father witnesses (see Matt. 6:1–18). In our Epistle arises the sage advice to servants or slaves, "Be obedient to them that are your masters according to the flesh, . . . as the servants of Christ, . . . with good will doing service, as [if] to the Lord, and not to men" (6:5–7). This is exactly the point made in Colossians: "Whatever you do, work at it with all your heart, as working for the Lord, not for men" (Col. 3:23 NIV). In Romans, Paul pulls away from service given by slaves and turns his readers to more general situations: "Not slothful in business; fervent in spirit; serving the Lord" (Rom. 12:11; see also 1 Cor. 12:5, "different kinds of service, but the same Lord," NIV).[24] In modern scripture, this concept links to how we treat the marginalized. We read that "inasmuch as ye do it unto the least of these, ye do it unto me" (D&C 42:38; see Matt. 25:40). More specifically, "inasmuch as ye impart of your substance unto the poor, ye will do it unto me" (D&C 42:31; see also D&C 56:16).

Not surprisingly, the Lord is the source of power and authority in the church. When Paul wrote his final salutations in his second letter to the Corinthian Saints, he noted that his absence was a good thing so that he would not "use sharpness" in calling them to repentance "according to the power [*exousia*] which the Lord hath given me" (2 Cor. 13:10). Earlier in that letter, Paul had held back from boasting about "our authority [*exousia*], which the Lord hath given us" (2 Cor. 10:8). In each of these passages, Paul insisted that this

---

22. Brown, *Testimony of Luke,* 1077–78.

23. Quell and Foerster, *TDNT,* 3:1086.

24. Quell and Foerster, *TDNT,* 3:1090–91.

power or authority was for "edification, and not for your destruction." In a word, the Lord granted authority to him and others to build up believers, not to tear them down (see the NIV translations of 2 Cor. 10:8 and 13:10).[25]

In our relationship with the Lord and because of who he is, we must do our best to stand worthily before him both here and hereafter. In this verse, we read the Apostle's words that we are to "walk worthy of the calling to which you were called" (4:1 NR; see also the Note below on "worthy"). Worthiness leads to blessings. In a prayer for the Saints at Colossae, Paul asked God that "they might be filled with the knowledge of [God's] will . . . that ye might walk worthy of the Lord . . . [with the specific blessings of] being fruitful in every good work, and increasing in the knowledge of God" (Col. 1:9–10). Paul took up the matter of unworthily partaking of the Eucharist or sacrament, a situation that he saw as most heinous. He declared that "whosoever shall eat this bread, and drink this cup of the Lord, unworthily, shall be guilty of the body and blood of the Lord," almost as if such people were participants in crucifying the Savior (1 Cor. 11:27).[26]

In the end, the Lord will come. He is the Coming One, and his arrival will impact everyone. On the occasion of his coming, when "the Lord [will] come, . . . [he] will bring to light the hidden things of darkness, and will make manifest the [evil] counsels of the hearts" (1 Cor. 4:5). Beyond this, as John the Baptist promised, "One mightier than I cometh, . . . he shall baptize you with the Holy Ghost and with fire" (Luke 3:16; see also Matt. 3:11; Mark 1:7–8; and Acts 19:4–6). Beyond these spiritual endowments, as the Psalmist sang and the multitude accompanying Jesus into Jerusalem shouted, "Blessed be the King that cometh in the name of the Lord [who will usher in] peace in heaven, and glory in the highest" (Luke 19:38; Ps. 118:26). When the Lord returns, those who "are alive and remain unto the coming of the Lord" will witness the moment that "the Lord himself shall descend from heaven with a shout . . . and with the trump of God: and the dead in Christ shall rise [and] . . . we which are alive . . . shall be caught up . . . to meet the Lord in the air: and so shall we ever be with the Lord" (1 Thes. 4:15–17; see the Notes on 1:6; 4:5, 17; 5:19, 22).[27]

---

25. Quell and Foerster, *TDNT*, 3:1091.

26. Quell and Foerster, *TDNT*, 3:1091.

27. Quell and Foerster, *TDNT*, 3:1091; Johannes Schneider, *TDNT*, 2:666–69; Brown, *Testimony of Luke*, 198, 877.

beseech: The verb παρακαλέω (*parakaleō*) exhibits a wide range of meanings. At base, it conveys the sense of calling someone to oneself.[28] In this passage, behind Paul's urgent request stands "the sphere of Jesus' saving power," an understanding that the Savior's powers are available to aid those whom the Apostle is addressing in this letter. It is clearly with this meaning that Paul unsuccessfully "besought the Lord thrice, that [the thorn in the flesh] might depart from me" (2 Cor. 12:8).[29] In his case, the Lord had evidently determined that Paul was not to "be exalted above measure" (2 Cor. 12:7). Even so, the Apostle stood within the circle of Christ's power to aid him (see the Note on 6:22).

walk: As we discovered in its first occurrence (see 2:2), the verb περιπατέω (*peripateō*) leads readers to how one conducts one's life, being aware, of course, that God has set the path (see Col. 1:10).[30] That notion is its first sense here, with the stipulation that a person lives life worthy of his or her calling. That is to say, the insertion of the expression "of the calling to which you were called" (4:1 NR) adds a further, richer dimension. The concern is not simply to proceed as God wants one to proceed. Because in the walk through life a church member comes to carry a responsibility, a calling, usually for the welfare of others, this means that the person's life must exhibit care and interest not just for one's own self but also for other persons whose lives can and will be impacted by calls to serve them. God's call to an investigator to walk with him is the same thing, even though it also means walking no longer "in darkness" but in "the light of life" (John 8:12; see also 1 Cor. 7:17 and Col. 1:10).[31] In sum, Paul is pointing to a life of service (see below in this Note and the Notes on 2:2, 9, 10; 4:17).

A second meaning, as we have discovered elsewhere (see the Note on 2:10), apparently grows out of sacred ceremony, out of a walk toward and within a place made sacred for special ritual acts and worship. Such movements are as old as Adam and Eve, who, as one account hints, followed a specific pathway and walked to a spot outside the Garden of Eden to worship and receive instruction. There they "called upon the name of the Lord, and they heard the voice of the Lord from the [sacred path]way [where they had walked] toward the Garden of Eden, speaking unto them"

---

28. Schmitz and Stählin, *TDNT*, 5:774; BDAG, 764.
29. Schmitz and Stählin, *TDNT*, 5:794.
30. Werner Foerster, *TDNT*, 1:380.
31. Seeseman and Bertram, *TDNT*, 5:944–45.

(Moses 5:4). The idea is that a cluster of passages in this letter evidently rests on physical movements that worshipers undertook in a ceremonial setting. Although not all eight occurrences of *peripateō* in Ephesians direct us to ceremony (see 2:2; 4:17 [twice]), the majority do (see the Notes on 2:10; 5:2, 8, 14, 15). Such actions appear readily in common settings, such as approaching Jerusalem from outside Judea, walking into the temple grounds during the week preceding any special holiday as part of the purification process, entering and exiting the Court of the Israelites for the slaughter of the lambs at Passover, and walking to the place of slaughtering within the temple's inner courtyard. Examples are easy to multiply. There is more.

The verbs "to put on" (6:11, 14, "having on"), "to take up [weapons]" (6:13, 16), and "to take" or "to receive" (6:17) open doors to the sacred actions of putting on or taking in hand God's garments and weaponry (see LXX Isa. 59:17, "[God] put on righteousness as a breastplate, and placed the helmet of salvation on his head"). Within the parameters of these verbs, a person dons holy clothing as an initial step in imitating God (see 5:1 NR) and taking up his cause in defeating "the rulers of the darkness of this world" (6:12; see also the Notes on 4:13, 20, 22, 24; 6:11, 13, 14, 17; introduction section XI; and appendix 1).

worthy: Very often, a term like "worthy" (ἄξιος, *axios*)—here in its adverbial form ἀξίως (*axiōs*)—is paired with the verb "to walk" (*peripateō*). Other expressions include statements like "walk in newness of life" (Rom. 6:4), "walk by faith" (2 Cor. 5:7), and "walk in the flesh" (2 Cor. 10:3).[32] Of itself, worthiness implies an enduring condition that characterizes the person and, not incidentally, strongly hints at that person's good works. On the other hand, unworthiness among believers raises a sharp concern, especially when an unworthy person partakes of the emblems of the sacrament or Eucharist. As Paul declares, "Whosoever shall eat this bread, and drink this cup of the Lord, unworthily, shall be guilty of the body and blood of the Lord. . . . For he that eateth and drinketh unworthily, eateth and drinketh damnation to himself" (1 Cor. 11:27, 29; see also 3 Ne. 18:28–29).[33] Why is this act so serious? Because by doing so such persons "crucify to themselves the Son of God afresh, and put him to an open shame" (Heb. 6:6; see also D&C 76:35; 132:27; and the Note above on "Lord").

---

32. Seeseman and Bertram, *TDNT*, 5:944.
33. Foerster, *TDNT*, 1:380.

vocation: The noun κλῆσις (*klēsis*) centers on a call or calling (4:1 NR). In New Testament hands, it typically features God's call to us to embrace the Christian life, to come to salvation (see 4:4; 1 Cor. 1:26; 2 Thes. 1:11; 2 Tim. 1:9; Heb. 3:1; and 2 Pet. 1:10).[34] But in three passages, the noun pertains to a person's calling in the church, like that which modern Latter-day Saints experience when called to serve. In his first letter to the Corinthian Saints, Paul instructed that "every man abide in the same calling wherein he was called," a passage that has to do with a church position (1 Cor. 7:20).[35] To be sure, the Apostle then slid into a discussion about servants or slaves receiving God's call (see 1 Cor. 7:21–24). But that does not blunt the initial thrust of 1 Cor. 7:20: persons "abide in the same calling," not seeking another that might bring more notoriety. For God has "set the members every one of them in the body [of Christ], as it hath pleased him." In fact, "those members of the body, which seem to be more feeble [spiritually], are necessary." Further, "those members of the body, which we think to be less honorable [in their modest callings], upon these we bestow more abundant honor" for their service (1 Cor. 12:18, 22–23; see also Heb. 5:4).

Next, this notion of a person being summoned to a specific calling or office in the church reposes on an important juxtaposition of two terms that Paul wrote when articulating his status as an apostle. The first, which shares the same root as *klēsis* above, is κλητός (*klētos*), whose sense is "called" or "invited" and serves as both a noun and a verb. The second is the noun for "apostle," *apostolos*. These two terms stand next to one another in two passages where they mean "called *to be* an apostle," where the italicized words "to be" are not in the Greek text but are needed to complete the idea (Rom. 1:1; 1 Cor. 1:1). Here we meet "a technical term [which] . . . suggests [a] calling to an office" (see the Notes on 1:18; 4:4).[36] To make the case even tighter, according to Clement of Rome, who may be the Clement mentioned in Philippians 4:3,[37] the two virtues that follow in our next verse (4:2), "lowliness and meekness," are required of bishops "and of anyone [else] who holds a leading position in the congregation."[38]

---

34. Schmidt, *TDNT,* 3:491–92; Barth, *Ephesians,* 1:454.

35. BDAG, 549; see also Louw-Nida, §33.314.

36. Schmidt, *TDNT,* 3:494; see also BDAG, 549, "calling to an office"; and Louw-Nida, §33.314, "summoned and commissioned."

37. Quasten, *Patrology,* 1:42–43.

38. Walter Grundmann, *TDNT,* 8:25; *First Clement* 44.3; 48.6, in *ANF,* 1:17, 18.

called: This verb, καλέω (*kaleō*), sits in the passive voice and thus points to God as the one who issues the call.[39] This principle is treated elsewhere in the New Testament within the reminder that "no man taketh this honor [of a calling] unto himself, but he that is called [participle of *kaleō*] of God, as was Aaron" (Heb. 5:4). As a matter of fact, this passage has to do with the call of Jesus to his messiahship; thereby it presents an example of how a calling should come from God.[40] The verb, of course, ties to the noun *klēsis*, which we have just dealt with (see also the Note on 4:4).

4:2 all: Usually translated "all" or "every" when paired with a substantive, in this passage the Greek adjective πᾶς (*pas*) bears the sense of "total" or "complete."[41] Hence, the virtues that are noted next are to be exercised in their fullest or purest expression, an aspect that should characterize the actions and attitudes of "the bishop" and other officers "in the congregation" (see the Note on 6:18).[42]

lowliness: Better translated as "humility," as in the NR,[43] the noun ταπεινοφροσύνη (*tapeinophrosynē*) can describe an ideal behavior or goal for a child when he or she is undergoing an education.[44] More than this, among the opportunities of serving others in a church setting, this noun revolves around a person's readiness to serve, which, importantly, "does not lift up itself above others."[45] Peter's directive to the readers of his first letter offered these words of counsel: "Be clothed in humility"—reproducing the same term, *tapeinophrosynē* (1 Pet. 5:5). The import, as we see, has to do with wearing our humility almost as an ever-present, ever-fresh piece of clothing while we avoid taking pride in our contrition. As we might expect, humility was not a sought-after virtue in the Greco-Roman world of Paul's era. But the Old Testament had raised it to a highly desired quality (see Isa. 57:15; 66:2; and Micah 6:8; see also Acts 20:19 and Col. 3:12).[46]

meekness: Another rendition for πραΰτης (*prautēs*) would be "gentleness" (NR).[47] In its adjectival form, Jesus says this of himself: "Take my yoke upon you and learn from me, for I am *gentle* and humble in heart" (Matt. 11:29 NIV,

---

39. Larkin, *Handbook*, 68; Merkle, *Guide*, 113.
40. Schmidt, *TDNT*, 3:488; BDAG, 503–4.
41. Bo Reicke and Georg Bertram, *TDNT*, 5:888.
42. Grundmann, *TDNT*, 8:25; *First Clement* 44.3; 48.6, in *ANF*, 1:17, 18.
43. BDAG, 989; Louw-Nida, §88.53.
44. Grundmann, *TDNT*, 8:25.
45. Grundmann, *TDNT*, 8:23.
46. Bruce, *Ephesians*, 75–76; Fowl, *Ephesians*, 130.
47. BDAG, 861; Louw-Nida, §88.59.

emphasis added; see also Matt. 5:5; 21:5). From this it follows that a believer's "meekness" or "gentleness" springs from the love that Jesus has offered to those who "labor, and are heavy laden" (Matt. 11:28). Although some naturally possess this virtue as a part of their character, for most people, donning meekness in its full Christian dress comes only as "the fruit of the Spirit," as one of God's gifts (Gal. 5:22–23; 6:1), a gift that is to be exhibited in a "quiet spirit" (1 Pet. 3:4).[48]

longsuffering: This characteristic (μακροθυμία, *makrothymia*) partially makes up who God is. It was his "patience" (NR) or "longsuffering" that put off punishing the wicked in the days of Noah and also that offered the gospel of repentance to those individuals while they were "spirits in [spirit] prison" (see 1 Pet. 3:19–20). Paul wrote about God's willingness to allow people to repent when he drew attention to "the riches of his . . . longsuffering [which] . . . leadeth thee to repentance" (Rom. 2:4; see also 2 Pet. 3:9). Christ, too, enjoys this virtue in his makeup. For it was he who showed forth in the Apostle "all longsuffering." What was its purpose? It was to serve as "a pattern to them which should hereafter believe on him to life everlasting" (1 Tim. 1:16).[49] Thus Christ was its model. To be sure, God's longsuffering is tied to his wrath, which hovers menacingly near those who dare to trivialize or turn their backs on his patience (see 1 Cor. 2:4–5; 9:22).[50] But the attribute of patience stands as the first virtue associated with love or charity, as we read, "Charity suffereth long" (1 Cor. 13:4). Longsuffering is also a trait of the missionary (see 2 Cor. 6:6). Finally, it is to be worn as an enlivening, special garment, "put on" and worn by those who receive it as a "fruit of the Spirit" (Col. 3:12; Gal. 5:22).[51]

forbearing: Here, the basic sense of the verb ἀνέχομαι (*anechomai*) is "to put up with."[52] But it means more than "to endure" events or persons that become trials. It has to do with "accepting one another" (NR), with genuine forgiveness toward those who may trespass against us (see 2 Cor. 11:19 and Col. 3:13). Even when Jesus' pique was aroused against his disciples for their failure to bring relief to a young boy who suffered seizures (see Matt. 17:17; Mark 9:19; and Luke 9:41), he patiently explained to them how they should proceed in such cases (see Matt. 17:19–21 and Mark 9:28–29).

---

48. Friedrich Hauck and Siegfried Schulz, *TDNT,* 6:650.
49. BDAG, 612–13.
50. Johannes Horst, *TDNT,* 4:382–83.
51. Horst, *TDNT,* 4:384.
52. BDAG, 78; Louw-Nida, §25.171.

This response follows a pattern of God restraining himself when his people deserved rebuke (see LXX Isa. 42:14; 64:12).[53] In the human case, believers are to accept "the word of exhortation" even when it disturbs (Heb. 13:22; see also Rom. 15:14) because, otherwise, they run the risk of not enduring "sound doctrine" and of turning "away their ears from the truth" (2 Tim. 4:3–4). Further, strengthened in the faith, when they are "reviled, [they] bless; being persecuted, [they] suffer it [*anechomai*]" (1 Cor. 4:12; see also 2 Thes. 1:4).[54]

in love: Love (ἀγάπη, *agapē*) always surmounts all other gifts from God. Among the fruits of the Spirit, it comes first (see Gal. 5:22–23). True love always expresses itself in sincerity (see Rom. 12:9–10). This said, Paul's language memorably presents its enduring traits: "Charity [*agapē*] suffereth long, and is kind; charity envieth not; charity vaunteth not itself, is not puffed up. Doth not behave itself unseemly, seeketh not her own, is not easily provoked, thinketh no evil; rejoiceth not in iniquity, but rejoiceth in the truth" (1 Cor. 13:4–6). In this light, we can agree wholeheartedly with the observations of Ethelbert Stauffer that love undergirds "a readiness for service and sacrifice, for forgiveness and consideration, for help and sympathy, for lifting up the fallen and restoring the broken, in a fellowship which owes its very existence to the mercy of God and the sacrificial death of Christ" (see 5:2; Philip. 2:1–3; and Col. 3:14–15).[55]

4:3 *Endeavoring:* This verb, the present active participle of σπουδάζω (*spoudazō*), can mean "to hurry." But in our passage it carries the sense "to make every effort."[56] Not surprisingly, it appears regularly in admonitions (see Heb. 4:11, "Let us labor therefore to enter"; 2 Pet. 1:10, "give diligence to make your calling and election sure"; etc.). In the context of this letter, Paul's readers are to pursue two main objectives, one of which possesses a communal focus and the other a personal goal. The first is to strive to preserve "the unity of Jews and Gentiles achieved by Christ" when he "abolished in his flesh the enmity" between the two peoples (2:15). The second has to do with each person seeking diligently to "be holy and without blame before [God] in love" (1:4).[57]

---

53. Heinrich Schlier, *TDNT*, 1:359.
54. BDAG, 78.
55. Quell and Stauffer, *TDNT*, 1:51.
56. BDAG, 939.
57. Günther Harder, *TDNT*, 7:565; the nonscriptural quotation is from this source.

to keep: Two of the meanings of τηρέω (*tēreō*) are "to guard" and "to preserve."[58] In one of its occurrences, it connects to the idea of sacred clothing, though with a metaphorical twist: "Blessed is he that watcheth, and keepeth his garments, lest he walk naked" (Rev. 16:15). In the Ephesians passage, "the unity of the Spirit" is already in force; it is not a future occurrence. Hence, the believers' task is to maintain or keep an existing unity.[59] Implicit, of course, is the notion that, without diligent attention, "the unity of the Spirit" can be lost.[60]

the unity of the Spirit: Because "the unity of the Spirit" comes to believers as a gift, these people are to do more than "treasure" it. They are to hold onto it with two-fisted energy.[61] In addition, because this unity is a gift, the possibility always exists that God will withdraw it, leaving the church an empty shell.[62] Two further matters present themselves in this expression, which we turn to next. One concerns the two occurrences of the noun "unity" in the New Testament (see 4:13), and the other revolves around whether or not the term "Spirit" should be capitalized.

unity: This unity (ἑνότης, *henotēs*) obliterates racial and national boundaries, much as the Mosaic Law tended to erase tribal loyalties. This oneness establishes an identity that rests on a shared belief in Christ and warmly embraces all. Within this unity, we meet no "strangers and foreigners, but [only] fellowcitizens with the saints, and [members] of the household of God" (2:19). All church members worship the one who will "lay down [his] life for the sheep," leading to the situation of "one fold, and one shepherd" (John 10:15–16). Such unity comes about because of the unity of the Father and Son, whose oneness draws in believers. In Jesus' words, this is "[so] that they may be made perfect in one" (John 17:23; see also John 17:21–22). Said another way, "both [the Son] that sanctifieth and they who are sanctified are all of one" (Heb. 2:11). Furthermore, "the [mixed] multitude of them that believed were of one heart and of one soul" (Acts 4:32).[63] Indeed.

We now focus on the two occurrences of *henotēs* in the New Testament, both found in this letter. Two matters arise. The first concerns the difference between the expressions "the unity of the Spirit" and "the unity of

---

58. BDAG, 1002; Louw-Nida, §§13.32; 37.122.
59. Harald Riesenfeld, *TDNT*, 8:143.
60. Muddiman, *Ephesians*, 180.
61. Contra Winger, *Ephesians*, 431.
62. Fowl, *Ephesians*, 132.
63. Ethelbert Stauffer, *TDNT*, 2:440.

the faith" (4:13). A little examination reveals that "the unity of the Spirit" comes as a divine gift, as noted above. On the other hand, "the unity of the faith" frames a result, not a gift, that emerges from the guiding hands of "apostles" and "prophets" whose task is to forge "the perfecting of the saints [and] . . . the work of the ministry" (4:11–12).

The second matter has to do with the rarity of the noun *henotēs* and its appearance only in Ephesians, and nowhere else in scripture, including the Septuagint.[64] In this light, a student might be tempted to conclude that the nonoccurrence of *henotēs* in others of Paul's letters leads us directly to another author for this Epistle. Under such a view, this situation with *henotēs* would be a key indicator that Paul did not write or dictate Ephesians. But this kind of observation presents a very thin fabric for dismissing Paul as the Epistle's author. In the first place, the gathered letters attributed to Paul form a very limited literary body. And if we were to accept the truncated view of some that Paul wrote only four letters—Romans, 1 and 2 Corinthians, and Galatians—the residue of Pauline Epistles from which to make a sound comparison is even more limited. As a counterweight, we notice that the noun "diversities" (the singular is διαίρεσις, *diairesis*), which stands opposite in meaning to "unity," occurs three times in 1 Corinthians 12:4–6 and appears only within these verses among Paul's letters. Under this glaring observation, the act of singling out the double appearance of *henotēs* in this Epistle cannot contribute to a case for an author other than Paul for Ephesians unless, of course, a person wanted to argue that Paul did not author 1 Corinthians because of the rare, triple occurrence of *diaresis* (see the Notes on 1:23; 3:8; 4:21; 5:27; 6:3, 5; and the Analysis of 3:1–13; 6:1–9).[65]

Spirit: To capitalize or not to capitalize this noun, that is the question, to borrow an expression. The majority opinion is to capitalize. For the minority, the reasoning hinges on the sentiment expressed in Philippians 1:27, "that ye stand fast in one [unifying] spirit [*pneuma*], with one mind striving together." But the reasoning in this verse, 4:3, is more complex and more connected to context. For a lowercase "spirit," the argument goes that the noun for "spirit" in 4:3 (*pneuma*) has been customarily capitalized because of its proximity to 4:4, "one body, and one Spirit," the proper way to render that line in 4:4. However, the material in 4:4–6—all focused on oneness— evidently came from a source like an early Christian recitation, which Paul was repeating. And this independent origin for 4:4–6 makes the case that

---

64. Merkle, *Guide,* 114.
65. Muddiman, *Ephesians,* 180–81.

pneuma in the expression "the unity of the spirit" need not be capitalized because it is concerned with the unity of the church and its members.[66] In contrast, the majority hold that *pneuma* is to be capitalized, for it refers to the work of the Holy Spirit in bringing unity among believers.[67] This power of the Holy Spirit to bring about unity springs from a commonly shared experience of divine revelation among believers that goes beyond or enriches an investigator's initial revelatory experience when coming to know that Jesus is the Christ (1:17; 3:5; see also the Notes on 2:18; 4:30).[68]

the bond of peace: The noun translated "bond" (σύνδεσμος, *syndesmos*) is extremely old in Greek literature and carries the basic sense of a connector or link, such as one sees in the joint of a machine that holds disparate parts together. Its meanings in Acts 8:23 ("the bond of iniquity") and Colossians 3:14 ("the bond of perfectness") stress varying situations or relationships that are joined by linking different qualities or characteristics by a third entity, the connector.[69] In the Acts passage, Simon is said to be in "the bond of iniquity," as if caught in confining shackles.[70] When we turn to the Colossians verse, charity acts as the lynchpin or clasp; that is, it serves as "the bond of perfectness."[71] In our passage, "the bond of peace" has to do with holding "the unity of the Spirit" together. To be sure, it is revelation that engenders the unity of the Spirit (see the Note above). But peace forms the connecting tissue of that unity.

peace: When we examine this noun (εἰρήνη, *eirēnē*), we discover a wide range of ideas. But only three seem applicable here, if peace is really the glue that holds unity in place as suggested above. In the first instance, Paul has already introduced the peace that prevails between believers of different backgrounds because of Christ: "For [Christ] is our peace, who hath made both [Jew and Gentile] one, and hath broken down the middle wall of partition." Christ did so "in his flesh," making "one new man [of the two peoples], so making peace" (2:14–15; see also Rom. 14:19). In the second case, we come upon peace with God. It is this kind of peace that lies behind the aged Simeon's classic wish after seeing the infant Jesus, "Now lettest thou thy servant depart [this life] in peace" (Luke 2:29). From Paul's pen

---

66. Muddiman, *Ephesians*, 180.

67. Barth, *Ephesians*, 2:428; Bruce, *Ephesians*, 76; Caird, *Letters*, 72; Lincoln, *Ephesians*, 237; Best, *Ephesians*, 365; Fowl, *Ephesians*, 132

68. Kleinknecht, Baumgärtel, Bieder, Sjöberg, and Schweizer, *TDNT*, 6:444–45.

69. Gottfried Fitzer, *TDNT*, 7:856–59.

70. Fitzmyer, *Acts of the Apostles*, 407; BDAG, 966.

71. BDAG, 966; Louw-Nida, §63.7.

comes the line "being justified by faith, we have peace with God through our Lord Jesus Christ" (Rom. 5:1). In another place, he wrote that "the peace of God, which passeth all understanding," comes to the person who willingly receives it (Philip. 4:7). In the third case, we run across the peace that takes up residence in one's soul. To the Corinthian Saints, Paul wrote the assurance that "God hath called us to peace" (1 Cor. 7:15). Later, to his readers in Rome he expressed the prayer that "the God of hope [may] fill you with all joy and peace" (Rom. 15:13). Finally, to church members in Colossae he expressed the wish that they would "let the God of peace rule in your hearts" (Col. 3:15).[72] In this light, God's peace, which is a gift of the Spirit (see Gal. 5:22), infuses congregations and individuals, elevating all above the nettlesome concerns of this life (see the Notes on 2:14, 15, 17; 6:15).

4:4 *one body:* The noun for "body" (σῶμα, *sōma*) occurs nine times in Ephesians (see 1:23; 2:16; 4:12, 16 [twice]; 5:23, 28, 30). In most cases in this letter, *sōma* pertains to the body of Christ, which is the church, as in this instance (see 1 Cor. 12:13, "by one Spirit are we all baptized into one body"). If, as the consensus holds, verses 4:4–6 consist of a hymn-like recitation of belief, then the idea of one body did not arise from fragmenting trouble within the church wherein the unity of believers in Asia was threatened. For instance, unity was undermined in the early second century when, among other challenges, Ignatius the bishop of Antioch evidently faced trouble from a rival congregation in his own city (see introduction section II).[73] Rather, in 4:4–6, we encounter a psalm-like affirmation of faith, composed as a celebration of oneness, that rests on a presentation of three characteristics twice, with an added final acknowledgment of God's place in eternity. The pattern is "one body, and one Spirit, . . . one hope," followed by "one Lord, one faith, one baptism." The final piece, which stands as number seven in the sequence, brings the recitation to a crescendo, "one God and Father of all" (4:4–6). Hence, no one comes upon a worrisome splitting of the church. Instead, we meet melodic lines of a festive recognition of unity.[74] With the Psalmist, we can thus sing, "How good and how pleasant it is for brethren [and sisters] to dwell together in unity" (Ps. 133:1; see also the Notes on 1:23; 2:16; 4:12, 16; 5:23, 28, 30).

---

72. Von Rad and Foerster, *TDNT,* 2:411–12.

73. Schoedel, *Ignatius of Antioch,* 10–11 and n. 62. Muddiman, *Ephesians,* 183, holds a different view.

74. Barth, *Ephesians,* 2:429, 462–72; Lincoln, *Ephesians,* 237–38; Best, *Ephesians,* 366; Muddiman, *Ephesians,* 181–82; Winger, *Ephesians,* 480–81.

one Spirit: In this term, we glimpse the Holy Ghost, here simply called *pneuma.* Opposed to him rides "the prince of the power of the air, the spirit [*pneuma*] that now worketh in the children of disobedience" (2:2). In our first introduction to the Holy Spirit in this letter, he is the one who has sealed believers with a firm "promise, which is the earnest of our [heavenly] inheritance" (1:13–14; see also 4:30). Additionally, the Spirit served as the unveiling power behind the divine secret that "is now revealed unto his apostles and prophets . . . that the Gentiles should be fellowheirs, and of the same body" (3:5–6; compare 1:17). Furthermore, the Spirit is God's agent in bringing about personal spiritual growth by vitalizing "with might . . . the inner man" (3:16; see also the Notes on 2:2, 18, 22; 3:16; 5:9).[75]

one hope: Though hope (ἐλπίς, *elpis*) here takes upon itself the garment of oneness, it actually wears several pieces of clothing. As we have elucidated elsewhere, hope dons the fabric of the end-time, the eschaton. In Psalm 16 we read, "My flesh also shall rest in hope. For thou wilt not leave my soul in hell" (Ps. 16:9–10, quoted in Acts 2:26–27). From the Proverbs, we hear the rustle of eschatological cloth in the words "When a wicked man dieth, his expectation shall perish: and the hope of unjust men perisheth" (Prov. 11:7). When Paul was unraveling the folds of the Resurrection, he wrote, "If in this life only we have hope in Christ, we are of all men most miserable" (1 Cor. 15:19). And so it goes.[76] With a slightly different twist, Paul unveiled the truth that Gentiles, before embracing Christ and his gospel, wasted away, "having no hope, and [were] without God in the world" (2:12). Though this hope certainly wraps itself around events of the eschaton, such as a promising resurrection that unbelieving Gentiles will miss (see 1 Thes. 4:13), it lays out a broader and more variegated tapestry (see Rom. 15:13, "[may] the God of hope fill you with all joy and peace").[77] For in their earlier life, "at that time," Gentiles found themselves undraped, unclothed as "aliens from the commonwealth of Israel," lacking the enfolding scriptural expectations that Jews enjoyed and that included the hope of God's intervention and guidance in their lives. In reality, those unbelieving Gentiles, uncovered before God, "were strangers from the covenants of promise" that God had caused to flow to Israelites for centuries (2:12; see also the Notes on 1:12, 18; 2:12).

---

75. Kleinknecht, Baumgärtel, Bieder, Sjöberg, and Schweizer, *TDNT,* 6:444–45.

76. See Job 6:11; Prov. 14:32; Acts 23:6; Col. 1:5; etc.; Alma 22:14; 25:16; 27:28; etc.

77. Bultmann and Rengstorf, *TDNT,* 2:531–32.

calling: This noun (κλῆσις, *klēsis*) mirrors the same term in 4:1 and may be one reason that 4:4–6 appears in this place, assuming a catchword connection through this term. But the context here, which draws all attention to oneness, invites the reader to think of a unity that is "above all, and through all, and in you all," as the Father is (4:6). Such oneness naturally leads readers to consider all who have come under the gospel's influence, including those who had languished in the spirit prison and had lately received a visit from Jesus in his spirit body. For among them has the gospel now been preached (see 1 Pet. 3:18–20; 4:6; see also Rom. 14:9 and Rev. 11:18).[78] Thus, in a sense, one's calling reaches beyond that person's current church assignment and into the world to come. And any such calling, naturally, is to repose on a divine commissioning (see Heb. 5:4; Philip. 3:14; and the Notes on 1:12, 18; 4:1, 5, 9, 10).[79]

4:5 *One Lord:* This term may introduce "the central line of the entire epistle," all folded into this verse.[80] Might we be hearing an echo of the prophesied day when "living water shall come out of Jerusalem" and when "there shall be one Lord, and his name one" (Zech. 14:8–9)? Possibly. Surely we hear the language of the *Shema,* "Hear, O Israel: The Lord our God is one Lord" (Deut. 6:4), which Jesus himself repeated (see Mark 12:29). Almost universally, the person who bears this title (ὁ κύριος, *ho kyrios*) is Christ.[81] The title immediately contrasts with the same one borne by the Roman emperor (see Acts 25:26).[82] But challenging the emperor is not the focus here. Rather, in a crisp declaration Paul affirmed that there is no other Lord, no other Messiah, no other Christ (see the Notes on 4:1; 5:19).

In addition, this expression scoops up other elucidating elements. In the first instance, Jesus is Lord because of his Resurrection and subsequent exaltation (see 1:20–22; Luke 24:34; Rom. 8:34; 10:9; 14:8–9; and Philip. 2:8–11).[83] And these two events, Resurrection and exaltation, always assume that his descent into the world of departed spirits occurred just

---

78. Friedrich, *TDNT,* 3:707–8.

79. Friedrich, *TDNT,* 3:712–13; Louw-Nida, §33.314.

80. Winger, *Ephesians,* 434.

81. The exceptions occur, for instance, in Jesus' parables such as the wheat and tares (see Matt. 13:27, "Sir"), the wicked husbandmen (see Mark 12:9), and the prepared servants (see Luke 12:36–37).

82. Winger, *Ephesians,* 435. Polycarp of Smyrna (died ca. AD 155) was the first Christian known to reject the title "Caesar is Lord" and be executed because of it. *Martyrdom of Polycarp* 8.2, in Schoedel, *Apostolic Fathers,* 5:62.

83. Quell and Foerster, *TDNT,* 3:1088–91; Otto Michel, *TDNT,* 5:212.

before them (see 4:8–9; Rom. 14:9; and 1 Pet. 3:18–20; 4:6). As Friedrich Büchsel has written, "Only as he who had been among the dead did Christ come to the right hand of God above all heavens, assuming over all spirits a position of power."[84] But there is more. All Christians everywhere knew about Christ's mission among the departed spirits and that this event linked intimately to his subsequent Resurrection and exaltation. That is why he was the one who could raise "a voice of gladness for the living and the dead" (D&C 128:19), was the one who possessed "the keys of hell and of death" (Rev. 1:18), and was the one "who shall judge the quick and the dead at his appearing" (2 Tim. 4:1; see also Acts 10:42 and 1 Pet. 4:5). It is because of his saving interaction with the dead that he "is gone into heaven, and [sits] on the right hand of God" (1 Pet. 3:22; see also Rom. 14:9; the Notes on 3:8, 10, 19; 4:9; 5:8; 6:10, 18; and the Analysis of 3:1–13; 4:1–16).

In the second case, he is the Lord and not the Father. This point is brought home when Paul wrote that "to us there is but one God, the Father, of (ἐξ, *ex*) whom are all things, . . . and one Lord Jesus Christ, by (δία, *dia*) whom are all things" (1 Cor. 8:6).[85] In this verse, the preposition ἐξ, *ex* (or ἐκ, *ek*) serves to indicate to readers the source, the originator, who is the Father (see Matt. 5:37, "cometh *of* evil"; John 4:22, "salvation is *of* the Jews"; emphases added; etc.).[86] The second preposition (δία, *dia*) discloses the agent (see Matt. 1:22, "spoken . . . *by* the prophet"; John 1:3, "made *by* him"; emphases added; etc.).[87] One important thing to notice is that the Father and the Lord Jesus Christ are not the same person and do not participate in the salvation process in the same ways.

This fact bursts into view most clearly in Christ's descent into the underworld to visit the realm of the dead and to inaugurate the preaching of the gospel among them, an event pointed to above (see also D&C 138:11–19). That was his mission, not another's. And the Apostle led his readers to the doors of the underworld when he wrote, "The expression 'he ascended,' what does it mean except that he also descended to the lower regions of the earth? He who descended [into the spirit world] is the very one who also ascended far above all the heavenly realms" (4:9–10 NR). To quote Albrecht Oepke's words again, "That a journey to the lowest regions

---

84. Büchsel, *TDNT,* 3:641; see also Oepke, *TDNT,* 2:424; and Hauck and Schulz, *TDNT,* 6:577–78.

85. Schrenk and Quell, *TDNT,* 5:1009.

86. BDAG, 296; Louw-Nida, §§89.3; 90.16.

87. Blass and Debrunner, *Greek Grammar,* §223(2); Louw-Nida, §90.4.

preceded that to the upper is seldom emphasized in the NT but everywhere presupposed" (see the Notes on 4:4, 9, 10; 5:8; 6:1, 9).[88]

one faith: One obvious import of this expression centers on the church. The term "faith" (πίστις, *pistis*) shows up in other contexts as a pointer to the church (see Acts 6:7; 13:8; 14:22; 2 Cor. 13:5; Gal. 1:23; etc.). In fact, leaving the faith will become a risk in the future, for "in the latter times some shall depart the faith, giving heed to seducing spirits, and doctrines of devils" (1 Tim. 4:1). This passage from 1 Timothy presents another nuance—namely, the content of belief. As we can grasp, the teachings or "doctrines of devils" will supplant those of faith. Earlier in that Epistle, we encounter the expression "the mystery of faith" (1 Tim. 3:9). Within a few lines, we come upon the content of faith which is totally mysterious and incomprehensible to an outsider. As one might expect, this content focuses on Christ: "Great is the mystery of godliness: God was manifest in the flesh, justified in the Spirit, seen of angels, preached unto the Gentiles, believed on in the world, received up into glory" (1 Tim. 3:16). This sort of statement stands close to the tradition that Paul had received from others about Jesus' transformation of the Passover into the sacrament or Eucharist (see 1 Cor. 11:23–26; see also 2 Thes. 2:15; 3:6). Thus, "one faith" can point both to the church and to the content of its teaching.[89]

This said, a person must not discount the idea that "one faith" has to do with faith in the Lord. Why not? Because the term "one faith" stands next to the expression "one Lord." And the tight, intertwined character of verses 4:4–6 surely rests on more than the concept of oneness or a lyrical and memorable set of lines. Further, the juxtaposition of Lord (*kyrios*) and faith (*pistis*) certainly does not arise from mere accident or from the poet's art. No, what we behold is a purposeful joining of Lord to faith, of proven master to trust.

one baptism: Although the noun for baptism (βάπτισμα, *baptisma*) occurs only once in Ephesians, its subtle presence is felt throughout the letter, from Jesus' offering "the forgiveness of sins" (1:7) to believers being joined "unto God in one body by the cross" (2:16). In practice, because baptism mirrors Jesus' death and Resurrection (see Rom. 6:3–6), this ordinance forms the access point to this "one body," the body of Christ, the church, wherein converts "are no more strangers and foreigners, but fellowcitizens

---

88. Oepke, *TDNT,* 2:424; see also Büchsel, *TDNT,* 3:640–42; and Hauck and Schulz, *TDNT,* 6:577–78.

89. Bultmann and Weiser, *TDNT,* 6:213.

with the saints" (2:19). This rite has borne various descriptions, all tied to the ministry of John the Baptist, such as "baptism of repentance" (see Acts 13:24; 19:4) and "baptism of repentance for the remission of sins" (Mark 1:4; Luke 3:3). This noun, *baptisma*, underlies the institution or ordinance as it existed in the early church, and also has to do with the act of immersing an investigator in water. In this light, we need to briefly treat the important passage in Hebrews that reads, "Not laying again the foundation of . . . the doctrine of baptisms" (Heb. 6:1–2). The singular of the term here translated "baptisms" is βαπτισμός (*baptismos*) and is therefore not the same as the Christian baptism. Instead, it pertains to Levitical cleansings, whether "of vessels or of the body" (see Mark 7:4, "the washing [*baptismos*] of cups"). We should not stop here.[90]

Any attention to baptism is naturally drawn to Paul's intriguing lines in 1 Corinthians. There he wrote, "Else what shall they do which are baptized for [ὑπέρ, *hyper*] the dead, if the dead rise not at all? why are they then baptized for [*hyper*] the dead?" (1 Cor. 15:29). The preposition *hyper* fundamentally has to do with an action done "on behalf of" a person or thing.[91] In this light, we find ourselves standing again with Jesus among the departed dead. This is the only conclusion that makes sense. For if "the gospel [was] preached also to them that are dead," then a path had to be cleared for those people to "be judged according to men in the flesh" (1 Pet. 4:6; see also Rev. 11:18). Christ cleared that path after he was "put to death in the flesh, but quickened by the Spirit: by which also he went and preached unto the spirits in prison" (1 Pet. 3:18–19; see also Rom. 14:9). The spirits' acceptance of that gospel message, coupled with baptism performed by proxies on their behalf, opened the gate whereby their "baptism doth also now save [them] . . . by the resurrection of Jesus Christ" (1 Pet. 3:21; see also the Notes on 3:10; 4:10).

Another important tie-in now unfurls before us. It concerns the people of Noah's age. As a group, the classic candidates for the spirit prison were Noah's contemporaries "who disobeyed long ago when God waited patiently in the days of Noah while the ark was being built" (1 Pet. 3:20 NIV). These people simply stretched God's patience to the breaking point. After their sudden deaths in the ensuing flood, their spirits ended up "in prison"

---

90. Albrecht Oepke, *TDNT*, 1:545; see also Frederick Fyvie Bruce, *The Epistle to the Hebrews*, The New International Commentary on the New Testament (Grand Rapids, Mich.: Eerdmans, 1964), 114–15.

91. Riesenfeld, *TDNT*, 8:512–13; BDAG, 1030; Louw-Nida, §90.36.

(1 Pet. 3:19). What then? In a clarifying response, modern scripture now steps to the fore. As background, the ancient prophet Enoch learned about the then-future flood in an extended vision. On that occasion, God said to Enoch concerning the people of that era, "Among all the workmanship of mine hands there has not been so great wickedness as among thy brethren" (Moses 7:36). Continuing, God informed Enoch that "these which thine eyes are upon shall perish in the floods." Perhaps worse, "I [God] will shut them up; a prison have I prepared for them" (Moses 7:38).[92]

Now enters the Savior into God's words: "That [Christ] which I have chosen hath pled before my face." And what did he plead for? That "he suffereth for their sins"—that is, for the sins specifically of those who perished in the flood. With deliverance offered to these people by the suffering One, if "they will repent in the day that my Chosen shall return unto me"—that is, after his Resurrection and after their days of "torment" (Moses 7:39)—then "all they that mourn [in the spirit prison] may be sanctified and have eternal life" (Moses 7:45). At this point, two lessons can be gleaned. First, the wicked people of Noah's day came to be seen as an example of what happens to such persons when they pass beyond the veil of mortality—they are shut up in "a prison" (Moses 7:38; see also D&C 38:5–6). Second, upon the condition of repentance such persons can receive at least a measure of redemption and "live according to God in the spirit" (1 Pet. 4:6; see also Rev. 11:18 and D&C 138:31–35).[93]

The idea that baptisms—whether our own baptisms or proxy baptisms—lead to freedom from the effects of death, especially spiritual death, rests in Paul's enlightened descriptions of the baptismal ordinance. For, in the language of death and burial, he wrote, "We are buried with [Christ] by baptism into death." There is more. Just "as Christ was raised up from the dead by the glory of the Father, even so we also should walk in newness of life" (Rom. 6:4). In different language, the Apostle wrote that in baptism believers are "buried with [Christ]." Further, through that baptism "ye are risen with him through . . . the operation of God, who hath raised [Christ] from the dead" (Col. 2:12). In this light, the person receiving baptism is united with Christ in his burial and Resurrection.[94] By extension, in proxy

---

92. This prison has been characterized variously: "the bottomless pit" (Rev. 9:1–2); "the state of . . . darkness, and a state of awful, fearful looking for the . . . wrath of God" (Alma 40:14); "chains of darkness" (D&C 38:5); "the captives who were bound" (D&C 138:31).

93. Draper, Brown, and Rhodes, *Pearl of Great Price,* 131–34.

94. Oepke, *TDNT,* 1:545.

baptism we are also joined with Christ in his concern for the departed spirits whom he visited between his burial and Resurrection (see the Notes on
3:8, 10, 19; 4:9, 10; 5:8; 6:10, 18; and the Analysis of 3:1–13; 4:1–16).

4:6 *One God and Father of all:* This line does not seem to relate to God
as master of the cosmos but rather to God as the One who stands at the
head of the community of believers because he has created it. It was under
his direction that Christ had "broken down the dividing wall, the hostility"
that divided Jew and Gentile, thus uniting them (2:14 NR). It was under his
direction that "all spiritual blessings in heavenly places" were planned for
in the grand premortal council (1:3). It was under his direction that Christ
granted the ineffable "access by one Spirit unto the Father" (2:18). This
access, of course, opened the gate for individuals to approach the Father
one-on-one (see the Notes on 2:18; 3:14, 15; and the Analysis of 3:14–21).[95]

One God: The seventh in the series that celebrates unity, this terminology sends the reader to the originator of every event and every blessing
that comes to a person in the life of faith and devotion. God's oneness links
to that of everyone else, including especially his Son (see John 10:30; 17:11,
21–23; Heb. 2:11; and 3 Ne. 11:27). In addition, it relates to the nothingness
of idols, as Paul reminds readers elsewhere: "We know that an idol is nothing . . . and that there is none other God but one" (1 Cor. 8:4). Further, the
concept behind this title directs us to the group of spiritual gifts that Paul
was about to list when he wrote that "there are diversities of operations,
but it is the same God which worketh all in all" (1 Cor. 12:6). Moreover, this
term fulfills the prophetic expectation that "I will walk among you, and
will be your God, and ye shall be my people" (Lev. 26:12; see also Jer. 30:22;
31:1, 33; 2 Cor. 6:16; Heb. 8:10; etc.).[96]

Father of all: In the human sphere, especially that of the ancient Israelites, this sort of appellation applies to only two—Adam and Abraham.
In the divine realm, it applies to one only, the heavenly Father of all.[97] To
be sure, from the following phrases ("above all . . . through all"), a person
might think that God's fatherhood has do with his involvement in creation (see 3:9, "who created all things").[98] But the thrust of the Old Testament, from the *Shema* of Deuteronomy 6:4 ("Hear, O Israel: The Lord our
God is one Lord") to lines from its last prophet Malachi ("Have we not all

95. Schrenk and Quell, *TDNT*, 5:1011–12.
96. Kleinknecht, Quell, Stauffer, and Kuhn, *TDNT*, 3:101–2.
97. Schrenk and Quell, *TDNT*, 5:974, 976.
98. Lincoln, *Ephesians*, 240.

one father? hath not one God created us?" [Mal. 2:10]), has been one of a personalized relationship with God (see Isa. 63:16; 64:8). And Ephesians features this dimension of God's interaction with this world. As we have noticed earlier, the Father "hath chosen us in him before the foundation of the world" (1:4). The "Father of glory" controls "all principality, and power, and might, and dominion, and every name that is named" (1:17, 21). The Father sent Christ to offer "redemption through his blood, the forgiveness of sins" (1:7). The Father "raised [Christ] from the dead, and set him at his own right hand in the heavenly places" (1:20). From the Father "every family in the heavenly realms and on earth derives its name" (3:15 NR). And through the Father believers are "strengthened with might by his Spirit in the inner man" (3:16; see also the Note on 2:18 and the Analysis of 3:14–21).

Within the embrace of the Father's relationship with his children rest certain principles that a person must understand. The linking of the title "God" with "the Father," as in this verse, conveys the status of lordship or sovereignty. The Father stands as the originator "of [Christ's] glorious grace which [God] showered upon us by his Beloved [Son]" (1:6 NR). This means that he directed Christ to give "himself for our sins, that he might deliver us from this present evil world," showing himself to be sovereign in bringing about our salvation (Gal. 1:4). The believer's act of "giving thanks always for all things" frames a reminder of the Father's power to control and manage all life (5:20). Moreover, employing his generous might, he can invite us to "be partakers of his holiness" (Heb. 12:10), a dimension of celestial reality which the Father controls and dispenses to the worthy. In an acknowledgment of his lordship, at "the end" Christ himself will deliver up "the kingdom to God, even the Father; when he shall have put down all rule and all authority and power" (1 Cor. 15:24). Besides all these, and perhaps soaring above them all, through God's unlimited love for us, he "will be a Father unto you, and ye shall be my sons and daughters, saith the Lord Almighty" (2 Cor. 6:18).[99] Happy day!

you: A number of important texts, including the earliest, $\mathfrak{P}^{46}$, omit the pronoun. A few later manuscripts substitute the pronoun "us," a clear gloss. The preferred reading omits both pronouns, "you" and "us."[100]

above all, and through all, and in you all: The last phrase should read "in all," leading us to the reading "above all . . . through all . . . in all" (see the Note above). The question to solve initially is whether the term translated

---

99. Schrenk and Quell, *TDNT,* 5:1010–11.
100. Metzger, *Textual Commentary,* 536.

"all" (plural of πᾶς, *pas*) is masculine or neuter. In the context, the unity of the church calls out to readers. That is, "one body" and "one faith" and "one baptism" together beckon readers inside the church (4:4–5). In this light, a person might favor the personal understanding of *pas* and read the term as masculine, a gender that embraces both male and female in Greek.[101] Why? Because the church represents people and welcomes them into its numbers. But, within Ephesians, the word *pas* in its neuter sense also regularly touches on the cosmos, on God's dominion. Let us take a look.

The term *pas* occurs fifty-two times in Ephesians. This high number should not surprise us because, for example, it appears thirty-four times in Philippians and thirty-nine times in Colossians. In view of its three occurrences at the end of this verse ("above all . . . through all . . . in all"), each touching on the created order in one way or another, it is plain that readers were looking at God as creator and custodian of our universe. Admittedly, in other passages the title "the Father" sends us to his relationship with his beloved son, "our Lord Jesus Christ" (1:3), and to his relationship with his sons and daughters who have become his possessions through "adoption as children unto himself through Jesus Christ" (1:5 NR).[102] But these dimensions are not in view in our verse. Rather, we learn that in the beginning the Father "created all things by Jesus Christ" (3:9; see also Heb. 2:10). Moreover, with the permission of the Father and as a prelude to his exaltation, Christ "ascended up far above all heavens, that he might fill all things" (4:10). Further, in the ceremony of exaltation, the Father "hath put all things under [Christ's] feet" (1:22). Additionally, during "the dispensation of the fulness of times" the Father will "gather together in one all things in Christ" (1:10). All of these examples revolve around the created order (see Rom. 11:36 and 1 Cor. 8:6; 15:28).

Not surprisingly, such language appears in modern scripture. With a focus on God the Father, the Lord revealed through the Prophet Joseph Smith that "he is above all things, and in all things, and is through all things, and is round about all things." How so? Because "all things are by him, and of him" (D&C 88:41). With a different subject—namely, Christ—elsewhere in the same document we meet language that mirrors that of 4:9–10: "He that ascended up on high, as also he descended below all things." At this point, he then achieved the objective that "he comprehended all things."

---

101. Smyth, *Greek Grammar,* §197a.

102. Winger, *Ephesians,* 436. See also Lincoln, *Ephesians,* 240; Best, *Ephesians,* 371; Fowl, *Ephesians,* 135.

In the midst of these declarations, we find that Christ's grasp of "all things" opened to him long ago the celestial role "that he might be in all and through all things, the light of truth" (D&C 88:6). This "light of truth" radiated extraordinary power, generating "the light of the sun" and "the light of the moon" and "the light of the stars" (D&C 88:7–9). Breathtakingly, this same light "proceedeth forth from the presence of God to fill the immensity of space" (D&C 88:12). Thus, God is its ultimate source, having released it in the creative processes. But that is not the end of the story. We encounter such light on a personal level too. For that same illumination "giveth you light [which] . . . enlighteneth your eyes [and] . . . quickeneth your understandings" (D&C 88:11). That is, this divine light helps all both to see the world and to grasp its spiritual components (see the Notes on 1:18; 4:18).[103]

4:7 *But:* The conjunction δέ (*de*) changes the direction of Paul's remarks both from "you" to "we" and from a unity of the whole to a oneness based on "each one of us" (NR)—that is, on the variety of individuals who make up the unity.[104]

unto every one of us: From an emphasis on unity that all share, including "one Spirit" that acts as a personal guide and "one baptism" that forms the entry point into the church (4:4–6), we arrive at a oneness that arises even in the midst of diversity. This unity steers separate persons as individuals to the self-elevating experience of "perfecting [themselves to be] of the saints" and engaging meaningfully in "the work of the ministry" (4:12). Furthermore, this oneness among church members points each of them to "the [deeper] knowledge of the Son of God" and, in every person's spiritual life, to ascension to "the measure of the stature of the fulness of Christ" (4:13). For those engaged in such efforts, progress toward these goals does not come at the same pace. Individual development does not need to coordinate with others as in a mobilized army.[105] In Peter's words, the rule is that "in every nation [the person] that feareth [God], and worketh righteousness, is accepted with him" (Acts 10:35).

is given: The passive of the verb δίδωμι (*didōmi*) directs readers to God as the giver. The verb itself connects to its partners in verses 4:8 and 4:11. Thus, the giving of grace in our verse links to Christ giving supernal "gifts

---

103. See Robinson and Garrett, *Commentary on the Doctrine and Covenants,* 3:100–102, 110–11; McConkie and Ostler, *Revelations of the Restoration,* 628–29, 634.

104. Lincoln, *Ephesians,* 241; Best, *Ephesians,* 375; Merkle, *Guide,* 122.

105. See Winger, *Ephesians,* 438, for a different view of unity that rests narrowly on spiritual gifts.

unto men" (4:8) which include but are not limited to giving "apostles" and other guiding officers to the church (4:11). All stretches back to the Father as the giver (see the Note on 1:22).

grace: In our prior reviews, we have learned that grace (*charis*) rests on a reciprocal relationship between a master and underling, with the master offering a generous gift which the servant is then obliged to try to match (see the Notes on 2:5, 8). In its ancient dress, *charis* does not come as a free gift.[106] With this in mind, it is evident that, according to this verse, the grace granted "unto every one of us"—that is, to current church members—is measured or controlled. It does not flow endlessly and without a recipient's obligation to God, its source. Though a minority of modern commentators want to hold onto a freely flowing grace that constantly bathes believers in its aromas,[107] a majority grasp that in this verse we are dealing with differences in the kinds and amounts of grace that God dispenses to his children. But the measurements are not haphazard. No. They have to do with "the work of the ministry" (4:12). Paul highlights this notion elsewhere. When writing about "many members in one body," he insisted that "all members have not the same office" (Rom. 12:4). Therefore, in serving others we each receive "gifts differing according to the grace that is given [to each of] us" (Rom. 12:6). In Paul's language, those "gifts," or responsibilities, may lie in prophesying, in ministering, in exhorting, or in presiding (see Rom. 12:6–8). Hence, "the grace which each believer has received for the discharge of his particular function in the community is proportionate" (see the Notes on 2:5, 8; 4:29).[108]

measure: This noun (μέτρον, *metron*) occurs three times in Ephesians, each with a different meaning (see 4:13, 16). In this verse, it concerns the distribution of the gift of grace. By writing the term *metron*, the Apostle has brought his readers to the view that each gift of grace is not the same. Instead, such gifts, even that of faith, differ from one person to another depending on how that person is serving in the kingdom (see Rom. 12:3, "God hath dealt to every man [and woman] the measure of faith"). Now to the question. If grace comes by measure to those who serve in God's kingdom, presumably the measurements "unto every one" are different for each.[109] The whole

---

106. Conzelmann and Zimmerli, *TDNT,* 9:373–74; Schmidt, *Relational Grace,* 100.

107. Winger, *Ephesians,* 438.

108. Bruce, *Ephesians,* 81. See also Lincoln, *Ephesians,* 241–42; Best, *Ephesians,* 375–76; Fowl, *Ephesians,* 136.

109. Gustav Stählin, *TDNT,* 3:350; Kurt Deissner, *TDNT,* 4:633–34; Bruce, *Ephesians,* 81; Fowl, *Ephesians,* 136.

matter hangs from the need of the person who serves, the necessity to serve as Christ would serve, to bless as he would bless. But not all service assignments are equal in the strength required, mental or physical, or in the endurance needed, spiritual or emotional, hence, the need for a divine measuring of gifts to the serving one (see the Notes on 4:13, 16).

Side by side with this rather obvious sense stands the further, more subtle question: Are there cases in which works are needed to make up any deficit in the measuring of grace? That is to say, does the gift of grace require the recipient to respond in some physical or mental way, notably, in the capacity of work? The answer has to be yes, certainly in the cases of serving in the church. For those callings are not for one's self-aggrandizement but for helping others. To illustrate, Paul came very close to prescribing a life of consecration when he wrote, "I beseech you . . . that ye present your bodies a living sacrifice, holy, acceptable unto God." Capping off this strong request, he wrote that such personal sacrifice "is your reasonable service" (Rom. 12:1, λογικὴν λατρείαν, *logikēn latreian*).[110] Pointedly writing "your bodies," he was requiring that believers offer all, with every bit of energy and time and skill that those bodies possess, to fill the measure of "your reasonable service." And the idea of reasonableness is not limited to human reason but embraces God's reasoning, which appears in Deuteronomy 10:12–21.[111] There we read that God requires us "to serve the Lord thy God with all thy heart and with all thy soul" (Deut. 10:12). That expectation for his people means mirroring him. Like him, believers are to look after "the fatherless and the widow" and love "the stranger, in giving him food and raiment." Why? The reason is direct: "Ye were strangers in the land of Egypt" whence God rescued his people (Deut. 10:18–19). That rescue operation attested to his willingness to serve them and grant gifts to them by bringing them "out of Egypt with a mighty hand . . . [showing] signs and wonders, great and sore" (Deut. 6:21–22).

the gift of Christ: Lest we forget, grace is a gift, pure and clear (see 3:7; Rom. 5:15, 17; 12:6; 15:15; 1 Cor. 1:4; 3:10; etc.). The appearance of the noun "gift" (δωρεά, *dōrea*) anticipates the giving of gifts in 4:8 and 4:11, all coming from Christ.[112] In fact, in the New Testament the term *dōrea* always touches on gifts of God and Christ to humans.[113] Importantly, such

---

110. BDAG, 587, 598; Thayer, *Lexicon*, 372, 379.
111. Hermann Strathmann, *TDNT*, 4:63–65.
112. Lincoln, *Ephesians*, 241; Larkin, *Handbook*, 73.
113. Büchsel, *TDNT*, 2:167.

gifts are shared not always directly from God and Christ but through other church members who are called to the ministry. These believers become the divine conduits for blessing God's children by giving their time and energy "for the perfecting of the saints, for the work of the ministry, for the edifying of the body of Christ" (4:12;[114] see the Notes on 4:8, 11).

4:8 *he saith:* The subject of this clause remains unclear. The issue is, Who or what is being quoted? Is it "he"—that is, David—or "it"—that is, the psalm? Most translations render the subject as neuter, "it," as in "it says" (NR). This is a standard way to cite scripture, although there are others. For example, in 5:14, the KJV translates the same verb, λέγει (*legei,* "she/he/it says"), as "he saith." But the universal preference is to point to what the scripture says by rendering the verb as "it says" (NR; see also Rom. 15:10 and Gal. 3:16). Of course, we regularly discover quotations from persons in Hebrews (see Heb. 1:5, 6, 7, 13; 2:6; etc.), quotations from God himself (see Rom. 9:15 and 2 Cor. 6:2, 16), words of David (see Rom. 4:7; 11:9), and lines from Isaiah (see Rom. 10:16; 15:12). For the rest, we come across the expression "the scripture says" (Rom. 4:3; 9:17; 10:11; 11:2; Gal. 4:30; 1 Tim. 5:18). Effectively, they all amount to the same thing: "the quoted words have divine authority."[115] Now the fun begins with the quotation of Psalm 68:18 (LXX 67:19; see also the Note on 5:14).

When he ascended up on high: This verse comes from Psalm 68, a psalm always associated with the Festival of Pentecost. Commentators generally agree about the meaning of this temporal clause. Quoted from Psalm 68:18, it has to do with Jehovah's ascent of Mount Zion (see Ps. 48:2),[116] which is termed "the hill of God" (Ps. 68:15). This ascent follows the rescue of his people from Egypt and his victory over foreign powers, events to which all of Psalm 68 refers. To be certain, debates about the origin of this psalm have been ongoing for decades.[117] But as the quoted line appears here, even allowing for Paul's adjustments to the text, the words aim directly at Christ and his ascension (see Acts 1:9). Naturally, quoting this line from Psalm 68:18 will bring to mind, especially among Jews, the generous attitudes and acts of Israel's God toward his people that are celebrated in this psalm. For example, "A father of the fatherless, and a judge of the widows, is God in his holy habitation" (Ps. 68:5). Besides enjoying guidance that leads to

---

114. Grundmann, Hesse, de Jonge, and van der Woude, *TDNT,* 9:558.
115. Lincoln, *Ephesians,* 242. See also Best, *Ephesians,* 378.
116. Caird, *Letters,* 74; Lincoln, *Ephesians,* 242; Muddiman, *Ephesians,* 188.
117. Barth, *Ephesians,* 2:473–74.

the temple, "his holy habitation," we encounter his unfathomable generosity to those on the margins of society, "the fatherless, and . . . the widows," treating them as individuals and not in a clump. Emphasizing how God values individuals and families, the Psalmist sings that lovingly "God setteth the solitary [persons] in families" (Ps. 68:6). Reaching out to those caught in the web of poverty, "thou, O God, hast prepared of thy goodness for the poor" (Ps. 68:10).

A person is reminded about Jesus, who, after calling the breadwinners of families into his service as disciples, granted them a huge haul of fish that, after being salted, would give their families food as well as fish to trade in the market "for months on end" (see Luke 5:4–10).[118] So it was again with Jesus, who raced through the night almost thirty miles from Capernaum to reach the village of Nain by the time the funeral procession emerged that bore the body of an only child, a son, of an obscure widow (see Luke 7:11–16).[119] So it was with Jesus who "must needs" (imperfect tense of δεῖ, *dei*, "it was necessary")[120] pass through Samaria (John 4:4), where he met an outcast Samaritan woman at Jacob's well and introduced her and her town's citizens to him and his gospel (see John 4:3–30). So it was with Jesus who stopped at a tree in Jericho and coaxed down a despised tax collector named Zaccheus, inviting himself into his home with the words "to day I must abide at thy house," bringing an unlooked-for blessing into the man's home and among his family members (see Luke 19:1–10).[121]

We cannot leave Psalm 68 without exploring the rich language that potentially applies to Christ, the Ascendant One. At his ascension into the heavens, "let the righteous be glad; let them rejoice before God: yea, let them exceedingly rejoice" (Ps. 68:3). In a line that can be read as hinting at Jesus' ascension, the Psalmist writes about "him that rideth upon the heavens of heavens" (Ps. 68:33). With his ascension to the side of the Father, Christ has become "our God [who] is the God of salvation" (Ps. 68:20). Celebrating his role as deliverer of those in the spirit prison, the Psalmist intones that "from the Sovereign Lord comes escape from death" (Ps. 68:20 NIV) and, more pointedly, "he bringeth out those which are bound with chains" (Ps. 68:6). Breathing in the aroma of temple worship, we come

---

118. Brown, *Testimony of Luke,* 274–81; S. Kent Brown, "The Savior's Compassion," *Ensign* 41, no. 3 (March 2011): 53–55.

119. Brown, *Testimony of Luke,* 363–68.

120. BDAG, 214; Thayer, *Lexicon,* 126.

121. Brown, *Testimony of Luke,* 851–58.

upon "the [sacred] mountain where God chooses to reign, where the Lord himself will dwell forever," even in the "temple at Jerusalem" (Ps. 68:16, 29 NIV). In an act of generous constancy, Christ "daily bears our burdens" (Ps. 68:19 NIV). As the son of peace, Christ is to "scatter ... the people that delight in war" (Ps. 68:30). Turning purposefully toward his followers, Christ presents himself as "the God of Israel ... that giveth strength and power unto his people. Blessed be God" (Ps. 68:35). Blessed indeed!

he led captivity captive: We can understand this expression in any of three ways. In each, Christ is the victor. The two words, a verb that occurs only here in the New Testament and a noun, share a common root (αἰχμαλωτεύω and αἰχμαλωσία, *aichmalōteuō* and *aichmalōsia*). This placing of similar sounds together is a characteristic of Semitic style and yields the idea "to take prisoners captive."[122] In a first understanding, the terms may center on Christ's victory over "death and hell," that, at Christ's arrival in the spirit world, were forced to deliver "up the dead which were in them." Thereafter, because Christ had taken possession of "the keys of hell and of death," under his control "death and hell were cast into the lake of fire" (Rev. 1:18; 20:13–14). In company with Satan, whom Christ will bind for a "thousand years" (Rev. 20:3), death and hell will be held captive away from the righteous.[123] In a second meaning, the words may revolve around Christ leading captive "principalities and powers" while making "a shew of them openly, triumphing over them" that bedevil people's lives (Col. 2:15;[124] see the Notes on 1:21; 3:10; 6:12). In a third sense, in light of the interest in Christ's descent into the underworld in 4:9–10, the expression may well pertain to Christ leading the former spirit captives out of their prison and into the fresh air of liberty.[125] This is the tone of Psalm 68:6: "he bringeth out those which are bound with chains."

gave gifts: Even though Paul was quoting Psalm 68:18, apparently from memory, his switch from the notion of receiving gifts, which we find in the Old Testament text ("thou hast received gifts for men"), to giving gifts as we discover here,[126] carries an important pair of meanings. First, the expression looks backward to 4:7, where we read that "unto every one of us is given grace" by the Father. In this earlier passage, we meet the treasured spiritual

122. BDAG, 31; Louw-Nida, §55.23–24; Larkin, *Handbook*, 75; Lincoln, *Ephesians*, 242.
123. Winger, *Ephesians*, 443.
124. Muddiman, *Ephesians*, 190; Merkle, *Guide*, 124.
125. Gerhard Kittel, *TDNT*, 1:196; Best, *Ephesians*, 382.
126. Barth, *Ephesians*, 2:472–76, offers an explanation for the reversal.

gift of his saving grace. Its mention quietly sends us to other spiritual gifts. Second, the other gift consists of church leaders who not only represent God but also faithfully pursue "the perfecting of the saints" and "the work of the ministry" (4:12).[127] This pairing of gifts that embrace both the spiritual sphere of God's grace and the ecclesiastical strength of the church shows how intimately intertwined they are in the community of faith. That is to say, spiritual gifts do not stand apart from church organization, and church organization does not exist simply to run the establishment. More to the point, Jesus' choosing of the Twelve and the Seventy possessed potential spiritual blessings for all believers, including but not limited to the undermining of Satan's kingdom (see Luke 10:18 and the Notes on 1:22; 4:7, 11).

In this connection, the fact that Psalm 68 was an important part of the Festival of Pentecost directs us to an intriguing linkage between the Twelve and spiritual gifts. We recall that the fledgling church's first public spiritual manifestation occurred during Pentecost. On that occasion, into the Jerusalem temple grounds "came a sound from heaven as of a rushing mighty wind," filling "all the house [temple]" where the throng had gathered. Almost instantly, "there appeared unto them cloven tongues like as of fire, and it sat upon each of [the Twelve]" (Acts 2:2–3). This was how things began that day. By its end, "there were added unto them [of the church] about three thousand souls" through baptism (Acts 2:41). Most of those baptized were from out of town. When these Jewish visitors returned home, they carried the memory of an unforgettable experience and surely told others, thus preserving the miraculous story and preparing the soil of distant souls for missionaries like Paul. That story was certainly known in Ephesus and the surrounding Christian branches in Asia Minor. And the Christianized Jews of that region had undoubtedly grown up knowing Psalm 68 and its attachment not only to Pentecost but also to that most remarkable day. Thus, Paul's citation of one of its verses would have brought to mind the well-known account of what happened at the most unusual celebration of that holy day in Jerusalem, complete with a miraculous spiritual manifestation being revealed through the Twelve, the earliest part of Christ's church organization.[128]

---

127. Grundmann, Hesse, de Jonge, and van der Woude, *TDNT,* 9:558; Best, *Ephesians,* 383; Merkle, *Guide,* 124.

128. S. Kent Brown, "Fire and Speaking in Tongues: What We Can Learn about the Pentecost Festival in Acts," in https://www.ldsliving.com/Fire-and-Speaking-in-Tongues -What-We-Can-Learn-About-the-Pentecost-Festival-in-Acts/s/91156.

Lest we turn away too quickly from this review of Psalm 68 and its attachment to Pentecost, we draw attention to a historical connection between Jesus, the one who ascended according to Paul's reading of Psalm 68:18, and the Pentecost festival during which the spiritual manifestation involving the Twelve occurred at the temple (see Acts 2). We all know that Pentecost, which means "fifty," falls fifty days after Passover. Jesus died at Passover time, rising from the tomb the following Sunday. This event was followed by his teaching of the Eleven during a forty-day period prior to his ascension (see Acts 1:3). Hence, at the moment of Jesus' ascension from the Mount of Olives (see Acts 1:12), forty-three or forty-four days had passed since the prior Passover, when Jesus died. At this same moment, many of the pilgrims who would be affected by the miracle at the Jerusalem temple a few days later had already begun to arrive and camp on the lower slopes of this tall mount. How so? Because all pilgrims traveling more than seventeen miles, which was the distance to the town of Modiin that lay west and north of Jerusalem, from "any direction" were obliged to arrive a week early for purification purposes, just as travelers to the city for Passover had to arrive early "to purify themselves" for that celebration (John 11:55; see the Note on 4:21).[129] Therefore, the Resurrected Christ was ascending to heaven from the top of the Mount of Olives when traveling devotees, who would soon celebrate Pentecost by singing Psalm 68 among other activities, were camping at the base of the mount. Surely some of these travelers were among Paul's readers of his letter to the Ephesians.

4:9 *he ascended:* The form of the verb (past tense of ἀναβαίνω, *anabainō*) virtually quotes the line in 4:8 from Psalm 68:18, illustrating that Paul saw an inner connection between the psalm and Jesus' ascent into heaven a few days before the Festival of Pentecost. His ascension, of course, occurred after his visit to the spirit prison and his Resurrection (see Acts 1:9; Rom. 14:9; Philip. 2:6–11; 1 Pet. 3:18–19; D&C 88:6; and the Note on 4:5).[130]

he also descended first into the lower parts of the earth: In sequence, Jesus' descent into the world of departed spirits happened before his Resurrection and ascension into heaven. On the question of how to understand this line, some commentators have interpreted it as focusing on Jesus'

---

129. *Mishnah Pesahim,* 9.1–2, in Danby, *Mishnah,* 148 and n. 6, quotation from 9.2. See also Christine Hayes, "Purity and Impurity, Ritual," in *Encyclopaedia Judaica,* ed. Michael Berenbaum and Fred Skolnik, 2nd ed., 22 vols. (Detroit: Macmillan Reference USA, 2007), 16:752–53.

130. Büchsel, *TDNT,* 3:641.

descent into the mortal world.[131] And that view has merit. One of its important elements is the assumed premortality of both Christ and all Earth's inhabitants who had also come from the upper regions.[132] However, the idea of "the lower parts of the earth" pulls in a different direction. As we have quoted from Albrecht Oepke earlier, "That a journey to the lowest regions preceded that to the upper is seldom emphasized in the NT but everywhere presupposed."[133] In a word, Jesus descended to the prison that held departed spirits.[134]

he also descended: Almost immediately, Jesus' quotation of Isaiah 61:1 in the Nazareth synagogue comes to mind: "The Lord hath anointed me . . . to proclaim liberty to the captives, and the opening of the prison to them that are bound" (cited in Luke 4:18). The insistence that we are dealing with a later Gnostic myth of Christ's descent to the earth is simply wrong.[135] For as we have just noted, his descent into Hades is everywhere assumed throughout the New Testament.[136] To that place, "he went and preached unto the spirits in prison" (1 Pet. 3:19; see also Rom. 14:9). In that place, he offered "the gospel . . . *also* to them that are dead." Within that space, he allowed the prisoners opportunity to "be judged according to men in the flesh, but live according to God in the spirit" (1 Pet. 4:6, emphasis added). The "also" (καί, *kai*) seems important, underscoring the idea that the departed spirits were now given the same chance as those on earth to accept the gospel and live by its principles. This observation places a deeper layer of interpretation on passages such as "the time of the dead, that they should be judged" (Rev. 11:18), a reference not just to deceased persons who lived while the gospel message was on the earth but also to those individuals who learned that

---

131. Büchsel, *TDNT,* 3:642; Lincoln, *Ephesians,* 244–47; Best, *Ephesians,* 385–86.

132. Johannes Schneider, *TDNT,* 1:523; Oepke, *TDNT,* 2:423.

133. Oepke, *TDNT,* 2:424; see also Sasse, *TDNT,* 1:679–80; Winger, *Ephesians,* 444.

134. The possibility of misunderstanding this scene as narrated in 1 Pet. 3:18–20 and 4:6 is readily visible in the judgment of Hauck and Schulz that the plural noun for *pneuma,* translated as "spirits" in 3:19, refers both "to the fallen angels," the so-called "sons of God" of Gen. 6:2 and 6:4, and "to the seduced souls of men" who were in need of deliverance; see Hauck and Schulz, *TDNT,* 6:577–78 and n. 84.

135. A view proposed by Büchsel, *TDNT,* 3:641; and Traub and von Rad, *TDNT,* 5:525–26.

136. Jeremias, *TDNT,* 1:148–49; Delling, *TDNT,* 1:488–89; Oepke, *TDNT,* 2:424; Friedrich, *TDNT,* 2:718–19; Oepke, *TDNT,* 3:213; Grundmann, *TDNT,* 3:399–401; Büchsel, *TDNT,* 3:641–42; Friedrich, *TDNT,* 3:707–8; Jeremias, *TDNT,* 3:746–47; Schneider, *TDNT,* 4:597–98; Bornkamm, *TDNT,* 4:821–22; Traub and von Rad, *TDNT,* 5:525–26, 533; Hauck and Schulz, *TDNT,* 6:577–78; Schweizer and Baumgärtel, *TDNT,* 7:1078–79.

message after death and, now standing on a level playing field, responded to it (see the Notes on 3:10; 4:8, 10).

Adding intensity to the importance of Jesus' descent, modern scripture builds out this scene with a revealing sketch about Jesus' ministry among deceased spirits. Coming as a vision to Joseph F. Smith, sixth president of The Church of Jesus Christ of Latter-day Saints, on Thursday, October 3, 1918, the day before he opened the fall general conference, his experience led him to view "the hosts of the dead, both small and great." Initially, he saw "an innumerable company of the spirits of the just, who had been faithful in the testimony of Jesus while they lived in mortality" (D&C 138:11–12). The spirits in this large gathering had been informed that "the Son of God" was about to arrive in "the spirit world, to declare their redemption from the bands of death" (D&C 138:16). Into "this vast multitude" the Christ finally came. While among them he declared "liberty to the captives . . . [and] preached to them the everlasting gospel." In a significant twist, "unto the wicked he did not go" (D&C 138:18–20). Because "the Lord went not in person among the wicked and the disobedient [he therefore] . . . from among the righteous [spirits] . . . appointed messengers . . . to go forth and carry the light of the gospel to them that were in darkness, even to all the spirits of men. . . . Thus was the gospel preached to those who had died in their sins" (D&C 138:29–30, 32). Hence, Christ inaugurated and then broadened his mission to the departed spirits through his authorized representatives in the spirit world (see the Notes on 3:8, 10, 19; 4:5; 5:8; 6:10, 18; and the Analysis of 3:1–13; 4:1–16).[137]

first: The best manuscripts, including $\mathfrak{P}^{46}$, the earliest, omit this term. It "appears to be a natural expansion introduced by copyists to elucidate the meaning."[138]

lower parts: The originality of the word for "parts" (μέρη, *merē*) is in question. Important manuscripts preserve it while others, including $\mathfrak{P}^{46}$, omit it. Its presence helps the meaning, whereas its absence means a translator has to supply a term like "regions" (NR) or "places."[139] The idea behind the word "lower" (κατώτερα, *katōtera*) bears on Jesus' descent to the spirit prison, which, as the ancients understood the matter, is located in the subterranean regions of the earth. As one might expect, the view is

---

137. Leaun G. Otten and C. Max Caldwell, *Sacred Truths of the Doctrine and Covenants*, 2nd ed., 2 vols. (Springville, Utah: LEMB, 1982–83), 2:393–97.

138. Metzger, *Textual Commentary*, 536.

139. Metzger, *Textual Commentary*, 537.

disputed whether this expression pertains to Jesus' descent to the region of deceased spirits. For, the argument runs, Jesus' descent would more likely be about his coming to this earth. The rub, it seems, is that "it is not clear how Christ's descent to hell would be tied to the giving of gifts to humans."[140] But that is exactly the point. Jesus' descent into Hades brought a long-expected gift of freedom to those in the spirit world, delivering them from spiritual bondage and placing them on the same footing as their fellow believers living on earth. This observation finds support in the basic sense of the verb διασώζω (*diasōzō*), translated "saved" in its passive form at the end of 1 Peter 3:20 in the KJV. Its fundamental meaning is "to deliver" or "to rescue."[141] As Johannes Horst reminds us, "the emphasis is not on the incidental illustration of the generation of Noah [in 1 Pet. 3:20] but on the present spiritual activity of the risen Lord" as the one who delivers.[142] That said, Horst obviously did not know the passage in modern scripture that, for the disobedient souls of Noah's day, God intended to prepare "a [spirit] prison" and "shut them up" in it, eventually offering them deliverance through "my Chosen" (Moses 7:38–39). This notation makes sense of the mention of Noah in 1 Peter 3:20. And such a linkage hints that Peter knew a source, now lost, that connected the unresponsive people of Noah's day to God's establishment of the spirit prison (see the Note on 4:5).

Modern scripture offers two further explanations of the image of the Descending One. The first paints the following picture: "He that ascended up on high, as also he descended below all things, in that he comprehended all things, that he might be in all and through all things, the light of truth" (D&C 88:6). Here we come upon a stunning measure of Christ's person and power. His physical ascent and descent actually occurred. But more happened during his experience than an enlightening education about how the cosmos works. Rather, by this ascent and descent he became "the light of truth." As appears plain, his ascent and descent were part of a plan to make him master of all creation, being "in all and through all things" (D&C 88:6; see also 4:6). He thereby became "the light of Christ . . . [which is] the light of the sun, and the power thereof by which it was made" (D&C 88:7). With this language, the experience of Jesus' ascent and descent attaches to the activity of creation and bends away from the act of redemption, which his

---

140. Fowl, *Ephesians*, 138; see also Schneider, *TDNT*, 1:523; Barth, *Ephesians*, 2:433–34; Lincoln, *Ephesians*, 244–47; Best, *Ephesians*, 383–86; Winger, *Ephesians*, 444–48.

141. BDAG, 237; Louw-Nida, §21.19.

142. Johannes Horst, *TDNT*, 4:386 n. 111.

descent into this world and into the world of imprisoned spirits brought about.[143] Perhaps this ascent and descent occurred during his creation of the earth and its associated activities. For, as is likely, he descended from the presence of the Father to the place of creation and then ascended again at the end of each creative period (see 3:9; Prov. 8:26–30; and Abr. 4:1, 27; 5:4).

A second explanation is hinted at in the words, "The Son of Man hath descended below them all" (D&C 122:8). The context for this line is suffering, specifically Joseph Smith's suffering when compared with that of Christ. With this line, we return to the matter of redemption, but with a focus on Jesus' suffering that led to our redemption. This line, as is clear, has to do with the sheer depth of Jesus' agony. It is not linked to his creative activities or to his descent into the world of departed spirits. This descent into pain took him into the crushing embrace of our sins heaped onto a sinless soul. To express what this experience was like lies beyond our abilities. But the Savior narrated this experience in another place, bringing readers to an awe-filled silence: "Which suffering caused myself, even God, the greatest of all, to tremble because of pain, and to bleed at every pore, and to suffer both body and spirit" (D&C 19:18; see also Luke 22:44; Mosiah 3:7; and Heb. 2:17–18; 4:15; 5:8–9).

In sum, the explanations of Christ's descent take several forms. First, it was associated with his creative activity with the result that he was "in all and through all things, the light of truth" (D&C 88:6). Second, it concerned his coming into this world when he "took upon him the form of a servant, and was made in the likeness of men" (Philip. 2:7). Third, his descent was one of allowing himself to be swallowed by "pains and afflictions and temptations of every kind," meaning that he would "take upon him the pains and sicknesses of his people . . . [including] death," thus defeating mortals' adversaries, pain and sin and death (Alma 7:11–12; see also Rom. 5:12). Fourth, he descended into the world of departed spirits to bring them both the gospel message and the opportunity to escape their own debilitating sins (see 1 Pet. 3:18–20; 4:6; see also Rom. 10:6–7; 14:9; Rev. 11:18; and the Notes on 3:10, 19; 4:4, 5).

the earth: The earth, of course, enjoys a special relationship with God, for it is his possession and creation through Christ (see 3:9; Ps. 24:1; and 1 Cor. 10:26). Although both the earth and heaven exist as spheres of God's activity and are spoken of in that manner (see Matt. 11:25; Luke 10:21; and Acts 17:24), they are distinct from one another. For instance, the earth is

---

143. Robinson and Garrett, *Commentary on the Doctrine and Covenants,* 3:100–101.

the place of types and shadows rather than real celestial things (see Mark 9:3; Col. 2:17; and Heb. 8:4–5; 10:1); it is the home of sins and abominations (see Mark 2:10 and Rev. 17:5); and it is the host of corruption and mortality (see Matt. 6:19–20; 1 Cor. 15:42–49, 53–54; etc.). Yet the two spheres, heaven and earth, remain closely connected (see Matt. 6:10 and Luke 2:14). That close link is underscored by actions undertaken on earth which then carry force in heaven. A person thinks almost reflexively of prayers uttered on earth that are heard in heaven (see Matt. 18:19 and James 5:16) and of sins forgiven on earth that are also forgiven in heaven (see 1:7; 4:32; Mark 2:10; and Luke 5:24). The flip side of this latter, of course, is retaining in the celestial realm the earthly sin of blasphemy against the Holy Ghost (see Matt. 12:31–32; and Luke 12:10). On the positive side of the ledger, Jesus entrusted Peter and the Twelve with keys that empowered them to bind or seal on earth, an act that would produce a corresponding binding or sealing in heaven. The reverse would also happen—an unbinding or loosing on earth would mean a loosing or untying in heaven (see Matt. 16:19; 18:18).[144] As we learn from multiple sources, this binding and unbinding has to do with measures taken inside the church's organization, particularly in the matter of ordinances, beginning with baptism and confirmation and ending with celestial marriages (see the Notes on 1:10; 6:3).[145]

4:10 *He that descended is the same also that ascended:* The identity of the Descending and Ascending One is not in doubt. This person is Jesus Christ, the Son of God. By writing this line, Paul has underscored that the One who "ascended up on high," written about in Psalm 68:18 (LXX Ps. 67:19) and quoted in 4:8, is in fact the Christ. Hence, Paul saw a messianic prophecy in the language of the psalm.[146] Moreover, he has emphasized that "for the Church there can be no chasm between heaven and earth."[147] The one who has descended and then ascended has welded them together in an undying union.

far above all heavens: The nearby citation of Psalm 68:18 sends us to God as the victor who has surmounted "all principality, and power, and might, and dominion, and every name that is named" (1:21).[148] The theme of victory is a major part of the message of Psalm 68, arising in its first lines. For there we read, "Let God arise, let his enemies be scattered [and] . . .

---

144. Sasse, *TDNT,* 1:679–80.
145. Brown, "Peter's Keys," 97–99.
146. Lincoln, *Ephesians,* 247.
147. Lincoln, *Ephesians,* 248.
148. Best, *Ephesians,* 387.

let the wicked perish at the presence of God" (Ps. 68:1–2). Threateningly, "God shall wound the head of his enemies" (Ps. 68:21). Moreover, at his presence in the past, "kings of armies did flee apace" (Ps. 68:12). This imagery invites readers to think of God's successful premortal battle to evict Satan from the halls of holiness.[149] The Old Testament had already enshrined this event in Isaiah's words: "How art thou fallen from heaven, O Lucifer, son of the morning! how art thou cut down to the ground" (Isa. 14:12). It was this one who had bragged, "I will ascend above the heights of the clouds; I will be like the most High" (Isa. 14:14). Instead, it was Jesus who "beheld Satan as lightning fall from heaven," his authorized representatives undercutting the aspiring, narcissistic devil (Luke 10:18). Eons before, through the aid of "Michael and his angels," the chosen Savior had "fought against the dragon . . . and his angels . . . [who] prevailed not; neither was their place found any more in heaven" (Rev. 12:7–8; see also Moses 4:1–4; Abr. 3:27–28; and D&C 29:36–38). As our verse affirms, only the Risen Christ had "ascended up far above all heavens." That act has led to universal rejoicing, even above the clouds: "rejoice, ye heavens, and ye that dwell in them" (Rev. 12:12; see also Deut. 32:43 and Isa. 44:23; 49:13).[150]

In an interesting turn, the Joseph Smith Translation substituted ten words for these four words, so its text reads: "into heaven, to glorify him who reigneth over all heavens" (JST 4:10). The texture in this reading sends readers to the Father, emphasizing that the Son ascended directly to him and not, vaguely, to a region "above all heavens." In the JST version, the ascension has become much more personal.

all heavens: Sitting visibly in the background of this term is the painting that heaven is not singular; it is multiple. To be sure, we often read "heavens" in scripture when the singular "heaven" would suffice. This state comes about because in Semitic tongues the term for heaven is plural, as in Hebrew (*shamayim*).[151] But the term "all heavens" does not center on just one heaven. Rather, we are looking at multiple heavens, as Paul's "third heaven" signified, hinting at even more (2 Cor. 12:2; see also 2 Cor. 5:1).[152] Of course, other religious movements pushed the notion that many heavens existed that were controlled by evil forces.[153] But early Christians did not embrace this kind of celestial view. That inimical forces roamed around

149. Traub and von Rad, *TDNT,* 5:533.

150. Traub and von Rad, *TDNT,* 5:533.

151. Bartelmus, *TDOT,* 15:205.

152. Traub and von Rad, *TDNT,* 5:525–26; Best, *Ephesians,* 387.

153. Traub and von Rad, *TDNT,* 5:525–26.

out there was a given, including the devils that tried to disrupt Jesus' ministry. But God had exercised a power that kept them in check, as 1:21–22 affirms ("all things under his feet"). More to the point, "he hath delivered us from the power of darkness, and hath translated us into the kingdom of his dear Son" (Col. 1:13). In the language of Peter, God "hath called you out of darkness into his marvelous light" (1 Pet. 2:9; see also the Notes on 1:10, 21; 2:2; 3:15; 6:9).

fill all things: We have met a similar expression in 1:23, "filleth all." The verb is the same (πληρόω, *pleroō*), though a different tense. And the term translated "all" or "all things" is identical (τὰ πάντα, *ta panta*). Because of where this expression leads—namely, to the apostles and prophets and other church representatives in the next verse—we have to reckon initially with the church as the recipient of Christ's filling action.[154] More to the point, his earthly and now heavenly activities have brought about a reconciliation between Gentile and Jew, making "in himself" of the two groups "one new man, so making peace" (2:15). He has thus offered to "both [peoples] . . . access by one Spirit unto the Father" (2:18; see also 2:11–22). Moreover, Christ's filling of the church opens the doors to its role as an instrument for carrying the gospel message not only to mortals but also to "the principalities and powers in heavenly places" (3:10)[155] as well as serving as an aid for the salvation of the spirits of the dead through vicarious baptism (see 1 Cor. 15:29[156] and the Notes on 3:10; 4:5, 8, 9).

Christ's ability to fill the church stems from his ability to fill the cosmos as the one who is "in and through all things, the light of truth" (D&C 88:6). With Jeremiah, we can quote the Lord's question, "Do I not fill heaven and earth?" (Jer. 23:24). God is the one who sustains his creation, even reaching into each individual's life. In electric language, he does so by "preserving you from day to day, by lending you breath, that ye may live and move and do according to your own will, and even supporting you from one moment to another" (Mosiah 2:21). The substance of this line is encapsulated within the Psalmist's questions: "Whither shall I go from thy spirit? or whither shall I flee from thy presence?" (Ps. 139:7). It is God's fulness in this sense that allows him to "gather together in one all things in Christ, both which are in heaven, and which are on earth" (1:10). But he is not identical with creation; he is not somehow suffused throughout the

---

154. Schweizer and Baumgärtel, *TDNT*, 7:1078 and nn. 500–501.
155. Schweizer and Baumgärtel, *TDNT*, 7:1078.
156. Riesenfeld, *TDNT*, 8:512–13.

cosmos. Rather, we find ourselves dealing with God's omnipresence, his omnipotence, and his loving willingness to insert his influence into the lives of believers (see Philip. 1:11; Col. 1:16, 20; Heb. 12:25;[157] Moses 1:39; and the Notes on 1:10, 23; 3:19; 5:18).

4:11 *he gave*: The past tense verb form ἔδωκεν (*edōken*) mirrors exactly the verb in 4:8 and shares the same tense and stem of the verb in 4:7, though not in the passive as in 4:7. Thus, the giving of church officers stands on the same continuum as the giving of grace in 4:7 and the giving of special "gifts unto men" in 4:8 (see 1 Cor. 12:28). What is added in this verse is the pronoun "he" or "himself" (αὐτός, *autos*). This addition lays stress on Christ as the giver—"he himself gave" or "he personally gave."[158] The expression "it was he who" (NR) brings us to the same end by putting emphasis on Christ as the Ever-Generous One (see the Notes on 1:22; 4:7, 8).

***apostles*:** By placing apostles at the first of his list, Paul openly splashes the enlivening, always moving waters of church organization, conceived and coordinated by God, onto his readers. After all, Jesus chose these men as his first leaders in his planned church, leaders whom he called "fishers of men" (Matt. 4:19; Mark 1:17; see also Luke 5:10), making of them his helpers to draw people into the truths of his gospel as into a net. With the exception of the Seventy (see Luke 10:1), these men were the only church officers known to be called directly and set apart by Jesus himself (see Matt. 10:1, 5–15; Mark 6:7–11; and Luke 9:1–5). And this number included Paul, who met the Christ, as he himself affirmed (see 3:2–4; 1 Cor. 9:1; 15:8–10; and Gal. 1:15–16).[159]

It is important to observe that in the early Christian church these apostles were the only general church officers. All others served local congregations. This concept lies behind the Risen Jesus' commission to the Eleven in Galilee days before his ascension. On that occasion, he said, "Go ye therefore, and teach all nations, baptizing them in the name of the Father, and of the Son, and of the Holy Ghost" (Matt. 28:19; see also Mark 16:15–16; Acts 1:8; and Morm. 9:22–23). In Paul's words, the apostles are "the foundation" upon which the church is built (2:20).[160] Moreover, these men, who had been sent by a direct divine commissioning, represented the senders, God and Jesus. In fact, as the Hebrew term *shaliach* (the equivalent of the

157. Delling, *TDNT*, 6:288–92; Traub and von Rad, *TDNT*, 5:517; Schweizer and Baumgärtel, *TDNT*, 7:1078 and n. 501.

158. Louw-Nida, §92.37; Merkle, *Guide*, 127.

159. Rengstorf, *TDNT*, 1:415, 423; Nibley, *Apostles and Bishops*, 1–23.

160. Rengstorf, *TDNT*, 1:423.

Greek *apostolos*) implies, the apostles stood in the place of the sender. As such, they were more than legal ambassadors who bore messages or carried out tasks.[161] Even the closest associates of the apostles, those whom Paul called "fellowlaborers," companions in preaching and administering, did not enjoy the direct call of Jesus (see Philip. 4:3; 1 Thes. 3:2; and Philem. 1:1, 24). Additionally, like those Old Testament figures sent to carry out tasks normally undertaken by God himself—Moses, Elijah, Elisha and Ezekiel[162]—the apostles were granted unusual powers, including casting out devils, taking up serpents, drinking poison with no effect, and healing the sick (see Mark 16:17–18 and Morm. 9:24; see also Acts 15:12; 19:11; 28:3–6; Rom. 15:18–19; 2 Cor. 12:12; Gal. 3:5; and 1 Thes. 1:5).

prophets: In the Old Testament, the term *shaliah* ("a sent one") regularly applied to the sending of prophets (see Ex. 3:10–15; Judg. 13:8; 2 Sam. 24:13; Isa. 6:8; 42:19; Jer. 7:25; 25:4; etc.).[163] Such persons, whom Paul featured here and at 2:20 and 3:5, are New Testament prophets and evidently stood in a supportive role when measured against the apostles. The untranslated Greek construction in this verse (μέν . . . δέ, *men . . . de*) clearly separates the two groups, making of them different church officers, with the *men* associated with "the apostles" and the *de* linked with "the prophets."[164] The suggestion that these individuals had "a foundational office, [but] not an ongoing role in the later church,"[165] is an admission of the loss of sacred authority and nourishment for church members (see Acts 13:1; 15:32; Rom. 12:6; 1 Cor. 12:28; 1 Thes. 5:20; Rev. 16:6; 18:20; etc.), bringing the early church into spiritual bankruptcy when these prophets passed out of existence (see the Notes on 2:20; 3:5).

Perhaps surprisingly, we possess an approximate date that such prophets last influenced early church members, about AD 145. That date centers on a man named Quadratus. Among modern historians he is justly celebrated as the first Christian apologist, who wrote a treatise defending Christianity and dedicated it to the Roman emperor Hadrian (AD 117–38). Quadratus

---

161. Rengstorf, *TDNT,* 1:414–15.

162. Rengstorf, *TDNT,* 1:419. Moses twice caused water to come out of a rock (see Ex. 17:6; Num. 20:8–11), Elijah raised a dead youth and brought rain (see 1 Kgs. 17:17–23; 18:30–45), Elisha opened a mother's womb and gave life to her dead son (see 2 Kgs. 4:8–37), and Ezekiel called dry bones to life (see Ezek. 37:1–14).

163. Frank-Lothar Hossfeld, F. van der Velden, and U. Dahmen, *TDOT,* 15:61–65; Mathias Delcor and Ernst Jenni, *TLOT,* 3:1333.

164. Smyth, *Greek Grammar,* §2904; Lincoln, *Ephesians,* 153.

165. Winger, *Ephesians,* 452.

may have presented his written work to the emperor when the latter was in residence in Asia Minor during AD 123–124 or 129.[166] Only one brief quotation from Quadratus's work survives, quoted by the fourth-century Christian historian Eusebius. In it, Quadratus wrote that during his own lifetime he had met people whom Jesus had healed and raised from the dead: "Some of them have survived even down to our own times," he declared.[167] What is important for our purposes is Eusebius's tag, writing that Quadratus, "as well as the daughters of Philip, was distinguished for the prophetical gift."[168] We meet these women in Acts 21:8–9, the "four daughters" of Philip "which did prophesy." As a capstone, Eusebius later reproduced a list of early prophetic personalities from an unnamed Christian author, mistakenly identified as Apollinarius of Hierapolis in Asia Minor (bishop AD 161–80).[169] This list, which included "the daughters of Philip" and Agabus, whom we encounter in Acts 11:28 and 21:10–11, ended with Quadratus's name.[170] That his name appeared last lays down a clear case that he was the last known Christian notable who bore the prophetic gift. After his death, that gift was utterly lost to the early church (see the Note on 2:20).

What about false prophets? Like Jeremiah, whom God warned about false prophets (see Jer. 23:21), Christian believers also received warnings from Jesus himself about such persons in their day. As early as the Sermon on the Mount, Jesus fulminated, "Beware of false prophets, which come to you [as if sent forth] in sheep's clothing, but inwardly they are ravening wolves" (Matt. 7:15). He further warned that, after his death and Resurrection, "many false prophets shall rise, and shall deceive many" (Matt. 24:11). More specifically, "there shall arise false Christs, and false prophets, and shall shew great signs and wonders; insomuch that . . . they shall deceive the very elect" (Matt. 24:24; see also Mark 13:22). In fact, a couple of generations later, already "there were false prophets also among the people" (2 Pet. 2:1–3), and "many false prophets [had] gone out into the world" (1 John 4:1). Yet to come was the false prophet associated with the beast of the book of Revelation, both of whom would receive a horrible punishment (see Rev. 19:20; 20:10).

---

166. Quasten, *Patrology*, 1:190–91; Frend, *Rise of Christianity*, 121, 235.

167. Eusebius, *Ecclesiastical History* 4.3.2, in *ANF*, 8:749.

168. Eusebius, *Ecclesiastical History* 3.37.1.

169. Quasten, *Patrology*, 1:228–29; see also Hugh Jackson Lawlor and John Ernest Leonard Oulton, trans., *Eusebius, Bishop of Caesarea: The Ecclesiastical History and the Martyrs of Palestine*, 2 vols. (London: SPCK, 1954), 1:162; 2:171, 173.

170. Eusebius, *Ecclesiastical History* 5.17.3.

evangelists: This term (εὐαγγελιστής, *euangelistēs*) presents two aspects. In its New Testament occurrences, on the one hand, it carries the meaning "a bringer of good tidings,"[171] a sense that shows its inner link to the noun translated "gospel" (εὐαγγέλιον, *euangelion*) and to the verb "to bring glad tidings" or "to proclaim good news" (εὐαγγελίζω, *euangelizō*).[172] In the New Testament, *euangelistēs* occurs three times. Besides its appearance in our verse, it is applied to Philip, called "the evangelist" (Acts 21:8), and to Timothy, also designated "an evangelist" (2 Tim. 4:5). Throughout the New Testament, the cluster of words linked to *euangelistēs* sends us to the proclamation of the gospel, directing us to both the act of preaching (see 2:17; 3:8; Luke 3:18; 4:18; Rom. 1:15; 10:15; etc.) and the message itself (see 1:13; 3:6; 6:15, 19; Matt. 24:14; 26:13; Mark 1:1, 14; Rom. 1:1, 9; etc.).[173] The noun *euangelistēs* bore this significance into the second century AD, with one important added concept. People known as evangelists came to be known as the successors to the apostles, a major step in the faltering effort to identify those who succeeded the Twelve and others like Paul. Over time, of course, the word "evangelist" grew attached to the authors of the Gospels.[174]

In its earliest sense, on the other hand, from a badly preserved inscription from the isle of Rhodes, the noun *euangelistēs* refers to "one who proclaims oracular sayings."[175] That is to say, this person declared future events that were hidden from those in the mortal world, beyond human view. This is precisely the function of a modern patriarch—to tell individual church members the things they otherwise could not see about their own futures from God's point of view, thus opening a window onto what that person may experience and become.[176] Such declarations come not to congregations or to the church as a whole but to individuals, one by one, person by person.

---

171. Thayer, *Lexicon*, 257.

172. BDAG, 402–3; Thayer, *Lexicon*, 256–57.

173. Friedrich, *TDNT*, 2:737; Fowl, *Ephesians*, 141.

174. Eusebius, *Ecclesiastical History* 5.10.2; see also 3.37.2–3; Friedrich, *TDNT*, 2:737; and Geoffrey W. H. Lampe, ed., *A Patristic Greek Lexicon* (Oxford: Oxford University Press, 1961), 559.

175. Friedrich, *TDNT*, 2:736; see also LSJ, 705, "proclaimer of oracular messages." The inscription was published in the series *Inscriptiones Graecae* by the Berlin-Brandenburg Academy of Sciences and Technology, vol. 12, no. 675.

176. According to a notation by Willard Richards about a discourse delivered between June 26 and July 2, 1839, Joseph Smith taught, "An evangelist is a patriarch even the oldest man of the Blood of Joseph or of the seed of Abraham, whereever the Church of Christ is established in the earth, there should be a patriarch for the benefit of the posterity of the Saints." "Discourse, between circa 26 June and circa 2 July 1839, as Reported by Willard

pastors: The first meaning of this noun is a shepherd or herdsman, whose basic task was to protect (ποιμήν, *poimēn*).[177] Throughout the Old Testament and the New, "shepherd" appears in metaphorical dress for persons who were to spiritually and physically care for and nourish others. In a most telling passage, the Lord complained about "the shepherds of Israel [who] ... do feed themselves" rather than "the flocks" (Ezek. 34:2). In words that disclose the divine expectations for God's shepherds, he charged that "the diseased have ye not strengthened; ... neither have ye bound up that which was broken, neither have ye brought again that which was driven away, neither have ye sought that which was lost; but with force and with cruelty have ye ruled them" (Ezek. 34:4). From the language throughout Ezekiel 34, it becomes plain that "the shepherds of Israel," though shirking their duties and worse, served at God's pleasure in positions of responsibility for his flock, for his people. So it was in New Testament times. Notably, Jesus called himself "the good shepherd" who, stunningly and in keeping with his deep commitment to the well-being of his flock, "giveth his life for the sheep." He thus set the ultimate example of sacrificing himself, his time, his energy, his life, for the sheep (John 10:11). That said, Jesus stated that, besides giving his all for the sheep, "I ... know my sheep" (John 10:14). Thus, for the real shepherd, more was required in the form of personal interactions and interest shown for the sheep. In this light, the pastors or shepherds of the New Testament, equivalent to modern bishops and branch presidents, bore an official responsibility for each person in the congregation as modeled by Jesus himself, as only our Ephesians verse here illustrates in the entire New Testament (see Heb. 13:20 and 1 Pet. 2:25; 5:2–4).[178]

teachers: In the Gospels, when the noun διάσκαλος (*didaskalos*) is applied to Jesus, the KJV translates it as "Master" (see Matt. 8:19; Mark 4:38; Luke 3:12; John 1:38; etc.), with one exception—when Nicodemus called Jesus "teacher [*didaskalos*]" (John 3:2). In the earliest church, teachers appear not to have an official responsibility to preside over their local congregations, like the pastors. Yet they hefted an important responsibility. They were both the transmitters of the doctrines of the church, bringing to members "the knowledge of the Son of God" (4:13), and the

Richards," 22, Joseph Smith Papers, https://www.josephsmithpapers.org/paper-summary/discourse-between-circa-26-june-and-circa-2-july-1839-as-reported-by-willard-richards/8.

177. BDAG, 843; Thayer, *Lexicon*, 527.

178. Joachim Jeremias, *TDNT*, 6:497–98; Lincoln, *Ephesians*, 250–51; Fowl, *Ephesians*, 141; Winger, *Ephesians*, 455–56.

guides who sought to help believers avoid "every wind of doctrine . . . and cunning craftiness" that might descend into their midst (4:14). In effect, they were the custodians of gospel truths and were as essential as any other officer of the church (see 1 Cor. 12:28). For it was they who enjoyed the spiritual gift of teaching (see Rom. 12:7; Moro. 10:10; and D&C 46:18). With this gift, they doubtless encouraged other believers' individual comprehension of the gospel so that their "understanding [was] enlightened" (1:18; see also D&C 121:42, "By . . . pure knowledge, which shall greatly enlarge the soul") and helped to broaden their comprehension of "what is the breadth, and length, and depth, and height" of Christ's love (3:18).[179]

4:12 *For the perfecting:* We finally arrive at the reasons God has given "unto every one of us . . . grace" (4:7) and has provided a church organization that brims with "apostles, . . . prophets, . . . pastors" and other needed individuals (4:11). Out of God's bounty has emerged such gifts, and they all have to do with "the edifying of the body of Christ," the church (4:12), and making "the whole body fitly joined together" (4:16). Thus joined and thus enriched, believers are brought to a place where they are able "to keep the unity of the Spirit in the bond of peace" (4:3). In sum, celestial work can now go on apace in the terrestrial church.

perfecting: The noun καταρτισμός (*katartismos*) presents an interesting picture. First, it appears only here in the New Testament. Second, its meanings range from equipping to preparing to training.[180] In a related verb form in Luke 6:40, it bears the sense "fully trained" rather than "perfect" as in the KJV: "Everyone who is fully trained will be like his teacher" (Luke 6:40 NR).[181] In our passage, 4:12, the noun paints the portrait of thoroughly preparing the Saints for their ministries, folding in all members, women and men alike, "till we all come in the unity of the faith" (4:13). That is, church leaders never assumed that recent converts had grasped all that they needed to while investigating the gospel; everyone required continuous training and education in doctrine and accepted procedures.

saints: In its most fundamental denotation, this noun ἅγιος (*hagios*) means "holy one," deriving its sense from the idea of holiness.[182] For church members, this common title "saints" stands as a goal to reach for, a status

---

179. Lincoln, *Ephesians*, 251; Fowl, *Ephesians*, 141.

180. LSJ, 910.

181. Brown, *Testimony of Luke*, 332, 343. See Gerhard Delling, *TDNT*, 1:476; BDAG, 526; Louw-Nida, §75.5.

182. Procksch and Kuhn, *TDNT*, 1:108.

to strive for. Wrapped tightly within the fabric of holiness is a person's state before God, before his altar in his sanctuary. The temple connection and its sacred clothing are always present with the term *hagios*, whether acknowledged or not. This is the significance of Paul's temple language wherein church members are to "present [their] bodies a living sacrifice, holy, acceptable unto God" (Rom. 12:1). If this statement about bodily sacrifice were not clear enough, he soon returned to it, but with a pointer to his efforts among Gentiles: "That the offering up of the Gentiles might be acceptable, being sanctified by the Holy Ghost" (Rom. 15:16). In another place he explained that "the temple of God is holy, which temple ye are" (1 Cor. 3:17).

In the light of these passages, it becomes apparent that one's body, not just one's mind and heart, serves as an important part of one's purifying sacrifice. It all has to do with the offering of a person's self, not of one's possessions.[183] This sort of sacrifice leads a person to "take up his cross" (Matt. 16:24), knowing full well that by hefting the cross one's path will lead to "persecutions and tribulations" and worse (2 Thes. 1:4). Such experiences did not come as surprises. No. As Paul wrote to the Thessalonian Saints, "When we were with you, we told you before that we [all] should suffer tribulation" (1 Thes. 3:4). Such tribulation may mean "that a man lay down his life for his friends" (John 15:13) or lay "down his life in [Christ's] cause, for [Christ's] name's sake" (D&C 98:13). These acts, of course, frame the ultimate sanctifying sacrifice of one's mortal body, the crowning act of consecration.

Paul did not leave himself out of the need for sacrifice. Rather, he wrote that "if I be offered upon the sacrifice and service of your faith, I joy, and rejoice with you all" (Philip. 2:17). He saw his life and ministry as one of complete consecration on the altar of holiness. It was Jesus himself who brought forward the need for purity or holiness: "Blessed are the pure [καθαρός, *katharos*][184] in heart: for they shall see God" (Matt. 5:8). In striving for holiness, a person seeks to become "holy and without blame" (1:4). Here the expression "without blame" means "without blemish," the requirement for an animal that is to be sacrificed at the temple. For the believer, it means to present oneself "unblameable in holiness before God"

---

183. Procksch and Kuhn, *TDNT*, 1:107–8.

184. In its basic sense here, the adjective καθαρός (*katharos*) refers not only to ritual purity (see Rom. 14:20; Titus 1:15) but also to innocence (see Acts 18:6, translated "clean"; 20:26). See Procksch and Kuhn, *TDNT*, 1:108.

(1 Thes. 3:13), with the phrase "before God" pointing to the sacred altar (see Alma 17:4, "before the altar of God . . . before him"; and the Notes on 1:4; 2:19; 3:18; 5:3).

work: The word ἔργον (*ergon*), which we meet elsewhere in this letter (see 2:9, 10; 5:11), directs readers to salvation itself. Throughout the New Testament, expressions like "the work(s) of God" and "the work(s) of the Lord" touch on the ultimate object of Christ's powers released both during his earthly ministry and through his Atonement. For example, especially from the fourth Gospel, we read Jesus' affirming words that "the works that I do in my Father's name, they bear witness of me" (John 10:25; see also John 4:34; 5:36; 9:3; 17:4). From Paul, we encounter his question "Are not ye my work in the Lord?" (1 Cor. 9:1; see also Rom. 14:20 and 1 Cor. 16:10; compare 1 Cor. 3:9 and Philip. 2:30).[185] Thus, "the work of the ministry" has to do with leading others to Christ and immersing them in the saving, sweet fragrances of salvation. Such work, of course, does not have to do with this life only, wherein people can hear and embrace the gospel message. It also has to do with the ministry that Christ organized among departed spirits in the spirit prison so that "they might be judged according to men in the flesh, but live according to God in the spirit" (1 Pet. 4:6; see also D&C 138:20–21, 30–37; and the Notes on 2:9, 10; 4:5, 9; 5:11).

ministry: Although the noun διακονία (*diakonia*) paints the ever-present picture of "waiting on tables," on the gospel canvas it portrays the highest of actions undertaken for the sake of others. When the Twelve made the decision that other church officers would handle "the daily ministration" for widows and they would devote themselves "to the ministry [*diakonia*] of the word" (Acts 6:1, 4), they were not ducking responsibility for the poor in their midst. Rather, they understood that winning souls to Christ carried monumental consequences for individuals. Because Paul grasped that ministering is a gift of grace, in his painting he could set it among the high spiritual gifts of prophecy and teaching (see Rom. 12:6–7) and add in the colorations of possessing the Spirit and rising to a place of righteousness as brightly colored consequences of personal ministering (see 2 Cor. 3:7–9).[186]

edifying: Translated "building" at 2:21, the noun οἰκοδομή (*oikodomē*) fundamentally pertains to the activity of building.[187] In Paul's hands, the

---

185. Bertram, *TDNT*, 2:642–43.
186. Hermann W. Beyer, *TDNT*, 2:87–88.
187. BDAG, 696–97; Louw-Nida, §§7.1; 42.34.

term revolves around spiritual encouragement and strengthening. In other words, it is about the building up or furtherance of both communal and individual spirituality. That is exactly the notion behind believers' embrace of God's special gifts, particularly the gift of prophecy. For in judging whether speaking in tongues or prophesying in church meetings brought the greater benefit to those who heard, Paul observed that "he that speaketh in an unknown tongue speaketh not unto men . . . for no man understandeth him." In contrast, "he that prophesieth speaketh unto men [and women] to edification [*oikodomē*], and exhortation, and comfort" (1 Cor. 14:2–3). To be clear, we understand from this latter passage that such prophesying included a large measure of exhortation. Then Paul tightened the vise by declaring that "greater is he that prophesieth than he that speaketh with tongues, . . . that the church may receive edifying [*oikodomē*]" (1 Cor. 14:5).[188] When paired with the image of building or constructing an edifice, the idea of edifying points both to an outsider—namely God, who builds and strengthens through spiritual aids—and to the members of a congregation, who reach out to edify and build up one another (see 1 Cor. 14:12, 26; and the Notes on 2:21; 4:16, 29).[189]

body: The church sits in the sights of this noun. The two, the body and the church, are one and the same. But they are more. "The Church is the earthly body of the heavenly Head [Christ]."[190] In the context of edifying or building up the spiritual capacity of church members, these members, or the body as a whole, strive to grow into Christ, to become as he is, maturing past their spiritual childhood. This concept lies beneath Paul's next words, "That we henceforth be no more children [but] . . . may grow up into him in all things, which is the head, even Christ" (4:14–15). With Christ's help, therefore, believers become the "perfect man [and woman]" (4:13), the "new man [and woman]" (2:15), enjoying the "peace" and reconciliation which Christ engenders between Jew and Gentile (2:14–16). All of these dimensions prepare believers for what is to come at the end of time, to become "heirs of God, and joint-heirs with Christ" (Rom. 8:17;[191] see also the Notes on 1:23; 2:16; 3:10, 21; 4:4, 12, 15, 16; 5:23, 27, 30).

---

188. Michel, *TDNT,* 5:145.
189. Barth, *Ephesians,* 2:440.
190. Schlier, *TDNT,* 3:680.
191. Schlier, *TDNT,* 3:680.

4:13 *come:* The verb καταντάω (*katantaō*) is richer than the simple "to come." It expresses the sense "to attain" or "to reach."[192] We see this verb, for instance, in the sentence "They arrived at Ephesus" (Acts 18:19 NIV; see also Acts 27:12). The thought is that a person reaches "the goal of a journey."[193] The meaning is transported to a different kind of goal though with the same idea, "to attain." In Paul's words we read, "If by any means I might attain [*katantaō*] unto the resurrection of the dead" (Philip. 3:11; see also Acts 26:7). This type of objective is set by God and involves personal participation by each believer,[194] whether living on earth or residing in the world of spirits.

unity: Paul now rounds back to the melodic theme that he had strummed earlier, that of oneness (ἑνότης, *henotēs*). Whether "one Spirit" or "one faith" or "One God and Father of all" (4:4–6), unity forms a main thrust of his remarks. What we see in this and surrounding verses are the grand results that grow out of the unity of believers, one with another. Among other things, these results bring about "the edifying of the body of Christ"; they grant "the knowledge of the Son of God"; and they lead to a spiritual maturity of believers so that they are "no more children" (4:12–14). But that is only part of the story. For, with Christ as the beginning and center points, the church has become "the new humanity whose author is Christ."[195] With his Father, with whom he is unified, he has shaped a new fellowship that, through his Atonement, offers to the initiated a united purpose in this life that aims ultimately at the next. This oneness transcends national and ethnic identities as well as city and neighborhood associations. As expressed in John's Gospel, "that also he [Christ] should gather together in one the children of God that were scattered abroad" (John 11:52; see also John 17:11, 21–23). Elsewhere, Paul spelled out this unity as a companion to constant endeavoring, a oneness that results when "ye stand fast in one spirit, with one mind striving together for the faith of the gospel" (Philip. 1:27; see the Note on 4:3).[196]

knowledge: This noun, ἐπίγνωσις (*epignōsis*), appears earlier at 1:17. It can refer to knowledge gained by experience or to understanding achieved by learning—that is, by mental effort.[197] The first kind of knowledge characterizes those in the highest heaven. The related verb ἐπιγινώσκω (*epiginō-skō*) illustrates this thought. While still in Galilee, Jesus said that "no man

---

192. BDAG, 523; Louw-Nida, §§13.16; 15.84.
193. Otto Michel, *TDNT,* 3:623.
194. Michel, *TDNT,* 3:623–24.
195. Ethelbert Stauffer, *TDNT,* 2:440.
196. Stauffer, *TDNT,* 2:440.
197. Louw-Nida, §28.2, 18; Merkle, *Guide,* 130.

knoweth [*epiginōskō*] the Son, but the Father; neither knoweth [*epiginōskō*] any man the Father, save the Son, and he to whomsoever the Son will reveal him" (Matt. 11:27).[198] From Jesus' saying, it is clear that such knowledge breathes out a divine origin, a celestial gift that comes not by study but by experience with personal revelation. The Apostle highlighted this message when he wrote that "we also . . . desire that ye might be filled with the knowledge of his will in all wisdom and spiritual understanding" (Col. 1:9). Coming to know the "will" of God, then, means eventually attaining to "all wisdom and spiritual understanding," a most remarkable state of being (see 5:17; Col. 2:2–3; and the Notes on 1:17; 3:18, 19; 5:5).

perfect man: The adjective τέλειος (*teleios*) occurs only here in Ephesians and is almost always translated in the KJV as "perfect" (see Matt. 5:48; Rom. 12:2; 1 Cor. 13:10; Philip. 3:15; etc.). It bears the sense of "complete" and "whole." In the world of temple sacrifices, for example, it centers on being "unblemished." When describing human actions and attitudes, it pertains to being "mature" and "dedicated." In a few New Testament passages, it touches on being "initiated."[199] That is to say, it has to do with persons who have received a special introduction to sacred truths in a holy place or sanctuary. Such people have received the supreme mysteries, as it were, "in distinction from the first stages" of belief.[200] To set this observation on a firm footing, we notice that Christ's actions took place in a "perfect [*teleios*] tabernacle, not made with hands" (Heb. 9:11), introducing us to a "heavenly sanctuary."[201] Even though Jesus' saving services to all were not enacted in the physical Jerusalem temple, it was as though they were. In this connection, we possess no mention in the New Testament of places where early church members may have participated privately in sacred ceremonies. But they surely did, as Paul's pointer to baptisms for the dead indicates (see 1 Cor. 15:29).

Scholarship has referred to Philippians 3:15 and Colossians 1:28 as passages that relate to initiation activities.[202] We read that "all of us who are initiated [deeper] into this faith should have this same attitude" (Philip. 3:15).[203] Further, Paul tasked missionaries with teaching in such a way "that we might [in time] bring everyone into a state of being initiated in Christ"

---

198. Louw-Nida, §28.2.

199. BDAG, 995–96; Louw-Nida, §11:18.

200. Gerhard Delling, *TDNT*, 8:67–69, quotation on 69.

201. Delling, *TDNT*, 8:77.

202. Delling, *TDNT*, 8:76; BDAG, 996; Louw-Nida, §11:18.

203. Louw-Nida, §11:18.

(Col. 1:28).[204] Plainly, the initial steps of faith and baptism were only the beginning. Another verse pushes itself into our view. As Paul wrote his final greetings to church members in Colossae, he mentioned that his fellow servant Epaphras was "always laboring fervently for you in prayers, that ye may stand perfect [*teleios*] and complete in all the will of God" (Col. 4:12). As quickly becomes clear, standing as an initiated person involves becoming "complete in all the will of God." This aspect of completeness is disclosed in the term for "man" (ἀνήρ, *anēr*) in this line, 4:13. The noun *anēr* leads us directly to an adult male—namely Christ—whereas the other noun often translated "man" or "men" in the New Testament (ἄνθρωπος, *anthrōpos*) represents more generally a "human being" (see 2:15; 3:16; 4:8, 22; etc.).[205] In this latter case, we find ourselves in the presence of one who, as an adult, whether man or woman, can embrace fully further covenants and divine teaching. This notion, naturally, contrasts with the "children" of 4:14.

Of course, some might object to the outline sketched above of a person initiated into a special ceremony or set of ceremonies that is only briefly hinted at within the New Testament. Such an objection would stress the mature or complete aspect of the church and its members in the term "perfect man" (see James 3:2). It would also emphasize that the real context of the term "perfect man" is framed chiefly by the interest in "unity" (4:3, 13), conferring the sense that the church as a whole strives to gain such perfection, and secondarily by the plain contrast between the adult *anēr* and the youthful "children" of 4:14.[206] In response, we notice that these elements are not the only framework that surrounds the idea of the "perfect man." In fact, other pieces of the context lead us to ceremony. Specifically, the verb at the beginning of 4:13 (*katantaō*) has to do with "reaching the goal of a journey."[207] With the quotation in 4:8 from Psalm 68, a psalm that has to do with a royal procession, and the imagery of special clothing in 4:22–24, the journey takes on the character of either royalty or marriage or both. Hence, the context for the "perfect man" brings us inside sacred ceremony, not just to the maturity of the church.[208] But the story does not end here.

---

204. Louw-Nida, §11:18.

205. BDAG, 79–82.

206. Van Roon, *Authenticity of Ephesians,* 319–25; Lincoln, *Ephesians,* 256; Best, *Ephesians,* 401; Winger, *Ephesians,* 467–68.

207. Michel, *TDNT,* 3:623.

208. Barth, *Ephesians,* 2:485–87.

We must also take account of the rich temple ties that appear throughout this letter and form an illumining pattern that cannot be dismissively set aside (see the Notes on 1:4, 6; 2:11, 18, 20, 21; 4:12, 20, 22, 24). Furthermore, obvious references to early Christian rituals occur in the collection of apocryphal texts discovered in 1946 or 1947 near the city of Nag Hammadi in Upper Egypt. Such references revolve around specific sacred acts such as a consecration by anointing with oil and a sacred marriage ceremony. The text that preserves a majority of these features is the Gospel of Philip. As becomes apparent, the Christian anointing bore strong resemblances to the anointing of Old Testament priests, and the marriage was both eternal and "available only to virgins and freedmen, that is to say, only to the worthy." Moreover, the marriage took place in a bridal chamber that stood in a special place in the temple, "the holy of the holies."[209] Finally, some of the earliest attestations of this adjective *teleios* and its accompanying nouns and verb send us to sacred rites that were intended to bring devotees inside the divine world, complete with instruction in holy truths and with pledges aimed at acceptable behavior and, unsurprisingly, at not revealing the nature and content of those rites.[210] In summary, all attempts to treat the term "perfect man" will always be perfumed by the aromas of sacred ceremonies (see the Notes on 2:6, 10; 4:1, 20, 22, 24; 5:2, 8, 14; 6:11, 13, 14; the introduction section XI; and appendix 1).

unto the measure of the stature of the fulness of Christ: If there ever were an expression in the New Testament that declared the possibility for ordinary church members to become as God now is, it is this one. Paul has succeeded in deftly framing what is almost unimaginable about human potential. To reach the stature of Christ in his fulness, in his perfection, goes beyond the Apostle's word-picture elsewhere that individuals can become "heirs of God, and joint-heirs with Christ" (Rom. 8:17). For that language sketches out an heirship, a celestial inheritance (see D&C 84:38, "all that my Father hath shall be given unto him"). Such passages address what the Saints will possess in the next life, not their inner, heavenly status as deities. Said another way, "Christ initiates a process of growth of which

---

209. S. Kent Brown, "The Nag Hammadi Library: A Mormon Perspective," in *Apocryphal Writings and the Latter-day Saints,* ed. C. Wilfred Griggs (Provo, Utah: BYU Religious Studies Center, 1986), 260–62, 275–77. For the anointing, consult the Gospel of Philip in James M. Robinson and Richard Smith, eds., *The Nag Hammadi Library in English,* 3rd rev. ed. (San Francisco: HarperCollins, 1990), 151; also 154–55; for the marriage and marriage chamber, see 151–52.

210. Delling, *TDNT,* 8:51, 58, 69.

He Himself is the goal and in which He Himself sets us," thus initiating and then shepherding the growth of each person "after [the ideal of] God" (4:24; see also the Note thereon).[211]

measure: In the case of the noun μέτρον (*metron*), we find ourselves face-to-face with a combining of the two senses that the term exhibits throughout the New Testament. In the first, we glimpse its spatial meaning, which deals with size or length. For instance, in talking about the field of labor that God himself had assigned to him, and acknowledging that it had limits which, significantly, stretched as far as Corinth, Paul wrote to the Corinthian church members that "our sphere is determined by the limit [*metron*] God laid down for us, which permitted us to come as far as Corinth" (2 Cor. 10:13 NEB). Second, Jesus highlighted its metaphorical sense when, in dealing with how we judge, he stated that "with the same measure [*metron*] that ye mete withal it shall be measured to you again" (Luke 6:38). Keeping these observations in mind, *metron* in our verse has to do with stature in the dual sense of not only height or loftiness but also the growth of the inner person. In both meanings, we are talking about "the sense of full measure"[212] of the individual when matched with Christ's stature (see the Note below and the Notes on 4:7, 16).

stature: From 3:17 ("rooted and grounded in love") through 4:16 ("increase of the body"), Paul has been moving in and out of images that relate to building and growth. This underlying pattern informs the notion of growing to a certain stature, in this case that of Christ. The noun ἡλικία (*hēlikia*) can mean "time of life." But it also represents "maturity" and "bodily stature."[213] In this context, the term has to do with stature, as in the case of Zacchaeus, the chief tax collector in Jericho: "he was little of stature [*hēlikia*]" (Luke 19:3). However, it is not as though Christ's stature is massive. On the contrary, his stature represents the aggregate of his status and relationship with his Father.

fulness: The question is whether this noun is quantitative or qualitative—that is, whether the Apostle was writing about the extent and texture of Christ's fulness or whether he had in mind Christ's inner fiber formed by both his mortal and immortal experiences. It seems to be the latter, lifting up before readers' eyes the maturity (*teleios*), spiritual and otherwise, that

---

211. Grundmann, Hesse, de Jonge, and van der Woude, *TDNT,* 9:558.
212. Kurt Deissner, *TDNT,* 4:632–34, quotation on 634.
213. BDAG, 435–36; Louw-Nida, §§67.151, 156; 81.4.

Christ had reached. On the believers' side, acquiring such maturity raises them to an adult station above the childhood level of the gospel so that they are no longer subject to being "tossed to and fro, and carried about with every wind of doctrine" and twisted by the "cunning craftiness" of those who would "deceive" (4:14). Happily, according to the Apostle, such maturity was within the grasp of his readers, allowing them each to "put on the new man [or woman]" (4:24).[214] And, remarkably, it was to rest on "the knowledge of the Son of God." This knowledge, of course, involved more than just knowing about Christ—that is, about his ministry, death, visit to the spirit prison, and Resurrection. It meant enjoying a revelatory relationship with the Son of God, a relationship of trust, a history of doing his will (see Rom. 15:29). Knowing the Son of God in a way that leads to God's fulness, as we expect, extends its roots into the Old Testament. There we discover that partaking of the tree of the knowledge of good and evil led in a blessed way to godlike knowledge (see Gen. 3:1–7, 22; and Moses 4:6–13, 28). Further, imitating the Messiah brought devotees to "the spirit of [heavenly] knowledge" (Isa. 11:2; see also Isa. 33:6[215] and the Notes on 1:10, 23; 3:19).

4:14 *children:* On one level, Paul has here featured children (singular νήπιος, *nēpios*) as a fitting contrast to the mature adult, the "perfect man" (4:13). In this passage, children, who stand in for naïve or immature adults, are vulnerable and can be swept up by deceit and false information (see 1 Cor. 3:1–2; 13:11; 14:20; and Gal. 4:3).[216] In one instance, God complained to Jeremiah that his people were "senseless children; they have no understanding." Moreover, willfully "they are skilled in doing evil; they know not how to do good" (Jer. 4:22 NIV). On the whole, however, scripture portrays children in a different light. To be sure, children are naïve and immature. But they are equipped with the ability to follow God's wishes and even take control of the promised land, unlike their seniors (see Deut. 1:39). Moreover, they can function like young Solomon, who received direction for a kingly reign (see 1 Kgs. 3:7; see also Isa. 7:15). Like the youthful Samuel, they are capable of coming to a deeper and clearer understanding of God's ways (see 1 Sam. 3:7, 19; see also Luke 1:80; 2:40; and Rom. 8:14–17).[217]

---

214. Delling, *TDNT,* 6:302.

215. G. Johannes Botterweck and Jan Bergman, *TDOT,* 5:464–65, 477.

216. Georg Bertram, *TDNT,* 4:918–19; Delling, *TDNT,* 6:302; Barth, *Ephesians,* 2:441; Lincoln, *Ephesians,* 257; Best, *Ephesians,* 404; Winger, *Ephesians,* 469.

217. Botterweck and Bergman, *TDOT,* 5:464, 469.

For Paul, children were in need of help, specifically in need of an education in the ways of God. For "when I was a child, I spake as a child, I understood as a child, I thought as a child." It was only "when I became a man, [that] I put away childish things" (1 Cor. 13:11). Hence, when we were children, "the law was our schoolmaster to bring us unto Christ." When "faith [in Christ] is come, we are no longer under a schoolmaster" because we have become mature (Gal. 3:24–25). In fact, in the broader society, "the heir, as long as he is a child, differeth nothing from a servant ... but is under tutors and governors until the time appointed of the [child's] father" (Gal. 4:1–2). According to Paul, in the gospel sense, the point of maturation arrives when believers "receive the adoption of sons [and daughters, and] ... God hath sent forth the Spirit of his Son into your hearts, crying, Abba, Father." The fatherhood of God has now become real. In that moment, "thou art no more a servant, but a son [or daughter]; and if a son [or daughter], then an heir of God through Christ" (Gal. 4:5–7).

With a completely different emphasis, Jesus affirmed that, in their innocence, children are susceptible to God's inspiration: "I thank thee, O Father, ... that thou hast hid these things from the wise and prudent, and hast revealed them unto babes (*nēpios*)" (Luke 10:21; Matt. 11:25; see also Matt. 21:16). It is modern scripture that presents real occurrences of inspiration coming to children and even infants (see 3 Ne. 26:14, 16–17, "even babes did open their mouths and utter marvelous things"). There is more. Jesus raised the bright image of the salvation of children when he declared to his Old World disciples that "except ye be converted, and become as little children, ye shall not enter into the kingdom of heaven" (Matt. 18:3). Moreover, "whosoever shall receive one of such children in my name, receiveth me: and whosoever shall receive me, receiveth not me, but him that sent me" (Mark 9:37; see also Matt. 18:5 and Luke 9:48). All of this centers on salvation being extended to children. For in another place we read that "all little children are alive in Christ" (Moro. 8:22), which means that "the blood of Christ atoneth for their sins" (Mosiah 3:16). Said another way, "little children are holy, being sanctified through the atonement of Jesus Christ" (D&C 74:7; see also Mosiah 15:25–26, "little children [do not] ... rebel against [Christ]"). Measured against the grand scale of creation, "children ... are whole from the foundation of the world" (Moses 6:54).

tossed to and fro: The Apostle has introduced here a scene of tempest on water. The verb that rests beneath this expression (κλυδωνίζομαι, *klydōnizomai*) pertains to raging waves and rough water. The noun κλύδων (*kludōn*) stands under the expressions "wave [*kludōn*] of the sea" in James 1:6 and "raging [*kludōn*] of the water" in Luke 8:24.[218] Paul, of course, was very familiar with storms at sea and the extreme danger and discomfort that they wrought. For he wrote that "thrice I suffered shipwreck, a night and a day I have been in the deep" (2 Cor. 11:25). These harrowing events did not occur in quiet water and did not include the subsequent wild ride on the Mediterranean Sea from the island of Crete to Malta when the grain ship Paul was a passenger on was caught and driven helplessly by an early winter storm (see Acts 27:5–44).[219]

doctrine: Fundamentally, the noun διδασκαλία, *didaskalia*, bears the meaning "teaching," pointing to both the act of teaching (see Rom. 12:7) and the subject that is taught (see Matt. 15:9; Mark 7:7; and Col. 2:22).[220] In its early appearances, including in the Septuagint, the word *didaskalia* touches on "the 'instruction' which comes from scripture" which was, as we discover in Romans 15:4, "written for our learning [*didaskalia*]." Importantly, because in Ephesians the term "every" modifies "wind" and not "doctrine," Paul was warning against currents that occasionally blow through the Ephesian church—that is, windy currents of doctrine that run against the historical outline of Jesus' ministry that he has set out in verses 4:4–11. Real events rest beneath Jesus' descent "into the lower parts of the earth" (4:9), his ascension "far above all heavens" (4:10), and his gifts not only of "grace" (4:7) but also of "apostles; and . . . prophets" and others for the church's ministry (4:11–12). For Paul, based on the historical record of Jesus' life and ministry, this one teaching, this unified "doctrine" of his life and ministry, acted as an anchor that would resist "every wind" that might blow against it.[221] This observation is buttressed by the definite article that appears with *didaskalia*, yielding the meaning "the doctrine." Putting a different trim in the sail and noticing that one object of believers is to "come in the unity of . . . the knowledge of the Son of God" (4:13), "the goal is certain knowledge of divine truth [about Christ] in contrast to the vacillation and variety of human opinion."[222]

---

218. BDAG, 550; Thayer, *Lexicon*, 350–51.

219. Williams, *Paul's Metaphors*, 197.

220. BDAG, 240; Louw-Nida, §33.224, 236.

221. Karl Heinrich Rengstorf, *TDNT*, 2:161–62, earlier quotation on 161. For a different view, see Williams, *Paul's Metaphors*, 206 n. 41.

222. Michel, *TDNT*, 3:624.

sleight: Beginning with this noun κυβεία (*kybeia*), whose earliest meaning centered on "dice-playing,"[223] Paul stacked up four nouns that all direct readers to intentional evil. These four include this word as well as those translated "cunning craftiness," "lie in wait," and "to deceive." In its metaphorical makeup, *kybeia* takes on the meaning of cheating at the game of dice. Hence, the words "the sleight of men" revolve around a purposeful, sinister motive.

cunning craftiness: Throughout the New Testament, the noun πανουργία (*panourgia*) appears in negative dress. As in Luke 20:23, the "craftiness" (*panourgia*) is always Satan-driven. In 2 Corinthians 12:16, while responding to an unwritten question with tongue in cheek, Paul wrote, "Being crafty, I caught you in guile." He implies that he had straddled the line between what is appropriate and what is not, and, acting in a cunning way, he achieved his end—to catch certain of his readers "in guile."[224]

lie in wait: The word μεθοδεία (*methodeia*) is not a verb. Rather, it is a noun that refers to scheming and perversion.[225] In 6:11, the only other passage in the New Testament where the term *methodeia* appears, this sort of scheming is said to go back to the devil himself. In our verse here, such seduction comes at believers from crafty, dishonest teachers who stand under the influence of the unseen world.[226] Paul's choice of *methodeia* leads readers to "a cunning process which seeks to deliver [believers] up to error."[227] What is more, it was Christ's experience not only of participating in mortality but also of descending "into the lower parts of the earth" and then ascending "far above all heavens" (4:9–10) that equipped him with the power to thwart such devilish deception (see Alma 7:11–12; D&C 122:5–8; and the Note on 6:11).[228]

to deceive: This English phrase does not rest on a Greek infinitive. Instead, it translates the expression ἐν πλάνῃ (*en planē*), whose meanings include "in error" and "by deceit."[229] The idea of error splits into an unintended error—that is, an erroneous belief (see 1 John 4:6)—and an intentional misleading of a person into error (see Rom. 1:27; Col. 2:8; and 2 Pet. 3:17).[230]

---

223. LSJ, 1004; BDAG, 573; Louw-Nida, §88.157.
224. Otto Bauernfeind, *TDNT,* 5:726.
225. BDAG, 625; Louw-Nida, §88.158.
226. Herbert Braun, *TDNT,* 6:245.
227. Michaelis, *TDNT,* 5:103.
228. Büchsel, *TDNT,* 3:642.
229. BDAG, 822; Thayer, *Lexicon,* 514–15.
230. Louw-Nida, §§31.8, 10; 88.262.

In this Ephesians verse, the plain sense concerns an obviously intentional deceit[231] as the prior piling up of three negative nouns tells readers. Again, Christ's giving of the "gifts" (4:8) of "grace" (4:7) and church officers (see 4:11), which links to his descent "into the lower parts of the earth" and his ascent "far above all heavens" (4:9–10), "equip[s] Christians for contending against seduction by [deceitful] teachers,"[232] of whom a few were already creating mischief in the church (see the Notes on 5:6, 8, 11; 6:11).

4:15 *speaking the truth in love:* The verb ἀληθεύω (*alētheuō*) has been understood in two ways. In its principal import, it means "to speak truth."[233] In a secondary sense, which commentators are happy to point out, it means "to deal truly" or "to live according to the truth."[234] In whichever way we understand the substance of this verb, a believer's actions are always to be undertaken "in love," a complete contrast to actions done "to deceive" (4:14). In fact, love is to undergird all interactions between church members and others, even those who operate by "cunning craftiness" (4:14). Moreover, it is only "in love" that the truth of the gospel will impact both members and nonmembers alike.[235]

grow up: Readers brush against the world of nature through the verb αὐξάνω (*auxanō*), as 4:16 will soon illustrate (see Luke 12:27, "Consider the lilies how they grow [*auxanō*]"; Matt. 6:28; Mark 4:8; and Luke 13:19).[236] But in our Ephesians verse, the verb escorts readers to the growth of individuals as well as of the church as a whole. In this metaphorical adornment, believers find an inviting goal facing them. Their spiritual objective takes them, astonishingly, to "the stature of the fulness of Christ" (4:13). Said more briefly, they are to grow "into him [Christ] in all things" (4:15).[237] This spiritual growth will assist church members to surmount the craftiness and deceit that Paul warned about in 4:14 (see Col. 1:10; 2:19; 1 Pet. 2:2; 2 Pet. 3:18; and the Note on 2:21).[238]

---

231. Braun, *TDNT*, 6:245.

232. Büchsel, *TDNT*, 3:642.

233. BDAG, 43; Louw-Nida, §33.251.

234. Gottfried Quell, Gerhard Kittel, and Rudolf Bultmann, *TDNT*, 1:251; Thayer, *Lexicon*, 26–27; Bruce, *Ephesians*, 88; Lincoln, *Ephesians*, 259; Winger, *Ephesians*, 471–72; for a different view, see Barth, *Ephesians*, 2:444; Best, *Ephesians*, 407.

235. Bruce, *Ephesians*, 89; Lincoln, *Ephesians*, 260; Winger, *Ephesians*, 472.

236. BDAG, 151; Louw-Nida, §23.188; Thayer, *Lexicon*, 84.

237. Barth, *Ephesians*, 2:445; Lincoln, *Ephesians*, 260; Best, *Ephesians*, 408; Muddiman, *Ephesians*, 207.

238. Braun, *TDNT*, 6:250.

into him: All agree that the phrase εἰς αὐτόν (*eis auton*) denotes the goal "whose referent is Jesus"[239]—that is to say, "the head, Christ" (4:15 NR). This unusual notion that the body, the church, grows into the head turned ancient medicine upside down, for it was thought that the bodies of infants grew out of their rather large heads.[240] Perhaps Paul was thinking that the church and its members grow not only into "the head"—that is, into "the measure of the stature of the fulness of Christ" (4:13)—but also out of its head, the Christ, as appears in 4:16, where the "increase of the body" is a natural outgrowth of "the effectual working in the measure of every [bodily] part" (see Col. 2:19).[241]

the head: As in 1:22, "the head" (κεφαλή, *kephalē*) is Christ. In that verse, we learn that he is the head because his Father had placed him in that role for the sake of the church, making "him to be the head over all things to the church" (see Col. 1:18 and the Note on 1:22). In the current verse, Paul has approached Christ's role from a different direction. Here Christ has become the goal, the standard, for the church and its members to seek and measure themselves to. A few lines earlier, the Apostle had written that Christ had given special officers to the church, including apostles, prophets, and evangelists (see 4:11), "for the perfecting of the [individual] saints." There is more to the story. He also appointed those officers "for the edifying of the body of Christ" as a spiritual and ecclesiastical unity (4:12). It is in this unity, this oneness (see 4:3, 13), that the church grows "into him, [into] ... Christ." It is in this unity that the church as a whole is able to resist any allurement to follow "the sleight of men" into deceit-filled paths.[242] It is in this unity that the congregation of the faithful are exalted "unto the measure of the stature of the fulness of Christ" (4:13).[243] It is in this unity that church members can expect "the King of glory [to] come" into their midst (Ps. 24:7, 9; see also the Notes on 1:22; 5:23).

4:16 *the whole body ... the body:* The Apostle has devoted this entire verse to the body (σῶμα, *sōma*), which embraces both the body of the church and, metaphorically, the body of Christ, with possible allusions to Christ's crucified and resurrected body.

---

239. Merkle, *Guide,* 132; see also Schlier, *TDNT,* 3:680; Lincoln, *Ephesians,* 261; Best, *Ephesians,* 408; Larkin, *Handbook,* 82; and Muddiman, *Ephesians,* 208.

240. Barth, *Ephesians,* 2:445; Winger, *Ephesians,* 473.

241. Muddiman, *Ephesians,* 208; see also Delling, *TDNT,* 8:518.

242. Braun, *TDNT,* 6:245, 250.

243. Schlier, *TDNT,* 3:680.

From whom: Of course, the reference is to Christ, whom Paul identified in the prior word in both the English and Greek texts. Because of him, "the whole body ... maketh increase"; that is, it grows (see the Note below). But what is "the whole body"? Is it the cosmos, or is it the church?

the whole body: At first glance, this expression seems aimed at the church as Christ's body. And that impression is most likely the case. A quick examination of what Paul has written in other letters confirms that he has long refined the message that church members constitute parts of Christ's body, the church. For example, tucked deep into his letter to the Romans, he observed that "we have many members in one body" but "all members have not the same office." Then, turning away from ecclesiastical matters, he uncovers more of his meaning: "We, being many, are one body in Christ, and every one members one of another" (Rom. 12:4–5). Clearly, the unification of the many into one rests in Christ.

This drumbeat can already be heard in one of the Apostle's earlier letters, 1 Corinthians. There, while discussing the meaning of the wine and bread of the Eucharist or sacrament, he introduced his thinking when he wrote, "Because there is one loaf, we, many as we are, are one body; for it is one loaf of which we all partake" (1 Cor. 10:17 NEB). After this tantalizing tidbit, he turned to unpacking his own thoughts: "For the body is not one member, but many" (1 Cor. 12:14). How so? In response, a person has only to think about how one entered that body, the church. It is "by one Spirit [that] ... we all [are] baptized into one body, whether we be Jews or Gentiles, whether we be bond or free" (1 Cor. 12:13; see also Gal. 3:27–28). After comparing church members to body parts—the foot, the hand, the ear, the eye (see 1 Cor. 12:15–17)—Paul continued his analogy by writing that even the most humble believers, the "more feeble" as he called them, "are necessary" in Christ's body (1 Cor. 12:22). Finally, addressing his readers directly, he concluded that "ye are the body of Christ, and members in particular" (1 Cor. 12:27).

Thus far, Christ's body is equivalent to the earthly church with its baptized members serving one another in different capacities. But what about those of the unseen world? Does Christ's body somehow involve them too? Do they form a church, a body of believers? The short answer is Yes. Two points are necessary to understand. First, according to 1:20–23, God exalted Christ, the head, to a status "far above all principality, and power, ... and hath put all things under his feet." Although the important element for believers was that Christ thereby became "the head over all things to the church," in the bigger picture he came to be the ruler of the universe, the master of the cosmos.[244] Somewhere within that space lies the place of departed spirits. Second, in the review of 3:10, we learned that the reach of the church into the world of spirits has become a reality, including among the wicked. It is in this capacity "that the Church is Christ's body [and] . . . herein the growth of the body takes place."[245] Growth, therefore, does not confine itself to the earthly church but also takes root and expands among "the spirits in prison" (1 Pet. 3:19), thereby penetrating "the cosmos" (see the Note on 3:10).[246]

When examining 2:16, we discovered that the "one body," because of its immediate tie to "the cross," points to Jesus' crucified body, squiring readers into the concrete reality of Jesus' death, as well as its spiritual impacts, and leading them away from metaphorical connections. For example, we do not say that the Crucifixion metaphorically stands for a convert's sudden change of behavior after accepting the gospel, effectively slaying that person's former life, which was lived "in the lusts of our flesh, fulfilling the desires of the flesh and of the mind" (2:3). Instead, we sense that the expression "the whole body" shares the sweetnesses of Jesus' now-resurrected body as the model of what will happen to all who have become members of the body of his church: "In the body of [Christ's] flesh through death, to present you holy and unblameable and unreproveable in his sight" (Col. 1:22; see the Notes on 1:23; 2:16; 3:10; 4:4, 12; 5:23, 30).[247]

fitly joined together: Occurring only here and in 2:21 in the New Testament, both instances presenting participial forms, this verb (συναρμο-λογέω, *synarmologeō*) appears to be Paul's creation. In 2:21, it has to do with the activity of building with stone. In 4:16, it relates to the growth of the body. The primary understanding is "to join together" (compare Col. 2:19, "supported and held together by its ligaments and sinews," NIV).[248] Standing inside the broader context of unity in this part of the letter (see 4:3, 13), such oneness unfolds and operates under the direction of "the head, even Christ" (4:15). This means that efforts "to act independently" do not occur under the guidance of "the head."[249] This sort of clamp on independence, especially forbidding innovations in ordinances, emerges

---

244. Schweizer and Baumgärtel, *TDNT*, 7:1078.

245. Schweizer and Baumgärtel, *TDNT*, 7:1078–79.

246. Schweizer and Baumgärtel, *TDNT*, 7:1081.

247. Schweizer, *TDNT*, 7:1077–78.

248. Christian Maurer, *TDNT*, 7:856; BDAG, 966; Merkle, *Guide*, 82, 133.

249. Bruce, *Ephesians*, 90.

as a major feature of the Resurrected Christ's visit to the New World. For there, after instructing his twelve newly called disciples in the proper way to baptize (see 3 Ne. 11:22–26), he appealed for unity and conformity in this matter by declaring that "the Father and I are one" and "as I have commanded you thus shall ye baptize" (3 Ne 11:27–28). Later he turned to the proper pattern for the sacrament, and, after blessing the bread and wine and supervising their distribution to the gathered multitude, he pressed upon his disciples that he was giving to them "a commandment that ye shall do these things" in a proper way because "whoso among you shall do more or less than these are not built upon my rock" (3 Ne. 18:12–13; see also the Notes on 2:21; 1:23). As we might expect, innovations were discouraged in more than ordinances. They were also forbidden in doctrinal teachings, whether, as examples, the surprising "worshipping of angels" (Col. 2:18) or laying overmuch stress on the gift of tongues (see 1 Cor. 14:1–33).

supplieth: Although translated as a verb, this term is a noun (ἐπιχο-ρηγία, *epichorēgia*) that is about support and provisioning.[250] In the KJV of Philippians 1:19, the word is translated "supply." In the secular world outside the New Testament, the related verb (ἐπιχορηγέω, *epichorēgeō*) points to the wealthy supporting the less well off.[251] In this light, a reader may sense a possible metaphorical meaning. That is to say, lying behind the idea of support rests a figurative sense that effectively features Christ as the generous person of means and his mortal followers as those who seek and need his support. Such a reciprocal relationship between Christ and his devotees, as we have already seen, stands forth as one of the main characteristics of the grand word "grace" (see the Note on 2:6).

working: We have come upon this noun (ἐνέργεια, *energeia*) and its verb (ἐνεργέω, *energeō*) in 1:19 and 3:20 respectively. Initially, it is important to notice that these terms articulate actions in the divine and demonic worlds (see the Note on 3:7). Next, the significance of the noun in this passage brings us inside the activities of Christ himself, "who grants the power of growth to each member" of his body, the church.[252] Our conclusion is that God and Christ are active participants both in the ongoing life of the church and in the lives of its individual members. Otherwise, the body is literally without life (see the Notes on 1:19; 3:20).

---

250. BDAG, 387; Louw-Nida, §35.31.
251. BDAG, 387.
252. Bertram, *TDNT,* 2:654.

measure: For the third and last time, we meet the word "measure" (μέτρον, *metron*) in this letter. As readers might expect, here this noun pulls up an important aspect that we have already met in the review of 3:7. The "measure of every part" sends readers to the fact that not all parts of the church—namely, its individuals and congregations, its established leaders and new converts—are equal in their needs when serving in the church and contributing to its growth. Here, Paul shows his sensitivity on this issue. For instance, we readily sense that the needs, both physical and spiritual, of apostles differ from those of teachers (see 4:11; the Notes on 4:7, 13).[253]

maketh increase: Consistent within this verse stands the idea of growth, specifically the growth of Christ's body, the church, as the rather rare noun αὔξησις (*auxēsis*) makes clear.[254] As we are reminded in the only other place where this noun occurs in the New Testament, "the Head, from which all the body . . . having nourishment . . . and knit together, increaseth with the *increase* of God" (Col. 2:19, emphasis added). This growth, of course, both expands from Christ and, remarkably, rises "into him" (4:15), enriching "the whole body" of the church and saving it (see 5:23, "he is the savior of the body").[255] Building on these thoughts, we notice that the growth is not one of natural expansion as one might observe in plants, animals and even humans. To be sure, in other passages the verb ποιέω (*poieō,* "to make," "to do"), occurring here, can carry the sense "to bring forth" (see Matt. 3:10; 7:17, 19; 13:26; Luke 13:9; James 3:12; etc.).[256] But the growth in our passage results from Christ, not natural processes. It is he who "permeates and dominates the whole" because of his redemption.[257] In a different vein, earlier in the letter the Apostle wrote the verb *poieō* to underline God's ability "*to do* immeasurably more than all we ask or imagine" (3:20 NIV, emphasis added). Paul thus established God's unlooked-for generosity (for miracles, see Acts 2:22; 15:12; 19:11; for the Atonement, 2 Cor. 5:21; see also the Note on 3:20).[258]

---

253. Stählin, *TDNT,* 3:350; Johannes Schneider, *TDNT,* 4:597; Deissner, *TDNT,* 4:634.

254. BDAG, 151; Thayer, *Lexicon,* 84.

255. Delling, *TDNT,* 8:518; Grundmann, Hesse, de Jonge, and van der Woude, *TDNT,* 9:557–58.

256. Braun, *TDNT,* 6:483–84.

257. Johannes Horst, *TDNT,* 4:566; see also Schweizer and Baumgärtel, *TDNT,* 7:1079.

258. Braun, *TDNT,* 6:464.

edifying: Although the noun οἰκοδομή (*oikodomē*) may exhibit "its more abstract sense" here,[259] the idea of some kind of a "structure" or "building" still bonds with it, even if lightly.[260] In a real sense, the "increase of the body" builds up not only the church at large but also each church member, thereby encouraging both the larger church and its individual members to engage meaningfully in "the work of the ministry" and to seek earnestly "the perfecting of the saints" (4:12). From modern scripture, we encounter the blending of references to a structure and to an elevating activity. Speaking about "the school of the prophets" in December 1832, the Lord promised that the school would "become a sanctuary, a tabernacle of the Holy Spirit to your edification" (D&C 88:137). Such edification might extend to an individual. For example, the Lord directed that "if any man among you be strong in the Spirit, let him take ... him that is weak, that he may be edified [and] ... become strong also" (D&C 84:106).

In most cases, by contrast, the act of edifying was to benefit the many. For instance, the Lord instructed that in a gathering everyone should "listen unto [a speaker's] sayings, that when all have spoken that all may be edified of all" (D&C 88:122; see also D&C 50:22; 97:5). As a further example, to church leaders the Lord gave "a commandment, that when ye are assembled together ye shall instruct and edify each other, that ye may know how to act and direct my church" (D&C 43:8; see also D&C 107:85). Almost mirroring the language of Paul, we read in another place that "the body hath need of every member, that all may be edified together, that the system may be kept perfect" (D&C 84:110). In sum, "that which doth not edify is not of God, and is darkness" (D&C 50:23; see also the Notes on 2:21; 4:12, 29).

love: In a word, the appeal to love here (*agapē*) stands as the culmination of the whole process of unifying the church while it grows, the underlying thrust of this section (4:1–16). This call to love echoes the appeal in 4:2, the beginning of this section, that church members accept "one another in love [*agapē*]" (NR). What is distinctive about this later appearance of *agapē* is that it pairs itself with the knowledge of the Son of God and the salvation that he offers. The act of grasping accurately his character and his ministry engenders a climate of unity and love among believers. We have already run into the high gift of being allowed "to know the love [*agapē*] of Christ,

---

259. Lincoln, *Ephesians*, 156.
260. Bruce, *Ephesians*, 90.

which passeth knowledge," in all its "breadth, and length, and depth, and height," with the object that believers "might be filled with all the fulness of God" (3:18–19). Further, within the broad need for unity as the church grows (see 4:3), a reader notices that such unity embraces gaining "the knowledge of the Son of God" (4:13) while engendering an "increase of the body [of the church] . . . in love." Elsewhere, the Apostle wrote that, in his efforts to aid church members in western Asia, "my purpose is that they may be . . . united in love [*agapē*], so that they may have the full riches of complete understanding, in order that they may know the mystery of God, namely, Christ" (Col. 2:2 NIV; see also Philip. 3:8; 2 Pet. 3:18; and 1 John 4:16–17).[261]

Analysis of 4:1–16

Paul has flipped a switch inside this section (4:1–16), pouring light onto the weighty matter of maintaining the oneness of the church even as it grows by scooping up people of very different backgrounds and interests. And what gives him authority to undertake such an appeal? To briefly answer, it is his imprisonment for their sakes as ordered by his master, Jesus Christ. For his non-Jewish readers, "I Paul [am] the prisoner of Jesus Christ for you Gentiles" (3:1). He then repeated for emphasis these words: "I therefore, the prisoner of the Lord" (4:1). Earlier on he had pled that readers "faint not at my tribulations for you" (3:13). The force of these pointers to his heaven-driven incarceration is monumental. Who will contradict him? Who will discount his afflictions on their behalf? No one. The table was now set for his plea for unity "in love" (4:2, 16).

In an acknowledgment of the diversity in his audience, the Apostle begged them "to keep the unity of the Spirit in the bond of peace" (4:3). It is that "bond of peace," acting as an internal glue within congregations, that could seep and spread out to the church as a whole, making it into "one body" (4:4). This kind of bonding did not arise because of some celestial arm twisting. Threats of force characterized the larger Roman world, not that of the church. Instead, within the membership of the church a person should come upon people who exhibit "all lowliness and meekness, with longsuffering, forbearing one another in love" (4:2).

The oneness of the church rested on seven simple characteristics set out in a passage that some see growing out of a confessional statement of sorts

---

261. Delling, *TDNT*, 6:311; Delling, *TDNT*, 7:764.

(see 4:4–6).[262] Even for an outsider, these distinctive Christian traits were readily visible. We have already run into the "one body" (4:4). This quality joined itself to others, including "one Spirit" of God and "one hope of your calling" (4:4). These three formed the undergirding attributes of the inner life and its Christian-shaped values, making the person into "the new man [or woman]" (4:24). How so? It was the individual's inward choice to belong to the "one body" of the church, which invited the "one Spirit" into one's spiritual life along with the "one hope of your calling." For a Christian person with eternal possibilities in the offing, these all led incrementally to decisions that conferred "righteousness and true holiness" on that individual (4:24).

The nature of the newly found life embraced "one Lord, one faith, [and] one baptism" (4:5). Plainly, these dimensions rested outside of a person's internal thoughts and beliefs. The "one Lord," of course, directed believers to Jesus Christ. Although "one faith" connects on one level to a person's belief, on another it had more to do with an early title of the church than might be suspected (see Acts 6:7; 13:8; 14:22; Rom. 1:5; 2 Cor. 13:5; Gal. 1:23; etc.). And "one baptism" was the unifying ordinance for all church members, no matter their backgrounds or habits. Naturally, a mental, physical, and emotional assent to these traits were required of all believers. But they resided outside one's inner soul.

The last of the seven was the "one God and Father of all, who is . . . in you all" (4:6). In this line, Paul paid proper tribute to the Father, the lord and master of everything. As the seventh in the list, the expression "one God and Father of all" shared the importance of the number seven, which carried special meaning and was sacred among the ancient Hebrews and others (see Gen. 2:3; Ex. 31:12–17; Heb. 4:4; etc.).[263] And, as the last in the series, a natural emphasis fell on it, bringing the reader to understand that it bore a significance beyond mere words. As creator, the Father towers "above all." As sustainer of creation, the Father's powers are suffused "through all." As guide for believers, the Father's influence is "in you all" (4:6).

Immediately after this recitation of oneness, Paul rivets his readers' attention on how this unity is to be achieved. It will not be by the unaided efforts

---

262. Barth, *Ephesians*, 2:429, 462–72; Lincoln, *Ephesians*, 228–29, 237–38; Muddiman, *Ephesians*, 181–82.

263. E. Otto, *TDOT*, 14:351–60; Jöran Friberg, "Numbers and Counting," in *ABD*, 4:1143–45.

of church members. Rather, they will need divine help. And they will get it. But it will not come in a massive flow of divine grace that is uniformly distributed to believers. No. Because "all members have not the same office" (Rom. 12:4), some serving as "apostles" and others as "pastors and teachers" (4:11), God needs to distribute his "grace according to the measure of the gift of Christ" (4:7). Though "we, being many, are one body in Christ," nevertheless God's gifts come to church members "differing according to the grace that is given to [each of] us" (Rom. 12:5–6). That is to say, God's grace comes in the divine strength and discernment that each person needs to receive in order to perform his or her task "for the perfecting of the saints, [and] for the work of the ministry" (4:12). In a word, gracious gifts come from God as he sees fit to distribute them for his purposes. Not all believers are the same, nor do their church assignments require the same celestial helps.

We now arrive at the scriptural underpinning of the whole segment. This scriptural passage, Psalm 68:18 (LXX Ps. 67:19), leads readers to a plethora of important concepts. In the Septuagint, the lines read: "Thou art gone up on high, thou hast led captivity captive, thou hast *received* gifts for man" (emphasis added). As quickly becomes clear, the Apostle has quoted the last words differently: "[He] *gave* gifts unto men" (4:8, emphasis added). This change switches the sense from God receiving gifts to dispensing them. But let us not quibble. Under inspiration, the Apostle is allowed to make adjustments (compare JS–H 1:36–39). The notion of God giving gifts uncovers one of the bright threads that is woven into the first half of chapter 4—God's generous gift of grace (see 4:7) and his essential gift of church officers (see 4:11). But that is not the whole story.

Paul's citing of the Psalm invites readers to consider the entire song. Its essence is that of Yahweh or Jehovah the triumphant, the Ascendant One who now rules in Jerusalem. Paul has imported this sense into his letter by quoting the line "[God] ascended up on high" to his throne (4:8). The immediate application to Jesus' ascent up to God's "right hand in the heavenly places" is obvious (1:20). But Paul then added the next thought, which happens to pertain to Jesus' ministry between his death and his Resurrection: "He also descended first into the lower parts of the earth" (4:9). Reading such a declaration, believers found themselves in the nether world—that is, in the realm of departed spirits. This is the place where the crucified Jesus offered salvation by organizing a missionary effort to those who had died without the law and to those who had wanted to repent of acts done in their mortal lives so "that they might be judged according to men in the flesh, but [from that moment on] live according to God in the spirit" (1 Pet. 4:6; see also Moses 7:38–39 and D&C 138:30–35). If we step to the side just one pace, we are able to see that the descent and ascent of Christ built the divine foundation for unifying what is done not only on earth but also in the spirit world and in heaven (see the Notes on 3:8, 10, 19; 4:5, 9; 5:8; 6:10, 18; and Analysis of 3:1–13).

Jesus' accomplishment in organizing a missionary effort among departed spirits was all-important (see D&C 138:30). Yet accessing salvation for these individuals was possible only when they received the essential ordinances of salvation through the vicarious actions of mortal church members, baptism being the key. That very issue was the point of Paul's questions to fellow believers in Corinth, questions whose answers they understood: "Else what shall they do which are baptized for the dead, if the dead rise not at all? why are they then baptized for the dead?" (1 Cor. 15:29).[264] Reading these questions takes readers into a large and spacious hall that is decorated in the colors and fabrics of sacred rituals. The first verse in our chapter lifts such a place to our view when we read "that ye walk worthy" (4:1; see also 2:10). Such walking, when paired with the verbs "to sit" (2:6) and "to stand" (6:11, 13, 14), draws the mind to sacred actions. There is more.

According to Colossians 3:12–13, church members are invited to "put on ... humbleness of mind, meekness, longsuffering; forbearing one another." These four virtues are exactly the same as those we come upon in 4:2: "Lowliness and meekness, with longsuffering, forbearing one another." In other words, we are to wear these virtues as though we had donned a holy garment with these characteristics sewn into it. Buttressing this idea is the observation that the same verb that stands in Colossians 3:12, "to put on," appears in 4:24 of Ephesians: "Put on the new man." But this does not exhaust the matter. For at 6:11, we discover: "Put on the whole armor of God" (see also 6:14; Rom. 13:12, "put on the armor of light," 14, "put ye on the Lord Jesus Christ"). Hence, as we track our way through Ephesians, we detect language that is at home in the world of sacred ceremony, including language that centers on the donning of special clothing in combination with the interests of walking, sitting and standing, all actions that themselves are at home within that decorated holy hall where sacred acts take place (see the Notes on 2:2, 6, 10; 4:1, 13, 22, 24; 5:2, 8, 14, 15; 6:11, 13, 14; and appendix 1).

---

264. Riesenfeld, *TDNT,* 8:512–13.

"Put on the New Man" (4:17–32)

King James Translation

17 This I say therefore, and testify in the Lord, that ye henceforth walk not as other Gentiles walk, in the vanity of their mind, 18 Having the understanding darkened, being alienated from the life of God through the ignorance that is in them, because of the blindness of their heart: 19 Who being past feeling have given themselves over unto lasciviousness, to work all uncleanness with greediness. 20 But ye have not so learned Christ; 21 If so be that ye have heard him, and have been taught by him, as the truth is in Jesus: 22 That ye put off concerning the former conversation the old man, which is corrupt according to the deceitful lusts; 23 And be renewed in the spirit of your mind; 24 And that ye put on the new man, which after God is created in righteousness and true holiness. 25 Wherefore putting away lying, speak every man truth with his neighbour: for we are members one of another. 26 Be ye angry, and sin not: let not the sun go down upon your wrath: 27 Neither give place to the devil. 28 Let him that stole steal no more: but rather let him labour, working with his hands the thing which is good, that he may have to give to him that needeth. 29 Let no corrupt communication proceed out of your mouth, but that which is good to the use of edifying, that it may minister grace unto the hearers. 30 And grieve not the holy Spirit of God, whereby ye are sealed unto the day of redemption. 31 Let all bitterness, and wrath, and anger, and clamour, and evil speaking, be put away

New Rendition

17 Therefore I say this, and testify to it in the Lord, that you no longer walk as the Gentiles walk, in the emptiness of their minds. 18 They are blind in their understanding, alienated from the life of God because of the ignorance that exists in them because of the hardness of their heart. 19 Having become callous, they have greedily given themselves over to licentiousness for the practice of every impurity. 20 But that is not the way you learned Christ—21 assuming you have heard about him and were taught by him, because the truth is in Jesus. 22 With regard to your former life, you were taught to put off the old person who is being corrupted by deceitful desires, 23 to be renewed in the spirit of your mind, 24 and to put on the new person who has been created by God in true righteousness and holiness.

25 So then, put off falsehood and let each one speak the truth with his neighbor, for we are members of one another. 26 "Be angry and do not sin." Do not let the sun go down on your anger, 27 neither give opportunity to the devil. 28 Let the thief no longer steal, but rather let him work, doing good with his own hands so that he may have something to share with the one who is in need. 29 Let no harmful word come out of your mouth, but whatever is good for the building up of the one in need, that it may impart grace to those who hear. 30 And do not offend the Holy Spirit of God, by whom you have been sealed for the day of redemption. 31 Let all bitterness, anger, wrath, shouting,

from you, with all malice: 32 And be ye kind one to another, tenderhearted, forgiving one another, even as God for Christ's sake hath forgiven you.

and slander be removed from you, along with all malice. 32 Be kind to one another, compassionate, forgiving each other just as God in Christ forgave you.

Notes on 4:17–32

4:17 *testify:* In this context, the verb μαρτύρομαι (*martyromai*) is much stronger than "to testify." Rather, it manifests "the meaning of [an] emphatic demand."[265] This sense is captured in Acts 2:40: "In these and many other words he *pressed his case* and pleaded with them" (NEB, translating the related verb form διαμαρτύρομαι, *diamartyromai*; emphasis added). From Paul in another place, we read of him "encouraging, comforting, and *urging* you to live lives worthy of God" (1 Thes. 2:12 NIV, translating all three verbs in the verse, unlike the KJV, which translates them as one; emphasis added). In three other passages, the verb *martyromai* carries the sense "to bear witness" (see Acts 20:26; 26:22; and Gal. 5:3).[266]

in the Lord: As we have grasped in the discussion on 4:1, Paul appears to be the inventor of this prepositional phrase (ἐν κύριῳ, *en kyriō*) as well as "in Christ" (see the Note on 4:1 and note 13 above).[267] Attached to these and other expressions like them rests the sense that those who are "in the Lord" or "in Christ" stand spatially removed from the first Adam, whose history has always been associated with death (see Rom. 5:14 and 1 Cor. 15:22), and that they have been escorted into the expanse inhabited by Christ and his Father. Further, those who live "in the law [of Moses]" or "under the law" reside in a circumstance that can only be described as "without the law"— that is, in a lawless state (see Rom. 2:12; 3:19–20; 1 Cor. 9:20–21; Gal. 4:4–5; 5:18; and the Notes on 4:1; 5:22).[268]

walk not: We have already met this verb (περιπατέω, *peripateō*) in 2:2, 2:10, and 4:1. In the last passage, 4:1, and this one, we encounter the sense that walking has to do with the conduct of one's life. But, as with the verb's appearance in 4:1, we also brush against the lingering, ever-present links— weak or not—to sacred ceremony. The fact that this verb occurs a second time in this verse strengthens the tie to individual behavior rather than to ritual (see the Note below and the Notes on 2:2, 10; 4:1; 5:2, 8, 15).

---

265. Hermann Strathmann, *TDNT,* 4:511; Louw-Nida, §33.319.
266. BDAG, 619; Louw-Nida, §33.223.
267. Oepke, *TDNT,* 2:541.
268. Oepke, *TDNT,* 2:542; BDAG, 85–86.

other Gentiles: The best manuscripts omit the word "other" (λοιπόν, *loipon*), including the earliest, 𝔓⁴⁶. The term *loipon* "is obviously an interpretative intrusion."[269] Throughout the New Testament, Gentiles (singular ἔθνος, *ethnos*) are to be distinguished from Jews.[270] Jews, of course, hold a special place in the history of salvation that is laid out in events from the Old Testament to the New. If we set aside the adjective *loipon,* "other," then in this verse the Gentiles represent those outside the faith, not the people to whom Paul was writing (see 3:1; 1 Cor. 1:23, where the better manuscripts read "Gentiles").[271] It is these nonmembers who "in time past . . . walked according to the course of this world, . . . in the lusts of our flesh, . . . and were by nature the children of wrath, [and] . . . were dead in sins" (2:2–3, 5). In Paul's lifetime, these people lived with their "understanding darkened . . . because of the blindness of their heart" (4:18; see also 1 Thes. 4:5).[272]

walk: Paul's statement before us concerns the behavior of Gentiles throughout their lives (περιπατέω, *peripateō*) and draws up a negative view of the personal conduct that characterized life outside the church and its teachings. After all, Gentiles' lives had led them into "the lusts of [their] flesh, fulfilling the desires of the flesh and of the mind" (2:3), and hence left them "alienated from the life of God" (4:18). More threatening, the devil "walketh about [*peripateō*], seeking whom he may devour" (1 Pet. 5:8). For Christians, on the other hand, their walk was to carry them into a "newness of life" (Rom. 6:4; see also John 8:12).[273] It was as if they were stepping onto a path that they had never beheld before. With their feet, they turned from the patterns of their prior lives and followed a completely different roadway.

Although we are now dealing with a metaphorical meaning, the notion of walking always brings up the companion thought of a space wherein a person can walk from place to place. It also involves the feet. One of the richest images of repentance in scripture has to do with turning the feet from the path of wickedness onto the path of righteousness.[274] One of the most striking instances involved the Lord himself repenting or turning away from a decision to "destroy Ephraim," the northern kingdom of Israel.

---

269. Metzger, *Textual Commentary,* 537.
270. BDAG, 276–77; Thayer, *Lexicon,* 168.
271. Metzger, *Textual Commentary,* 480.
272. Bertram Schmidt, *TDNT,* 2:370–72; BDAG, 602–3.
273. Seeseman and Bertram, *TDNT,* 5:944–45.
274. M. Graupner and Heinz-Josef Fabry, *TDOT,* 14:475, 480; Bertram, *TDNT,* 7:715, 717, 719, 723, 726–27.

Hosea wrote that the Lord had declared, "Mine heart *is turned* within me, my repentings are kindled together. I will not execute the fierceness of mine anger, I will not return to destroy Ephraim" (Hosea 11:8–9, emphasis added; see also Jer. 18:8).[275] For his part, the prophet Elijah became an instrument in God's hands to turn his people back to paths leading away from the god Baal and toward the God of their ancestors. For before the fire fell from heaven, Elijah affirmed in his prayer, "Thou [God] *hast turned* their heart back again" to their forebears "Abraham, Isaac, and . . . Israel" (1 Kgs. 18:36–37, emphasis added; see also Mal. 4:5–6).

On another level, God commanded the former Hebrew slaves, "Turn ye not unto idols, nor make to yourselves molten gods" (Lev. 19:4; see also Ezek. 14:6). Turning or walking toward God brought needed blessings, as we see in Moses' words: "When thou art in tribulation, . . . if thou turn to the Lord thy God, . . . he will not forsake thee, . . . nor forget the covenant of thy fathers" (Deut. 4:30–31). God reiterated this promise by declaring, "The Lord thy God will make thee plenteous . . . for good . . . if thou turn unto the Lord thy God with all thine heart, and with all thy soul" (Deut. 30:9–10; see also 2 Chr. 7:14–15; Neh. 1:8–9; Isa. 31:6; etc.). According to scripture, this kind of promise was fulfilled at least once in the case of Rehoboam, king of Judah, "when the king entered into the house of the Lord, [and] . . . humbled himself, the wrath of the Lord turned from him, . . . and also in Judah things went well" (2 Chr. 12:11–12; see also 2 Kgs. 23:25 and 2 Chr. 15:3–4). As Isaiah assured his listeners, this sort of turning or repenting can bless entire communities: "The Redeemer shall come to Zion, and unto them that turn from transgression in Jacob" (Isa. 59:20).

The opposite sense also applies—that is, turning or walking away from heavenly help. In the negotiations between the two and a half tribes that were to settle on the eastern bank of the Jordan River and those that would inhabit the western bank, those from the east insisted that they would not set up an altar to compete with the one standing next to the sacred tabernacle at Shiloh: "Far be it from us to rebel against the Lord and turn away from him today by building an altar for burnt offerings . . . other than the altar of the Lord our God that stands before his tabernacle" (Josh. 22:29 NIV). This decision was made early on in the history of the twelve tribes' acquisition of the land of Canaan for their own. But things did not go so well thereafter.

---

275. Klaus Dieter Seybold, *TDOT,* 3:426–27.

Before the Assyrian army captured Samaria, capital of the northern kingdom, Israel, the Lord had warned the Israelites "by all the prophets, and by all the seers, saying, Turn ye from your evil ways" (2 Kgs. 17:13). But the people did not listen. Because they had "walked in the statutes of the heathen" (2 Kgs. 17:8), "in the ninth year of Hoshea [king of Israel] the king of Assyria took Samaria, and carried Israel away into Assyria," thus inaugurating the dispersion of the lost tribes of Israel (2 Kgs. 17:6). The year was 722 BC.[276] Two and a half centuries later, following the reforms of Ezra, the Levites led a large public confession at the temple and declared, among other things, that "they have not served thee [God] in their kingdom, . . . neither turned they from their wicked works" (Neh. 9:35). In sum, "The people turneth not unto him that smiteth them, neither do they seek the Lord of hosts" (Isa. 9:13; see also Jer. 3:10; 34:16; and Ezek. 3:19–20).

In the New Testament, we discover a similar pattern with verbs of turning. On the negative side, we bump into Paul's stern and searching questions to church members in Galatia who had begun to wander. He wrote, "Now that you know God . . . how is it that you are turning back to those weak and miserable principles? Do you wish to be enslaved by them all over again?" (Gal. 4:9 NIV; see also 2 Tim. 4:4). During his defense before the Jerusalem Sanhedrin, Stephen uttered a grim reminder about how Moses fared among his people: "Our fathers would not obey [him], but thrust him from them, and in their hearts turned back again into Egypt" (Acts 7:39; see also Heb. 12:25). Thereafter we encounter the disheartening words about people in the era of the early church: "Some are already turned aside after Satan" (1 Tim. 5:15). Perhaps the saddest words written about former believers wandering into the grasp of apostasy appear in this line: "All they which are in Asia be turned away from me" (2 Tim. 1:15).

Of course, during the initial forward thrust of missionary work and its immediate aftermath, we witness a different state of affairs. The promise of good times ahead rested snugly within the angel's words to Zacharias about the promised son who would be known as John the Baptist. In his role as forerunner of the Messiah, "many of the children of Israel shall he turn to the Lord their God" (Luke 1:16). During Peter's extended trip from Jerusalem to the coastal town of Joppa, or Jaffa, he passed through the small city of Lydda where he met "a certain man named Aeneas" who had been bedridden "eight years, and was sick of the palsy," being paralyzed. After Peter

---

276. John Bright, *A History of Israel,* 3rd ed. (Philadelphia: Westminster Press, 1981), 275.

healed him of his malady, not only Aeneas but also "all that dwelt at Lydda and Saron ... turned to the Lord" (Acts 9:33, 35). In complimenting the Thessalonian Saints after spending a mere three weeks preaching in their city (see Acts 17:2), the Apostle Paul wrote that these good people had "turned to God from idols to serve the living and true God" (1 Thes. 1:9). When Paul appeared before King Agrippa and Bernice in the Caesarean palace where the governor of Judea, Festus, resided, the Apostle affirmed that he had been called by Jesus himself "to open [the Gentiles'] eyes, and to turn them from darkness to light, and from the power of Satan unto God" (Acts 26:18). Other examples crop up, particularly in the book of Acts (see Acts 11:21; 14:15; 15:19; 26:20; and the Notes on 2:2, 10; 4:1, 13; 5:2, 8, 15).

vanity: Expressing a sense of futility and emptiness, the noun ματαιότης (*mataiotēs*) sends us to the vanity of the world, which lodges in a person's mind rather than in one's property and wealth.[277] In the term before us, Paul has echoed the Lord's saying that is quoted by Jeremiah and aimed at ancient Judah: "What iniquity have your fathers found in me [the Lord], that they ... have walked after vanity, and are become vain?" (Jer. 2:5).[278] The Apostle has here applied "vanity" to Roman society. His critique of Gentile life without the true God also appears at the opening of his letter to the Romans: "When they knew God, they glorified him not as God, neither were they thankful; but became vain in their imaginations, and their foolish heart was darkened" (Rom. 1:21). In a word, without God they had embraced "the nothingness of man" (see Rom. 8:20; 2 Pet. 2:18; and Moses 1:10, "man is nothing").[279]

mind: Paul seems not to have in mind an individual's intellectual capacity. Rather, in this context, the noun νοῦς (*nous*) tends toward the notion of "mind-set."[280] In utter contrast to heathen spiritual comprehension stands the Christian, into whose mind and soul has come "the love of Christ, which passeth knowledge" (3:19; see also Philip. 4:7). That is not all. Such a believer, owing to his or her "understanding being enlightened," has come to grasp "what [are] the riches of the glory of [God's eternal] inheritance in the saints" (1:18). This is, plain and simple, revealed knowledge to the mind—that is, "the knowledge of him [God]" (1:17).[281] He is the same who

277. BDAG, 621; Louw-Nida, §65.37.
278. Barth, *Ephesians,* 2:499.
279. Otto Bauernfeind, *TDNT,* 4:523.
280. Best, *Ephesians,* 417.
281. Behm and Würthwein, *TDNT,* 4:958–59.

came to Paul: "By revelation he [God] made known unto me the mystery" of the embrace of Gentiles into the kingdom (3:3; see also the Notes on 1:17, 18; 3:3, 9).

4:18 *the understanding:* This verse and the next (4:19) blend together because each treats the actions of "other Gentiles" (4:17), not the Gentiles whom the Apostle was addressing. This said, the application of the noun translated here as "understanding" (διάνοια, *dianoia*), which occurs in one other verse in this letter, runs to spiritual bankruptcy. For in 2:3, "the [wicked] desires of the flesh and of the mind" come under scrutiny. As in this earlier case, *dianoia* in our verse dredges up the darkness of pagan life. So it is elsewhere. Gentile church members had "once [been] ... alienated from God and were enemies in your minds [*dianoia*]" toward both God and church members "because of your ill behavior" (Col. 1:21 NIV). Owing to a human person's natural disposition to mock and discount spiritual realities (see "natural man" in 1 Cor. 2:14 and Mosiah 3:19), this tendency can be reversed only when "the Son of God has awakened in us the mind and given our thinking the orientation to know God, to receive His revelation, [and] to share fellowship with Him."[282] This is the pith of the statement: "We know that the Son of God is come, and hath given us an understanding [*dianoia*], that we may know him that is true" (1 John 5:20). Similarly, this thought burrows inside the words which are a rough quotation of Jeremiah 31:33: "I [God] will put my laws into their mind [*dianoia*], and write them in their hearts" (Heb. 8:10; see also Heb. 10:16 and the Note on 2:3).

darkened: As we have already noticed, a condition of darkness hovered above unenlightened Gentiles. Not only were they "vain in their imaginations," but also "their foolish heart was darkened" (Rom. 1:21). Lying behind such statements rests the notion of a lack of light rather than, say, blindness. For that is what we meet in Romans 13:12, which Paul has addressed to fellow church members: "The night is far spent, the day is at hand: let us therefore cast off the works of darkness, and let us put on the armor of light." Said another way, "ye were sometimes darkness, but now are ye light in the Lord: walk as children of light" (5:8). In similar language, we encounter the lines "ye are all the children of light, [and] ... are not of the night, nor of darkness" (1 Thes. 5:5). Menacingly, this darkness possesses a power that requires God's help to escape (see Col. 1:12–13).[283] In this connection, it is important to recall that the devil's power or authority

---

282. Behm and Würthwein, *TDNT,* 4:967.
283. Hans Conzelmann, *TDNT,* 7:442–43; contra Best, *Ephesians,* 419.

is allowed but limited by God, as the devil himself admits to Jesus in the wilderness: "All this power [*exousia*] . . . is delivered unto me" (Luke 4:6).[284]

being alienated: Irony hovers here. Speaking in broad terms, humankind is alien to the celestial world, and those who inhabit that world— namely, God and Christ—are alien to this world. In a manner of speaking, the person who comes to God through his Son thereafter becomes alien to this world, the world in which that person has residence. This crossing of boundaries comes about through the Son, who left his home on high and descended into the physical world with the express purpose of drawing believers out of this world and into his. Although this departure does not occur at the moment of baptism or when the person receives sacred ordinances, effectively that individual becomes more and more oriented toward heavenly realities and less and less toward earthly concerns (see Col. 1:21; D&C 36:6; 38:31; and the Note on 2:12).[285]

the life of God: This expression is most intriguing. Does it mean a godlike life that one discovers when a convert to the teachings of Christ? Or does it mean God's life, the life that he lives? Most commentators slip by the question, not raising it to the level of discussion.[286] Others who undertake a review of these words scratch their heads and rub their eyes when trying to say that Paul does not have in mind God's life. Barth holds that the words are "puzzling." He solves this puzzle by associating the expression with "righteousness," a linkage that appears elsewhere in the Apostle's letters. For instance, "if Christ be in you, the body is dead because of sin; but the Spirit is life because of [Christ's] righteousness" (Rom. 8:10). In other words, death results from sin because "the wages of sin is death" (Rom. 6:23). Life in its eternal dress comes about through Christ's righteousness (see Rom. 6:16–19 and Gal. 3:21–22).[287] Eadie insists that God's life derives "from the operation and indwelling of the Holy Ghost."[288] Fowl takes up the matter in a different manner. The real meaning of the words "the life of God" is "participation in God's own life"—that is, to enjoy life as he does, eternally and happily.[289] Fair enough. But the expression invites more, much more.

---

284. Foerster, *TDNT,* 2:567–68.

285. Stählin, *TDNT,* 5:28–30.

286. For example, Caird, *Letters,* 79; Lincoln, *Ephesians,* 277–78; Best, *Ephesians,* 420; Winger, *Ephesians,* 508.

287. Barth, *Ephesians,* 2:502.

288. John Eadie, *A Commentary on the Greek Text of the Epistle of Paul to the Ephesians,* 2nd ed. (Grand Rapids, Mich.: Baker Book House, 1979), 338.

289. Fowl, *Ephesians,* 148.

Firstly, it is important to notice that this life (ζωή, *zōē*) possesses the highest value, far above all earthly wealth combined. Jesus clarified this to hearers, and turned their eyes toward heavenly realities, when he asked, "What shall it profit a man, if he shall gain the whole world, and lose his own soul?" (Mark 8:36; see also Matt. 16:26 and Luke 9:25). The repercussions of losing one's heavenly life, even after huge successes in mortal life, were almost beyond comprehension. But this observation does not discount mortal life in the least, for it is worth everything to each person. Hence, the resuscitation of life, say, through becoming well, is universally welcomed. That is why Jesus' healings brought so much relief not just to the recipients but also to the persons' families and associates. Moreover, the acts of Jesus in restoring life created a climate of rejoicing and, occasionally, even disbelief (see Mark 2:12; 5:42; Luke 7:16; and John 4:46–53).[290]

If, then, life is so precious and living life well carries celestial possibilities, what is the payoff in the eternities? The short answer is living "the life of God"—that is to say, living life as he lives it, no more, no less. Each of us is to become as he is. Scriptural descriptions vary, but they all point in the same direction. Paul wrote to church members in Rome, "The Spirit itself beareth witness with our spirit, that we are the children of God: and if children, then heirs; heirs of God, and joint-heirs with Christ" (Rom. 8:16–17). Modern scripture says it in a different way: "He [or she] that receiveth me receiveth my Father; and he [or she] that receiveth my Father receiveth my Father's kingdom; therefore all that my Father hath shall be given unto him [her]" (D&C 84:37–38). These people "shall pass by the angels, and the gods, . . . to their exaltation and glory in all things, . . . which glory shall be . . . a continuation of the seeds forever and ever" (D&C 132:19). In a word, such individuals will enjoy eternal increase in their families forever. "Then shall they be gods, because they have no end; . . . then shall they be above all, because all things are subject unto them. . . . They have all power" (D&C 132:20).

ignorance: The question with this noun (ἄγνοια, *agnoia*) is whether it signifies a person's willful turning away from saving knowledge or an innocent, unintentional lack of understanding. As one might guess, in the larger Roman and Jewish societies, this question carried legal overtones. If it bore the meaning of deliberate action, then *agnoia* stands at the base of evil, which can include everything from the lack of civilized behavior to intentional sinning. This sort of ignorance risks God's punishment. In the words of modern scripture, "because they yield unto the devil and choose works of darkness rather than light, therefore they must go down to hell" (2 Ne. 26:10). If, on

---

290. Von Rad, Bertram, and Bultmann, *TDNT,* 2:862.

the other hand, a person simply does not know, then he or she stands inno-cent until true knowledge arrives (see 1 Cor. 15:34 and 1 Pet. 1:14). In both cases, the ignorant person does not possess the knowledge of God and thus the understanding that can lead to salvation.[291] In our verse, Paul evidently has cut Gentiles some slack, not imputing sinister motives to their lack of knowledge (see Acts 17:30).[292] But he does not let them entirely off the hook, as the next line and the next verse illustrate. Besides, in another place Paul wrote of Gentiles, "The invisible things of [God] from the creation of the world are clearly seen, . . . even his eternal power and Godhead; so that they are without excuse" (Rom. 1:20).

blindness of their heart: Truth be told, the noun translated "blindness" (πώρωσις, *pōrōsis*) really means "hardness" (NR). To be sure, it means "blindness" in the sense of "dullness" or "insensitivity."[293] We meet this term in the account of Jesus healing the man with the withered hand in a syna-gogue. On that occasion, when Jesus sensed that some in the congregation held jaded feelings about him healing on the Sabbath, he "looked round about on them with anger, being grieved for the hardness [*pōrōsis*] of their hearts" (Mark 3:5). The only other appearance of this word in the New Testament occurs at Romans 11:25, where Paul was explaining the evident reluctance of Jews to embrace the gospel, holding that the Gentiles will come into the kingdom before Jews arrive in large numbers: "Israel has experienced a hardening [*pōrōsis*] in part until the full number of the Gen-tiles has come in" (NIV; see also the Notes on 1:18; 4:6).

The heart (καρδία, *kardia*) is a different matter, for it is the place in the human psyche that God can influence, that his Spirit can penetrate, if a per-son is willing.[294] It is the heart, in a figurative sense, that is hardened in other New Testament passages. At times, the hardened heart belongs to Jesus' disciples, thus preventing them from understanding some important truth (see Mark 6:52; 8:17). In other instances, it is the hearts of the disciples' fel-low Jews that are hardened (see John 12:40 and Rom. 11:7). For, according to Paul, a veil of unbelief hangs between them and the truths of the gospel revealed through the Old Testament (see 2 Cor. 3:14–15; see also the Notes on 5:19; 6:5).[295]

---

291. Rudolf Bultmann, *TDNT,* 1:116–19.
292. Contra BDAG, 13.
293. Karl Ludwig Schmidt and Martin Anton Schmidt, *TDNT,* 5:1022–23; BDAG, 900.
294. Friedrich Baumgärtel and Johannes Behm, *TDNT,* 3:612–13.
295. Schmidt and Schmidt, *TDNT,* 5:1026–27.

4:19 *being past feeling:* Paul has written the perfect participle of ἀπαλγέω (*apalgeō*) and has thus presented both a past situation and a continuing condition. That is, these "other Gentiles" (4:17) had long ago plunged into lives of insensitivity to both human and divine stimuli, with no letup.[296] In effect, they have ceased to feel discomfort at any act of depravity.[297] For what follows presents a series of three nouns that are regularly associated with unrestrained sexual activity.[298] Although not all commentators see sexual depravity alone festering inside these nouns,[299] they have ignored the widespread degradation in the larger Roman empire that reached such a pitch that, in one instance, it drew the attention of the emperor Augustus (31 BC–AD 14), who saw the need to officially curb such unchaste actions, with little effect.[300] As an added note, a few ancient manuscripts preserve one or another different verb with the general sense of "despairing," depending on the manuscript. But the earliest and best manuscripts preserve the participle of *apalgeō*, "dead to feeling," offering the best reading to us.[301]

have given themselves over: Whether it was "God [who] gave them up" to vile actions (Rom. 1:26), or whether it was individuals who "have given themselves over" to immoral acts, the result was the same. The verb common to these two passages (παραδίδωμι, *paradidōmi*)[302] pertains to a surrendering of the will to devilish powers (see Acts 7:42). This was the case with Judas: "Then entered Satan into Judas," exercising control over the failing apostle (Luke 22:3).[303] Modern scripture paints a two-step process of how demonic powers overcome a person's will. First, it has to do with those "that will harden their hearts." If they continue in this path, "they are [then] taken captive by the devil, and [in the process] led by his will down to destruction," allowing themselves to be wrapped tightly in "the chains of hell" (Alma 12:11; see also 2 Ne. 2:27; 26:10; Alma 34:33–35; 40:13; etc.; and the Notes on 5:2, 25).

---

296. Best, *Ephesians,* 421.

297. BDAG, 96.1; Louw-Nida, §25.197.

298. Lincoln, *Ephesians,* 279; Muddiman, *Ephesians,* 215.

299. Barth, *Ephesians,* 503–4; Best, *Ephesians,* 423; Fowl, *Ephesians,* 148–49; Winger, *Ephesians,* 510.

300. Everitt, *Augustus,* 238–40.

301. Metzger, *Textual Commentary,* 537; BDAG, 96.1; Merkle, *Guide,* 140.

302. BDAG, 762.1.b.

303. Büchsel, *TDNT,* 2:169–70; Schmidt and Schmidt, *TDNT,* 5:1026 n. 5.

lasciviousness: The noun ἀσέλγεια (*aselgeia*) leads a reader to a person who fractures "all bounds of what is socially acceptable."[304] "Licentiousness" (4:19 NR) is a good rendition of this word.[305] As one might anticipate, such a term appears in lists of degrading activities. For example, in Jesus' catalog of vices, we learn that "out of the heart of men, proceed evil thoughts, adulteries, . . . deceit, [and] lasciviousness [*aselgeia*]," which "defile the man" (Mark 7:21–22, 23). Not a whit behind, the Apostle has set down "the works of the flesh" to be "adultery, fornication, uncleanness, [and] lasciviousness [*aselgeia*]," among others (Gal. 5:19). For Paul, licentiousness was a plague that affected current church members, at least in Corinth. For he worried that "when I come again [to Corinth] . . . I shall bewail many which . . . have not repented of the . . . lasciviousness [*aselgeia*] which they have committed" (2 Cor. 12:21; see also Jacob 3:12 and Alma 16:18).

all uncleanness: As the translations "uncleanness" or "impurity" (NR) clearly hint, the term ἀκαθαρσία (*akatharsia*) was related to ceremonial impurity in its Old Testament and Jewish contexts. We hear Jesus' sharp words spoken to "scribes and Pharisees, hypocrites," whom he compared to "whited sepulchres," and thus to sources of ritual uncleanness in their persons. These, he sneered, "are within full of dead men's bones, and of all uncleanness [*akatharsia*]" (Matt. 23:27). But this meaning quickly turned to "moral impurity which excludes man from fellowship with God."[306] The beginning of this shift becomes apparent in Paul's quotation of Isaiah 52:11 at 2 Corinthians 6:17: "Come out from among them, and be ye separate, saith the Lord, and touch not the unclean thing [*akatharsia*]; and I will receive you." In another place, the Apostle begged his Roman readers that, "as ye have yielded your [bodily] members [as] servants to uncleanness [*akatharsia*] and to iniquity [in the past,] . . . even so now yield your members [as] servants to righteousness unto holiness" (Rom. 6:19; see also 1 Thes. 4:7). Hence, Christians had moved away from the Jewish notion of ritual uncleanness and addressed themselves to moral cleanness and purity (see the Notes on 5:3, 5).[307]

greediness: The NR has rendered the prepositional phrase "with greediness" (ἐν πλεονεξίᾳ, *en pleonexia*) as the adverb "greedily." The noun that lies in this phrase is customarily associated with a drive to acquire material

---

304. BDAG, 141; see also Thayer, *Lexicon,* 79–80.
305. Otto Bauernfeind, *TDNT,* 1:490; Louw-Nida, §88.272.
306. Rudolf Meyer and Friedrich Hauck, *TDNT,* 3:428.
307. Meyer and Hauck, *TDNT,* 3:428–29.

possessions at any cost, whether by violence or by cunning.[308] In this instance, the noun *pleonexia* exhibits a fundamental meaning outside of illicit sexual relations. We encounter this meaning in Jesus' words to a man who sought his intervention in a dispute about the distribution of property between himself and his brother. To the man's appeal, Jesus answered, "Beware of covetousness [*pleonexia*]: for a man's life consisteth not in the abundance of the things which he possesseth" (Luke 12:15). In Jesus' words recorded in another place, he enshrined the principle in the following line: "Ye cannot serve God and mammon" (Luke 16:13; see also the Notes on 5:3, 5).[309]

4:20 *But ye:* This turn of phrase is strong, pulling our attention away from the reprobate Gentile world and back to the faithful Gentiles who had embraced Christ and his church.[310]

ye have not so learned Christ: The vocabulary of this verse and the next is suggestive of a school of sorts.[311] But no one believes that a formal Christian school existed in Ephesus or the surrounding area. Generally, commentators believe the sense has to do with the education that an investigator underwent on the way to baptism.[312] But is that the end of the story? It seems not. In the first place, the language is unique in the Pauline Epistles. In a word, it is completely unexpected. This characteristic of language leads us to Paul as the author. No one would have dared to write in this way if he were imitating the Apostle. The freshness of the expression can go back only to him.[313]

Second, the context exhibits links to ritual, ritual that goes beyond baptism. For directly after verses 4:20–21, we read about putting off "the old man" and putting on "the new man" (4:22, 24). This language of taking off and putting on a garment, as we have already seen, brings us into direct contact with sacred ceremony (see the Notes on 2:10; 4:1, 13, 20, 22, 24; 5:2, 8, 14; 6:11; and appendix 1). Hence, learning Christ in the way that Paul indicates involved more than catechetical instruction for the new investigator. It evidently also included learning through sacred ceremony. Such a level of acquaintanceship with Christ immediately reminds a person of Jesus' words not long before he and his disciples began their walk to Gethsemane: "This is life eternal, that they might know thee the only true God,

---

308. Gerhard Delling, *TDNT,* 6:271–72; Louw-Nida, §§25.22; 88.144.
309. Delling, *TDNT,* 6:271.
310. Larkin, *Handbook,* 89; Winger, *Ephesians,* 511; Merkle, *Guide,* 140.
311. Barth, *Ephesians,* 2:504, 529–30.
312. Lincoln, *Ephesians,* 279–80; Winger, *Ephesians,* 511.
313. Muddiman, *Ephesians,* 215–16; see also Caird, *Letters,* 80.

and Jesus Christ, whom thou hast sent" (John 17:3). Hence, the context demands that we see more going on than merely "room for growth."[314]

This deeper meaning arises in an unlooked-for corner of Paul's letters. A close look at 1 Corinthians yields a most interesting morsel. We discover that Paul put forward at least two levels of understanding, one called milk and another called meat. In an uncomplimentary observation about certain Corinthian Saints, he wrote: "I could not address you [when I was among you] as spiritual but as worldly—mere infants in Christ." What was the result? "I gave you milk, not solid food, for you were not yet ready for it. Indeed, you are still not ready" (1 Cor. 3:1–2 NIV). This same distinction between simpler and richer spiritual experiences appears in a more noted passage in Hebrews. In a review of people slipping into disbelief from belief, we read, "You have gone back to needing milk, and not solid food. Truly, anyone who is still living on milk cannot digest the doctrine of righteousness because he is still a baby" (Heb. 5:12–13 Jerusalem Bible). We then learn that "grown men can take solid food; their perceptions are trained by long use to discriminate between good and evil" (Heb. 5:14 NEB). Plainly, we meet different levels of understanding, variances within sacred instruction and learning. And the grasp of the higher level comes only to those whose "perceptions are trained by long use to discriminate." Said another way, long spiritual experience counts both in church gatherings and in other sacred settings (see the Notes on 2:10; 4:1, 13, 20, 22, 24; 5:2, 8, 14; 6:11; the introduction section XI; and appendix 1).

Third, to "learn Christ" surely begins with someone preaching Christ and another person hearing the message (see Rom. 10:14, 17). To state the obvious, the process of learning Christ involves a continual pursuit of living as Christ would ask a believer to live. This is the force of a notable change in the Joseph Smith Translation, where we find "learned" substituted for "heard" in the next verse (JST 4:21). But there is more. Amidst all of this human effort to come to Christ and to embrace him and his teachings resides revelation, pure and simple. For in another place the Apostle wrote: "God hath revealed them unto us by his Spirit: for the Spirit searcheth all things, yea, the deep things of God" (1 Cor. 2:10). In a word, the Holy Spirit knows and reveals "the things of God" to those who will receive them (1 Cor. 2:11). Albrecht Oepke grasped the principle accurately when he wrote that "the apostle's sense of revelation reaches a giddy height in this

---

314. Fowl, *Ephesians*, 150.

passage."[315] Indeed, especially if we take into account "the third heaven" of 2 Corinthians 12:2 (see the Notes on 1:9, 17; 3:3).

Fourth, this revelation is initiated by the one who teaches Christ and his gospel. The learner does not know initially that revelation is available or even encouraged but will soon learn. Such revelation, as the language of this verse suggests, leads both the investigator and church member directly to Christ. Because these experiences play out on such a high plane, a plane that connects seekers to God and his Son, it goes almost without saying that the initiator of this process, the missionary, stands as God's spokesperson. In a word, "'Christ' himself 'speaks in' those proclaiming him."[316] Said another way in the language of modern scripture, "whether by mine own voice or by the voice of my servants, it is the same" (D&C 1:38; see also Isa. 50:10; 1 John 4:6; D&C 21:5; and the Note on 4:21).

learned: The verb μανθάνω (*manthanō*) bears the general meaning of learning, whether from instruction or through experience, including an increase of understanding.[317] The connection of this verb to the noun for disciple is obvious (μαθητής, *mathētēs*). For a disciple is one who follows and learns from a master.[318] It is in this light that the apostle wrote the words "learned Christ." That is to say, the emphasis falls on the hearing, not on the teaching. It is the disciple and believer, therefore, onto whom the responsibility falls for learning or understanding the deep things of Christ and thus developing "the inner life."[319]

Christ: Significantly, the name Christ, here with the definite article (τὸν Χριστόν, *ton Christon*), could be translated "the Christ" or "the Messiah." Further, it appears in the accusative case. So, one might ask, what is special about that? The short answer is that the case makes all the difference, for it underlines the fact that Christ is the object of one's learning. Paul was not making reference to the message about him. Yes, learning Christ involved an acquaintance with the traditions handed down about him, such as his inauguration of the Eucharist or sacrament during the Last Supper (see 1 Cor. 11:23–26). But there is more. In learning Christ, a believer comes into direct contact with the Savior through revelation, no intermediaries present.[320]

---

315. Oepke, *TDNT*, 3:584.
316. Barth, *Ephesians*, 2:530.
317. BDAG, 615; Thayer, *Lexicon*, 388–89.
318. Karl Heinrich Rengstorf, *TDNT*, 4:417, 419, 441–42, 445–46; BDAG, 609–10.
319. Rengstorf, *TDNT*, 4:410, 442, quotation on 442.
320. Lincoln, *Ephesians*, 279–80; Winger, *Ephesians*, 511.

4:21 *ye have heard him, and have been taught by him:* As with the prior verse, 4:20, this verse and the following three (4:22–24) present teachings that are found in few places, if any, in Paul's letters, drawing us to the conclusion that Ephesians was authored by the Apostle and not an imitator (see the Notes on 1:23; 3:8; 4:3; 5:27; 6:3, 5; and the Analysis of 3:1–13; 6:1–9).[321] That said, the opening line, as will be evident to any reader, has drawn a lot of attention from scholars. For it is plain that none of Paul's readers had been among the hearers of Jesus when a mortal man, save perhaps a tiny handful of individuals. The first verb, "to hear" (ἀκούω, *akouō*), is key. When this verb takes an accusative object, it means "to hear the thing itself or the person directly."[322] We read lines such as "thou hearest the sound" (John 3:8) and "they heard not the voice" (Acts 22:9; see also Matt. 12:19; Rev. 5:11; etc.). Hence, the KJV translation is correct: "ye have heard him." Some commentators, sensing the apparent impossibility of hearing the Resurrected Jesus' voice directly, opt for a translation "heard about him" or the like.[323] But more is hovering in the air than merely hearing about Christ.

Any suggestion that a few in Paul's readership had heard Jesus teach is clearly remote, though not impossible. It is also possible that a handful had heard and met members of the Twelve on the day of Pentecost (see Acts 2). How so? Because Israelite men were required to attend three celebrations per year in Jerusalem, if they were able—Passover, Pentecost, and Tabernacles (see Ex. 23:14–17; 34:18–24; Deut. 16:16; and 2 Chr. 8:18). Typically, those who lived at a great distance would attend only one of the celebrations when circumstances allowed. In this light, it is likely that some Jewish men and Gentile proselytes from western Asia Minor had gone to Jerusalem for the Passover when Jesus died, arriving a week beforehand, as Jesus did. Why arrive early? Because all pilgrims who lived farther than seventeen miles from the capital city were required to arrive early for purity reasons (see John 11:55 and the Note on 4:8).[324] Those who traveled from western Asia Minor would thus have been on hand when Jesus taught in the temple and when he was tried and crucified in a very public manner.

---

321. Muddiman, *Ephesians,* 215–16, 218.

322. BDAG, 37; Thayer, *Lexicon,* 22–23.

323. Houlden, *Paul's Letters from Prison,* 318; Lincoln, *Ephesians,* 280; Fowl, *Ephesians,* 151; Merkle, *Guide,* 141; Blass and Debrunner, *Greek Grammar,* §173, citing only this passage, Eph. 4:21.

324. *Mishnah Pesahim,* 9.1–2, in Danby, *Mishnah,* 148 and n. 6; see also Hayes, "Purity and Impurity, Ritual," in Berenbaum and Skolnik, *Encyclopaedia Judaica,* 16:752–53.

Naturally, the passage of three decades or more from Jesus' Crucifixion to the date of Paul's composition of this letter would have thinned the ranks of any who had been present during that fateful Passover and the purification week before it. The tiny number, if any, who remained alive would not be enough for Paul to write these words in 4:21 as if to all his readers.

The same can be said for the day of Pentecost seven weeks after Jesus' execution, wherein the Twelve were very much involved with the extraordinary, unexpected activities at the temple, where "about three thousand souls," mostly from out of town, were added to the numbers of Christian believers (Acts 2:41; see also the Note on 4:8). Although those people from Asia and other provinces in what is now modern Turkey were singled out for special mention (see Acts 2:9–10),[325] the chance that these persons had lived until the writing of the letter to the Ephesians is small and does not explain why Paul has evidently addressed his remarks to all his readers. Into this gap has stepped the Joseph Smith Translation. The Prophet Joseph Smith changed the verb "heard" to "learned," altering the basic sense to learning about Christ, rather than having heard his voice, which was a near impossibility (JST 4:21).

Having eliminated the likelihood that any more than a small handful of people in Paul's audience might have personally heard Jesus teach in Jerusalem or interacted with members of the Twelve during the following Pentecost, we must now face the question from another viewpoint: What did Paul mean when he wrote, "Ye have heard [Christ]"? To answer, Paul's claim rests on something that he had written elsewhere: "You will have the proof you seek of the Christ who speaks through me" (2 Cor. 13:3 NEB). In effect, "Christ himself is heard in those who proclaim him."[326] We have already bumped into this concept in modern scripture: "Whether by mine own voice or by the voice of my servants, it is the same" (D&C 1:38). A further illustration arises from God's promise to Moses that the "many waters . . . shall obey thy command as if thou wert God" (Moses 1:25). This principle rests inside the words of God to the prophet Nephi after he had surveyed the gloomy situation among his people: "I will make thee mighty in word . . . even that all things shall be done unto thee according to thy word" (Hel. 10:5; see also the Note on 4:20).

---

325. Cornell and Matthews, *Atlas of the Roman World,* 150–51.

326. Best, *Ephesians,* 427; see also Eadie, *Commentary on the Greek Text,* 343; Bruce, *Ephesians,* 93; Winger, *Ephesians,* 512.

him: As noted above, the verb *akouō*, "to hear," takes the accusative case of the thing heard, whether a voice or some other noise.[327] The pronoun αὐτόν (*auton*) lies in the accusative case and underlines an event of hearing Christ directly as pointed to by the expression "whether by mine own voice or by the voice of my servants" (D&C 1:38).

taught by him: This verbal line, which recounts Jesus' teaching of Paul's audience, governs what is coming in the next three verses, 4:22–24. In each of those verses stands an infinitive that serves as the main verb—"put off," "be renewed," "put on." The grammatical makeup of these verses requires that the infinitives become imperatives as the KJV has rendered them.[328] But an English-speaking reader quickly grasps the intended sense if we render them as infinitives: "taught by him . . . to put off . . . to be renewed . . . to put on" (4:21–24 NR).

as: The sense of this adverb (καθώς, *kathōs*) is most likely causal, to be rendered "since" or "because" (NR) rather than the comparative "just as."[329] We encounter this meaning for *kathōs* elsewhere in Paul's letters. For instance, to the Corinthians he wrote, "In him you have been enriched . . . because [*kathōs*] our testimony about Christ was confirmed in you" (1 Cor. 1:5–6 NIV). Elsewhere, he observed that God had given Gentiles "over to a depraved mind," an act he undertook "since [*kathōs*] they did not think it worthwhile to retain the knowledge of God" (Rom. 1:28 NIV; see also John 17:2 and 1 Cor. 5:7, where the KJV translates *kathōs* "as"; and Philip. 1:7, "Even as").

truth: This occurrence of "truth" (ἀλήθεια, *alētheia*) in Ephesians has occasioned much discussion. Why? Because *alētheia* resides "in Jesus," and because commentators are divided whether the noun *alētheia* is the subject or predicate of the line. This latter issue arises because *alētheia* does not appear with a definite article, the lack of which commonly points to a predicate in a sentence. Simply asked, does the expression mean "[the] truth is in Jesus" or "[we find] truth in Jesus"? In the first case, we meet an absolute statement much like we find in John 14:6, where Jesus declared of himself, "I am the way, the truth, and the life." In the second instance, it is possible to see Jesus as a source of truth, but not of all truth. This latter is hardly a

---

327. BDAG, 37; Thayer, *Lexicon*, 22–23.

328. Lincoln, *Ephesians*, 283–84; Best, *Ephesians*, 430–31, 435; Larkin, *Handbook*, 92; Merkle, *Guide*, 142.

329. BDAG, 493; Thayer, *Lexicon*, 314–15; Best, *Ephesians*, 429.

meaning that we could ascribe to the Apostle.[330] We can excuse Pilate for uttering his throwaway question in the prisoner Jesus' presence, "What is truth?" (John 18:38), a frivolous question that doubtless came from his days as a Roman schoolboy.

A further dimension arises from the lack of the definite article with *alētheia*. Although it is true that the absence of a definite article should typically direct us to a predicate, it need not be so. Abstract nouns serving as subjects in sentences are not uncommon, and certainly not uncommon in Paul's letters.[331] Hence, a proper rendition could be either "truth is in Jesus" or "the truth is in Jesus." Certainly, both senses would occur to Paul's Greek-reading audience.

It is now time to take up Pilate's flippant question, "What is truth?" (John 18:38), and see whether it is possible to discover meaning in the term *alētheia*. Out of the gate, we immediately step into a living landscape that surrounds Jesus as the source of God's truth. We peek into Romans for a first glimpse: "Unto them that are contentious, and do not obey the truth [*alētheia*], but obey unrighteousness, [there comes] indignation and wrath" (Rom. 2:8). In this passage, the word *alētheia* relates both to Jesus as truth's source and to true principles of behavior. The people whom Paul has written about here disobey both Jesus and his teachings. Similarly, when Peter and others waffled at Antioch in Paul's presence by withdrawing from a meal with Gentile church members, Paul scolded them for not walking "uprightly according to the truth [*alētheia*] of the gospel" (Gal. 2:14). Plainly, *alētheia* consists of the guiding principles present in the gospel. But, additionally, Jesus is the source of those principles, and thus Peter and his fellows had clearly turned away from Jesus and his welcoming embrace of all peoples (see John 1:17, "grace and truth came by Jesus Christ"; 2 Cor. 11:10; 1 Thes. 2:13; 1 John 3:19; and Moses 1:6, 32).[332]

From modern scripture comes this statement from the Risen Jesus: "I am the Spirit of truth" (D&C 93:26). Hence, he couples himself with truth both as his personal virtue and as a fundamental element of his personality, whose grasp of eternity allows him to say, "Truth is knowledge of things as they are, and as they were, and as they are to come" (D&C 93:24). There is more. From a lost record of John the Baptist, the Resurrected Christ quoted this line about himself: "The light and the Redeemer of the world; the Spirit of

---

330. Best, *Ephesians*, 429.

331. Blass and Debrunner, *Greek Grammar*, §258.

332. Quell, Kittel, and Bultmann, *TDNT*, 1:242.

truth" (D&C 93:9). Moreover, presenting more clarity are additional words from the Baptist: "I, John, bear record that I beheld his glory, as the glory of the Only Begotten of the Father, full of grace and truth, even the Spirit of truth, which came and dwelt in the flesh" (D&C 93:11). Such language lays emphasis on Jesus' mortality as the arena wherein his character as truth-bearer became fully mature and visible (see the Notes on 5:9; 6:14).

Jesus: The conversation around this name focuses on its appearance without the name-title Christ. Its occurrence here stands as one of the very few instances of Paul writing the name Jesus by itself.[333] The question is, Does this mean anything special? The answer is, Probably. The places where the name Jesus occurs by itself in Paul's letters either centered on the mortal Jesus or revolved around his death and Resurrection. So it is in our Ephesians passage. For example, when writing of severe persecution, the Apostle observed that "we who are alive are always being given over to death for Jesus' sake, so that his [earthly] life may be revealed in our mortal body" (2 Cor. 4:11 NIV; see also 2 Cor. 4:10). In another passage, after writing poetically about Jesus "being found in fashion as a man," thus tying Jesus to mortality, Paul went on to declare that "God also hath highly exalted him [from his human state], and given him a name which is above every name: that at the name of Jesus every knee should bow" (Philip. 2:8–10). The polished connections to Jesus' death and Resurrection are enshrined in these assuring words: "Knowing that he which raised up the Lord Jesus shall raise up us also by Jesus" (2 Cor. 4:14). Even more clear are the following lines: "If the Spirit of him that raised up Jesus from the dead dwell in you, he that raised up Christ from the dead shall also quicken your mortal bodies by his Spirit" (Rom. 8:11).[334]

4:22 *That ye:* It may be notable that the Joseph Smith Translation replaces these two words with the authoritative words "and now I speak unto you," so that the whole thought is this: "And now I speak unto you concerning the former conversation." But Joseph Smith was not finished. For he inserted the phrase "by exortation" into the middle of the verse, adding more authority, and set the expression "that ye put off" immediately afterward so that the line in the middle now reads, "By exhortation, that ye put off the old man, which is corrupt" (JST 4:22). Hence, by additions and relocations, the JST offers a clearer sense of this verse.

---

333. See Rom. 3:26; 8:11; 1 Cor. 12:3; 2 Cor. 4:5, 10, 11, 14; 11:4; Philip. 2:10; 1 Thes. 1:10; 4:14.

334. Werner Foerster, *TDNT,* 3:289.

put off: The verb ἀποτίθημι (*apotithēmi*) leads us directly into the baptismal font.[335] And this action is governed by the verb "have been taught by [Christ]" in the prior verse. The conclusion, therefore, is that a major thrust of Jesus' teaching was that people accept baptism (see John 3:5). To be sure, the idea of taking off—the basic meaning of the verb *apotithēmi*[336]—the old garments and habits of one's prior life, when a person was without Christ, presents the figurative meaning for this verb—that a person discard the old ways (see Rom. 13:11–13 and Col. 3:5–8). It is also the case that references to taking off old clothing before baptism and putting on new afterward do not appear until the second century AD.[337] Yet the abundant references and allusions to ceremony throughout this letter stand as markers of the act of changing out of one's street clothes for baptism. That action of disrobing out of one's old garments is, literally and concretely, putting off the old person,[338] just as baptism is a tangible experience. For examples we need go no farther than the letter to the Romans. In that missive, we come upon the words that those who "were baptized into Jesus Christ were baptized into his death . . . planted together [in the water] in the likeness of his death . . . knowing this, that our old man is crucified with him, that the body of sin might be destroyed" (Rom. 6:3, 5–6; see also Col. 2:11–12; 3:9).

Two dimensions of the infinitive form of *apotithēmi* arrest our attention. First, it stands in the past tense, the aorist in Greek. Hence, as others have observed, it points to a one-time experience in the past, a once-for-all action, and brings believers to a full abandonment of the old self that is completed in the process of repentance and baptism. Such an experience lifts a person out of a passive and into an active role, resulting in a hoped-for decisive and permanent change.[339] Second, in three successive verses, the infinitives for "put off" and "be renewed" and "put on" really represent imperatives—that is, Paul's directives to his readers.[340] Why is that important? Because they also exhibit a sense of continuity along a path that, once begun, draws believers along to deeper and richer vistas. This is what one commentator has called an "ongoing transformation of believers' habits of thinking, feeling, and perceiving."[341] But the story does not end here.

---

335. Seesemann, *TDNT*, 5:719.
336. BDAG, 123–24.
337. Lincoln, *Ephesians*, 284–85; Best, *Ephesians*, 433.
338. Muddiman, *Ephesians*, 218.
339. Barth, *Ephesians*, 2:505, 541–42; Lincoln, *Ephesians*, 284–85.
340. Lincoln, *Ephesians*, 283–84; Best, *Ephesians*, 430–31, 435; Larkin, *Handbook*, 92; Merkle, *Guide*, 142.
341. Fowl, *Ephesians*, 152.

The notable change of shucking off the old person comes as a result of repentance and baptism. But the character of what happens next does not rest totally on a foundation of holding onto one's faith in the face of challenges. It is that, certainly. But the process of renewal is richer than this. For it is aided by the reception of the Holy Ghost and the remaking of covenants undertaken at baptism by partaking of the Eucharist or sacrament. The first of these becomes evident in the experience of Jesus himself when, after his baptism, "the Holy Ghost descended . . . like a dove upon him" (Luke 3:22; see also Matt. 3:16; Mark 1:10; and 2 Ne. 31:8). In the words of Christ, "He that is baptized in my name, to him will the Father give the Holy Ghost, like unto me" (2 Ne. 31:12). Out of Peter's mouth came the words "Repent, and be baptized every one of you in the name of Jesus Christ . . . and ye shall receive the gift of the Holy Ghost" (Acts 2:38). From John the Baptist, who spoke prophetically about Jesus, we encounter, "He shall baptize you with the Holy Ghost, and with fire" (Matt. 3:11; see also Mark 1:8; Luke 3:16; John 1:33; and Acts 1:5; 19:4–6).

Concerning the second matter, that of renewing covenants made at baptism, we must establish that baptism generates a covenant between believers and God. Alma the Elder made the case most clearly. After reviewing the inner pledge that a person makes when receiving baptism, which includes being "willing to bear one another's burdens . . . and to stand as witnesses of God at all times," Alma affirmed that in receiving baptism a person has "entered into a covenant with [God], that ye will serve him and keep his commandments" (Mosiah 18:8–10). Fair enough. The next step consists in renewing that covenant, an aspect that Paul's words in another place hint at strongly. For when he wrote about "the cup of blessing" that links participants to "the blood of Christ" (1 Cor. 10:16), it is evident that regularly partaking of that cup in a sacrament setting offered much more than simple refreshment, whether physical or spiritual, for the cup "conveys blessing," enriching us in a deep, spiritual way.[342]

Modern scripture makes this clear as well. About a year after Jesus' Resurrection and ascension, and long before Paul penned any of his letters, the Savior appeared as the Risen Christ in the New World, where he introduced the sacrament to his followers and explained its future, ongoing purposes. The emblems of his body and blood, he said, were to be distributed "unto the people of my church, unto all those who shall believe and be baptized in my name." Moreover, partaking of the sacrament "shall be a

---

342. BDAG, 408, s.v. "εὐλογία"; see also Draper and Rhodes, *Paul's First Epistle to the Corinthians*, 489.

testimony unto the Father that ye do always remember me," which leads to having "my spirit to be with you" (3 Ne. 18:5, 7). Was this to be a one-time experience? No. For "this shall ye *always observe to do,* even as I have done," when his followers were to meet the next time and the time after that (3 Ne. 18:6, emphasis added). Specifically, with an emphasis on doing, "I [the Lord] give unto you a commandment that ye shall *do* these things." Further, "if ye shall *always do* these things blessed are ye" (3 Ne. 18:12, emphasis added). Hence, partaking of the sacramental emblems meant that, on the part of believers, they always remember the redeeming sacrifice of Jesus at his death, and, on the Lord's part, he will bless believers with his Spirit.

One further item needs tending. One commentator confidently declared, "Further changes of clothing [after baptism] will not be needed for us to reach our goal."[343] Really? What, then, are we to do with the Apostle's directive that appears later in this letter: "Put on the whole armor of God" (6:11; see also 6:14; Rom. 13:12; and 1 Thes. 5:8)? From this imperative to put on divine, protective garments, it becomes evident that more is involved in a Christian's life than passing through baptism as the sole, needed experience for discarding the old person and its unwanted habits. Other teachings and ordinances apply. An example from an early Christian text written in its original form before AD 200 may shed light on what such people underwent in their worship. The Gospel of Thomas, a document in the Coptic language found in full in Upper Egypt, presents a series of sayings of Jesus to his disciples. Most of these sayings are preserved in the New Testament Gospels, though in a rather different form. In this Gospel, Jesus and his followers do nothing and go nowhere. It is all talk. The sayings are connected chiefly by catchwords or repeating expressions.[344] Such catchwords aided the memorization of the sayings. Conclusion? The Gospel of Thomas was evidently a document memorized by several people who recited from memory, in front of an audience, the questions from Simon Peter and Matthew and Thomas and others, to which a person representing the Risen Jesus responded. It was like a live play, complete with the main characters, that was designed to inform those in the audience about the sacred teachings of Christ (see the Notes on 1:20; 4:13, 23, 24; 6:11; and appendix 1).[345]

---

343. Fowl, *Ephesians,* 153.

344. Helmut Koester and Thomas O. Lambdin, "The Gospel of Thomas," in Robinson and Smith, eds., *Nag Hammadi Library in English,* 124.

345. We meet this sort of play in ancient Egyptian religious ceremonies, complete with staging dependent on a temple's architecture. See Siegfried Morenz, *Egyptian Religion,* trans. Ann E. Keep (Ithaca, N.Y.: Cornell University Press, 1973), 84, 86, 219.

former conversation: In the context, the reference centers on a Gentile believer's former pattern of living, as the noun ἀναστροφή (*anastrophē*) tells us (see 2 Pet. 2:7).[346] Like here in 4:22, the related verb in 2:3 describes the lives of Jews who had remained in disobedience. Paul was even willing to turn the term's negative side against himself when sketching his former life before meeting Christ (see Gal. 1:13, "my previous way of life," NIV). That former life had dulled him to the spiritual enticements of Christ because of, as Peter expressed it, the "tradition from [our] fathers" (1 Pet. 1:18;[347] see also the Note on 2:3).

the old man: Age is not the factor; the change from one's former self is. The noun translated "man" (ἄνθρωπος, *anthrōpos*) touches on women too, because it embraces all of humanity, not just a male or group of men.[348] In that earlier state, as a plethora of New Testament passages have affirmed, evil acts clasped Gentiles in their claws, leading them to "fornication, uncleanness, [and] inordinate affection" as well as to "anger, wrath, [and] . . . filthy communication out of [their] mouth" (Col. 3:5, 8; see also Gal. 5:19–21; Col. 1:21; Titus 3:3; and 1 Pet. 1:14; 4:3).[349] In the end, "our old man is crucified with [Christ], that the body of sin might be destroyed." What was the result? "That henceforth we should not serve sin" (Rom. 6:6). God be praised! (See Ether 8:26 and the Notes on 2:15; 3:16; 4:13, 24.)

corrupt: The adjective actually derives from a present passive participle of the verb φθείρω (*phtheirō*), which is about the deterioration of a person's inner life.[350] The basic sense of the present tense centers on the ongoing, ever-slippery slide into "the moral rot" of the larger society.[351]

deceitful: The first recorded act of deceit, of course, was the devil's trickery with Eve. Hence, readers find themselves standing at the edge of the Garden of Eden and peering inside to get a glimpse of Eve in her struggle with the question of whether to partake of the forbidden fruit.[352] In truth, she saw beyond the deception of the person who stood before her and truly grasped her options. For that is the monumental meaning of the verb "to see" in Genesis 3:6: "When the woman *saw* that the tree was good for food, . . . and a tree to be desired to make one wise, she took of the fruit thereof,

346. BDAG, 73; Louw-Nida, §41.3.
347. Bertram, *TDNT*, 7:717.
348. BDAG, 81–82; Louw-Nida, §§9.1–2.
349. Stählin, *TDNT*, 2:925.
350. BDAG, 1054.
351. Winger, *Ephesians,* 515; see also Lincoln, *Ephesians,* 286; and Muddiman, *Ephesians,* 219.
352. Muddiman, *Ephesians,* 219; Winger, *Ephesians,* 515.

and did eat" (emphasis added; see also Moses 4:12). Most significantly, this verb is the same that describes God's sight. For example, "God saw the light" and "God saw that it was good" and "God saw every thing" (Gen. 1:4, 12, 31). What is the message? In plain terms, it is that, during that moment when she faced Satan, Eve saw as God saw, that she knew with divine clarity the course she had to follow (see the Note on 5:31).[353]

Beside this, we come to the full frightful flower of deception that the devil and his allies place before unwary souls. Those allies include human agents, unconverted Gentiles in this case. The expression before us (τὰς ἐπιθυμίας τῆς ἀπάτης, *tas epithymias tēs apatēs*) can be rendered literally "the desires for deception," indicating that some in Paul's wider society sought to deceive (see D&C 89:4, "conspiring men"). The noun translated as the adjective "deceitful" (ἀπάτη, *apatē*) carries two meanings. One has to do with pleasure, the other with deceitfulness.[354] A person stumbles onto the ambiguity between these different meanings in Jesus' parable of the sower. In the KJV, we read "the deceitfulness of riches," but the RSV translates this expression "the delight in riches" (Matt. 13:22; Mark 4:19). Both are correct, and Jesus may well have meant his audience to think of both senses. But like Peter, who criticized those "sporting themselves with their own deceivings while they feast with you" and having their "eyes full of adultery" (2 Pet. 2:13–14), Paul in our verse intended to paint the noun *apatē* in a truly dark and negative light.

lusts: Although a reader might consider the noun "lusts" to be an overly strong translation of this term (singular ἐπιθυμία, *epithymia*), which points to one's "desires,"[355] it is exactly right. In a few passages, the noun *epithymia* and its corresponding verb (ἐπιθυμέω, *epithymeō*) are associated with the desire for good things, such as food (see Luke 15:16; 16:21) or heavenly secrets (see Matt. 13:17; Luke 17:22; and 1 Pet. 1:12) or any good outcome (see Philip. 1:23; 1 Tim. 3:1; and Heb. 6:11). Otherwise, they are linked to evil desires, to undisciplined urges. A short sample would incorporate "the lusts" of "the mortal body" (Rom. 6:12) and "the lust of the flesh, and the lust of the eyes" (1 John 2:16), "fleshly lusts" (1 Pet. 2:11) and "worldly lusts" (Titus 2:12). Such desires, such lusts, can dwell in individuals and control them (see Matt. 5:28 and the Note on 2:3).[356]

---

353. Draper, Brown, and Rhodes, *Pearl of Great Price*, 43–45.
354. Albrecht Oepke, *TDNT*, 1:385; BDAG, 99.
355. BDAG, 372; Louw-Nida, §25.12, 20; Thayer, *Lexicon*, 238–39.
356. Friedrich Büchsel, *TDNT*, 3:170–71.

4:23 *be renewed:* The present infinitive of the verb "to renew" (ἀνανεόω, *ananeoō*), here in the passive voice,[357] centers on a constantly active process, because of the present tense, that does not shut off. It is governed by the verbal expression "ye . . . have been taught by [Christ]" (4:21), reminding readers about the Christ who has taught them about the necessity to be constantly renewed (see 2 Cor. 4:16).[358] The question is, How does that renewal take place? As we have learned above, the biggest factors are the reception of the Holy Ghost and the regular renewal of one's baptismal covenant by partaking of the sacrament or Eucharist. It is in this renewal of the covenant wherein we "present [our] bodies a living sacrifice, holy, acceptable unto God" that we are "transformed by the renewing of [our] mind" (Rom. 12:1–2). The regular influence of the Holy Spirit, even if intermittent, brings believers to rely on the promise of the Resurrected Christ that "ye shall have my Spirit to be with you" (3 Ne. 18:7). By this means, church members can experience "the ongoing transformation of believers' habits of thinking, feeling, and perceiving."[359] Significantly, this change "is finally accomplished on them rather than through them," one by one, person by person. The activator "of the renewal is obviously Christ Himself" (see the Notes on 4:22, 24).[360]

the spirit of your mind: The celestial improvement of the mind comes about with several aids. In the first place, the faithful Christian lives with the assurance of being sealed "with that holy Spirit of promise." That experience, undergone in this life, "is the earnest of our inheritance" with God (1:13–14; see also 4:30, "the holy Spirit . . . sealed [you] unto the day of redemption"; 2 Cor. 1:22, "sealed us, and given the earnest of the Spirit"; and Gal. 3:13–14). There is more. Revelation plays a role, exhibiting its powers in revealing "the knowledge of [God]" to the seeker (1:17) and in disclosing the mystery of his will to his servants, the "holy apostles and prophets" (3:5). These events go beyond "the basic knowledge of the Christ event" that all investigators learn about. Further, the language of 6:17 features scripture as a major element when we learn that "the sword of the spirit" is "the [written] word of God."[361] Hence, the study of scripture leads to a spiritual endowment (see the Notes on 1:13, 14, 17; 3:5).

---

357. Larkin, *Handbook,* 92–93; Merkle, *Guide,* 143.

358. Behm and Würthwein, *TDNT,* 4:958; Barth, *Ephesians,* 2:505, 507.

359. Fowl, *Ephesians,* 152.

360. Johannes Behm, *TDNT,* 4:901.

361. Kleinknecht, Baumgärtel, Bieder, Sjöberg, and Schweizer, *TDNT,* 6:444; see also Bultmann, *TDNT,* 1:708.

4:24 *the new man, which after God is created in righteousness and true holiness:* Any review of this verse must deal with the question, Does this notion not tie to the idea of humans becoming like God? In particular, the phrase "after God," which can be rendered "just as God" or "in accord with (the pattern of) God" (κατὰ θεόν, *kata theon*),[362] seems to say that we model ourselves after him, acquiring along the way "righteousness and true holiness" (see 5:2, 8, 9; and the Note below).

put on: As in the prior two verses, this verb (ἐνδύω, *enduō*), an infinitive that stands for an imperative, depends on 4:21: "ye have . . . been taught by [Christ]." Therefore, inside the teaching from Christ rests the obvious instruction to "put on the new person" (4:24 NR). In light of the verb's link to baptism (see the Note on 4:22), we expect to see the idea of getting into new clothes,[363] a notion verbalized in the after-baptism ordinance of partaking of the sacrament or Eucharist. And we are not disappointed. For in the prayer uttered over the bread we hear this line: "That they are willing to take upon them the name of thy Son" (Moro. 4:3; D&C 20:77; see also D&C 109:22, "that thy name may be upon them"). This language points to the donning of a garment, to putting on a piece of clothing. In the sacramental prayer, a person is to get into and wear the name of Christ, as if wearing a piece of holy clothing. So it was with Paul's instruction to the Saints in Rome: "Put ye on [*enduō*] the Lord Jesus Christ" (Rom. 13:14; see also Gal. 3:27, "put on [*enduō*] Christ"; and 1 Thes. 5:8). The thought of wearing a spiritual garment of celestial power sits in Jesus' directive to his disciples just before his ascension: "Stay in the city then, until you are clothed [*enduō*] with the power from on high" (Luke 24:49, Jerusalem Bible). It is possible to multiply examples of the figurative meaning.

The literal sense also lingers nearby. It ties to the notion that new clothes elevate a person, whether illustrating a new status in one's employment or a special place in one's society.[364] One has only to notice that angels exiting the heavenly temple were "clothed [*enduō*] in pure and white linen" (Rev. 15:6). This kind of elevation by what one wears, or lack thereof, is presumed in Jesus' parable of the Great Supper. In Jesus' retelling of the story, all the hastily invited guests were in the wedding hall "when the king came in to the see the guests." What greeted his gaze was "a man which had not on [*enduō*] a wedding garment." The story then rounded on this man who

---

362. BDAG, 513.
363. BDAG, 333.2.a.
364. Barth, *Ephesians,* 2:540–41.

lacked proper clothing. Because of his lack, he was taken away "and cast ... into outer darkness" (Matt. 22:11, 13). Obviously, the proper garment would have made all the difference.

One inescapable conclusion of our brief review tells us that the individual who puts on the new person now stands fully in God's image.[365] The parts of *enduō*, figurative and literal, each aim at this conclusion. The spiritual endowment of power that a person realizes when donning Christ, as if putting on a garment, is real and elevating, even energizing. We listen to the words of Paul to the Colossian church members, writing that they "have put on [*enduō*] the new man, which is renewed in knowledge after the image of him that created him" (Col. 3:10). Putting "on the Lord Jesus Christ" forms the apex of a Christian's efforts to escape "the works of darkness, and ... put on [*enduō*] the armour of light" (Rom. 13:14, 12). The literal comes into play as well, for the literal meaning stands just to the side of what Paul wrote about celestial defensive clothing, "putting on [*enduō*] the breastplate of faith and love" (1 Thes. 5:8) and, in different words, "having on [*enduō*] the breast plate of righteousness" (Eph. 6:14). Each of these is subsumed in "the whole armour of God" (6:11; see also Rev. 1:13; 15:6; 19:14). There is more.

The verb *enduō* shares connections with two other verbs that exhibit ties with sacred acts and sacred clothing. In Ephesians, *enduō* shows up in this verse, 4:24, and in 6:11 ("put on") and 6:14 ("having on"). The instances in chapter 6 have to do with putting on and wearing God's armor, effectively God's clothing. These deeds are made holy because they involve a believer in donning God's garments. The second verb, meaning "to take up [weapons]" (ἀναλαμβάνω, *analambanō*), occurs at 6:13 and 6:16.[366] Again, the term pertains to the church member's effort to grasp and hold what belongs to God. The third verb is δέχομαι (*dechomai*), which appears at 6:17 and exhibits the meanings "to receive" or "to take."[367] Here, too, the believer takes in hand and places on the body items belonging to God, making those actions holy (see the Notes on 4:22, 24; 5:20; 6:11, 13, 14, 16, 17; the Analysis of 6:10–20; and appendix 1).

the new man: The "new man" is not the same as the "inner man" (3:16). The "inner man," as we have learned, has to do with a person's inner core, which is fortified and edified after baptism. Such strengthening comes

---

365. Joachim Jeremias, *TDNT,* 1:366; Heinrich Seesemann, *TDNT,* 5:719.

366. Delling, *TDNT,* 4:8; BDAG, 66.2.

367. BDAG, 221.1; see Lincoln, *Ephesians,* 452.

about through a pattern of ceremonial experiences that elevate the individual and bring that person closer to being like God, made possible in part by partaking of the sacrament or Eucharist (see 2 Cor. 4:16). In a different vein, the "new man" directs us first to the newly baptized person, fresh and clean and innocent before God. But that is only part of the story. For the recently baptized person is now to step onto the path that leads to apotheosis, or becoming like God. All of this happens in "the sacramental sphere."[368]

The grand exemplar, of course, is Jesus Christ. He is the Redeemer of both the individual and the church as a whole, uniting both Jew and Gentile (see 2:15; 4:13). Perhaps the most complete statement occurs in another place. There we read: "Seeing that ye have put off the old man . . . and have put on the new man, which is renewed in knowledge after the image of him that created him" (Col. 3:9–10; see also 2 Cor. 5:17–18, "a new creature"). God, of course, is the creator of the new person. But Christ has joined him as co-creator. We meet the proper relationship in words that speak of God, "who created all things by Jesus Christ" (3:9; see also 2:10).[369] The "knowledge" spoken of in Colossians 3:10, as we might expect, derives from a celestial realm; it is not earthly (see the Notes on 3:18, 19; 4:13). Passing farther along this path, we notice that "we have borne the image of the earthly [person]" because of our mortality. But, in the next life, "we shall also bear the image of the heavenly" (1 Cor. 15:49). Naturally, that image belongs to the Father and the Son. In their image, steadfast believers are more than "created after God's image."[370] In the ultimate sense and in the final scene, like Abraham, Isaac, and Jacob, these people will "sit upon thrones, and are not angels but are gods" (D&C 132:37). This is "because they have no end; therefore shall they be from everlasting to everlasting, . . . because all things are subject unto them" (D&C 132:20; see also D&C 76:58–60; and the Note on 4:22). In the language of the New Testament, faithful believers will become "partakers of the divine nature, having escaped the corruption that is in the world" (2 Pet. 1:4; see also the Note on 3:16).

after God: The phrase "after God" (κατὰ θεόν, *kata theon*), whose plain imports are "after (the ideal of) God" or "following in God's path," can embrace a number of ideas, mainly because the preposition *kata* possesses a rich set of meanings. In this instance, it is attached to the accusative *theon,* the noun for God in an objective case. And the messages among the

---

368. Jeremias, *TDNT,* 1:366.
369. Jeremias, *TDNT,* 1:366.
370. Seesemann, *TDNT,* 5:719.

399 occurrences of *kata* with an accusative noun in the New Testament are extremely varied. Among these denotations, we can eliminate all but two. In the context, the preposition surely does not mean "toward" or "to," "along" or "through," "during" or "for the purpose of," "in relation to" or "with respect to," all meanings of the term.[371] Two other senses fit. One can be understood as "in accord with" or "in the manner of."[372] That is to say, we can read the line as "put on the new man, which in accord with [the pattern of] God, is created in righteousness," or "put on the new man, which in the [celestial] manner of God, is created in righteousness." This sense for *kata* appears elsewhere in the Apostle's letters, including Ephesians. For example, we encounter, "In time past ye walked *according to* the course of this world, *according to* the prince . . . of the air" (2:2, emphasis added). Further, "the Spirit intercedes for the saints *in accordance with* God's will" (Rom. 8:27 NIV, emphasis added; see also Rom. 15:5). In a passage that reproduces exactly our phrase, *kata theon,* we read, "Ye were made sorry *after a godly manner*" (2 Cor. 7:9, emphasis added; see also 2 Cor. 7:11; 11:17; and Col. 3:10).

The other likely implication for *kata* bears the thought "as" or "just as." We meet this sense in Galatians 4:28: "We, brethren, [*just*] *as* Isaac was, are the children of promise" (emphasis added).[373] In the light of these two meanings, it becomes evident that Paul was saying that we put on the new person, who, remarkably, is after God's pattern or after God's character. This "new man," as Paul has written, accords with God's divine design, which, because it was created and shaped by him, brims with "righteousness and true holiness." As is now apparent, the implication runs to God's children becoming exactly like him. We bump forcefully into this thought later in Ephesians: "Therefore, be imitators of God" (5:1 RSV). Said another way, "Christ initiates a process of growth of which He Himself is the goal and in which He Himself sets us" (see 4:15–16 and the Notes on 4:13; 5:1).[374]

is created: The passive, as elsewhere, sends us to God as the actor, the creator.[375] The verb κτίζω (*ktizō*) concerns both the creation of the natural world and the new creation which a person enters upon at baptism—that is, allowing oneself to be sculpted "after the image of him that created him"

---

371. BDAG, 511–13.

372. BDAG, 512.5.a.α; Louw-Nida, §89.8; Thayer, *Lexicon,* 328.3.c.α.

373. BDAG, 513.5.b.α.

374. Grundmann, Hesse, de Jonge, and van der Woude, *TDNT,* 9:558.

375. Merkle, *Guide,* 144.

(Col. 3:10). The mention of the word "image" recalls very directly this term in Genesis 1:26–27. On one level, the new person, created by God, has become like Adam and Eve.[376] Those distant ancestors were formed by God and, for a time, enjoyed his company (see Gen. 1:28–30; 2:16–17, 19; 3:9–19; Moses 2:28–30; 3:16–17; 4:15–25; and Abr. 5:11–13, 16). With the aid of Christ, Adam and Eve have escaped their old life, punctuated by sin and death, and have emerged as new persons. For, "if by one man's [Adam's] offence death reigned by one; much more they which receive abundance of grace . . . shall reign in [heavenly] life by one, Jesus Christ" (Rom. 5:17). Christ's gracious, atoning act extended not only to those who came after him in time but also to Adam and Eve and their faithful descendants. Now, for Paul's readers, "the new man" becomes a new Adam and a new Eve. Following a path blazed by Christ, the new person grows to be like "the second man [Christ who] is the Lord from heaven" (1 Cor. 15:47). What has wrapped its arms around the believer is "a new relation to God,"[377] changing everything (see the Notes on 2:10, 15).

righteousness and true holiness: This expression is better rendered "true righteousness and holiness" (NR). Literally, it reads "righteousness and holiness of the truth."[378] But the phrase "of the truth" bears the sense of an adjective. In one vein, righteousness (δικαιοσύνη, *dikaiosynē*) has to do with a person's relationships with other people in this life. This is one of the fruits of the Spirit that aids an individual's interactions with others (see 5:9). In a quotation from Psalm 112:9, Paul wrote, "He [the good person] hath dispersed [his goods] abroad; he hath given to the poor: his righteousness remaineth for ever" (2 Cor. 9:9). The notion of holiness (ὁσιότης, *hosiotēs*), on the other hand, turns fully toward heavenly realities. It is this idea that sits behind the following: "I will therefore that men pray every where, lifting up holy hands, without wrath and doubting" (1 Tim. 2:8). Hence, the expression "true righteousness and holiness" presses forward with both terrestrial and celestial force (see the Notes on 5:9; 6:14).[379]

The only other New Testament passage where the noun "holiness" (*hosiotēs*) occurs is in Luke 1:75, where it is also paired with the term for "righteousness" (*dikaiosynē*). In that context, holiness and righteousness characterize the one—John the Baptist, in this case—who comes "before

---

376. Barth, *Ephesians*, 2:509; Lincoln, *Ephesians*, 287.
377. Foerster, *TDNT*, 3:1034.
378. Eadie, *Commentary on the Greek Text*, 353.
379. Eadie, *Commentary on the Greek Text*, 353; Larkin, *Handbook*, 94.

[God]," before his altar, and is the recipient of the "holy covenant" and "the oath" made by God with Abraham. Thus equipped, he will be able to "serve [God] without fear . . . all the days of our life" (Luke 1:72–75). The plural pronoun "our" in these lines pertains to a wider group of recipients, beyond the Baptist, who will become heirs of Abraham's oath and covenant.

4:25 *Wherefore:* Paul pivots again, as before, pulling away from sublime doctrinal discussion in the preceding verses and turning his attention to proper behavior. Commentators differ about the next section, whether it extends to 5:2 or 5:5. Ultimately, it makes little difference. That said, the appearance of the conjunction διό (*dio*) weaves together both the following exhortations and his prior discussion about putting off the old person and pulling on the new.[380] Readers will now hear his practical instructions. His appeals, usually in the form of a list, mirror what we find in other letters.[381] In Ephesians, we come across no deeply serious acts of evil. It seems that the most serious problems that church members faced were how to deal with a fellow believer accused of stealing (see 4:28) and how to respond to church members pushing their own agendas (see the Notes on 5:6, 7, 11).

putting away lying: The participle translated "putting away" is from the same verb that underlies the infinitive "put off" in 4:22 (ἀποτίθημι, *apotithēmi*). Hence, the Apostle has now transferred the act of putting away "the old man" of 4:22 to that of putting away one of the deepest ingrained tendencies in a human's nature, to lie. The effort to avoid lying has to be as conscious and purposeful as the acts of unstrapping, unbuttoning, unwinding, and untying articles of clothing. A good reason exists for not lying. Each church member has united with other believers in the body of Christ, the church. Therefore, each is an integral part of "the whole body [of Christ which is] fitly joined together and compacted" for the mutual benefit of all (4:16). Any breach of this unity creates a fracture that runs through an entire congregation.[382]

Approaching lying from a different angle, we observe that God "cannot lie" (Titus 1:2). Compared to his rock-hard truth, all humanity stands as a pack of liars. For in their unenlightened state, they "changed the truth

---

380. Larkin, *Handbook*, 97; Merkle, *Guide*, 146.

381. See Rom. 1:29–31; 1 Cor. 5:10–11; 6:9–10; 2 Cor. 6:3–8; 12:20–21; Gal. 5:16–23; Col. 3:8–14; 1 Tim. 1:9–10; etc.

382. Lincoln, *Ephesians*, 300–301.

of God into a lie, and worshiped and served the creature more than the Creator" (Rom. 1:25). As a custodian of the gospel and a representative of God himself, Paul could assert, "I say the truth in Christ, I lie not" (Rom. 9:1; see also Gal. 1:20, "I lie not"). Another dimension rears its prickly head. It is that during the events of the end-time, "that Wicked [one will] be revealed ... after the working of Satan with all power and signs and lying wonders" (2 Thes. 2:8–9). Hence, a grand deceptive lie will sit at the base of a trickster's power. Because duped individuals "received not the love of the truth [from God,] ... God shall send them strong delusion, that they should believe a lie," to their eternal hurt (2 Thes. 2:10–11).[383] Thus, a false cabal will draw them on to a vacant reward.

neighbour: A quotation from LXX Zechariah 8:16 has brought this noun into Paul's words. It reads, "Speak truth every one with his neighbor." A person's neighbor (πλησίον, *plēsion*) has been an object of concern since the days of Moses when the Lord declared, "Thou shalt love thy neighbor as thyself" (Lev. 19:18). Jesus picked up this thread in his own teaching (see Matt. 19:19; Mark 12:31; and Luke 10:27). Paul, too, drew attention to this old commandment (see Rom. 13:9 and Gal. 5:14). Within the larger Jewish society, one discovers a debate about who one's neighbor really is. In the Sermon on the Mount, Jesus pushed himself into this fray by criticizing a current thought that a person could "love [the] neighbor, and hate [the] enemy." His response? "Love your enemies, bless them that curse you, do good to them that hate you," and so forth. Hence, in Jesus' view, neighbors included enemies who "despitefully use you, and persecute you." Concerning those who are hard to love, "pray for them" (Matt. 5:43–44). The classic story that illustrated who one's neighbor really is was Jesus' parable of the Good Samaritan (see Luke 10:25–37). Lying at the base of that story rests the "sense of divine sonship"[384]—the idea that we are all God's children.

members of one another: In its first conception, the term for "member" (μέλος, *melos*) brings us to individuals' physical bodies.[385] We see this meaning, for example, in Paul's words "The body is not one member, but many" (1 Cor. 12:14), which are followed by his review of the body's members such as "the foot" and "the ear" and "the eye" (1 Cor. 12:15–16; see also 1 Cor. 12:18–20). Paul understood that our bodies form the conduits to evil acts. Adopting the image of slave owners, he noted to his Roman readers

---

383. Hans Conzelmann, *TDNT*, 9:601.
384. Heinrich Greeven and Johannes Fichtner, *TDNT*, 6:316–17.
385. BDAG, 628; Louw-Nida, §8.9.

that, in the past, "ye have yielded your members servants to uncleanness and to iniquity." In this light, he pled, "Even so now yield your members servants to righteousness unto holiness" (Rom. 6:19; see also Rom. 6:13). For his Jewish readers, the Mosaic law, with its plethora of paths to sin, stimulated "the flesh" and awakened "our sinful passions, aroused by the law, [which] were at work in our members to bear fruit for death." With God's help, "we are discharged from the law, dead to that which held us captive, so that we serve . . . in the new life of the Spirit" (Rom. 7:5–6 RSV; see also Rom. 7:23).[386]

The other thought is figurative and linked to members of Christ's body, the church. We occasionally stumble upon a mixing of the literal and metaphorical. For instance, "we have many members in one body, and all members have not the same office" (Rom. 12:4; see also "the tongue" in James 3:5–6). In our Ephesians passage, 4:25, we face a figurative meaning tied to membership in the church: "we are members one of another." An almost identical idea occurs in Romans: "We, being many, are one body in Christ, and every one members one of another" (Rom. 12:5).[387] Above all, we must not forget that Christ "permeates and dominates the whole" (see the Note on 5:30).[388]

4:26 *Be ye angry, and sin not:* This line is a quotation from LXX Psalm 4:5 (Ps. 4:4 Hebrew Bible and KJV). How to deal with this double imperative (verbs ὀργίζω, *orgizō*, and ἁμαρτάνω, *hamartanō*) has long puzzled commentators. Does the line concern the correction of another believer who has wandered?[389] Does it allow one to become angry as long as the pique goes away before the sun sets?[390] Does it counsel against a nursed resentment?[391] Does it permit indignation on behalf of other believers?[392] Does it encourage a person to exhibit anger on God's behalf?[393] The problem for any of these solutions arises in 4:31 where we read: "Let all bitterness and wrath, and anger . . . be put away from you." Jesus himself set the

---

386. Johannes Horst, *TDNT,* 4:561, 566.

387. BDAG, 628; Louw-Nida, §63.17.

388. Horst, *TDNT,* 4:566; see also Grundmann, Hesse, de Jonge, and van der Woude, *TDNT,* 9:557–58.

389. Lincoln, *Ephesians,* 302.

390. Muddiman, *Ephesians,* 225; Fowl, *Ephesians,* 156; Winger, *Ephesians,* 521.

391. Eadie, *Commentary on the Greek Text,* 357; Bruce, *Ephesians,* 96; Lincoln, *Ephesians,* 301.

392. Barth, *Ephesians,* 2:513.

393. Kleinknecht, Grether, Procksch, Fichtner, Sjöberg, and Stälin, *TDNT,* 5:419 n. 266; Best, *Ephesians,* 450.

bar: "Whosoever is angry with his brother shall be in danger of [God's] judgment" (3 Ne. 12:22; Matt. 5:22 differs in its language). His words leave no wiggle room. James mirrors Jesus' words: "Everyone should be quick to listen . . . and slow to become angry, for man's anger does not bring about the righteous life that God desires" (James 1:19–20 NIV). Other examples occur elsewhere.[394] In the final grappling, it is not possible to determine exactly what the Apostle meant except that, in light of the rest of the verse, any outburst of anger was to be quickly subdued.

The Joseph Smith Translation offers an intriguing adjustment to this line. The Prophet Joseph Smith reframed these words into a question which reads: "Can ye be angry, and not sin?" (JST 4:26). With one brief stroke, the JST lifts away all questions about the meaning of the puzzling expression, letting the reader know that anger in any of its forms is a sin.

Modern scripture addresses a form of anger only once, that of firm reproval. Perhaps surprisingly, a statement of the Lord allows a person to reprove another individual "betimes with sharpness." But we immediately run into a barrier. A person can exhibit pique only "when moved upon by the Holy Ghost." No one has a free pass to show any form of anger toward another. Moreover, even when the Holy Ghost moves the person to express disapproval, that utterance must be followed instantly by "showing forth . . . an increase of love toward him whom thou hast reproved." Why? Now the high ground shifts to the one who received the reproval and away from the person who uttered it. The demonstration of the "increase of love" is so that the person receiving the reproof does not "esteem thee to be his [or her] enemy." Without the expression of love toward the reproved person, the one who expressed the disapproval now stands in the wrong. On the other hand, communicating "an increase of love" will let the reproved person "know that thy faithfulness is stronger than the cords of death" (D&C 121:43–44; see also the Notes on 4:29; 5:11, 13).

let not the sun go down: This requirement is as old as the Mosaic law. It surfaced in the demand that an employer pay a day-laborer the salary coming to him before "the sun shall go down upon it" or "upon him" (Deut. 24:15). No postponement of payment was allowed. For if that happened to a poor person and "he cry against thee unto the Lord," then the refusal of payment, frighteningly, became a celestial matter. In that case, in the eyes of God "it be sin unto thee," with wrathful divine consequences to

---

394. See Prov. 15:1, 18; 22:24; 29:8; Eccl. 7:9; Gal. 5:19–20; Col. 3:8; 1 Tim. 2:8; Titus 1:7.

follow (see Luke 12:4–5 and Heb. 10:31). That situation lies behind Paul's words here.

4:27 *place:* The noun τόπος (*topos*) most often focuses on a location, whether a place or a building.[395] In our case, however, its meaning concerns opportunity or chance.[396] We encounter this sense once elsewhere in Paul's letters. In a discussion of a church member taking vengeance against someone who had wronged that person, the Apostle first pled that the believer "live peaceably with all men." Then he instructed, "Avenge not yourselves, but rather give place [*topos*] unto [God's] wrath" because "I will repay, saith the Lord" (Rom. 12:18–19, loosely quoting Deut. 32:35; see also Ps. 94:1 and Prov. 24:29). With the denotation of opportunity or chance, we find *topos* in the mouth of Festus, the governor of the Judean province, when explaining to King Agrippa why Paul would not be going back to Jerusalem for trial in front of Jewish magistrates. To those magistrates, who had agitated to get Paul back in Jerusalem, Festus had said earlier that "it is not the Roman custom to hand over any man before he . . . has had an opportunity [*topos*] to defend himself against their charges" (Acts 25:16 NIV). The last instance of this meaning of *topos* in the New Testament concerns Esau's failed effort to get back the birthright blessing (see Gen. 27:30–40). We read these words: "When [Esau] wanted to inherit this blessing, he was rejected. He could bring about no change [*topos*] of mind, though he sought the blessing with tears" (Heb. 12:17 NIV).

the devil: We have already come upon this personality in 2:2 and will do so again at 6:11 and 6:16. He has been with humankind "from the beginning," having distinguished himself as "a murderer" (John 8:44). The allusion doubtless has reference to the killing of Abel, an act plotted by Cain and Satan (see Moses 5:29–32, 38). The Genesis text does not preserve this detail, although it is hinted at in John 8:44: "the devil . . . was a murderer from the beginning" (see also Hel. 6:27 and Ether 8:15). In short, the devil holds sway throughout the earth, and people are generally powerless to escape his influence because he is "the god of this world" (2 Cor. 4:4). However, he possesses power over humankind only as allowed by God (see Luke 4:6). Notably, the coming of Christ—both the promise of his coming and his actual arrival—changed everything for the devil. The Savior's activities and those of his authorized servants have not only weakened but shattered the devil's base of operation. Jesus said to his seventy

---

395. BDAG, 1011.
396. Helmut Köster, *TDNT,* 8:205–6; BDAG, 1012; Louw-Nida, §71.6.

disciples upon their return from their preaching missions, "I beheld Satan as lightning fall from heaven" (Luke 10:18). So great were the cracks in the devil's dominions that, decades after Jesus' Atonement, John could write to youthful church members in Asia Minor, "Ye have overcome the wicked one" (1 John 2:13). To the Saints residing in Thessalonica, Paul declared that "the Lord is faithful, and he will strengthen and protect you from the evil one" (2 Thes. 3:3 NIV).[397] Victory will become so total that "the God of peace will soon crush Satan under your feet" (Rom. 16:20 NIV;[398] see also the Notes on 2:2; 6:11, 16).

4:28 *Let him that stole:* With these words, the Apostle led his readers into the world of bad and good actions through the next few verses, the good intended to correct and overcome the bad. To set up his review, he began with a real crime, stealing. The law of Moses had already inveighed against this action: "Thou shalt not steal" (Ex. 20:15; see also Lev. 19:11 and Deut. 5:19). Paul now moved into his reform program for those guilty of stealing. Even if, in fact, this verse directs us into the world of slavery, as noted just below, the principle of honest work applies to all, wherever individuals may be on the economic ladder.

steal no more: This appeal brings the modern reader into direct contact with the bottom rung of ancient society. Particularly among slaves, stealing and thievery were common practices.[399] A person requires little imagination to grasp why this was so among a terribly depressed group of people who lacked access to any of the services and goods that made life tolerable for even the lowest class of society. In the context, the stealing seems to have nothing to do with sexual transgression. Rather, the matter had to do with covetousness and the illicit acquisition of another's property.[400] Such a thought lies behind Paul's question to his Roman readers: "Thou that preachest a man should not steal, dost thou steal?" (Rom. 2:21; see also 1 Pet. 4:15). His question opened up the issue to more than the lower classes represented in a congregation; its grasp also reached those who held responsible positions in the citizenry. Perhaps the most enduring consequence of such acts rests in the betrayal of the fellowship of trust and love within a Christian community.[401]

---

397. Von Rad and Foerster, *TDNT,* 2:79–80.
398. Werner Foerster and Knut Schäferdiek, *TDNT,* 7:161–62.
399. Caird, *Letters,* 82; Lincoln, *Ephesians,* 303.
400. Gerhard Delling, *TDNT,* 6:271–72.
401. Herbert Preisker, *TDNT,* 3:755; Barth, *Ephesians,* 2:515–16.

labour: Because of the present tense, this present tense, third-person imperative—a form usually translated "let him" or "may she"—of the verb κοπιάω (*kopiaō*) ushers in the senses of beginning and continuing. That is, within one thought the Apostle was urging his readers both to begin and to continue to work diligently and to avoid the temptation to steal.[402] One of the meanings of the verb *kopiaō* is "to grow weary."[403] Like many verbs, it exhibits both literal and figurative denotations. On the literal side, for instance, we read that Jesus, having reached Jacob's well, "wearied [*kopiaō*] as he was with his journey, sat down beside the well" (John 4:6 RSV; see also 1 Cor. 4:12). The same idea appears in the following words, with an added nod to the end-time to be enjoyed with Jesus himself: "Come unto me, all ye that labor [*kopiaō*], and are heavy laden, and I will give you rest" (Matt. 11:28). The verb *kopiaō* also bears the related thought of "wearing oneself out." This is the import of the verb in our passage here.[404] We see this sense in Peter's words to Jesus next to the shore of the Sea of Galilee when, sitting together in a fishing boat, he said, "Master, we have toiled [*kopiaō*] all the night, and have taken nothing: nevertheless at thy word I will let down the net" (Luke 5:5; see also Matt. 6:28).

In its metaphorical clothing, we frequently see the verb *kopiaō* and its associated noun κόπος (*kopos*) in Paul's Epistles when he was writing about the burden that he had taken up for Christ. One sample occurs in 1 Thessalonians 2:9: "Ye remember, brethren, our labor [*kopos*] and travail . . . [when] we preached unto you the gospel of God." On one level, he understood his labors as a measure of personal satisfaction. When making a point about "false apostles" who had come to Corinth, he wrote, "Are they ministers of Christ? . . . I am more; in labors [*kopos*] more abundant, in stripes above measure, in prisons more frequent" (2 Cor. 11:13, 23; see also 1 Cor. 15:10). But he also grasped that he was not alone in his labors. For God had braced him up and multiplied his efforts to bring people to Christ. This notion lies visibly in the foreground when he wrote about his hope "that we may present every man mature in Christ.[405] For this I toil [*kopiaō*], striving with all the energy which he mightily inspires within me" (Col. 1:28–29 RSV). At the end, he hoped that his labors would bear

---

402. Merkle, *Guide*, 149.

403. BDAG, 558.

404. Friedrich Hauck, *TDNT*, 3:828–29; BDAG, 558.

405. The KJV reads "Christ Jesus" at the end of Col. 1:28. But the best manuscripts, including the earliest, 𝔓⁴⁶, do not preserve the name Jesus. See Aland and others, *Novum Testamentum Graece*, 525.

eternal fruit for himself "that I may rejoice in the day of Christ, that I have not run in vain, neither laboured [*kopiaō*] in vain" (Philip. 2:16; see also 1 Thes. 3:8).[406]

working with his hands: The Apostle's plan sought to repatriate those who, for whatever reasons, had kept their lives going by thievery, even if they also had to work with their hands. Of course, he knew that old patterns would be difficult to change. But he could look to Christ for genuine aid to help believers quash old habits and routines and adopt new ones. In general, such work does not match the "good works" that flow from one's faith (see 2:10 and Acts 26:20). What Paul had in mind in our passage is physical labor that improves a person's status, whether slave or free. He himself pursued honorable, physical labor so that he, as an itinerant preacher, would not have to depend on gifts from others (see Acts 20:34; 1 Cor. 4:12; 1 Thes. 2:9; and 2 Thes. 3:8). He expected this kind of behavior from fellow church members. If we listen, we hear him say with reference to what he had taught the Thessalonians when he was among them, "That ye study to be quiet, and to do your own business, and to work with your own hands, as we commanded you" (1 Thes. 4:11). This counsel did not accomplish all that he had hoped. When he wrote again, he included these lines: "When we were with you, this we commanded you, that if any would not work, neither should he eat" (2 Thes. 3:10). What had generated this straight talk? "We hear that there are some which walk among you disorderly, working not at all." What was the Apostle's response? In setting out his solution, he invoked the name of "our Lord Jesus Christ," making the matter one of ultimate status with God: "Them that are such we command and exhort by our Lord Jesus Christ, that with quietness they work" (2 Thes. 3:10–12). By these means, believers would become useful servants to masters and upright members of their societies, thus bringing to church members a much-needed positive reputation within their communities.[407]

hands: A person's hands (plural of χείρ, *cheir*) bear the brunt of physical work, and thus form an ennobling part of the body. As we have seen in the paragraph above, hands also tie to the work of Christ on earth (see 2 Thes. 3:12). Besides physical work that produces enough to feed a family and creates an abundance that allows a believer to give "to him that needeth," "hands" link directly to holy acts (see Acts 6:6; 8:17). Whether Paul thought about the connection between having clean hands and performing sacred tasks we cannot know. But a connection there is. In the Gospels, the examples

---

406. Hauck, *TDNT,* 3:829.

407. Bertram, *TDNT,* 2:649–50; Preisker, *TDNT,* 3:755 n. 3; Perkins, *Ephesians,* 108–9.

of Jesus healing by the touch of his hands are many. Jesus transferred his powers to the Twelve and Seventy (see Luke 9:1; 10:1); hence, we run into accounts of disciples healing people by the touch of their hands. In one of the earliest instances, we follow Peter and John toward the Court of the Women at the Jerusalem temple. At the approach, they met a "man lame from his mother's womb." This unnamed man, asking alms of temple visitors, met the gaze of the two apostles. After Peter invoked "the name of Jesus Christ of Nazareth . . . he took [the lame man] by the right hand, and lifted him up: and immediately his feet and ankle bones received strength," healing him (Acts 3:2, 6–7; see also Acts 9:36–41). Paul himself was healed of blindness by the laying on of hands by the reliable Ananias, who came to the future apostle at God's behest (see Acts 9:10–18).[408] There is more.

By the laying on of hands, church leaders conferred divine power on those being set apart for a special work. Following the pattern set down by Jesus with the Twelve (see Luke 9:1), leaders of the congregation at Antioch, who were titled "prophets and teachers," "laid their hands on" Paul and Barnabas and "sent them away" on what we have come to know as Paul's first missionary journey (Acts 13:1, 3). Luke's account lays emphasis on several key factors that guided those church leaders. In the first place, they were fasting when "the Holy Ghost said, Separate me Barnabas and Saul for the work whereunto I have called them." By such words, fasting and the direction of the Holy Ghost emerge from this experience as essential ingredients. Afterwards, they "fasted [again] and prayed" before sending the two missionaries on their way (Acts 13:2–3). The lesson? The story makes crystal clear that, first, the guidance of God's Spirit and, second, the seeking of that guidance through fasting and prayer before laying hands on Paul and Barnabas were the grand spiritual keys that underlay the ordinance of the laying on of hands (see the Notes on 2:20; 4:11).[409]

the thing which is good: This expression rests on a simple noun and its definite article (τὸ ἀγαθόν, *to agathon*) that a translator can render "the good." This fact has given rise to an understanding of "the good" as "the progress of the gospel."[410] Readers might also take the noun to refer to "honest work."[411] As tantalizing as these ideas may be, it seems better to think that the next line defines "the good": "that he may have to give to him that needeth."[412]

---

408. Lohse, *TDNT,* 9:431–32.
409. Lohse, *TDNT,* 9:433.
410. Muddiman, *Ephesians,* 228.
411. Best, *Ephesians,* 454–55; Larkin, *Handbook,* 100–101.
412. Barth, *Ephesians,* 2:517; Lincoln, *Ephesians,* 304; Merkle, *Guide,* 150.

to give to him that needeth: Of all the kindnesses that one person who has can offer to another who has not, the gift of necessities ranks very high. We now see the aim of the Apostle's program to take stealing out of a thief's life. Such a transformative undertaking and the person's inner experience of joy when giving such a gift cannot be measured by human means. Especially among slaves, through their diligent work for masters and mistresses and through scraping together even the smallest of extras, they were to practice charity by giving to others who were in need, as though these people were not themselves in need. If the poorest people could be charitable, so could everyone else (see the "poor widow" of Luke 21:1–4). One is almost left speechless. For the giver, "conduct like this will be a sure proof of a changed heart."[413]

4:29 ***Let no corrupt communication proceed:*** With these words, Paul stepped away from the tough world of crime and escorted readers into the sphere where spoken words predominate[414]—all kinds of words, both good and bad. For good reasons, as we shall see, he sought to excise the bad words from the speech of his fellow Saints.

no: As this term (πᾶς, *pas*) appears here, without a definite article and bound to the following noun translated "word" (λόγος, *logos*), it bears the sense of "none at all." No exceptions are allowed. Period.[415]

corrupt communication: This pair of Greek words (λόγος σαπρός, *logos sapros*) dredge up a common characterization of words that carry malice. All languages exhibit this kind of negative thrust, a thrust aimed at causing hurt or misdirection or misrepresentation. This last is exactly what readers find at 5:6: "erroneous words" (NR). We compare expressions such as "flattering words" (1 Thes. 2:5) and "malicious words" (3 John 1:10). For Christians, however, genuine words come from God. Such words come by revelation. More than this, they send us to the one who uttered them, to God himself.[416] Hence, words matter. How much? The next lines tell us, not only on the human side but also on the divine. Believers need to hear words that are "good for the building up of the one in need" and "do not offend the Holy Spirit of God" (4:29–30 NR; see also the Notes on 5:4, 6).[417]

---

413. Bruce, *Ephesians*, 98; see also Preisker, *TDNT*, 3:755 n. 3.

414. Debrunner, Kleinknecht, Procksch, Kittel, Quell, and Schrenk, *TDNT*, 4:101–2.

415. Reicke and Bertram, *TDNT*, 5:888.

416. Debrunner, Kleinknecht, Procksch, Kittel, Quell, and Schrenk, *TDNT*, 4:101–2.

417. Rudolph Bultmann, *TDNT*, 4:322; Otto Bauernfeind, *TDNT*, 7:97.

proceed out of: In general, the verb ἐκπορεύομαι (*ekporeuomai*) displays the meaning "to go out" or "to come forth."[418] It describes both good and bad actions. On the good side, we hear about those whose hearts resonated with the preaching of John the Baptist and "went out to him [from] Jerusalem, and all Judea" (Matt. 3:5). In the sphere of God's powers to be manifested at the end-time, "out of his mouth goeth a sharp sword, that with it he should smite the nations" (Rev. 19:15; see also Rev. 1:16). In the resurrection, the dead will hear God's voice and "come forth" (John 5:29). On the bad side, we listen to Jesus' words to a multitude to whom he declared: "Not that which goeth into the mouth defileth a man; but that which cometh out of [*ekporeuomai*] the mouth, this defileth a man." A few moments later, Jesus repeated his point with an unusual fist-pounding emphasis: "Those things which proceedeth out of [*ekporeuomai*] the mouth come forth from the heart; and they defile the man" (Matt. 15:11, 18).[419] This was precisely Paul's point.

mouth: The mouth (στόμα, *stoma*), of course, brings up a number of scenes, both literal and spiritual. As we might expect, in some contexts the mouth is equated with speech (see Luke 1:64 and Acts 1:16).[420] This equivalency is virtually the case in James's complaints about the tongue and the mouth. We hear his strong declamations: "The tongue is a fire, a world of iniquity ... [so] that it defileth the whole body, ... an unruly evil, full of deadly poison. Therewith bless we God ... and therewith curse we men." In summary, James wrote, "Out of the same mouth proceedeth blessing and cursing." Finally came James's sober appeal: "My brethren, these things ought not so to be" (James 3:6, 8–10).

The reason that "these things ought not so to be" was because for centuries the mouth had enjoyed a special status in religious events and sacred settings. In ancient Egyptian religion, for example, the ceremony that opened the mouth not only of the statues of deities but also of the dead in mummified form was to enliven the person while residing in the next world.[421] In the Old Testament, God opened his mouth and spoke words of creation that we read in the couplets "God said" and "God called" (see Gen. 1:3, 5, 6, 8, 9, 10, 11; etc.). In the creation of humankind, begun with Adam, through his mouth God "breathed into [Adam's] nostrils the breath

---

418. Friedrich Hauck and Siegfried Schulz, *TDNT,* 6:579; BDAG, 308–9.
419. Hauck and Schulz, *TDNT,* 6:579.
420. Louw-Nida, §§33.74–75.
421. Konrad Weiss, *TDNT,* 7:694; Morenz, *Egyptian Religion,* 155, 219–20, 319 n. 77.

of life" (Gen. 2:7). In the matter of prophetic speech, the mouth of the one called to be a prophet was sanctified, and then the person spoke the words of God. For instance, Isaiah's mouth was cleansed by a hot coal from the incense altar in the heavenly temple, and then he was sent by the Lord with a divine message (see Isa. 6:7, 9–10). Similarly, the Lord "touched [Jeremiah's] mouth," thus installing "my words in thy mouth" (Jer. 1:9). On his part, Ezekiel ate the words of God, ingesting them so that he became effectively the mouthpiece of God (see Ezek. 3:1–3). With these divine associations of the mouth, it is no wonder that the Apostle expressed concern about how believers conducted communication (see the Note on 6:19).

the use: The noun (χρεία, *chreia*) is the same that we have met in the expression in 4:28, translated in the KJV as "him that needeth" and better rendered "the one who is in need" (NR). Its basic sense is "need" or "lack."[422] Those who lack, we might presume, are fellow church members. But that need not be so. Outsiders are also worthy of a believer's good conduct, including both generosity (see 4:28) and edifying conversation. These kinds of behaviors are the interior, rock-hard indicators of Christian love,[423] whether visible to others or not.

edifying: As in 4:12 and 4:16, the meaning of the noun οἰκοδομή (*oikodomē*) pertains to the building up of both individuals and one's congregation.[424] In this case, the building up of one's fellow believers and one's congregation involves a sensitivity to different "measures and stages of faith."[425] That is the thought that lies behind the granting of grace or a gift.[426] In other passages, Paul connected edification to authority. There he insisted that his apostolic authority, "which the Lord hath given us," was intended to edify, to build up, and "not for your destruction" (2 Cor. 10:8; see also 2 Cor. 13:10). The essence of his words mirrors that in modern scripture where we learn that "no power or influence can or ought to be maintained by virtue of the priesthood, only by persuasion, by long-suffering, by gentleness and meekness, and by love unfeigned," even when sharpness may seem to be called for (D&C 121:41). In that eventuality, it must be driven only "by the [inspiration of the] Holy Ghost," with a

---

422. BDAG, 1088; Louw-Nida, §57.40.
423. Lincoln, *Ephesians,* 304.
424. BDAG, 696.1.b.α.
425. Gustav Stählin, *TDNT,* 6:715.
426. Both Barth, *Ephesians,* 1:272, and Lincoln, *Ephesians,* 156, hold that the edifying is aimed at the entire church, an impossible task for any individual who hears this letter read.

demonstration "afterwards [of] an increase of love toward him whom thou hast reproved" (D&C 121:43; see also the Notes on 2:21; 4:12, 16).

grace: This grace is not precisely the same as that which we meet in 3:2 and 3:7, although the same verb, which means "to give" (δίδωμι, *didōmi*), stands together with *charis* in the earlier two passages and this one. The grace noted in 3:2 and 3:7 comes directly from God. The grace mentioned in our passage goes to "the [speaker's] hearers." Thus, the imparted gift is not salvation (see 2:8). Rather, its inner spring lifts listeners up and edifies them. This sense stands close to the angel's words to Mary, "Thou hast found favor [*charis*] with God" (Luke 1:30), and to Luke's summary of Jesus' youth, that he "increased in wisdom and stature, and in favor [*charis*] with God and man" (Luke 2:52; see also Luke 2:40 and Acts 7:10).[427] The beneficiaries of such favors, of such gifts, are "the hearers" with whom the giver forms a reciprocal relationship that edifies both.[428] In truth, the *charis* consists of not only the gift of hearing but also that of believing, as we read: "After you *heard* the word of truth . . . and *believed*—you were sealed by the Holy Spirit of Promise" (1:13 NR, emphasis added; see the Notes on 2:5, 8; 4:7).[429]

4:30 *grieve not:* Recognizing that the verb λυπέω (*lypeō*) offers the meaning "to offend" or "to insult,"[430] a reader senses behind this verb that the "Spirit of God" can be saddened by anyone who turns away from the joy and gladness of the gospel message and pivots back to "the old person" (4:22 NR), thereby giving "place to the devil" (4:27) and uttering "corrupt communication" out of the mouth (4:29). On God's part, he feels after us in love. Said one way, "the God proclaimed in Ephesians is not an unmoved mover."[431] Said another, "in all their affliction [the Lord] was afflicted" (Isa. 63:9).[432] In a word, human insults, human offenses, human troubles affect God. From an era earlier than Isaiah, the prophet Hosea shined a light on God's feelings for his wayward children, the people of northern Israel, whom he had to punish: "How shall I give thee up, Ephraim? how shall I deliver thee, Israel? . . . Mine heart is turned within me." Out of his deep feelings of love, God determined not to make an end of Israel. We listen to his words: "My repentings are kindled together. I will not execute the fierceness of mine anger, I will not return to destroy Ephraim: for I am

---

427. Conzelmann and Zimmerli, *TDNT,* 9:392.
428. Conzelmann and Zimmerli, *TDNT,* 9:373–78.
429. Barth, *Ephesians,* 2:520.
430. Rudolf Bultmann, *TDNT,* 4:322; BDAG, 604; Louw-Nida, §25.275.
431. Barth, *Ephesians,* 2:548.
432. Barth, *Ephesians,* 2:549.

God, and not man; the Holy One in the midst of thee" (Hosea 11:8–9). A century and a half later, as God watched the people of Judah slide into apostasy, he inspired Jeremiah to declare on his behalf, "Woe is me for my hurt! my wound is grievous: but I said, Truly this is a grief, and I must bear it" (Jer. 10:19; see also Jer. 4:19 and Moses 7:28, "the God of heaven . . . wept"). Like the pictures in these early sources, Paul portrays God as one who possesses deep and lasting love.[433]

holy Spirit of God: Undoubtedly, this personality is the Holy Ghost, the one grieved by the wicked actions and words of believers. In a much earlier era, that of the Exodus, God "in his love and in his pity . . . redeemed [the Hebrew slaves]; and he bare them, and carried them all the days of old" (Isa. 63:9). But as was the usual story, "they rebelled, and vexed his holy Spirit." As a result, "he was turned to be their enemy, and he fought against them" (Isa. 63:10). So it is in this letter. Through his Spirit, God is willing to nourish and carry his people, making both Gentiles and Jews "fellowheirs, and of the same body, and partakers of his promise in Christ" (3:6). More than this, his Spirit has "sealed [them] unto the day of redemption" (4:30). However, such a divine seal can be lost without vigilance (see Matt. 13:5–6; Mark 4:5–6; Luke 8:6; Heb. 2:1; 3:12; and the Notes on 1:13; 2:18; 5:19).[434]

The matter of blaspheming against the Holy Ghost falls close to the topic in this verse, though a more grave offense. Jesus warned against this kind of sin when he intoned that "blasphemy against the Holy Ghost shall not be forgiven unto men" (Matt. 12:31; see also Mark 3:29 and Luke 12:10). What exactly does "blasphemy against the Holy Ghost" mean? The Epistle to the Hebrews offers the one helpful answer: "It is impossible for those who were once enlightened, and have tasted of the heavenly gift, and were made partakers of the Holy Ghost, . . . if they shall fall away, to renew them again unto repentance; seeing they crucify to themselves the Son of God afresh, and put him to an open shame" (Heb. 6:4, 6; see also Heb. 10:29). A more nuanced response reposes in modern scripture. There we read the Risen Christ's words that "blasphemy against the Holy Ghost . . . is in that ye commit murder wherein ye shed [Christ's] innocent blood, and assent unto my death, after ye have received my new and everlasting covenant, saith the Lord God" (D&C 132:27). To put it another way, "the innocent blood is that of Christ; and those who commit blasphemy against the Holy Ghost . . . thereby 'crucify to themselves the Son of God afresh, and put

---

433. Lincoln, *Ephesians*, 306–7.
434. Sjöberg and Schweizer, *TDNT*, 6:445; see also Heinrich Schlier, *TDNT*, 1:513–14.

him to an open shame.' (Heb. 6:6.) They are, in other words, people who would have crucified Christ, having [all] the while a perfect knowledge that he was the Son of God" (see Alma 39:6).[435]

ye are sealed: As we have learned in the discussion on 1:13, the act of sealing (verb σφραγίζω, *sphragizō*) and the use of the seal itself (noun σφραγίς, *sphragis*) exhibit a long history and relate to the need to certify the authenticity of goods and communiques.[436] In the gospel context, the seal comes from God's Spirit and follows baptism. In a figurative sense, it is compared to circumcision, which Abraham received after exercising faith and attaining a level of righteousness, but not before (see Rom. 4:8–13). Also like circumcision, there was a physical aspect for the Christian believer—namely, receiving an anointing: "God establishes us with you in Christ and has anointed us, who sealed us and gave us his Spirit in our hearts as a promise" (2 Cor. 1:21–22, Wayment). At some point after a convert had found faith, had repented and accepted baptism, and had come to stand justified before God—in other words, had been made upright by him—the person then received an anointing that spiritually marked him or her as God's possession.[437]

Both in the past and in the future, a seal or mark has formed an important identifier, or will become such. For example, the Hebrew slaves daubed blood from a slaughtered lamb on their exterior doorframes to escape God's final plague that was to rush down upon the Egyptians (see Ex. 12:7, 12). As a second example, God instructed one of the angels who had charge of Jerusalem to pass "through the midst of the city, through the midst of Jerusalem, and set a mark (ות, *taw*)[438] upon the foreheads of the men that sigh and that cry for all the abominations that be done in the midst thereof" (Ezek. 9:4). This mark of the letter *taw* on the forehead looked like an *X* when written in Ezekiel's day. Those who bore this seal or mark would be spared when the city was emptied of its inhabitants (see Ezek. 9:5–9). Likewise, in the future, the servants of God are to receive such a mark on their foreheads to preserve them from God's wrath in the last days (see Rev. 7:3; 9:4; 14:1; 22:4). This kind of sealing stands in stark contrast with the seal or mark of the beast given to those who do business in his way (see

435. Bruce R. McConkie, *Doctrinal New Testament Commentary,* 3 vols. (Salt Lake City: Bookcraft, 1965–73), 3:345.

436. Fitzer, *TDNT,* 7:939–50; BDAG, 980–81; Thayer, *Lexicon,* 609.

437. Fitzer, *TDNT,* 7:949–50.

438. BDB, 1063.

Rev. 13:16; 14:9; 20:4). In fact, his mistress, the harlot "who personifies all worldly abominations," wears a long name written on her forehead like a seal (see Rev. 17:5;[439] see also the Note on 1:13).

unto: This preposition (εἰς, *eis*) denotes time in this setting, particularly a span of time "until the day of redemption." Thus it is better translated "until" or "for," as in "for the day of redemption" (NR; see also Philip. 1:10, "till the day of Christ").[440]

day: As in the Gospels, the "day" (ἡμέρα, *hēmera*) for Paul belongs to Christ. Often, Christ's day is about his return, his Second Coming. The expressions "day of the Lord" and "day of our Lord Jesus" illustrate this observation. We read that church members in Thessalonica knew "perfectly that the day of the Lord so cometh as a thief in the night" (1 Thes. 5:2; see also 1 Thes. 5:4). Heartwarming is Paul's promise that steadfast believers will be "blameless in the day of our Lord Jesus Christ," an obvious reference to the Second Coming (1 Cor. 1:8; see also 2 Cor. 1:14; 6:2, "day of salvation"). Reaching farther back in time, the Savior's words pierced the air as he anticipated his own death: "The days will come, when the bridegroom shall be taken from them, and then shall they fast" (Mark 2:20; see also Matt. 9:15 and Luke 5:35). With a focus on his Second Coming, Jesus said these words to his disciples on the Mount of Olives: "After the tribulation of those days shall the sun be darkened, . . . and then shall appear the sign of the Son of man in heaven: . . . and they shall see the Son of man coming in the clouds of heaven" (Matt. 24:29–30). The day of the First Resurrection is to accompany the Second Coming (see 1 Thes. 4:16–17) and, in John's Gospel, is called "the last day" (John 6:39–40, 44, 54; 11:24;[441] see the Notes on 5:16; 6:13).

redemption: As we learned in the discussion of this noun (ἀπολύτρωσις, *apolytrōsis*) in the Note on 1:7, the roots of redemption reach back into Old Testament times wherein one person could redeem another—a captive, a prisoner, a slave—by the payment of an agreed-upon sum.[442] For instance, to redeem a person—often a youth—who had been sold into slavery in order to pay a debt, the Mosaic law set out rules for redeeming or freeing the slave, with the clear understanding that all involved in the transaction were themselves God's servants or slaves because he had redeemed his

---

439. Carl Schneider, *TDNT*, 4:635–37, quotation on 637.
440. Oepke, *TDNT*, 2:426–27.
441. Gerhard von Rad and Gerhard Delling, *TDNT*, 2:952–53.
442. Procksch and Büchsel, *TDNT*, 4:352.

people from Egypt (see Lev. 25:47–54). Thus, God himself had exercised redeeming power on behalf of his people. As the Psalmist sang in gratitude for God's assistance, "Let the words of my mouth, and the meditation of my heart, be acceptable in thy sight, O Lord, my strength and my redeemer" (Ps. 19:14; see also Ps. 78:35).

As indicated above, for Israelites the laws of redemption rested on the fact that God, exercising a legal right, had gone into Egypt, redeemed his people, and brought them out. The Hebrews belonged to him, and the Egyptians had put them into bondage without any arrangement with the Hebrews' master, the Lord God.[443] Hence, with no little pique, God informed Moses that "I will rid [all of] you of their bondage, and I will redeem [all of] you with a stretched out arm, and with great judgments" (Ex. 6:6). Importantly, God did not have to do this—except for the covenant with Abraham that he would give the land of Canaan to his descendants (see Gen. 15:18; 17:7–8; see also Gen. 26:2–5; 28:13–15). Even so, his actions were driven by his mercy, as we hear Moses sing following the Israelites' escape, "Thou in thy mercy hast led forth the people which thou hast redeemed" (Ex. 15:13).

When we swing around to the New Testament, we find the tapestry adorned with different colors and woven with various textures. The Old Testament world of redeeming slaves and captives fades from view. In its place stands Jesus Christ, both the redeemer and the redemption. That is to say, outside of Christ we find no redemption that "has its own intrinsic life and power apart from His person."[444] In Paul's language, believers are "justified freely by [God's] grace through the redemption [*apolytrōsis*] that is in Christ Jesus" (Rom. 3:24). Said more directly, "of [God] are ye in Christ Jesus, who of God is made unto us wisdom, and righteousness, and sanctification, and redemption [*apolytrōsis*]" (1 Cor. 1:30). Thus, one may say, through his Father's power Christ is the personification of redemption and its eternal blessings that come to believers "in personal fellowship with Him."[445]

For the Apostle, the Savior's redemption, his Atonement, reaches into believers' lives here and now, drawing in powers beyond their own (see the Notes on 1:9; 2:7, 16; 3:16). Moreover, the redemption impacts one's physical body, making it everlasting. Paul understood that the redeeming

---

443. David Daube, *The Exodus Pattern in the Bible* (London: Faber and Faber, 1963), 42–46.

444. Procksch and Büchsel, *TDNT,* 4:354.

445. Procksch and Büchsel, *TDNT,* 4:353–54, quotation on 354.

powers of Christ touch the physical world, with a precise promise about human bodies. When speaking about longing for salvation, he wrote that "even we ourselves groan within ourselves, waiting for . . . the redemption of our body" (Rom. 8:23). What he meant was that "this corruptible [body] must put on incorruption, and this mortal [body] must put on immortality" (1 Cor. 15:53; see also Rom. 8:21 and 1 Cor. 15:42–44). In other words, the assured immortality of all persons will be spent in physical bodies. The story goes on. In Paul's words, "the Lord Jesus Christ . . . shall change our vile body, that it may be fashioned like unto his glorious body" (Philip. 3:20–21).[446] May it be so!

One last element needs attention. There exists a view that Christ's redemption does not involve a payment or the satisfying of a ransom.[447] This is where the Restoration makes a firm, clear contribution. Paul forms the starting point. We stand very close to the idea of payment in his words "Christ hath redeemed us from the curse of the law, being made a curse for us" (Gal. 3:13). The same can be said of his assertion that "God sent forth his Son . . . to redeem them that were under the law, that we might receive the adoption of sons" (Gal. 4:4–5). Besides the rich idea of sonship touched on here (see the Note on 1:5), the combined two passages center on a payment made in accord with the Mosaic law, or any set of laws, whose strictures entrap people in lives of sin. Christ's payment freed people from the captivity of having to worry about breaking one rule or another. We listen to the mortal Jesus speaking to acquaintances in the Nazareth synagogue about his Father's commissioning act: "[God] hath sent me . . . to preach deliverance to the captives, . . . to set at liberty them that are bruised" (Luke 4:18). More striking, perhaps, is the line "the man Christ Jesus, who gave himself as a ransom for all men," coupled with "our great God and Savior, Jesus Christ, who gave himself for us to redeem us from all wickedness" (1 Tim. 2:6 NIV; Titus 2:14 NIV).

To make the case more clear, modern scripture lays out a picture of the Savior paying a price by taking upon himself the transgressions and sins of those who will follow him. How otherwise shall we understand his words in Gethsemane, "My soul is overwhelmed with sorrow to the point of death," as our sins crashed down onto him (Mark 14:34 NIV)? Just moments earlier, he had begun "to be sore amazed, and to be very heavy" (Mark 14:33).[448] From what was he recoiling? From the pains of payment for sin. We turn to

---

446. Procksch and Büchsel, *TDNT,* 4:352.

447. Procksch and Büchsel, *TDNT,* 4:354–55.

448. For a different slant, JST Mark 14:36 states that it was the disciples who "began to be sore amazed, and to be very heavy."

the book of Alma, where we read Alma's words to his wayward son Corianton: "The plan of mercy could not be brought about except an atonement should be made." What did that plan of mercy consist of? "God himself atoneth for the sins of the world, to bring about the plan of mercy, *to appease* the demands of justice" (Alma 42:15, emphasis added). This appeasement was a payment to satisfy the justice that required each person to suffer for her or his transgressions. Other passages are relevant.

A famous speech by a soon-to-be-executed prophet named Abinadi declared that Christ was "filled with compassion towards the children of men; standing betwixt them and justice; having broken the bands of death, [having] taken upon himself their iniquity and their transgressions, having redeemed them, and satisfied *the demands of justice*" (Mosiah 15:9, emphasis added; see also Alma 34:16, "mercy can satisfy the demands of justice, and encircles them in the arms of safety"). And what are these "demands of justice"? Without Christ's redemption, the human family would lie in the grasp of "that awful monster, death and hell, and the devil, and the lake of fire and brimstone, which is endless torment" (2 Ne. 9:26; see also Alma 42:24, "justice exerciseth all his demands, and also mercy claimeth all which is her own"). There is more.

We look to the book of Ether, where we listen to the premortal Redeemer's words to the brother of Jared: "Behold, I am he who was prepared from the foundation of the world to redeem my people . . . and they shall become my sons and my daughters" (Ether 3:14). Further, in reference to Christ's redeeming death, we learn that believers "are they whose sins he has borne; these are they for whom he has died, to redeem them from their transgressions" (Mosiah 15:12; see also D&C 133:53). In different words, "He offereth himself a sacrifice for sin, to answer the ends of the law, unto all those who have a broken heart and a contrite spirit" (2 Ne. 2:7). Furthermore, "the Son of God suffereth according to the flesh that he might take upon him the sins of his people, that he might blot out their transgressions according to the power of his deliverance" (Alma 7:13). Clearly implied is a payment for sins, a payment for transgressions, a payment that Christ made by suffering for those transgressions and sins. But Christ's redemption, which opens the doors into heaven, has a limit: "Behold, he cometh to redeem those who will be baptized unto repentance, through faith on his name" (Alma 9:27). For "unto none else can the ends of the law be answered" (2 Ne. 2:7; see also Alma 11:40).

With a hope-filled turn, we discover that Christ's redeeming powers paid the price for the fall of Adam and Eve and, through his Resurrection, reversed its horror-filled consequence of endless death for all. An outline of events runs thus: "By Adam came the fall of man. And because of the fall of man came Jesus Christ, . . . and because of Jesus Christ came the redemption of man" (Morm. 9:12). To explain further, "the fall came by reason of transgression; and because man became fallen they were cut off from the presence of the Lord." Redemption was therefore needed. "Wherefore, [Christ's redemption] must needs be an infinite atonement—save it should be an infinite atonement this corruption could not put on incorruption." In fact, "this flesh must have laid down to rot . . . to rise no more" (2 Ne. 9:6–7). In a majestic turnaround, "the death of Christ bringeth to pass the resurrection, which bringeth to pass a redemption from an endless sleep, from which sleep all men shall be awakened by the power of God when the trump shall sound" (Morm. 9:13; for the extended reach of the Atonement, see the Notes on 1:7, 9; 2:7, 16; 3:16, 20; and the Analysis of 1:3–14; for the Atonement as a vicarious act, see 5:2, "given himself for us"; see also 5:25).

4:31 *all:* By introducing the following lists of vices and virtues in verses 4:31 and 4:32, Paul has now departed from the urgent appeals that he wanted his audience to conform to—no stealing, no evil speaking, no knowingly offending God's Spirit—and turned to faults and qualities that characterize the "old person" and the "new person" (4:22, 24 NR; see also Col. 3:8–9). What is so striking is the motivation for abandoning the evil acts and embracing the virtues: God's indescribable forgiveness.[449] In this connection, the word "all" (πᾶσα, *pasa*) applies to all five of the following faults, the phrase "with all malice" carrying its own *pasa*. Incidentally, Paul introduces brief lists at 2 Corinthians 12:20, Galatians 5:19–20, and Colossians 3:8, with the Colossians passage matching more closely the Ephesians register.[450]

bitterness: The noun πικρία (*pikria*) denotes not only a bitter taste in one's mouth about a prior event or personal encounter but also a "sharp, intense resentment" against a person's neighbor.[451] From a review of the list in this verse, one senses that *pikria* and the other vices arise from anger.[452]

wrath: If there is a difference between this noun (θυμός, *thymos*) and the next (ὀργή, *orgē*), that variation generally is slight. The term *thymos* sends readers to "a state of intense anger, with the implication of passionate outbursts."[453] A person glimpses this meaning in Luke 4:28: "All they in the

---

449. Barth, *Ephesians*, 2:521.
450. Muddiman, *Ephesians*, 229.
451. Wilhelm Michaelis, *TDNT*, 6:125; Louw-Nida, §88.201.
452. Best, *Ephesians*, 460; Winger, *Ephesians*, 529.
453. Louw-Nida, §88.178; see also BDAG, 461.

synagogue ... were filled with wrath [*thymos*]." In other contexts, *thymos* and *orgē* intensify each other. Writing about God's judgment, Paul observed that "unto them that are contentious [will come God's] ... indignation [*orgē*] and wrath [*thymos*]" (Rom. 2:8; see also Rev. 16:19, "fierceness of his wrath"; 19:15, "fierceness and wrath").[454] The Stoics may have grasped the difference between the two nouns, holding that *thymos* denoted "an initial explosion of rage" and *orgē* "a more settled feeling of gnawing hostility" (see the Notes on 2:3; 5:6).[455]

anger: Ancient readers understood this noun (ὀργή, *orgē*) as pointing to anger against another person or persons. That sense surely lies behind the apostolic hope that fellow Christians not lift up unholy hands while praying, hands that have lashed out at others: "I will therefore that men pray every where, lifting up holy hands, without wrath [*orgē*] and doubting" (1 Tim. 2:8).[456] In Jesus' Sermon on the Mount, he was blunt about anger and its manifestations: "Whosoever is angry with his brother ...[457] shall be in danger of the judgment" (Matt. 5:22).

The devil is the worst offender, exhibiting undiminished hostility while seeking to destroy God's kingdom. In a scene featuring a red dragon representing Satan and a woman representing Christ's church,[458] we read that "the dragon was wroth with the woman, and went to make war with the remnant of her seed, which keep the commandments of God" (Rev. 12:17).[459] The human representation of satanic anger against Jesus, then an infant, was Herod the king. In a scene tied to the visit of "the wise men," we read that "Herod, when he saw that he was mocked of the wise men, was exceeding wroth, and sent forth, and slew all the children that were in Bethlehem" (Matt. 2:16). Switching subjects, on the side of God's anger, one can see

---

454. Büchsel, *TDNT,* 3:167–68; Kleinknecht, Grether, Procksch, Fichtner, Sjöberg, and Stälin, *TDNT,* 5:384.

455. Lincoln, *Ephesians,* 308; see also Kleinknecht, Grether, Procksch, Fichtner, Sjöberg, and Stälin, *TDNT,* 5:384 n. 6.

456. Louw-Nida, §88.173.

457. In this ellipsis, the KJV reads "without a cause," translating a single Greek word (εἰκῇ, *eikē*). But a number of important ancient manuscripts and early Christian authors omit it, including the earliest manuscript (𝔓⁴⁶) and also the Vulgate. Hence, it is probable "that the word was added by copyists" to Jesus' words. Metzger, *Textual Commentary,* 11. Notably, the Resurrected Christ's Sermon at the Temple at 3 Nephi 12:22 omits this expression, making all the difference. The message? No reason, real or apparent, justifies anger at another person.

458. Draper and Rhodes, *Revelation of John the Apostle,* 431–32, 435–37.

459. Draper and Rhodes, *Revelation of John the Apostle,* 474–75.

a clear indication of the angry, divine weight that will descend on a person who lures young persons into sin in these ominous words from Jesus: "Temptations to sin are sure to come; but woe to him by whom they come! It would be better for him if a millstone were hung round his neck and he were cast into the sea, than that he should cause one of these little ones to sin" (Luke 17:1–2 RSV;[460] see the Notes on 2:3; 4:26; 5:6).

clamour: Among the subject matters of this noun (κραυγή, *kraugē*) are that of weeping (see Rev. 21:4, "neither sorrow, nor crying [*kraugē*]") and crying out in joy, like Elisabeth did when Mary came to her home (see Luke 1:42). But in our passage, 4:31, readers find themselves face-to-face with "people shouting back and forth in a quarrel."[461] It is this kind of outcry that exploded in a meeting of the Sanhedrin that Paul was forced to attend in order to tell the story of his arrest within the temple grounds. As soon as he said, "of the hope and resurrection of the dead I am called in question[,] . . . there arose a great cry," with the representatives of the Pharisees and Sadducees shouting at one another at the tops of their lungs (Acts 23:6, 9).[462] The Pharisees believed in a resurrection, the Sadducees did not. Paul knew that and planted the seed for the shouting match.

evil speaking: The noun is "blasphemy" (βλασφημία, *blasphēmia*). In one of its meanings, the term has to do with reviling or defaming.[463] The seriousness of such an act appears in the archangel Michael's refusal to "bring against [the devil] a railing accusation [*blasphēmia*]" when disputing "about the body of Moses." Rather than do so, he carefully avoided reviling the devil and said instead, "The Lord rebuke thee" (Jude 1:9).[464] Nevertheless, people have reviled God and Christ. For example, in response to the punishment poured out onto the earth by the fifth angel in John's revelation, those affected "gnawed their tongues for pain, and blasphemed the God of heaven" (Rev. 16:10–11; see also Rom. 2:24 and Rev. 16:9, 21). The "beast" who rose out of the sea in the same revelation defamed more than God: "He opened his mouth in blasphemy against God, . . . and his tabernacle, and them that dwell in heaven" (Rev. 13:6; see also 1 Tim. 6:1 and Titus 2:5).

Even though the New Testament uniformly presents blasphemy as an act or utterance that violates the Father's power and majesty, accusations of such actions were, perhaps surprisingly, leveled at Jesus during the last

---

460. Kleinknecht, Grether, Procksch, Fichtner, Sjöberg, and Stälin, *TDNT*, 5:420–21.
461. BDAG, 565; see also Louw-Nida, §25.138.
462. Walter Grundmann, *TDNT*, 3:903.
463. BDAG, 178; Louw-Nida, §33.400.
464. Hermann W. Beyer, *TDNT*, 1:623.

hours of his mortal life. In these instances, the term *blasphēmia* does not occur in the accounts but is present implicitly. The first event occurred during the hearing before Jewish authorities in the high priest's house. There, Jesus was blindfolded and struck "on the face." Then the gathered men shouted at him and demanded, "Prophesy, who is it that smote thee?" (Luke 22:64). It was a clear defaming of Jesus' prophetic powers. In a second occurrence, the crowd at the cross "that passed by reviled him, wagging their heads." They, of course, taunted him that he exercise his powers, if he truly was "the Son of God, [and] come down from the cross" (Matt. 27:39–40; see also Mark 15:29–30 and Luke 23:35–37). The third incident happened in the same place when one of the criminals hurled the challenge to Jesus: "If thou be Christ, save thyself and us" (Luke 23:39;[465] see also the Note on 4:30 for blasphemy against the Holy Ghost).

with all malice: This final phrase indicates to the reader that the preceding list of five vices is incomplete. How so? Because the noun translated "malice" (κακία, *kakia*) is a general term for evil or wickedness.[466] As one commentator observed, almost in the spirit of Lehi's teachings, "κακία is the reality of this cosmos" (see 2 Ne. 2:11–13).[467] On its practical face, the disruption of our relationship with God will inevitably lead to our disruption with fellow believers. From the Apostle, we possess these words: "Because they have not seen fit to acknowledge God, he has given them up to their own depraved reason. This leads them to break all rules of conduct." And what was the consequence? In time, "they are filled with every kind of injustice, mischief, rapacity, and malice [*kakia*]" (Rom. 1:28–29 NEB). It is only through the creation of a community of believers that people have a chance to combat and permanently discard these kinds of wicked behaviors, as we see in the next verse.[468]

4:32 *be ye kind:* Paul has now reversed directions and pulled our attention to the kinds of virtues that will undergird congregations filled with church members.[469] When dealing with a similar list elsewhere, he drew forward the image of putting on a garment (see Col. 3:12). Here, in 4:32, he wrote the imperative of γίνομαι (*ginomai*), "to be" or "to become," in order to make a point about his readers' inner characters, their inner qualities. A person's nature of being "kind" (χρηστός, *chrēstos*)[470] derives from

465. Beyer, *TDNT,* 1:622–23.
466. Barth, *Ephesians,* 2:522–23; BDAG, 500.1.
467. Walter Grundmann, *TDNT,* 3:484.
468. Grundmann, *TDNT,* 3:484.
469. Lincoln, *Ephesians,* 309.
470. BDAG, 1090.3.b.α and β; Louw-Nida, §88.68.

a Heavenly Father who also is kind, as Jesus himself reminded us. We hear his words: "Love ye your enemies, and do good, . . . for [God] is kind [*chrēstos*] unto the unthankful and to the evil." And what was to be the reward? "Ye shall be the children of the Highest." In this lofty place, believers will "therefore [be] merciful, as your Father also is merciful" (Luke 6:35–36; see also Rom. 2:4).[471]

tenderhearted: This adjective (εὔσπλαγχνος, *eusplanchnos*) occurs in only one other passage in the New Testament, with an unusual translation in the KJV: "Be ye all of one mind, . . . love as brethren, be pitiful [*eusplanchnos*]" (1 Pet. 3:8). It would be better to render this term as "compassionate" (NR) or something similar.[472] The noun from which *eusplanchnos* is derived (σπλάγχνα; *splanchna*) refers to entrails. The KJV renders this noun "bowels" in Philippians 2:1: "If there be therefore any consolation in Christ, . . . if any bowels [*splanchna*] and mercies. . . ." Because this noun has to do with the human heart motivating compassionate acts, the following translation of the last clause in the Philippians verse is preferred: "if any tenderness [*splanchna*] and compassion" (NIV; see also Luke 1:78; James 5:11; and 1 John 3:17).[473]

forgiving: The verb (χαρίζομαι, *charizomai*) that underlies this present participle is mirrored at the end of the verse, where it attributes forgiveness to God himself. The initial meaning of the verb relates to "giving as a favor." Forgiving or pardoning represents an extended sense of giving.[474] Jesus led the way by requiring that his hearers "love your enemies, bless them that curse you, do good to them that hate you" (Matt. 5:44; see also Luke 6:35; Matt. 18:21–35; and 2 Cor. 12:13).[475] Although the word "forgiveness" does not occur in these words of Jesus, it forms the underpinning pillar of all such actions. So it was in Christ's giving of himself for us.[476] Believers have to remember that Christ's earlier forgiveness of them frames and predates their own forgiving efforts.[477] That is the very thought behind receiving "redemption through his blood," which brought the unspeakable "forgiveness of sins" (1:7). But after receiving this breathtaking, healing forgiveness, is all settled? Not according to the Savior. His modeling of prayer tells

---

471. Konrad Weiss, *TDNT,* 9:488.
472. BDAG, 413; Louw-Nida, §25.51.
473. Helmut Koester, *TDNT,* 7:556–57.
474. Conzelmann and Zimmerli, *TDNT,* 9:396; BDAG, 1078.3; Louw-Nida, §40.10.
475. Bruce, *Ephesians,* 100.
476. Conzelmann and Zimmerli, *TDNT,* 9:397.
477. Grundmann, Hesse, de Jonge, and van der Woude, *TDNT,* 9:559.

followers that seeking God's forgiveness continues: "Give us day by day our daily bread. And forgive us our sins" (Luke 11:3–4; see also Matt. 6:11–12).

even as: In a majority of cases, the adverb καθώς (*kathōs*) represents a comparison as in the English "just as." But here it bears the causal meaning "because."[478] Hence, the line should read, "forgiving each other because God in Christ forgave you" (NR). The causal clause that begins with "because" in our verse now links forward to the "therefore" (οὖν, *oun*) of 5:1.[479] The result? Believers become "imitators of God" (5:1 NR) as a result of God forgiving them and allowing them to stand clean before him. Church members cannot become like him without him purging their sins (see the Notes on 5:1, 2).

God: Naming God the Father in this context, especially in relation to Christ, does not arise haphazardly. On the contrary, it is the Father who fully invested his Son with all the powers and authority necessary to represent him from "before the foundation of the world" (1:4) to the moment that the Father "set him at his own right hand in the heavenly places [and] . . . put all things under his feet" (1:20, 22).[480]

for Christ's sake: The expression consists of the simple prepositional phrase ἐν Χριστῷ (*en Christō*), which is most readily rendered "in Christ" (NR). We have noticed elsewhere that this phrase was likely invented by Paul to suit his needs (see the Notes on 2:7, 10; 3:6).[481] To render this phrase more roundly, we might write, "in and through Christ." After all, Jesus came from God (see John 8:42; 13:3; 16:28; etc.), and the Father is with him (see Matt. 1:23 and John 3:2). Hence, it is a small step to say that God "works in Him," granting him "all power."[482]

forgiven: The verb here (χαρίζομαι, *charizomai*) takes us back to the prior participle of this same verb. The difference, of course, arises because the first acts of forgiveness mentioned in this verse emerge from believers; the second forgiveness comes from God through Christ. This latter fact alone serves as a sweetened motivation for the believer to forgive others, because the freshening forgiveness from God, soon to arrive, underscores a "divine initiative" on his part toward followers.[483]

---

478. BDAG, 494.3.
479. Wilhelm Michaelis, *TDNT,* 4:671.
480. Kleinknecht, Quell, Stauffer, and Kuhn, *TDNT,* 3:102–4.
481. Oepke, *TDNT,* 2:541.
482. Kleinknecht, Quell, Stauffer, and Kuhn, *TDNT,* 3:103.
483. Barth, *Ephesians,* 2:521; Muddiman, Ephesians, 230. The quotation is from Muddiman.

you: An alteration among manuscripts has produced a variant reading between "you" and "us" who are recipients of God's forgiving gift. The difference seems to be accidental, resulting from the audible similarity between the two pronouns in Greek. Certainly, because the main verb at the beginning of the verse is a second plural imperative; "you" (plural) is original.[484]

Analysis of 4:17–32

Paul spins around from his treatment of Jesus' descent and ascension, followed by his handling of ecclesiastical matters (see 4:1–16), and invites readers to walk behind him into the world of good and evil, which, whether wanted or not, continues to touch church members, as chronicled in these verses (see 4:17–32). Since the days when they first heard the voice of Christ through the voices of his preaching servants, they have been taught to walk in the path blazed by the Savior. The Apostle will encourage believers to continue on that roadway, eventually stepping into the forgiving arms of the Father.

A number of Paul's readers, notably Gentiles, stood close enough to their old lives of "vanity" and "ignorance" (4:17, 18) that they needed a stern reminder to stand farther away from old habits and to thoroughly "put off . . . the old man" who was plagued by "deceitful lusts" (4:22). In these verses, he wrote in general terms, begging them to "walk not as other Gentiles walk," with their "understanding darkened" and suffering from "the blindness of their heart" (4:17–18). Such persons in the world were "past feeling" in the truly human sense and had permanently and cripplingly stooped to "lasciviousness" and "greediness" (4:19). For converts, "ye have not so learned Christ" (4:20).

A continuing careful reading of Paul's lines escorts a person into a room made dim by light-absorbing images. These images, in contrast to the general, unpleasant language that he employed in verses 4:17–19, picture specific, objectionable actions by church members in Ephesus and beyond, hinting at his familiarity with individual cases of transgression. He first turned his attention to "lying," the practice that undercuts all personal relationships. He begged that "every man [speak] truth with his neighbor" (4:25), an important standard that Jesus himself had set decades earlier (see Matt. 5:37). Following this appeal, in second place arose one of

---

484. Metzger, *Textual Commentary,* 538.

the most puzzling of sentences ever written by the Apostle. It concerned anger, a destabilizing outburst by someone that could pull apart a branch of the church: "Be ye angry, and sin not" (4:26). To be sure, his next line made the point that any anger should be short-lived: "Let not the sun go down upon your wrath." But "be angry" anytime? This imperative is all the more puzzling because of the approaching directive to "let all bitterness, and wrath, and anger . . . be put away from you" (4:31). One solution may emerge from modern scripture, wherein a church member reproves another, but only "when moved upon by the Holy Ghost" and only when "showing forth afterwards an increase of love toward him whom thou hast reproved" (D&C 121:43). Anger is not allowed except under the most stringent and tight limits.

The Apostle was not finished. Evidently, he had become aware of a church member, most likely a poor slave, who was augmenting his living by stealing. What to say? Paul was not at a loss for words: "Let him that stole steal no more." What was this poor person to do? Go to work, said the Apostle, "working with his hands" so that he could create enough extra, likely a tiny overage for a very poor person, "to give to him that needeth" (4:28). Charity is required of all, including those with the least. Then Paul addressed "corrupt communication" or harmful words, knowing by experience that Saints should speak "that which is good" that leads to "edifying" one another (4:29). One major thing more, and this was the gravest of offenses: "Do not offend the Holy Spirit of God" (4:30 NR). Besides the offending person standing in the middle of the highway where God's wrath is bearing down at breakneck speed, that individual risked losing "the day of redemption," the grandest of all God's gifts (4:30; see also the Note thereon).

Almost as an afterthought, Paul drew up a list of deeply objectionable attitudes and actions, each arising from an angry temperament. Believers should surmount or discard these. He produced similar lists at Colossians 3:8 and elsewhere in his letters (see 2 Cor. 12:20 and Gal. 5:20). Each of these behaviors—"bitterness . . . wrath . . . anger . . . clamor . . . evil speaking . . . malice" (4:31)—has the power to undo the communal unity within a branch of the church. The overarching motive for jettisoning such behaviors is the sweet forgiveness that comes from God (see 4:32). Importantly, Paul paired that forgiveness with being "renewed in the spirit of your mind" and putting "on the new person" (4:23–24). Besides these, church members were to put "away lying, [and] speak every man truth with his neighbor," thereby not giving "place to the devil" (4:25, 27). Such acts would lead to the treasured unity among believers, "for we are members one of another" (4:25).

Within these verses, as elsewhere in this letter, sit references to ritual acts. The two most prominent notations direct believers "to put off the old person" and "to put on the new person" (4:22, 24 NR). The connections to taking off clothes and putting them on are obvious. A person might suggest that these expressions are metaphorical in nature. That person would be correct. But the cluster of literal actions sits not far away. And links to actual, ceremonial movements of disrobing and robing are strengthened by other allusions and pointers to ceremonies inside this Epistle. One of those lies in verse 4:20, where the Apostle writes, "Ye have not so learned Christ." This line is not a reference to the initial instruction directed at an investigator, "Jesus Christ and him crucified" (1 Cor. 2:2), or to putting "on Christ" at baptism (Gal. 3:27). Rather, he has referred backward to the actions and behaviors of unredeemed Gentiles in 4:18–19 ("darkened ... alienated ... past feeling"), items suitable to continuing instruction after baptism. Then he has pointed forward to putting off "the old person" and putting on "the new person" (4:20, 22 NR), with clear hints at sacred ritual (see 6:11, 13). At a minimum, modern readers come upon the language of the continuing renewal of the baptismal covenant celebrated weekly in the Eucharist or sacrament: "That they are willing *to take upon them* the name of thy Son" (Moro. 4:3; D&C 20:77, emphasis added; see also the Notes on 2:10; 4:13, 20, 22, 24; 5:2, 8, 15; 6:11; and appendix 1).

Becoming "the new person" (4:24 NR) opens other possibilities for the individual—namely, becoming like God himself. This eventuality appears in the prepositional phrase "after God." As we discovered in the review of 4:24, the notion embedded in this phrase is something like "after the manner of God" or "after the character of God." Persons who pursue this grand possibility come to possess "righteousness and true holiness" (4:24) and become "imitators of God" (5:1 NR). A reader of the KJV would not see this sense in 5:1, where a person reads the words "followers of God," a totally different meaning that drifts toward discipleship rather than toward a pattern in life that seeks to imitate God (see the Notes on 4:24; 5:1–2). Such a pattern of living will bring believers to an inner place where they are able to not "give place to the devil" (4:27). After the devil is removed from their lives at baptism, people need to replace his influences with other edifying powers such as the Holy Ghost. This thought lies precisely behind Jesus' words about "the unclean spirit" who was forced "out of a man" and later, returning to its former haunt, found that the man's soul had been "swept and garnished" but nothing put in its old place. Not shy, the spirit invited "seven other spirits more wicked than himself" to move in with him, "and the last state of that man [was] worse than the first" (Luke 11:24–26).[485]

As with earlier sections of this letter, we discover the dominating, magisterial presence of God the Father. Since the beginning of the Epistle, when Paul invoked "the will of God" in his apostleship (1:1), the rhythm of praising God has not let up. Within these verses (4:17–32), he is mentioned four times, the last being the most important. We initially meet nonmember Gentiles who are "alienated from the life of God" and who possess no "understanding" of him (4:18). Next we encounter the phrase "after God" (4:24), which invites church members to a life of imitating their God in word and action, as the following verses illustrate. Next, God is mentioned in the need not to grieve or offend "the Holy Spirit of God" (4:30 NR), a most serious transgression that involves a believer turning away from the only spiritually secure habitat in the universe. The final notation has to do with God's ineffable forgiveness (see 4:32), a wondrous celestial grant that cleanses and continues to cleanse throughout a person's life. The reference to God's forgiving clamps an emphatic stamp on the prior verses.

Finally, a word about Paul's authorship of these lines. Muddiman has drawn attention to the unique character of verses 4:20–24. All of the talk about learning "Christ" and "the truth is in Jesus" and "the new person" and "the old person" stands without parallel in the Apostle's other letters. The liveliness and freshness of the language do not send readers to a later imitator of the Apostle, who would want to keep his expressions within the bounds of words and style that one finds in Paul's other Epistles. Rather, readers encounter unpredictable expressions, which Paul was capable of writing, that send them to the Apostle himself as their author (see the Notes on 1:23; 3:8; 4:3; 5:27; and the Analysis of 3:1–13, 6:1–9).[486]

---

485. Brown, *Testimony of Luke*, 571–75.

486. Schmidt, *TDNT*, 3:511; Bruce, *Ephesians*, 12; Merkle, *Guide*, 94; Muddiman, *Ephesians*, 145–47, 156, 215–16, 218.

Chapter 5

INTRODUCTION

Paul propelled forward his concerns with proper Christian behavior, pushing them to new heights. As even a cursory reading will make clear, he ultimately, and even desperately, wanted to clothe his readers in "the whole armor of God" so they would be "able to withstand in the evil day" and be "able to quench all the fiery darts of the wicked [one]" (6:11, 13, 16). The Apostle knew that his beloved Saints faced the onslaught of "the rulers of the darkness of this world [and] . . . spiritual wickedness in high places" (6:12). Rely on God? Of course. Bind that reliance on God with reservoirs of personal behavior and spiritual strength? Most definitely. Simply stated, in order to be "children of light," believing readers needed to cultivate "goodness and righteousness and truth" and have "no fellowship with the unfruitful works of darkness" (5:8–9, 11). It is evident that Paul was trying to fortify his fellow Saints for a massive, looming storm that would sink the ship of the church into a grave of watery chaos and apostasy.

As we have come to expect, Paul has maintained the rhythmic cadence that leads our ears and hearts to God the Father and his unparalleled place in both human affairs and heavenly matters. From the beginning, God has stood as the one whom believers are to imitate, to pattern their inner and outer selves after (see 5:1 NR). The effort to imitate God involves looking to Christ as another exemplar, whose love brought him to give "himself up for us as a fragrant offering and sacrifice to God" (5:2 NR). That is to say, the infusion of God's love into believers' lives, modeled on Christ's loving actions, will naturally steer them into acts of charity for others, sacrificing time and energy for nonmembers and fellow Saints alike. Naturally, behaving in the opposite manner will drive away the possibility of "any inheritance in the kingdom of Christ and of God" (5:5). In fact, those whose practices make them into "the children of disobedience" will draw down "the wrath of God" upon themselves (5:6). For believers, overall, God's unmatched gifts will reverentially turn them to give "thanks always for all things unto God and the Father in the name of our Lord Jesus Christ" (5:20).

Notably, the shunning of the vices that Paul lists in verses 5:3–5 and the avoidance of "the unfruitful works of darkness" (5:11) and other questionable practices, such as acting "unwise" and allowing oneself to be entrapped by strong drink (5:17–18), take on the character of "works" that Saints are to undertake. To be sure, earlier in this letter the Apostle declared that "we are [God's] workmanship, created in Christ Jesus unto good works" (2:10). Much of chapters 4 and 5 is taken up in discussing good works and the conscious setting aside of evil practices. One conclusion is that believers' access to divine grace does not give them a completely free pass into heaven with nothing required except to show up (see the extended Notes on "grace" at 2:5 and 2:8; and the Notes on 2:10; 4:1; and 4:30 on "redemption").

One of the most nettlesome passages in scripture appears in the lines of chapter 5—the submission of wives to their husbands (see 5:22–33). Although one of the chief aspects revolves around a sacred marriage with Christ at its center, the puzzle remains about Paul's insistence that "wives, submit yourselves unto your own husbands" (5:22). Some of the surprise dissipates at the Apostle's injunction to husbands that they "ought . . . to love their wives as their own bodies" because "no man ever yet hated his own flesh; but nourisheth and cherisheth it" (5:28–29). Further, it is the man who is obliged to leave "his father and mother, and . . . be joined unto his wife," a plain acknowledgment that he goes to her, not she to him at their marriage (5:31). Even though these words from Paul lay important responsibilities on husbands, the sense of partnership in marriage seems to be undercut by the Apostle's injunction to wives. But that is not the whole story, as will become apparent in the Notes on 5:22–33.

Most commentators link the early verses of chapter 5 with the last verses of chapter 4, as a whole cloth. The most preferred joins 5:1–2 to the end of chapter 4.[1] This comes about because the same present imperative form of the verb "to be" (γίνομαι, *ginomai*) occurs in 4:32 and 5:1, tying the two verses together. Moreover, the conjunction translated "therefore" (οὖν, *oun*) in 5:1 "is inferential" and "draw[s] out the consequences of the preceding exhortations (4:25–32)."[2] The attempt to make all the material in 5:1–20 connect directly to the end of chapter 4 has found little support.[3]

---

1. Houlden, *Paul's Letters from Prison,* 320, 322–23; Caird, *Letters,* 83; Lincoln, *Ephesians,* 310–12; Best, *Ephesians,* 465–66; Fowl, *Ephesians,* 161; Merkle, *Guide,* 154–55.

2. Merkle, *Guide,* 154; see also BDAG, 736.1.a.

3. Muddiman, *Ephesians,* 210.

"BECOME THEREFORE IMITATORS OF GOD" (5:1–2)

King James Translation

1 Be ye therefore followers of God, as dear children; 2 And walk in love, as Christ also hath loved us, and hath given himself for us an offering and a sacrifice to God for a sweetsmelling savour.

New Rendition

1 Become therefore imitators of God, as beloved children. 2 And walk in love, just as Christ loved us and gave himself up for us as a fragrant offering and sacrifice to God.

Notes on 5:1–2

5:1–2: The sense of the context of these verses demands that they be understood to connect closely to the last lines of chapter 4. The inferential conjunction "therefore" (οὖν, *oun*) ties off what Paul had just written about setting aside all intemperate actions, including what a person may say, and nurturing kindness and forgiveness. The enduring model, of course, is God himself (see 4:29–32).

5:1 *Be:* Throughout coming verses, Paul has shown himself to be a "teacher," a role that he noted in his list of church officers in 4:11.[4] That observation, however, did not excuse him from his lofty responsibilities as an apostle. Far from it. He must and would still verbalize his witness about the Christ who offered "himself . . . a sacrifice to God" (5:2) and who helped believers escape "the prince of the power of the air . . . that now worketh in the children of disobedience" (2:2). The imperative of the verb "to be" or "to become" (γίνομαι, *ginomai*) matches exactly the imperative in 4:32 and thus bridges us from the God who forgives to the God who loves (see 5:2).[5]

therefore: This inferential conjunction οὖν (*oun*) carries the thought of Paul's previous instructions into the following result. In other words, a warm response to his appeal that "ye [be] kind one to another, . . . forgiving one another, even as God . . . hath forgiven you" (4:32) will result in his readers becoming "imitators of God" (5:1 NR).[6]

followers: This noun (plural of μιμητής, *mimētēs*), which means "imitator,"[7] appears only here in the New Testament with the sense of imitating God. Its associated verb (μιμέομαι, *mimeomai*) occurs four times, usually rendered in the KJV with the meaning "to follow" (see 2 Thes. 3:7, 9; Heb. 13:7;

---

4. Rengstorf, *TDNT,* 2:158.
5. Lincoln, *Ephesians,* 310; Best, *Ephesians,* 465; Winger, *Ephesians,* 533–34.
6. BDAG, 736.1.a.; Merkle, *Guide,* 154.
7. BDAG, 652.

and 3 John 1:11). The noun *mimētēs,* customarily translated "followers" in the KJV, regularly has to do with imitating Paul (see 1 Cor. 4:16; 11:1; and 1 Thes. 1:6) or "the churches" (1 Thes. 2:14; compare Heb. 6:12 and 1 Pet. 3:13). Wilhelm Michaelis engineered his best effort to say that, in our passage, the term *mimētēs* points to an obedient "disciple,"[8] or to a follower, even though the entire weight of the term's history in the Greek language presses down onto the meaning "imitator."[9] He was not convincing. Hence, the consistent translation of the word as "follower" in the KJV has to be discarded. His concern was that mentioning God in 5:1 construed "the reference to God as though God were set up as a model," something that he could not imagine because the Father is so far beyond human reach.[10] But that is exactly the message (see Philip. 3:21, "like unto his glorious body"; 1 John 3:2, "we shall be like him"; 3 Ne. 27:27, "even as I am"; Moro. 7:48, "we shall be like him").

The question arises, Whom better might one emulate than Heavenly Father? Can a person find something inherently wrong with imitating God? To be sure, we possess no direct window to look through so that we witness God's life and activities. But his Son represents the Father in every important way, mirroring him as we find hinted at in 5:2 (see 2:4 and 6:23 for God's love reflected in the Son's love in 5:2; see also Rom. 8:39 and the Note on 5:2). This is the substance of the exchange between Jesus and his disciples Thomas and Philip at the Last Supper. When answering Thomas's question about how to find him after death, Jesus responded: "If ye had known me, ye should have known my Father also." If so, then "from henceforth ye know him, and have seen him" (John 14:7). Not grasping what Jesus had just said, Philip begged Jesus to "shew us the Father." In reply, Jesus said to Philip, "He that hath seen me hath seen the Father" (John 14:8–9). To be clear, imitating the Father involves a third party—namely, Jesus. How so? Because Jesus mediates or reveals God to believers, including the almost unfathomable "length, and depth, and height" of his love (3:18), and because "through him we both [Jew and Gentile] have access . . . unto the Father" (2:18). If the relationship were one of discipleship, only two persons would be required, the leader and the follower.[11] This is not the end of the matter.

---

8. Michaelis, *TDNT,* 4:671–73.

9. LSJ, 1134; the varied senses all link to "imitator"—an artist "who impersonates characters, as an actor or poet" or an "imposter."

10. Michaelis, *TDNT,* 4:671.

11. Barth, *Ephesians,* 2:591.

The Apostle's command to be "imitators of God" (5:1 NR) threads its way through succeeding verses, which are more than a patchwork of commands. One of the keys has to do with a person putting away old practices noted in 5:3–6, because at one time all believers, especially Gentiles, were caught in "being alienated from the life of God" (4:18). With the aid of Christ's love, which came to readers as "an offering and a sacrifice to God" (5:2), church members can avoid being "partakers" of enticing items that "the children of disobedience" serve up (5:6–7). As "imitators of God," the "dear children" (5:1 NR) not only reprove "the unfruitful works of darkness" (5:11) but hold onto "the light" (5:13). Embracing light does not recommend itself just because it scuttles "darkness" (5:11), but because the light has vanquished the dark and revealed its soul-sagging works (5:13). There is more.

The shout "Awake!" to the one who sleeps spiritually rouses the listless to "arise from the dead," not in a literal sense but from a state as if they were dead (5:14). As an illustration, elsewhere Paul referred to both a metaphorical dying and real death: "If in union with Christ we have imitated his death [in baptism], we shall also imitate him in his resurrection." What is more, "we believe that having died with Christ we shall return to life with him" (Rom. 6:5, 8, Jerusalem Bible). The point? Imitating God requires action, not passivity, which lifts believers to a higher state of living life, as if resurrected. Readers are also urged to be "wise," not acting "as fools." Why? "Because the days are evil," and therefore believers must come to a heavenly-enlightened "understanding what the will of the Lord is" (5:15–17). Finally, individuals must swivel away from the debilitating allure of "wine" and instead "be filled with the Spirit." And how is that to be done? By singing. The singing is not to be of barroom choruses but of "psalms and hymns and spiritual songs, . . . making melody in your heart to the Lord" (5:18–19). Thus, imitating God opens an almost endless horizon of activities and behaviors that draw believers into "giving thanks always for all things unto God and the Father" (5:20; see also the Notes on 4:24, 32).[12]

dear children: We encounter the adjective here translated "dear" (ἀγαπητός, *agapētos*) at the scene of Jesus' baptism, "Thou art my *beloved* Son" (Mark 1:11, emphasis added), and his transfiguration, "This is my *beloved* Son" (Mark 9:7, emphasis added). Of course, this does not mean that Paul was addressing his readers as if they enjoyed the same status as the Son of

---

12. Barth, *Ephesians*, 2:592.

God. Why not? Because *agapētos* appears often as a term of endearment in the Apostle's letters (see Rom. 16:5, 8, 9, 12; 1 Cor. 15:58; 2 Cor. 12:19; Philip. 4:1; etc.).[13] That said, the context in Ephesians, with readers' attentions purposefully and almost suddenly drawn to the lofty invitation to become "imitators of God" (NR), lifted up the prospect that believers could enjoy the distinction of "beloved" in God's eyes. Such a status does not mean that church members stand on the same celestial ground that Christ does. Far from it. However, this kind of perch rests firmly on the trajectory that Christ's heavenly elevation pioneered. In this sense, the adjective *agapētos* carries the sense of "only" or "only beloved" or "the one I love."[14] To capture this sense, we appeal to an expression that illustrates the dazzling position of a true disciple, "where I [Christ] am, there ye may be also" (John 14:3).

The mention of God and "children" (τεκνόν, *teknon*) raises the matter of God's family. Readers have already taken in this subject in 3:14–15, where mention of "every family in the heavenly realms and on earth" links to "the Father," who has given his name to those families (NR). Indeed, "through Jesus Christ," children have undergone a divine "adoption . . . unto [God] himself" (1:5 NR). All of this language wraps itself around the concept of celestial families, of which the "dear children" are an integral part. Although one might argue that Paul was merely addressing his readers by this term, much like he called Saints in Corinth his "beloved sons" (1 Cor. 4:14), because he was their spiritual father,[15] and his "beloved brethren" (1 Cor. 15:58), the context demands a more robust meaning. For his readers "are beloved children incorporated into God's family."[16] They are not less (see the Note on 3:15).

5:2 *walk:* Earlier we came across this verb (περιπατέω, *peripateō*) at 2:2, 10, 4:1, and 4:17 and will encounter it twice more at 5:8 and 5:15. In some of these passages, the meaning of "walk" features a distinctive ritual connection (see the Notes on 2:2, 10; 4:1, 17). Here it does not, except perhaps in the sense that a person's walk through life is to imitate Christ, who "hath given himself . . . *an offering and a sacrifice* to God" (5:2, emphasis added; see also Rom. 12:1, "present your bodies *a living sacrifice* . . . unto God," emphasis added). This high and lofty pattern of loving, for which individuals must "pray unto the Father with all the energy of heart, that ye may

13. BDAG, 7.2; Louw-Nida, §25.45.
14. BDAG, 7.1; Louw-Nida, §§25.45; 58.53.
15. Winger, *Ephesians,* 535; Perkins, *Ephesians,* 114.
16. Fowl, *Ephesians,* 161; see also Schrenk and Quell, *TDNT,* 5:1017–19.

be filled with this love" (Moro. 7:48), stands completely opposed to the rampant selfishness that motivates "fornication, and all uncleanness, [and] . . . filthiness" (5:3–4; see also 1 Thes. 4:1–12). This observation about competing paths that lead to love and selfishness respectively brings readers close to the principle of the "two ways"[17] enunciated by Jesus in the Sermon on the Mount: "Wide is the gate, and broad is the way, that leadeth to destruction, and . . . strait is the gate, and narrow is the way, which leadeth unto life" (Matt. 7:13–14). The language of 5:8 captures this thought very succinctly: "Ye were sometimes darkness, but now are ye light in the Lord." A similar idea arises from 5:15: "See then that ye walk circumspectly, not as fools, but as wise."

In the gospel sense, a believer's walk in a celestial-like life begins at baptism, which marks the end of that person's walk in "the course of this world" (2:2; see also 1 Cor. 3:3; and Col. 3:7). The pattern of a church member's walk moves that person into a "newness of life" that is tangible and real (Rom. 6:4; see also John 8:12, "shall have the light of [celestial] life"; 2 Cor. 6:16, "I [God] will . . . walk in them"; and D&C 84:33, "the renewing of their bodies"). Choosing the right path with its gate and eschewing the other path and its gate meant that a committed individual walked "not after the flesh, but after the Spirit" (Rom. 8:4). For the believer, the flesh "is no longer the lord of the baptized" (see 2 Cor. 10:2–3; Gal. 5:16; and the Notes on 2:2, 10, 4:1, 17; 5:8, 15, 26).[18]

in love: The noun translated "love" (ἀγάπη, *agapē*) occurs ten times in Ephesians.[19] Without trying to be exhaustive but respecting Paul's concept of *agapē*, we notice that the nature of divine love announced immediately after this phrase had been framed by Christ, who "hath loved us, and given himself for us" (5:2). Two dimensions are at play. The first connects God's love for us to Christ's love for us. Fundamentally, they are the same; Paul makes no distinction between them. At the end of a long review of the character of heavenly love (see Rom. 8:32–37), we run across these lines: "I am convinced that neither death nor life, neither angels nor demons, . . . neither height nor depth, nor anything else in all creation, will be able to separate us from the love of God that is in Christ Jesus our Lord" (Rom. 8:38–39 NIV). Elsewhere we discover the following words in the Apostle's correspondence to the Thessalonian Saints: "May our Lord Jesus Christ

---

17. Michaelis, *TDNT*, 5:73–75, quotation on 73.
18. Seeseman and Bertram, *TDNT*, 5:944–45, quotation on 945.
19. See 1:4, 15; 2:4; 3:17, 19; 4:2, 15, 16; 5:2; 6:23.

himself and God our Father, who loved us[,] . . . encourage your hearts and strengthen you in every good deed and word" (2 Thes. 2:16–17 NIV).[20]

The second dimension links the identity of God's love and Christ's love with love that arises from death, specifically from Christ's death.[21] We read that "God demonstrates his own love for us in this: While we were still sinners, Christ died for us" (Rom. 5:8 NIV). It is Christ's sacrificial death, undertaken in love, and God's loving orchestration of it (see John 3:16), that vaults believers into "a readiness for service and sacrifice, for forgiveness and consideration, for help and sympathy, for lifting up the fallen and restoring the broken, in a fellowship which owes its very existence to the mercy of God and the sacrificial death of Christ."[22] Emerging from these almost melodious lines we hear the following echoes in scripture: "Succor the weak, lift up the hands which hang down, and strengthen the feeble knees" (D&C 81:5; see also Job 4:3–4; Isa. 35:3; and Heb. 12:12). In a perfect harmonious blend, we listen to Paul's elevating song: "Charity [*agapē*] suffereth long, and is kind; charity envieth not; charity vaunteth not itself, is not puffed up. Doth not behave itself unseemly, *seeketh not her own*" (1 Cor. 13:4–5, emphasis added). This kind of love or charity comes to no one naturally but is "bestowed upon all who are true followers of [God's] Son" (Moro. 7:48; see also the Notes on 2:4; 3:19; 5:25).

Christ also hath loved us: This expression unfolds Christ's true relationship with his disciples, his imitators. From the beginning, God's love, explicitly stated or implicitly present, has perfumed the relationship of God and his children.[23] Love was certainly present in an overflowing way when "the Holy Ghost fell on Adam, . . . saying [in the name of the Son and in covenantal language]: I am the Only Begotten of the Father from the beginning, . . . that as thou hast fallen thou mayest be redeemed, and all mankind, even as many as will" (Moses 5:9). The celestial promise in these words, laden with love, brought forward a rush of emotion in Adam, who inspiringly declared that "again in the flesh I shall see God" (Moses 5:10). Eve's feelings of gratitude matched her husband's when she almost sang, "Were it not for our transgression we never should have had seed, and never should have known . . . the joy of our redemption" (Moses 5:11). Moreover,

20. Quell and Stauffer, *TDNT,* 1:49.

21. Barth, *Ephesians,* 2:684–87.

22. Quell and Stauffer, *TDNT,* 1:49, 51, quotation on 51.

23. Quell and Stauffer, *TDNT,* 1:27.

God's love for his children pours out of his later covenant with Abraham wherein, on his side, he promised that "in thee [Abraham] shall all the families of the earth be blessed" (Gen. 12:3; see also Gen. 18:18; 22:18; and Abr. 2:9–11). It may be worth noting that this is the most quoted passage from the brass plates in the Book of Mormon (see 1 Ne. 15:18; 22:9; 3 Ne. 20:25, 27; see also 2 Ne. 29:14; Morm. 5:20; and Ether 13:11).

Within the pages of the Old Testament we glimpse gems of how individuals are to love neighbors and enemies alike, all resting on God's love for his people. Jesus was the one who articulated this relationship for humans: "Love your enemies, bless them that curse you, do good to them that hate you." Why? Because God the Father, in arranging this earth to serve as home for all his children, "maketh his sun to rise on the evil and on the good, and sendeth rain on the just and on the unjust" (Matt. 5:44–45; see also Luke 6:27–29, 35–36). From Proverbs we hear, "If thine enemy be hungry, give him bread to eat; and if he be thirsty, give him water to drink" (Prov. 25:21). This instruction sits atop a prior set of God's commands given to the earlier freed Hebrew slaves: "If thou meet thine enemy's ox or his ass going astray, thou shalt surely bring it back to him again." Furthermore, "if thou see the ass of him that hateth thee lying under his burden, and wouldest forbear to help him, thou shalt surely help with him" (Ex. 23:4–5). Paired with such instructions, we find these requirements for relationships with neighbors, all resting on God's love for his people: "Thou shalt not see thy brother's ox or his sheep go astray, and hide thyself from them: thou shalt in any case bring them again unto thy brother. . . . In like manner shalt thou do with his ass; and so shalt thou do with his raiment" (Deut. 22:1, 3).[24]

Paul was certainly aware of the love of God manifested in these commandments and covenants. But, for him, the example of genuine and truly selfless love rested in Christ's saving act and in the Father's gift of him to the world. In his words recorded in this verse, "Christ also hath loved us, and [as a result] hath given himself for us an offering and a sacrifice to God." Said another way, "God demonstrates his love for us, because while we were still sinners Christ died for us" (Rom. 5:8, Wayment). Thus, out of death, specifically Christ's redeeming death, came the greatest manifestation of love (see the Note on 2:4).[25]

---

24. Quell and Stauffer, *TDNT*, 1:26.
25. Barth, *Ephesians*, 2:684–87.

given himself for us: This line embodies within it two important doctrines. One pertains to vicarious action, especially that which Jesus performed on behalf of both believers and nonbelievers. The second relates to salvation, a state that is to come only to the faithful. Let us approach this expression by reversing its parts. In examining the short prepositional phrase "for us" (ὑπέρ ἡμῶν, *hyper hēmōn*), readers soon discover that it plays the key role for grasping the vast implications of what Jesus has done for those who follow and imitate him. "Jesus in His death vicariously took upon Himself . . . the mortal curse,"[26] doing so for all. The vicarious nature of his act comes alive in the phrase *hyper hēmōn,* whether translated with the thought "for our benefit" or "in our place,"[27] with the firm emphasis on "in our place" or "taking our place." As such, on one level the words carry the sense of Jesus serving as a substitute "for us," taking our place.[28] Hence, in this brief prepositional phrase readers come upon the doctrine of vicarious action for both the living and the dead.

The original linkage of the phrase *hyper hēmōn* to Christ's suffering and death appears to arise in Paul's language about its edible memorial—that is, the bread of the Eucharist or sacrament. Through the Apostle, we listen to Jesus' words at the Last Supper: "Take, eat: this is my body, which is broken *for you*" (1 Cor. 11:24, emphasis added; see also Luke 22:19, "given for you").[29] In the case of Jesus' "offering and sacrifice" (NR), the impact stretches across all creation. In the case of human participation in vicarious actions, it extends only to the realm of the dead (see 1 Cor. 15:29, "why are they . . . baptized for the dead?"[30]; compare Matt. 16:19, "whatsoever thou shalt bind on earth"). In this verse, the image is one of a sacrifice that removes the stench of believers' sins from the nostrils of the Father, both in this world and the next, turning them into "a fragrant offering . . . to God" (NR). In two other passages, the representations are different but amount to the exactly same thing.

At Galatians 3:13, we perceive that Paul has drawn upon the institution of slavery as a comparison. This comparison deals with slavery to the Mosaic law and the fact that the law pins sin upon believers even though they strive against it. Simply stated, "Christ redeemed us from the curse of the

---

26. Harald Riesenfeld, *TDNT,* 8:509.
27. BDAG, 1030.A.1.γ; Louw-Nida, §90.36; Larkin, *Handbook,* 107; Winger, *Ephesians,* 536.
28. Lincoln, *Ephesians,* 312; Merkle, *Guide,* 155; Winger, *Ephesians,* 536.
29. Riesenfeld, *TDNT,* 8:510–11; Lincoln, *Ephesians,* 312.
30. Riesenfeld, *TDNT,* 8:512–13.

law by becoming a curse for us" (NIV). The verb translated "redeemed" here (ἐξαγοράζω, *exagorazō*) means to bring about "the release or freedom of someone by a means which proves costly to the individual causing the release."[31] Framed differently, the image goes back to the freeing of a slave with a net economic loss to the owner.[32] Another comment is important. It is not that Christ was "made a curse for us" as in the KJV. He willingly became a curse, putting himself under the curse of sin that stood in need of a purging sacrifice, which he undertook for our sins (see Heb. 9:14). In another place, furthermore, he became "sin for us (*hyper hēmōn*), who knew no sin; that we might be made the righteousness of God in him" (2 Cor. 5:21). In both Galatians 3:13 and 2 Corinthians 5:21, the phrase "for us" is the same as in our Ephesians passage, *hyper hēmōn*. Just as in 5:2, in these two other passages we understand *hyper hēmōn* to mean "taking our place," thus completing the vicarious sense of Jesus' offering (see the following verses that employ *hyper* as a preposition, making firm the notion of Jesus' vicarious service: 2 Cor. 5:14–15, "for all"; Gal. 1:4, "for our sins"; Gal. 2:20, "for me"; 1 Tim. 2:6, "for all"; and Titus 2:14, "for us"; see also the Note on 4:30 on "redemption" and the Note on 5:25).

We now turn to the first expression, "given himself," noticing the same wording at 5:25, except the verb and pronoun are reversed in the Greek text. The verb translated "given" is παραδίδωμι (*paradidōmi*) in both passages and occurs in the aorist or simple past tense. This term is better translated "to hand over" or "to deliver up."[33] This sense drives home the point that it was Jesus who willingly delivered himself up as a sacrifice. The Father stood behind him, but Jesus' love and will escorted him into his self-offering.[34] In other words, Jesus and heaven were in charge of his Atonement, as he declared to Pilate: "Thou couldest have no power at all against me, except it were given thee from above" (John 19:11). Two matters arise. The first has to do with Judas. The same verb, *paradidōmi*, described Judas's betrayal of Jesus as we read in Mark: "Judas Iscariot, one of the twelve, went unto the chief priests, *to betray* him unto them" (Mark 14:10, emphasis added; see also Matt. 26:16, 21; Mark 14:42; Luke 22:4, 6; John 18:2, 5;

---

31. Louw-Nida, §37.131; see also Raymond T. Stamm, "The Epistle to the Galatians," in *The Interpreter's Bible,* ed. George Arthur Buttrick, 12 vols. (New York: Abingdom Press, 1953), 10:509.

32. Riesenfeld, *TDNT,* 8:509.

33. BDAG, 761.1.

34. Caird, *Letters,* 83; Fowl, *Ephesians,* 161.

etc.).[35] Thus, in our passage the Apostle's readers were taken back to events that engulfed the mortal Jesus. In this light, Paul's use of this term surely associated in his readers' minds Judas's treachery with Jesus' suffering and death, his Atonement—an awful yet wonderful pairing of events.[36] This observation sends us to an item of interest, this one about the verb δίδωμι (*didōmi*), which underlies *paradidōmi*. While *paradidōmi* means "to hand over," *didōmi* means "to give."[37]

We find ourselves reclining at the Passover meal with Jesus and his Twelve Apostles the evening before his arrest. Hence, as in the prior paragraph, Jesus was still engaged in events that were ongoing during the last full day of his life. At the beginning of the meal, after Jesus, the host, blessed the unleavened bread,[38] he then broke the bread and "gave unto them, saying, This is my body which is given for you" (Luke 22:19). Twice *didōmi* appears in these lines, the first in the simple past tense, "he . . . gave." In the other occurrence, *didōmi* lies as a present, passive participle in the words "given for you," meaning that in this moment and in the future the power of "my body" is being given continually as a strengthening, elevating blessing for his disciples, all of them.[39] The language lifts up and puts a vicarious meaning onto Jesus' words and subsequent actions. This dimension finds reinforcement in the preposition ὑπέρ (*hyper*), which occurs in the phrase "given for [*hyper*] you" and means in this context "in place of" or "on behalf of."[40] The participle and the preposition, plus its pronoun, become "given on your behalf" or "given in your place."

---

35. BDAG, 762.1.b; Louw-Nida, §37.111.

36. Best, *Ephesians*, 469; Larkin, *Handbook*, 107; Muddiman, *Ephesians*, 231; Winger, *Ephesians*, 536.

37. BDAG, 242; Thayer, *Lexicon*, 145.

38. Alfred Edersheim, *The Temple: Its Ministry and Services as They Were at the Time of Jesus Christ* (Grand Rapids, Mich.: Eerdmans, 1983), 241–42; S. Kent Brown, "Jesus' First Visit to the Temple," in *The Temple: Symbols, Sermons, and Settings, Proceedings of the Fourth Interpreter Foundation Matthew B. Brown Memorial Conference "The Temple on Mount Zion," 10 November 2018,* ed. Stephen D. Ricks and Jeffrey M. Bradshaw (Orem, Utah: Interpreter Foundation, forthcoming).

39. Bednar, "In the Strength of the Lord," 121–28; Rasmus, "Enabling Power of the Atonement," 18–21; see also Eising, *TDOT*, 4:349, 353–55; Grundmann, *TDNT*, 2:313–16; Oepke, *TDNT*, 2:542–43; Braun, *TDNT*, 6:464.

40. I. Howard Marshall, *The Gospel of Luke,* The New International Greek Testament Commentary (Grand Rapids, Mich.: Eerdmans, 1978), 803–4; Joseph A. Fitzmyer, *The Gospel according to Luke,* 2 vols., vol. 28 of the Anchor Bible (New York: Doubleday, 1981, 1985), 2:1401.

One further important coloration appears on the canvas of Jesus' vicarious act. Specifically, it derives its textures and hues from the language in 5:2 and 5:25 that we have been reviewing—that is, "given himself for us" and "gave himself for it [the church]." These two passages present the idea of an Atonement whose saving power is focused on and offered to those inside God's fold and not to others.[41] We reached this conclusion when reviewing the term "redemption" at 4:30. An examination of passages that feature *hyper* makes this observation solid. The first is the most simple. In Galatians, Paul wrote about "the Son of God, who loved me, and gave himself for [*hyper*] me" (Gal. 2:20). Paul, of course, stood within the band of believers. Earlier in that same letter, he had written the line "our Lord Jesus Christ, who gave himself for [*hyper*] our sins" (Gal. 1:4). Yes, Christ paid for the sins of all, but those transgressions that were actually forgiven belonged to believers: "We [believers] have redemption through his blood, the forgiveness of sins" (Eph. 1:7). This thought finds confirmation in words about the second coming: "The glorious appearance of our great God and Savior, Jesus Christ, who gave himself for [*hyper*] us to redeem us from all wickedness and to purify for himself a people that are his very own" (Titus 2:13–14 NIV). The meaning is plain. Christ's redemption of our transgressions was "to purify for himself a people" whose numbers consisted of believers, not nonbelievers.

Two other passages preserve the words "for all," opening the possibility that Christ's saving Atonement included all people. It did include all, saving them from the grasp of mortal death. But a close look suggests that his Atonement offered spiritual powers to disciples only, a distinct outcome from the proffered salvation. In the First Epistle to Timothy we read about "God our Savior, who desires all men to be saved and to come to the knowledge of the truth." For these "the man Christ Jesus . . . gave himself as a ransom for [*hyper*] all" (1 Tim. 2:3–6 RSV). Above all, "our Savior . . . desires all men to be saved." But that will not happen. That saving power will flow only to those who respond to the message that Paul and others preached (see 1 Ne. 15:33–35; 2 Ne. 9:21–23; and Hel. 14:17–18). The Apostle's second letter to the Corinthians holds these words: "One has died for [*hyper*] all." But does this line mean that all, irrespective of their response to the Savior, have unobstructed access to salvation? We read further that "he died for [*hyper*] all, that those who live [celestially] might live no longer for themselves but for him who for their sake died and was raised" (2 Cor. 5:14–15

---

41. Barth, *Ephesians,* 2:557; Fowl, *Ephesians,* 161.

404 *The Epistle to the Ephesians*

RSV). In this passage, "those who live" will focus their spiritual sight "no longer [on] . . . themselves" but on "him who for their sake died and was raised." Clearly, these people stand within the circle of steadfast believers (see John 11:25–26, "he that believeth in me . . . shall . . . live [eternally]").

In summary, the language "given himself for us" in this passage and "gave himself for it [the church]" at 5:25 stand forth as clear pointers, perhaps the clearest in the New Testament, to two important teachings. The first has to do with the vicarious nature of Jesus' act undertaken specifically for believers, elevating them to heaven in a saved condition. The second relevant doctrine concerns the focused character of salvation. It will not reach all, for some will turn their backs on it. Instead, only the devout will be brought to salvation, a number that includes children and those who die without knowing the gospel (see Moro. 8:22 and D&C 128:5; 138:31–34; compare Acts 17:30). As we have already learned, "behold, he cometh to redeem those who will be baptized unto repentance, through faith on his name" (Alma 9:27). For "unto none else can the ends of the law be answered" (2 Ne. 2:7; see also Alma 11:40–42; the Notes on 4:19; 5:25; 6:18, 19; and the Note on "redemption" at 4:30).

a sacrifice: This term (θυσία, *thysia*) first pulls readers inside the sacred space of the temple. To be sure, Christ's sacrifice occurred away from the temple, and thus in this verse his sacrifice reposes on metaphorical grounds. But the tie still exists, underlining the holiness of his Atonement. For believers who are the recipients of Christ's action, two important ingredients bubble to the surface when applying his sacrifice to their lives. First, Jesus' suffering and death formed a one-time event (see Heb. 9:12, 26, 28; 10:10, 12–13). He, of course, was the sacrifice "when he offered up himself" (Heb. 7:27). His act meant that disciples no longer needed to offer sacrifices at the temple to restore their relationship with God. In contrast, priests, including the high priest once a year on the Day of Atonement, needed to offer regular sacrifices in order to preserve the connection of fellow Jews to heaven (see Heb. 7:27; 9:7, 25; 10:1, 3, 11). Second, the Christian's life became one of sacrifice, whether engaging in the work of the ministry (see Rom. 15:16, "the offering up of the Gentiles might be acceptable") or supporting other needy Saints in material ways (see Philip. 4:18, "the things . . . sent from you . . . a sacrifice acceptable"). This approach to living life before God was "the direct opposite of the offering of the life of another [creature] in cultic sacrifice" which reared itself on the deaths of sacrificial animals (see the Note on 1:7).[42]

---

42. Johannes Behm, *TDNT*, 3:185.

a sweetsmelling savour: In the Old Testament, the roots of a "sweet savor" nestle deep inside the acts of sacrifice, and they point to an anthropomorphic God who can smell.[43] We pick up this experience on God's part when Noah "offered burnt offerings on the altar" that he had set up "and the Lord smelled a sweet savor." Next, Noah's acceptable sacrifice led the Lord to say "in his heart, I will not again curse the ground any more for man's sake; . . . neither will I again smite any more every thing living, as I have done" (Gen. 8:20–21). Thus, Noah's action brought about a celestial blessing for all future citizens of the earth. Though virtually all subsequent references to "sweet savor" touch on sacrifices offered on altars (see Ex. 29:18, 25; Lev. 1:9, 13, 17; Num. 15:3, 13, 14; etc.), in Paul's hands they relate in some way to Christ while, at the same time, clinching the Apostle's words ever more tightly to temple rituals (for sacred ceremonies, see the Notes on 2:10; 4:1, 13, 20, 22, 24; 5:8, 14; 6:11, 13, 14; and appendix 1).[44]

Even though the adjective for "sweet-smelling" (εὐωδία, *euōdia*) in its three occurrences in the New Testament always sends us to a metaphorical meaning, including in our verse, it holds onto its original linkage to temple sacrifices.[45] We read that "we are unto God a sweet savour [*euōdia*] of Christ, [both] in them that are saved, and in them that perish" (2 Cor. 2:15). How can it be that Christ's sweet savor wafts over both the "saved" and "them that perish"? In response, Paul makes it clear that the power of God to react to one's "sweet smelling" acts can propel that person toward salvation. Fair enough. Yet the acceptability of an individual's sacrifice or good works leans against the person's inner attitude, whether done "with real intent" or not (Moro. 7:6; 10:4). If not, then the effort fails and becomes "the savour of death unto death" rather than "the savour of life unto life" (2 Cor. 2:16; see also Moro. 7:6–10, "it profiteth him nothing"). Back on the positive side, the Apostle called the material gifts of the Philippian Saints to the poor church members of Jerusalem "an odor of sweet smell [*euōdia*], a sacrifice acceptable, wellpleasing to God" (Philip. 4:18). In this light, it is evident that the sweet savor that pleases God braids an almost palpable cable between earth and heaven as well as laying out "one of the constant perceptible marks of the invasion of the terrestrial world by the supraterrestrial."[46]

---

43. Albrecht Stumpff, *TDNT,* 2:809.
44. Stumpff, *TDNT,* 2:810.
45. BDAG, 417; Thayer, *Lexicon,* 264.
46. Stumpff, *TDNT,* 2:810.

"Walk as Children of Light" (5:3–20)

King James Translation

3 But fornication, and all uncleanness, or covetousness, let it not be once named among you, as becometh saints; 4 Neither filthiness, nor foolish talking, nor jesting, which are not convenient: but rather giving of thanks. 5 For this ye know, that no whoremonger, nor unclean person, nor covetous man, who is an idolater, hath any inheritance in the kingdom of Christ and of God. 6 Let no man deceive you with vain words: for because of these things cometh the wrath of God upon the children of disobedience. 7 Be not ye therefore partakers with them. 8 For ye were sometimes darkness, but now are ye light in the Lord: walk as children of light: 9 (For the fruit of the Spirit is in all goodness and righteousness and truth;) 10 Proving what is acceptable unto the Lord. 11 And have no fellowship with the unfruitful works of darkness, but rather reprove them. 12 For it is a shame even to speak of those things which are done of them in secret. 13 But all things that are reproved are made manifest by the light: for whatsoever doth make manifest is light. 14 Wherefore he saith, Awake thou that sleepest, and arise from the dead, and Christ shall give thee light. 15 See then that ye walk circumspectly, not as fools, but as wise, 16 Redeeming the time, because the days are evil. 17 Wherefore be ye not unwise, but understanding what the will of the Lord is. 18 And be not drunk with wine, wherein is excess; but be filled with the Spirit; 19 Speaking to yourselves in psalms and hymns and spiritual songs, singing and making melody in your heart

New Rendition

3 But do not let sexual immorality, any kind of impurity, or covetousness even be mentioned among you, as is fitting for saints. 4 Neither allow filthy behavior, foolish talk, or coarse joking— things which are not proper—but rather, gratitude. 5 For of this you can be sure: no fornicator, unclean, or covetous person (such a person is an idolater) has an inheritance in the kingdom of Christ and of God. 6 Let no one deceive you with erroneous words, for because of such things God's wrath comes upon the children of disobedience. 7 So do not become fellow partakers with them. 8 For you were once darkness, but now you are light in the Lord. Walk as children of light 9 (for the fruit of the light lies in all goodness and righteousness and truth), 10 proving what is pleasing to the Lord. 11 And do not take part in the fruitless works of darkness, but rather expose them. 12 For their actions that occur in secret are shameful even to mention. 13 But everything exposed by the light becomes visible, 14 for everything made visible is light. This is why it says, "Awake, O sleeper, rise from the dead, and Christ will shine upon you." 15 So look carefully to how you walk, not as unwise people but as wise, 16 making the most of your time, because the days are evil. 17 Therefore, do not become foolish, but understand what the will of the Lord is. 18 And do not get drunk with wine, in which is debauchery, but fill yourselves with the Spirit, 19 speaking to one another with psalms, hymns, and spiritual songs.

to the Lord; 20 Giving thanks always for all things unto God and the Father in the name of our Lord Jesus Christ;

Sing and make music in your heart to the Lord, 20 always giving thanks for everything to our God and Father in the name of our Lord Jesus Christ.

Notes on 5:3–20

5:3 *But:* The conjunction δέ (*de*) swivels readers away from the topic of Christ's love embedded in his atoning act and draws their focus onto behaviors that will surely push persons away from the Atonement, specifically actions associated with sexual promiscuity.[47] Paul is saying that no one should underestimate the power of such acts and associated thoughts to trap an individual within deep spiritual darkness.

fornication: As will become clear from the discussion of related vices in verses 5:3–5, the indulgences in all these practices touch one way or another on immoral sexual gratification. The noun here (πορνεία, *porneia*) chases down actions from adultery to fornication to activities with prostitutes.[48] This sense pervades most New Testament references to this act (see Acts 15:20, 29; 21:25; Rom. 1:29; 1 Cor. 5:1; etc.). As is well known, from the Old Testament came the figurative notion that apostasy in its many forms was equivalent to fornication or adultery. From the frightful practice of torturing children in the worship of the foreign god Molech (see Lev. 18:21; 20:2–5; Jer. 32:35; etc.) to imbibing idol worship (see Deut. 31:16; Judg. 2:17; Jer. 3:2–9, 13, 20; 5:7; 13:27; etc.) to sacrificing children born to adulterous relationships consummated in pagan rites (see Isa. 57:3–6; Ezek. 16:35–43; 23:43–49; and Ps. 106:34–39), all such actions were characterized by God as an adulterous breach of his covenant with the people of Israel.[49] A like meaning resides in notices about the harlot in the book of Revelation. There we read about "the great whore that sitteth upon many waters: with whom the kings of the earth have committed fornication" (Rev. 17:1–2). She is called "Babylon[,] . . . that great city [which] . . . made all nations drink of the wine of the wrath of her fornication" (Rev. 14:8; see also Rev. 18:3; 19:2).[50]

---

47. Bruce, *Ephesians,* 102; Lincoln, *Ephesians,* 321–22.

48. BDAG, 854; Lincoln, *Ephesians,* 321; Fowl, *Ephesians,* 164–65.

49. Seth Erlandsson, *TDOT,* 4:101–4; David Noel Freedman and Bruce E. Willoughby, *TDOT,* 9:116–18.

50. Thayer, *Lexicon,* 531–32.

Back to *porneia,* this sin carried strong consequences for early Christians. The number of times that the Apostle inveighed against it, especially to Gentile readers, marks *porneia* out as an act that dragged one's soul downward, along with the branch of Christians of which the guilty party was a member. Jews, including Christianized Jews, had already adjusted their lives to the prohibitions in the Decalogue against adultery and coveting a neighbor's wife or husband (see Ex. 20:14, 17; and Deut. 5:18, 21). So the issue impacted almost exclusively Gentiles.[51] In a related vein, even though Paul taught that "God hath shewed it [the truth] unto [Gentiles]" so that "the invisible things of him from the creation of the world are clearly seen" (Rom. 1:19–20), he knew that Gentiles were plagued by idolatry. That is, they "changed the glory of the uncorruptible God into an image made like to corruptible man, and to birds, and fourfooted beasts" (Rom. 1:23). He knew that hard behind idolatry—the most nettlesome of sins because it denied a true understanding of the Father—rushed sexual license. Instead of restraining them, "God also gave them up to uncleanness through the lusts of their own hearts, to dishonor their own bodies between themselves." In a word, "God gave them up unto vile affections" (Rom. 1:24, 26). All of that—idolatry and "vile affections"—Paul sought to expunge. He grasped fully that the "toleration of the offender makes the whole church guilty." That is why, when he learned of a situation in Corinth, he not only drew attention to it by writing, "There is fornication among you," but he also demanded that church members "put away from among yourselves that wicked person," a person who had pursued intimacies with "his father's wife" (1 Cor. 5:1, 13; see the Notes on 4:19; 5:5).[52]

uncleanness: We learned earlier that this state (ἀκαθαρσια, *akatharsia*) dealt with ritual impurity in Old Testament times, with the meaning migrating to moral uncleanness in the New Testament era (see the Note on 4:19). In Paul's custody, it has taken on a dual aspect, first of an immoral quality that is met by holiness and second of sexual impropriety. The expression "all uncleanness," as at 4:19, nods toward all kinds of immoral actions. For example, writing about "the infirmity of your flesh," the Apostle held that "ye have yielded your [bodily] members [as] servants to uncleanness and to iniquity." The recipe for resistance was to "yield your [bodily] members

---

51. Friedrich Hauck and Siegfried Schulz, *TDNT,* 6:593.

52. Hauck and Schulz, *TDNT,* 6:593–94, quotation on 593. The "father's wife" was a second spouse rather than the man's mother. See Draper and Rhodes, *Paul's First Epistle to the Corinthians,* 264.

[as] servants to righteousness and holiness" (Rom. 6:19). The need for holiness, the antidote to uncleanness, reaches deep into the family, as Paul affirmed. How does this happen? "The unbelieving husband is sanctified by the wife, and the unbelieving wife is sanctified by the husband." What about the children? With a parent of holiness in the home, "now are they [the children] holy" (1 Cor. 7:14).

In our verse, *akatharsia* leans toward sexual immorality. How so? The matter turns on its association with *porneia,* "fornication." These two terms pair off with one another in four other passages that come from Paul's hand: "For this is the will of God . . . that ye should abstain from fornication [*porneia*]" because "God hath not called us unto uncleanness [*akatharsia*], but unto holiness" (1 Thes. 4:3, 7). Here we see that "holiness" stands in the mix. When listing the "works of the flesh," the Apostle generated a long ledger, at the top of which stood "adultery, fornication [*porneia*], [and] uncleanness [*akatharsia*]" (Gal. 5:19). To the Corinthian Saints, he worried that, during a planned visit to them, he would "bewail many which have sinned already, and have not repented of the uncleanness [*akatharsia*] and fornication [*porneia*] . . . which they have committed" (2 Cor. 12:21). As a fourth proof that Paul saw these two sins as closely linked, he urged readers that, in light of Christ's future appearance "in glory" and the fact that they would "appear with him," they should "put to death, therefore, what is earthly in you: fornication [*porneia*], impurity [*akatharsia*], passion, evil desire," and so forth (Col. 3:4–5 RSV).[53] A final passage repeats *akatharsia* and hints at *porneia.* To the Roman church members, the Apostle wrote that, because of the idolatry among earlier generations of Gentiles, "God also gave them up to uncleanness [*akatharsia*] through the lusts of their own hearts, to dishonor their own bodies between themselves" (Rom. 1:24; see also the Notes on 4:19; 5:5).[54]

covetousness: At its heart, the term πλεονεξία (*pleonexia*) is about "striving for material possessions."[55] This meaning roosts beneath Jesus' words to a man desiring a full share of his inheritance: "Beware of all types of greed [*pleonexia*], because a person's life is more that the quantity of his possessions" (Luke 12:15, Wayment). As we soon learn, Paul took this sense into the arena of fraudulent actions, writing the verb πλεονεκτέω (*pleonekteō*),[56] which is related to *pleonexia*: "No one should wrong [*pleonekteō*] his

---

53. Lincoln, *Ephesians,* 279, 321.
54. Meyer and Hauck, *TDNT,* 3:428–29.
55. Delling, *TDNT,* 6:271.
56. BDAG, 824.

brother or take advantage of him. The Lord will punish men for all such sins" (1 Thes. 4:6 NIV). Indeed, the Apostle sought to remove all striving for material gains, including denigrating "the covetous" as persons who "go out of the world" in the company of "the fornicators of this world [and] . . . with idolaters" (1 Cor. 5:10; see also 1 Cor. 5:11).[57]

When the meaning of *pleonexia* shaded into "sensual desire," at the center of the stage the idea of "immoderation in food and intoxicating drink" came alive. We witness this in Paul's question and its answer. He first asked, "Know ye not that the unrighteous shall not inherit the kingdom of God?" Then his answer came, sweeping along "drunkards [and] . . . revilers" as those unfit to "inherit the kingdom of God." With these ne'er-do-wells stood "fornicators [and] . . . idolaters [and] . . . adulterers," all wrapped together in a tidy, noxious bundle (1 Cor. 6:9–10).[58] In the light of 1 Cor. 5:10–11 and 6:9–10, *pleonexia* in our verse "should also be taken as the sort of unrestrained sexual greed whereby a person assumes that others exist for his or her own gratification" (see the Notes on 4:19; 5:5).[59]

named: So great was the effort not to be attracted to or touched by sin, especially illicit sexual activities, that Paul demanded that church members not even repeat the names of transgressions.[60] Obviously, on one level naming bore a sacred quality. How so? Because the Apostle pushed naming into God's domain. Earlier in this Epistle Paul disclosed that "I kneel before the Father (from whom every family in the heavenly realms and on earth derives its name)" (3:14–15 NR). From another viewpoint, "God names all families, and is thus Father of all; for it is the father's affair to give names."[61] Even in the case of Adam naming the animals, his action was under God's direction (see Gen. 2:19–20; Moses 3:19–20; and Abr. 5:20–21).

becometh: The impersonal verb πρέπει (*prepei,* from πρέπω, *prepō*), a term that occurs only four times in the New Testament, carries the meaning "to be fitting" or "to be suitable."[62] Between our verse and Matthew 3:15 there arises a question of whether early Christians possessed a written code or memorial of some sort according to which "Jesus was bound to be baptized," something that Marcus Barth argued against.[63] In Matthew's Gospel,

---

57. Delling, *TDNT,* 6:271.
58. Delling, *TDNT,* 6:271–72; the quotations are from 6:271.
59. Lincoln, *Ephesians,* 322; see also Caird, *Letters,* 84; Merkle, *Guide,* 159; and Winger, *Ephesians,* 553; see Louw-Nida, §88.144, on the sense of exploitation.
60. BDAG, 714.2; Lincoln, *Ephesians,* 322; Best, *Ephesians,* 476–77.
61. Hans Bietenhard, *TDNT,* 5:282.
62. BDAG, 861; Thayer, *Lexicon,* 535. See also Matt. 3:15; 1 Cor. 11:13; Heb. 2:10.
63. Barth, *Ephesians,* 2:560.

we hear Jesus say to John the Baptist before receiving baptism, "It *becometh* us to fulfill all righteousness" (Matt. 3:15, emphasis added). Even though no written document is known from the earliest church that described how and where Jesus was to be baptized, a very clear celestial expectation existed. Significantly, the essence of Jesus' baptism reposes in modern scripture. In a long passage about the nature and necessity of baptism, the prophet Nephi asked his readers about the prophetic divine demand that Jesus receive baptism at the hands of "that prophet," John the Baptist. He responded that Jesus needed "to be baptized by water, to fulfil all righteousness." To what end? In answering, Nephi placed Jesus' baptism on the highest of plateaus, that of his personal holiness. For "notwithstanding he being holy, he showeth unto the children of men that, according to the flesh he humbleth himself before the Father, and witnesseth unto the Father that he would be obedient unto him in keeping his commandments" (2 Ne. 31:4–5, 7). Our question to Nephi bears on the nature of "his [the Father's] commandments." Did they come orally or in written form? The clearest clue arises from John's Gospel. After establishing that the Baptist "was a man sent from God," the Gospel writer then quoted John as saying, "He that sent me to baptize with water . . . *said* to me" (John 1:6, 33, emphasis added). Plainly, John came baptizing "with water" because of oral instructions from a divine personality. It is a simple step to conclude that Jesus came to John owing to celestial oral instructions too.

saints: In this verse, the occurrence of this noun (plural of ἅγιος, *hagios*) carries a different feel from its other appearances in this letter, whether as the noun "holy one" or "saint," or as the adjective "holy."[64] In our context, the noun appears without a definite article, thus laying a subtle emphasis on the special character of these individuals, a holiness that has become a part of who they are. These people represent more than a glad-handing fellowship. Rather, they constitute a clustering of the vigilant, charitable faithful.[65] In their own way, they have come to mirror the Savior, who himself was holy (see Mark 1:34; Luke 1:35; 4:34; John 6:69;[66] and the Notes on 2:19; 3:18; 4:12).

5:4 *filthiness:* Paul now trains his eye on the sins of speech, a topic that he touched on at 4:29: "Let no corrupt communication proceed out of your mouth, but that which is good to the use of edifying." Although

---

64. Ephesians 1:1, 4, 13, 15, 18; 2:19, 21; 3:5, 8, 18; 4:12, 30; 5:27; 6:18. See BDAG, 10–11; Louw-Nida, §§11.27; 88.24.

65. Lincoln, *Ephesians*, 322.

66. Procksch and Kuhn, *TDNT*, 1:101–2. The preferred reading from the best manuscripts of John 6:69 is "thou art the Holy One of God." Metzger, *Textual Commentary*, 184.

the very rare noun αἰσχρότης (*aischrotēs*) generally pertains to shameful behavior,[67] in this verse it links to bad speech because of its connection to the following two terms, which have to do with sinful conversation. In its turn, the obscenity of *aischrotēs* colors those next two nouns and frames them as "foolish talk and coarse joking about sex."[68] Hence, in 5:3 Paul has pointed out illicit sexual acts, naming them as he asks his readers not to do, and in 5:4 he ties rough speech to the same degrading world. A reader cannot miss the contrast between the divine self-sacrifice of Christ noted in 5:2 and the evil self-indulgence outlined in 5:3–5 (see the Notes on 4:29; 5:6).

foolish talking: Like its two partners that come before and after, this noun appears only here in the New Testament. The meaning of μωρολογία (*mōrologia*) is "foolish or stupid talk."[69] Jesus raised this matter and quickly paired it with anger. Mirroring the laws of his day, Jesus declared that "whosoever is angry with his brother . . . shall be in danger of the judgment . . . but whosoever shall say, Thou fool, shall be in danger of hell fire" (Matt. 5:22; 3 Ne. 12:22). As is plain, calling another person a "fool" brought on the more severe punishment, whether deserved or not. However, when pushed, Jesus called Pharisees and scribes "fools." Partly, it was because of their μωρολογία, hairsplitting in this case. With divine override, he called them "blind fools," because they had become caught up in questions like whether the temple or the gold stored in the temple's treasury was more important. Derisively, he asked, "Which is the more important, the gold, or the sanctuary which sanctifies the gold?" (Matt. 23:17 NEB). When he saw foolishness masquerading as a sanctifying, informing intelligence, he did not back away from bringing offenders up short (see the Notes on 4:29; 5:6, 15).[70]

jesting: As in the case of the prior two nouns, εὐτραπελία (*eutrapelia*) is found only here in the New Testament and presents the meaning of "coarse or vulgar speech."[71] To be sure, in the wider world this term often bore the positive meaning "pleasantry or humor," but not always.[72] In Paul's reckoning, it offered its negative side to believers. One can almost hear the echoes of terms like "loud laughter" and "evil speaking" in this and the prior two nouns.

---

67. BDAG, 29; Louw-Nida, §88.149. According to Rudolf Bultmann, this noun occurs only in Attic Greek literature and in this New Testament passage. *TDNT,* 1:191.

68. Lincoln, *Ephesians,* 322–23; the quotation is from 323; see also Barth, *Ephesians,* 2:561; Larkin, *Handbook,* 109; Merkle, *Guide,* 160.

69. BDAG, 663; Louw-Nida, §33.379.

70. Georg Bertram, *TDNT,* 4:842, 844–45.

71. BDAG, 414; Louw-Nida, §33.34.

72. Thayer, *Lexicon,* 263; Lincoln, *Ephesians,* 323; Best, *Ephesians,* 479; Larkin, *Handbook,* 109; Merkle, *Guide,* 160; Winger, *Ephesians,* 554.

are not convenient: The verb ἀνῆκω (*anēkō*) sits in the imperfect tense, the tense of past customary action. With its negative οὐκ (*ouk*), it pushes forward the sense "is not proper."[73] Framed differently, it denotes "that which does not belong." In the context, it "is opposed to" what "is fitting for saints" (5:3 NR).[74]

giving of thanks: The term εὐχαριστία (*eucharistia*) denotes "the rendering of thanks" as well as pointing to the Eucharist or sacrament itself.[75] Even if one judges that this noun conveys only the sense of giving thanks, it still attracts the fragrances of the sacramental ordinance, complete with its remembrance of Christ's atoning act and the recipient's pledge never to forget him (see 3 Ne. 18:5–7). This cluster of connections can be found lying in the associated verb at 1:16 and 5:20. It is this sacramental ordinance, the Eucharist, received with "real intent," that braces the individual "against the wiles of the devil" (6:11) and strengthens that person "according to the power that worketh in us" (3:20), even "the exceeding greatness of [God's] power" (1:19). Thus armed, the person possesses the power to resist the behaviors listed in this verse and the prior one (see 5:3 and the Notes on 1:16; 5:20).

5:5 *this:* The pronoun τοῦτο (*touto*) wraps itself around all of the evil traits listed in this verse and the prior two (5:3–4). Paul's audience knows that he knows that they know that all such activities are out of bounds for church members. But they are willing to receive his counsel, and he is more than willing to give it. Within these verses, 5:3–5, we come upon the limitations for a person to obtain a celestial inheritance. Not present but certainly implicit are the "good works" that are an essential ingredient for receiving an inheritance, as 2:10 affirms: "Which God hath before ordained that we should walk in them" (see the Notes on 1:11, 18; 2:10).

ye know: The construction is unusual, with a finite verb meaning "to know" along with a participle from a different root that also signifies "to know" (ἴστε γινώσκοντες, *iste ginōskontes,* derivatives of οἶδα, *oida,* and γινώσκω, *ginōskō,* respectively),[76] a recipe for strong emphasis. The debate concerns whether the finite verb is an indicative or an imperative. If indicative, the meaning is "you certainly know." If imperative, we get the sense "know this!" The firmer case comes down on the side of the indicative meaning, "you certainly know," because Paul was stressing something that his readers were

---

73. Blass and Debrunner, *Greek Grammar,* §358; see also BDAG, 79.2.
74. Heinrich Schlier, *TDNT,* 1:360.
75. BDAG, 416.2 and 416.3.
76. BDAG, 199–201, 693–94; Thayer, *Lexicon,* 117–18, 174.II.1–2.

already aware of. No surprises here. In either case, the construction mirrors a Hebrew word arrangement, illustrating that Paul was drawing, consciously or unconsciously, on his Jewish background.[77]

Although a first glance may tell readers that the Apostle was inviting their gaze to a normal, undifferentiated scene of improper, sinful behaviors, in its makeup the vista offered a view of "a knowledge which accepts the consequences of knowledge." In other words, the one who knows also knows that this knowledge brought expectations of proper attitude and action. Jesus articulated this dimension in his words "If the goodman of the house had known in what watch the thief would come, he would have watched, and would not have suffered his house to be broken up" (Matt. 24:43). That is, if the owner had known, he would have prepared to protect his property. When charity weaves itself into the vista, then we see the following result: "I was an hungered, and ye gave me meat: I was thirsty, and ye gave me drink: I was a stranger, and ye took me in" (Matt. 25:35). The one who knows also knows what to do and what will result. In an oft quoted passage that deals briefly with trials, James wrote about this kind of knowledge: "Knowing [*ginōskontes*] this, that the trying of your faith worketh patience" (James 1:3; see also James 5:20[78] and the Notes on 1:17; 3:18, 19; 4:13).

whoremonger: The noun here is πόρνος (*pornos*), "a male prostitute or fornicator."[79] In Paul's informed view, the stakes for such persons were grim. As he stridently reminded his Corinthian readers, "the unrighteous shall not inherit the kingdom of God . . . neither fornicators [plural of *pornos*] . . . nor adulterers" (1 Cor. 6:9). The Apostle was inveighing against those who pursued immoral acts.[80] Jesus, on the other hand, raised the bar even higher by declaring that "whosoever looketh on a woman to lust after her hath committed adultery with her already in his heart" (Matt. 5:28). Both Christ and Paul brought the understanding that, after an investigator receives baptism and the gift of the Holy Ghost, "your body is the temple of the Holy Ghost which is in you" because "ye are bought with a [measureless] price: therefore glorify God in your body, and in your spirit, which are God's" (1 Cor. 6:19–20). In the world of believers, a person's body, a person's life, constituted the offering that replaced the animal and vegetative sacrifices of

---

77. Merkle, *Guide*, 161; Blass and Debrunner, *Greek Grammar*, §422.
78. Rudolf Bultmann, *TDNT*, 1:704.
79. BDAG, 855; Thayer, *Lexicon*, 532.
80. Hauck and Schulz, *TDNT*, 6:593.

the past, thus bringing a person's need to remain pure to a highly personal and tangibly physical level.[81] As Paul reminded his Roman readers, their "bodies [were] a living sacrifice, holy, acceptable unto God, which is your reasonable service" (Rom. 12:1; see also the Notes on 4:19; 5:3).

unclean person: The simple adjective ἀκάθαρτος (*akathartos*) nestles beneath these two English words, carrying the meaning "unclean." In the New Testament, the Greek term took its bearings from the Old Testament, where it directed readers to that which was not to touch God or anything associated with him, particularly in a ritual setting.[82] In a move toward metaphorical meanings, a number of ill practices were gathered up in Leviticus 18:24–30 and given the label "defiled," with consequences even for the land that God called his own. That is, the presence of defiled persons made the land unclean, causing "the land itself" to vomit "out her inhabitants" (Lev. 18:25).[83] An easy step brings a reader to see that the "unclean person" of our verse will not receive "any inheritance in the kingdom of Christ and of God." In another passage wherein Paul offers a rough quotation of Isaiah 52:11, we encounter the words "come out from among them, and be ye separate, saith the Lord, and touch not the unclean thing; and I will receive you" (2 Cor. 6:17;[84] see also the Notes on 4:19; 5:3).

covetous man: Like the prior two nouns, *pornos* and *akathartos,* Paul has personified the individuals who have indulged themselves in "covetousness" (*pleonexia*; 5:3) by writing the noun πλεονέκτης (*pleonektēs*), "greedy person."[85] In the three other occurrences of this noun in the New Testament, it is always associated with "fornicators" (*pornos* in its plural form; see also 1 Cor. 5:9–11; 6:9–10). This is not impressive company. Among those who want more than they already possess are found both rich and poor. In modern scripture we read, "Wo unto you rich men, that will not give your substance to the poor." Within a few lines, we discover the words "wo unto your poor men . . . whose bellies are not satisfied [and] . . . whose eyes are full of greediness" (D&C 56:16–17). One of the chinks in the spiritual armor of early Latter-day Saints living in Missouri appears in the words "I, the Lord, am not well pleased with the inhabitants of Zion, for . . . their eyes are full of greediness. These things ought not to be, and must be done

81. Procksch, *TDNT,* 1:108.
82. G. André and Helmer Ringgren, *TDOT,* 5:331, 337; BDAG, 34; Thayer, *Lexicon,* 21.
83. André and Ringgren, *TDOT,* 5:337–38.
84. Meyer and Hauck, *TDNT,* 3:428–29.
85. BDAG, 824; Louw-Nida, §25.23.

away from among them" (D&C 68:31–32). Here we find the clear recognition that persons of greed within the community of believers assist in "the ravaging of all human relationships," thus undoing the spiritual ties that bind people one to another (see the Notes on 4:19; 5:3).[86]

idolater: According to Colossians 3:5, "covetousness [*pleonexia*] . . . is idolatry." In this light and in the light of our present verse, an idolater (εἰδωλολάτρης, *eidōlolatrēs*) shares the bad characteristics of the greedy person[87] and, perhaps, those of the "whoremonger" and "unclean person" as well.[88] More than this, such an individual denies the powers and influences of God, whether secretly or openly. An important passage in modern scripture describes an idolater as a person who "walketh in his own way, and after the image of his own god, whose image is in the likeness of the world" (D&C 1:16). In the words of the mortal Jesus, "ye cannot serve God and mammon" (Matt. 6:24; Luke 16:13).

hath: The question is whether the present tense of ἔχω (*echō*), "to have," refers to an already-possessed inheritance that steadfast believers now enjoy, or whether it bears a future sense that vaults readers into the distant world where they are to possess their eternal inheritances. Opinions vary. If one considers the question in the light of "the absolute assurance of hope," then everlasting realities are already present.[89] For instance, Paul elsewhere wrote to believers: "Now that you have been set free from sin[,] . . . the return you get [*echō*[90]] is sanctification and its end, eternal life" (Rom. 6:22 RSV). Again, "if our earthly house of this tabernacle were dissolved, we have [*echō*] a building of God, . . . eternal in the heavens," already prepared (2 Cor. 5:1). On the other hand, the future meaning is in full display in the lines "the unrighteous shall not inherit the kingdom of God" (1 Cor. 6:9) and "they which do such things [just listed] shall not inherit the kingdom of God" (Gal. 5:21; see also Rom. 8:23).[91]

On the side asserting that believers already possess heavenly gifts rests the "redemption through his [Christ's] blood, the forgiveness of sins" (1:7). We read elsewhere the instruction to "hold that fast which thou hast, that no man take thy crown" (Rev. 3:11; see also Rev. 2:25).[92] That said, the matter

---

86. Delling, *TDNT*, 6:272.
87. Friedrich Büchsel, *TDNT*, 2:380; Delling, *TDNT*, 6:271; Lincoln, *Ephesians*, 324–25; Best, *Ephesians*, 481; Merkle, *Guide*, 162.
88. Barth, *Ephesians*, 2:563–64; Winger, *Ephesians*, 556.
89. Hanse, *TDNT*, 2:825.
90. BDAG, 421.3.c.
91. Hermann and Foerster, *TDNT*, 3:782–83.
92. Barth, *Ephesians*, 2:564.

is resolved more satisfactorily when we understand the present tense of a verb both to picture a present reality and to paint a portrait of what is to come.[93] Hence, a person's present possession of an "inheritance in the . . . Kingdom" and a future possession are not mutually exclusive.[94] In the few passages reviewed above, church members clearly stood on much higher ground than their unbelieving contemporaries who flailed at life while entwined in "deceitful lusts" (4:22). Moreover, their eternal prospects were and will be infinitely richer (see John 5:24 and 1 John 3:15; 5:12).

inheritance: The story of inheritance begins with Abraham, whose possessions were all moveable so he could respond instantaneously to God's command "Get thee out of thy country . . . unto a land that I will shew thee" (Gen. 12:1; Abr. 2:3). That was the case until he purchased from the sons of Heth for four hundred shekels of silver a piece of ground where he could bury his wife, Sarah (see Gen. 23:2–20). From that moment on, land became a real commodity that could be inherited like moveable property. Even so, inheritance took upon itself a metaphorical shimmer, moving one's real inheritance from the earth to the heavens. For instance, the last verse in the book of Daniel reads: "But go your way till the end; and you shall rest, and shall stand in your allotted place at the end of the days" (Dan. 12:13 RSV). In an intriguing trajectory of this notion of receiving one's inheritance "at the end of days," the Septuagint reading of the last expression brings the "allotted place" or inheritance into the heavenly world: "You shall rest, and shall stand in your glory [*doxan*] at the end of days" (LXX Dan. 12:13; see also LXX Ps. 15:5–6 [Ps. 16:5–6 KJV]).[95]

From this place, it is an easy jump to the New Testament concept of inheriting heavenly realities, of becoming an heir of God and Christ. In a passage noted before, Paul wrote that "the Spirit itself beareth witness with our spirit, that we are the children of God: and if children, then heirs; heirs of God, and joint-heirs with Christ" (Rom. 8:16–17). Such a prospect lifts a person's gaze in an instant from the terrestrial world to the celestial. In other words, "the concept of the kingdom of God and of the inheritance is freed from all earthly limitations and qualifications."[96] Spatial thoughts that have to do with land and property fall away, and readers come across the prospect of inheriting "the riches of [God's] glory" (1:18; see also Rom. 8:17), an "[everlasting] blessing" (1 Pet. 3:9), salvation (see Heb. 1:14), and

93. Blass and Debrunner, *Greek Grammar,* §323.
94. Best, *Ephesians,* 481–82.
95. Werner Dommershausen, *TDOT,* 2:455.
96. Hermann and Foerster, *TDNT,* 3:782.

"eternal life" (Titus 3:7). Perhaps the most stunning of promises has to do with married couples becoming "heirs together of the grace of [eternal] life" (1 Pet. 3:7).

Even though Jesus promised the meek that they would "inherit the earth" (Matt. 5:5), in that far-off moment the earth will enjoy a celestialized state and will be the place of God's kingdom (see Isa. 65:17; Rev. 21:1; Ether 13:9; D&C 29:23–24; 63:21; 77:1; 76:63; 88:17–26; etc.). Keeping in mind the character of an eternal inheritance, one grasps that "it is God's rule or reign, which lavishes on man [and woman] the inconceivable riches of the divine life,"[97] breathtakingly bringing "his [and her] lot [into] the council of God" (see the Notes on 1:14, 18; and appendix 2).[98]

kingdom: Only here does this noun appear in Ephesians (βασιλεία, *basileia*).[99] Such a kingdom needs both a king and subjects. Of course, absent from the subjects will be the fornicators, the unclean, and the greedy (see 5:5; 1 Cor. 6:9–10; and Gal. 5:19–21). As we have just established above, subjects in God's kingdom will be heirs, "the children of God" (Rom. 8:16), not servants or slaves. Believers will be spiritually "born of him [Christ] and [will] have become his sons and daughters" (Mosiah 5:7; see also Gal. 4:5–7 and James 2:5). More than this, these heirs will rule and reign with God. We hear Jesus' words at the end of a parable spoken on the Mount of Olives: "His lord said unto him [the steady steward], Well done, thou good and faithful servant: thou hast been faithful over a few things, I will make thee ruler over many things" (Matt. 25:21; see also Matt. 25:23 and Luke 19:17). With even more descriptive language, the Revelator wrote about "Jesus Christ . . . that loved us, and washed us from our sins in his own blood, and hath made us kings and priests unto God and his Father" (Rev. 1:5; see also 5:10).

of Christ and of God: This extended prepositional phrase is unusual because it occurs nowhere else in Paul's writings, and because it seemingly assigns one kingdom to Christ and another to God (see Rev. 11:15, "the kingdom of our Lord and of his Christ," NIV). It may be that "*the kingdom is Christ's here and God's hereafter.*"[100] If so, we encounter a fundamental continuity, a unity, between the two.[101] Christ's kingdom came from his Father, and Christ gives to his true disciples "a kingdom." We listen to Jesus'

---

97. Hermann and Foerster, *TDNT,* 3:783.

98. Albrecht Oepke and Karl Georg Kuhn, *TDNT,* 5:299.

99. BDAG, 168–69.

100. Caird, *Letters,* 85, italics in original.

101. Hermann Kleinknecht, Gerhard von Rad, Karl Georg Kuhn, and Karl Ludwig Schmidt, *TDNT,* 1:581; Lincoln, *Ephesians,* 325.

words spoken during the Last Supper: "I appoint unto you a kingdom, as my Father hath appointed unto me" (Luke 22:29). As a matter of fact, the kingdoms that came to Jesus' followers actually flowed as gifts from the Father: "Fear not, little flock," said Jesus, "for it is your Father's good pleasure to give you the kingdom" (Luke 12:32).[102]

Perhaps as important is the explicit affirmation of the deity of Jesus Christ. This status lies just under the earlier language to the effect that the Father "raised him from the dead, and set him at his own right hand in the heavenly places" (1:20). We also discover this affirmation in John's Gospel—"the Word was God" (John 1:1)—and in the quoted lines from LXX Psalm 44:6 (Ps. 45:7 Hebrew Bible; Ps. 45:6 KJV)—"unto the Son he saith, Thy throne, O God, is for ever and ever: a sceptre of righteousness is the sceptre of thy kingdom" (Heb. 1:8).[103] Examples could be multiplied.

5:6 *deceive:* Paul adjusted the eyes of his readers so that they could see the current world and its inhabitants more clearly. Some in their society at Ephesus spoke "erroneous words" (NR), which he knew well after spending so much time among them (see Acts 19:10; 20:31). Others crowded them with "darkness," as they had done with believing Gentiles before they had found Christ (5:8). These persons he labeled "the children of disobedience" in both this verse and 2:2. Upon these would come "the wrath of God," not sparing (see Col. 3:5–6).[104]

Among the nonvirtues that Paul had just listed, deceiving (ἀπατάω, *apataō*) exacted a high price in the ancient world. The charge of deception was what brought Socrates to his end. Deceit was the underlying claim of the false witnesses against Jesus who in the early-morning hearing claimed that he had asserted, "I will destroy this temple that is made with hands, and within three days I will build another made without hands" (Mark 14:58; see also Matt. 26:61). The question in our passage is, Who spoke deceitfully? Church members? Gentile outsiders? It is possible that such deceit existed among believers. After all, "practices and beliefs of the pagan world will have continued to be present in the church and be the more dangerous if arguments supporting them came from within the community," a blazing harbinger of hot coals that would eventually flare up into a full-flamed apostasy.[105] Whether such deceit would come from outside the church would

---

102. Kleinknecht, von Rad, Kuhn, and Schmidt, *TDNT,* 1:587.
103. Barth, *Ephesians,* 2:565.
104. Fowl, *Ephesians,* 168–69.
105. Best, *Ephesians,* 484; contra Lincoln, *Ephesians,* 325.

depend on how deeply impressed believers were with the social and religious machinery that promoted the worship of Diana at her spectacular temple that lay northeast a mere mile and a half from the heart of Ephesus. It was this sort of thing that Paul preached against while in the city, kindling the built-up anger of the silversmiths, who fashioned Diana trinkets to sell and who drove the Apostle away for good (see Acts 19:23–41; and the Notes on 4:14; 6:11).

vain words: If, indeed, such words (κενοῖς λόγοις, *kenois logois*) were coming from those who paraded themselves about as Christians, the situation in Ephesus was more dire than might be supposed. Are we looking at the beginnings of the situations pictured in the lines "our trouble which came to us in Asia . . . insomuch that we despaired even of life" (2 Cor. 1:8)? Very possibly. The sense of the singular *kenos* is "empty" or even "erroneous" or "untrue."[106] In light of Paul's plea not to be deceived, the latter meaning of "erroneous" is surely closer to the truth, bearing "a warning against heresy" within the church.[107] This is apparently why persons who deceived the Saints will, ominously, inherit "the wrath of God." The Apostle's concern here reminds one about the struggles mirrored elsewhere over matters that impacted true teachings: "fables and endless genealogies, . . . vain jangling [and] . . . the law [which] is good if a man use it lawfully" (1 Tim. 1:4, 6, 8–10).

Perhaps significantly, such "words" (plural of λόγος, *logos*) are all vocal, not written.[108] Words spoken to injure another were considered more severe than actions that affected the property of others. We read about "sins of the tongue" such as "enticing words" (Col. 2:4), "filthy communication" (Col. 3:8), "vain jangling" (1 Tim. 1:6), and "godless chatter" (1 Tim. 6:20 NIV; see also 2 Tim. 2:23 and Titus 3:9).[109] In an earlier period, Jesus had criticized pretended truths that rested on supposed spiritual subtleties. His aroused ire can be heard behind his lashing words: "Woe unto you, scribes and Pharisees, hypocrites! for ye . . . for a pretense make long prayer" of many words (Matt. 23:14). More precisely, "you also say, 'If anyone swears

---

106. BDAG, 539; Best, *Ephesians,* 485; Louw-Nida, §72.10.

107. Bertram, *TDNT,* 4:844; see also Johannes Schneider, *TDNT,* 2:674: "The appearing of Christ will be preceded by apostasy." New Testament references to a looming crisis among early believers include such passages as Mark 13:5, 22 (Matt. 24:5, 24; Luke 21:8); Acts 20:29–30; Gal. 1:6; 3:1; 2 Thes. 2:3–4; 1 Tim. 1:6; 4:1; 2 Tim. 2:18; 3:1, 5; 4:4; Titus 1:16; 2 Pet. 2:1; 1 John 2:18; 4:1; Jude 1:4; and Rev. 2:2.

108. Debrunner, Kleinknecht, Procksch, Kittel, Quell, and Schrenk, *TDNT,* 4:102.

109. Bertram, *TDNT,* 4:844.

by the altar, it means nothing; but if anyone swears by the gift on it, he is bound by his oath.'" Then he asked, "Which is greater: the gift, or the altar that makes the gift sacred?" (Matt. 23:18–19 NIV). As an ebony capstone of sorts, Jesus warned these men that "ye also outwardly appear righteous unto men, but within ye are full of hypocrisy and iniquity" (Matt. 23:28). With this, Jesus' judgment had circled back to the initial thought that transgressions of the tongue remain worse than those of the hands and feet (see the Notes on 4:29; 5:4).[110]

wrath: It is not that "the wrath of God will fall [only] on unbelievers (Col. 3:6; Eph. 5:6)."[111] As we saw above, the problem for the church seemingly lay not so much among nonmembers or unbelievers but among deceivers who were within the fold, at least temporarily. This is evidently why the fearsome wrath (ὀργή, *orgē*) of God would surely come. To be sure, "the wrath [*orgē*] of God is revealed from heaven against *all* ungodliness and unrighteousness of [all] men." Why? "Because that which may be known of God is manifest in them; for God hath shewed it unto them." Hence, "they are without excuse" (Rom. 1:18–20, emphasis added).

In a different vein, the question arises whether God's wrath is limited in duration. That is, does his anger spend itself in an event, or series of events, or does it percolate over long stretches of time, perhaps forever? The roots of the matter spring up in Old Testament passages that have to do with the expected and dreaded "day of the Lord," a day that promises massive disruption and punishment. To cite one example, we hear the shrill cry "The great day of the Lord is near, it is near, and hasteth greatly. . . . That day is a day of wrath, a day of trouble and distress, a day of wasteness and desolation, a day of darkness and gloominess, a day of clouds and thick darkness" (Zeph. 1:14–15). John the Baptist threw this image toward his audiences, particularly the religious authorities of his day: "O generation of vipers, who hath warned you to flee from the wrath [*orgē*] to come?" As he assured, his message was designed to get his hearers to "bring forth therefore fruits meet for repentance" (Matt. 3:7–8; see also Rom. 2:4–5). Jesus too pressed upon his disciples in his sermon on the Mount of Olives the fact that this wrath would eventually swallow Jerusalem: "When ye shall see Jerusalem compassed with armies, then know that the desolation thereof is nigh." The next part of his warning persisted among his followers for another forty years, saving their lives when they fled from the city as directed by a

---

110. Bertram, *TDNT,* 4:842, 844–45.
111. Schneider, *TDNT,* 2:674.

revelation received by church leaders.[112] For, he almost shouted, "let them which are in Judea flee to the mountains; and let them which are in the midst of it depart out" (Luke 21:20–21). The Christians fled Jerusalem, settling in Pella, a town on the east bank of the Jordan River just south of the Sea of Galilee. There they rode out the war in relative tranquility.

So far, God's wrath has been confined to an event or series of events such as the Romans' successful prosecution of the war against rebellious Jewish partisans in AD 66–70, capturing Jerusalem at the end.[113] Jesus also pictured such situations in parables. For instance, in the story of a "certain man [who] made a great supper, and bade many," the host's generosity and goodness were rebuffed by invited guests who declined at the last minute. One had "bought a piece of ground," another had "bought five yoke of oxen," and a third had "married a wife, and therefore I cannot come." Naturally, at this news, the man became "angry [the verb related to *orgē*]" and directed his servant to invite as guests "the poor, and the maimed, and the halt, and the blind," the spiritually receptive (Luke 14:16–21). The underlying goodness of the host in Jesus' story is precisely what Paul emphasized when he asked, "Despisest thou the riches of his [God's] goodness and forbearance and longsuffering; not knowing that the goodness of God leadeth thee to repentance?" (Rom. 2:4). Here we grasp that God's preference is to move his children by means of gifts of gentleness and kindness rather than through threats of retribution.[114]

Whirling back to the question of God's limitations on his wrath, we notice that, in Jesus' parable of the unforgiving servant, "in anger [the verb related to *orgē*] his master turned him over to the jailers . . . until he should pay back all he owed" (Matt. 18:34 NIV). Importantly, although the servant faced the impossible task of paying his debts while in prison, he did not face annihilation. If we move Jesus' earthly story into the heavens, it becomes clear that God will not destroy a wicked person's self or soul, but will subject it to an awful punishment of some kind.[115] A key passage occurs in Paul's first letter to the Thessalonians. There he presented the fate of Jewish opponents who had pushed back hard against Paul's message in Thessalonica and then carried their fight against him to Berea, a town fifty miles distant (see Acts 17:5, 13). Of them, the Apostle wrote that they forbade

112. Eusebius, *Ecclesiastical History* 3.5.3.
113. Kleinknecht, Grether, Procksch, Fichtner, Sjoeberg, and Stählin, *TDNT,* 5:430.
114. Kleinknecht, Grether, Procksch, Fichtner, Sjoeberg, and Stählin, *TDNT,* 5:442.
115. Kleinknecht, Grether, Procksch, Fichtner, Sjoeberg, and Stählin, *TDNT,* 5:444.

"us to speak to the Gentiles [in Thessalonica and Berea] that they might be saved, to fill up their sins alway: for the wrath [*orgē*] is come upon them to the uttermost" (1 Thes. 2:16). What is a reader to think?

The next question centers on the final prepositional phrase, which the KJV renders "to the uttermost" (εἰς τέλος, *eis telos*). Most translations understand the phrase to mean "at last," as if those hateful persecutors were at that moment bearing God's punishment. The phrase does not mean "forever" or the like. Hence, the meaning pertains to an outpouring of God's wrath for a controlled, limited time, not indefinitely.[116] This is exactly the essence of the Lord's words to Joseph Smith: "I am endless, and the punishment which is given from my hand is endless punishment, for Endless is my name." Moreover, "eternal punishment is God's punishment" (D&C 19:10–11). Therefore, when we come upon "endless punishment" or "eternal punishment," we are not learning about punishment or wrath without an end, without a time component. Instead, we are discovering the keeper of the time (see the Notes on 2:3; 4:31).

the children of disobedience: As we have learned above, this verse, 5:6, may revolve a good deal around a nascent apostasy, with so-called Christians leading the efforts to deceive their former fellow-believers. In their case, they were not "alienated from the life of God through the ignorance that is in them" (4:18). They knew, but seemed not to believe that God knew, of their deceit. Hence, Paul's writing of this same expression at 2:2 differs from the one here. At 2:2, the Apostle wrote about the devilish influences that had pushed and pulled Gentile converts before they came to Christ, when they "walked according to the course of this world, [and] according to the prince of the power of the air." In those days, they unknowingly fulfilled "the desires of the flesh and of the mind," whatever those desires might have been (2:3; see also Col. 3:4–11).

The apparent deceivers in our passage evidently stood against the knowledge that had come to them from heavenly heights, a spiritually fatal misstep. After their initial experience with God's Spirit as fresh investigators, some surely had come to enjoy "the spirit of wisdom and revelation in the knowledge of [God]" (1:17). Some had spent enough time with Paul to "understand [his] knowledge in the mystery of Christ" (3:4). Further, some had come to "comprehend with all saints . . . the love of Christ, which passeth knowledge" (3:18–19). The common denominator in all these statements is knowledge, a heaven-directed understanding

---

116. Kleinknecht, Grether, Procksch, Fichtner, Sjoeberg, and Stählin, *TDNT,* 5:434.

that introduced the then-believers into chambers of celestial treasures. Why might they have turned away? Jesus answered the question best on this topic: "Some [seed] fell upon a rock; and as soon as it was sprung up, it withered away, because it lacked moisture. And some fell among thorns; and the thorns sprang up with it, and choked it" (Luke 8:6–7). For the purposes of any review, the expression "the children of disobedience" here contrasts sharply with the "dear children" of 5:1 (see the Note on 2:2). In fact, the expression "the children of disobedience" hints strongly that these people had once sat within the kingdom as children, as inheritors of God's gifts.

5:7 *partakers:* Like the case at 3:6, the term συμμέτοχος (*summetochos*)[117] makes better sense as "fellow partaker" (NR). Unlike the same noun at 3:6, in 5:7 the word has a distinctly negative meaning. In our verse, we pick up Paul's appeal that his readers not join themselves to deceivers who apparently sit in their ranks, Jews or Gentiles.[118] Regrettably, the fellowship hinted at has evidently been broken by those who have deceived and driven away mutual trust. Lost to such people is "the heavenly calling" and the companionship of "the Apostle and High Priest of our profession, Christ Jesus" (Heb. 3:1). Thunderous in the ears of any inside deceiver are the words "It is impossible for those who were once enlightened, and have tasted of the heavenly gift, and were made partakers of the Holy Ghost, . . . if they shall fall away, to renew them again unto repentance; seeing they crucify to themselves the Son of God afresh, and put him to an open shame" (Heb. 6:4, 6). The blight resting on these individuals darkens: "of how much sorer punishment . . . shall he [she] be thought worthy, who hath trodden under foot the Son of God, and hath counted the blood . . . wherewith he was sanctified, an unholy thing" (Heb. 10:29; see also the Notes on 3:6; 4:30).[119]

5:8 *were:* The verb is the imperfect form of "to be" (εἰμί, *eimi*) and thus bears the sense "used to be" or "had been" in a past situation.[120]

darkness: This verse presents a typical contrast between light and darkness, a contrast fully at home in the Judaism of Paul's day. On one level, darkness (σκότος, *skotos*) refers readers to a kingdom or sphere of evil that has attached itself to this world. For example, at the time of his arrest, Jesus

---

117. BDAG, 958; Louw-Nida, §57.8; Thayer, *Lexicon*, 596.
118. Hanse, *TDNT*, 2:831 n. 5; Best, *Ephesians*, 486.
119. Hanse, *TDNT*, 2:831–32.
120. Blass and Debrunner, *Greek Grammar*, §330; BDAG, 285.5.

said to "the chief priests, and captains of the temple, and the elders" in the arresting party, "This is your hour, and the power of darkness [*skotos*]" (Luke 22:52–53). They were somehow the owners or custodians of a darkness whose frightening power they held in their hands at least temporarily. In the words of the Resurrected Christ addressed to Paul, however, one senses a subtle shift from the notion of a coordinated kingdom of darkness that is possessed by Christ's enemies to the concept of this world as a place of gloom that is to be escaped: "Rise and stand upon thy feet," commanded the Savior. "Now I send thee, to open their [the Gentiles'] eyes, and to turn them from darkness [*skotos*] to light, and from the power of Satan unto God" (Acts 26:16–18).[121] The aspect that unites the two thoughts arises from a very simple idea. An individual or group can fall under the influence of Satan, who seeks to dominate them, bringing on spiritual darkness and eventual captivity. Luke wrote, "Then entered Satan into Judas. . . . And he . . . communed with the chief priests and captains, how he might betray him unto them" (Luke 22:3–4). From that moment until Jesus' arrest, Judas was fully a servant of the devil (see Alma 34:35; D&C 10:20–22, 26–27; and the Notes on 2:2; 5:11; 6:12).

now are ye light in the Lord: Astonishment hangs all over this line. Why? Because the Apostle's readers are said to be light, not enlightened as at 1:18; 3:9; and 5:14. In our passage, they are not recipients of divine light or "the children of light" (1 Thes. 5:5; see also John 12:36). Instead, they are light just as John declared that "God is light" (1 John 1:5) and Christ affirmed that he himself is light. "I am the light of the world," Jesus intoned. But unlike Paul's words here, Jesus stated that "he that followeth me shall not walk in darkness, but shall have the light of life" (John 8:12). That is, the steadfast disciple will come to possess "the light of life," not be the light itself (see D&C 50:24, "he [and she] that receiveth light, and continueth in God, receiveth more light"). So what was Paul really saying?

On one level, it is possible for evil to transform itself into what masquerades as light. The Apostle himself wrote that, in his day, "false apostles" had changed "themselves into the apostles of Christ." Just as worrisome, "Satan himself [was] transformed into an angel of light" (2 Cor. 11:13–14). This concept was at home in the Judaism of Paul's day.[122] Centuries later, illustrating a continuity across time, Joseph Smith wrote that "the voice of Michael on the banks of the Susquehanna [River], [identified] the devil

121. Hans Conzelmann, *TDNT,* 7:442 n. 175.
122. Conzelmann, *TDNT,* 9:345.

when he appeared as an angel of light" (D&C 128:20). But in our verse, 5:8, light and darkness are clearly not both controlled for an evil purpose but are separated, and, according to the Apostle, his readers consisted of light itself. How shall we explain this concept?

The natural beginning place is the letter of Ephesians itself. Herein lies a key that appears in an unlooked-for corner. After correctly touting grace, a pure gift, as the door to salvation (see 2:8), Paul then wrote that "we are his [God's] workmanship, created in Christ Jesus unto good works, which God hath before ordained that we should walk in them" (2:10). Readers must keep in mind two important truths. First, humankind enjoys a celestial origin. They constitute God's everlasting "workmanship." That message sits deep inside the story of creation because humans are "in [God's] image, after [God's] likeness . . . male and female" (Gen. 1:26–27; Moses 2:26–27; Abr. 4:26–27). Second, in addition to sharing their enduring, heavenly origins, people are capable of improvement on a grand, supernal scale. If not, why did the Apostle write, "created in Christ Jesus unto good works . . . that we should walk in them" (2:10)?[123]

Naturally, the faithful do not measure up to Christ as a source of light. About him we read that "the [heavenly] city had no need of the sun, neither of the moon, to shine in it: for the glory of God did lighten it, and the Lamb [Christ] is the light thereof" (Rev. 21:23; see also Isa. 60:19, "the Lord shall be unto thee an everlasting light"). Yet in the spirit of improvement of the inner self, Paul has written that believers "have discarded the old nature with its deeds and have put on the new nature, which is being constantly renewed in the image of its Creator and brought to know God" (Col. 3:9–10 NEB). According to modern scripture, church leaders in Missouri during 1838 were to "shine forth, that [their] light may be a standard for the nations" (D&C 115:5). Three and a half years earlier Warren Cowdery was promised that "if he continue to be a faithful witness and a light unto the church I [Christ] have prepared a crown for him in the mansions of my Father" (D&C 106:8). The basic thought beneath such passages points to light within. And how does this come about? The process is gradual, not all at once. In one passage we read that "that which is of God is light; and he [and she] that receiveth light, and *continueth in God, receiveth more light*; and that light groweth brighter and brighter until the perfect day" (D&C 50:24, emphasis added). In other words, "if your eye be single to my glory, your whole bodies shall be filled with light, and there shall be no darkness

---

123. Conzelmann, *TDNT,* 9:347.

in you; and that body which is filled with light comprehendeth all things" (D&C 88:67; see also Matt. 6:22–23; Luke 11:34–36; and the Notes on 1:18; 2:10; 3:9; 5:13).

now: By writing this temporal adverb νῦν (*nun*), Paul vaults his readers into an array of gospel truths. In one sense, "now" is about the coming of new celestial knowledge. In an individual case, we hear the aged Simeon respond to seeing the infant Jesus at the Jerusalem temple. After anticipating this experience for years, he was finally able to say, "Lord, now [*nun*] lettest thou thy servant depart in peace, according to thy word" (Luke 2:29). In a broader sense, the mystery hidden for ages about the Gentiles' entry into God's kingdom "now" was "made known unto me [Paul]" and "unto his holy apostles and prophets" (3:3, 5). In another sense, the "now" represents one's new life in the gospel, something that a believer did not enjoy before embracing Christ. In the new moment, a person felt rescued from a former life of "the lusts of our flesh" (2:3) and spiritual "uncleanness" (5:3). "Now" believers emerged "strengthened with power in the inner person through his Spirit" (3:16 NR; see also Rom. 5:11).[124]

In our verse, 5:8, the matter is different. It refers to a new relationship with God. Earlier in our letter, Paul wrote, "At that time ye were without Christ, . . . having no hope, and without God in the world: but now [*nuni*, a variant spelling of *nun*[125]] in Christ Jesus ye . . . are made nigh by the blood of Christ" (2:12–13). Peter framed the idea clearly: "Once you were not a people, but now [*nun*] you are the people of God; once you had not received mercy, but now [*nun*] you have received mercy" (1 Pet. 2:10 NIV). With an emphasis on the current situation of the Roman Saints, Paul wrote that "we also joy in God through our Lord Jesus Christ, by whom we have now [*nun*] received the atonement" (Rom. 5:11; see also Rom. 11:28–31). In a negative pivot, but with the same result, the Apostle framed a question for his Galatian readers: "Formerly, when you did not know God, you were slaves to those who by nature are not gods. But now [*nun*] that you know God . . . how is it that you are turning back to those weak and miserable principles?" (Gal. 4:8–9 NIV). At issue, of course, was his readers' new relationship with God, which they had enjoyed following their conversions, but had now abandoned for something of far less value (see the Notes on 3:5, 10).[126]

---

124. Stählin, *TDNT,* 4:1117–18.
125. Stählin, *TDNT,* 4:1106.
126. Stählin, *TDNT,* 4:1117.

in the Lord: All in this verse makes sense with the addition of this phrase (ἐν κυρίῳ, *en kyriō*). It is the Lord who makes all else possible, including believers becoming sources of light. Paul was the likely inventor of such phrases as "in the Lord"[127] in his effort to capture this very sense for his audience—nothing celestial happens without the aid of Christ the Lord. Nothing. Rooted under this observation grows "the view of Christ as a universal personality." He is the cosmic Lord, not only in the present but also in the past and future. With him, in contrast to Adam and the first creation, a second creation has sprung to life, one that leads through a series of personal experiences and through historic time to a place at God's side in heaven at the end of time as we know it (see the Note on 4:1).[128]

walk: In the review of 5:2, we touched briefly on the principle of the two ways. Our verse, 5:8, invites a further examination, because the notion of the two ways rests comfortably in the opposites darkness and light. Jesus articulated his thought about dual pathways in his Sermon on the Mount when he said, "Wide is the gate, and broad is the way, that leadeth to destruction, and . . . strait is the gate, and narrow is the way, which leadeth unto life" (Matt. 7:13–14; see also 3 Ne. 27:33). The idea is that we walk along one path or the other, through one gate or the other, leading us, the travelers, toward good or ill. Whether or not the path goes inside an enclosure such as a city wall cannot be determined from the brief context with which Jesus surrounds the saying.[129] The entry onto the narrow path may well also involve expending a significant amount of energy, as hinted in a saying of Jesus found elsewhere on a similar subject: "Strive to enter in at the strait gate" (Luke 13:24). There Jesus "summons man to exert all his own powers" to get through the gate.[130]

In effect, Jesus was inviting his audience to become his disciples by making the irreversible decision to follow his way, his path. After all, he is "the way, the truth, and the life: no man [or woman] cometh unto the Father, but by me" (John 14:6). Earlier in the Sermon on the Mount, in order to make his saying secure by highlighting two different approaches to building, Jesus made the following point about those who respond to his

---

127. Oepke, *TDNT*, 2:541.

128. Oepke, *TDNT*, 2:542.

129. Michaelis, *TDNT*, 5:71; Joachim Jeremias, *TDNT*, 6:922–23. Both authors assume that the paths led into the interior of a city rather than to destinations outside the city gates. The metaphorical destinations, heaven or hell, can be thought of as either outside or inside city walls.

130. Michaelis, *TDNT*, 5:75.

message: "Whosoever heareth these sayings of mine, *and doeth them,* I will liken him unto a wise man, which built his house upon a rock." In contrast, "every one that heareth these sayings of mine, *and doeth them not,* shall be likened unto a foolish man, which built his house upon the sand" (Matt. 7:24, 26, emphasis added). Jesus planted the sign posts deep in the earth for the person who would see and become a disciple. Furthermore, Jesus' talk about the two ways framed a summons to repentance. That is the force of Jesus' introductory imperative, "Enter ye in at the strait gate" (Matt. 7:13). Such an act, such an effort to meet his demands for discipleship, was required before wiggling through the tight, packed gate and stepping onto the narrow path.[131]

These demands of discipleship and repentance, when followed, lead an investigator out of the darkness and into the light, perhaps for the first time in that person's life. This kind of walk into the light may be spiritually blinding at first, but gradually grows into a walk through heavenly gardens and celestial vistas. Naturally, the illuminated landscape offers to an individual's view other possibilities for next steps. Moving among the sights that present themselves to the viewer are the "walk worthy of God" and the "walk worthy of the Lord" (1 Thes. 2:12; Col. 1:10) as well as walking "worthy of the calling to which you were called" (4:1 NR).[132] Such worthiness, of course, implies possessing the behaviors and attitudes that Paul lists in 1 Thessalonians 4:2–12—staying away from sexual sins, dealing honestly with others, practicing "brotherly love," and tending to "your own business." That said, pairing the ideas of pursuing worthiness and entering a narrow, tight gate presents promising possibilities.

Revelation that dispels darkness generally comes to the worthy. Angels often serve as carriers of revelation, of celestial knowledge. One thinks, for example, of the angel who came to both Zacharias and Mary, bearing God's tidings (see Luke 1:11, 19, 26). Of Zacharias, Luke wrote that he and his wife, Elizabeth, were "both righteous before God" (Luke 1:6). The angel himself called Mary "highly favored" and affirmed that "the Lord is with thee" (Luke 1:28). As a result, both Zacharias and Mary found themselves on paths constructed by God, on pathways aimed at destinations that God himself had sculpted. Then the two of them, along with Elizabeth, stepped into a divine light and left the darkness behind them, enfolding their lives into God's purposes, which were to prepare for and to bring his Son into the world.

---

131. Michaelis, *TDNT,* 5:74–75.
132. Seesemann and Bertram, *TDNT,* 5:944.

Speaking metaphorically, that Son would unlock dark, forbidding gates and lighten paths in ways that would allow followers to spend eternity with him, "that where I am, there ye may be also" (John 14:3).

In a word, Jesus' efforts formed a rescue operation, rescuing "every one of you from his [or her] iniquities" (3 Ne. 20:26). This lifesaving effort did not confine itself to the mortal citizens of this world. No. It reached into the world of departed spirits too (see Rom. 14:9; 1 Pet. 3:18–20; 4:6; and Rev. 11:18). For this task, heaven recruited faithful followers of the Son who, for instance, were "baptized for the dead" (1 Cor. 15:29).[133] Further, the earthly actions of the Twelve were to stretch across boundaries and into the heavens, as Jesus declared to Peter and his fellows: "Whatsoever ye shall bind on earth shall be bound in heaven: and whatsoever ye shall loose on earth shall be loosed in heaven" (Matt. 18:18; see also Matt. 16:19). One of the happy consequences was that those eternal, departed spirits of dead persons "might be judged according to men in the flesh, but live according to God in the spirit" (1 Pet. 4:6; see also Rev. 11:18). This labor on behalf of the dead would free those souls from the dark powers of Satan, allowing them to bathe in celestial light (see the Notes on 2:2, 10; 4:1, 9, 10, 17; 5:2, 15).[134]

children of light: Unlike other scriptural sources aimed at Israelites, Paul has now wrapped his arms around Gentiles as well as Jews.[135] The expression contrasts with "the children of disobedience" in 5:6. This latter already had a history in the Old Testament under various titles: "children of wickedness" (2 Sam. 7:10), "children of iniquity" (Hosea 10:9), "the son of wickedness" (Ps. 89:22), "a son that causeth shame" (Prov. 10:5), and "the children of Belial" (Deut. 13:13; etc.).[136] The words "children of light" mirror Jesus' title for followers in his parable of the unjust steward. There he unflatteringly compared them to "the children of this world [who] are ... wiser than the children of light" (Luke 16:8). Jesus' point had to do with the focused intensity with which "the children of this world" pursue their worldly, personal aims, in comparison to the rather easygoing manner of "the children of light" in running after theirs. By

---

133. Riesenfeld, *TDNT,* 8:512–13.

134. Jeremias, *TDNT,* 1:148–49; Friedrich, *TDNT,* 2:718–19; Oepke, *TDNT,* 3:213; Grundmann, *TDNT,* 3:399–401; Büchsel, *TDNT,* 3:641–42; Friedrich, *TDNT,* 3:707–8; Jeremias, *TDNT,* 3:746–47; Schneider, *TDNT,* 4:597–98; Hauck and Schulz, *TDNT,* 6:577–78.

135. Procksch and Kuhn, *TDNT,* 1:106.

136. Herbert Haag, Jan Bergman, and Helmer Ringgren, *TDOT,* 2:151, 153.

contrast, when we come to 5:8, the "children of light" have already put "darkness" behind them and are enjoying their experience as "light in the Lord" (see John 8:12; 1 Thes. 5:5, "Ye are all the children of light, and the children of the day"; and the Notes on 2:10; 5:6).[137]

5:9 *the fruit of the Spirit:* This expression is identical to that in Galatians 5:22. A number of early manuscripts read "the fruit of the light" (NR). Even though the earliest text, $\mathfrak{P}^{46}$ (c. AD 200), and others read "the fruit of the Spirit," the alternate reading "the fruit of the light" enjoys support from a wide range of manuscripts, including $\mathfrak{P}^{49}$ from the third century, and is likely the original reading. The prevailing view centers on a copyist's evident effort to harmonize our verse, 5:9, with Galatians 5:22.[138]

fruit: John the Baptist held up the metaphor of fruit (καρπός, *karpos*) and peeled back its skin to reveal the consequences of a person's lack of response to the message of repentance in the face of God's approaching wrath: "Bring forth therefore fruits worthy of repentance, . . . every tree . . . which bringeth not forth good fruit is hewn down, and cast into the fire" (Luke 3:8–9; see also Matt. 3:8, 10). Jesus too appealed to the imagery of fruit in his teaching, presenting it as a visible result of a person's inner intentions. In the Sermon on the Mount he declared that "every good tree bringeth forth good fruit; but a corrupt tree bringeth forth evil fruit. . . . Wherefore by their fruits ye shall know them" (Matt. 7:17, 20; see also Matt. 12:33; Luke 6:43–45; and John 15:2). Noble inner intentions bring believers to a more abundant life, as Jesus disclosed in the parable of the sower. There he spoke of seed that "fell on good ground, and did yield fruit [*karpos*] that sprang up and increased; and brought forth, some thirty, and some sixty, and some an hundred" (Mark 4:8; see also Matt. 13:8 and Luke 8:8).[139]

In Paul's correspondence, the gears meshed differently. On one level, those whom he introduced to the gospel, and who had seized it, became his fruit. To the Roman Saints, whom he had not yet met, he expressed the desire "that I might have some fruit among you also, even as among other Gentiles" (Rom. 1:13; see also Philip. 1:22). With a twist, and with an obvious reference to the results of missionary work, the Apostle asked, "Who planteth a vineyard, and eateth not of the fruit thereof?" (1 Cor. 9:7; see also 2 Tim. 2:6). To his friends in Philippi, in a passage that comes close to the meaning "the fruit of the Spirit" or "the fruit of the light," Paul wrote

---

137. Brown, *Testimony of Luke*, 750–51.
138. Metzger, *Textual Commentary*, 539–40.
139. Friedrich Hauck, *TDNT*, 3:615.

about their generosity when sending a gift to the impoverished Saints in Judea, saying, "I seek the fruit that increases to your credit" (Philip. 4:17 RSV). Here, "fruit" is a virtual synonym to sanctification (see James 3:18, "the fruit of righteousness").[140]

the Spirit: As we have already seen, this term was most probably inserted by a later scribe who sought to harmonize the expression to "the fruit of the Spirit" in Galatians 5:22.[141] After all, in the Galatians passage, Paul had listed the fruits that come from the Spirit, and nowhere else had he written about the fruit of light. But the weight of the manuscript evidence supports the words "the light" (NR; see also the Notes on the Spirit at 2:2, 18, 22; 3:3, 16; 4:4).

goodness: Here the noun ἀγαθωσύνη, *agathōsynē*, is God's possession, which he bestows on the faithful, as we see in Paul's words: "we pray continually that our God will make you worthy of his call, and by his power fulfill all your desires for goodness [*agathōsynē*] and complete all that you have been doing through faith" (2 Thes. 1:11, Jerusalem Bible). The notion that *agathōsynē* comes from God also arises in this line: "The fruit of the Spirit is love, joy, . . . goodness, faith" (Gal. 5:22).[142] Such goodness stands palpable among church members, even bringing them to willingly accept admonishment of each other. Paul wrote, "I myself also am persuaded of you, my brethren, that ye also are full of goodness, filled with all knowledge [of celestial things, therefore] able also to admonish one another" (Rom. 15:14).[143]

righteousness: The term δικαιοσύνη (*dikaiosynē*) links to obedience as if an inner cable inseparably binds the two together. Pursuit of obedience leads to holiness. The Apostle taught these doctrines clearly when he prepared the matter by asking the question, "Do you not know that if you present yourselves as obedient slaves, you are slaves of the one whom you obey, whether to sin which results in death, or to obedience which results in righteousness?" His complimentary answer declared, "You were set free from sin and became enslaved to righteousness." What difference did this new status make? It meant that his readers "now present your members as slaves to righteousness, leading to holiness." The end of the story is "that you are free from sin and enslaved to God, [and] you produce fruit leading to holiness and its end,

---

140. Hauck, *TDNT*, 3:615.
141. Bruce, *Ephesians*, 106; Metzger, *Textual Commentary*, 539–40.
142. Merkle, *Guide*, 164–65.
143. Walter Grundmann, *TDNT*, 1:18.

an eternal life" (Rom. 6:16, 18, 19, 22, Wayment). In a word, "righteousness [is] the living power which overcomes sin" (see the Notes on 4:24; 6:14).[144]

Even though *dikaiosynē* did not make the list of heaven-sent fruits in Galatians 5:22–23, it does in our verse, 5:9. And it shines out as a divine characteristic that comes from light. At its base, it describes the relationship of God as ruler or king and his people as his subjects. God's righteousness, which characterizes his nature, guides him in his relationship with his children, particularly in offering salvation to them (see Deut. 32:4, 35–36; Hosea 2:19; and Micah 7:9).[145] He is not capricious as the Roman gods were, regularly surprising their subjects and leaving priests and devotees scrambling to determine what those gods wanted in order to placate them. Rather, on the Christian side, Christ had exemplified God's righteousness by being "put forward as an expiation [through] his blood, to be received by faith. This was to show God's righteousness, because in his divine forbearance he had passed over former sins." Further, all this "was to prove . . . that [God] himself is righteous and that he justifies him who has faith in Jesus" (Rom. 3:25–26 RSV).[146]

truth: Paul steered clear here of the almost unending Greek discussions on the meaning of truth. Those interests were foreign to his interest in "the truth [which] is in Jesus" (4:21). Instead, truth is bound up with how a person responds to it. In the negative arena, Paul stated that "the wrath of God is revealed from heaven against all . . . who hold the truth in unrighteousness" (Rom. 1:18). This kind of declaration recalls the concern with apparent deceivers within the ranks of Christian believers in 5:6. The truth noted in 6:14 can be worn by a believer-soldier as a defense against "spiritual wickedness in high places" and "the evil day" (6:12–13). The truth in this verse, 5:9, derives from light and thus unfolds to view a "divine reality."[147] This thought reminds one of another line from modern scripture: "Truth is knowledge of things as they are, and as they were, and as they are to come" (D&C 93:24). The concept of the linkage between truth and light, as we find in our verse, finds ballast when we read that "truth shineth. This is the light of Christ." That light—namely, Christ—"is in the sun, and the light of the sun, and . . . in the moon, and is the light of the moon, and . . . also the light of the stars." That "light which shineth, which giveth you light, is

---

144. Gottfried Quell and Gottlob Schrenk, *TDNT,* 2:209.

145. Quell and Schrenk, *TDNT,* 2:195.

146. Quell and Schrenk, *TDNT,* 2:203.

147. Oepke and Kuhn, *TDNT,* 5:308.

through him who enlighteneth your eyes, [and] . . . quickeneth your understandings" (D&C 88:7–9, 11). On this view, the light of Christ illumines all reality and all celestial truth (see the Notes on 4:21; 6:14).

5:10 *Proving:* The verb δοκιμάζω (*dokimazō*), here in participle form and governed by the verb "walk" in 5:2,[148] carries the sense of putting an item to the test to determine its genuineness.[149] In other words, "what is acceptable unto the Lord" can be known by every individual who will put the Lord's word to the test.[150] As Jesus reminded his critics, "If any man will do his [God's] will, he shall know of the doctrine [διδαχή, *didachē*, 'teaching'[151]], whether it be of God, or whether I speak of myself" (John 7:17). In another place where he adopts language similar to verse 5:10, Paul encouraged his Roman readers to be "transformed by the renewing of your mind, that ye may prove [*dokimazō*] what is that good, and acceptable, and perfect, will of God" (Rom. 12:2; see also Gal. 6:4). In the syntax of this passage, all of this effort is to be done as a believer undertakes to "walk" in a way that tests the genuineness of whether "Christ also hath loved us, and hath given himself for us an offering and a sacrifice to God" (5:2). In the end, each person is to come to a decision about the Atonement based on revelation flowing from "him that is able to do exceeding abundantly above all that we ask or think, according to the [divine] power that worketh in us" (3:20).

acceptable: Almost uniformly in the New Testament, the adjective εὐάρεστος (*euarestos*) sets out what is acceptable or "well pleasing" to God.[152] Here it serves as a predicate nominative. Throughout Paul's letters, *euarestos* displays varying nuances. For example, we catch the glinting colors of the consecrated life in his words, "Ye present your bodies a living sacrifice, holy, acceptable [*euarestos*] unto God" (Rom. 12:1; see also 2 Cor. 5:9). In the instance of donations made by Philippian church members to impoverished members in Judea, Paul caught the aromas of charitable giving when he wrote about "an odor of a sweet smell, a sacrifice acceptable, well pleasing [*euarestos*] to God" (Philip. 4:18). Service also stands among the acceptable activities before God, including when it draws the attention of outsiders, as the Apostle affirmed: "He that in these things serveth Christ is acceptable [*euarestos*] to God, and approved of men" (Rom. 14:18; see

---

148. Lincoln, *Ephesians*, 328; Larkin, *Handbook*, 115.
149. BDAG, 255.1; Louw-Nida, §27.45; Merkle, *Guide*, 165.
150. Werner Foerster, *TDNT*, 2:561.
151. BDAG, 241; Thayer, *Lexicon*, 144–45.
152. Werner Foerster, *TDNT*, 1:457; Delling, *TDNT*, 8:77 n. 60; BDAG, 403; Louw-Nida, §25.94.

also Heb. 13:21). Moreover, the obedient actions of children bring God's approval, as we read: "Children, obey your parents in all things: for this is well pleasing [*euarestos*] unto the Lord" (Col. 3:20).[153] Thus, a person's acceptability before God can take various forms, from charitable acts to service to obedience to the consecrated life.

5:11 *have no fellowship:* The smoldering question that readers face in this verse and the following lines turns on whether these words involve people inside or outside the circle of believers. In a word, do the challenges detailed in these verses press on Christians from the wider Roman world or from their fellow church members? We have learned in the discussion of 5:6–7 that Paul was apparently staring down, and was encouraging his readers likewise to stare down, a growing concern within believers' ranks. It almost goes without saying that pressure from outside usually brings unity and cohesion, whereas pressure from within routinely leads to disunity and disarray. The argument that Paul sought to make the church into "an appealing alternative to the world" carries some merit.[154] But the idea of a congregation that glistened in the Aegean sunlight and was purposely polished to offer an appealing alternative to the worship of Diana at her spectacular temple a mile and a half away from downtown Ephesus does not fly very high. Even if the church members across Asia Minor brought honor to themselves as upright citizens and thus attracted nonmembers to the doors of their meetinghouses, calling those Gentile outsiders "darkness" (5:8) and "the children of disobedience" (5:6) presents a heavy burden to lift for those who make these verses refer to believers' neighbors.[155] Rather, the difficulties that these words addressed were possibly internal. It makes little sense that Christians were to "reprove" or publicly confront unwanted beliefs and behaviors of their Gentile acquaintances.[156]

The verb translated "have fellowship" is another *syn-* term (συγκοινω-νέω, *synkoinōneō*; see 5:7 and the Notes on 2:5, 22; 4:16) that bears the meaning "to participate with" or "to associate with."[157] At its base, we meet Paul's strong appeal that "the people of God must leave Babel lest they share in its sins and the resultant judgment (Rev. 18:4)."[158] More than this, the Apostle's readers had to avoid "being alienated from the life of God"

---

153. Foerster, *TDNT*, 1:457.
154. Fowl, *Ephesians*, 171.
155. Fowl, *Ephesians*, 170–71; see also Lincoln, *Ephesians*, 329–30.
156. Barth, *Ephesians*, 2:570; Best, *Ephesians*, 492–94.
157. BDAG, 952.1.a; Louw-Nida, §34.4; Thayer, *Lexicon*, 593.
158. Friedrich Hauck, *TDNT*, 3:804.

after holding it in their hands (4:18). Said another way, their lives were to aim to "put on the new man, which after [the pattern of] God is created in righteousness and true holiness" (4:24). No other standard would do.[159]

unfruitful works of darkness: Producing the adjective "unfruitful" (ἄκαρπος, *akarpos*)[160] mirrors in a negative tone "the fruit" in verse 5:9. Out of a scene of stark bareness comes a lifeless portrait of certain "trees whose fruit withereth, [are] without fruit, [are] twice dead, [and are] plucked up by the roots" (Jude 1:12). This was the bleak horticultural view. Next came the metaphorical view wherein the subject stood front and center as completely "useless," totally "unproductive."[161] This judgment, of course, arose in Jesus' mournful prediction about the sower's seeds that "are sown among thorns . . . [that is,] the cares of this world, and the deceitfulness of riches [choking] . . . the word, and it becometh unfruitful [*akarpos*]" (Mark 4:18–19; see also Matt. 13:22–23). In one of the most unkind cuts against his Corinthian detractors who were riding a self-inflated crest of speaking in tongues, Paul pulled up a double critique that had to do not only with praying but also with saying the prayer in an unknown tongue. We hear his words: "If I use this gift [of speaking in tongues] in my prayers, my spirit may be praying but my mind is left barren [*akarpos*]" (1 Cor. 14:14, Jerusalem Bible). From the Apostle's viewpoint, speaking in tongues, even in prayer, left the speaker without understanding about what he or she had just said. Hence, both the unknown language and the prayer itself were *akarpos,* fruitless (see Titus 3:14; 2 Pet. 1:8; Alma 5:36; and the Notes on 2:2, 10; 4:12; 5:9).

works: A noun that appears in three other places in this letter (*ergon*; see 2:9, 10; 4:12), here it is draped in dark hues. The matter is not a lack of action or work. The issue concerns "human work in the sense of vanity and sinfulness."[162] Elsewhere, Paul had observed, "The night is far spent, the day is at hand." Then came his appeal: "Let us therefore cast off the works of darkness, and let us put on the armor of light" (Rom. 13:12). Perhaps oddly, he did not take up the idea of good works in this message from his letter to the Romans and offered no alternative to sable actions. Nor did he when mentioning "works of the flesh" (Gal. 5:19) or "wicked works" (Col. 1:21). Nor did other authors. Instead, the usual fare focused firmly on the negative.

---

159. Gerhard Friedrich, *TDNT*, 3:699.
160. Hauck, *TDNT*, 3:616; BDAG, 35; Louw-Nida, §23.202.
161. Louw-Nida, §65.34.
162. Bertram, *TDNT*, 2:645.

We read of "the works of the devil" (1 John 3:8) and "evil deeds" (2 John 1:11), of "ungodly deeds" (Jude 1:15) and "unlawful deeds" (2 Pet. 2:8). The only exception to the illuminating influence of good works when noting evil deeds occurs in a review of Cain and Abel. After recalling that Cain "belonged to the evil one and murdered his brother," John asked, "Why did [Cain] murder [Abel]? Because his own actions were evil and his brother's were righteous" (1 John 3:12 NIV).[163] It is as if dark works extinguish works of light, a grim prospect unless resisted (see the Notes on 2:9, 10; 4:12).

darkness: In this verse, darkness (σκότος, *skotos*) fundamentally touches on conversion, or the lack thereof. We take in Paul's hope-filled words that "ye, brethren, are not in darkness. . . . Ye are all the children of light, and the children of the day" (1 Thes. 5:4–5; see also Acts 26:18 and 1 Pet. 2:9, "Him who hath called you out of darkness into his marvelous light").[164] The darkened state arises because the doer of "the unfruitful works of darkness" has either not truly been converted or has seriously drifted from the faith. Such persons have now slipped so far that the Apostle could write that they themselves are "darkness"—that is, its personification (5:8).[165] As an entity, darkness has the power to hide its sinister character. But, at the Last Judgment, "the Lord [will] come, who both will bring to light the hidden things of darkness, and will make manifest the counsels of the [sinners'] hearts" (1 Cor. 4:5; see also Rom. 2:16).[166] It is important to notice that, owing to its nature, "darkness has 'works,' but no 'fruit.'"[167] The lack of self-perpetuating life is most striking (see the Notes on 5:8; 6:12).

reprove: Among the preferred meanings of the verb ἐλέγχω (*elenchō*) are "to expose" or "to rebuke."[168] In broad terms, it means "to show someone his [or her] sin and to summon him [or her] to repentance"—that is, "to correct."[169] In our verse, 5:11, the act of correcting appears to lie between two people (see Matt. 18:15, "between thee and him alone"). It is not a public matter that involves a congregation or a large number within the community.[170] Latter-day Saints, of course, live under specific instructions from God that pertain to private situations of one person correcting another.

---

163. Bertram, *TDNT,* 2:645.

164. Conzelmann, *TDNT,* 7:442.

165. Lincoln, *Ephesians,* 329.

166. Conzelmann, *TDNT,* 7:442.

167. Winger, *Ephesians,* 564.

168. BDAG, 315.1; Louw-Nida, §33.417; Thayer, *Lexicon,* 202–3.

169. Friedrich Büchsel, *TDNT,* 2:474 and n. 8.

170. Büchsel, *TDNT,* 2:474.

Near the end of a long revelation to Joseph Smith while he was incarcerated in the jail at Liberty, Missouri, God spoke words that repeated the English verb that appears here in the KJV: "*Reproving* betimes with sharpness, . . . and then showing forth afterwards an increase of love toward him whom thou hast *reproved*" (D&C 121:43, emphasis added). But as the Father laid out the matter, the "increase of love" was not enough. All relationships inside the kingdom, particularly those that involve a presiding officer and another, are to be undertaken "by persuasion, by long-suffering, by gentleness and meekness, and by love unfeigned." This ideal is only possible when, instead of the correcting party acting out of frustration or pique, that person is "moved upon by the Holy Ghost" (D&C 121:41, 43). No freelance reproving is permissible. Otherwise, God, who sends the Holy Ghost in such situations, will soon or later make his displeasure known. And only by the "increase of love" will the corrected individual "know that thy faithfulness is stronger than the cords of death" (D&C 121:44; see also the Notes on 4:23, 29; 5:13).

5:12 *it is a shame:* In the Greek word order, this expression (αἰσχρόν ἐστιν, *aischron estin*) occurs near the end of the line, not at the beginning. The cluster of Greek words associated with *aischros* all are about baseness, disgrace, and shame.[171] With his words in 5:12, Paul draws himself up to his full authoritative height to discourage church members from discussing shameful acts in any conversation. Notably, one may think that an inherent contradiction exists between reproving a fellow believer with words (see 5:11) and not speaking about evil at all. But no contradiction exists here.[172] Corrections that come from church governance are not the same as a gossipy whisper. In our passage, "those who glibly discuss and censure evil deeds are declared as guilty as the objects of their scorn."[173] Saying this much, it is important to note that the Apostle does not enter into a discussion about whether darkness possesses its own allure for the weak and unsuspecting. That is not his purpose here.[174]

those things which are done: The passive participle of the verb γίνομαι (*ginomai*), plus a definite article, serves as the direct object of the other verb in the sentence, "to speak." The general sense of *ginomai* revolves around the idea "to come into existence." In the context of 5:12, it carries

---

171. Rudolf Bultmann, *TDNT*, 1:189–91.
172. Caird, *Letters*, 85.
173. Barth, *Ephesians*, 2:572.
174. Lincoln, *Ephesians*, 330.

the meaning "to be made" or "to be performed."[175] Hence, "actions" (NR) fits the meaning well.

of them: The prepositional phrase ὑπ᾽ αὐτῶν (*hyp᾽ autōn*) bears the sense "by them," sending us to the agents of dark deeds. This phrase forms the final suggestion that the unnamed persons in Paul's mind may have been flipped believers. Why? Because "the immoral lifestyle of non-Christian Gentiles was unrestricted and blatantly evil (cf. 4:17–19, 22) and thus their deeds do not need to be done in secret."[176]

in secret: Besides the metaphor of darkness and light, the Apostle now turns his appeal to a comparison of the secret and the divinely disclosed.[177] The dreary secrecy pursued apparently by ne'er-do-wells in the Church contrasts sharply with the revelation that God had recently entrusted "unto me" and "unto his holy apostles and prophets by the Spirit," bringing into the bright light of full disclosure "that the Gentiles should be fellowheirs" with Jews in the kingdom (3:3, 5–6). In the first place, there was no Spirit in the actions of the doers of darkness. All was done in a corner, out of the revealing glare of the light. Rather, they had set themselves up to become recipients of "the wrath of God [that is to be poured out] upon the children of disobedience" (5:6). So frightening will this event be that the guilty will plead "to the mountains, Cover us; and to the hills, Fall on us" (Hosea 10:8).

Jesus repeated this language when addressing citizens of Jerusalem as he lugged the wooden bar of the cross to the place of his execution. He knew the dire future of the city and the desperation that would invade the hearts and minds of its citizens. Especially to the women he said, "Weep not for me, but weep for yourselves, and for your children. [In] . . . the days [that] are coming . . . they [will] begin to say to the mountains, Fall on us: and to the hills, Cover us" (Luke 23:28–30). According to the book of Revelation, all who have worked in secret, from the most important people to the least, from "the kings of the earth [to] . . . every bondman," will become so hopeless because all routes leading away from "the wrath of the Lamb" are so thoroughly blocked that they will beg "the mountains and the rocks, Fall on us, and hide us from the face of him that sitteth on the throne" (Rev. 6:15–16; see also 1 Tim. 5:25 and Alma 36:12–15).[178] Thus was to be the fate of those whose "works were in the dark" (Moses 5:51).

---

175. BDAG, 197.2.a; Thayer, *Lexicon,* 116.4, 116.5.d; Larkin, *Handbook,* 117.

176. Merkle, *Guide,* 166.

177. Merkle, *Guide,* 166.

178. Oepke and Meyer, *TDNT,* 3:976.

5:13 *all things that are reproved:* Modern translations of Ephesians, following the lead of edited Greek texts, including the Society for Biblical Literature's text, divide this verse differently. For example, the Revised Standard Version and the New English Bible mirror the King James Version. But the Jerusalem Bible, the New International Version, and the SBL text separate verses 5:13 and 5:14 after the expression "made manifest by the light." The impact is very slight.[179]

By repeating the verb *elenchō* from 5:11, here in a passive participle form with the meaning "to expose" or "to correct," Paul engaged again the pressing need of correction, this time with the sense of exposing "works of darkness" (5:11).[180] That need will not go away quietly. The most important ally in any such action will be light. In fact, because in the Greek text the phrase "by the light" comes immediately after the verb *elenchō,* the question arises whether to understand the light as the instrument for exposing darkness or the tool for making manifest, for making visible. The two ideas are basically the same in this verse.[181] Commentators are virtually split evenly on whether to attach "by the light" to one verb or the other. The issue turns on a small point, whether "light" was part of the needed reproof or correction in 5:11.[182] The answer is no, although "light" was noted a few lines earlier (see 5:8), and darkness, the opposite of light, appears in 5:11. Yet it seems better to attach the light's work here to the exposing: "Everything exposed by the light becomes visible" (NR; see also the Notes on 4:23, 29; 5:11).

made manifest: Within a line, this verb (φανερόω, *phaneroō*) will appear again. In this context, it means "to make visible" or "to expose."[183] The object of the divine uncovering consists of dark, evil deeds. The perpetrators are not just inclined to wickedness. They have chosen their benighted course knowingly. As Jesus declared to Nicodemus, "Men loved darkness rather than light" (John 3:19).[184] Although the sense "to appear" hovers nearby, calling up the idea of a vision or dream, the meaning loops around to being made completely visible in a physical, concrete sense. We are not talking about a visionary or dream-like state wherein darkness fades gradually from view. The celestial light that turns fully on evil works

---

179. Best, *Ephesians,* 496.

180. Friedrich Büchsel, *TDNT,* 2:474 and n. 8; BDAG, 315.1; Louw-Nida, §33.417; Thayer, *Lexicon,* 202–3.

181. Conzelmann, *TDNT,* 9:353 and n. 358.

182. Lincoln, *Ephesians,* 330–31.

183. BDAG, 1048.1.b; Louw-Nida, §24.19; Thayer, *Lexicon,* 648.

184. Conzelmann, *TDNT,* 9:353.

will leave no corner unexposed, no shadow unerased. Besides the thought of exposure, one detects a triumphant note, almost an audible anthem, wherein God and his forces overcome and put darkness in its eternally loathsome place (see Job 2:1–7; 2 Thes. 2:7–10; D&C 19:2–3; 121:4; and the Notes on 1:21; 3:10).

by the light: As we observed above, this prepositional phrase evidently links to *elenchō*, "to expose" or "to correct," rather than to *phaneroō*, "to make visible." But the difference in meaning is slight whether we say "everything exposed by the light becomes visible" (NR) or "everything exposed becomes visible by the light."

is light: Standing by itself, unhinged from even a definite article, and tied to the subject of the sentence by a form of the verb "to be" (ἐστιν, *estin*), the solitary predicate noun "light" (φῶς, *phōs*) invites inquiry. Who or what is this light, this illumining power that lightens "everything" (NR)? The shortest answer is Christ. He is Light, with a capital letter. But more may be in the mix. The "whatsoever" in "whatsoever doth make manifest" (KJV) hides the word πᾶν (*pan*), a term that stands as an object of the present passive participle of *phaneroō* and bears the meanings "all" or "every(thing)."[185] The literal rendition would be "everything that is brought to light is light."[186] Curling back to 5:8, we read that believers themselves had become "light in the Lord," a most unusual statement, as we discovered. But that state involves a process that each individual undergoes. At the end, the faithful person becomes like the Father and the Son, each of whom is the personification of light (see 1 John 1:5 and John 8:12). But that may not be the whole story. Embedded deep within such principles rests the companion principle of repentance. Somewhere a door stands open to the person trapped in darkness. Somehow Christ's Atonement reaches the deepest depths that a soul can sink to and can lift it to the heavens. As the Risen Savior once declared of himself, "The Son of Man hath descended below them all. Art thou greater than he?" (D&C 122:8).

Two examples of repentance will illustrate. The first arises within modern scripture. The account relates to a man named Zeezrom who led an effort in a settlement called Ammonihah to undercut the preaching of men named Alma and Amulek. Featured as "the foremost to accuse Amulek and Alma [and] . . . being one of the most expert among them [Ammonihah's citizens]" (Alma 10:31), Zeezrom was in the grasp of the "adversary," the

---

185. BDAG, 782–84, s.v. "πᾶς"; Thayer, *Lexicon*, 491–93.
186. Best, *Ephesians*, 496.

devil, who astonishingly had "exercised his power in [Zeezrom]" (Alma 12:5). But during the second of Alma's two sermons in the city, "Zeezrom began to inquire of them diligently, that he might know more concerning the kingdom of God" (Alma 12:8). Eventually, Zeezrom accepted baptism at Alma's hand and "began from that time forth to preach unto the people" (Alma 15:12). The second example comes from Luke's Gospel. A publican stood in the Jerusalem temple courtyard at some distance from a self-important Pharisee and, in Jesus' recounting, "would not lift up so much as his eyes unto heaven, . . . saying, God be merciful to me a sinner." Jesus' judgment? "I tell you, this man went down to his house justified[,] . . . for every one . . . that humbleth himself [in repentance] shall be exalted" (Luke 18:13–14). Yes, enlightenment awaits the repentant sinner (see 1 Pet. 2:9, "out of darkness into his marvelous light").

5:14 *Wherefore he saith:* Paul has leaned into a quotation that he judged would make his point, as he had at 4:8. But where did the following quote make its home? It is surely not scriptural. Quality guesses have ranged from apocryphal sources tied to Elijah or Jeremiah to a source farther afield. Most commentators believe that the next lines likely derive from a Jewish source or from a now-unknown early Christian hymn. Presumably, the Apostle's readers enjoyed some acquaintance with the passage that he cited. But its origin has not been established.[187]

he saith: At 4:8, this very expression introduced a quotation from Psalm 68:18. Likewise, its appearance in James 4:6 ushered in a paraphrased passage of scripture, Proverbs 3:34. The verb (λέγει, *legei*) could also be translated as "it says" (NR), the preferred rendition (see the Note on 4:8).[188] The three lines unfold as follows in the KJV:

> Awake thou that sleepest,
> and arise from the dead,
> and Christ shall give thee light.

In the New Rendition, we read:

> Awake, O sleeper,
> rise from the dead,
> and Christ will shine upon you.

187. Oepke and Meyer, *TDNT,* 3:990; Gerhard Delling, *TDNT,* 8:500–501; Barth, *Ephesians,* 2:574–75; Lincoln, *Ephesians,* 318–19, 331–32; Best, *Ephesians,* 497; Muddiman, *Ephesians,* 242–43; Winger, *Ephesians,* 567.

188. Debrunner, Kleinknecht, Procksch, Kittel, Quell, and Schrenk, *TDNT,* 4:110.

Awake: The imperative of ἐγείρω (*egeirō*) directs readers either to baptism or to the Resurrection or perhaps to both. This verb also brings readers inside the three-line celebration of the renewal of life as shown above. Paul's appeal to these three lines must rest on their familiarity to his intended audience, though the lines show up nowhere else in ancient literature. Very possibly consisting of a fragment of an early Christian hymn composed to accompany the ordinance of baptism,[189] the song picks up language from Isaiah 26:19 ("Awake and sing, ye that dwell in dust") and 60:1–2 ("Arise, shine; for thy light is come").[190] There is more.

The command to awake hints plainly at a follow-on action: to stand up (see the Note on "arise" below). Of course, on a spiritual level a person stands up "from the death and sleep of sins."[191] In Ephesians, this takes the form of arising and firmly standing "against the wiles of the devil" (6:11) and in preparation for "the evil day" (6:13). The plural verbs in these passages indicate that this effort is undertaken by both individuals and congregations, having the sense of collective action by a group of believers. Hence, standing up in a physical sense, and putting on spiritual armor, pertains to persons standing as individuals together with others in a worship setting designed to endow them with power to resist and overpower "the rulers of the darkness of this world" and "spiritual wickedness in high places" (6:12). This kind of scene lies behind the Apostle's words to King Agrippa. First, he said, "I *stand* and am judged." Judged for what? He was under a darksome indictment both because of his "hope of the promise made of God unto our fathers" and because of his faith "that God should raise the dead" (Acts 26:6, 8, emphasis added). Therefore, he took a stand. With God on his side, "I *stand* here *and testify* to small and great alike . . . that the Christ would suffer and [would be] . . . the first to rise from the dead" (Acts 26:22–23 NIV, emphasis added). It is obvious that after collapsing "to the earth" at suddenly hearing the voice of Jesus when on the road to Damascus, Paul was empowered to "rise, and stand upon thy feet," thereafter to become "a minister and a witness . . . of these things which thou hast seen" (Acts 26:14, 16). Clearly Paul had been endowed with power not only to stand before Agrippa and the other dignitaries in the room but especially

---

189. Caird, *Letters,* 86; Muddiman, *Ephesians,* 243; Merkle, *Guide,* 167–68.

190. Even though the Septuagint version of these verses is quite different, some important Greek verbs appear. For instance, "The dead shall rise [ἀνίστημι, *anistēmi,* the third verb in 5:14], and they that are in the tombs shall be raised [passive of *egeirō*], and they that are in the earth shall rejoice" (LXX Isa. 26:19). Again, "thy light is come, and the glory of the Lord is risen upon thee" (LXX Isa. 60:1), exhibiting links to "Christ shall give thee light" (5:14).

191. Walter Grundmann, *TDNT,* 7:652 n. 40.

to bear witness of the Christ to "the Gentiles, unto whom now I send thee" (Acts 26:17).[192]

thou that sleepest: In the vocative case,[193] which is the case for "exclamations and direct address,"[194] the verb's form is a participle employed as a singular predicate noun. The verb is καθεύδω (*katheudō*) and presents the ideas "to sleep" or "to be indifferent" with the extended meaning "to be dead."[195] In its figurative sense, as here, it focuses on spiritual indifference. In another letter, the only one wherein Paul repeated this verb, he mixed the metaphorical with the literal. We listen to his words: "Let us not sleep [*katheudō*], as do others; . . . they that sleep [*katheudō*] sleep [*katheudō*] in the night; . . . whether we wake or sleep [*katheudō*], we should live together with him" (1 Thes. 5:6–7, 10). Both in these lines and in the poetic trill of our letter, the notion of death, especially spiritual death, hovers nearby.[196]

arise: The command to stand up follows naturally the imperative, "Awake!" The verb ἀνίστημι, *anistēmi*, in its transitive form can point to bringing a person back from the dead. In its intransitive meaning, it conveys the senses not only of getting up but also of rising from the dead, its meaning here.[197] Beyond this, the results of arising and standing on one's feet point to revelation, an enlightening burst of knowledge. How so? For starters, Paul had undergone this experience. We hear his rehearsal spoken to King Agrippa. Out of the "light from heaven, above the brightness of the sun," the Apostle said, came the audible commands of the Risen Christ: "Rise, and stand upon thy feet" (Acts 26:13, 16). In Paul's case, the standing position was evidently important because so much celestial information burst upon him as he stood: "I have appeared unto thee . . . to make thee a minister and a witness . . . of these things which thou hast seen . . . to open [the Gentiles'] eyes, and to turn them from darkness to light, and from the power of Satan unto God" (Acts 26:16, 18). Hence, it was in a standing position that Paul received from the Christ his commission to impart heavenly light to his hearers.[198] It is a small step to a ritual act wherein a participant, standing, receives sacred knowledge. All of this peeks out from behind the

---

192. Grundmann, *TDNT*, 7:652–53.

193. Larkin, *Handbook*, 120; Merkle, *Guide*, 168.

194. Smyth, *Greek Grammar*, §1283.

195. BDAG, 490; Louw-Nida, §§23.66, 104.

196. Barth, *Ephesians*, 2:575; Lincoln, *Ephesians*, 332; Best, *Ephesians*, 498; Williams, *Paul's Metaphors*, 93, 107 n. 77; Winger, *Ephesians*, 567–68.

197. BDAG, 83.2, 7.

198. Grundmann, *TDNT*, 7:653 n. 42; Conzelmann, *TDNT*, 9:347–48.

Apostle's words to his Ephesian readers as he prays for God's illuminating, revelatory power to be with them: "May he enlighten the eyes of your mind so that you can see . . . what rich glories he has promised the saints . . . and how infinitely great is the power that he has exercised for us believers" (1:18–19, Jerusalem Bible; see also 1 Cor. 4:5; 2 Tim. 1:10; for ceremonial links, see the Notes on 1:20; 2:2; 4:13; 5:2, 8, 15; 6:11, 13, 14; and appendix 1).

dead: The figurative sense of "dead" (νεκρός, *nekros*) is to be preferred over the literal.[199] In one vein, sins engender death, the physical death. Paul reminded his Roman readers, "As by one man sin entered into the world, and death by sin; and so death passed upon all men, for that all have sinned" (Rom. 5:12). Likewise, sins also lead to a spiritual death: "You, being dead in your sins[,] . . . hath he quickened together with him, having forgiven you all trespasses" (Col. 2:13). Again, "even when we were dead in sins, [God] hath quickened us together with Christ" (2:5; see also 2:1). The quickening, of course, brings a believer to the door of eternal life within the embrace of a family. For that very principle was stressed in Jesus' parable of the prodigal son. We hear the joy-filled voice of the young man's father saying, "This my son was dead, and is alive again; he was lost, and is found." Later, when discussing the younger son's return with the older brother, the father tried in that tense moment to soothe the older's pique by affirming that "this thy brother *was dead,* and is alive again; and was lost, and is found" (Luke 15:24, 32, emphasis added). Just as the father in this story was master of his formerly dead, returning son, so Christ serves as the master of those who earnestly come to him, including those in the spirit world who respond positively to the Savior's message carried among them (see Rom. 14:9; 1 Pet. 3:18–20; 4:6; Rev. 11:18; D&C 138:29–34; and the Notes on 3:8, 19).[200]

Physical death is temporary and will be rectified for all at the Resurrection. Spiritual death can be temporary, depending on a person's response to the gospel message.[201] On the other hand, life is ongoing, never ending. However, in the ultimate sense, some life adds up to less than it should. For example, living "in the flesh" represents a step down from living "in Christ." One glimpses Paul's ranking of the two types of lives in these words: "I live; yet not I, but Christ liveth in me: and the life which I now live in the flesh I

---

199. BDAG, 667–68.A.2 and B.2; Louw-Nida, §74.28.

200. Büchsel, *TDNT,* 3:641–42; see also Jeremias, *TDNT,* 1:148–49; Friedrich, *TDNT,* 2:718–19; Oepke, *TDNT,* 3:213; Grundmann, *TDNT,* 3:399–401; Friedrich, *TDNT,* 3:707–8; Jeremias, *TDNT,* 3:746–47; Schneider, *TDNT,* 4:597–98; Hauck and Schulz, *TDNT,* 6:577–78.

201. Bultmann, *TDNT,* 4:893–94.

live by the faith of the Son of God, who . . . gave himself for me" (Gal. 2:20; see also Rom. 7:24; 2 Cor. 5:15; and Philip. 1:22). Thus, enfolded inside the embrace of Christ a person lives life on a higher plane. This life, which exhibits a heavenly quality, stands on a continuum with the eternal life that steadfast believers will eventually receive. In scriptural language, this life (ζωή, *zōē*) often appears without any adjective to describe it. In those instances, "life" means celestial life, both here and hereafter (see the Notes on 1:20; 2:1, 5).[202]

Christ: Paired in the Greek text with a definite article, yielding "the Christ" or "the Messiah" or "the Anointed One," this reference to him gathers up each previous mention. Of course, we shall run into this title further on in the letter. But this verse, 5:14, enshrines the last of the poetic passages in Ephesians that celebrate Christ in specific ways (see 1:3–14; 2:4–7, 14–18; 3:14–21). In the first passage, 1:3–14, believers receive "all spiritual blessings" through Christ "the beloved," including, for each person, an "adoption . . . to [God] himself" and "the forgiveness of sins" (1:3, 5–7). On the macro level, "in the dispensation of the fulness of times [God will] . . . gather together in one all things in Christ, both which are in heaven, and which are on earth" (1:10). According to the next poetic section, 2:4–7, at the end-time "we who were dead in sins [will be] . . . quickened . . . together with Christ [and] . . . sit together in heavenly places in Christ Jesus" (2:5–6).

The third cluster of verses, 2:14–18, pushes Christ forward as the grand reconciler both between humans and their God and between Jews and Gentiles. It was he who "hath broken down the middle wall of partition" between the two peoples. Fitting this pattern, it was he who made "in himself of twain one new man, so making peace . . . that he might reconcile both unto God in one body by the cross." As a result, "through him we both have access by one Spirit unto the Father" (2:14–16, 18). In the middle of the letter, the fourth passage, 3:14–21, celebrates Christ's love. For through his love believers are "able to comprehend with all saints what is the breadth, and length, and depth, and height [of] . . . the love of Christ, which passeth knowledge" (3:18–20).[203] Upon all of these principles and insights rests the crowning statement in our line: "Christ shall give thee light," endless and stretching ever outward (5:14; see also the Notes on 3:17, 19).

---

202. Gerhard von Rad, Georg Bertram, and Rudolf Bultmann, *TDNT*, 2:863–64.
203. Grundmann, Hesse, de Jonge, and van der Woude, *TDNT*, 9:559–60.

give thee light: The underlying verb (ἐπιφαύσκω, *epiphauskō*), in the future tense, occurs only here in the New Testament, with the sense "to shine upon."[204] Thus, a clear rendition would be "Christ will shine upon you" (NR). It is not unreasonable to think that Paul has given the light a name: Christ. For he is often described in this way (see John 1:9; 8:12, "I am the light of the world"; 9:5; 2 Cor. 4:6; etc.).[205] If so, Paul is not far from that mark. For the plain meaning of these words concerns the source of light, that which both illuminates the universe and enlightens individuals. Modern scripture captures these meanings best in an almost rhythmic set of lines. After mentioning the "other comforter [who] is the same that I promised unto my disciples, as is recorded in the testimony of John," the divine voice rhapsodized about him, saying, "He that ascended up on high [is] . . . the light of truth; which truth shineth." This is not the whole story. For the shining light "is the light of Christ." Furthermore, "he is in the sun, and the light of the sun . . . as also he is in the moon, and is the light of the moon . . . as also the light of the stars."[206] What is more, "the light which shineth, which giveth you light, is through him who enlighteneth your eyes, which is the same light that quickeneth your understandings." This "light proceedeth forth from the presence of God to fill the immensity of space" (D&C 88:3, 6–9, 11–12). Therefore, the light emanating from Christ carries both a physical component, one that we can see and that aids our ability to see, and a spiritual or intellectual dimension that assists our understanding (see Luke 24:31–32, 45;[207] and the Note on 5:8).

5:15 *See:* Paul has turned back to his mode of instructing his readers by inserting the imperative of βλέπω (*blepō*), which in this context can carry the sense "to keep your eyes open"[208] or "to watch out for, to pay attention to" (see Philip. 3:2).[209] We must be open to the possibility that Paul may have been playing with his readers, having just talked about light (see the Notes on 5:8, 14). This is his verb of choice when he leads readers into a set of instructions on behavior. For example, when he took up the matter of eating meats sacrificed to idols in the wake of his readers' newly found liberty in Christ, he wrote, "Take heed [*blepō*] lest by any means this liberty of

---

204. BDAG, 386; Thayer, *Lexicon*, 246.
205. Barth, *Ephesians*, 2:573; Best, *Ephesians*, 499.
206. Contra Muddiman, *Ephesians*, 243.
207. Brown, *Testimony of Luke*, 1124–26, 1135.
208. BDAG, 179.6.c.
209. Louw-Nida, §27.58.

yours become a stumblingblock to [other church members] that are weak" (1 Cor. 8:9). Later in the same letter, after a brief review of serious missteps by the ancient Hebrews, he counseled, "Wherefore let him that thinketh he standeth take heed [*blepō*] lest he fall" (1 Cor. 10:12).[210]

then: The conjunction οὖν (*oun*) presents the force of "therefore," tying back to the prior discussion of light and dark and drawing a conclusion that reaches into a believer's behavior, both now and in the future.

walk: We come upon the last occurrence of the verb περιπατέω (*peripateō*), a term that we have run into on seven previous occasions (see 2:2, 10; 4:1, 17 [twice]; 5:2, 8). In this instance, the verb clearly stands in the metaphorical stream wherein Paul encouraged readers to walk or to live "not as fools, but as wise [persons]." That said, the aspect of a sacred walk never stands far away. Not surprisingly, an important treatment of this dimension shows up in the Epistle to the Hebrews. The question centers on whether the access offered by Jesus into the holy sanctuary consists in any way of passing through a physical gate—that is, actually walking into a holy place. The answer is, Yes and no. Why? Because the key passages can be read both metaphorically and literally. Our focus now comes to rest on Hebrews 9:8 and 10:19-20.[211] A more refined question deals with the relationship between the nouns εἴσοδος and ὁδός (*eisodos* and *hodos*) in 10:19-20, whose respective meanings are "an entrance"[212] and "a path or way."[213] Although the plain sense sends us to an access opened by Christ wherein lies a new relationship with God, the context breathes out a physical walk into the sanctuary (see Heb. 9:1-5)—not the sanctuary in Jerusalem but the sanctuary "not made with hands" that is yet real (Heb. 9:11).

The key words for detecting an undertone of ceremony lie in the line "a new and living way [*hodos*]" (Heb. 10:20). This pathway, of course, was blazed by Christ. In fact, believers "through the blood of Jesus have the right to enter [*eisodos*] the sanctuary" (Heb. 10:19, Jerusalem Bible). It is in dissecting the line "a new and living way" that the physical or action aspect becomes visible. The Greek term translated "new" is not the common word rendered "new" in ancient literature, although it can be translated that way. In its earliest meanings, πρόσφατος (*prosphatos*) pertained to an

---

210. Best, *Ephesians*, 502; Merkle, *Guide*, 171.
211. Michaelis, *TDNT*, 5:75-78.
212. Thayer, *Lexicon*, 188. Almost universally, the noun *eisodos* in Heb. 10:19 is rendered "to enter" in translations of the Bible, as in the KJV.
213. BDAG, 294.1, 691.1; Thayer, *Lexicon*, 437-38.

undecomposed body or a freshly killed animal.[214] Detecting an allusion to Jesus' crucified body is a very short step. The same goes for the participle translated "living" that draws into its clasp Jesus' resuscitated body. The manifest physicality in these terms, each tied to Jesus' Atonement, directs readers to an active walk along the now-marked pathway into a place of holiness and sacred celebration, "into the holiest [place] of all" (Heb. 9:8), into "the sanctuary" where holy ordinances can be received (Heb. 10:19 Jerusalem Bible; see also the Notes on 2:2, 10; 4:1, 13, 17, 20, 22, 24; 5:2, 8, 14; 6:11, 13, 14).

circumspectly: The question at hand is one of word order in the text. The answer will tell us whether the adverbs ἀκριβῶς and πῶς (*akribōs* and *pōs*) tie to the verb "to see" or "to walk." The earliest manuscript, 𝔓[46], and a number of other important texts preserve *akribos* ("circumspectly" or "carefully")[215] close to the verb "to see." A cluster of later manuscripts pair this adverb with the verb "to walk," leading to the KJV translation, which stresses the circumspect walk.[216] Thus the better rendition reads, "Look carefully [*akribōs*] to how [*pōs*] you walk" (NR). This translation connects firmly to the prior imperative "to walk" at the end of 5:8, bringing a sense of unity to the whole passage.[217]

fools: Becoming wise in the ultimate sense is a gift of God. It is he who "hath abounded toward us in all wisdom" (1:8), and it is "the God of our Lord Jesus Christ [who will] . . . give unto you the spirit of wisdom" (1:17). No other source will do, especially the wisdom of the world. For "God [has] made foolish the wisdom of this world" (1 Cor. 1:20). Further, "the wisdom of their wise men shall perish" (Isa. 29:14). What is more, the fool (ἄσοφος, *asophos*) dwells on the opposite side from divinely imparted wisdom. A smattering of Old Testament passages illustrate this point. We read, "The fool hath said in his heart, There is no God" (Ps. 14:1; see also Ps. 53:1). Again, in total spiritual oblivion, "fools make a mock at sin" (Prov. 14:9). As a result, "the fool walketh in darkness" (Eccl. 2:14).

That said, with God's aid converts are brought out of the foolishness of the world and into the realm of wisdom, as we have just noticed. But Paul knew that spiritual danger lurked. He was already aware that some believers had turned their backs on the truth in Christ and thereafter had

---

214. LSJ, 1529; Thayer, *Lexicon*, 550.
215. BDAG, 39; Thayer, *Lexicon*, 24.
216. Metzger, *Textual Commentary*, 540.
217. Bruce, *Ephesians*, 108–9.

become "unwise" (5:17). Perhaps surprisingly, the way to blunt and even repair such foolishness is through good works. "For," Peter reminded his readers, "[it] is the will of God, that with well doing ye may put to silence the ignorance of foolish men" (1 Pet. 2:15; compare Col. 4:5).[218] In sum, good works, especially those undertaken toward the foolish, will draw their admiration and reassure them "that thy faithfulness is stronger than the cords of death" (D&C 121:44; see also the Notes on 4:29; 5:6).

wise: For one to become wise in the divine measurement, which includes coming to know God, that person must be the recipient of revelation. As Paul pleaded in his first prayer embedded in this letter, "[May] the God of our Lord Jesus Christ . . . give unto you the spirit of wisdom and revelation in the knowledge of him" (1:17). Said another way, the Apostle prayed elsewhere "that ye might be filled with the knowledge of his will in all wisdom and spiritual understanding" (Col. 1:9). Clearly, wisdom and knowledge nestle together and come to an individual by divine disclosure.[219] A truly wise person is one who knows by divine means. Such knowledge, of course, consists of coming to know "the mystery of [God's] will" and the overarching "purpose of him who worketh all things after the counsel of his own will" (1:9, 11; see also Col. 1:26–27).[220] Grasping the grandeur of God's designs would surely engender wisdom in one's mind. But there is another aspect. That feature remains highly personal and involves an individual coming to know what God's will is for herself or himself. As Paul wrote later in this chapter, "Be ye not unwise, but understanding what the will of the Lord is" (5:17; see also Acts 22:14). This grasp of celestial knowledge for oneself is exhibited in Paul's very direct comprehension that he was "an apostle of Jesus Christ, by the will of God" (1:1; see also 2 Cor. 1:1). An important example of this status goes back to a prophet named Nephi. To him God said, "Blessed art thou, Nephi, for [thou] . . . hast sought my will, and to keep my commandments[, and] . . . thou shalt not ask that which is contrary to my will" (Hel. 10:4–5; see also D&C 76:10 and the Notes on 1:8, 17; 3:10; 5:17).

5:16 Redeeming: The English verb "redeem" is unexpected. Yet it is an accurate rendition of the participle of ἐξαγοράζομαι (*exagorazomai*). Rather than envisioning a payment that one makes to redeem a person or an item of property, like paying a ransom, the idea is "to make a wise

---

218. Georg Bertram, *TDNT,* 9:231–32.
219. Georg Bertram, *TDNT,* 4:847.
220. Ulrich Wilckens and Georg Fohrer, *TDNT,* 7:523.

and sacred use of every opportunity for doing good, so that zeal and well-doing are as it were the purchase-money by which we make the time our own."[221] Thus, the verb *exagorazomai* presents the sense "to make the most of" (NR; see also Col. 4:5 NIV, "make the most of every opportunity";[222] and the Note on 4:30 on "redemption").

time: Any mention of this noun (καιρός, *kairos*), which occurs four times in this letter (see 1:10; 2:12; 6:18), regularly raises to view a moment or period of crisis that demands resolute action or decision, including the end-time, which brings its own set of crises.[223] The meaning does not shade into the figurative but "stands for the opportunities offered by [the passage of] time."[224] Moreover, such a time is "divinely ordained" or planned for, emphatically so. But a more subtle melody is playing here. It is the urgent "demand of the καιρός, which recurs with each moment of the Christian life, and which in its instantaneousness requires of the Christian that he [or she] should recognize it and concretely fulfil its demand . . . in the exercise of brotherly love."[225] This is exactly Paul's sentiment when he wrote about life's obligations, such as taxes and mutual respect: "Owe no man anything, but to love one another" (Rom. 13:8). With the time available to us, he held, the one obligation is to love others, fulfilling the law "Thou shalt love thy neighbor as thyself." For "love worketh no ill to his [or her] neighbor: therefore love is the fulfilling of the law." Then came the Apostle's strong reminder to his readers that "knowing the time [*kairos*], that now it is high time to awake out of sleep: for now is our salvation nearer than when we [first] believed" (Rom. 13:9–11). Furthermore, "the night is far spent, the day is at hand: let us therefore cast off the works of darkness, and let us put on the armor of light" (Rom. 13:12). And how do we accomplish this? By acts of love (see the Notes on 1:10; 6:18).[226]

days: The plural initially pushes forward the sense of time and its passage, such as in the expression "all the days of our life" (Isa. 38:20).[227] In its earlier occurrence in this letter, the word "day" (ἡμέρα, *hēmera*) brought readers to the happy prospect of "the day of redemption" (4:30). In our

---

221. Thayer, *Lexicon*, 220.

222. BDAG, 343.2; Louw-Nida, §65.42.

223. BDAG, 498.3.a and b.

224. Friedrich Büchsel, *TDNT*, 1:128; see also Gerhard von Rad and Gerhard Delling, *TDNT*, 2:953.

225. Gerhard Delling, *TDNT*, 3:460.

226. Delling, *TDNT*, 3:460.

227. Magne Saebø, Wolfram von Soden, and Jan Bergman, *TDOT*, 6:9, 16–17, 21.

passage, 5:16, the earlier, once-welcome character of "day" now comes to wear a gloomy gown. This aspect should not have surprised Paul's readers. For scripture is full of notices of "the day" or "the days" that will bring serious consequences, especially for the wicked. One such line consists of the words "the day of the Lord" (Isa. 2:12; 13:9; Joel 1:15; 2:1, 11; Amos 5:18; etc.). Jeremiah is known for his words "the days come" when turning to a bleak future event. For instance, we glimpse "the days [that shall] come, saith the Lord, that I will do judgment upon [Babylon's] graven images" (Jer. 51:52; see also Jer. 9:25; 19:6; 48:12; 49:2; etc.). Notably, he also spread a layer of hope-filled future repeating these same words, such as when he prophesied about the coming Messiah: "The days come, saith the Lord, that I will raise unto David a righteous Branch, and a King [from him] shall reign and prosper" (Jer. 23:5; see also Jer. 23:7–8; 30:3; 31:31; etc.; and the Notes on 4:30 on "redemption"; and 6:13).

evil: Readers regularly run across the adjective πονηρός (*ponēros*) in the New Testament. It frames the idea of wicked or evil or base.[228] In our verse, however, it is associated with an era yet to come, the end-time. Those days will be *ponēros*. But days will arrive sooner, introducing severe difficulties for believers in the near future, stretching their faith and faithfulness. On this point, Jesus warned his Twelve that in their lifetimes enemies "shall lay their hands on you, and persecute you. . . . Ye shall be betrayed both by parents, and brethren, and kinsfolks, and friends; and . . . ye shall be hated of all men for my name's sake" (Luke 21:12, 16–17). Such scenes would lead Paul to write about "this present evil [*ponēros*] world" (Gal. 1:4). For he had experienced ill treatment in various cities. For instance, from his effort to preach the gospel in Thessalonica we learn that he and his converts were harassed by "certain lewd [*ponēros*] fellows of the baser sort" (Acts 17:5; see also Matt. 5:11, "say all manner of evil [*ponēros*] against you falsely").

The Apostle knew, of course, that other, distant days were coming that would test the resolve of believers. From the days of Moses, Israelites had lived with his prophecy that "evil will befall you in the latter days" (Deut. 31:29). At the end, as we read elsewhere, "evil [*ponēros*] men and seducers shall wax worse and worse, deceiving, and being deceived" (2 Tim. 3:13). But all is not lost, because God is in charge. In the classical passage that treats Jehovah's power we find that "I form the light and create the dark. I make good fortune and create calamity" (Isa. 45:7, Jerusalem Bible). Even though some commentators want to restrict the sense of this verse to Jehovah's

---

228. BDAG, 851.1; Thayer, *Lexicon*, 530.2.b.

intent to rescue his people from their Babylonian overlords,[229] the language reaches far beyond a promised historical event into the heavenly world. In concert with this observation stands the notion that, even though "the days are evil" according to 5:16, and are "darkened by the woes of the end-time,"[230] the Saints will surmount the darkness. Residing in a place where "there shall be no night ... and they need no candle, neither light of the sun ... [and] they shall reign for ever and ever" (Rev. 22:5; see also 1 Thes. 5:5; Rev. 5:10, "we shall reign on the earth"; and the Notes on 1:10; 4:30; 6:13).

5:17 *Wherefore:* By writing the prepositional phrase διὰ τοῦτο (*dia touto*), Paul has brought his readers to a place where he can draw a conclusion or two based on his remarks in 5:15–16 that rhythmically tap out a warning about a desolate future.[231]

unwise: Although the root of this term (ἄφρων, *aphrōn*) differs from that for "fools" in 5:15 (*asophos*), they are close synonyms.[232] Regrettably, church members can fall back into foolishness even after escaping.[233] This observation apparently brings readers back inside the church to look for those who have turned themselves away from gospel truths and have sought to turn others in the same direction (see 2 Cor. 11:19). This foolishness, this lack of wisdom, leads to the lamentable loss of "understanding what the will of the Lord is," with no safety straps to grasp. In our verse, the contrast is between "unwise" and "understanding," whereas in 5:15 "fools" and "wise" stand at opposite ends. The difference is subtle but real. The contrast between "fools" and "wise" sends us into the world of the Old Testament, where wisdom consists of practical applications of lessons learned through experience while foolishness pushes away such lessons to pursue a different course. In our verse, 5:17, the "unwise" were not setting aside practical matters but have deliberately pivoted away from the far more weighty "will of the Lord," putting their eternal futures in deep jeopardy (see Rom. 12:2).

understanding: The form of the verb συνίημι (*syniēmi*) is imperative. Hence, the rendition "understand" (NR) is correct. The meaning of this term shades into an intellectual grasp of an issue or topic in contrast to emotional empathy.[234] In a word, each individual believer has a responsibility to come to understand, not just through his or her feelings but by an

---

229. Christoph Dohmen and D. Rick, *TDOT,* 13:576.

230. Günther Harder, *TDNT,* 6:554.

231. Merkle, *Guide,* 173.

232. Bertram, *TDNT,* 9:231; Lincoln, *Ephesians,* 342.

233. Bertram, *TDNT,* 9:231.

234. BDAG, 972; Thayer, *Lexicon,* 605.2.

intellectual effort, "the mystery of [God's] will . . . which he hath purposed in himself" (1:9)—that is, God's master plan of salvation for all his children, both living and dead. This said, each person does not arrive at this situation by personal diligence alone. No. For it is "the Lord [who will] give thee understanding in all things" (2 Tim. 2:7).[235] A heavenly gift is required.

will: This noun (θέλημα, *thelēma*) has appeared five times already in Ephesians[236] and will occur one more time (see 6:6). Coming to grasp the divine will, with celestial aid, forms one of the most significant steps that a believer can undertake and achieve. The vista that opens in front of a devotee is truly breathtaking and inspiring, featuring salvation for all of God's children, living or dead.[237] In this case, we hasten to point out, God's will is at work "in individual cases," not in the universal sense.[238] Hence, in a manner bathed in quiet, eternal reassurances, we perceive that God's will wraps itself around each believer, bringing purpose to every person's life, not just to the church as a whole or even to specific congregations.

But this act of revealing the divine will to individuals carries consequences for those who learn God's intentions for themselves but thereafter do not fully pursue them. Jesus himself drove home this principle in a parable that highlighted "that servant, which knew his lord's will, and . . . neither did according to his will." What was his fate? He was to "be beaten with many stripes." In contrast, "he that knew not, and did commit things worthy of stripes, shall be beaten with few stripes" (Luke 12:47–48). Clearly, the one who knows more bears more responsibility for proper action (see D&C 82:3). This concept lies behind the reach of Jesus' atoning power to those who sin ignorantly: "His blood atoneth for the sins of those who . . . have died not knowing the will of God concerning them, or who have ignorantly sinned" (Mosiah 3:11; see also 2 Ne. 9:25–27).

When we turn to Paul, we understand that in his case he was positioned to "know [God's] will" after his vision of the Christ (Acts 22:14), something that was completely fresh and new to him even though as a Jew he had previously thought he knew (see Rom. 2:18). This novel comprehension lifted the Apostle to a new height, a height that required him "not [to] be conformed to this age," not to fall under the pervasive influences of his era. Rather, after experiencing Christ, he became "transformed by

---

235. Hans Conzelmann, *TDNT*, 7:896; Georg Bertram, *TDNT*, 9:227; Louw-Nida, §32.26.

236. Ephesians 1:1, 5, 9, 11; 2:3 ("the desires").

237. Schweizer and Baumgärtel, *TDNT*, 7:1078–79.

238. Schrenk, *TDNT*, 3:58.

the renewing of [his] mind, so that [he could] determine what the will of God is" (Rom. 12:2, Wayment; see also Col. 1:9).[239] Obviously, the stakes had suddenly become higher than they had been a few minutes before the Resurrected Jesus appeared to him on the road to Damascus (see the Notes on 1:1, 5; 2:3; 6:6).

5:18 *drunk:* The imagery of drunkenness, with its total loss of self-control, stands in utter contrast to the personal control that leads to being "filled with the Spirit."[240] We can discover no reason from the meaning of this verb (μεθύσκω, *methyskō*) to connect it to a supposed concern on Paul's part with church members' possible participation in pagan cults or Dionysian ceremonies. Nor does it appear that believers were carrying on inappropriately in their personal lives. Instead, because the Apostle has paired concerns with darkness and drunkenness elsewhere, it seems that we are looking at a metaphor for self-indulgence that has grown naturally out of his earlier remarks about the dark and the night (see 5:8, 11). To the Thessalonians, he wrote, "They that be drunken are drunken in the night. But let us, who are of the day, be sober, putting on the breastplate of faith and love" (1 Thes. 5:7–8). Similarly, in another place he appealed, "Let us therefore cast off the works of darkness, and let us put on the armor of light." That was not the whole story, because he then begged, "Let us walk honestly, as in the day; not in rioting and drunkenness" (Rom. 13:12–13).[241]

wine: The mention of wine (οἶνος, *oinos*) makes the image all the more vivid, especially because all readers were acquainted with wine and its containers, big and small. Although wine was not forbidden, because it was a beverage safe from diseases transmitted by water, Paul knew that drinking it in the presence of weaker Saints could create troubling consequences. In his letter to Roman church members he wrote, "It is good neither to eat flesh, nor to drink wine, nor any thing whereby thy brother stumbleth, or is offended, or is made weak" (Rom. 14:21).[242] The message? Let the inner strengths and weaknesses of fellow Saints be your guides.

excess: This noun form (ἀσωτία, *asōtia*) bears the bleak sense of "reckless abandon" or "debauchery,"[243] with an emphasis on "wild and disorderly rather than extravagant or voluptuous living."[244] It is this meaning that we ascribe to the prodigal son, who, in Jesus' parable, became known for his

---

239. Schrenk, *TDNT*, 3:57.

240. Herbert Priesker, *TDNT*, 4:548; Delling, *TDNT*, 6:291.

241. Lincoln, *Ephesians*, 343–44.

242. Heinrich Seesemann, *TDNT*, 5:164–65.

243. BDAG, 148.

244. Werner Foerster, *TDNT*, 1:507.

"riotous living" and spending his inheritance on "harlots" (Luke 15:13, 30; see also Titus 1:6 and 1 Pet. 4:4).[245]

filled: This passive imperative of πληρόω (*pleroo*) fills two functions. First, the passive directs us to God as the One who fills, the same who "fills [*pleroo*] everything in every way" (1:23 NIV) and who grants to believers "the fulness [*pleroma*] of Christ" (4:13). Second, the verb pushes forward the idea of filling "with a content."[246] In this case, because God is the acting agent, the content is heavenly—namely, the Spirit. The command to "be filled" draws down onto readers the obligation to live their lives in such a way "that they may always have his Spirit to be with them," with the emphasis on "always" (Moro. 4:3; D&C 20:77).

God's activity of filling, whether it has to do with the cosmos (see 1:23; 4:10), or with Christ (see D&C 93:12–14, 16), or with us (see 3:19; 4:13; and D&C 93:20), has enriched the relationship between the heaven and the earth. Certainly, "by him were all things created, that are in heaven, and that are in earth, visible and invisible" (Col. 1:16). More than this, under God's direction Christ has wrought a reconciliation of "all things unto himself[,] . . . things in earth, or things in heaven" (Col. 1:20). This reconciliation patched up the strained relationship between humans on the one side and God on the other, a situation that had existed since the days of Adam and Eve. The Apostle wrote that "when we [humans and God] were enemies, we were reconciled to God by the death of his Son" (Rom. 5:10). As a result, God "in the dispensation of the fulness [*pleroma*] of times [will] . . . gather in one all things in Christ, both which are in heaven, and which are on earth" (1:10; see the Notes on 1:23; 3:19; 4:10, 13).[247]

with the Spirit: The question here concerns how to accurately render this prepositional phrase (ἐν πνεύματι, *en pneumati*). Because the word for Spirit (πνεῦμα, *pneuma*) is in the dative case, three options present themselves. The first and least attractive is to render the phrase "in the Spirit," a so-called "dative of sphere." The second and most widely accepted is "by the Spirit," a "dative of means" wherein the filling is done by an agent, "the Spirit." The third possible rendition is "with the Spirit" (KJV, NR), an appeal to a "dative of content."[248] Onto these three options the sacramental

---

245. Foerster, *TDNT*, 1:507.

246. Delling, *TDNT*, 6:291.

247. Traub and von Rad, *TDNT*, 5:517.

248. Merkle, *Guide*, 174–75; see also Delling, *TDNT*, 6:291 n. 27; and Blass and Debrunner, *Greek Grammar*, §172.

prayers direct light. We hear the words "That they may always have his Spirit to be *with* them" (Moro. 4:3; D&C 20:77, emphasis added; see also Moro. 5:2 and D&C 20:79, "that they may have his Spirit to be *with* them," emphasis added). It is one thing to be filled "by the Spirit," wherein the Spirit supplies the content. It is quite another to be filled "with the Spirit" when talking about the constant companionship of the Holy Ghost or Holy Spirit (see D&C 121:46).

One further coloration should be splashed onto the canvas. This one touches on revelation. Although believers are "to be strengthened with might by his Spirit in the inner man [and woman]" (3:16), the key both for entering God's kingdom and for progressing within that space consists of "revelation in the knowledge of him" (1:17). After all, revelation "unto me" (3:3) and "unto his holy apostles and prophets" (3:5) informed church leaders that God intended to bring Gentiles into his fold, expanding everything. All of this revelatory activity went well beyond "the basic knowledge of the Christ event" that missionaries were teaching to investigators. In a word, revelation was the spiritual life force that was feeding the church.[249]

Spirit: The power of the Spirit (*pneuma*) manifests itself in an inviting variety of ways. To start at the beginning, investigators learn that "if ye shall ask [in prayer] with a sincere heart, with real intent, having faith in Christ, [God] will manifest the truth of [the gospel] unto you, by the power of the Holy Ghost." Moreover, "by the power of the Holy Ghost ye may know the truth of all things" (Moro. 10:4–5). Such experiences, of course, are deeply personal. In addition, the Spirit is the dispenser of spiritual gifts, including healing, prophecy, and speaking in tongues (see 1 Cor. 12:4–10; Moro. 10:8–16; and D&C 46:10–27). The legacies of the Spirit fit within the following words of Paul: "The signs of an apostle were wrought among you in all patience, in signs, and wonders, and mighty deeds" (2 Cor. 12:12). There is more.

The Spirit also brings reassurance about the heavenly hereafter. Jesus' Resurrection forms the linchpin. For by rising from the dead, he produced the guarantee of an immortal future. At the front of the line, one's physical body is promised redemption. Calling this assurance "the firstfruits," Paul wrote that "not only [all creatures], but ourselves also, which have the firstfruits of the Spirit [are] . . . waiting for the adoption, to wit, the redemption of our body" (Rom. 8:23). That guarantee is made secure by believers' deliverance "from the bondage of corruption into the glorious liberty of the children of

---

249. Kleinknecht, Baumgärtel, Bieder, Sjöberg, and Schweizer, *TDNT*, 6:444.

God" (Rom. 8:21; see also 2 Cor. 1:22; 5:5). Additionally, reassurances about the future include the inheritance in the next life, as we have already seen in our letter. For "that holy Spirit of promise" has "sealed" the steadfast "which is the earnest of our inheritance" (1:13–14;[250] see also the Notes on 1:13; 2:18; and especially 4:30).

5:19 *Speaking to yourselves:* Paul now arrives at his counsel for tempering church services. As if his sharp contrast between being drunk and being "filled with the Spirit" (5:18) were not enough, he plows the furrow deeper by adding to the Spirit-filled side of the ledger the singing of "psalms and hymns and spiritual songs."[251] The envisioned context for these activities, as presented by the line "speaking to yourselves," reposes clearly inside church services,[252] although church members could certainly sing religious songs individually and in their homes.

psalms and hymns: The noun "psalm" (ψαλμός, *psalmos*) is rather more common in the New Testament than the noun "hymn" (ὕμνος, *hymnos*), registering seven occurrences[253] to two. In 5:19, Paul was not talking about the biblical psalms, which carried their own divine weight as scripture (see Luke 24:44), but Christian compositions that evidently preserved characteristics of the Bible's psalms. Unfortunately, the New Testament presents few possible samples, and most of them are disputed. One instance that all agree is a Christian psalm or hymn composed from beginning to end to celebrate Christ's ministry occurs in Philippians 2:6–11.[254] During Jesus' lifetime and the earliest days of the Christian movement, disciples sang the biblical psalms (see Matt. 26:30 and Mark 14:26; the "hymn" consisted of the second part of the Hallel Psalms, Ps. 114–18). It was only later that Christian composers went to work under inspiration. How do we know that they were inspired? The answer lies in Paul's language, much of which appears in his letter to the Colossians.

At their base, "the Lord" was the person praised in these musical scores (5:19). Elsewhere, Paul's words buttress this observation when he wrote about "singing with grace in your hearts to the Lord" (Col. 3:16). Thus we find a reference to hymns to Christ. More than this, the music was regarded highly enough that it supplemented the spoken words of instruction and

250. Kleinknecht, Baumgärtel, Bieder, Sjöberg, and Schweizer, *TDNT,* 6:422.
251. Preisker, *TDNT,* 4:548.
252. Gerhard Delling, *TDNT,* 8:498.
253. See 5:19; Luke 20:42; 24:44; Acts 1:20; 13:33; 1 Cor. 14:26; Col. 3:16.
254. Delling, *TDNT,* 8:499–501.

testimony in church services: the Apostle wrote about "teaching and admonishing one another in psalms and hymns and spiritual songs" (Col. 3:16). One of the chief objectives of such music, whether freshly composed or not, focused on "all things [being] done unto edifying" in church meetings (1 Cor. 14:26). Importantly, not all singing was congregational. A believer who had composed a song was allowed and even encouraged to sing it in church services (see 1 Cor. 14:15, 26).[255] The clinching piece has to do with the expression translated "spiritual songs" (5:19; Col. 3:16). The word "spiritual" (πνευματικός, *pneumatikos*) pertains through and through to the divine world, to God's world, not to our world.[256]

One further question presses for an answer. Were any of these psalms and hymns from the Old Testament psalter? More precisely, were any of these psalms being sung at the Jerusalem Temple? The answer is, Very probably. Within the first few years following Jesus' death and Resurrection, Christian worshipers surely sang selections from the Old Testament that were at home in the temple.[257] They possessed little else. But the pieces of information that come to us from Ephesians 5:19 and the First Epistle to the Corinthians and the Epistle to the Colossians indicate that Christian musicians soon began to create their own compositions that came to focus clearly on the Christ and his stunning gifts (see Philip. 2:6–11). After all, the majority of Old Testament psalms did not allow believers to express themselves freely when praising the Lord Jesus Christ (see the Note on 6:4).

spiritual songs: Little difference likely existed between Christian psalms, hymns, and songs, although Paul mentioned all three here and at Colossians 3:16.[258] As we have seen, they regularly celebrated "the Lord," the Christ (5:19; Col. 3:16). In this connection, the noun for "songs" (plural of ᾠδή, *ōdē*) is about hymns that touched on Jesus' Atonement: "Thou was slain, and hast redeemed us to God by thy blood" (Rev. 5:9). In another we hear the words of praise from "the song of the Lamb": "Great and marvelous are thy works, Lord God Almighty; just and true are thy ways, thou King of saints" (Rev. 15:3).[259] These two samples may point at music sung

---

255. Delling, *TDNT*, 8:498–99.

256. Heinrich Schlier, *TDNT*, 1:164–65; Kleinknecht, Baumgärtel, Bieder, Sjöberg, and Schweizer, *TDNT*, 6:437.

257. Margaret Barker, *The Great High Priest: The Temple Roots of Christian Liturgy* (London: T&T Clark, 2003), 141–42.

258. Lincoln, *Ephesians*, 345–46; Best, *Ephesians*, 511.

259. BDAG, 1101.

by a choir. As we have also seen, the adjective "spiritual" (*pneumatikos*) takes singers and hearers alike into the celestial heights.[260]

What kinds of instruments might musicians have played to accompany congregational and solo music? Depending on one's ability to play, the options presented a wide variety, mostly confined to stringed instruments and woodwinds. Presumably, trumpets and percussive pieces were not played in church services, although that is unsure. Of stringed devices, a musician might play something with several strings or as few as one, a lyre, a harp, or a cithar, relying on picking with fingers or strokes with a bow. Woodwinds also offered a variety, anything from a simple flute to an aulos, an instrument similar to a clarinet or oboe.[261] The sound and harmony of the singing was perhaps much like the current Coptic music of Egypt.[262]

in your heart: The tie between being "filled with the Spirit" (5:18) and experiencing the joy in one's heart that leads to singing stands boldly forth in this phrase.[263] In antiquity, the heart was thought to be the seat of understanding where a person's thoughts, good or ill, sprang to life.[264] In Mary's case, after hearing the words of the shepherds, she "kept all these things, and pondered them in her heart" (Luke 2:19; see also Luke 2:51). When Jesus' disciples became embroiled in a quarrelsome private conversation about "which of them should be greatest," he became aware, "perceiving the thought of their heart" (Luke 9:46–47; see also Luke 5:22; 24:38). Paul mirrors the same view of the heart as the place of comprehending and thinking. We read that "God . . . hath shined in our hearts, to give the light of knowledge of the glory of God" (2 Cor. 4:6). Here the heart is the recipient of God's illuminating light, his heavenly understanding. That said, in modern scripture the Resurrected Jesus said that "my soul delighteth in the song of the heart; yea, the song of the righteous is a prayer unto me" (D&C 25:12; see also the Notes on 4:18; 6:5).

---

260. Schlier, *TDNT*, 1:164–65; Kleinknecht, Baumgärtel, Bieder, Sjöberg, and Schweizer, *TDNT*, 6:437.

261. James Frederick Mountford and Reginald Pepys Winnington-Ingram, "Music," in *OCD2*, 709–11; Victor H. Matthews and Ivor H. Jones, "Music and Musical Instruments," in *ABD*, 4:930–39.

262. Ragheb Moftah, Marian Robertson, Martha Roy, and Margit Tóth, "Music, Coptic," in *The Coptic Encyclopedia,* ed. Aziz S. Atiya, 8 vols. (New York: Macmillan, 1991), 6:1715–47.

263. Lincoln, *Ephesians*, 345–46.

264. Baumgärtel and Behm, *TDNT*, 3:606–7, 612.

to the Lord: In the two Greek words translated "to the Lord" (τῷ κυρίῳ, *tō kyriō*), Paul has disclosed that the Christian hymns known to him offered praise to Christ, becoming hymns to Christ and songs "in which Christ makes himself heard."[265] Moreover, all in Christianity stand reverently within the name-title of Christ. Singing underscores this, adding one more avenue for expressing thanks to him (see the Notes on 4:1, 5).[266]

5:20 *Giving thanks:* One matter to examine concerns whether the giving of thanks (εὐχαριστέω, *eucharisteō*) satisfies itself in "singing and making melody" (5:19) or whether implicitly linked to the verb is the celebration of the Eucharist or sacrament. Two passages from New Testament letters appear to envision the verb *eucharisteō* describing the ordinance of the Eucharist. In a context of worship, the Apostle instructed his Philippian friends that "in every thing by prayer and supplication with thanksgiving [*eucharisteō*] let your requests be made known unto God" (Philip. 4:6). Similarly, we read: "I exhort therefore that . . . supplications, prayers, inter-cessions, and giving of thanks [*eucharisteō*], be made for all men" (1 Tim. 2:1). The view that the Eucharist was not a regular feature of Christian wor-ship until late in the first century[267] purposely discounts Paul's instructions about this ordinance in his first letter to the Corinthian Saints, written about AD 55 or 56.[268] The clincher that the Eucharist was a well-established and regular worship practice anchors itself in Paul's concern for believers who partook of the sacrament "unworthily." We read, "Whosoever shall eat this bread, and drink this cup of the Lord, unworthily, shall be guilty of the body and blood of the Lord." That is, "he [or she] that eateth and drin-keth unworthily, eateth and drinketh damnation to himself [or herself]" (1 Cor. 11:27, 29). It is plain that this kind of concern would hardly arise for discussion if Christians were partaking of the Eucharist, say, once a year at Easter or on some other special annual date. The regular character of the ordinance drives the need to address the issue of worthiness or its lack (see JST Mark 14:24, "as oft as ye do this ordinance, ye will remember me"; and the Notes on 1:16; 5:5).

---

265. Schlier, *TDNT,* 1:164–65; Delling, *TDNT,* 8:498. The quotation comes from Schlier, *TDNT,* 1:165.

266. Hans Bietenhard, *TDNT,* 5:274.

267. Hans Conzelmann, *TDNT,* 9:414–15 and n. 78; Lincoln, *Ephesians,* 347; Muddi-man, *Ephesians,* 249.

268. Bruce, *Paul: Apostle of the Heart Set Free,* 475; Winger, *Ephesians,* 589–90.

for all things: The idea behind the preposition ὑπέρ (*hyper*) sends us to "on account of" or "because of." It manifests this sense often in expressions of praise or thanks. On one occasion, Paul asked of his critics, "If I take part in the [unbeliever's] meal with thankfulness, why am I denounced because of [*hyper*] something I thank God for?" (1 Cor. 10:30 NIV). In another place, he wrote, "The Gentiles might glorify God for [*hyper*] his mercy" (Rom. 15:9 RSV; see also Acts 5:41; 9:16; etc.).[269] Although the term translated "all things" (plural of πᾶς, *pas*) could be thought of as a reference to "all people," it is much more likely to be neuter in its meaning, signaling "all things" (see 1 Thes. 5:18, "in every thing give thanks").[270] Within this letter, Paul has made reference to a series of blessings for which a believer should be giving thanks. One thinks, for example, of our "redemption through his blood, the forgiveness of sins" (1:7); of our "understanding being enlightened" so that we "know what [are] . . . the riches of the glory of his inheritance" (1:18); of Christ's Resurrection "from the dead" and his elevation to God's "own right hand in the heavenly places" (1:20), with us seated next to him (see 2:6); of the welcoming of Gentiles into God's fold (see 2:11–22; 3:6); and of the gift of apostles, prophets, and other church officers "for the edifying of the body [church] of Christ" (4:11–12).[271]

God and the Father: The KJV translators sensed that the thanksgiving nature of this verse was strengthened by this line in combination with the expression "in the name of our Lord Jesus Christ." In fact, this latter expression precedes the line "God and the Father" in the Greek text. In a series of passages in Paul's letters, the combination of God and Father always brings us to lofty, often solemn, words of thanksgiving or praise. Thus we read about Christ "who gave himself for our sins . . . according to the will of God and our Father; to whom be glory for ever and ever" (Gal. 1:4–5; see also Col. 1:17). We can almost hear the Apostle's voice dictating the soaring, rhythmic line, "The God and Father of our Lord Jesus Christ, which is blessed for evermore" (2 Cor. 11:31). In his affirmation that believers have left behind their beliefs in multiple pagan gods, Paul wrote to his Corinthian readers a passage laced with thanksgiving to the effect that "to us there is but one God, the Father, of whom are all things, and we in him; and one Lord Jesus Christ, by whom are all things, and we by him" (1 Cor. 8:6).[272]

---

269. Riesenfeld, *TDNT,* 8:514–15; BDAG, 1031.A.c.2.
270. Best, *Ephesians,* 513; Merkle, *Guide,* 176.
271. Best, *Ephesians,* 513.
272. Schrenk and Quell, *TDNT,* 5:1007.

Such expressions stand out not only because of their obvious links to thanksgiving and praise but also owing to the fact that New Testament authors generally preferred to frame God the Father in Old Testament terms. Hence, we read the title "the God of Abraham, and of Isaac, and of Jacob, the God of our fathers" (Acts 3:13; see also Matt. 22:32; Mark 12:26; Luke 20:37; and Acts 7:32). The simple "God of our fathers" appears in Acts 5:30 and 22:14. Elsewhere we come upon references to "the God of Israel" (Matt. 15:31; Luke 1:68, "the Lord God of Israel"). In Old Testament fashion, we meet "our God" (Luke 1:78; Rev. 7:12; 19:5; compare Mark 12:29 and Acts 2:39, "the Lord our God") and "my God" (Rom. 1:8; 2 Cor. 12:21; Philip. 1:3; 4:19; etc.). Even in the presence of such an array of titles, God the Father was now God of "the church of God" (Acts 20:28;[273] see also the Notes on 2:18; 3:14; 5:1; and the Analysis of 3:14–21).

the name: The mention of the name (ὄνομα, *onoma*) of Jesus Christ "implies an official gathering of the Church in the name of Christ for worship."[274] This name also opens door after door for the believer who seeks an entry to heaven. The most important consists of his power to save. As Peter declared to a gathering of Jewish notables in Jerusalem, "there is none other name [than Jesus Christ] under heaven given among men, whereby we must be saved" (Acts 4:12).[275] This truth echoes across modern scripture again and again. In a quotation from an angel, cited by King Benjamin in the Book of Mormon, we discover a similar statement: "There shall be no name given nor any other way nor means whereby salvation can come unto the children of men, only in and through the name of Christ, the Lord Omnipotent" (Mosiah 3:17; see also 2 Ne. 25:20; 31:21). Within the framework of the Old Testament, the prophet Hosea presented the future Savior in the following way: "I am the Lord thy God from the land of Egypt, and thou shalt know no god but me: for there is no savior beside me" (Hosea 13:4). Hosea's quotation from "the Lord thy God" undergirds the idea that the God who rescued the Hebrew slaves is Jesus Christ, the Savior of humankind.

Analysis of 5:1–20

All commentators pair verses 5:1–2 with the latter verses of chapter 4. This linkage is an easy exercise because of the appearance of οὖν (*oun*) in 5:1, which means "therefore" and, in a summarizing way, clearly ties back to

---

273. Kleinknecht, Quell, Stauffer, and Kuhn, *TDNT,* 3:101.
274. Muddiman, *Ephesians,* 249.
275. Bietenhard, *TDNT,* 5:274.

chapter 4, particularly to 4:32, where we read Paul's plea that "ye [be] kind one to another, tenderhearted, forgiving one another, even as God for Christ's sake hath forgiven you." This appeal, with Christ nestled inside as the forgiving one, fits snugly as an introduction to his following entreaty that believers be "followers of God . . . and walk in love, as Christ also hath loved us, and hath given himself for us" (5:1–2). Besides being the forgiving one, Christ is also the loving one. At this point, 5:3, Paul altered the tenor of his remarks, turning round on acts of bad behavior that mortally wound a devotee's standing with God.

However, a person can read verses 5:1–2 differently, because in a real sense they stand as a prologue to what Paul will write in 5:3–20.[276] Specifically, the emphasis on being "imitators of God" (5:1 NR) threads its way through the following verses, preparing readers for the imperative to "walk in love, as Christ also hath loved us" (5:2), and to avoid even mentioning spiritually crippling activities such as "fornication, . . . uncleanness, . . . covetousness, [and engaging in] . . . foolish talking" (5:3–4). Imitating God pulls believers away from deception and the ever-sapping power of darkness, instead ushering them into the embrace of divine light (see 5:6–14). Imitating God lifts devotees into the heights of wisdom, where they understand "what the will of the Lord is" and the blessing of being "filled with the Spirit" (5:15–18). Finally, imitating God brings such a pitch of joy that only "singing and making melody in your heart" will do (5:19–20).

A reader soon notices that verses 5:1–20 rest on a series of opposites, an approach that aids memory. But taller than memory stand the principles that grow out of believers becoming "imitators of God" (5:1 NR). In front of them blossom the flowers of walking "in love"—not just any expression of love but one that imitates that of "Christ [who] also hath loved us, and hath given himself for us an offering and a sacrifice to God" (5:2). Recipients of this gift could clearly discern the counterfeits of love—namely, "sexual immorality, any kind of impurity, or covetousness" (5:3 NR). Onto those who wittingly or unwittingly pursued such courses of action "cometh the wrath of God" in all its fury (5:6). Paul's painting shows more.

Following his treatment of love and its counterfeits, Paul pushes into our sight light and its counterweight, darkness. Admitting that his Gentile readers "were sometimes darkness" in their earlier lives, he assures them that "now are ye light in the Lord" (5:8), a breathtaking prospect. Why?

---

276. Barth, *Ephesians*, 2:585.

Because believers, no matter how much they cultivate goodness, cannot be equated with God and his Son, each of whom is thought of as a source of light (see 1 John 1:5, "God is light"; and John 8:12, "I am the light"). Rather, Paul's statement in 5:8 relates to an eternal eventuality, a promised destiny. For the moment, believers "walk as children of light" (5:8). As he wrote in another place, "Ye are all the children of light, and the children of the day: we are not of the night, nor of darkness" (1 Thes. 5:5). As we learn from modern scripture, "he that receiveth light, and continueth in God, receiveth more light; and that light groweth brighter and brighter" (D&C 50:24). Even more impressive are the lines "If your eye be single to my glory, your whole bodies shall be filled with light, and there shall be no darkness in you." Besides the personal effort implicit in the words "if your eye be single," we come upon God's gracious effort of filling our "whole bodies . . . with light." There is more. At the end of this process comes the majestic result—namely, "that body which is filled with light comprehendeth all things" (D&C 88:67).

Such comprehension, of course, links closely with wisdom, which, not surprisingly, holds an honored spot opposite folly. Although the Apostle did not repeat the noun for wisdom (σοφία, *sophia*) in verses 5:1–20, and mentioned it only elsewhere in Ephesians (see 1:8, 17; 3:10), it surely stood in the back of his mind as he wrote about being "wise" and "unwise" (5:15, 17). As all understand, wisdom was discovered and thereafter revealed by God; wisdom also participated with him in the creation of the earth (see Job 28:23–28 and Prov. 8:22–30). Notably, it is from modern scripture that believers learn about the close meshing of "the Spirit of the Lord" and the paths that wisdom has blazed for humankind. In a voice filled with warning, King Benjamin cracked a whip of sorts over the heads of listeners when he declared that "if ye should transgress and go contrary to that which has been spoken, that ye do withdraw yourselves from the Spirit of the Lord, that it may have no place in you to guide you in wisdom's paths[,] . . . the same cometh out in open rebellion against God" (Mosiah 2:36–37). Elsewhere, wisdom gains the character of a benevolent ruler on whom many have turned their backs. In the words of King Limhi, with darkness hovering within his spoken lines, "How blind and impenetrable are the understandings of the children of men; for they will not seek wisdom, neither do they desire that she should rule over them" (Mosiah 8:20).

The last contrast of this section has to do with being filled, a topic that Paul has taken up elsewhere in this letter (see 1:23; 3:19; 4:10, 13). The two sides of the dividing line take on a physical and a spiritual form. On the one side stands drunkenness "with wine"; on the other reposes being "filled with the Spirit" (5:18). The opposition of the two conditions could not be more stark. On the one hand appears the common sight of inebriated persons around town who have lost all control of speech and actions. On the other travel individuals who enjoy full control of their physical and spiritual lives, possessing the ability "to give to him [or her] that needeth" (4:28) and basking in the light of the gospel "as children of light" (5:8).

At the end, with "singing and making melody in [their] heart[s]," they raise their joyous voices, mirroring to the faithful a heavenly happiness that gives "thanks always for all things unto God and the Father in the name of our Lord Jesus Christ" (5:19–20). At times of joy, voices raised in song provide the deepest, most meaningful expression of "giving thanks" (5:20). Nothing else will do. Such an experience lifts one out of the destructive world of "vain words" (5:6) and lands one in the bosom of God. Indeed!

One issue that begs for settlement arises from reference to those who "deceive you with vain words" (5:6). Did such persons stand outside the church or inside? If, as suggested in the Notes on 5:6–7 and 5:11, the enemies apparently lurked within the church, then Ephesians may not have been "the peaceful epistle" that Barth had supposed.[277] That said, if at the time apostate or heretical teachings were an overpowering threat to believers in Ephesus and nearby branches, then Paul would have pushed the matter to the front of his letter as he did in his Galatian correspondence. There, within a few lines of his usual opening, he plunged deep into the apostate threat, to wit, "I marvel that ye are so soon removed from him that called you into the grace of Christ unto another gospel" (Gal. 1:6). He did not do so in Ephesians. Hence, the threat, though serious, was evidently not beyond control or remedy. Only time would tell.

"Husbands, Love Your Wives" (5:21–33)

King James Translation

21 Submitting yourselves one to another in the fear of God. 22 Wives, submit yourselves unto your own husbands, as unto the Lord. 23 For the husband is the head of the wife, even as Christ

New Rendition

21 Submit to one another out of reverence for Christ. 22 Wives, submit to your husbands as to the Lord, 23 for the husband is the head of the wife as Christ is the head of the church—he himself

---

277. Barth, *Ephesians,* 1:43; see also Fowl, *Ephesians,* 8.

is the head of the church: and he is the saviour of the body. 24 Therefore as the church is subject unto Christ, so let the wives be to their own husbands in every thing. 25 Husbands, love your wives, even as Christ also loved the church, and gave himself for it; 26 That he might sanctify and cleanse it with the washing of water by the word, 27 That he might present it to himself a glorious church, not having spot, or wrinkle, or any such thing; but that it should be holy and without blemish. 28 So ought men to love their wives as their own bodies. He that loveth his wife loveth himself. 29 For no man ever yet hated his own flesh; but nourisheth and cherisheth it, even as the Lord the church: 30 For we are members of his body, of his flesh, and of his bones. 31 For this cause shall a man leave his father and mother, and shall be joined unto his wife, and they two shall be one flesh. 32 This is a great mystery: but I speak concerning Christ and the church. 33 Nevertheless let every one of you in particular so love his wife even as himself; and the wife see that she reverence her husband.

being the savior of the body. 24 Now as the church submits to Christ, so also wives should submit to their husbands in every way. 25 Husbands, love your wives, just as Christ loved the church and gave himself up for her 26 to sanctify her—having cleansed her through the washing of water with a promise—27 that he might present to himself a glorious church, not having stain or wrinkle or any such thing, but holy and blameless. 28 In the same way, husbands ought to love their wives as their own bodies. He who loves his wife loves himself. 29 For no one ever hated his own flesh, but nourishes it and cherishes it, even as Christ does the church, 30 since we are members of his body. 31 "For this reason a man will leave his father and mother and be joined to his wife, and the two will become one flesh." 32 This is a great mystery, but I am speaking about Christ and the church. 33 In any case, let each one of you love his wife as himself, so that the wife may reverence her husband.

Notes on 5:21–33

5:21 *Submitting yourselves:* This verse, with its present middle participle of ὑποτάσσω (*hypotassō*) and with the meaning "subjecting oneself,"[278] continues the string of participles in prior verses. This means that grammatically verse 5:21 belongs to what precedes. But it belongs also to what follows because of the sense of the verb "to submit," which sits at the base of verses 5:21–33.[279] Its structural connection is to the verb "be filled" (5:18)

---

278. Delling, *TDNT,* 8:40; Larkin, *Handbook,* 129; Merkle, *Guide,* 177; contra BDAG, 1042.1.b.β, which takes the participle as a passive.

279. Barth, *Ephesians,* 2:608–9; Lincoln, *Ephesians,* 352; Fowl, *Ephesians,* 186; contra Muddiman, *Ephesians,* 256.

and fills out the pattern of participles—"speaking," "singing and making melody" (5:19), and "giving thanks" (5:20).[280]

The question arises: Submitting to whom? Does the term translated "one to another" (dative plural ἀλλήλοις, *allēlois*) have to do with church members submitting to each other for any and all reasons? By twisting and turning, some argue for this meaning.[281] Or are we looking at a passage that governed ecclesiastical matters wherein believers submitted, say, to their "pastors" (4:11 and the Note thereon)?[282] Although there is good reason to prefer the latter since otherwise chaos would reign in a branch, the next verse sends us into the world of marital relationships, not ecclesiastical. Thus our passage differs markedly from 1 Corinthians 11:3–15, where the matter has to do with the propriety of women participating in church meetings with their hair uncovered. In Paul's view, within the expectations of the broader society they should not do so.[283] It also differs substantially from Paul's treatments in 1 Corinthians 7:2–16 and 7:25–40 that deal with the questions of whether to marry and to what degree that decision may impact one's ability to enter missionary service.

fear: The noun φόβος (*phobos*) manifests a range of meanings depending on the context. The notions of "fear" and "terror" are absent here, whereas "reverence" fits (NR).[284] In brief, "this is an attitude that looks to Christ in awe at his overwhelming love and at his power." Moreover, "the specific relationships within marriage that are set out are also to flow from and be an expression of such [awe]."[285] Said another way, "Christ's enemies are subjected to him involuntarily (Eph. 1:20–22; Phil[ip]. 2:10); Christians are subordinate to him . . . with a willing heart" (see the Note on 6:5).[286]

God: The preferred reading is "Christ" (NR). Some late manuscripts preserve "Jesus Christ"; the KJV title "God" comes from medieval manuscripts and late Christian writers.[287]

5:22 *Wives:* With this verse, we step into the home, a sacred place. A spirit of reverence is required of readers and commentators alike. Some

---

280. Larkin, *Handbook,* 129–30; Merkle, *Guide,* 170–71, 177.

281. Lincoln, *Ephesians,* 365; Muddiman, *Ephesians,* 257; Fowl, *Ephesians,* 186–87.

282. Winger, *Ephesians,* 601.

283. Draper and Rhodes, *Paul's First Epistle to the Corinthians,* 518–42.

284. BDAG, 1062.2.b; Louw-Nida, §53.59; Thayer, *Lexicon,* 656; Best, *Ephesians,* 518; contra Horst Balz and Günther Wanke, *TDNT,* 9:217.

285. Lincoln, *Ephesians,* 367.

286. Winger, *Ephesians,* 602–3.

287. Best, *Ephesians,* 518; Aland and others, *Novum Testamentum Graece,* 512.

have suggested that the following verses rest on a Hellenistic "house table," *Haustafel* in German, which sets out the responsibilities of family members, including slaves.[288] But, even if Paul was acquainted with this kind of rule collection, he has bent it to serve Christian concepts. For it appears that Paul has addressed marital and family matters in a special light—in the home, we have the best chance to become "imitators of God" (5:1 NR), and there we are to "walk in love, as Christ also hath loved us" (5:2).

The most intriguing and important question is, Where do wives stand on the scale of personal relationships inside homes? Other questions attach themselves to this one. For example, do wives enjoy a different status at home from that in the church? How much of Paul's remarks grew out of his cultural conditioning and how much arose from inspiration? Do his ideas have anything to do with standards in the modern church? In framing a set of responses, we begin with Jesus.

Jesus. Gaining a clear sense about how Jesus measured the value of women, particularly widows, pushes itself to the fore. Such valuation, it seems obvious, turns a celestial key for assessing the long view of women and wives, because Christ "hath loved [all of] us, and hath given himself for [all of] us an offering and a sacrifice to God" (5:2).

The first place to look is Luke's narrative of Jesus' ministry in Galilee, his first field of labor. Luke made certain that we knew the central role of the Twelve when he wrote that Jesus "went throughout every city and village, preaching ... the kingdom of God: and the twelve were with him" (Luke 8:1). Immediately after this note he added, "Certain women, which had been healed of evil spirits and infirmities ... ministered unto him of their substance" (Luke 8:2–3). Hence, linked to the Twelve was a group of women devoted to Jesus who traveled in his entourage and, out of their own purses, met his and his disciples' needs.[289] Within the sphere of Jesus' earthly ministry, these were heady days for those women. Moreover, it was this group of women who served the last supper and went early in the morning to tend to Jesus' body, which had lain in a tomb over the weekend.[290] Besides becoming the first witnesses of Jesus' Resurrection, these women were made into divine messengers by one of the angels whom the women met at the empty tomb: "Go quickly, and tell his disciples that he is risen from the dead" (Matt. 28:7).

---

288. Caird, *Letters,* 88; Barth, *Ephesians,* 2:608–9; Lincoln, *Ephesians,* 358–61, 367; Best, *Ephesians,* 521–27; Fowl, *Ephesians,* 187; see also Balz and Wanke, *TDNT,* 9:217.

289. Oepke, *TDNT,* 1:787.

290. Brown, *Testimony of Luke,* 395–400, 985, 987, 1094–95, 1099–1101, 1106–10, 1112.

Although the Twelve and others did not believe their news, still the Resurrected Christ, through his angel, had entrusted this most important task to these women.

Besides this capstone on Jesus' earthly ministry, other occurrences underline the importance of women, not just as women but as God's beloved and deserving daughters. Again we turn to Jesus. On the margins of society stood poor widows. Jesus drew the attention of his disciples to a widow while in the Court of the Women in the Jerusalem temple. While his hard-working disciples were captured by the beauty of the temple and by those who brought impressive gifts to its treasury, Jesus saw a poor widow approach one of the thirteen chests that were set out in the courtyard to receive gifts. After she cast in her "two mites," Jesus observed "that this poor widow hath cast in more than they all" because "she of her penury hath cast in all the living that she had" (Luke 21:2–4). In sum, she was the true disciple, having given all that she possessed to God's house.[291]

Another incident brings out Jesus' active response toward those on the margins of society, specifically toward a widow who had just lost her only child, a son. On one day, Jesus and his followers were in Capernaum on the north shore of the Sea of Galilee. By the next morning, he had reached Nain, a village some thirty miles distant, clearly implying that he and his disciples had walked through much of the night to reach the place. When the funeral procession emerged from the village, he stopped it. He spoke reassuringly to the widow, saying, "Weep not." He then touched the bier and commanded, "Young man, I say unto thee, Arise." Immediately, the dead man was restored to his grieving mother, solving a big problem for her. For without her son, she had no source of income. In time, after spending her dowry, she would have become the poorest of the poor. Jesus knew of her desperate situation from afar. He came all that distance specifically to bring life-stabilizing assistance to her (Luke 7:11–16).[292]

A third example leads us to an oft-divorced woman. On one of Jesus' return trips from Jerusalem to Galilee in the company of his disciples, he passed through Samaria, a land whose inhabitants held Jews in low esteem. John wrote that Jesus "must needs go through Samaria" (John 4:4). That is, a divine necessity lay upon Jesus to travel that way rather than along the customary route through the Jordan Valley. Stopping at Jacob's well at noon,

---

291. Brown, *Testimony of Luke*, 932–35.
292. Brown, *Testimony of Luke*, 363–67.

his disciples went into the nearby village to purchase food. At that juncture, a woman of the town walked to the well to fetch water. Jesus asked for a drink, opening a conversation with the woman. As their communication went on, Jesus promised the woman "a well of water springing up into everlasting life." She then said, "Sir, give me this water, that I thirst not." He replied, "Go, call thy husband." When she said that she was not married, Jesus then revealed to her that he knew her marriage situation: "Thou hast had five husbands; and he whom thou now hast is not thy husband." Most commentators fix their attention on Jesus' act of guiding the conversation so that he could disclose his knowledge of her marital circumstance. They therefore lose track of his invitation that she bring her husband so that she and he could partake of "this water" that Jesus was offering. The point? Jesus' gift that would lead to "everlasting life" was available to her only in the company of her husband—that is, inside a family setting. In such a setting, she would not be the lesser party; she was to be an equal partner in receiving the Savior's gift. The husband was not the key; he was simply one of two equivalent parts (see John 4:3–30; and the Note on 3:15).

A fourth account further rounds out the picture of Jesus' views on women and wives. He repeated two short parables, one about a man and one about a woman, a common pairing in Luke's Gospel. In the first, he compared "the kingdom of God" to a man who planted "a grain of mustard seed [in] . . . his garden" (Luke 13:18–19). In the second, he likened "the kingdom of God" to "a woman" who kneaded "leaven" inside "three measures of meal, till the whole was leavened" (Luke 13:20–21). Jesus' short stories laid emphasis on the kingdom of God and the man and woman who figured in his brief narratives. Yes, in the first instance the seed grew into "a great tree" where "the fowls of the air lodged," showing the open, welcoming character of the kingdom (Luke 13:19). And yes, in the second the "three measures of meal," about fifty pounds of flour, were made ready to bake in a raised state, a pointer to the sufficiency of God's kingdom (Luke 13:21). Each of the activities—working in the garden and working in the kitchen—were normal household tasks, underscoring the connection of God's kingdom to home and hearth. But in the retelling, Jesus had completely changed the face of his contemporary social system. Rather than men alone playing the leading roles in Jesus' kingdom, as in the larger Near Eastern and Roman societies, women were and are to enjoy equal access to all its blessings.[293]

---

293. Oepke, *TDNT,* 1:784–85; Brown, *Testimony of Luke,* 665–68.

A few sayings of Jesus are also relevant. On one occasion, when he was reviewing how certain persons of elevated standing like to be greeted, he instructed his disciples, "Neither be ye called masters; for one is your Master, even Christ. But he that is greatest among you shall be your servant" (Matt. 23:10–11). Although this saying bears directly on church governance, it also can be applied to family situations. At the Last Supper, after the disciples fell into a heated discussion about "which of them should be accounted the greatest," Jesus intervened. Like in the other situation, Jesus reminded his followers that "the kings of the Gentiles exercise lordship over them. . . . But ye shall not be so: but he that is greatest among you, let him be . . . as he that doth serve . . . [for] I am among you as he that serveth [διακονέω, *diakoneō*]" (Luke 22:25–27; see also Matt. 20:25–28 and Mark 10:42–45). Here, too, the chief application has to do with presiding in the church. But Jesus' words also fit within the home, because women typically are those who wait upon others, and Jesus obviously expected his disciples to become involved in serving, including in the home.[294]

Another sample comes from the Sermon on the Mount. Jesus was very clear about the thoughts of men and the need to protect women from evil intentions. When he addressed the matter of adultery, he spoke plainly: "I say unto you, That whosoever looketh on a woman to lust after her hath committed adultery with her already in his heart" (Matt. 5:28). Jesus understood the human psyche and how certain men think about women. One example concerned divorce. In his response to a group of Pharisees who asked, "Is it lawful for a man to put away his wife for every cause?" Jesus answered in a way that leveled the field for women victimized by the actions of cavalier husbands. Citing the creation account and the eternal duration of the first marriage, performed by God himself, that of Adam and Eve, Jesus declared, "What therefore God hath joined together, let not man put asunder." To further answer his questioners, he made the point that "Moses because of the hardness of your hearts suffered you to put away your wives: but from the beginning it was not so" (Matt. 19:3, 6, 8). From these two instances, Jesus obviously sought to elevate women and protect them from the ill behavior of wanton strangers and husbands.

A last instance frames a striking illustration of Jesus with women. As he bore his cross to the place of his execution, he called out in one final, desperate attempt to get the attention of people who, forty years hence, would be overwhelmed by the attack and siege of the Roman army. To whom did he

---

294. BDAG, 229.2.b; Louw-Nida, §§35.19; 46.13.

address his pleas? To the "women," those in the gathered crowd who followed his steps. To them he appealed, "Daughters of Jerusalem, weep not for me, but weep for yourselves and for your children. For, behold, the days are coming, in the which they shall say ... to the mountains, Fall on us; and to the hills, Cover us" (Luke 23:27–30). Why cry out to the women? Because Jesus knew that they would listen, whereas others in the citizenry would not. Among the women he would find receptive ears and hearts (see the Note on 6:2).[295]

Paul. When we review Paul's experiences and letters, we find a corpus limited largely to 1 Corinthians. Of course, we know about Lydia, the seller of purple fabrics whom Paul and his companions taught and baptized in Philippi. She was the Apostle's first convert in Europe who opened her home to him and his companions until their departure (see Acts 16:12–15, 40). When we turn to 1 Corinthians, we discover that it was evidently written as a response to a message from a trusted woman named Chloe, whose representatives likely were Stephanus, Fortunatus, and Achaicus (see 1 Cor. 16:17–18). These men had apparently told the Apostle about "divisions" and "contentions" within the Corinthian congregation (1 Cor. 1:10–11). It seems likely that "this lengthy and doctrinally rich [letter] identifying the destructive ramifications of disunity is evidence of Paul's respect for a woman's perceptions in spiritual matters."[296]

As we have noticed earlier, the passage 1 Corinthians 11:3–15 deals with the question of whether a woman should participate in church meetings with her head uncovered, the kind of issue that would arise within the context of established worship patterns in Roman and Jewish religions. On the back side of this matter appears the fact that women who covered their heads certainly participated in church services, whether singing, preaching, bearing witness, praying, or even prophesying. Women were not excluded from these sorts of activities (see 1 Cor. 11:13).[297]

Chapter 7 of 1 Corinthians presents a different situation. Here Paul treated a variety of matters—to wit, intimacy in marriage (see 1 Cor. 7:1–6), remarriage (see 7:7–9), divorce (see 7:10–11), marriage to an unbeliever

---

295. Brown, *Testimony of Luke*, 1072–76.

296. Camille Fronk, "Submit Yourselves ... as unto the Lord," in *Go Ye into All the World: Messages of the New Testament Apostles*, ed. Ray L. Huntington, Jerome M. Perkins, Thomas A. Wayment, and Patty A. Smith, 31st Annual Sidney B. Sperry Symposium (Salt Lake City: Deseret Book, 2002), 102; see also Frederick Fyvie Bruce, *New Testament History* (Garden City, N.Y.: Anchor Books, 1972), 325–26.

297. Oepke, *TDNT*, 1:787; Fronk, "Submit Yourselves ... as unto the Lord," 108; Draper and Rhodes, *Paul's First Epistle to the Corinthians*, 533–34.

(see 7:12–16), circumcision and uncircumcision (see 7:17–19), slaves (see 7:20–24), those called to the ministry (see 7:25–35), engaged couples (see 7:36–38), and remarriage of widows (see 7:39–40).[298] Nothing there applies directly to our verse, 5:22, and the submission of wives to husbands. The topic of the long center section, 1 Corinthians 7:25–35, received an assist from the Joseph Smith Translation, because at the beginning of 7:29 the Prophet inserted, "But I speak unto you, who are called unto the ministry." Believers were not to undertake this ministry inside the Corinth branch. Instead, they were to "be sent forth unto the [preaching] ministry" outside Corinth, just as modern missionaries are sent away from their homes. At the end of this verse, Joseph Smith added, "For ye are called and chosen to do the Lord's work" (1 Cor. 7:29 JST). Thus, the center portion, 1 Corinthians 7:25–35, has to do with missionary work. And ideally that missionary effort was to be carried out by single persons. For "he that is unmarried careth for the things that belong to the Lord, how he may please the Lord." On the other hand, "he that is married careth for the things that are of the world, how he may please his wife," an activity that was perfectly normal for a married man (1 Cor. 7:32–33). Paul made the same point about an "unmarried woman" who was eligible to engage in missionary work (see 1 Cor. 7:34). He wanted his missionaries to "attend upon the Lord without [the] distraction" of husband or wife (1 Cor. 7:35).

The one outlier occurs in 1 Thessalonians. Here Paul affirms that the "instructions we gave you [came] through the Lord Jesus" (1 Thes. 4:2 RSV). Hence, no less a person than the Savior was his authority. And what were those instructions? Just these: "This is the will of God, your sanctification: that you abstain from unchastity" (1 Thes. 4:3 RSV). Thus, the inexpressible quality of holiness became available to his readers only through chastity. The opposite side of the coin from resisting unchastity was to marry. In an almost mirror image of what he wrote in 1 Corinthians 7:2 ("because of the temptation to immorality, each man should have his own wife and each woman her own husband" [RSV]), Paul declared "that each one of you know how to take a wife [σκεῦος, *skeuos*[299]] for himself in holiness and honor, not in the passion of lust like heathen who do not know God" (1 Thes. 4:4–5 RSV; see also 1 Pet. 3:7).

---

298. Draper and Rhodes, *Paul's First Epistle to the Corinthians*, 333.

299. Although *skeuos* is usually rendered "vessel" or "object," here and in 1 Pet. 3:7 this noun clearly has to do with a married woman. See Christian Maurer, *TDNT*, 7:367; BDAG, 928.3; Louw-Nida, §10.55.

In the end, a reader is left with the impression that women, married or single, enjoyed significant opportunities for participation and service inside the congregations to which Paul wrote. And they enjoyed his admiration. In an odd statement near the end of 1 Corinthians, he writes, "Let your women keep silence in the churches" (1 Cor. 14:34). This passage has historical problems and was not originally from the Apostle.[300] In this light, it becomes apparent that Paul did not contradict his notice that women prayed regularly in congregational meetings (see 1 Cor. 11:13). Instead, he saw them as partners in the ongoing labors of the church.[301] As he wrote elsewhere, "There is neither male nor female: for ye are all one in Christ Jesus" (Gal. 3:28; see also Col. 3:11).

Old Testament. In the earliest form of the Mosaic law, we come upon these lines: "Honor thy father *and thy mother*: that thy days may be long upon the land which the Lord thy God giveth thee" (Ex. 20:12, emphasis added). Into this important commandment the wife and mother has been drawn and elevated with the husband and father in a family. To be sure, women were esteemed in a lower status than men in the Old Testament.[302] Yet, under this law, neither the father nor the mother stood in front of the other. Under this law, a child was obliged to honor both parents. There is more. In what is called the Covenant Code, Exodus 20–23, of which the Ten Commandments are a part, we hear God's voice: "He that smiteth his father, *or his mother,* shall be surely put to death" (Ex. 21:15, emphasis added). Again comes the divine warning: "He that curseth his father, *or his mother,* shall surely be put to death" (Ex. 21:17, emphasis added). The pairing of the wife with the husband in these legal statements has elevated the woman to the status of one receiving respect and honor in God's eyes (see the Note on 6:2).[303]

The diminished status of the ancient woman in marriage becomes evident in God's words to the fallen Eve: "In sorrow thou shalt bring forth children; and thy desire shall be to thy husband, and he shall rule over thee" (Gen. 3:16; see also Moses 4:22). But it was not so from the beginning. In the Genesis story, the man and woman, Adam and Eve, stood together as equals. Yes, the man was created first, out "of the dust of the

---

300. The passage 1 Corinthians 14:35–36 exhibits textual problems, not the least of which is whether it was ever a part of Paul's letter. See Oepke, *TDNT,* 1:787 n. 55; Metzger, *Textual Commentary,* 499–500.

301. Ben Witherington III, "Women (NT)," in *ABD,* 6:959.

302. Falk, *Hebrew Law in Biblical Times,* 109–11.

303. Schrenk and Quell, *TDNT,* 5:964–65.

ground" (Gen. 2:7), and the woman was created second, out of "one of [the man's] ribs" (Gen. 2:21). But this situation was merely a matter of "primacy of age," not a subordinate position. That latter sort of differentiation characterized the relationship of the man and the woman with the animals which are under the dominion of the humans (see Gen. 1:26, 28; Moses 2:26, 28; Abr. 4:26, 28). After all, it was God who created them "male and female" with no discernible difference in status before him (Gen. 1:27;[304] see also Moses 2:27 and Abr. 4:27).

Roman Society. Little has survived from Roman times about women's activities in the household. Although the Roman empress was hardly the measure of commoners' lives, Livia, Augustus's wife, offers small glimpses into women's routines. For example, a wife would apply cosmetics, if she could afford them, before leaving her house. She was in charge of the wardrobes of her children and the medicines that were given to family members during illnesses. In a word, she was to look after her husband and children. She did not concern herself with her husband's affairs, including how he produced income to support the family. In fact, if she became involved with her husband's business, she ran the risk of coming to the notice of others and acquiring a reputation, whether good or bad.[305] It was a rare woman who owned and maintained any kind of property, although Priscilla, the wife of Aquila and friend of the Apostle, was a partner with her husband in the enterprise of sewing twill (see Acts 18:2–3; see also Rom. 16:3 and 1 Cor. 16:19). Moreover, along with her husband, she became a mentor to a man from Alexandria in Egypt named Apollos "and expounded unto him the way of God more perfectly" (Acts 18:26).

Summary. From the review above, which is not exhaustive by any means, the modern reader sees plainly that women stood side by side with men as citizens of God's kingdom.[306] Yes, their roles were different. None, for instance, became "apostles" or "pastors" (4:11). But like Tabitha, a woman whom Peter raised from the dead (see Acts 9:40–41), they enjoyed well-earned reputations for "always doing good and helping the poor" (Acts 9:36 NIV). In their marriages with nonmembers, they brought heavenly blessings into their homes. As Paul wrote, "The unbelieving husband is sanctified by the [believing] wife." Moreover, their children were thought to be "holy" (1 Cor. 7:14).

---

304. N. Panagiotis Bratsiotis, *TDOT*, 1:225–29, quotation on 227.
305. Everitt, *Augustus*, 251–55.
306. Oepke, *TDNT*, 1:362.

submit yourselves: The oddity of this verse arises from the fact that this verb does not occur here, nor does any other verb. The sense has migrated from 5:21. Hence, the idea of a wife submitting herself to her husband bathes itself in the perfumes of "reverence for Christ" and not in the noxious smells of coerced actions (5:21 NR).[307] To add a touch of contemporary attitudes, Jewish scholarly thoughts toward even speaking with women appear in the following: "The Sages have said: He that talks much with womankind brings evil upon himself and neglects the study of the Law and at the last will inherit Gehenna [hell]."[308] This kind of attitude is nowhere present in any of Paul's statements about women and wives. In fact, he was "the first to insist that the discrimination against . . . women had been made obsolete by Christ (Gal. 3:28; Col. 3:11)."[309]

The meaning "to submit oneself" (middle voice of *hypotassō,* as in 5:21) was Paul's clear intent. He was not going "to tamper with the basic structure of ancient society."[310] Yes, most marriages were arranged between parents. And yes, frequently the bride and groom had not met before their wedding. But a Christian wife's submission was not to occur because marriage demanded it of her. Ideally, like her husband who wanted to please her, she desired that "she may please her husband" (1 Cor. 7:34). Surely she entered into marriage with the understanding that her husband would take the lead in many aspects of their lives together. But, with the concept of Christ as the bridegroom in the verses that follow, the believing woman entered marriage as one who had already surrendered herself to Christ. Her groom was to care for and watch over her.[311] That said, in the ancient church, we find women under the authority of their husbands (see Col. 3:18; Titus 2:5; and 1 Pet. 3:1, 5).[312] The ever-persistent question is whether they willingly submitted, as Jesus did to his parents (see Luke 2:51, "was subject [*hypotassō*] unto them"). For Paul, that question was answered yes, as long as they were enfolded within the ministering influence of Christ.[313] It is worth observing at this juncture that "we never hear from the lips of Jesus a derogatory word concerning woman," and that Jesus set the woman "at the side of man as equally a child of God."[314]

307. Fronk, "Submit Yourselves . . . as unto the Lord," 104, 107; Draper and Rhodes, *Paul's First Epistle to the Corinthians,* 336, 342.

308. *Mishnah Aboth,* 1.5, in Danby, *Mishnah,* 446.

309. Caird, *Letters,* 88.

310. Caird, *Letters,* 88.

311. Ethelbert Stauffer, *TDNT,* 1:656; see also Barth, *Ephesians,* 2:710.

312. Oepke, *TDNT,* 1:362–63; Oepke, *TDNT,* 1:785.

313. Fowl, *Ephesians,* 187; Winger, *Ephesians,* 603; Merkle, *Guide,* 177.

314. Oepke, *TDNT,* 1:785.

This view is at home in the modern church. Reaching back to Adam and Eve, we can say that "they understood that their earthly purpose and eternal goal were identical [while] . . . learning to labor in love and righteousness together." Over time, "females in many societies became subservient to males rather than side-by-side partners." With the Restoration, "men and women began to realize anew the importance and potential of working as partners, authorized and directed in this sacred labor [of families] by Him." In a word, "our roles [as husbands and wives] are complementary rather than competitive." In the end, "women do possess distinctive, divine gifts and are given unique responsibilities, but those are not more— or less—important than men's gifts and responsibilities."[315]

Before becoming president of The Church of Jesus Christ of Latter-day Saints, Elder Russell M. Nelson declared, "We need each married sister to speak as 'a *contributing* and *full* partner'[316] as you unite with your husband in governing your family." Clearly, he envisioned a "full" partnership between parents. There is more. To the women he appealed, "We . . . need your strength, your conversion, your conviction, your ability to lead, your wisdom, and your voices." More precisely, "We need women who are devoted to shepherding [all of] God's children along the covenant path toward exaltation; women who know how to receive personal revelation, . . . women who know how to call upon the powers of heaven to protect and strengthen children and families; women who teach fearlessly" (see the Note on 5:31).[317]

your own husbands: A reader might think that Paul was concerned about some kind of dalliance among Christian wives. Nothing could be farther from the truth. Because Christ and the church stand in the center of the picture in these verses, almost overpowering any other image, the not-so-subtle message has to do with a believer's unswerving allegiance to Christ the Lord.[318] The noun here rendered "husbands" (plural of ἀνήρ, *anēr*) almost always relates to men rather than husbands. The KJV wording draws readers into a discussion about husbands and wives rather than about men and women.[319]

---

315. Jean B. Bingham, "United in Accomplishing God's Work," *Ensign* 50, no. 5 (May 2020): 60–61, 63.

316. Citing Spencer W. Kimball, "Privileges and Responsibilities of Sisters," *Ensign* 8, no. 11 (November 1978): 106, emphasis in original.

317. Russell M. Nelson, "A Plea to My Sisters," *Ensign* 45, no. 11 (November 2015): 96–97.

318. Lincoln, *Ephesians,* 368; Muddiman, *Ephesians,* 258; Fowl, *Ephesians,* 187; Merkle, *Guide,* 182.

319. Oepke, *TDNT,* 1:361–62.

The modern church has added clarity to the husband's roles. To be sure, as President Howard W. Hunter reminded a large gathering of men and boys, "of necessity there must be in the Church and in the home a presiding officer (see D&C 107:21)." Yet a husband must bear in mind that "a man who holds the priesthood accepts his wife as a partner in the leadership of the home and family with full knowledge of and full participation in all decisions relating thereto." He is not a lone tone-setter in his home. Rather, "together with your wife, you determine the spiritual climate of your home." Ominously, "for a man to operate independent of or without regard to the feelings and counsel of his wife in governing the family is to exercise unrighteous dominion." In a positive light, "a man who holds the priesthood looks upon marriage as a sacred privilege and obligation." In ultimate terms, "next to your own salvation, brethren, there is nothing so important to you as the salvation of your wife and children."[320] Indeed.

as unto the Lord: The term translated "Lord" (κύριος, *kyrios*) aims directly at Christ. It has nothing to do with husbands, who some may consider to be lords to their wives.[321] By repeating this title, Paul raised marriage onto a lofty platform. Throughout this and the following verses, the husband is lifted to a place of imitating Christ, of doing what Christ would do. By the same stroke, a wife enjoys the same heights because she enters marriage in a state of "reverence for Christ" (5:21 NR). The whole context brings us inside a "holy marriage" (ἱερὸς γάμος, *hieros gamos*), a celestial marriage, one that rests on the powers and blessings of the Lord.[322] Within the sacred nature of this kind of marriage, the nurture of "children . . . is well pleasing unto the Lord" (Col. 3:20).

Jesus' parable of the ten virgins breathes much the same air as Paul's words. The possible meanings of this parable are many. One of the most obvious is the warning that, after a delay, the bridegroom will come suddenly just as the Lord will come suddenly a second time (see Matt. 25:13). Another pertains to the lack of preparation by five of the virgins, leaving them on the outside looking in (see Matt. 25:8–9). A third, which rests on the edge of the story, understands that the bridegroom is the coming "Son of man" (Matt. 25:13) and that the wedding involves him. Little effort is required to grasp that the heavenly bridegroom, here the returning Lord

---

320. Howard W. Hunter, "Being a Righteous Husband and Father," *Ensign* 24, no. 11 (November 1994): 49–51.

321. Lincoln, *Ephesians,* 368; Best, *Ephesians,* 533.

322. Stauffer, *TDNT,* 1:656; Schweizer, *TDNT,* 7:1079; Kent R. Brooks, "Paul's Inspired Teachings on Marriage," in Huntington and others, *Go Ye into All the World,* 89–94.

who greets the young women who themselves are prepared and worthy for the wedding, is entering into a marriage adorned with celestial furnishings (see Isa. 62:5;[323] and the Notes on 4:1, 17).

5:23 *For:* The conjunction ὅτι (*hoti*) introduces a causal clause that explains what Paul had just written in 5:22.[324]

the head: In the two earlier references to "head" (κεφαλέ, *kephalē*) in Ephesians, the head is Christ and the body is the church (see 1:22–23; 4:15–16). Besides the body or the church owing obedience to Christ, its members' allegiance to him is directed to the one who, under the guidance of the Father, created all things (see 2:10; 3:9). Thus, the existence not only of the church but especially of the entire created order grew out of the Savior's actions. And it was he who, following his Father's counsel, guaranteed that believers will enjoy an eternal life together within families, specifically within "every family" (3:15 NR). Boldly stated, the concept of family stands very close to the notion of the *kephalē*, the Christ.[325] This thought underlies the expression "the household of God" (2:19). As one might suspect, the term translated "household" (οἰκεῖος, *oikeios*) has everything to do with families and relatives.[326]

Additionally, including everyone within the gospel net means bringing in women and children. For how else shall we understand the statement, "One God and Father of all, who is above all . . . and in you all" (4:6)? If one of the objects of creating a church organization is to insure that "we all come in the unity of the faith," shall we set aside families as not fitting within the term "all" (4:13)? Clearly, all members of all families are welcome (see 6:24). Paul kept this doctrine connected to the marriage bond when he wrote that, avoiding the pitfalls of "unchastity[,] . . . each one of you know how to take a wife for himself in holiness and honor" (1 Thes. 4:3–4 RSV; see also 1 Pet. 3:7). This is nowhere more apparent than in his trenchant criticism of Gentiles who had adopted ways that militated against honored marriage practices (see Rom. 1:24–28 and the Note on 2:19).[327] The question then becomes, What does this set of observations have to do with "the husband" who is said to be "the head [*kephalē*] of the wife" and the "children" (6:1)? The answer is, Everything.

---

323. Joachim Jeremias, *TDNT,* 4:1104.

324. BDAG, 732.4; Larkin, *Handbook,* 131; Merkle, *Guide,* 182.

325. Schlier, *TDNT,* 3:680–81.

326. BDAG, 694; Louw-Nida, §10.11; Thayer, *Lexicon,* 439; see also Schrenk and Quell, *TDNT,* 5:962 n. 96.

327. Maurer, *TDNT,* 7:367.

In the first place, at the beginning of a relationship with Christ, any comparison to the Savior lays on a man or husband the everlasting necessity to try to follow Christ's lead, to conform himself to Christ's example in good times and bad. Such action will lead him into the embrace of the Father, an embrace that will "protect [him] from the evil one" (John 17:15 NIV). In the second, the husband and wife are brought to a unity with God and his Son: "That they *all* may be one; as thou, Father, art in me, and I in thee, that they also may be one in us" (John 17:21, emphasis added). In the third, the language in 5:23 elevates the husband to a spot inhabited by Christ. The term *kephalē* connects both to Christ's body and particularly to his role as head of all things. The husband does not at the moment enjoy the status as head of all things. But a promise of such a status lingers in *kephalē*, pointing the husband forward to the time when it will be said of him and his wife, "as it is written [in Ps. 82:6], they are gods" (D&C 76:58; see also John 17:24, "be with me where I am"; D&C 132:20, 37; and the Notes on 1:22; 4:15, 16).

the head of the wife: With these words, Paul gave shape to his analogy: as Christ is "the head of the church," so the husband is "the head of the wife." The analogy, of course, does not fit one hundred percent. Why? Because the relationship between Christ and the church is not the same as that between a married man and woman. For instance, Christ is the source of life and growth of the church (see 4:15). As we read elsewhere, Christ stands as "the Head, from whom the whole body . . . grows as God causes it to grow" (Col. 2:19 NIV). But the husband is not the source of life-sustaining growth for his wife.[328] Yet, in other ways, his efforts to join himself to Christ and to imitate him qualify the man to take his place in the family as one who leads out, linking arm in arm with his wife (see the Note above). Moreover, as a following verse (5:25) will show, Christ's love enfolds all else. His love is unique, and therefore the man's love is to model itself after that of Christ.[329] This means that his love is one that sacrifices for his wife as we have already encountered: "Christ also hath loved us, and hath given himself for us as an offering and a sacrifice to God" (5:2).[330]

even as: The two conjunctions ὡς καί (*hōs kai*) produce a more-than-normal comparison, bumping the heft of "as" to "even as." Paul has thereby laid emphasis on the second part of his analogy, stressing Christ's headship. The force of the expression underscores Christ's leadership as the one that

---

328. Winger, *Ephesians*, 605 n. 33.

329. Barth, *Ephesians*, 2:613–14.

330. Winger, *Ephesians*, 605–6.

counts most, the one that makes other guiding roles effective. For, without him, a husband's involvement with his wife tumbles downward into an insensitive dominion untouched by the beauties and promises of a celestial, everlasting relationship.

head of the church: In Christ's case, this role was conferred on him by his Father, who "gave him as head over all things in the church" (1:22 NR). Initially, we notice that the church formed a new entity among the nations of the earth. The church did not match any nation but existed separately and nobly apart. And the church consisted of its members, who "each must intercede for and suffer with the others";[331] as Paul wrote elsewhere, "If one member suffers, all suffer together" (1 Cor. 12:26 RSV; see also Gal. 6:2, "bear ye one another's burdens"; and Mosiah 18:8–10, "willing to bear one another's burdens").

In the Old Testament, God's headship is framed as fatherhood, with all of the emotional and intimate nature that characterizes the relationship between parent and child. To Jeremiah, God directed, "Thou shalt call me, my Father; and shalt not turn away from me" (Jer. 3:19). But things did not work out in this manner. Schooled in how humans treated one another, Malachi asked, "Have we not all one father? hath not one God created us?" Then he came to the nub of the problem: "Why do we deal treacherously every man against his brother?" (Mal. 2:10). Obviously, God's heavenly affection for his people as their Father was bearing little earthly fruit. Yet "his hand is stretched out still" (Isa. 9:12; see also Isa. 5:25; 9:17, 21; 10:4). This sentiment rests snugly inside Christ's headship over the church. The insight of God as Father and Christ as Son and Head stands as "the supreme insight of biblical faith" (see the Notes on 1:22, 23; 5:24).[332]

saviour: The line wherein this noun (σωτήρ, *sōtēr*) sits—"and he is the saviour of the body"—introduces a new point. Up to this moment, the analogy has been between Christ and husbands in their connections to the church and wives respectively. The conjunction "and" in the KJV is not in the Greek text. The genuine force of the line really is "Christ is, indeed, the Saviour of the body" (NEB). The appeal to *sōtēr,* which occurs only here in Ephesians, is striking. As background, *sōtēr* is a relatively rare term in the New Testament, appearing twenty-four times, with ten of those in the Pastoral Epistles (1 and 2 Tim.; Titus).[333] The appearance of *sōtēr* injects a

---

331. Stauffer, *TDNT,* 2:439–40.

332. Schrenk and Quell, *TDNT,* 5:973–74, quotation on 974.

333. Luke 1:47; 2:11; John 4:42; Acts 5:31; 13:23; Eph. 5:23; Philip. 3:20; 1 Tim. 1:1; 2:3; 4:10; 2 Tim. 1:10; Titus 1:3, 4; 2:10, 13; 3:4, 6; 2 Pet. 1:1, 11; 2:20; 3:2, 18; 1 John 4:14; Jude 1:25.

second focus into the following verses, a focus that rests on Christ as Savior (see 5:25–27, 30).[334]

Introducing *sōtēr* into the mix also brings with it a radiance of glory (*doxa*). All humans begin at the same point: "All have sinned, and come short of the glory [*doxa*] of God" (Rom. 3:23). One main difference between the redeemed and unredeemed resides in an eventual "glorious body," just like the one that the Resurrected Christ possesses. As Paul wrote to his friends in Philippi, "The Savior [*sōtēr*], the Lord Jesus Christ . . . shall change our vile body, that it may be fashioned like unto his glorious body" (Philip. 3:20–21). Again, God "called you by our gospel, to the obtaining of the glory of our Lord Jesus Christ" (2 Thes. 2:14). Thus, glory in bodily form makes all the difference in eternity. That this process of obtaining glory was happening among his fellow Saints can be seen in these words from the Apostle: "[Those] whom he did foreknow, he also did predestinate [foreordain] to be conformed to the image of his Son, . . . and [those] whom he justified, he also glorified" (Rom. 8:29–30).[335] No matter how carefully Paul worked his comparison between husbands and Christ, the Savior's glory distanced him from any one-to-one comparison. That said, the day will come when honorable, believing men who "love their wives" (5:28) will be "justified [and] . . . also glorified" (Rom. 8:30).

body: Christ is the one who saves the "body" (σῶμα, *sōma*)—that is, the church. In this and following verses, we detect no sense that Christ's body links figuratively to all creation as one senses in 1:22–23.[336] The church, like Christ, is to engage in a ministry to the world of demonic actions—both seen and unseen—in which it is placed (see 3:10), as did Jesus (see Col. 2:15). Its struggle "against spiritual wickedness in high places" takes place both in the physical world and in the world of departed spirits. To aid in this effort, the church is organized into branches, which "are builded together for an habitation of God through the Spirit" (2:22). This line frames an affirmation that church work is often most effectively pursued in congregations, not just among single members. And, of course, growth comes about through "the head, even Christ: from whom the whole body fitly joined together and compacted . . . maketh increase of the body" (4:15–16; see also Col. 2:19[337] and the Notes on 1:23; 2:16; 4:4, 12, 16; 5:28, 30).

---

334. Foerster, *TDNT,* 7:1016,
335. Foerster and Fohrer, *TDNT,* 7:993.
336. Schweizer and Baumgärtel, *TDNT,* 7:1078.
337. Schweizer and Baumgärtel, *TDNT,* 7:1078–79.

5:24 *as the church is subject unto Christ:* With this line, Paul has extended his comparison, this time focusing on Christ as the presiding officer in the church and husbands as presiding persons in their homes. As Christ's body, the church has taken up a number of functions and characteristics that directly affect husbands and wives. In brief, within its numbers are those who have received "the adoption of children by Jesus Christ to himself" without regard to gender (1:5); church members have witnessed Christ breaking "down the middle wall of partition" between Jews and Gentiles (2:14); through Christ all church members enjoy "access by one Spirit unto the Father" (2:18); "after [the pattern of] God," church members are "created in righteousness and true holiness" (4:24); with Christ's aid, the church is to "be holy and without blemish," imparting these virtues to believers (5:27; see also 1:4); and, perhaps highest of all, "Christ also loved the church, and gave himself for it," bathing all its members in that love (5:25).[338] The unending emanation of love best explains the reason for church members being "subject unto Christ."

In the language of the Old Testament, the church is made up of those "that follow after righteousness, . . . that seek the Lord." To them God said, "Look unto the rock whence ye are hewn" (Isa. 51:1). The Psalmist sang about "my father, my God, and the rock of my salvation" (Ps. 89:26). In Paul's discussion of the Israelites eating manna—their "spiritual meat"—and drinking water that came out of a rock, he observed that the "spiritual Rock that followed them" in their desert experience "was Christ" (1 Cor. 10:3–4). In the earliest reference to the Messiah as a rock, we read: "I am Messiah, . . . the Rock of Heaven, which is broad as eternity; whoso cometh in at the gate and climbeth up by me shall never fall" (Moses 7:53). It is a simple step to move from Christ as the rock to his church as a rock that assists in sustaining and lifting its members. In this connection, it is the rock of revelation that undergirds the church (see Matt. 16:17–18 and the Note on 5:23).

the wives: A person should understand that wives and women are never excluded from the Spirit and its heavenly gifts, as the three lists in scripture demonstrate. In the KJV, the translation of 1 Corinthians 12:7 is misleading: "The manifestation of the Spirit is given to every man." Neither of the Greek nouns for "man" appears in this verse. Rather, the sense is more clearly set out thus: "To each one the manifestation of the Spirit is given for the common good" (1 Cor. 12:7 NIV). The same can be said of the KJV rendition of 1 Corinthians 12:11, "Dividing to every man severally as he will." No noun

---

338. Schmidt, *TDNT,* 3:510; see also Delling, *TDNT,* 8:45.

for "man" occurs in this verse either. In the intervening list of spiritual gifts, no preference is given to men or to women (see 1 Cor. 12:8–10). We find the same pattern in the two other presentations of spiritual gifts (see Moro. 10:8–18 and D&C 46:8–29). They do not feature men or man. In Moroni 10:17, we read the words "every man," which bears the sense of "every person." Likewise, "every man" appears in D&C 46:16, also with the obvious meaning of "every person." As a guiding touch, the expressions "the children of men" and "the children of God," which include both genders, are also found (D&C 46:15, 26; see also the Note on 5:22). To be sure, the spiritual gift of discernment is to come to presiding officers of the church, such as "the bishop" and "elders[,] . . . lest there shall be any among you professing and yet be not of God" (D&C 46:27). This latter gift, then, was for men who preside in the church. Otherwise, women are always in the picture as beneficiaries of all spiritual gifts.

in every thing: This prepositional phrase (ἐν παντί, *en panti*) elucidates an important concept. Surely Paul was not advocating that a wife "submit to her husband in matters that are clearly sinful or contrary to God's commands." Peter and other members of the Twelve had already set the standard when they declared that "we ought to obey God rather than men" (Acts 5:29). Obedience to celestial standards served as the Christian measuring stick. Even though "there may be exceptions, the focus of the passage is on the importance of the wife's *willing* submission to the leadership of her husband."[339]

5:25 *love your wives:* Now we begin "an elucidation" of the last line of 5:23.[340] It may seem odd that the verb "to love" is ἀγαπάω (*agapaō*), the verb that undergirds all descriptions of Christian service and aid. Of course, its noun is *agapē*, which is consistently translated "love" or "charity." It is this love that arrives with the reception of the Spirit, as Paul wrote in another place: "The fruit of the Spirit is love [*agapē*]" (Gal. 5:22). It is this love that is the companion of God's mercy, for "God, who is rich in mercy" pours out "his great love [*agapē*] wherewith he loved [*agapaō*] us" (2:4). It is this love that bends the believer toward those who need assistance: "by love [*agapē*] serve one another" (Gal. 5:13). It is this love that stands beneath the timeless commandment, "Thou shalt love [*agapaō*] thy neighbor as thyself" (Gal. 5:14, quoting Lev. 19:18).[341] The question is, Why apply

---

339. Merkle, *Guide,* 183, emphasis added.
340. Foerster and Fohrer, *TDNT,* 7:1016.
341. Quell and Stauffer, *TDNT,* 1:50–51.

this verb to marital love? The answer: for all of the characteristics just cited, and more. For such love is drenched in the divine care for others.

During the far reaches of time, God made the Israelites his daughter or wife. Therefore, it made a difference how she responded to him and to her neighbors. Even when she behaved like Gomer, the wife of the prophet Hosea, and left the prophet for another man—that is, for another god or pantheon of gods—God said in a forgiving voice, "I will allure her, and bring her into the wilderness, and speak comfortably unto her" (Hosea 2:14). To those who had drawn themselves far from God, he would say, "Thou art my people; and they shall say, Thou art my God" (Hosea 2:23). When faced with thrashing ancient Israel for her sins, God turned away in graciousness and forgiveness and asked, "How shall I give thee up, Ephraim? how shall I deliver thee, Israel? . . . mine heart is turned within me, my repentings are kindled together." Then he answered his own questions, "I will not execute the fierceness of mine anger, I will not return to destroy Ephraim: for I am God, and not man; the Holy One in the midst of thee" (Hosea 11:8–9; see also Ps. 89:30–34). More than a hundred years later, God pledged himself to bear the pain and disappointment that the kingdom of Judah had caused him (see Jer. 10:19). These scenes, which portray God's lenient love for his daughter or wife, became the benchmarks for the love that God's people should expect from him and that they should expect from one another.[342] All of this is directly relevant to marriage.

We shall learn in verse 5:27 what the Messiah intends his church to become—his bride. We read the Apostle's words: "That he [Christ] might present the church to himself in splendor, without spot or wrinkle or any such thing, that she might be holy and without blemish" (RSV). Paul's language harks back to God's presentation of the newly created Eve to Adam. There we encounter the words "[the Lord God] brought her unto the man" (Gen. 2:22). In this case, the man Adam had a helper, a matchmaker of sorts, in the person of the Lord God, who introduced Eve to her soon-to-be husband. In the case of Christ and the church, which was now his bride, no matchmaker assisted like at Jewish weddings. Christ took on the full responsibility of bringing the bride, the church, into existence.[343] For this is the sense of the verb translated "to present" (παρίστημι, *paristēmi*): "to cause to exist" or "to raise up."[344] Therefore, as Christ has lovingly brought

---

342. Schrenk and Quell, *TDNT,* 5:972–73.
343. Barth, *Ephesians,* 2:678–81.
344. Louw-Nida, §13.83; contra BDAG, 778.1.c, "to render."

his betrothed to a perfected state, one "without spot or wrinkle . . . that she might be holy and without blemish" (5:27 RSV), so the husband is to lovingly open the door to his wife to become "holy and without blemish" before him and before her Maker (see the Notes on 2:4; 5:2, 27, 28).

loved the church: For a second time in this verse, we meet the verb *agapaō*, "to love." In the heart of the Messiah-King, the love for the church, his bride, is without bounds. He does not exercise "rights of lordship over her; he takes responsibility for her."[345] What bride would not rejoice over a bridegroom like Christ, who exhibits constant love and care for his betrothed? It was the Psalmist who sang of Christ in his premortal role as one more steady than family relationships: "Though my father and my mother forsake me, the Lord will take me into his care" (Ps. 27:10 NEB).[346]

The grand proof of Christ's love for the church was his death. The love manifested thereby reached all the way to the top, to the Father: "For God so loved the world, that he gave his only begotten Son." And why did God give this gift? It was so "that whosoever believeth in him should not perish, but have everlasting life" (John 3:16). Thus, death and love became intertwined in Jesus' atoning act. Indeed, "greater love hath no man than this, that a man lay down his life for his friends" (John 15:13). But this saying of Jesus pointed directly at his soon-to-occur Atonement and, more distantly, to martyrs who gave up their lives rather than deny their faith. Perhaps oddly, Jesus' death presented the most ineffable of expressions of love: because of his following Resurrection, Christ was able to draw everyone through the fearsome veil of death and into a newness of life. Christ's act demonstrated that his love for his fellow creatures was not for just this life but extends into eternity. This observation applies directly not only to Christ's love for the church but also to a spouse's love for her or his spouse (see the next Note).[347]

gave himself for it: The verb παραδίδωμι (*paradidōmi*) also occurs at 4:19 and 5:2. In the Note on 5:2, we learned that this verb ties to Judas's betrayal of Jesus. In a totally different sense, the verb concerns the handing on of Christian doctrines and tradition, orally at first and only later in written form. For example, Paul directed his Corinthian readers to "keep the ordinances, as I *delivered* them to you" (1 Cor. 11:2, emphasis added). Later,

---

345. Stauffer, *TDNT,* 1:656; see also Amy Blake Hardison, "Unity and Atonement in Ephesians," in Huntington and others, *Go Ye into All The World,* 120–27.

346. Schrenk and Quell, *TDNT,* 5:974.

347. Barth, *Ephesians,* 2:684–87.

when featuring the institution of the Eucharist or sacrament at the Last Supper, the Apostle wrote, "I have received of the Lord that which also I *delivered* unto you" (1 Cor. 11:23, emphasis added).[348]

More germane to our passage (5:22), Christ's "offering and sacrifice to God" (5:2) has transported believers to an inner conviction that life is lived no longer for themselves but for the sake of Christ and his purposes. As Paul reminded his Roman readers, "Whether we live, we live unto the Lord; and whether we die, we die unto the Lord: . . . we are the Lord's" (Rom. 14:8). As Christ "hath loved us, and hath given himself for us" (5:2)—that is, for church members—so those same people who "are members of his body, of his flesh, and of his bones" (5:30) are to "subject [themselves] unto Christ" (5:24) so that "he might sanctify and cleanse [them] with the washing of water" (5:26).[349] Though these lines sound a triumphant note, Christ's painful path to this position of sanctifying power was prophesied centuries beforehand, as early Christians grasped. In Isaiah's words, "The Lord gave him up [*paradidōmi*] for our sins" (LXX Isa. 53:6). The prophet continued: "His soul was delivered [*paradidōmi*] to death: and he was numbered among the transgressors; and he bore the sins of many, and was delivered [*paradidōmi*] because of their iniquities" (LXX Isa. 53:12).[350]

The prepositional phrase "for it" (ὑπὲρ αὐτῆς, *hyper autēs*) brings readers back to the preposition *hyper* that appeared in 5:2 in the phrase "for us." This latter phrase almost matches what Jesus said to his disciples at the last supper, declaring, "This is my body which is given *for you*" and "This cup is the new testament in my blood, which is shed *for you*" (Luke 22:19, 20, emphasis added; see also 1 Cor. 11:24). The difference lies in "for you" and "for us." The first phrase, "for you," repeats Jesus' language as uttered by the One who instituted the Eucharist. The second phrase, "for us," reflects the human viewpoint as recipients of the bread and wine of the sacrament. This said, how do we come to the phrase "for it" in 5:25? One solution presents itself in the words that had come down to Mark as the description of the Last Supper and Jesus' institution of the Eucharist, particularly the wine: "This is my blood of the new testament, which is shed *for many*" (Mark 14:24). It is a simple step to understand that the "many" came to be the "church." Hence, in the deep background of the phrase "for it" in this verse reposes the words

---

348. Büchsel, *TDNT,* 2:171.
349. Bultmann, *TDNT,* 3:19–20.
350. Walther Zimmerli and Joachim Jeremias, *TDNT,* 5:706.

of Jesus memorably spoken during the Last Supper (see the Notes on 4:19; 5:22; 6:18, 19).[351]

5:26 *sanctify:* In the Old Testament, sanctification of humans (priests, judges, kings) came about by dousing the head with holy oil, whose composition imparted holiness (see Ex. 30:23–25 and Lev. 8:11–12). The same kind of generous anointing conferred holiness on objects such as the temple altar and the temple vessels (see Ex. 30:26–29). This sort of sanctification had come to an end with the fall of Jerusalem and its temple to the Babylonians in 587 BC.[352] It is significant that Jesus did not try to revive these practices. Instead, he added a liquid that would carry a sacred dimension among his followers—namely water, specifically water for immersion baptisms. Even though this verse bears on the sanctification of the church, the application of its language relates to individuals because the church consists of united believers.

Receiving baptism shaped an important first step in the sanctification process. All was physical, not figurative. Jesus, of course, set out the path to sanctification through his Atonement: "Jesus also, that he might sanctify the people with his own blood, suffered without the gate [of Jerusalem]" (Heb. 13:12). Sanctification is a state of spiritual reality, and this becomes visible in Paul's observation in his Corinthian correspondence about the marriage of a member and a nonmember spouse. There he declared that "the unbelieving husband is sanctified by the [believing] wife, and the unbelieving wife is sanctified by the [believing] husband." If it were not so, the "children" born to their union would be "unclean; but now they are holy" (1 Cor. 7:14). Just as intriguing is the thought that sanctification can begin before birth, when a person may be foreordained or set apart, as Jeremiah was: "Before thou camest forth out of the womb I sanctified thee, and I ordained thee a prophet unto the nations" (Jer. 1:5; see also Gal. 1:15 for Paul).[353]

The verb "to sanctify" (ἁγιάζω, *hagiazō*) can also mean "to consecrate."[354] The main question has to do with its relationship to the next verb, an active participle of καθαρίζω (*katharizō*), meaning "to cleanse" in the sense of a moral cleansing.[355] The presence of the participle may involve prior action, suggesting the church was cleansed before it was sanctified. Or it may center

---

351. Riesenfeld, *TDNT*, 8:510–11.

352. Milgrom, *Leviticus 1–16*, 516–19.

353. Procksch and Kuhn, *TDNT*, 1:111–12; see also Meyer and Hauck, *TDNT*, 3:429.

354. BDAG, 10.2.

355. BDAG, 488.3.b.

on events that happened simultaneously. But this latter seems fraught with difficulties.[356] Why? Because cleansing appears to be a single act, such as the cleansing from sin that occurs at baptism. On the other hand, sanctification occurs over a long period of time (see the Note on 2:19).[357]

cleanse: This cleansing (participle of καθαρίζω, *katharizō*) is performed with water, as a reader discovers in the next line. But this cleansing was nothing like that portrayed in the Old Testament, where almost all concern centered on external cleanness (see Matt. 23:25–26 and Luke 11:41). Jesus showed the way by turning away from such concerns, even touching people with diseases, actions that should have rendered him unclean. But he allowed himself such touching because it had no effect on him, the Son of God.[358] For instance, in one of his earliest miracles, he cleansed a man who "was full of leprosy" by touching him (Luke 5:12–13; see also Matt. 8:1–3 and Mark 1:40–42). Later, at a meal in a Pharisee's home, he allowed himself to be touched by "a woman [from] the city, which was a sinner"; she proceeded "to wash his feet with tears, and did wipe them with the hairs of her head, and kissed his feet" (Luke 7:37–38), sending the host into a tizzy (see Luke 7:39). Why? Because Pharisees laid great value on ritual cleanness, and, in the eyes of the host, the woman was obviously unclean.[359]

Following Peter's lead, other church leaders pushed aside ritual cleanness as a measure of a person's standing before God, especially as Gentiles began to receive baptism. Peter's first lesson occurred in the house of his friend, Simon the Tanner of Joppa. There a vision burst on him as he prayed, demonstrating that the unclean animals that Jews had avoided— "all manner of fourfooted beasts of the earth, and wild beasts, and creeping things"—God had now declared to be suitable for eating. The divine voice declared, "What God hath cleansed, that call not thou common" (Acts 10:12, 15). Almost immediately following the vision, men representing a Roman centurion knocked at Simon's door with a request that Peter come with them to meet their Gentile master, a man named Cornelius, who had also received a heavenly vision. As a result, the Gentile master and his friends and family received baptism (see Acts 10:1–8, 47–48). The final upshot of the experience of Peter and others was that cleanness before God

---

356. Merkle, *Guide,* 184–85.

357. Meyer and Hauck, *TDNT,* 3:425, 429–30; see also Procksch and Kuhn, *TDNT,* 1:111–12.

358. Meyer and Hauck, *TDNT,* 3:425.

359. Meyer and Hauck, *TDNT,* 3:424.

became a matter of the heart, not of rules that had to do with the external world.[360] And a person's heart is at its cleanest at the moment of baptism, an ordinance which itself carries cleansing power (see John 3:25–26; Heb. 10:22; 1 Pet. 3:21; 2 Pet. 1:9; and D&C 39:10). Baptism marks the end of an individual's participation in "the course of this world" (2:2; see also 1 Cor. 3:3 and Col. 3:7) and moves the person into a "newness of life" that is concrete, affecting one's physical body (Rom. 6:4; see also John 8:12; 2 Cor. 6:16;[361] D&C 84:33, "the renewing of their bodies"; and the Note on 5:2).

the washing of water: The noun translated "washing" (λουτρόν, *loutron*) appears only here and at Titus 3:5 in the New Testament. The term is related to ritual washings known from the earliest Greek literature and from the Old Testament.[362] But in our verse, 5:26, it carries a completely different sense. In those earlier eras, *loutron* pertained to one's external relationship with the divine world, to humans' connections with the gods through sacrifices and gifts. In the New Testament, it links hard and fast to "the forgiveness of sins, according to the riches of [God's] grace," a completely different connection (1:7; see also Col. 1:14).[363] On another level, *loutron* sends a reader to the act of being washed clean in the blood of Christ. That individual, as if living inside a dead body that is often characterized as lifeless "garments," is washed in Christ's blood but with the sure promise of celestial life (see 1 John 1:7, "the blood of Jesus Christ . . . cleanses us from all sin"; Rev. 1:5; 5:9; 7:14; Alma 5:21; 3 Ne. 27:19, God's "kingdom [consists of] . . . those who have washed their garments in my blood"; and the Note on 6:14).

Water also cleanses. This liquid, of course, can pose a danger, as two of Jesus' miracles around the Sea of Galilee illustrate. The first miracle happened on the day that Jesus and the Twelve sailed from Capernaum to the east shore of the lake to meet the Gergesenes. A storm arose while Jesus slept in the bow of the boat. Most of the Twelve were fishermen and knew that the storm posed trouble. In desperation, they awoke Jesus and begged for his help. His words spoken to the boisterous wind, and the wind's response, have echoed across the centuries: "Peace, be still. And the wind ceased, and there was a great calm" (Mark 4:39). In the second instance, Jesus had just dismissed the five thousand people whom he had miraculously fed with

---

360. Meyer and Hauck, *TDNT*, 3:424–25.
361. Meyer and Hauck, *TDNT*, 3:429–30; Lincoln, *Ephesians*, 375.
362. BDAG, 603; Thayer, *Lexicon*, 382.
363. Albrecht Oepke, *TDNT*, 4:303.

the assistance of the Twelve. Daylight was almost gone when he sent his disciples in a boat across the northern end of the lake to Capernaum while he climbed up a mountain to pray. During the night, as the Twelve were struggling to row the boat against a strong headwind from the west, Jesus came walking to them on the sea. After Jesus assured them that he was not "a spirit," Peter wondered aloud if he could meet the approaching Savior. When Jesus said, "Come," Peter stepped out of the boat and onto the surface of the roiling water. His daring experiment lasted only a few moments; Jesus soon had to rescue him from sinking into the ebony waters. In both of these cases, Jesus immediately talked to the disciples about their "little faith" (Matt. 8:26; 14:29, 31). Plainly, faith was the supporting launchpad of such events, and Jesus called his followers to faith that would help them to sail above the waters that threatened to engulf them (see Matt. 9:2; Mark 2:5; and Luke 5:20).[364]

Most commentators agree that the reference to water is a pointer to baptism.[365] But a problem presents itself: it is evident that Paul is talking about the baptism of the whole church.[366] Does he envision an archetype, the one representing the many or vice versa? Very possibly. As Caird argued, "Language reminiscent of baptism is being used to describe something more comprehensive and universal."[367] And what might that be? To be sure, mentioning "the word" seems to point to the baptismal prayer uttered in Christ's name (see the Note below). Hence, we find ourselves in possession of another connection to baptism. Naturally, for believers baptism represents a "comprehensive and universal" linkage to other church members. What else? Might we be staring at holy acts undertaken for and on behalf of those in the world of departed spirits that bring us to a "more comprehensive and universal" achievement of church members? Surely that is exactly what the Apostle was referring to when he wrote, "What shall they do which are baptized for the dead, if the dead rise not at all? why are they then baptized for the dead?" (1 Cor. 15:29).[368] Proxy ordinances performed for dead persons, such as baptism and the bestowal of the gift of the Holy Ghost, elevate the goals of the church to a point of making

---

364. Leonhard Goppelt, *TDNT,* 8:323.

365. Goppelt, *TDNT,* 8:331; Bruce, *Ephesians,* 116; Houlden, *Paul's Letters from Prison,* 333–34; Barth, *Ephesians,* 2:624; Lincoln, *Ephesians,* 375–76; Best, *Ephesians,* 543; Fowl, *Ephesians,* 189; Perkins, *Ephesians,* 134; Winger, *Ephesians,* 611.

366. Caird, *Letters,* 89; Houlden, *Paul's Letters from Prison,* 333.

367. Caird, *Letters,* 89.

368. Riesenfeld, *TDNT,* 8:512–13.

"known by the church the manifold wisdom of God" to "the principalities and powers in heavenly places" (3:10; see also the Note thereon and D&C 124:29–39; 127:6–7; 128:1–25). A blessed work.

by the word: Again, most commentators agree that this term (ῥῆμα, *rhēma*) points to the words spoken in the baptismal ordinance.[369] Those words cannot be recovered from the New Testament, but they appear in a record that rests on Jesus' words spoken and preserved in the New World (see Moro. 2:1; 4:1, "according to the commandments of Christ"). This is certainly how we must view the baptismal prayer among Old World Christians: "It goes back to God and Christ, and thence derives its efficacy."[370] The noun *rhēma* is not the same as *logos* and usually directs us to something said orally.[371] Elsewhere it is equated to the gospel preached orally: "The word [*rhēma*] of the Lord endureth for ever. And this is the word [*rhēma*] which by the gospel is preached unto you" (1 Pet. 1:25;[372] see also the Note on 6:17).

5:27 *present:* With this verse, we pick up the next-to-last comment on the final line of 5:23, "he himself being the savior of the body [of the church]" (NR). The saving power of Christ will, of course, be manifested universally at his Second Coming. In that moment, he will "present to himself a glorious church" (5:27 NR).[373] As we have discovered in the Note on 5:25, the verb rendered "to present" (παρίστημι, *paristēmi*) can mean "to cause to exist" or "to raise up."[374] In this setting, it also bears the sense "to present," as in the case of a best man presenting the bride to her groom on their wedding day.[375] Paul saw himself playing that role between the church and Christ. He wrote to the Corinthian Saints, "I arranged for you to marry Christ so that I might give you away as a chaste virgin to this one husband" (2 Cor. 11:2, Jerusalem Bible). The reception of this heavenly bride who has no external "spot, or

---

369. Goppelt, *TDNT,* 8:330; Bruce, *Ephesians,* 116; Houlden, *Paul's Letters from Prison,* 334; Lincoln, *Ephesians,* 376; Fowl, *Ephesians,* 189; Perkins, *Ephesians,* 134; Winger, *Ephesians,* 611.

370. Oepke, *TDNT,* 4:304.

371. BDAG, 905.1; Louw-Nida, §§33.9, 98; Thayer, *Lexicon,* 562–63.

372. Debrunner, Kleinknecht, Procksch, Kittel, Quell, and Schrenk, *TDNT,* 4:116.

373. The "it" which appears in the KJV reading "present it" is misleading because "it" stands in the masculine gender (αὐτός, *autos*) and points to Christ, reinforcing the pronoun "himself" and emphasizing "Christ's personal involvement." Merkle, *Guide,* 185; see also Larkin, *Handbook,* 135. The "it" has nothing to do with the "church" (ἐκκλησία, *ekklēsia*), which is feminine in gender.

374. Louw-Nida, §13.83; contra BDAG, 778.1.c, "to render."

375. Jeremias, *TDNT,* 4:1106.

wrinkle" and is inwardly "holy and without blemish" will involve all believers, male and female, Jew and Gentile, who enjoy "access by one Spirit unto the Father" (2:18). In that scene, Christ will warmly embrace his bride in her perfected state just as husbands are to lovingly enfold their wives into their eternal embraces and together "go on unto perfection" (Heb. 6:1; see also the Notes on 2:4; 5:2, 25, 27, 28).

As noted above, the grand moment when Christ presents (*paristēmi*) "to himself a glorious church" will be at the end-time. Although the emphasis may seem to repose on the spotless and holy character of the church in that coming scene, the undergirding stress really connects to the suddenness with which this time will arrive. For the underlying image is of the arrival of the bridegroom to claim his bride. Jesus' parable of the ten virgins illustrates the essence. Even though many lessons can be extracted from this story, including the lack of preparation on the part of the five foolish virgins and the evident wisdom of the five prepared young women, the deep thrust of the parable revolves around the sudden coming of the bridegroom at an unknown hour and the judgment that accompanies his arrival. This judgment welcomes five of the virgins into the marriage festivities and cuts off the other five. So it is with others of Jesus' stories, including the parable of the thief who comes at night (see Matt. 24:42–44 and Luke 12:39–40), the story of the servants who are watchful for their master's arrival (see Mark 13:33–37; see also Luke 12:35–38), and the story of the wise and slothful servants (see Matt. 24:45–51). Hence, the fundamental, bedrock message is preparedness.[376]

A reader also catches hints of formality and structure in the divine world when Christ presents "to himself a glorious church" (NR). This is not to be a random event. Celestial formality pushes itself forward in various ways, from "Gabriel, who stands before God" (Luke 1:19, Wayment) to "every knee" bowing "at the name of Jesus" (Philip. 2:10) to standing at attention "before the judgment seat of Christ" (Rom. 14:10)[377] to presenting our "bodies a living sacrifice, holy, acceptable unto God" (Rom. 12:1). This last passage, Romans 12:1, features the same verb, *paristēmi*, "to present." We have already encountered Paul's intent to hand off the church to Christ

---

376. Jeremias, *TDNT*, 4:1104–5; see also Foerster and Fohrer, *TDNT*, 7:1016 and n. 67.

377. Modern scripture adds to the image of the final judgment by saying that people will be "brought" before God or Christ as if escorted by a bailiff. See 1 Ne. 15:33; Alma 5:18; 11:2, 43; 12:8, 12; 24:15; 36:15; 40:21; Hel. 14:15; D&C 98:28; 123:7.

when he wrote, "I have espoused you [church members] to one husband, that I may present [*paristēmi*] you as a chaste virgin to Christ" (2 Cor. 11:2). But in our passage, 5:27, Christ needs no best man to present the Church to him because, significantly, he is the one who acts and fills that role. In another place, when writing about God's intent to raise us from the dead, Paul declared, "He which raised up the Lord Jesus shall raise up us also by Jesus, and shall present [*paristēmi*] us with you" at the end-time (2 Cor. 4:14; see also Col. 1:22, "to present [*paristēmi*] you holy and unblameable"; Col. 1:28, "present [*paristēmi*] everyone perfect in Christ," NIV). Hence, scripture portrays heaven as a place of order and, like a mirror, the earthly kingdom of God is also to undertake its affairs in an orderly fashion.[378] In that heavenly order, the bride does not go seeking her groom, nor does she acquire her "own holiness." Rather she relies totally on Christ, and she, with her cadre of believers, "will in all things grow up into him who is the Head, that is, Christ" (4:15 NIV).[379] More than this, the bride is to appear without "spot, or wrinkle," a clear indicator that she is to be properly adorned and made up for her special ceremony (see Rev. 19:8 and Ezek. 16:10–14).[380]

glorious: The meaning of this adjective (ἔνδοξος, *endoxos*) breaks in one of two ways, depending on what it refers to. On the one hand, it refers to the "glorious" or "splendid" nature of the one who possesses such a quality in himself—namely, God. Other persons with this personal texture may include those from the celestial world or their actions (see LXX Ex. 34:10 and LXX Job 5:9; 9:10). On the other hand, it centers on a measure of eminence or esteem conferred by another person or persons. That is, the exceptional caliber is not native to the person but has been acquired because of the often flattering viewpoints of others (see 1 Cor. 4:10).[381] In the case of the "glorious church," both senses present themselves. For Christ will confer on her a "glorious" appearance and will clothe her with heavenly beauty. After all, he is her "beautician."[382] Thereafter internally she will be celestially "glorious" forever. As we have read earlier in a paean of praise to the Father, the church is to rest comfortably within the everlasting divine circle: "To [God] be glory in the church and in Christ Jesus throughout all generations, for ever and ever" (3:21 NIV).

---

378. Bo Reicke and Georg Bertram, *TDNT,* 5:840–41.

379. Fowl, *Ephesians,* 190.

380. Fowl, *Ephesians,* 190–91.

381. Von Rad and Kittel, *TDNT,* 2:254; BDAG, 332–33; Louw-Nida, §§79.19; 87.6.

382. Best, *Ephesians,* 546; Winger, *Ephesians,* 613.

church: One of the puzzles that arises in Ephesians concerns the many ways that Paul described the church. Early in the letter, the church is called Christ's "body" (1:23). More than that, Christ is said to be its "head" (1:22; 5:23). Moreover, the church depends on "the Lord" for its nourishment (5:29) and its growth (see 4:16). Finally, the church has become Christ's wife (see 5:26–27). This set of characteristics goes far beyond what Paul has written about the church as Christ's body in Romans 12:4–5 and 1 Corinthians 12:12–27.[383] What are we to conclude? The answer begs to be heard. No imitator or admirer of the Apostle would have ever dared to paint outside the lines that Paul had sketched on the canvas of his other letters. Such an act would have immediately labeled the imitator's work as a fraud. Let us admit that the work before us is from Paul's hand. He is the only person who would write an epistle with this kind of expansive and rich detail (see the Notes on 1:23; 3:8; 4:3, 21; 5:27; 6:3, 5, 21; and the Analysis of 3:1–13; 6:1–9).[384]

spot, or wrinkle: With these two terms (σπίλος and ῥυτίς, *spilos* and *rhytis*) we come face-to-face with permanent marks on the skin, on the body's exterior.[385] Even though *spilos* and *rhutis* also hand to us the metaphorical sense of "the church's moral purity and excellence,"[386] a reader is still drawn to the thought of no blemish or physical scar on the bride. She is perfect in her appearance in every way (see Rev. 12:1) and ready for the formality of her wedding.

holy and without blemish: The two terms (ἅγιος and ἄμωμος, *hagios* and *amōmos*) that underlie this expression appeared earlier in Ephesians as characteristics of those who are chosen by God (see 1:4). The noun for holiness or sanctification, related to *hagios,* is ἁγιασμός (*hagiasmos*) and describes a quality of God and Christ (see 1 Cor. 1:30). In fact, believers are summoned to holiness, as Paul affirmed: "For God hath not called us unto uncleanness, but unto holiness [*hagiasmos*]" (1 Thes. 4:7). At least a measure of this attribute can be acquired with the aid of God's Spirit. As the Apostle wrote to his Thessalonian converts, "God chose you from the beginning to be saved, through sanctification [*hagiasmos*] by the Spirit and [by] belief in the truth" (2 Thes. 2:13 RSV; see also 1 Pet. 1:2, "through sanctification [*hagiasmos*] of the Spirit"). To those same Thessalonian friends

---

383. Schmidt, *TDNT,* 3:510.
384. Schmidt, *TDNT,* 3:511; Bruce, *Ephesians,* 12; Merkle, *Guide,* 94; Muddiman, *Ephesians,* 215–16, 218, 145–47, 156.
385. BDAG, 938, 908; Thayer, *Lexicon,* 584, 564; Best, *Ephesians,* 546.
386. Merkle, *Guide,* 186.

Paul wrote about choosing a bride: "Each one of you [should] know how to take a wife for himself in holiness [*hagiasmos*] and honor, not in the passion of lust like heathen who do not know God" (1 Thes. 4:4 RSV). Here we glimpse the role that holiness should play in courting and choosing a wife.

The notion of being "holy" sits on a higher plane than being free from a blemish. The one centers on an inner quality; the other initially referred to an exterior condition present on the skin. Naturally, concern with blemishes pulls readers inside the walls of the temple, where priests with blemishes could not participate in holy ordinances (see Lev. 21:17–23) and blemished animals could not serve as sacrifices (see Lev. 22:20–25).[387] As we might expect, over time the word *amōmos* acquired the metaphorical meaning of "blameless."[388] In its figurative meaning, the loftiest pointer is to God himself: "As for the Mighty One, his way is blameless [*amōmos*]: . . . he is a protector to all that put their trust in him" (LXX 2 Kgs. 22:31 [2 Sam. 22:31 KJV]). This blamelessness is to settle on Christians before the judgment, thus offering the church and its members to Christ "without blemish," without blame in any form (see 2 Cor. 11:2;[389] the Notes on 1:4; 5:22; and the Analysis of 1:3–14).

5:28 *So:* The adverb οὕτως (*houtōs*) bears the sense "in this manner."[390] Its appearance effectively looks back and says that Christ's love for the church, as outlined in verses 5:25–27, has become the model for a husband's love of his wife. Because Paul had written earlier about a husband loving his wife (see 5:25), he has created here a point of high emphasis. In other words, as Christ has loved the church, so a man should love and treasure his wife.[391]

ought: At this moment, Paul has set aside his interest in the church as Christ's bride and has turned back to the relationship of husbands and wives. To drive home his point about the heartfelt intensity of a husband's love for his wife, he has written the verb ὀφείλω (*opheilō*), which means "to owe" in its basic sense. In this passage, it bears the sense of "one must" or "one ought" because it is joined to a following infinitive.[392] What was his point? That believing men owe their wives their deepest affection, their total loyalty, their most noble efforts in their marriages. No marriage of

387. Hauck, *TDNT,* 4:830–31; Winger, *Ephesians,* 614.
388. BDAG, 56.
389. Hauck, *TDNT,* 4:831; Jeremias, *TDNT,* 4:1104–5 and n. 50.
390. BDAG, 741.1; Thayer, *Lexicon,* 468.1.
391. Lincoln, *Ephesians,* 378; Winger, *Ephesians,* 614–15.
392. BDAG, 743.2.a.β.

convenience here; no marriage just to produce offspring; no marriage centered chiefly on sexual relationships, though that is to be an important ingredient: "A man should give his wife what is due sexually, and likewise a wife to her husband. The woman does not have authority over her own body, but her husband does. Likewise, the husband does not have authority over his own body, but his wife does" (1 Cor. 7:3–4, Wayment). The obligations set out by the Apostle are not by way of commandment, which was how they typically came from Jesus, but by way of how a person experiences the path to salvation and life with God.[393]

love their wives: Here Paul has repeated the verb "to love" (ἀγαπάω, *agapaō*) that he wrote in 5:25 and has again applied it to marital affection. As we noticed in the Note on 5:25, the related noun is *agapē*, a term that embraces the elevated character of God's love that awaits those who will receive it. And a person who bears inwardly God's love will surely find all relationships enriched beyond words to express.[394] Paul, of course, expressed the unbounded nature of God's love. We read: "Charity [*agapē*] suffereth long, and is kind; charity envieth not; charity vaunteth not itself, is not puffed up. Doth not behave itself unseemly, seeketh not her own, is not easily provoked, thinketh no evil; . . . never faileth" (1 Cor. 13:4–5, 8). As eloquent as these lines are, Paul may have saved his best for the Saints in Rome. A person needs only to think of a married couple facing the tugs and pulls that snipe at a marriage to see the relevance of the Apostle's lines: "Who shall separate us from the love [*agapē*] of Christ? shall tribulation, or distress, or persecution, or sword? . . . I am persuaded that neither death, nor life, nor angels, nor principalities, nor powers, nor things present, nor things to come, nor height, nor depth, nor any other creature, shall be able to separate us from the love [*agapē*] of God, which is in Christ Jesus our Lord" (Rom. 8:35, 38–39; see also Gal. 5:6, 13–14 and the Notes on 2:4; 5:2, 25, 27).

own bodies: Christ possesses his body into eternity. It will be ever with him. It represents much of who he is, because in its makeup remain the wounds of his crucifixion, the proof of his suffering and death that were vicariously undertaken for all (see John 20:24–28 and 3 Ne. 11:13–15). Christ's personal body, as a person might describe it, is not the same as the church, also called his body (see 1:23; 4:4, 12, 16; 5:23). But he treasures

---

393. Friedrich Hauck, *TDNT*, 5:563–64.
394. Quell and Stauffer, *TDNT*, 1:50–51.

both. Only a short step separates Christ's eternal regard for his personal body and a person's acute regard for her or his own body. Even if an individual's love of body boils down to self-preservation, that person will preserve the body at any cost.[395] Such intensity surely rests beneath Paul's words here. Hence, a man's vivid desire to preserve his body, here described as "love," should stretch itself to enfold his wife into its embrace (see the Notes on 1:23; 2:16; 4:4, 12, 16; 5:2, 30).

loveth himself: The measure for how a man loves himself takes its mark from how deeply and committedly he loves his wife. No mystery lingers here. As spelled out in the Note above, Christ serves as the model.[396] The reflexive pronoun "himself" (ἑαυτόν, *heauton*) mirrors the reflexive pronouns that Paul applied to Christ elsewhere in the letter. The first has to do with Christ's unifying influence, a point of reference that centers directly on marriage: "That he might create through himself the two into one new human, thus making peace" (2:15 NR; see 5:31, quoting LXX Gen. 2:24). The second leads to Christ's sacrifice not for himself but for believers: "Christ also hath loved us, and hath given himself for us an offering and a sacrifice to God" (5:2). Such a selfless act brings readers to an important ingredient in marriage: sacrificing time and energy for one's spouse. The third instance is similar. The difference lies in Christ's sacrifice for individuals as in 5:2 and his sacrifice for the church as a body or as a whole wherein he exhibited an elevating capacity, a trait welcome within the bond of marriage. We read: "That he might present to himself a glorious church, not having stain or wrinkle ... but holy and blameless" (5:27 NR). May husbands always act their part.

5:29 *hated:* The verb that means "to hate" or "to detest" (μισέω, *miseō*) can be aimed at earthly things (see John 3:20, "the light"; Heb. 1:9, "iniquity"; Rom. 7:15; and Jude 1:23) or groups (see Rev. 2:6, "the Nicolaitans") or individuals (see Matt. 5:43, "thine enemy"; Luke 19:14; John 15:25; etc.).[397] In this context, the verb crisply and intentionally contrasts with the verb "to love" (see 5:25, 28), throwing each into relief because of the presence of the other. The net effect is to lay "sharply upon the husband the duty of loving his espoused wife."[398]

---

395. Winger, *Ephesians,* 616.
396. Stauffer, *TDNT,* 1:656.
397. BDAG, 652.1.b.
398. Otto Michel, *TDNT,* 4:692.

flesh: Hating one's flesh (σάρξ, *sarx*) is highly unusual. During his agony suffered in the Garden of Gethsemane, Jesus told his disciples that "the flesh is weak" (Matt. 26:41; Mark 14:38). But this concept differs from the notion of "sinful flesh" that Jesus took upon himself when he became mortal (Rom. 8:3; see also Rom. 8:8, 13; Gal. 5:17; 1 Pet. 3:21; etc.). Hating one's flesh seems more at home in the modern world, which is plagued by "bulimia, self-loathing, and [some] suicidal depression."[399] A reader does get a sniff of an ascetic strain of Christian living that has located itself in Asia Minor in the letter to the Colossians. When Paul wrote about re-adopting "principles of this world," he noted rules such as "Do not handle! Do not taste! Do not touch! . . . Such regulations indeed have an appearance of wisdom, with their . . . harsh treatment of the body, but they lack any value in restraining sensual indulgence" (Col. 2:21, 23 NIV). But this is only a hint and not the full-blown asceticism that began to creep into the Christian world during the second century. Still, the insistence on keeping one's flesh or body properly nourished and cared for stands against any abuse of oneself (see 5:29).[400]

The highlighting of *sarx* as making up the body of the church, an unusual concept,[401] doubtlessly prepared readers for its reappearance a few lines later in the quotation from Genesis (see 5:31).[402] There it touches on the uniting of men and women in matrimony, wherein they become "one flesh" (Gen. 2:24). The thought of "one flesh," therefore, connects to the human world and its marriage practices. The expression "all flesh" can pertain to all humankind or to all living creatures, including both animals and humans.[403] In the realm of "all flesh," God is in charge, and onto his children he can pour out his Spirit. In a compelling passage, we read, "I [God] will pour out my spirit upon *all flesh*; and your sons and your daughters shall prophesy" (Joel 2:28, emphasis added). According to the Old Testament, God controlled all "flesh," not only granting and preserving life (see Job 10:11–12) but also restoring flesh to the bones of the dead (Ezek. 37:1–10). It is this cluster of ideas that have embedded themselves into the notion of loving and taking care of one's flesh or body. For the flesh of one's body is God's domain (see the Notes on 2:3, 11, 15; 5:30, 31; 6:5, 12).[404]

---

399. Winger, *Ephesians,* 616; see also Best, *Ephesians,* 549.
400. Lincoln, *Ephesians,* 379.
401. Schweizer, Baumgärtel and Meyer, *TDNT,* 7:137.
402. Best, *Ephesians,* 549; Larkin, *Handbook,* 138; Merkle, *Guide,* 187.
403. Bratsiotis, *TDOT,* 2:319.
404. Bratsiotis, *TDOT,* 2:330–32.

nourisheth and cherisheth: These verbs (ἐκτρέφω and θάλπω, *ektrephō* and *thalpō*) underlined how Christians viewed the human body and its treatment as the church moved forward into ever-varying communities of the world. These verbs also brought an emphasis onto how a husband is to care for his wife.[405] To be sure, these actions do not suggest that "all a husband needs to do is to provide food and clothing for his wife."[406] They imply much more. The fact that the verb *ektrephō* appears again in 6:4, this time tied to raising children, and *thalpō* in 1 Thessalonians 2:7, there connected to the work of a nurse who has care of a family's children, opens the door to the care of young people as well as to the care of one's wife. That said, there is no reason to push forward the misguided idea that Paul was writing about "a child-bride," whether a person or the church, "who is being brought to maturity by the bridegroom's care."[407] No, the existence of a marriage contract that repeated these two verbs when describing the obligation of the groom, though in reverse order from 5:29—"to cherish and nourish and clothe her"—stands as confirming evidence that Paul certainly had marriage in mind (see the Note on 6:4).[408]

even as: The adverbial conjunction καθώς (*kathōs*) stands here in its comparative sense.[409] Therefore, it should be rendered "even as" or "just as." Paul is therewith tying an ever-tighter knot that, no matter what, Jesus loves in an inseparable way his church and his people within it.

the Lord: The best manuscripts do not read "the Lord" but instead read "Christ" (NR) with the definite article (ὁ Χριστός, *ho Christos*), implicitly representing the Semitic meaning, "the Messiah." As the Messiah, he died "for the ungodly," even "for us" (Rom. 5:6, 8), being "raised up from the dead by the glory of the Father" (Rom. 6:4). Because of that Resurrection, "Christ . . . dieth no more; death hath no more dominion over him" (Rom. 6:9). Our baptisms mean that we "have been baptized into Christ [which allows us to] put on Christ" as if we were putting on a celestial garment (Gal. 3:27; see also Moro. 4:3 and D&C 20:77; 109:22), and, with it wrapped around us, can live with him forever (see Rom. 6:22; 8:13–17; Gal. 6:8; etc.). At the end, "in the dispensation of the fulness of times [God will] gather

---

405. Bruce, *Ephesians,* 118.

406. Best, *Ephesians,* 550.

407. Lincoln, *Ephesians,* 379.

408. Cited by Lincoln, *Ephesians,* 379–80; Best, *Ephesians,* 550; and Muddiman, *Ephesians,* 267–68.

409. BDAG, 493.1; Louw-Nida, §64.14.

together in one all things in Christ, both which are in heaven, and which are on earth" (1:10; see also 1 Cor. 15:28).[410]

the church: In Ephesians and Colossians, a reader of the New Testament comes upon "a specific doctrine of the Church,"[411] a feature that does not show up in others of Paul's letters. Yes, the church appears as Christ's body elsewhere, even featuring certain officers such as apostles and prophets (see Rom. 12:4–5 and 1 Cor. 12:12–31). But we learn more in Ephesians, much more. For example, we turn to our letter to learn that God "gave" the church and its organization "for the perfecting of the saints, for the work of the ministry, for the edifying of the body of Christ" (4:11–12). For individuals, this meant coming to grasp "the knowledge of the Son of God" and reaching "the measure of the stature of the fulness of Christ" (4:13). In Ephesians we discover that Christ is the head of the church (see 1:22; 4:15; and Col. 1:18; 2:10), an important disclosure about his enduring relationship with the church and its members. As its head, Christ presides over the church (see 5:24). Moreover, he loves infinitely and, in that love, has given himself to the church that it may be "holy and without blemish" (5:27; see also 1:4; 5:25). Furthermore, as a virtual parent, he "nourisheth and cherisheth it" (5:29).[412] Hallelujah!

5:30 *For:* The conjunction ὅτι (*hoti*) presents the reason why something is so. Hence, the sense of *hoti* becomes "because" or "since" (NR).[413] That is to say, Christ has nourished and cherished believers because they are "members of his body." If they stand to the side of his body—that is, outside the church—they receive no such nourishment. Because believers have drawn near to Christ, his Father has shown "the exceeding riches of his grace in his [fathomless] kindness toward [them]" (2:7).

we are: The first-person plural of the verb "to be" (εἰμί, *eimi*) appears to frame the Apostle's effort to say to his Gentile readers that, in an unlooked-for way, they were in that very moment recipients of God's gracious care through his Son.[414] That was the warm meaning of them being "fellow-citizens with the saints" (2:19).

---

410. Quell and Foerster, *TDNT*, 3:1090–91.

411. Schmidt, *TDNT*, 3:509.

412. Schmidt, *TDNT*, 3:509; Grundmann, Hesse, de Jonge, and van der Woude, *TDNT*, 9:556–58; see also Merkle, *Guide*, 188.

413. BDAG, 732.4; Merkle, *Guide*, 188.

414. Lincoln, *Ephesians*, 380.

members: This is the only place in Ephesians where Paul called devotees "members" (plural of μέλος, *melos*)[415] of Christ's "body." Earlier, he had termed the growing group of believers "members one of another" (4:25). But the sense is not the same. In the earlier passage, the stress lay on the enriching fellowship within the church. Here, in 5:30, we glimpse a subtle emphasis on individuality, on a person's uniqueness that is surprisingly not suppressed within "the household of God," a massive collective (2:19; see also 1 Cor. 6:15; 12:27). After all, "Christ's care of the church is always his care of the individuals composing it" (see the Notes on 4:16, 25).[416]

body: For the last time in Ephesians, the noun for "body" appears (σῶμα, *sōma*). As in 5:23, Christ's body links both to the church and to marriage. Because the addressees of the Epistle are chiefly Gentiles, their place within Christ's body came about by preaching. When they heard God's word through missionaries, they were "afar off" but soon became "nigh" (2:17). In those bygone days, they "were without Christ, being . . . strangers from the covenants of promise, having no hope, and without God in the world" (2:12). However, "ye who sometimes were far off are made nigh by the blood of Christ" (2:13). Thus, an unexpected thunderclap crashed graciously and generously when Christ made Jews and Gentiles "into one" and created "through himself the two into one new human" (2:14–15 NR). It is this essential oneness that makes up his *sōma*. In a word, "he denieth *none* that come unto him, black and white, bond and free, male and female; . . . and all are alike unto God, both Jew and Gentile" (2 Ne. 26:33, emphasis added; see also the Notes on 1:23; 2:16; 4:4, 12, 16; 5:23, 28).

of his flesh, and of his bones: This line was likely not in Paul's original letter.[417] The options are two. (1) This line was not in the original copy of Ephesians and the verse ended with the possessive pronoun "his" (αὐτοῦ, *autou*), referring to "his body." The manuscripts that omit the expression include the earliest, 𝔓[46]. (2) A more impressive group of texts preserve this line, a line that bears the interpretative meaning "some of his flesh and bone."[418] If this expression forms an addition, which is likely, the words were evidently added later in anticipation of the quotation of LXX Gen. 2:24 in the next verse, 5:31, and the memory of Eve as "bone of my bones,

---

415. BDAG, 628; Thayer, *Lexicon*, 397.
416. Best, *Ephesians*, 551.
417. Metzger, *Textual Commentary*, 541; Bruce, *Ephesians*, 119.
418. Muddiman, *Ephesians*, 268, italics removed.

and flesh of my flesh" in Genesis 2:23. Perhaps oddly, the terms "flesh" and "bones" are reversed from the Genesis story. Importantly, nothing in Paul's writings that compares Christ's body and the church hints at the thought of church members being Christ's bones.

5:31 *For this cause:* With this phrase (ἀντὶ τούτου, *anti toutou*) that introduces a quotation from LXX Genesis 2:24,[419] Paul plunged his readers into the creation account, a story perhaps known only imperfectly among Gentiles (see Matt. 19:5 and Mark 10:7–8). But that did not stop him. After all, the Old Testament supplied the norms for much of Christian living. And Gentiles had to become acquainted with it. The phrase is properly translated as "for this cause."[420]

a man leave his father and mother: The image presents a young bridegroom leaving his parents and, with his new bride, beginning a home of their own. An important question is whether Paul has read this verse from Genesis in an allegorical sense. Why? Because if he did, we can detect a Mother in Heaven behind the passage. On only two occasions did Jesus treat marriage matters allegorically.[421] In the first instance, he answered a question from a group of scribes and Pharisees about why his disciples did not fast. To them he replied, "As long as [my disciples] have the bridegroom with them, they cannot fast. But the days come when the bridegroom shall be taken away from them, and then shall they fast" (Mark 2:19–20; see also Matt. 9:15 and Luke 5:34–35). We should notice that, even though Jesus employed the image of a bridegroom to describe himself, he was applying it to a situation that would soon develop when "he would be taken away from them." The second allegory, the parable of the ten virgins, also pointed to him. The picture the allegory paints is of the Second Coming. In the run-up to the judgment of his followers and others—that is, the "ten virgins" (Matt. 25:1)—"the bridegroom tarried," throwing plans out of sorts for the time being (Matt. 25:5). Later, of course, "the bridegroom came" and the wedding festivities began (Matt. 25:10). This time, Jesus' focus was not on the frightful future when "he would be taken away from" his followers but on the end-time.

---

419. Schweizer, Baumgärtel, and Meyer, *TDNT,* 7:137. The quotation is almost exact except for the missing Greek possessive pronouns "his" before both "father" and "mother"; see Lincoln, *Ephesians,* 380.

420. Friedrich Büchsel, *TDNT,* 1:372.

421. Contra Jeremias, *TDNT,* 4:1101–4.

Paul also brought marital allegory into his correspondence. To his Corinthian readers, he wrote, "I promised you to one husband, to Christ, so that I might present you as a pure virgin to him" (2 Cor. 11:2 NIV). In this passage, the Apostle thought of himself as the groom's best man, who would take charge of the promised bride and deliver her to him in purity on their wedding day. Here, too, we come upon Christ as the bridegroom and the large collection of his followers as the bride.[422] The question now becomes, Might Paul have been thinking of allegory when he quoted LXX Genesis 2:24 at 5:31? Other commentators shout an emphatic no.[423] But when Paul calls this Genesis verse "a great mystery" (5:32), he swings the gate open.

An examiner must admit at the outset that it is impossible to capture all the thoughts and intents of the Apostle as he wrote verses 5:22–33. Yet Paul has left a clear guide to much of what he was thinking. Even a quick perusal of these lines brings a reader to a stunning set of insights. The Apostle has compared the relationship between a husband and wife to that of Christ and the church. He has framed that relationship in unbounded love. He has seen that Christ's love and care for the church will "sanctify and cleanse it." That cleansing, he assured his readers, will come about "with the washing of water" and "by the word"—that is, by the scripture and its enduring power (5:26). Thus washed and adorned, all of which has pointed to a sacred marriage, the church will stand before her bridegroom under the wedding canopy without "stain or wrinkle or any such thing," being "holy and blameless" throughout eternity (5:27 NR). With a final flourish, Paul affirmed that "we are members of his body," an image that can be understood only in a figurative sense (5:30). In this brief summary, we have been walking on metaphorical ground, not on soil and stones. We are now ready for a heightened sense of metaphor: allegory.[424]

---

422. Jeremias, *TDNT*, 4:1104–5.

423. Jeremias, *TDNT*, 4:1105; Lincoln, *Ephesians*, 380.

424. As we see in the later Hymn of the Pearl, we can understand the lines from LXX Gen. 2:24 quoted in 5:31 to apply allegorically to the coming of Jesus and to his union with his band of followers, the church. Even though the hymn was non-Christian in origin, its appearance in the apocryphal *Acts of Thomas* assures us that Christians saw in it a story that pointed to the Christ's descent into the world, leaving his parents behind, as well as to the descent of anyone else from a premortal heavenly home. See the *Acts of Thomas*, 108–13, in Edgar Hennecke and Wilhelm Schneemelcher, eds., *New Testament Apocrypha*, trans. R. McL. Wilson and others, 2 vols. (Philadelphia: Westminster Press, 1963, 1965), 2:498–504.

We have to ask, How do the words from LXX Genesis 2:24 match with Christ and his beloved, the church? The answer appears in two words: through allegory. In this view, the man who left his father and mother to take his bride and begin a new, sanctified life was, naturally, Christ.[425] Who else is in view? No one. As Paul made very plain, "I speak concerning Christ and the church" (5:32). Now the allegorical element needs clarity. The bridegroom who left his parents to join his bride is both a real man and allegorically the Savior. The father and mother mentioned in LXX Genesis 2:24 are also real. But can they represent someone else in an allegorical sense? Yes, they can, in fact, embody someone different in the context of our letter, a requirement for allegory. Certainly, that is the case with "his father," an earthly man. This person allegorically stands in for God the Father. Next up is "his mother." Like "his father," this earthly mother in LXX Genesis 2:24 must represent someone different, someone celestial, to match the father. Hence, we find ourselves standing at the gate of Christ's mother, the Mother in Heaven.[426] As Paul wrote in the next verse, "This is a great mystery" (5:32).[427] It is also breathtaking.

be joined: The verb is the future passive of προσκολλάω (*proskollaō*) with the meaning "will be joined" and the added sense of "to begin an association with someone."[428] The passive points to God as the one who brings the couple together in marriage. How so? As the language found in Genesis 3:12 describes ("the woman whom thou [God] gavest to be with me"), "God himself is responsible for establishing marriage." That is apparent in the verb translated "thou [God] gavest" (נתן, *natan*), which underscores among other things the covenant dimension of the union of Adam and Eve (see Prov. 2:17, "the covenant of her God").[429] A question arises whether the verb envisions the two becoming as if a single personality. The answer is no. The reasons appear in our letter. Earlier Paul had called the unifying of Jew and Gentile "his [Christ's] body, the fulness of him that filleth all

---

425. Jeremias, *TDNT*, 1:366.

426. Philo of Alexandria (c. 20 BC to AD 50) treated LXX Gen. 2:24 allegorically, making the father into "God the Father of the universe" and the mother into "wisdom, the Mother of all things." *Allegorical Interpretation* 2.49, in *Philo I*, trans. F. H. Colson and G. H. Whitaker, Loeb Classical Library (Cambridge, Mass.: Harvard University Press, 1971), 255, cited in Best, *Ephesians*, 553.

427. Bornkamm, *TDNT*, 4:823: "The μυστήριον ['mystery'] is thus the allegorical meaning of the OT saying [from LXX Gen. 2:24]."

428. Louw-Nida, §34.22; see also BDAG, 881–82.

429. Bratsiotis, *TDOT*, 1:227.

in all" (1:23). As if to emphasize this point, he later wrote that "Gentiles should be fellowheirs, and of the same body" with Jews (3:6). Further, Paul pointed to "the new person" who was to embrace all, Jew and Gentile (4:24 NR). Yet amidst all this talk about unity, he quietly affirmed essential differences when he wrote that "through him we both [Gentile and Jew] have access by one Spirit unto the Father" (2:18). Clearly, the Apostle did not see men and women becoming essentially the same in marriage, which is the highest expression of unity (see the Note on 5:22).[430]

unto: The preposition πρός (*pros*) here carries the meaning of movement over a physical distance, of motion toward someone or something.[431] This sense fits the thought of a bridegroom and a bride coming together in marriage.

wife: Like the Greek γυνή (*gynē*), the Hebrew אשה (*ishah*) can mean either an unmarried woman or a wife, depending on the context.[432] For an ancient person acquainted with the Bible, this term *ishah,* written first in Genesis 2:22, would come to heft the lofty expectations of Proverbs 31:10–31. In those verses, a reader encounters the highest of praise for a noble wife. In those lines, we hear of "a virtuous woman [whose] . . . price is far above rubies." In her marriage, "the heart of her husband doth safely trust in her" (Prov. 31:10–11). She "worketh willingly with her hands [and] . . . she riseth also while it is yet night and giveth meat to her household" (Prov. 31:13, 15). Moreover, "she stretcheth out her hand to the poor; yea, she reacheth out her hands to the needy" (Prov. 31:20). Of her character, "strength and honor are her clothing." Additionally, "she openeth her mouth with wisdom; and in her tongue is the law of kindness" (Prov. 31:25–26). Within her family, "her children arise up, and call her blessed; her husband also, and he praiseth her." For "a woman that feareth the Lord, she shall be praised" (Prov. 31:28, 30).

In a different vein, the expression "his wife" (Gen. 2:24) is much warmer than "the woman" in the Lord God's address to Eve in Genesis 3:12. This latter passage, of course, arose after Eve had partaken of the fruit of the tree of the knowledge of good and evil, therefore after the fall. But let us not be mistaken. Even though we read elsewhere in the New Testament that "the woman [Eve] being deceived was in the transgression" (1 Tim. 2:14), this is not the whole story. The key lies in the verb "to see" (ראה, *ra'a*).

---

430. Barth, *Ephesians*, 2:641.
431. Bo Reicke, *TDNT*, 6:721; BDAG, 874.3.a.γ; Larkin, *Handbook*, 140.
432. BDAG, 208–9; Bratsiotis, *TDOT*, 1:224–25.

From the plain sense of the Genesis text, Eve saw as God saw. Although the devil sought to deceive the woman at the critical moment of her decision whether to partake of the fruit, she saw her options clearly. We hear the familiar cadences of the report: "God saw [*ra'a*] the light, that it was good" (Gen. 1:4; see also Gen. 1:10, 12, 18, 21; etc.). Then came the scene in the garden with the woman and the serpent. On the question of whether to eat the fruit of the tree of the knowledge of good and evil, the serpent's smooth voice assured the woman, "God doth know that in the day ye eat thereof, then your eyes shall be opened, and ye shall be as gods, knowing good and evil." What was the woman's reaction? "When the woman saw [*ra'a*] that the tree was good for food . . . and a tree to be desired to make one wise, she took of the fruit thereof, and did eat" (Gen. 3:5–6). The use of the verb *ra'a* to spell out the actions of God and the woman was not coincidental. Its presence in the narrative shows a carefully crafted intent. In that moment of moments, with the woman facing the decision of the ages, she saw as God himself saw, with his celestial sight and discernment. She made her decision in the full light of heaven's brightness (see Gen. 21:19; 2 Kgs. 6:17; Prov. 20:12; and the Notes on 4:22; 5:22; 6:2).[433]

one flesh: This expression, of course, pertains to the first marital intimacy between a new husband and wife.[434] There is more. The idea of "flesh" introduces readers to the transitory nature of human life. The enlivening element in life is not the flesh but "the breath of life" (Gen. 2:7; 6:17; see also Job 12:10, "the breath of all mankind"). The impermanent quality of "flesh" resides in its reduction to dust after death (see Gen. 3:19; Job 34:15; and Eccl. 12:7).[435] In a figurative sense, however, the words "one flesh" can also point "to a higher union with the Lord."[436] Not surprisingly, this thought directs a reader to oneness, to "the single and unique." For example, often a person's trajectory through life is decided by one big decision. We look to the stories of the rich young ruler and of Mary, sister of Martha, for confirmation (see Mark 10:21 and Luke 10:42). The simple commandment to love embraces within itself the divine will (see Matt. 5:44–46; Luke 6:27–29, 35; and Gal. 5:14). To break one tenet of the law means being "guilty of all" (James 2:10). The disciples' watching for "one hour" would have made a huge difference

---

433. Draper, Brown, and Rhodes, *Pearl of Great Price,* 43–45.
434. Schmidt, *TDNT,* 3:823.
435. Bratsiotis, *TDOT,* 2:328.
436. Stauffer, *TDNT,* 2:435.

for the suffering Jesus (Matt. 26:40; Mark 14:37). This singularity takes on a sinister tone when Jesus said to the arresting party, "This is your hour, and the power of darkness," underscoring the vast consequences of making the wrong decision in that "hour" (Luke 22:53).[437]

One other coloration pushes itself forward. It centers on the permanence of the flesh in the eternal scheme of things. Paul's line to his Corinthian acquaintances gives focus to this matter. He wrote, "This I say, brethren, that flesh and blood cannot inherit the kingdom of God" (1 Cor. 15:50). Elsewhere, when reporting on the vision of Christ that burst upon him while he was going to Damascus, he recorded, "I conferred not with flesh and blood" (Gal. 1:16). From these two passages, it appears that flesh does not have a place in the celestial world. Case closed? Hardly. Rather, the combination of "flesh and blood" sends readers to the condition of mortality, because, in scriptural language, blood carries the life in a human or animal. People are reminded of this when, in passages that deal with ingesting blood at meals, they read, "The blood is the life; and thou mayest not eat the life with the flesh" (Deut. 12:23), and the "flesh with the life thereof, which is the blood thereof, shall ye not eat" (Gen. 9:4). In this light, the noncelestial element is blood, not flesh. Clarification arises in Paul's words to his friends in Philippi: "We look for the Savior, the Lord Jesus Christ: who shall change our vile body, that it may be fashioned like unto his glorious body" (Philip. 3:21). The crowning observation comes from Jesus himself when, during a post-Resurrection appearance to his gathered disciples, he invited them to "handle me, and see; for a spirit hath not flesh and bones, as ye see me have" (Luke 24:39). As modern commentators have assured us, "Christ is the true example of this [eternal] union of spirit and flesh."[438]

5:32 great: This adjective (μέγας, *megas*) occurs only here in Ephesians, but is splashed liberally throughout the New Testament. A better translation of the line in which it appears might be "this mystery is great" (Wayment), adding emphasis to the character of the mystery.[439] The greatest of Christ's gifts is love, *agapē*. Readers first encounter Paul's admonition to "seek for the greater [comparative of *megas*] gifts" (1 Cor. 12:31, Wayment) and then run into his judgment: "Now abideth faith, hope, charity

---

437. Stauffer, *TDNT*, 2:435.
438. Schweizer, Baumgärtel, and Meyer, *TDNT*, 7:147.
439. Lincoln, *Ephesians*, 380; Winger, *Ephesians*, 620.

[*agapē*], these three; but the greatest [superlative[440] of *megas*] of these is charity [*agapē*]."[441]

mystery: In our letter, the "mystery" has revolved around the acceptance of Gentiles into the church, a feature of the kingdom that had been disclosed only in the days of Paul and the other apostles (see 3:3–6). But the discussion of marriage in 5:22–31 has shifted the meaning of "mystery" to that of the allegorical meaning of LXX Genesis 2:24 quoted in 5:31, a passage that holds a "mysteriously concealed prophecy of the relation of Christ to the ἐκκλησία ['church']."[442] And within this allegorical understanding of the Genesis verse readers perceive that the mother whom the bridegroom leaves to marry his bride stands for the Heavenly Mother (see the Note on 5:31).[443] Even though some commentators reject this idea,[444] the allegorical interpretation of the prior verse, 5:31, is the only one that makes sense.[445] Thus, we find ourselves staring at the Heavenly Mother, who is a part of the "great mystery" (see the Notes on 1:9; 3:4, 9; 6:19).

Christ: Although the man who leaves "his father and mother" can represent Christ when LXX Genesis 2:24 is understood allegorically (5:31), Christ, of course, was not a mythical figure. Although he has been elevated by the Father to stand as "the head over all things to the church" (1:22), he walked and talked as a mortal man. Although his characteristics can be made to suit almost any person's tastes, he was fully historical and individual. Although examples from his life and ministry may be fitted into patterns that seek to inform and elevate the behavior of fellow humans, he walked on the earth, stepping onto dirt and rocks. Although his teachings can be molded into a myriad of lessons, he sat and reclined on the ground with followers and admirers, accepting meals and other helpful items for his work. In a word, he was fully human. He was like us. But, unlike us, he came to earth with a power and grace that offered "redemption through his blood, the forgiveness of sins" (1:7), and, through the Holy Spirit, "access

---

440. By the New Testament era, the superlative form of adjectives had largely gone out of style; in their place stood the comparative, which functioned as a superlative depending on the context. See Blass and Debrunner, *Greek Grammar,* §§60, 244.

441. Walter Grundmann, *TDNT,* 4:531.

442. Bornkamm, *TDNT,* 4:823; see also Caird, *Letters,* 89.

443. Philo of Alexandria titled the mother in LXX Gen. 2:24 as "wisdom, the Mother of all things." *Allegorical Interpretation* 2.49, cited by Best, *Ephesians,* 553.

444. Jeremias, *TDNT,* 4:1105; Lincoln, *Ephesians,* 380.

445. Bornkamm, *TDNT,* 4:823; Barth, *Ephesians,* 2:643–44; Muddiman, *Ephesians,* 270.

... unto the Father" (2:18). All this he did in a real time and a real place.[446] All one has to do is think of the cross and the tomb.

the church: Pairing the church with Christ, as throughout prior verses (see 5:23–27), draws up the question whether the church forms and controls the only path to salvation. The short answer is yes. Said another way, "in Ephesians Christology and soteriology are sustained by ecclesiology"; that is, Jesus' saving powers are ministered through the existence and work of the church.[447] No outside road leads to the unfathomable riches of heavenly rewards (see 3:16, 20). Not only has Christ loved the church and adorned her so that she is "holy and without blemish" (5:27), but he has placed within her "your order" (Col. 2:5). That is, within the church a person finds divine patterns of worship and celestial ordinances that pull believers closer and closer to an everlasting destiny of fellowship with the Father and the Son. Here one discovers fellow believers who have devoted themselves to assisting in "the perfecting of the saints, [and] for the work of the ministry" (4:12). Here one comes upon "the foundation of the apostles and prophets, Jesus Christ himself being the chief cornerstone" (2:20). Here one experiences the fellowship of those who, in their consecrated lives, "are builded together for an habitation of God through the Spirit" (2:22). As a first physical, concrete step, "believers are taken up into this event by baptism."[448]

5:33 *love his wife even as himself:* With this verse, Paul has rounded off his review of the relationships of husband and wife, of Christ and the church. Against the tide of his surrounding culture, he has demanded that husbands love and care for their wives on the model of Christ having loved the church and given himself for it (see 5:2, "hath loved us, and hath given himself for us"). This language, of course, was all directed toward husbands. The Apostle's words centered first on the men. The wives came in for his entreaty only at the end of the verse.[449]

Two dimensions appear immediately. The one, as just noted, involved the husband loving his wife as Christ has loved the church, a point that Paul made in 5:25. This second mention of the need for husbands to love

---

446. Grundmann, Hesse, de Jonge, and van der Woude, *TDNT*, 9:557.

447. Grundmann, Hesse, de Jonge, and van der Woude, *TDNT*, 9:556.

448. Grundmann, Hesse, de Jonge, and van der Woude, *TDNT*, 9:559.

449. Lincoln, *Ephesians*, 384; Matthew O. Richardson, "Ephesians: Unfolding the Mysteries through Revelation," in Huntington and others, *Go Ye into All the World*, 140–42.

wives certainly adds heft to the earlier passage, like a loud bang. The second dimension directs a reader to the need for husbands to love their wives as they love themselves, the essence of Paul's remarks in 5:28 when he demanded that men ought "to love their wives as their own bodies." He was smart enough to know that people would do anything to avoid injury or illness in their bodies. That intense will was to be matched by the same intensity in how men treat their wives, how they love them. Besides, scripture stands at the base of such a requirement, as we read in Leviticus 19:18: "Thou shalt love thy neighbor as thyself."[450] In a word, "the wife is the husband's primary and exemplary neighbor."[451]

that: The adverb that lies beneath this English term is ἵνα (*hina*).[452] It points to an unexpressed verb like "to desire" (θέλω, *thelō*) or "to admonish" (διαστέλλομαι, *diastellomai*) as we find in Mark 8:15: "He [Jesus] admonished [the disciples]" (Wayment).[453] Why is this important? Because Paul's intent becomes clear. The syntax here breathes the air of what the Apostle wrote elsewhere, "I speak not by commandment," when appealing to church members to offer generous gifts to fellow Saints in need (2 Cor. 8:8). This stance contrasts sharply with his declaration to the Thessalonian believers that his preaching rested on the "commandments we gave you by the Lord Jesus" and "by the word of the Lord" (1 Thes. 4:2, 15). In our passage, 5:33, the sense stands on his trust and hope that wives would respect and reverence their husbands because they wanted to, not because he required it of them.[454] This position differs markedly from Paul's three strong commands that husbands love their wives (see 5:25, 28, 33).

reverence: In 5:21, we came upon the noun *phobos*, which almost always means "fear." We discovered that in that context it bore the meaning "reverence."[455] In our verse, 5:33, we meet the verb associated with *phobos*. It is φοβέω (*phobeō*). Its form in this verse does not seem to be a real imperative but rather a strong invitation.[456] Perhaps oddly, some commentators try to argue that the basic meaning of this verb, "to fear," fits well with what Paul has been discussing. That is, women are to fear their husbands just as

---

450. Lincoln, *Ephesians*, 384.

451. Barth, *Ephesians*, 2:719.

452. Smyth, *Greek Grammar*, §2498; Thayer, *Lexicon*, 302.1.

453. Larkin, *Handbook*, 143.

454. Barth, *Ephesians*, 2:648.

455. BDAG, 1062.2.b; Louw-Nida, §53.59; Thayer, *Lexicon*, 656; Best, *Ephesians*, 518; contra Horst Balz and Günther Wanke, *TDNT*, 9:217.

456. Barth, *Ephesians*, 2:648; Larkin, *Handbook*, 143.

both husbands and wives fear Christ, with a slightly less fearful sense that leans toward an elevated "respect."[457] In response, one can ask, where is the love for Christ? Is it to be overpowered by believers' fear of him? If so, where does the line fit that speaks of "the love of Christ, which passeth knowledge" (3:19)? And where is the wife's love for her husband? In any of its forms, fear does not equate to love. Hence, it seems plain that Paul is not appealing for a scaled-down fear, such as an obsequious obedience or, perhaps worse, an elevated anxiety not to offend. He really is asking that women reverence husbands who love them.[458] As we read in another translation of 5:33, "Each one of you [husbands] must also love his own wife as he loves himself, so that his wife may respect her husband" (Wayment; see also the Note on 5:21).

Analysis of 5:21–33

In these verses, Paul has escorted his readers into the world of family relationships, particularly that of husband and wife. Importantly, he has made that journey arm in arm with Christ. Like most, he was out of his depth and needed help. The kind of help that he sought, the kind of example that he needed, lay in Christ's enriching, nourishing, and guiding involvement with the church and its members. As he had already expressed in Ephesians, through Christ came "redemption [and] . . . forgiveness" (1:7); through Christ came a firm yet compassionate governance, because the Father had given "him as head over all things in the church" (1:22 NR); through Christ's breaking "down the middle wall of partition" between Gentile and Jew, all could live in harmony (2:14); "through [Christ] we both [Jews and Gentiles] have access by one Spirit unto the Father" (2:18); under Christ, believers were protected by "the chief cornerstone," which is the last stone inserted into a structure (2:20); within Christ's edifice, believers and their church reposed in "the building fitly framed together [that] groweth unto a holy temple" (2:21); through celestial revelation, devotees came "to know the love of Christ, which passeth knowledge" (3:19); and through the church's teachings believers grasped that "Christ also hath loved us, and hath given himself for us [as] an offering and a sacrifice to God" (5:2).

---

457. Balz and Wanke, *TDNT*, 9:217; Bruce, *Ephesians*, 120; Barth, *Ephesians*, 2:648; Lincoln, *Ephesians*, 384–85, 389–90; Best, *Ephesians*, 559; Fowl, *Ephesians*, 192; Winger, *Ephesians*, 625–26.

458. BDAG, 1060–62.2.b; Thayer, *Lexicon*, 655–56.3.

Yes, Paul thought of women as subordinate to men (see 5:22, 24). This fact should not surprise us, because this situation was embedded in his Roman and Jewish societies. Two points are relevant. First, on the Apostle's part he directed husbands to love their wives, not to rule over them.[459] Second, in the last line of this chapter he pled with wives to "reverence" their husbands. He did not command them (see the Note on 5:33). For husbands, as we have noticed in the paragraph above, their model is "Christ [who] also hath loved us, and hath given himself for us [as] an offering and a sacrifice to God" (5:2). This language drives up the standard for men to the height that their love and devotion to their wives will lead them to sacrifice all for them, even surrendering their lives for their wives.[460] At this point, Paul pushed beyond his contemporaries and showed himself not to be a parrot of contemporary marriage traditions, as different as they were from one another. For no one else taught this kind of fidelity and devotion on the man's part.[461]

From Paul's backyard blew the winds of the Old Testament, strong and at times fierce. Within the pages of that collection of texts resided God's commandments regarding mothers and wives. And those commandments came with hard-fisted capital penalties for violating them. A person simply turns toward the Ten Commandments to get a first glimpse of the heated cauldron almost ready to boil. The words of God rushed down the slopes of Mount Sinai, apparently within the hearing of the Hebrews (see Ex. 20:21): "Honor thy father and thy mother," the words thundered. Graciously, God held out the specific blessing and the myriad other blessings that would accompany the obedient one if a person would so honor father and mother: "That thy days may be long upon the land which the Lord thy God giveth thee" (Ex. 20:12). But lying just to the side of this scene lurked God's punishment for anyone who violated this command and would thereby upset the delicate balances inside a family.[462] The penalty showed up a few lines later when God warned that a person who "smiteth his father, or his mother" or "curseth his father, or his mother, shall surely be put to death" (Ex. 21:15, 17). The weight of such commands that paired father and mother, husband

---

459. Lincoln, *Ephesians*, 387.
460. Lincoln, *Ephesians*, 389.
461. Winger, *Ephesians*, 634–35.
462. Raymond F. Collins, "Ten Commandments," in *ABD*, 6:384, citing the work of Anthony Phillips, holds to the view that the threat of death as a penalty for dishonoring father and mother in Ex. 20:12 links to penalties associated with other acts of mistreatment of parents.

and wife, lifted the woman to a place of honor and respect in both her family's esteem and in God's sight.[463]

The appearance of LXX Genesis 2:24 at 5:31 naturally draws a reader's attention. Why? Because Paul treated this passage allegorically, calling it "a great mystery" and opening up the interpretation of the "man" who "is joined unto his wife" and "his father and mother" to persons other than Adam and Eve and their offspring. As matters were spelled out in the treatment of 5:31, this approach allows an interpreter to see Christ in the "man" who is "joined to his wife" and to glimpse the church in the "wife." In concert with this view, the "father" represents God the Father from whom Christ came. What about the "mother" in this scene? The most natural answer comes to rest on a Mother in Heaven (see the Note on 5:31).[464]

A further texture needs review. This set of verses directs any reader to the view that Christ has placed his sanction upon marriage, equating it to the sacred act of creating and nourishing his church. By this means, both the church and marriage have become holy paths to God. They each, as spiritual companions of one another, grant "access by one Spirit unto the Father" (2:18). Together they allow believers to know God, "who is able to do immeasurably more than all we ask or imagine" (3:20 NIV). In sum, marriage has continued to be a holy relationship with God at its head, as it was in the beginning (see Gen. 3:12, "the woman whom *thou [God] gavest* me," emphasis added; see also the Note on 5:31). A reader therefore concludes that Paul has not held or encouraged any ascetic tendency that believers should remain single.[465]

A final observation has to do with the issue of whether Paul was the author of Ephesians. As we set out the case in the discussion of 5:27, the author has to be the Apostle. The portrait of the church in Ephesians is much richer and more complex than in any other New Testament source. It is unimaginable that an untethered author of the first or second century would paint a picture of the church in such rich tones and then claim that it belonged to Paul (see the Notes on 1:23; 3:8; 4:3, 21; 5:27; 6:21; and the Analysis of 3:1–13; 6:1–9).[466]

---

463. Schrenk and Quell, *TDNT,* 5:964–65.
464. Philo of Alexandria, *Allegorical Interpretation* 2.49.
465. Bruce, *Ephesians,* 118–19; Lincoln, *Ephesians,* 388.
466. Schmidt, *TDNT,* 3:511; Bruce, *Ephesians,* 12; Merkle, *Guide,* 94; Muddiman, *Ephesians,* 215–16, 218, 145–47, 156.

Chapter 6

INTRODUCTION

Marriages—that of husband and wife and that of Christ and the church, his bride—create a wide, family-centered arc that loops around children and others inside the home: servants or slaves in this case. Never deviating, the standard for families nestles upon the warm, soft rugs of "the nurture and admonition of the Lord" and of "doing the will of God from the heart" (6:4, 6). Swiveling away from marriage and family matters, Paul then began his last appeal to readers that they individually "be strong in the Lord" and that each seek and receive "the power of his might" (6:10). With such a crucial need for inner strength and an accompanying outpouring of divine help, readers sensed that an ebony, filmlike cloud was blowing toward them, like an enveloping, sticky darkness. This coal-black essence did not represent the world of "flesh and blood" but rather "spiritual wickedness in high places" (6:12). And it was not approaching with the gentleness of a light breeze but with the fury of a hurricane. Hence, almost shouting, Paul drove home the need for believers to "put on the whole armour of God, that ye may be able to stand against the wiles of the devil" (6:11). Hopefully, it was not too late.

With no exceptions, all is Christ-centered in matters of the home. Yes, Paul employed the title "the Lord" throughout the early verses of this chapter (see 6:1–9). But as we found out in our review of "Lord" at 4:1, this title appears almost always in the Apostle's moral instructions. Further, "Lord" bears deep connections to the Old Testament; but in the New Testament, it always pertains to Christ. And so it does in these verses. Hence, we can easily substitute the name Christ wherever the title "the Lord" occurs. As an illustration, fathers are to "bring [children] up in the nurture of [Christ]" (6:4). Nothing is lost in substituting "Christ" for "the Lord." Further, in the Apostle's directives to servants and slaves, he urged them to "render service with good will, as if you were serving [Christ], not people" (6:7 NR). The thoroughgoing identity of "Christ" and "the Lord" becomes apparent amidst these verses when we read, "Servants, be obedient to them that are your masters . . . as unto Christ" (6:5). In summary, Paul portrayed the household as one committed to an unwavering loyalty to Christ and his teachings. In addition, the identity of the Lord of the Old Testament and Christ of the New Testament becomes secure. They are the same person (see the Note on 4:1).

Closely tied with Paul's emphasis on the Lord in homes stand his revealing words on prayer. Following his extended discussion about arming oneself for the Herculean struggle "against the rulers of the darkness of this world" (6:12; see also 6:11–17), he begged that his readers pray "with all perseverance" (6:18), writing the noun προσκαρτέρησις (*proskarterēsis*), which carries the meaning of firm, strong persistence in the face of difficulty.[1] This term underscores in vivid colors the approaching days of severe difficulty for the church. How can we be sure that this was the case? Because the Apostle pled that church members pray "for all saints" and for "me" (6:18–19). Such a request for strong, persistent praying, Paul knew, would infuse him and his fellow Saints with the needed heavenly power in their last stand "against the wiles of the devil [and] . . . spiritual wickedness in high places" (6:11–12). He knew that, for this effort, he needed to "speak boldly, as I [and they] ought to speak" (6:20). He sensed the necessity that he and his fellow Saints bring into the fold as many as possible before the rushing, descending, sable cloud snuffed out the light.

This chapter also presents pointers to sacred ceremony. One can hardly avoid strong allusions to holy actions in the verbs "to put on" (6:11, 14, "having [put] on"), "to stand" (6:11, 13, 14), "to take up" (6:13, 16), and "to take" (6:17). The reader encounters the verbs "to walk" and "to sit" earlier in Ephesians and here again is escorted into a sacred chamber festooned with heavenly actions that lead to an intensely personal relationship with the Father and the Son (see the Notes on 2:10; 4:13, 20, 22, 24; 5:2, 8, 14; 6:11, 13–14; and appendix 1).

Within Paul's outline of relationships between masters and slaves, all Christ-centered, it becomes quickly apparent that he was not a social critic or reformer (see 6:5–9). In his heaven-driven ministry, he had adopted a single focus that rested on preaching "Jesus Christ, and him crucified" (1 Cor. 2:2). All else was secondary. Simply stated, he did not blanch at one human being owning another and totally controlling that person's life and even death. For the Apostle, the principal matter had to do with how a believer treated another person in the wider world. He was fully aware

---

1. BDAG, 881; Louw-Nida, §68.68.

of Old Testament laws that governed master-slave relationships and that violation of one of those laws by a master would eventually bring an out-pouring of God's anger (see Deut. 23:21 and Eccl. 5:2, 4–5; see also 2 Cor. 5:10–11 and Heb. 10:31). That said, he expected the best behavior from both Christian slaves and Christian masters. Concerning slaves, when serving their masters, they were to be "as the servants of Christ, doing the will of God from the heart" (6:6). Concerning masters, they were to avoid even "threatening" their slaves. For, as the Apostle warned, "Your Master also is in heaven; neither is there respect of persons with him" (6:9).

"DOING THE WILL OF GOD FROM THE HEART" (6:1–9)

King James Translation

1 Children, obey your parents in the Lord: for this is right. 2 Honour thy father and mother; (which is the first commandment with promise;) 3 That it may be well with thee, and thou mayest live long on the earth. 4 And, ye fathers, provoke not your children to wrath: but bring them up in the nurture and admonition of the Lord. 5 Servants, be obedient to them that are your masters according to the flesh, with fear and trembling, in singleness of your heart, as unto Christ; 6 Not with eyeservice, as menpleasers; but as the servants of Christ, doing the will of God from the heart; 7 With good will doing service, as to the Lord, and not to men: 8 Knowing that whatsoever good thing any man doeth, the same shall he receive of the Lord, whether he be bond or free. 9 And, ye masters, do the same things unto them, forbearing threatening: knowing that your Master also is in heaven; neither is there respect of persons with him.

New Rendition

1 Children, obey your parents in the Lord, for this is right. 2 "Honor your father and your mother"—which is the first commandment with a promise— 3 "that it may be well with you and that you may live long on the earth." 4 And fathers, do not provoke your children to anger; instead, bring them up in the discipline and admonition of the Lord. 5 Slaves, obey the masters of your flesh with fear and trembling in the sincerity of your heart as you do to Christ, 6 not only while being watched—like people-pleasers—but as slaves of Christ, doing the will of God from the heart. 7 Render service with good will, as if you were serving the Lord, not people, 8 because you know that if each person (whether slave or free) does something good, it will be repaid by the Lord. 9 And masters, do the same things to them, dispensing with threats, because you know that you have the same Lord in heavenly realms, and there is no favoritism with him.

Notes on 6:1–9

6:1 *Children:* This noun, the plural of τέκνον (*teknon*), generally relates to a descendant from another person, like a child from a parent.[2] Such children, here tied to a family, are not the same as the "children" in 4:14, where we find the plural of νήπιος (*nēpios*), a noun that centers on the age or legal status of a young person.[3] That said, the fact that children can "obey [their] parents" illustrates that Paul had in mind children who had likely reached the "years of discretion,"[4] an expression that resembles the Latter-day Saint designation "the years of accountability" (D&C 20:71; 137:10). This observation, however, does not remove the possibility that, in worship settings, "infants would be present in their mothers' arms"[5] (see the Note on 6:4).

Because Paul addressed children directly, he obviously expected them to join their families when worshiping, even taking part "in crucial events in the life of the community" (see Acts 21:5). Moreover, because he valued them so highly, all believing parents understood clearly that they were never to participate in the odious practice of abandoning infants or small children. Such an act was simply beyond anything that a Christian parent might even think of doing.[6]

obey your parents: In both Roman and Jewish societies, the authority of the father was absolute in the lives of his children. His influence reached deep into behavior in the home, into education, and into the child's choice of a skill or other work.[7] But for Christians, this authority was to be governed and shaped by both the parents' and the child's relationships to the Lord. No part of the parent-child involvement was to be exercised outside the realm of the Lord's potency. On the one hand, all parental guidance was to be conducted "in the Lord." On the other, a child would also be obeying the Lord while obeying his or her parents, as is the case in Judaism.[8]

obey: Appearing in Ephesians for the first time, the verb ὑπακούω (*hypakouō*) bears the sense of obeying after paying attention to directions. Thus, the gathered crowd in the Capernaum synagogue remarked that

---

2. BDAG, 994.1.a; Louw-Nida, §§10.28, 36; see also Lincoln, *Ephesians,* 403.

3. BDAG, 671.1.b.α.

4. Oepke, *TDNT,* 5:650; see also Lincoln, *Ephesians,* 403; Fowl, *Ephesians,* 192; and Merkle, *Guide,* 195.

5. Oepke, *TDNT,* 5:650.

6. Oepke, *TDNT,* 5:650–51, quotation on 650.

7. Lincoln, *Ephesians,* 398–402.

8. Schrenk and Quell, *TDNT,* 5:975; Lincoln, *Ephesians,* 402–3; contra Larkin, *Handbook,* 144; Winger, *Ephesians,* 657–58.

Jesus "gives orders to evil spirits and they obey [*hypakouō*] him" (Mark 1:27 NIV; see also the Note on 6:5).[9]

in the Lord: This phrase underlines the fundamental ingredient in the relationship between parents and children in Christian homes (see Luke 2:51). Presumably, even if one parent or the other was not a believer, the Lord remained the essential feature for harmony in the home, a harmony that hoped for a complete, eventual union of all family members under the influence of Christ (see 1 Cor. 7:12–14).

According to the textual evidence, some manuscripts omit this phrase. But the majority, including the earliest, $\mathfrak{P}^{46}$, retain it. It may have been omitted to keep from placing a limit on how and when a child would obey, complying only when parents' wishes were from the Lord.[10] In any event, the phrase appears to be genuinely original.

right: Although the adjective δίκαιος (*dikaios*) is customarily translated "righteous" and its verb connects to God's justification of individuals through their faith (see Luke 18:14; Rom. 3:24, 28, 30; 5:1; Gal. 3:24; etc.), in verse 6:1 it bears on one level the meaning "the right thing to do." This sense emerges in a beloved passage where Paul wrote, "Whatsoever things are true, whatsoever things are honest, whatsoever things are just [*dikaios*], whatsoever things are pure, . . . think on these things" (Philip. 4:8).[11] On another level, its sense goes beyond "natural law"—that is, "the right thing to do"—and ties to "the righteous divine order enjoined by the commandment" quoted in the very next verse.[12] This dimension takes its profound character from the phrase "in the Lord,"[13] the controlling person (see Col. 3:20, "well pleasing unto the Lord"). Loyalty to any other higher authority is not in view.

6:2 *Honour thy father and mother:* The quotation matches exactly the original wording in the Septuagint translation of Exodus 20:12. The divine reward for honoring parents is spelled out in the next verse, 6:3, although it reads differently from the Old Testament text: "That it may be well with thee, and that thou mayest live long on the earth." Like Paul, Jesus repeated

---

9. BDAG, 1028.1; Louw-Nida, §36.15; Thayer, *Lexicon,* 638.2; Winger, *Ephesians,* 655–56.

10. Metzger, *Textual Commentary,* 541–42; Best, *Ephesians,* 564; Larkin, *Handbook,* 144–45; Merkle, *Guide,* 196.

11. BDAG, 247.2; Louw-Nida, §66.5; Lincoln, *Ephesians,* 403; Merkle, *Guide,* 196; contra Winger, *Ephesians,* 658.

12. Quell and Schrenk, *TDNT,* 2:188.

13. Schrenk and Quell, *TDNT,* 5:1004 and n. 352.

the commandment to honor parents when he taught the rich, young ruler (see Matt. 19:19; Mark 10:19; and Luke 18:20). On another occasion, Jesus spelled out the penalty for dishonoring parents as it appears in Exodus 21:17: "Let him die the death" by stoning (Matt. 15:4; Mark 7:10).

father: The commandment to honor one's father brings forward a pair of conditions that surround the concept of fatherhood. In one, we glimpse the strong, emotional bonds that bind children to their father. In general, their ties to him are enriched by feelings that are directed to him and to him alone. Even if a child's feelings are those of anger or frustration, that child will suppress them because of the commandment rather than allowing them to erupt. The proof of this observation emerges from the fact that the Old Testament records no instance of patricide. In the other, the teaching that God is a father sprinkles fatherhood with a divine aura. A significant step in this direction arises from the idea that God has a people who are his responsibility, like a father has a family: "The Lord's portion is his people; Jacob is the lot of his inheritance" (Deut. 32:9). More direct is the Psalmist's statement "All of you are children of the most High" (Ps. 82:6).[14] Again, we hear God's voice through Jeremiah: "I am a father to Israel, and Ephraim is my firstborn" (Jer. 31:9; see also Isa. 63:16 and the Notes on 2:18; 3:14).

To continue, the title "God the Father" underscores the fact of God's fatherhood. The notion of God as father emerges out of two defining events. The first was the creation of the world, and the second was the redemption of the Hebrew slaves from Egypt. In the first, the connection to the creation, we hear the words of Isaiah: "O Lord, thou art our father; we are the clay, and thou our potter; and we all are the work of thy hand" (Isa. 64:8). More than a century later, Jeremiah quoted similar words: "O house of Israel . . . as the clay is in the potter's hand, so are ye in mine hand" (Jer. 18:6). In the second, the tie to the Exodus, we hear the voice of God: "Ye are the children of the Lord your God . . . and the Lord hath chosen thee [in Egypt] to be a peculiar people unto himself" (Deut. 14:1–2; see also Ex. 19:4–6 and Deut. 4:20; 7:6–8).

mother: Jesus was interested in both the nuclear, physical family and the family created by the brotherhood and sisterhood of believers. His mother stood front and center. For example, Jesus' concern for his mother appears in John's narration of the scene at the cross, where Jesus entrusted the care of his mother to the disciple "whom he loved" by saying, "Woman, behold thy son" (John 19:26). In the other vein, he previously made clear his intent

---

14. Schrenk and Quell, *TDNT,* 5:964–66.

to create a family from his disciples when, as his mother and brothers stood on the edge of a gathered crowd, "he stretched forth his hand toward his disciples, and said, Behold my mother and my brethren! For whosoever shall do the will of my Father, . . . the same is my brother, and sister, and mother" (Matt. 12:47, 49–50; see also Mark 3:31–35 and Luke 8:19–21).[15]

Another treasured picture arises from the marriage at Cana with Jesus' mother and his disciples present (John 2:1–11). Nowhere in John's Gospel does the name Mary occur. When John wrote about Mary and Jesus together, he typically penned "his mother," with no further elaboration. It was not needed. (see John 2:5, 12; 19:25–26). On the occasion of recounting the marriage in Cana, however, he called Mary "the mother of Jesus" (John 2:1, 3). Wilhelm Michaelis termed this expression "almost as a proper name." Yes, indeed. Even today, Middle Eastern people will call a mother by the name of her first son, "mother of so-and-so." Hence, John presented to his readers the name by which Mary was known in her community and beyond—"the mother of Jesus"—even though friends and family knew her name perfectly well[16] (see Moses 8:12, "the mother of Japheth"; and the Notes on 5:22, 31).

first commandment with promise: The appearance of the noun "promise" (ἐπαγγελία, *epangelia*) occurs for the fourth and last time in Ephesians (see 1:13; 2:12; 3:6). Its companion word "commandment" (ἐντολή, *entolē*) appeared at 2:15. The term *entolē* usually pertains to one of the Old Testament commandments and often to one of the Ten Commandments, as it does here. The idea that it is the first among the Ten Commandments to spell out a promise cannot be true. Why not? Because two earlier commandments in the list of ten append either a promise or a clear sense of celestial blessedness. To be specific, the command not to make a graven image concludes with God's promise that he will show "mercy unto thousands of them that love me, and keep my commandments" (Ex. 20:6). Next, after commanding the Israelites to "remember the sabbath day, to keep it holy," God declared that he had "blessed the sabbath day, and hallowed it" (Ex. 20:11). In this light, what did Paul mean when he wrote "the first commandment with promise"? In reply, this commandment to honor father and mother "has a special significance by reason of the promise annexed" to it in 6:3 (see the Notes on 2:12, 14–15; 3:6).[17]

---

15. Wilhelm Michaelis, *TDNT,* 4:643.

16. Michaelis, *TDNT,* 4:643.

17. Gottlob Schrenk, *TDNT,* 2:552; see also Lincoln, *Ephesians,* 404; Fowl, *Ephesians,* 193.

6:3 *That:* The quotation is almost precisely taken from the Septuagint of Exodus 20:12 except for the verb in the second part of the verse translated "mayest live" and the omitted ending of the Exodus verse, "which the Lord thy God givest thee" (see also LXX Deut. 5:16). Prior to quoting the Exodus passage, Paul had presented two reasons to children to obey their fathers—because of their commitment as Christians "in the Lord" and because obeying was the "right and proper thing to do" (6:1). The lines from the Ten Commandments now offered a third reason, so "that it may be well with thee." Latched onto this third reason came a fourth, that "thou mayest live long on the earth" (6:3).[18]

The conjunction "that" (ἵνα, *hina*) introduces a purpose clause, a clause that sets out why something was undertaken or done ("for the purpose of"). As is evident, the intent of obeying the commandment brings good things to the obedient, good things that are promised and ensured by God, underscoring the reason why a person would follow the directive.[19]

The argument that Paul would not cite such a verse because he lived during the era of high expectation that the Lord would return soon and therefore the idea of believers living long on the earth did not fit the anticipated near return of Christ simply fails.[20] Such a view does not take into account the fact that, during Paul's lifetime, he knew "Christians whose exemplary obedience was nevertheless rewarded by poverty and premature death, starting with Paul himself."[21] Moreover, this kind of viewpoint willfully overlooks what the Apostle himself wrote to his Thessalonian converts. Because a question had arisen about the timing of Christ's return, the issue in play here, he replied in plain language: "Let no one deceive you by any means, because that day [of Christ's return] will not come until the apostasy comes first and the man of lawlessness, who is the son of perdition, is revealed" (2 Thes. 2:3, Wayment). Paul himself understood that a long delay would ensue, and he wrote clearly about that delay (see 2 Thes. 2:1–2; the Notes on 1:23; 3:8; 4:3, 21; 5:27; 6:5; and the Analysis of 3:1–13; 6:1–9).

mayest live: Living life presented its hazards, as Paul's imprisonment illustrated for his readers (see 3:1, 13; 4:1; 6:20). Therefore, "to live" or "to be" (future tense of εἰμί, *eimi*) must carry some incentive. Part of the incentive must have been to engage in winning souls while standing "against

---

18. Lincoln, *Ephesians,* 404.
19. Stauffer, *TDNT,* 3:330; Larkin, *Handbook,* 146; Merkle, *Guide,* 197.
20. Lincoln, *Ephesians,* 406.
21. Muddiman, *Ephesians,* 274; see also Fowl, *Ephesians,* 194.

the wiles of the devil [and] . . . against spiritual wickedness in high places"
(6:11–12). To undertake a harvest of souls as the curtain began to come
down would have been exhilarating and enlivening to persons who sought
the eternal welfare of family and acquaintances. Of course, the challenges
would have been daunting, perhaps almost beyond endurance, because
"the evil day" was surely coming (6:13). But, as Jesus reminded his gathered
Eleven, "greater love hath no man than this, that a man lay down his life
for his friends" (John 15:13). In Paul's words, "I beseech you therefore . . .
that ye present your bodies a living sacrifice, holy, acceptable unto God"
(Rom. 12:1). Beyond this, it is worth observing that living an extended life
offered opportunity to honor those to whom honor and deference was
due—namely, one's parents by taking care of them in their old age just as
the commandment enjoined.

long: The adjective μακροχρόνιος (*makrochronios*) occurs only here
in the New Testament with the meaning "long duration" or "long-lived."[22]
Because the focus rested on living on the earth, a reader was not looking at
a reminder of eternal life. The whole texture of the passage is earthy, of this
world (see 6:5, "masters according to the flesh").[23]

the earth: Reference to the earth (γῆ, *gē*) in LXX Exodus 20:12 and Deuteronomy 5:16 directs readers to the promised land (see Acts 7:3 and Heb.
11:9). But by omitting the line "which the Lord your God giveth thee," Paul
made the heritage of the Saints much larger than the land of Canaan, which
was promised to the ancient Hebrews. The church members were to be like
Abraham, "the heir of the world" (Rom. 4:13). In a word, they were to enjoy
"the entire earth and its fruits"[24] (see the Notes on 1:10; 4:9).

The first line in the biblical text discloses the connection between the
earth and God's activities: "In the beginning God created the heaven and
the earth" (Gen. 1:1). As we learn elsewhere, this creative activity involved
Christ as a coagent (see 3:9; Ps. 24:1; and 1 Cor. 10:26). A pointer to his role
and to a Mother in Heaven appear in the plural pronouns "us" and "our" in
God's declaration of his plan: "Let *us* make man in *our* image, after *our* likeness . . . male and female" (Gen. 1:26–27, emphasis added; compare Moses
2:26–27, "mine Only Begotten"; and Abr. 4:26–27). Even though the earth
is the sphere of human affairs, like Christ, citizens of the earth have come
from a heavenly home and are "strangers and pilgrims on the earth [who]

---

22. LSJ, 1075; Thayer, *Lexicon,* 387.
23. Lincoln, *Ephesians,* 405; Merkle, *Guide,* 197.
24. Winger, *Ephesians,* 661; see also Lincoln, *Ephesians,* 405; Best, *Ephesians,* 567–68.

... seek a [celestial] country" (Heb. 11:13–14). Thus, the earth is the place of transitory events and actions with only modest value except for those who navigate this life with Christ's aid (see 2:12–13). That situation on the earth will change when God fashions new heavens and a new earth, with both getting an extreme makeover (see Isa. 65:17; 66:22; 2 Pet. 3:13; Rev. 21:1;[25] and the Note on 4:9).

6:4 *fathers:* For their children, fathers were responsible for their education and for building their skills, both religious and secular. Paul and his fellow Christians had inherited this role from both their Hellenistic and Jewish cultures. Embracing Christ did not turn fathers from this duty but rather intensified it. In fact, the importance of fathers educating their children brought Paul to say, "Though ye have ten thousand instructors in Christ, yet have ye not many fathers." In fact, for the Apostle, there were two fathers. The one was biological and the other was himself: "For in Christ Jesus I have begotten you through the gospel" (1 Cor. 4:15; see also Philip. 2:22 and 2 Thes. 2:11–13).[26] This pointer to fathers' roles in the gospel education of their children underscores their key function as the force for the steadiness and growth of the Christian faith, which their children would carry out. This observation gathers its proof by linking the fathers' roles with the Lord's.[27]

The suggestion that the term "fathers" draws up the idea of mothers as well is undercut by the perfectly good noun "parents" (plural of γονεύς, *goneus*) that Paul had just written in 6:1. If he had meant parents, he would have written the word. Hence, it is fathers who receive the Apostle's admonition, not mothers.[28] Fathers are to exercise their authority over their children as God does over his children, in love and fairness (see 6:9).[29]

provoke not . . . to wrath: The imperative of the verb παροργίζω (*parorgizō*), which bears the sense "to make angry,"[30] does not indicate that this behavior by fathers was then a difficulty, let alone an ongoing problem.[31] The most frequent occurrences of *parorgizō* in the Septuagint have to do

---

25. Sasse, *TDNT*, 1:678–80.

26. Georg Bertram, *TDNT*, 5:624–25; Schrenk and Quell, *TDNT*, 5:949, 1005–6; Lincoln, *Ephesians*, 406.

27. Schrenk and Quell, *TDNT*, 5:1004.

28. Lincoln, *Ephesians*, 406; Best, *Ephesians*, 568; Merkle, *Guide*, 198; Winger, *Ephesians*, 661–62.

29. Winger, *Ephesians*, 662.

30. BDAG, 780; Louw-Nida, §88.177.

31. Merkle, *Guide*, 198.

with provoking the Lord (see LXX Deut. 4:25; 31:29; 32:21; LXX Judg. 2:12; LXX 3 Kgs. 14:9, 15 [1 Kgs. 14:9, 15 KJV]; etc.). Bible-reading fathers would have been aware of this verb's association with that kind of provocation and would have sensed that Paul wrote the verb to send a strong message.

Another message lies amidst these early verses of chapter six. It touches on reciprocal relationships. Paul had written that children should obey their parents and that this obedience should reflect the obedience that those same children should exhibit toward God, a notion clearly implicit in his quotation of the divine command to honor one's father and mother (see 6:1–2). In an almost dancing motion, he then twirled around to fathers, with perhaps mothers and his prior insistence that children obey parents in mind. He now made the case that, for children's obedience, fathers were to proceed with gentleness, not demands; with encouragement, not with anger; with love unfeigned, not with provocation.[32] After all, anger will "give place to the devil" (4:27).

bring them up: The verb ἐκτρέφω (*ektrephō*), here in the imperative, also occurred in 5:29, where it was translated "nourishes" (NR). There, it focused on self-preservation or self-elevation. In this passage, 6:4, it has found an object in the children with the meaning "to rear" or "to bring up" (see Luke 4:16; Acts 7:21; and 1 Tim. 5:10).[33] Paul's encouragement that fathers raise their children properly hints that he does not expect the end-time to arrive anytime soon. Life is to go on as normal (see the Notes on 5:29; 6:3).[34]

nurture: The noun παιδεία (*paideia*) almost always links to the meaning "education" or "training."[35] Although the instruction envisioned here did not discount secular education, the fact that the fathers were believers wraps an informative Christian covering around the experience for children.[36] The content of the training was to anchor their souls to "the Lord." Assumed in this activity is the observation that these children had reached the "years of discretion"—that is, an age wherein they could grasp the difference between right and wrong—could understand mature concepts, and could also participate fully in the worship life of their branch of the church (see "age of accountability" in D&C 20:71; 137:10; see also "accountable"

---

32. Bruce, *Ephesians,* 122.
33. BDAG, 311.2; Louw-Nida, §35.51.
34. Best, *Ephesians,* 570.
35. BDAG, 748.1.
36. Bertram, *TDNT,* 5:624.

in Moro. 8:10).[37] No one knows the exact educational content of the children's instruction. Even when paired with the next noun, "admonition," we are left to surmise the content.[38] However, hints lie around in Ephesians that begin to form an image. But they do not offer a sketch of what children would have learned or experienced in local schools. What we glimpse is their religious training, doubtless received mostly in their homes. In the view of modern scripture, parents "that teach [children] not to understand the doctrine . . . the sin be upon the heads of the parents" (D&C 68:25).

First, believers' children learned "psalms and hymns and spiritual songs" (5:19). Margaret Barker holds the viewpoint that these musical selections came from temple worship at Jerusalem rather than "from the synagogue."[39] Christians, of course, had no hymns ready at hand when Jesus ascended into heaven. Except for early Christian compositions that remain unknown, the music for worship had to come from someplace. For example, the "hymn" that Jesus and the Eleven sang together at the end of the Last Supper consisted of the final four Hallel psalms, Psalms 115–18 (see Matt. 26:30 and Mark 14:26; they had already sung the first two at the beginning of the Passover meal).[40] Earlier that afternoon, a Levitical choir had sung those six pieces, Psalms 113–18, three times in the temple as men and boys ritually slaughtered the lambs that would be roasted for the Passover celebration.[41] Thus, such psalms served as worship aids in settings as diverse as the temple and private gatherings of worshipers outside the temple (see the Note on 5:19).

Second, in Ephesians we come upon the reality of "light," specifically light that comes from Christ (5:14). In this letter, Paul has called believers "children of light" and has written that they were "light in the Lord" (5:8). As such, they were to avoid and reprove "the unfruitful works of darkness" (5:11). All of this, as we learned in the Note on 5:8, points to a light that persons possess innately. But this light has to be coaxed into full flower in part by instruction. Of course, that blossoming comes about principally because "Christ shall give thee light" (5:14). This process is also helped by a person keeping his or her eye single toward God's glory, as in "when

---

37. Oepke, *TDNT*, 5:650; see also Lincoln, *Ephesians*, 403; Fowl, *Ephesians*, 192; Merkle, *Guide*, 195.

38. Best, *Ephesians*, 569.

39. Barker, *Great High Priest*, 141; contra Victor H. Matthews, "Music and Musical Instruments," in *ABD*, 4:934.

40. *Mishnah Pesahim*, 10:5–6, in Danby, *Mishnah*, 151 nn. 2–4.

41. Edersheim, *Temple*, 223–24.

thine eye is single, thy whole body also is full of light." If, on the other hand, "thine eye is [fixed on] evil, thy body also is full of darkness" (Luke 11:34; see also Luke 11:36 and Matt. 6:22). The sense arises from the observation that what a person takes in through the eyes directly influences behavior. And an education guided by a believing father or other Christian teacher will have introduced a child to the realm of revealed truth, to the world of celestial light.

This understanding of light ties to the temple, not to the synagogue nor to pagan institutions. In the first place, the Holy of Holies was thought of as a place of light even though it was completely dark inside. How so? Because, as Ezekiel learned, this room was the place of God's chariot-throne, which glowed with fire (see Ezek. 1:26–28; 10:4, 18; 11:22–23, where "the midst of the city" sends readers to the Holy of Holies). Likewise, Daniel saw in vision "the Ancient of days," namely God, "whose garment was white as snow, and the hair of his head like the pure wool: his throne was like the fiery flame" (Dan. 7:9). Within the earthly temple burned bright lights at the ends of the seven arms of the giant candlestick, the menorah, that were kept burning all day and all night in the holy place (see Ex. 27:20–21). In expressions suffused with temple imagery, those who are "called . . . out of darkness into his marvelous light" become "a chosen generation, a royal priesthood, an holy nation, a peculiar people" (1 Pet. 2:9).[42] Those were worthy goals for children.

Third, in their religious education, children would naturally have learned about Christ. Paul informed readers of Ephesians about some of the most important characteristics of Christ. He is the one in whom, "in the dispensation of the fulness of times," God will "gather together in one all things . . . both which are in heaven, and which are on earth" (1:10; see also Col. 1:17).[43] He is the one who has brought about "redemption through his blood, the forgiveness of sins" (1:7). He is the one who has "abolished in his flesh the enmity" between Jew and Gentile (2:15). He is the one who has offered to all "access by one Spirit unto the Father" (2:18). He is "the chief corner stone" in "the household of God" (2:19–21). He is the creator of "all things" under the direction of his Father (3:9; Col. 1:16). And, as all children in the church had learned, Paul himself was the recipient of a special revelation from Christ (see 3:2–4, 7–9).

---

42. Barker, *Great High Priest*, 185–87.
43. Barker, *Great High Priest*, 249.

Without trying to be exhaustive, it is possible to expand this list to include other doctrines and principles that the Apostle has touched on in Ephesians and that would frame suitable topics for the religious education of children. Such a register would embrace the majesty of God the Father, a theme that Paul has displayed in bright hues throughout the letter (see 1:3–6, 9–11, 19–22; 2:1, 4–7, 10; 3:2–3, 15, 20; etc.). The docket would include how children are to treat parents and domestic helpers (see 6:1–3, 9). The listing would incorporate how to face personal trials and the looming apostasy (see 5:6–7, 11–12; 6:11–13, 18). Not least, the registry would bear on the value of scripture (see 6:17, "the word of God") and the rewards promised for faithful living (see 1:11, 14; 2:4–7, 18–22; 3:6, 16–20; 4:7, 23–24; 5:14; and the Note on 6:1).

admonition: The term νουθεσία (*nouthesia*) differs little from *paideia* except to say that it usually characterizes corrective oral instruction that serves to warn or exhort. The translation "admonition" is correct.[44] In another place, Paul wrote that Old Testament events that displayed God's wrath "happened to them as examples and were written down as warnings [*nouthesia*] for us" (1 Cor. 10:11 NIV). The key for fathers is to admonish without "provoking or embittering."[45]

of the Lord: As in other passages in Ephesians, Paul has acknowledged "the Lord" as the agent who makes things happen (see 2:21; 5:8, 19, 22, 29; 6:1, 8, 10). With the addition of the phrase "of the Lord," readers have learned that the Lord is "the ultimate instructor who works through the father."[46]

6:5 Servants: The noun is the plural of δοῦλος (*doulos*) and appears here for the first time in the letter. It will occur twice more in this chapter (see 6:6, 8, "bond"). The meaning of the singular is "a male slave."[47] In this spot, the term opens a new paragraph. Paul is obviously not addressing just any group of slaves but those who have embraced the Christian faith. Significantly, beginning with Jesus, these people have always been welcomed in the gospel as equal to other followers. Why? Because all are in need of Christ's redeeming powers. None can escape worldly influences, no matter their rank or earthly circumstance. Jesus' words "No man [or woman] can serve two masters" applies particularly to a person's relationship to him

44. BDAG, 679; Thayer, *Lexicon*, 429; Merkle, *Guide*, 198.

45. Johannes Behm and Ernst Würthwein, *TDNT*, 4:1021.

46. Best, *Ephesians*, 569.

47. Karl Heinrich Rengstorf, *TDNT*, 2:48; BDAG, 259–60; Louw-Nida, §87.76; Thayer, *Lexicon*, 157–58.

(Matt. 6:24; see also Luke 16:13). Paul solved the dilemma for Christian slaves by mandating that they perform their "service, as to the Lord" (6:7). In effect, these enslaved people were to serve the Lord by faithfully serving their masters, as if "doing the will of God from the heart" (6:6). Hence, for a believer, service of any kind stands on the same level as other types of service. There is no difference. Said another way, "the primary goal of the slave won for Christ is not the attainment of freedom; it is that as a slave he [or she] should live unto the Lord like all those for whom He died" (see Rom. 14:7–13; 2 Cor. 5:15;[48] and the Notes on 4:1; 6:6).

We must turn to a different observation. A careful reading of the situation of slaves as envisioned in the following lines, 6:5–8, leads a person to conclude that "Paul shows himself to be naïvely innocent of the practicalities of slave-ownership." To be sure, he had observed slaves and slave masters in their interactions. But he was surely not an owner because nothing in the New Testament even remotely hints at such a status. Thus, this naïveté on the Apostle's part "is one further reason for attributing the slave sections of Colossians and Ephesians to his own hand"[49] (see the Notes on 1:23; 3:8; 4:3, 21; 5:27; 6:3; and the Analysis of 3:1–13; 6:1–9).

be obedient: This verb is exactly the same as in 6:1 (ὑπακούω, *hypakouō*) and is employed in narrating how demons and nature respond to Jesus' commands. We read the reaction of a crowd to Jesus casting out "an unclean spirit" from a man attending a synagogue service: "With authority commandeth he even the unclean spirits, and they do obey [*hypakouō*] him" (Mark 1:23, 27). Incidentally, from this scene, a person gains a sense about the generous character of the worshipers at the synagogue, who allowed the bedeviled man into their midst for a Sabbath meeting. In a second example, we run upon the disciples' response to Jesus calming the wild winds and waves on the Sea of Galilee: "They feared . . . and said one to another, What manner of man is this, that even the wind and sea obey [*hypakouō*] him?" (Mark 4:41; see also Matt. 8:27 and Luke 8:25).[50] This verb also applies to a believer's march to salvation, as Paul reminded his friends in Philippi: "As ye have always obeyed [*hypakouō*], not as in my presence only, but now much more in my absence, work out your own salvation with fear and trembling" (Philip. 2:12; see also the Note on 6:1).[51]

---

48. Rengstorf, *TDNT*, 2:270–72, quotation on 272.
49. Muddiman, *Ephesians*, 280.
50. Gerhard Kittel, *TDNT*, 1:223.
51. Kittel, *TDNT*, 1:224.

masters: The noun κύριος (*kyrios*) is the same as that applied to Christ when calling him Lord. The obviously different meaning arises because of the secular context (compare the religious tone in 6:9, "your Master . . . in heaven" is Christ). Throughout the New Testament, *kyrios* in secular settings bears the sense of master, owner, or lord. We come across this meaning in Jesus' parable of the wicked husbandmen, who physically abused the owner's representatives and, frighteningly, killed the heir. Jesus then asked the question, "What shall therefore the lord [*kyrios*] of the vineyard do?" (Mark 12:9). In a different story about planting and harvesting, this time about a fig tree, the owner was discouraged that the tree had not produced fruit within three years and wanted to cut it down. His more optimistic "dresser of his vineyard" pled, "Lord [*kyrios*], let it alone this year also, till I shall dig about it, and dung it" (Luke 13:7–8). When Paul wanted to make a point about heirship, he wrote about the heir, "a child," who, because of his youth and owing to his legal status, "differeth nothing from a servant, though he be [the future] lord [*kyrios*] of all" (Gal. 4:1).

In contrast, God is also called *kyrios* but almost exclusively in quotations from and allusions to the Old Testament. For instance, when Mary began her song, called the Magnificat, she sang, "My soul doth magnify the Lord [*kyrios*]" (Luke 1:46). As Jesus stood before the congregation in the Nazareth synagogue, he announced who he was by quoting the lines from Isaiah 61:1–2: "The spirit of the Lord [*kyrios*] is upon me, because he hath anointed me to preach . . . the acceptable year of the Lord [*kyrios*]" (Luke 4:18–19). When Jesus referred to himself as the capstone, he asked, "Haven't you read this scripture: 'The stone the builders rejected has become the capstone; the Lord [*kyrios*] has done this, and it is marvelous in our eyes'?" (Mark 12:10–11 NIV). When Jesus and his entourage crossed the Mount of Olives on their way to Jerusalem, fellow travelers "cried, saying, Hosanna; Blessed is he that cometh in the name of the Lord [*kyrios*]" (Mark 11:9). When Peter and John recounted what happened during their hearing before the Jerusalem Sanhedrin, they quoted to their fellow believers Psalm 2:1–2: "The kings of the earth stood up, and the rulers were gathered together against the Lord [*kyrios*], and against his Christ" (Acts 4:25–26). Each of these occurrences of *kyrios,* and more, point to God the Father.[52]

---

52. Quell and Foerster, *TDNT,* 3:1086–87. See Matt. 27:10; John 12:38; Acts 2:20–21, 34; 13:10; Rom. 4:8; 9:28; 11:34; 15:11; 1 Cor. 1:31; 3:20; 10:22, 26; 2 Cor. 3:16; etc.

Latter-day Saints should not be surprised that in quoted scripture "the Lord" can refer to God the Father. Three instances will make the case. In a long quotation of the Father's words recorded in 3 Nephi 16, the Resurrected Christ pulled language from Micah in reference to the Gentiles and their role in gathering God's people at the end-time. In a passage that features the actions of the Father, we read, "I will not suffer my people, who are of the house of Israel, to go through among them, and tread them down, saith the Father" (3 Ne. 16:14). These words echo those in Micah 5:8 that are ascribed to "the Lord" in Micah 5:10: "The remnant of Jacob shall be among the Gentiles ... as a young lion ... who, if he go through, both treadeth down, and teareth in pieces." The image of victorious Israelites is basically the same. The difference is that, in 3 Nephi 16:14, the Father "will *not* suffer my people ... to go through among [the Gentiles], and tread them down" (emphasis added). A second example brings more clarity. In a virtual quotation of Isaiah 52:12, Christ omitted "the Lord" from Isaiah's words and substituted "the Father" in 3 Nephi 21:29. We read, "The Lord will go before you" (Isa. 52:12), but "I will go before them, saith the Father" (3 Ne. 21:29). The matter becomes even more plain elsewhere in 3 Nephi 21. In this chapter, we run across an extended quotation from Micah 5:8–14, with additions from the Savior himself. In a clear sample, we read in Micah 5:10, "It shall come to pass in that day, *saith the Lord,* that I will cut off thy horses" (emphasis added). In quoting this very passage, the Risen Christ rendered it in these words: "It shall come to pass in that day, *saith the Father,* that I will cut off thy horses" (3 Ne. 21:14, emphasis added). Hence, an Old Testament saying attributed to "the Lord" is put in the mouth of "the Father" in the Book of Mormon (see the Note on 6:9).

according to the flesh: This phrase secures the secular character of *kyrios,* translated as "masters" (see the Note above).[53] In contrast, we read later about "your Master ... in heaven" (6:9). The difference is obvious. What Paul meant to do was to place obedience to one's earthly master on the same continuum as obedience to the heavenly master, adding the phrase "as unto the Lord."[54] But this point should not encourage readers to see masters "according to the flesh" as representatives of the celestial Lord. Far from it. "Rather, in their service to their [mortal] masters, slaves are to see the opportunity to serve Christ and to perform their work as if they were doing it for Christ."[55]

---

53. Fowl, *Ephesians,* 196; Merkle, *Guide,* 202.
54. Merkle, *Guide,* 202.
55. Lincoln, *Ephesians,* 421.

flesh: Forming a further pillar for the case that "masters" in this verse are secular, the noun σάρξ (*sarx*) pertains in another context to those who "in time past [were] Gentiles in the flesh [and who] . . . were without Christ . . . and without God in the world" (2:11–12). Into the believing Gentiles' lives came "Christ Jesus [who] . . . made them nigh by the blood of Christ" (2:13).[56] The physical reality of Christ's blood has created an unspeakable difference in the lives of believing Gentiles. One of the blessings that has come to them is that "the enmity" between them and Jews has been "abolished in [Christ's] flesh" (2:15; see also the Notes on 2:3, 11, 15; 5:29–31; 6:12).

with fear and trembling: This prepositional phrase occurs in two other letters (see 2 Cor. 7:15 and Philip. 2:12). The preposition translated "with" (μετά, *meta*) appears in connection with objects and things more regularly than with persons.[57]

The noun "fear" (φόβος, *phobos*) describes generally a slave's attitude toward an earthly master, even if the two are on good terms. For Paul, in another passage, this attitude forms an element of respect or "reverence" (see 1 Cor. 2:3 and the Note on 5:21).

The next noun, "trembling" (τρόμος, *tromos*), lifts up interesting connections. This term carries the meaning of "quivering" or "trembling."[58] This sense certainly fits within the world of slaves because they know that their masters and mistresses possess enormous power over their lives. And they would likely tremble uncontrollably, at least inwardly, if a person with that kind of power turned against them. Notably, trembling also flowers in contact with divinity. We come upon the response of the woman plagued by "an issue of blood twelve years" when Jesus called her into the midst of the gathered crowd through which she had pushed in order to touch his garment to be healed. We read that "when the woman saw that she was not hid, she came trembling, and falling down before him" (Luke 8:43, 47; see also Mark 5:33).[59] A second example comes from the experience of the former Hebrew slaves as they gathered at the foot of Mount Sinai and heard God's voice. Their experience of witnessing "the thunderings, and the lightnings, and the noise of the trumpet, and the mountain smoking" is cataloged in these words: "When the people saw it, they removed, and stood afar off"

---

56. Schweizer, Baumgärtel, and Meyer, *TDNT,* 7:136.
57. Grundmann, *TDNT,* 7:772; Louw-Nida, §89.109.
58. BDAG, 1016; Louw-Nida, §16.6.
59. Brown, *Testimony of Luke,* 431–35.

(Ex. 20:18). The issue has to do with the term translated "removed" in the KJV. The Hebrew verb נוע (*nua*) at base means "to sway back and forth." In this Exodus passage, it bears the sense "to tremble," as it does when the temple's threshhold shook during Isaiah's vision (see Isa. 6:4) and the gods of Egypt trembled at the approach of the Lord (see Isa. 19:1).[60] On a spiritual level, all of this, the fear and the trembling, come down to an ongoing, submissive humility in God's sight and presence.[61]

singleness: The noun ἁπλότης (*haplotēs*) conveys the senses "sincerity" and "generosity." The translation "singleness of heart" in our verse, 6:5, captures its essence.[62] A reader encounters this meaning in passages such as Paul's instructions about how individuals should apply their heavenly endowments in the service of others: "If it is giving, let him [and her] give with sincerity [*haplotēs*]" (Rom. 12:8, Wayment); and such as the Apostle's praise of the Saints of Macedonia, who gave beyond their means to relieve the poor in far-off Judea: "We want you to know about the grace that God has given the Macedonian churches. Out of the most severe trial, their overflowing joy and their extreme poverty welled up in rich generosity [*haplotēs*]" (2 Cor. 8:1–2 NIV).

heart: In the Old Testament, the heart (לב, *lev*) was the seat or center of a person's understanding, emotions, and motivations. We meet a classical passage in God's words to the prophet Hosea when describing that he intended to bring Israel, his wayward bride, back to himself. He declared, "I am going to lure her and lead her out into the wilderness and speak to her heart [*lev*]." Plainly, he wanted to take her back into the wilderness to begin anew his covenant that he had established with her at Sinai. His effort was intended to appeal to the Israelites' intellect by persuasive talk, to their emotions by speaking to their hearts, and to their motives by enticing them to turn their energies and thoughts back to him. Not to be lost is the disruptive physical act of moving back into the desert. At the end of this process, God hoped, "She will call me 'My husband,' no longer will she call me 'My Baal'" (Hosea 2:14, 16, Jerusalem Bible). What do these words all mean? That God's "unconditional love is the only requirement for the healing of faithlessness and shows his punishment to be an act of love."[63]

---

60. Helmer Ringgren, *TDOT,* 9:294.
61. Balz and Wanke, *TDNT,* 9:217.
62. Otto Bauernfeind, *TDNT,* 1:386–87; BDAG, 104.
63. Heinz-Josef Fabry, *TDOT,* 7:418.

All of these traits of the heart migrated into the New Testament. In Ephesians, the heart (καρδία, *kardia*) is the place where religious sensibilities reside, where the divine can penetrate, where "Christ may dwell in your hearts by faith" (3:17). Remarkably, Jesus taught that the "pure in heart" will be able to "see God" and receive divine "rest" (Matt. 5:8; 11:29). Further, the "good man out of the good treasure of his heart bringeth forth that which is good." Regrettably, the "evil man out of the evil treasure of his heart bringeth forth that which is evil" (Luke 6:45). In the end, as Paul earnestly prayed, "May [God] strengthen your hearts so that you will be blameless and holy in the presence of our God and Father when our Lord Jesus comes with all his holy ones" (1 Thes. 3:13 NIV). Obviously, the Apostle's desire focused on the heart of the redeemed (see the Notes on 4:18; 5:19).[64]

as unto Christ: Everything that the Apostle has written in verses 6:5–8 hangs on this phrase and those like it: "as the servants of Christ" (6:6) and "as to the Lord" (6:7).[65] Even in the workaday world, every situation that a slave encounters will present a celestial, Christ-driven flow within it, something that the slave can experience either in eternal terms or in terms of the here and now (see Mosiah 24:15, "submit cheerfully and with patience to all the will of the Lord").

6:6 *eyeservice:* The unusual noun ὀφθαλμοδουλία (*ophthalmodoulia*) occurs only here and in Colossians 3:22, with the meaning "service that is performed only to make an impression in the owner's presence."[66] This approach to service for a master or mistress stands in contrast to service "from the heart." For the slave to take on tasks merely in order to please, but with a hidden, grudging attitude, cankers that person's soul and leaves the slave bereft of a lofty "dedication and with no sense of inner obligation to the master for the sake of God and of Christ."[67] Hence, the slave, a precious soul to God, is lost.

menpleasers: This term, the plural of ἀνθρωπάρεσκος (*anthrōpareskos*), directs us to a "fawner," to one who curries the favor of other people.[68] This inclination, "born of fear and quite natural in slaves," latches onto the human world, where power is visibly manifested, and, generally, where people turn their backs on God.[69] Implicit is the sense that, when the attention of the master or mistress is turned away, the slave "acts differently"

---

64. Baumgärtel and Behm, *TDNT*, 3:612–13.
65. Schrenk and Quell, *TDNT*, 5:1004.
66. BDAG, 744; see also Thayer, *Lexicon*, 469.
67. Karl Heinrich Rengstorf, *TDNT*, 2:280.
68. BDAG, 80; Thayer, *Lexicon*, 46.
69. Werner Foerster, *TDNT*, 1:456; Winger, *Ephesians*, 667.

(see Matt. 24:45–51 and Luke 12:41–46).[70] Elsewhere, Paul has written about pleasing others and thereby not pleasing God. In his frustration directed against his Galatian converts, who were then swerving away from the gospel message, he thundered, "Do I now persuade men, or God? or do I seek to please men? for if I yet pleased men, I should not be the servant of Christ" (Gal. 1:10; see also 1 Thes. 2:4).

servants of Christ: The Christian viewpoint framed servanthood in a different way from how the external world pictured it. By Paul's reckoning, all believers are servants or slaves of Christ and were slaves to sin before conversion, including Christian masters and mistresses whose "Master also is in heaven" (6:9). We read the Apostle's words to the Christians in Corinth: "He who was called in the Lord as a slave is a freedman of the Lord. Likewise he who was free when called is a slave of Christ. You were [all] bought with a price" (1 Cor. 7:22–23 RSV). Even though Paul seems to be saying that the slave convert is free, that is true only on a spiritual level. For "if you present yourselves as obedient slaves, you are slaves of the one whom you obey, whether to sin which results in death, or to obedience which results in righteousness." With palpable relief, Paul states, "Thanks be to God . . . that you were set free from sin and became enslaved to righteousness" through Christ (Rom. 6:16–18, Wayment;[71] see also Acts 20:19; Rom. 1:1, "a servant of Jesus Christ"; 2 Cor. 4:5; Gal. 1:10; Philip. 1:1; Col. 4:12; and the Notes on 4:1; 6:5).

doing: The participle of ποιέω (*poieō*) plays up "the importance of practical observance"; that is to say, it intensifies the importance of works.[72] Ultimately, the object of believers is to do what God commands and not to do that which is forbidden. This notion derives from the Old Testament and receives support within the New. From the mouth of the man born blind to whom Jesus gave his sight, we hear his response to the Savior's detractors: "We know that God heareth not sinners: but if any man be a worshipper of God, and doeth [*poieō*] his will [like Jesus], him he heareth" (John 9:31). Inevitably, heavenly "fruits" will accompany such works, including "customs" that seem strange to nonmembers (see Acts 16:20–21). For repentance and its motives are set up to produce such outcomes. To "the Pharisees and Sadducees," John the Baptist hissed, "O generation of vipers, who hath warned you to flee from the wrath to come? Bring forth therefore fruits meet for repentance."[73] Indeed! (See the Notes on 2:3; 6:8.)

---

70. Muddiman, *Ephesians*, 279; Lincoln, *Ephesians*, 421.

71. Rengstorf, *TDNT*, 2:274.

72. Braun, *TDNT*, 6:479.

73. Matt. 3:7–8; see also Matt. 21:43; Braun, *TDNT*, 6:479.

will of God: As we have noticed in the prior note, the duty of all believers is to do the will of God. That imperative did not go away for slaves, no matter how easy or harsh their situation. It was God's will that dominated the lives and actions of all Christians. This had been the theme since the early days of Jesus' ministry: "Not every one that saith unto me, Lord, Lord, shall enter into the kingdom of heaven; but he that *doeth the will* of my Father which is in heaven" (Matt. 7:21, emphasis added). Later from Jesus' own mouth came the words, "Whosoever shall *do the will* of my Father which is in heaven, the same is my brother, and sister, and mother" (Matt. 12:50, emphasis added; see also Luke 12:47).[74]

will: Even though the meaning of the noun θέλημα (*thelēma*) can shade into "desire" (see 1 Cor. 7:37),[75] God's desires and his will line up perfectly. As a divine expression that sits on the continuum that links "desire" and "will," the following lines from modern scripture express God's intent: "This is my work and my glory—to bring to pass the immortality and eternal life of man" (Moses 1:39). This saying represents the macro view, the big picture. But God's will also operates in the micro world, in the lives of individuals. That fact emerges from the experience of Paul with the Resurrected Christ on the road from Jerusalem to Damascus. In a muscular manifestation of God's will for an individual, the Apostle received the following about his future ministry among Gentiles during the initial vision: "Now I send thee, to open their eyes, and to turn them from darkness to light, and from the power of Satan unto God, that they may receive forgiveness of sins, and inheritance among them which are sanctified by faith that is in me" (Acts 26:17–18). Continuing the personal focus on Paul, we encounter Ananias, the faithful man who blessed Paul to receive his sight. The Lord told Ananias before he even met Paul that Paul was "a chosen vessel unto me, to bear my name before the Gentiles, and kings, and the children of Israel" (Acts 9:15). From Ananias came these words during his blessing: "The God of our fathers hath chosen thee [Paul], that thou shouldest know his will [*thelēma*], [and] . . . be his witness unto all men of what thou hast seen and heard" (Acts 22:14–15).

Although no one's experiences in life will even approximate those of Paul, each person has a specific place in God's design which is unique to that individual, like the differing parts of the body (see Rom. 12:4 and 1 Cor. 12:12–31). As Paul wrote in another place, "It is God who works in [each of] you to will and to act according to his good purpose" (Philip. 2:13 NIV). The key is God's will that is realized through every believer. The results will

---

74. Winger, *Ephesians*, 667.

75. Louw-Nida, §25.2.

be astonishing, with God himself both "working in you that which is well pleasing in his sight, through Jesus Christ" (Heb. 13:21) and transforming every person "by the renewing of your mind, so that you determine what the will of God is, what is good, acceptable, and perfect" (Rom. 12:2, Wayment). To the Saints in Corinth, Paul wrote in very personal tones that "now we [each] see through a glass, darkly; but then face to face" (1 Cor. 13:12;[76] see also the Notes on 1:1, 5; 2:3; 5:17; 6:8).

from the heart: The phrase may be better rendered "from the soul [ψυχή, *psychē*]." Although "from the heart" seems to capture the meaning,[77] the translation "from one's very being" is intriguing and suggests the deep inducement whereby Paul wanted to motivate slaves.[78] As Gottlob Schrenk wrote, "This doing [from the heart] is the epitome which provides the impulse for the whole conduct of life."[79] What is more, this "doing the will of God from the heart" comes down to "the giving of that which constitutes life, e.g., time, energy, and health."[80] In sum, serving "from the heart" means that believing persons consecrate their time, property, and talents to serve and benefit others.

6:7 *good will:* As laid out here, the thought of "good will" or "eagerness" (εὔνοια, *eunoia*) takes on the flavor of a subordinate to a master.[81] Over time, the noun *eunoia* had occurred in a variety of contexts, from marriage contracts to treaties and from descriptions of the goodwill of rulers toward their subjects to statements of affection between relatives. As we have already witnessed, in Paul's hands a slave's eagerness to serve a master or mistress rested on a religious foundation, on a commitment to do the right thing because, in the long view, actions undertaken with ill intent— that is, not "as [if] to the Lord"—would be settled in a celestial courtroom on Judgment Day.[82]

doing service: The participle of δουλεύω (*douleuō*) here means "performing the duties of a slave."[83] Paul has employed a verb with a secular past but added a spiritual twist. To illustrate, we read his words to the Roman Saints about sin: "Our old man is crucified with [Christ], that the body of sin might

---

76. Schrenk, *TDNT,* 3:58.

77. Best, *Ephesians,* 578.

78. Winger, *Ephesians,* 667.

79. Schrenk, *TDNT,* 3:58.

80. Georg Bertram, Albert Dihle, Edmond Jacob, Eduard Lohse, Eduard Schweizer, and Karl-Wolfgang Tröger, *TDNT,* 9:648.

81. BDAG, 409.2; Louw-Nida, §25.72.

82. Johannes Behm and Ernst Würthwein, *TDNT,* 4:972–73.

83. BDAG, 259.2.

be destroyed, that henceforth we should not serve [*douleuō*] sin" (Rom. 6:6). In lines addressed to the believing Jews in the same city, he wrote the following about the Mosaic law: "Now we are delivered from the law . . . that we should serve [*douleuō*] in newness of spirit, and not in the oldness of the letter" (Rom. 7:6).

as to the Lord: Continuing the exalting image observed in other verses, this phrase paints in the brightest and most colorful hues the one who serves because of his or her righteous actions (compare "as unto Christ" [6:5], "as the servants of Christ," and "from the heart" [6:6]). The application of the principle to all kinds of service by believers, aimed at members and non-members alike, is readily apparent.[84] To the individual, the path is clear: "As ye have therefore received Christ Jesus the Lord, so walk ye in him" (Col. 2:6). Such a posture, effectively dedicating our lives' actions to "Christ Jesus the Lord," acknowledges that, on the grand, cosmic scale, "he is before all things, and by him all things consist" (Col. 1:17). Said another way that entwines with his Atonement, he is the one who, "through the blood of his cross, [will] . . . reconcile all things unto himself . . . whether they be things in earth, or things in heaven" (Col. 1:20). In Christ's case, "when all things shall be subdued unto him, then shall the Son also himself be subject unto him that put all things under him, that God may be all in all" (1 Cor. 15:28). Hence, an individual's willingness to do "as to the Lord" is enfolded into a divinely driven pattern that fulfills "the will of God" (6:6; see also Mosiah 24:15, "submit cheerfully and with patience to all the will of the Lord").[85]

6:8 *Knowing:* This kind of construction, a participle of perception followed by "that," identifies the readers as the recipients of Paul's instructions rather than those who are the objects of his words, slaves in this case (compare 6:9).[86] This wording casts Paul's net wider and enfolds all his letter's recipients.

good thing: Paul has now led his readers to rewards for good behavior.[87] They are based, as one might expect, on good things done. Although it is not possible to distinguish in Paul's term (ἀγαθόν, *agathon*)[88] between good actions done because they were required by the mistress or master and good deeds performed without instruction, both types of good performance will bring forth rewards for good things accomplished.

---

84. Schrenk and Quell, *TDNT,* 5:1004.
85. Quell and Foerster, *TDNT,* 3:1090.
86. Muddiman, *Ephesians,* 280; contra Best, *Ephesians,* 578–79.
87. Lincoln, *Ephesians,* 422–23; Merkle, *Guide,* 204.
88. BDAG, 3.1.b and 4.2.b; Thayer, *Lexicon,* 3.

any man: The NR captures the real sense of the distributive pronoun ἕκαστος (*hekastos*) by rendering it "each person."[89] Hence, Paul's focus is trained on the one, on the individual (see the Note on 6:6).

doeth: In prior verses, readers bumped into "doing the will of God" (6:6) and "doing service" (6:7). The verb here is a form of the verb ποιέω (*poieō*), as in 6:6, though in the subjunctive mood. Once again, the stress is on works, pure and simple. In the Old Testament, the matter was framed by the concept of obeying in contrast to the perfunctory offering of sacrifices. To the headstrong King Saul, the prophet Samuel almost roared, "To obey is better than sacrifice, and to hearken than the fat of rams" (1 Sam. 15:22). Through the prophet Hosea, God declared, "I desired [acts of] mercy, and not sacrifice; and the knowledge of God more than burnt offerings" (Hosea 6:6). The feat of inching toward God's altar, whether in an act of worship or in an effort to be close to the holy, does not override the need to obey. Jesus hit this concept hard when he warned that "many will say to me in that day, Lord, Lord, have we not prophesied in thy name? and in thy name have cast out devils? and in thy name done many wonderful works? And then will I profess unto them, I never knew you: depart from me, ye that work iniquity" (Matt. 7:22–23). The basic message is that it does not matter how close we may sit to the divine or to those in power. What matters is that, in obeying, we do the works of God, the good things. We meet the negative elsewhere: "He that doeth wrong shall receive for the wrong which he hath done" (Col. 3:25; see also 2 Cor. 5:10 and the Notes on 2:3; 6:6).[90]

the same: The Greek text features the demonstrative pronoun τοῦτο (*touto*), which means "this thing" or "this one."[91] Its referent is ἀγαθόν (*agathon*), the "good [heavenly] thing." The pronoun *touto*, of course, centers on the divine reward. A reader must remember that doing the "good thing" means doing things in God's way, according to "the will of God" (6:6). With divine help, a person's charitable and dutiful actions make a deeper and more lasting impact. This essence arises from Paul's earlier words: "We are [God's] workmanship." This means that believers were "created in Christ Jesus unto good works" that mesh with a divine design. That framework of heavenly assisted efforts "God hath before ordained that we should walk in them" (2:10). It is by becoming "children of light" (5:8) that believers enjoy the multiplied effect of their good works and therefore

---

89. BDAG, 298.b; Thayer, *Lexicon,* 192.
90. Braun, *TDNT,* 6:479.
91. BDAG, 740–41; Thayer, *Lexicon,* 466–67.

stand as recipients of God's grand rewards.[92] On the level of a slave's life, the promise holds out a reward in the next life if not in this. It is important to add that Paul's words do not hint at freedom or manumission for a slave.[93]

receive of the Lord: Here, Paul identified the source of real rewards. That source did not consist of any earthly person or institution. Rather, he labeled the source as "the Lord," who, in his infinite love, "gave himself up for us as a fragrant offering and sacrifice to God" (5:2 NR). It is Christ the Lord who is "the concrete reality of divine love and . . . the true victory over hate," a condition that must have existed in the hearts of many slaves toward masters and mistresses.[94]

receive: In this context, the middle voice of the verb κομίζω (*komizō*) presents the sense "to get (for oneself)" or "to receive (for oneself)"[95] and throws open the door to the notion of a reward for good works.[96] Although commentators will not acknowledge this possibility, the entire thrust of this section of the letter trends in this direction. One notices the emphasis on doing good things in another place: "We must all appear before the judgment seat of Christ so that we may each receive [*komizō*] what is due according to the things that have been done in the body, whether good or evil" (2 Cor. 5:10, Wayment; see also Col. 3:25).

6:9 *masters:* Finally, Paul has come to adjust his focus onto slave owners. And these owners were not just anyone. They surely were Christians.[97] By turning his attention to them, the Apostle exerted more than subtle pressure on these believing people not only to treat their slaves decently but even very generously. In 6:5, the same noun appears, *kyrios.* Its occurrence there gave off an aura of superiority to which others were to submit. As an example, after Philippi had been rattled by a nighttime earthquake that freed Paul, his companion Silas, and all the other prisoners inside the jail, in an unexpected turn, the jailer asked, "Sirs [*kyrios*], what must I do to be saved?" (Acts 16:30). The tables had been turned, and the one in charge was suddenly not in charge. His respectful address to Paul and the others illustrates that he understood the nature of the change (see the Note on 6:5).[98]

---

92. Herbert Preisker and Ernst Würthwein, *TDNT,* 4:723.
93. Bruce, *Ephesians,* 125; Fowl, *Ephesians,* 196; Winger, *Ephesians,* 669.
94. Michel, *TDNT,* 4:689.
95. BDAG, 557.3; Louw-Nida, §57.136; Thayer, *Lexicon,* 354.4.
96. Contra Winger, *Ephesians,* 668.
97. Rengstorf, *TDNT,* 2:270.
98. Quell and Foerster, *TDNT,* 3:1086.

do: The drumroll continues. For the third time in the last four verses, 6:6–9, Paul has pushed the verb "to do" (ποιέω, *poieō*) into his set of instructions. By now, all readers had noticed that doing "the will of God" (6:6) and doing the "good [celestial] thing" (6:8) were sounding an almost audible, rhythmic pattern, a pattern that could not be stilled. One of the blessings that "doing" leads to is revelation. At the Feast of Tabernacles, Jesus said in the Jerusalem temple, "My doctrine is not mine, but his that sent me. If any man [or woman] *will do his will,* he shall know of the doctrine, whether it be of God, or whether I speak of myself" (John 7:16–17, emphasis added). As is plain, Jesus promised that the doer of God's will can look forward to a heavenly endowment of knowledge (see the Notes on 6:6, 8).

the same things: The plural demonstrative pronoun and its definite article (τά αὐτά, *ta auta*) actually stand before the verb "to do" in the Greek text, thus emphasizing their importance, and form its direct object. A question arises whether this term refers back to the "good thing" of 6:8 for which masters will be rewarded or to the virtues enjoined on slaves in verses 6:5–8, such as "singleness of your heart" (6:5) and "doing the will of God from the heart" (6:6).[99] Whatever the answer may be, Paul's point pertains to owners acting with goodwill toward their slaves, recognizing that they all eventually have to face "the same Lord in heavenly realms" (6:9 NR) and give an accounting of their stewardships. In effect, "both masters and slaves are to be guided by the same principles" (see Col. 4:1).[100] Not incidentally, the relationship of master and slave is reciprocal but not the same for each by any means. This simple observation grows out of the fact that the owners are not asked to obey another human.[101]

forbearing: The participle of ἀνίημι (*aniēmi*), which presents the sense "to cease from" or "to stop altogether,"[102] may have struck slave owners not only as odd but even as interfering with their rights as heads of households. But Paul was not cowed in the least by what people might think of him and his instructions. To illustrate, when writing about noxious "contentions among [Corinthian church members]," the Apostle almost rhapsodized, "I thank God that I baptized none of you, but Crispus and Gaius" (1 Cor. 1:11, 14). A second example will suffice. When Paul wrote about Jewish

---

99. Larkin, *Handbook,* 153; Merkle, *Guide,* 204–5.
100. Gustav Stälin, *TDNT,* 3:355.
101. Merkle, *Guide,* 205.
102. BDAG, 83.3; Louw-Nida, §68.43.

missionaries, whom he called "false prophets, deceitful workers," who had taught in the Corinthian congregation, he asked, "Are they Hebrews? so am I. Are they Israelites? so am I. Are they the seed of Abraham? so am I. Are they ministers of Christ? . . . I am more; in labors more abundant, in stripes above measure, in prisons more frequent, in deaths oft" (2 Cor. 11:13, 22–23). The gist comes down to Paul wanting Christian slave owners, because they were believers, to cease treating their slaves badly, including making threats against them.

threatening: The noun ἀπειλή (*apeilē*) means "threat" with the expanded sense of menacing words "that one will cause harm to someone, particularly if certain conditions are not met."[103] What is a Christian owner to do about punishment if no threats are allowed? As Best observed, "If Christian owners are to lay aside threats, they must also lay aside the punishments which would follow."[104] Said differently, Paul was "asking them to view their slaves as brothers and sisters in Christ."[105] The question then arises, How can an owner control his slaves? For, as the reader will discern with a little thought, the owner loses leverage over the slave. The matter is perhaps made more complex when, in a Sunday meeting, the owner and slave worship together and partake of the same bread and from the same wine cup of the Eucharist or sacrament. For slave owners, the answer could not have been easy. But the Apostle's expectation was clear. A slave's treatment in the home of a Christian was to be measurably better than in a pagan home. And a little more thought would tell an owner that threats and belittling outbursts would lead slaves to serve only with "eyeservice" and would discourage them from making genuine efforts "from the heart" (6:6). Incidentally, Rudolf Bultmann judged that the words "dispensing with threats" (6:9 NR) forms "a choice expression."[106]

Master: The better translation for *kyrios* here is "Lord" (NR) to be consistent with other occurrences of this title for Christ. As in the earlier appearances of this noun, appealing to this title added an infinite measure of "profundity" to Paul's words, lending authority to what he wrote.[107] As Lord, Jesus now occupied the place at the Father's "own right hand in the heavenly places," thus elevating him as Judge of all (1:20; see also 1 Cor. 4:4;

---

103. Louw-Nida, §33.291; see also BDAG, 100.
104. Best, *Ephesians,* 581; see also Fowl, *Ephesians,* 197.
105. Winger, *Ephesians,* 670.
106. Rudolf Bultmann, *TDNT,* 1:367.
107. Schrenk and Quell, *TDNT,* 5:1004; Quell and Foerster, *TDNT,* 3:1090. The quoted term is from 5:1004.

2 Tim. 4:1, 8; and Heb. 10:30). This is exactly Paul's message in this verse. More than that, the Son has taken up the impartial character of the judging responsibility from God, who is the highest judge. From Peter's correspondence, we encounter, "Ye call on the Father, who without respect of persons judgeth according to every man's work" (1 Pet. 1:17). Paul's line written to the believers in Rome breathes the same air: "There is no respect of persons with God" (Rom. 2:11).[108] The meat of the matter rests on Christ acting as an impartial judge too (see the Notes on 4:5; 5:22, 29–30; 6:1, 7–8, 10).

heaven: The pairing of heaven and earth as God's domain enjoys a long history. During a moment of a personal pledge, Abraham obliged his chief servant, Eliezer, to "swear by the Lord, the God of heaven, and the God of the earth, that thou shalt not take a wife unto my son [Isaac] of the daughters of the Canaanites" (Gen. 24:3). In prayer, Jesus himself uttered the words, "I thank thee, O Father, Lord of heaven and earth" (Matt. 11:25; see also Luke 10:21). When Jesus addressed the "Lord of heaven and earth" as "Father," he lifted the emphasis away from God as creator and placed the main stress on God as the bringer of the covenant, which opened the gate to salvation. That said, we are not to turn our backs on heaven as an object of God's creative activities. We read that he was joined by his Son by whom "were all things created, that are in heaven, and that are in earth, visible and invisible . . . all things were created by him" (Col. 1:16).[109]

In harmony with God's creative role and his covenantal gift stands heaven as the place from which judgment will come. For it will come in the person of Christ when he returns. This sense is surely implicit in the account of Christ's ascension. On that occasion, "while they [the Eleven] looked steadfastly toward heaven as he went up, behold, two men stood by them in white apparel." These two announced that "this same Jesus, which is taken up from you into heaven, shall so come in like manner as ye have seen him go into heaven" (Acts. 1:10–11). To be more clear, the sense that heaven sends down judgment presents itself in Paul's words to his Thessalonian friends. He wrote, "The Lord himself shall descend from heaven with a shout . . . and the dead in Christ shall rise first." What else? "Then we which are alive and remain shall be caught up together with them in the clouds . . . and so shall we ever be with the Lord" (1 Thes. 4:16–17). Does not the last line capture the sense that a judgment has taken place in connection with Jesus' descent that will allow the righteous to "ever be with

---

108. Lincoln, *Ephesians,* 424.
109. Traub and von Rad, *TDNT,* 5:516.

the Lord"?[110] The fact that the Lord possesses judging power should be enough to bring Christian slave owners into conformity with Paul's words in this verse (see the Notes on 1:10; 3:15; 4:10).

respect of persons: The noun προσωπολημψία (*prosōpolēmpsia*) anciently resided in a person's respect paid to another by the first person lowering the gaze "to the ground" or sinking "to the earth." Unlike humans, God does not bow before others and thereby acknowledge their persons (see Deut. 10:17 and 2 Chr. 19:7). God held up this standard as a beacon to his people, especially judges, when he stated, "Ye shall not respect persons in judgment; but ye shall hear the small as well as the great; ye shall not be afraid of the face of man; for the judgment is God's" (Deut. 1:17; see also Rom. 2:11). James has provided the odious consequences for church members who show obsequious "respect." He wrote, "If there come unto your assembly a man with a gold ring, in goodly apparel . . . and ye have respect to him that weareth the gay clothing, and say unto him, Sit thou here in a good place," something is not right. In contrast, if "there come in also a poor man in vile raiment . . . and [you] say to the poor . . . sit here under my footstool; are ye not then partial in yourselves?" (James 2:2–4). Yes. Regrettably, "ye have despised the poor" (James 2:6). Unlike these church members, God has "chosen the poor of this world [who are] rich in faith, and heirs of the kingdom" (James 2:5).[111] In light of these passages, slave owners were far, far better off if they treated their servants as Paul directed rather than risking antagonizing the Lord himself, who cares nothing about their earthly status.

Analysis of 6:1–9

Within a few short verses, 6:1–9, Paul has led readers inside an ancient home, complete with children and slaves. We should not lose sight of the home-oriented theme that dominates this section, including the last half of chapter 5 (see 5:22–33). Commentators delight in claiming that these verses derive from a household code of sorts. That is why Paul glided smoothly from topic to topic, all of which have to do with the management of the home. Never mind that the similar section in Colossians, beginning with the husband-wife relationship, which is also said to rest on a household tabulation, is much shorter and less religious in its orientation. The section on slaves presents an exception. In Colossians 3:22–25, the

---

110. Traub and von Rad, *TDNT,* 5:524.
111. Eduard Lohse, *TDNT,* 6:779–80, quotation on 779.

instructions to slaves differ, particularly at the end, where the Apostle wrote, "He [the slave] that doeth wrong shall receive for the wrong which he hath done." The total opposite sits in Ephesians, promising "that whatsoever good thing any man doeth, the same shall he receive of the Lord, whether he be bond or free" (6:8). Moreover, in Colossians God's "no respect of persons" is applied to slaves rather than to slave owners, a very odd sentiment (Col. 3:25; Eph. 6:9). All of these items raise the question of how much Paul was slavishly following a household listing of duties for each resident of the home.

While on the subject of slaves, it is clear that Paul shows a streak of naïveté about how slaves experienced life. In Muddiman's words, "Paul shows himself to be naïvely innocent of the practicalities of slave-ownership." Although he must have known stories shared by enslaved brothers and sisters, he seems not to have stood close to their unrelentingly challenging lives, rising early and retiring late, working long hours and meeting the whims of uncaring mistresses and masters. As Muddiman observed, "This is one further reason for attributing the slave sections of Colossians and Ephesians to his [Paul's] own hand" and not to another, anonymous person.[112]

In a related vein, in 6:2–3, the citation of Exodus 20:12 has brought forward the idea that the Apostle would not have cited this passage with its promise of living a long life "on the earth" because he lived in an era when the Lord was expected back at any moment.[113] That notion also fails. Again, it is Muddiman who makes the key observation. He wrote that Paul knew "Christians whose exemplary obedience was nevertheless rewarded by poverty and premature death, starting with Paul himself."[114] Furthermore, the insistence that Paul believed that the Lord's coming was just around the corner denies the plain sense of his words to his Thessalonian friends. As we can see, this issue had come up and he had answered it. "Let no one deceive you by any means," he wrote, "because that day [of Christ's return] will not come until the apostasy comes first and the man of lawlessness, who is the son of perdition, is revealed" (2 Thes. 2:3, Wayment). He then went on to say, "Don't you remember that when I was with you I used to tell you these things?" (2 Thes. 2:5 NIV). The Apostle knew that a long delay was in the works (see the Notes on 6:3, 5).

---

112. Muddiman, *Ephesians*, 280.
113. Lincoln, *Ephesians*, 406.
114. Muddiman, *Ephesians*, 274; see also Fowl, *Ephesians*, 194.

An unusually heavy emphasis falls on "doing" in these verses. It first emerges in words addressed to slaves. Paul wrote about these people "doing the will of God from the heart" rather than allowing themselves to be trapped into the groveling lives of "menpleasers" (6:6). As if he had not said enough, he wrote about slaves "doing service, as to the Lord, and not to men" (6:7). The Apostle was lifting the gaze of slaves from the sometimes unbearable vicissitudes of their grinding lives to a lofty, celestial pinnacle that would be theirs when their lives ended. But he was not finished. He next turned to slave owners. To them he wrote, "Do the same [service] for them, not threatening them." Why? "Because you know that there is the same Lord in heaven for both of you, and there is no partiality with him" (6:9, Wayment). Of course, the owners surely liked being the wolf instead of the lamb in the tranquil scene painted by Isaiah (see Isa. 11:6). But in the eternal scheme, it is the Lamb that has the power (see John 1:29, 36, "the Lamb of God"; Rev. 5:6, 8; etc.).

In one sense, the instructions to each group of believers in 6:1–9 could be seen as mirroring the expectations in the broader, surrounding culture. But readers would be mistaken to leave matters there. Plainly, Paul took things to a much higher level, a level that is perfumed with the pleasing aromas of heaven. What is at stake is nothing less than each person's eternal destiny, rich or poor, "bond or free" (6:8). To that end, next to each step of everyone's path stands the gracious, assisting Lord. But he does not simply cheer on believers as they pass by. He also makes demands, and those demands involve more than simple belief. In fact, they push readers to do something ennobling to the self, something helpful to others. In other words, Christ the Lord expects all to engage in mutually beneficial works. For example, we encounter "obey your parents" (6:1), "bring them up" (6:4), "doing the will of God" (6:6), "doing service" (6:7), and "do the same things unto them [your slaves]" (6:9). This disclosure by the Apostle about the necessity of works in the eternal scheme of things is one of the most significant in the whole letter.

Another distinctive contribution reposes in the treatment of all as responsible persons before the Lord, including children and slaves. Evidently, Paul judged that the children had reached the "years of discretion"[115] or "the age of accountability" and were therefore in a position to make a contribution to the worship life in their branches. Their education, particularly

---

115. Oepke, *TDNT*, 5:650; see also Lincoln, *Ephesians*, 403, 409; Fowl, *Ephesians*, 192; and Merkle, *Guide*, 195.

as it came from their fathers, was to center on honoring their parents (see 6:1–3) and on the teachings of Christ—that is, "the nurture and admonition of the Lord" (6:4). In the case of slaves, like those in pagan households, they were to "be obedient to them that are your masters according to the flesh" (6:5). But the comparison ended there. For Christian slaves lived with higher expectations placed upon their heads. They were to serve their mistresses and masters "in singleness of your heart, as unto Christ" (6:5). As if this were not clear enough, Paul piled on more. Rather than act as "menpleasers" around those whom they served, they were to perform their tasks "as the servants of Christ" (6:6). Said another way, their labors, no matter how rigorous, were to be undertaken "with good will [while] doing [their] service, as to the Lord" (6:7).

Fathers and slave owners alike, though they exercised authority in their homes, also faced high expectations. Paul laid fathers under the injunction to "provoke not your children to wrath." Without subtlety, his demand underscored the notable, celestial value that children possess. Curbing parental prerogatives, it may seem, brought the Apostle to step way over an unapproachable threshold. But the Apostle was more than willing to hop across that barrier and hold parents, especially fathers, from anything that could be construed as mistreatment of their children. As we have noted, fathers were to focus chiefly on raising and educating their children "in the nurture and admonition of the Lord" (6:4). After all, those children would become the church and community leaders in the next generation. In other words, the parents' gift to that coming generation consisted of their children.

Slave owners stood on similar terrain with regard to their human possessions. Paul required that they stop threatening their charges, leaving them only with the option of appealing to their slaves' better selves (see 6:9). As a result of their self-restraint in their relationships with their slaves, they would get helpers who would serve "in the singleness of [their] heart" and "not with eyeservice" (6:5–6). Beyond this, they were to treat their slaves "in the same way" (6:9 NIV) that they expected the Lord to "reward each one for whatever good they do" (6:8 NIV). Although Paul's directive surely surprised slave masters, it was the natural outcome of putting everything into the Lord's lap. For Christian slaves were "as fully members of the Christian community as their masters."[116] Significantly, in his role as judge, "there [is no] respect of persons with [Christ]" (6:9).

---

116. Lincoln, *Ephesians,* 424.

In the end, the Lord towers above all as the standard setter and guarantor of divine rewards for all classes of people. The major clue arose from his welcome to Gentiles. Those people had been "dead in trespasses and sins" (2:1). Their lives had been besotted with "the lusts of [their] flesh" (2:3). But completely unexpectedly, "now in Christ Jesus ye who sometimes were far off are made nigh by the blood of Christ" (2:13). This breaking down of the barrier, "the middle wall of partition between" Jew and Gentile (2:14), spread out the banquet for all to enjoy, no matter their status in this life. For that status would surely change in the next. In fact, the change in status had already begun with all becoming disciples of Christ, thereby being "no more strangers and foreigners, but fellowcitizens with the saints, and of the household of God" (2:19).

"Put on the Whole Armour of God" (6:10–20)

King James Translation

10 Finally, my brethren, be strong in the Lord, and in the power of his might. 11 Put on the whole armour of God, that ye may be able to stand against the wiles of the devil. 12 For we wrestle not against flesh and blood, but against principalities, against powers, against the rulers of the darkness of this world, against spiritual wickedness in high places. 13 Wherefore take unto you the whole armour of God, that ye may be able to withstand in the evil day, and having done all, to stand. 14 Stand therefore, having your loins girt about with truth, and having on the breastplate of righteousness; 15 And your feet shod with the preparation of the gospel of peace; 16 Above all, taking the shield of faith, wherewith ye shall be able to quench all the fiery darts of the wicked. 17 And take the helmet of salvation, and the sword of the Spirit, which is the word of God: 18 Praying always with

New Rendition

10 Finally, become empowered in the Lord and in his mighty strength. 11 Put on the full armor of God so that you may be able to stand against the schemes of the devil, 12 because our battle is not against blood and flesh, but against the rulers, the authorities, and the cosmic lords of this darkness, and against the spiritual forces of evil in the heavenly realms. 13 Therefore, take up the full armor of God so that you may be able resist them on the evil day, and having done everything, to stand. 14 Stand, therefore, having girded your waist with truth, having put on yourself the breastplate of righteousness, 15 and having fitted your feet with the readiness of the gospel of peace. 16 In addition to all this, having taken up the shield of faith, with which you will be able to extinguish all the flaming arrows of the evil one, 17 so receive the helmet of salvation and the sword of the Spirit, which is the word

all prayer and supplication in the Spirit, and watching thereunto with all perseverance and supplication for all saints; 19 And for me, that utterance may be given unto me, that I may open my mouth boldly, to make known the mystery of the gospel, 20 For which I am an ambassador in bonds: that therein I may speak boldly, as I ought to speak.

of God. 18 With every prayer and plea, pray at all times in the Spirit, and in it be watchful in all perseverance and entreaty for all the saints. 19 And pray for me that, when I open my mouth the word may be given to me to make known fearlessly the mystery of the gospel, 20 for which I am an ambassador in chains, and that I may speak about it freely, as I should speak.

Notes on 6:10–20

6:10 *Finally:* The expression τοῦ λοιποῦ (*tou loipou*) introduces a summing up of Paul's instructions that he began in 4:1. By his account, believers were to equip themselves in God's armor for a final showdown with evil, trying to avert a full-blown apostasy. Their success would have less to do with moral qualities than with an infusion of God's aid that would come as a result of "praying always with all prayer and supplication" (6:18).[117]

my brethren: This endearing address (ἀδελφοί μου, *adelphoi mou*) is surely a late addition to a limited number of texts. It is omitted by the best manuscripts, including the earliest, 𝔓[46]. A scribe may have thought it necessary to insert the expression to draw all readers together at the beginning of a new and final section.[118]

be strong: This passive imperative of ἐνδυναμόω (*endynamoō*) presents the meaning "to become strong." The passive character of the verb directs us to the Lord as the one who grants inner strength ("the power of his might").[119] His strengthening power that was released to each member was to fortify every person for the struggle against the nascent apostasy that had already begun, as indicated by the present tense of the verb.[120] The joining of verbs and nouns that convey the sense of the divine endowment of energy and strength to believers occurs at 1:19, where the grand proof of God's power manifested itself in the Resurrection of Christ from the dead (see 1:20).

The rock-hard nature of Christ's power and might is perceptible to those whose "eyes of your heart [are] enlightened, [that] you may know ... the surpassing greatness of his power toward us, the ones who believe" (1:18–19

---

117. Oepke and Kuhn, *TDNT,* 5:300–302.
118. Best, *Ephesians,* 589.
119. BDAG, 333.2.b; Louw-Nida, §74.7; Merkle, *Guide,* 210.
120. Grundmann, *TDNT,* 2:313–14; Oepke and Kuhn, *TDNT,* 5:301–2.

NR). Thus, a revelatory gift wove itself through each person's grasp of Christ's ability to strengthen them beyond their natural resilience, tapping into "the spirit of wisdom and revelation in the knowledge of him" (1:17).[121] But the required inner strength would exceed that of putting "on the new man [and woman]" in an enjoyment of spiritual nourishment through divine knowledge (4:24). Rather, church members needed a measure of muscular power to undertake the "wrestle . . . against the rulers of the darkness of this world" (6:12). Physical, bodily strengthening would be required (see 3:16, "to be strengthened with might"; and the Note on 1:19).[122]

in the Lord: As we have noted elsewhere, this sort of phrase was most likely created by Paul to carry his messages of strength that resides in the Lord. Here, his intent centered on the inner strengthening of believers by Christ's power. For without it, they would fail in their "struggle against the threatening powers of darkness" (see the Notes on 1:1; 2:7, 10; 3:6; 4:1, 17, 32; 5:8).[123]

power: This noun (κράτος, *kratos*) occurs one other time in this letter in the expression "the working of his mighty power [*kratos*]" (1:19). Pairing this term with the next noun, ἰσχύς (*ischys*), as in 1:19, packages the divine fury required to overcome "the rulers of the darkness of this world" and "spiritual wickedness in high places" (6:12). On one level, Christ's power has set itself to deliver believers from their earthly vicissitudes; on another, his might must remain intact through the last great battle for the souls of men and women (see Rev. 20:7–10 and D&C 88:110–15).[124] The appearance of *kratos* in Mary's Magnificat, when taken in its context, underlines in bright colors the irresistible, overpowering majesty of God. We read, "He hath shewed strength [*kratos*] with his arm; he hath scattered the proud in the imagination of their hearts." More than this, in an act of social justice, "he hath put down the mighty from their seats, and exalted them of low degree." In a similar vein, "he hath filled the hungry with good things; and the rich he hath sent empty away" (Luke 1:51–53;[125] see the Notes on 1:18–19).

---

121. Bednar, "In the Strength of the Lord," 121–28; Rasmus, "Enabling Power of the Atonement," 18–21; see also Eising, *TDOT,* 4:349, 353–55; Grundmann, *TDNT,* 2:313–16; Oepke, *TDNT,* 2:542–43; Braun, *TDNT,* 6:464, who has discussed Elisabeth and Mary (see also Luke 1:25, 49).

122. Oepke and Kuhn, *TDNT,* 5:301.

123. Oepke and Kuhn, *TDNT,* 5:302; Oepke, *TDNT,* 2:541.

124. Oepke and Kuhn, *TDNT,* 5:302.

125. Wilhelm Michaelis, *TDNT,* 3:907–8.

might: The term ἰσχύς (*ischys*), like the prior noun *kratos,* touches on power and might. In sources outside the New Testament, it revolves around "the power of prayer" and "the power of truth."[126] Hence, it carries the sense of a power inherent in quiet, private actions that involve prayer and the celebration of truth. But the noun *ischys* also bears a community sense, where a group of Saints benefits from God's might. We listen to Peter's words: "If anyone serves [others], he should do it with the strength [*ischys*] God provides, so that in all things God may be praised through Jesus Christ" (1 Pet. 4:11 NIV).[127]

This power, this might, lies exactly at the flash point between Christ and Satan. When Jesus was criticized for casting out devils by the power of Beelzebub, the devil, he shot a warning missile across the bow of his critics to not get things wrong. He declared, "If I with the finger of God cast out devils, no doubt the kingdom of God is come upon you." Then he led his hearers inside the devil's house: "When a strong man [Satan] armed keepeth his palace, his goods are in peace." But matters took a serious downturn "when a stronger [Christ] than he [Satan] shall come upon him, and overcome him." The result? Christ "taketh from him all his armour wherein he [Satan] trusted" (Luke 11:20–22). The "goods" that the devil lost in this contest included the souls of those whom he had influenced but Jesus was able to recover, including the departed dead (see the Notes on 3:8, 10, 19; 4:5, 9; 5:8; 6:18; and the Analysis of 3:1–13; 4:1–16).[128]

6:11 *Put on:* The verb ἐδνύω (*enduō*), here a plural imperative, appears for a second time in Ephesians and will occur a third (see 4:24; 6:14). With the basic meaning "to put on" or "to clothe oneself,"[129] the term can be applied to putting on Christ. Paul wrote, "Rather, clothe yourselves [*enduō*] with the Lord Jesus Christ" (Rom. 13:14 NIV; see also Moro. 4:3, "take upon them the name of thy Son"; D&C 20:77; 2 Ne. 1:23, "put on the armor of righteousness"; and D&C 109:22, "that thy name may be upon them"). In the Romans passage, the meaning is metaphorical, as it is in the sacramental prayer. But Paul's directive in Ephesians clearly touches on the physical

---

126. BDAG, 484.

127. Grundmann, *TDNT,* 2:313–14; Grundmann, *TDNT,* 3:399.

128. Jeremias, *TDNT,* 1:146–49; Delling, *TDNT,* 1:488–89; Friedrich, *TDNT,* 2:718–19; Oepke, *TDNT,* 3:213; Grundmann, *TDNT,* 3:399–401; Büchsel, *TDNT,* 3:641–42; Friedrich, *TDNT,* 3:707–8; Jeremias, *TDNT,* 3:746–47; Schneider, *TDNT,* 4:597–98; Bornkamm, *TDNT,* 4:821–22; Traub and von Rad, *TDNT,* 5:525–26, 533; Hauck and Schulz, *TDNT,* 6:577–78; Schweizer and Baumgärtel, *TDNT,* 7:1078–79; Brown, *Testimony of Luke,* 568–70, 573.

129. BDAG, 333.2.a; Louw-Nida, §49.1.

act of clothing oneself. Even though the gear that he lists hereafter points to military hardware, that gear belongs to God. Therefore, dressing in it becomes a sacred act and connects to other shimmering celestial ceremonies wherein believers put on holy garments.[130] That is to say, the worshiper puts on God's garments; this clothing does not come to the devotee as a divine gift. It is clothing dried, spun, woven, and sewn in this world, clothing worn in sacred settings. In a related vein, the link to heavenly realities burgeons in Jesus' words to his disciples after an all-night session with them: "Stay in the city of Jerusalem until you are clothed [*enduō*] with power from on high" (Luke 24:49, Wayment). Paul tied this off nicely in a reference to a new, physical robing in the next life: "This corruptible must put on [*enduō*] incorruption, and this mortal must put on [*enduō*] immortality" (1 Cor. 15:53; see also 2 Cor. 5:1–4).[131] But that is not the whole story.

The verb *enduō* anticipates other verbs in coming verses.[132] Besides the repetition of *enduō* at 6:14 ("having on"), readers encounter ἀναλαμβάνω (*analambanō*), which bears the sense "to take up [weapons]" and occurs at 6:13 and 6:16.[133] They also meet δέχομαι (*dechomai*), which shows up at 6:17 and presents the meanings "to receive" and "to take."[134] Each of these verbs ties to deeds of putting on God's armor or his divine garments. The believer effectively has taken in hand what belongs to God and placed it on his or her body, an activity made holy because the items belong to the Father. Thus, the broad context of verse 6:11 drives home the point that readers find themselves in the midst of strong notices of sacred actions and holy ceremonies (see the Notes on 2:10; 4:13, 20, 22, 24; 5:2, 8, 14; 6:13–14, 16–17; and appendix 1).

whole armour: The noun πανοπλία (*panoplia*) on one level features the armor worn by a Roman soldier—pounded, scraped, cut, fitted, cinched, tied, and strapped on. Jesus referred to this armor when he spoke about the "stronger [Christ]" taking from the "strong man [the devil] . . . all his armour [*panoplia*] wherein he trusted" (Luke 11:21–22; see also the Note on 6:10).[135] On another level, the term represents a metaphor of God's enduring, spiritual protection. Such a metaphor brings readers into contact with God's power that can infuse a person in the unending struggle

---

130. Contra Oepke, *TDNT*, 2:320.
131. Wilckens, *TDNT*, 7:691.
132. Lincoln, *Ephesians*, 452.
133. Delling, *TDNT*, 4:8; BDAG, 66.2.
134. BDAG, 221.1; see Lincoln, *Ephesians*, 452.
135. BDAG, 754.1 and 2; Thayer, *Lexicon*, 476.

"against principalities, against powers, against the rulers of the darkness of this world" (6:12). Said another way, "the night is far spent, the day is at hand: let us therefore cast off the works of darkness, and let us put on [*enduō*] the armour of light" (Rom. 13:12).

The wearing of God's armor equates to wearing his garment.[136] Obviously, this action is not possible in a literal sense. But in ceremony, a devotee in a representative manner can "put on incorruption" and can "put on immortality," thus blunting the threats associated with death (1 Cor. 15:53–54). But death does not come up for review in Ephesians. With God's armor, believers will triumph. The lack of a lancet or spear, not mentioned in these verses, will not deter them. Even though the "wicked" will fight at a distance, shooting "fiery darts" or "flaming arrows" (6:16), Christians will have to fight hand-to-hand (see "wrestle" in 6:12) in order to overcome, as the reference to the short sword in 6:17 clearly indicates.[137] This will be no easy task (see the Notes on 5:16; 6:13, 17).

be able: An infinitive of the verb δύναμαι (*dynamai*), this word carries the plural nature of the earlier verb *enduō*. Hence, Paul was appealing to the community of believers to stand fast together rather than one by one.[138] The verb carries the meaning "to be capable."[139] The ability to withstand demonic and other unsavory pressures, of course, comes from Christ's power. For through his Atonement, he has overcome the world and its troubles, as he reminded his disciples a few hours before his arrest: "In the world ye shall have tribulation: but be of good cheer; I have overcome the world" (John 16:33).

to stand: The verb is an infinitive of ἵστημι (*histēmi*) and can mean "to stand up" as well as "to stand up against" or "to resist."[140] Appearing for the first time in Ephesians, it will occur twice more (see 6:13–14). The chief sense in this verse, 6:11, is "to resist," as it is in 6:13. But in 6:14, the meaning shades into an upright position of a person who models God's clothing, a very different view of standing. One of the Apostle's warnings revolved around the need to stand and resist because a person may slip and fall from his or her spiritual perch (see the Notes on 5:14; 6:13–14).[141]

---

136. Oepke and Kuhn, *TDNT,* 5:301.
137. Oepke and Kuhn, *TDNT,* 5:301; Merkle, *Guide,* 212.
138. Grundmann, *TDNT,* 2:313–14.
139. BDAG, 262.
140. BDAG, 482.B.3 and 5.
141. Grundmann, *TDNT,* 7:652.

wiles: The noun μεθοδεία (*methodeia*) features the meaning "craftiness" or "deceit" in all its negative dress.[142] Such deceitfulness captured nonbelievers "in the lusts of [their] flesh" (2:3) and drove them "to and fro" so that they found themselves snagged by "every wind of doctrine, by the sleight of men, and cunning craftiness" (4:14). As people came to faith, Christ's power to deliver them from their blighted situation flowed to them from his Atonement, including his descent "into the lowest parts of the earth," where he rescued captive souls as an essential step in delivering all who would turn to him (4:9; see also Rom. 14:9, "Lord both of the dead and living"; 1 Pet. 3:18–20; 4:6; and Rev. 11:18).

The term *methodeia* does not focus on some sort of intellectual haze, a kind of methodological confusion. In its only two occurrences in the New Testament, both in Ephesians, it produces the sense of a "planned and conscious" approach to an issue, bringing to bear the full weight of evil. Hence, the devil does not sit as a nonparticipating bystander who merely observes and cheers on the fulminating forces of wickedness. No. As "the prince of the power of the air" (2:2), he has inaugurated "a cunning process which seeks to deliver [all] up to error."[143] More than this, God does not produce error to test believers. That role belongs to the devil. As James reminded his readers, "Let no man say when he is tempted, I am tempted of God: for God cannot be tempted with evil, neither tempteth he any man" (James 1:13; see also the Notes on 4:9, 14).[144]

the devil: The devil (διάβολος, *diabolos*) was a preexistent personality who sought to hijack the Father's plan to send a redeemer to the earth to save the Father's children. In modern scripture, we read, "Satan . . . came before me, saying—Behold, here am I, send me, I will be thy son, and I will redeem all mankind, that one soul shall not be lost, and surely I will do it; wherefore give me thine honor" (Moses 4:1). Besides his demand that the Father share his divine honor, the promise that he would "redeem all mankind, that one soul shall not be lost," cut against the free will that God had built into his plan (see 2 Ne. 2:26–27, "they are free to choose"). We hear the Father's voice: "Because that Satan rebelled against me, and sought to destroy the agency of man . . . and also, that I should give unto him mine own power; by the power of mine Only Begotten, I caused that he should be cast down" (Moses 4:3; see also Abr. 3:27–28 and D&C 29:36–39). In

---

142. BDAG, 625; Thayer, *Lexicon*, 395–96.
143. Michaelis, *TDNT*, 3:102–3, quotation on 103. Also see Bauernfeind, *TDNT*, 5:726.
144. Heinrich Seesemann, *TDNT*, 6:29; Braun, *TDNT*, 6:245.

another place, "The great dragon was cast out, that old serpent, called the Devil, and Satan, which deceiveth the whole world: he was cast out into the earth, and his angels were cast out with him" (Rev. 12:9). In this terrestrial place, he and his minions have created havoc and tried to undo all that the Father and his Son have put in place for human salvation (see the Notes on 2:2; 4:27).[145]

6:12 *wrestle:* The word πάλη (*palē*) is a noun and bears the meaning "fight," particularly a wrestling contest.[146] The contest that Paul envisioned is a "part of the great final battle which has already begun." Seizing the plain sense of the noun, one must admit that the struggle involves physical effort, not just mental or spiritual. The Apostle appealed elsewhere to this sort of titanic struggle. To the Roman church members, he wrote, "The day is at hand: let us therefore . . . put on the armour of light" (Rom. 13:12). Again, "Let us, who are of the day, be sober, putting on [*enduō*] the breastplate of faith and love; and for an helmet, the hope of salvation" (1 Thes. 5:8).[147]

flesh and blood: The expression in the Greek text is "blood and flesh" and directs readers to the world as people experienced it and away from the world of God's Spirit. Paul was effectively saying that a believer need not turn to the typical ways of dealing with the ever-hostile physical world, such as through magic or joining mystery cults. The world served up challenges, yes, but the real, enduring problems for Christians arose out of the unseen world,[148] as they had for Jesus during his ministry. For in his experience, he was opposed at almost every turn by nasty demons who were invisible to everyone else. As an example, in the Capernaum synagogue on a Sabbath, "a man with an unclean spirit . . . cried out, saying, Let us alone; what have we to do with thee, thou Jesus of Nazareth? art thou come to destroy us?" (Mark 1:23–24; see also Luke 4:33–35). Of course, synagogue members knew that this unnamed man in their midst was spiritually blighted. But they had no idea how to deliver him from his tormenting spirit, as his unrelieved, continuing situation illustrates. It was Jesus who understood the man's plight and rescued him from what Paul called "spiritual wickedness in high places" (see the Notes on 2:3, 11, 15; 5:29, 30–31; 6:5).[149]

---

145. Von Rad and Foerster, *TDNT,* 2:79–80; Foerster and Shäferdick, *TDNT,* 7:161–62.
146. Louw-Nida, §39.29; Thayer, *Lexicon,* 474.
147. Heinrich Greeven, *TDNT,* 5:721.
148. Behm, *TDNT,* 1:172; Lincoln, *Ephesians,* 443.
149. Delling, *TDNT,* 1:489.

principalities: This noun (ἀρχή, *archē*) has occurred twice before (see 1:21; 3:10). In each instance, the term in the singular represents a personality who inhabits the unseen world. In this verse, it stands for the first of three invisible opponents that Christians will face. Whether tentatively called "gods many, and lords many" (1 Cor. 8:5) or "the host of heaven" (Acts 7:42), the individuals mentioned in 1:21 and 3:10 obviously differ from one another. In 1:21, the personalities wear a sable tunic of sorts, dark and sour, evil in their core. In 3:10, by contrast, the characters are capable of redemption by the aid of "the church" after gaining access to "the manifold wisdom of God." With one exception, whenever *archē* refers to an entity or person, it pertains to the invisible world. That exception rests in Luke 12:11 and has to do with Roman "magistrates." In a mildly puzzling passage, Paul has linked the world of angels with that of principalities: "I am persuaded, that neither death, nor life, nor angels, nor principalities [*archē*] . . . shall be able to separate us from the love of God" (Rom. 8:38–39). But it is not clear how angels and principalities fit together.[150] In any event, Jesus has surmounted all those who opposed him, whether in this world or the next, because he has triumphed over their leader: "Now is the judgment of this world: now shall the prince of this world be cast out" (John 12:31), and "the prince of this world is judged" (John 16:11; see also Matt. 25:41 and the Notes on 1:21; 2:2; 3:10; 4:8).[151]

powers: Paul has presented a second unseen opponent by repeating the noun ἐξουσία (*exousia*). It appears here for the fourth and last time in Ephesians (see 1:21; 2:2; 3:10). By writing it, Paul has brought readers inside his most dire warning about believers' futures. Yes, Christ has overpowered Satan as we have seen in the prior Note (see John 12:31; 16:11). Yes, the "powers" (*exousia*) are under his control. But in exercising vigilance, church members must understand that they have received their celestial status as a gift, not as something that they have snatched for themselves. This is the thrust of the language of "having preordained us for adoption as children unto himself through Jesus Christ, according to the benevolence of his will" (1:5 NR).[152] Such high and holy gifts, when clasped firmly by devotees, will lead to exaltation and away from the soul-draining "principalities" and "powers." As Paul declared almost breathlessly, even though "we were dead in sins, [God] hath quickened us together with Christ . . .

---

150. Delling, *TDNT,* 1:483.
151. Delling, *TDNT,* 1:489; Werner Foerster, *TDNT,* 2:17; Traub and von Rad, *TDNT,* 5:526.
152. Foerster, *TDNT,* 2:566.

and hath raised us up together, and made us to sit together in heavenly places in Christ Jesus" (2:5–6). For the steadfast, "the Lord God will disperse the powers of darkness from before you" (D&C 21:6; see also the Notes on 1:21; 2:2; 3:10; 4:8).

the rulers of the darkness of this world: The line "the rulers . . . of this world" rests on a single noun and its definite article, the plural of ὁ κοσμοκράτωρ (*ho kosmokratōr*). The singular noun carries the meaning "world-ruler,"[153] and the expression is better translated "the cosmic lords of this darkness" (NR). Because the term *kosmokratōr* appears only here in the New Testament, an interpreter faces the difficulty of determining exactly where this sort of personality fits within the invisible world. A marginal hint shows up in modern scripture wherein Joseph Smith directed church members to hold onto their memories of the severe persecutions that they had suffered in the state of Missouri. He wrote that "we should waste and wear out our lives in bringing to light all the hidden things of darkness." In this case, the Saints had experienced all the lightlessness that one person could receive from another. Such darksome horrors "are truly manifest from heaven," placing their retribution in the hands of God (D&C 123:13). If the *kosmokratōrs* envisioned in this verse had indeed interfered in the mortal lives of believers, their future was a gloomy one because "it is a fearful thing to fall into the hands of the living God" (Heb. 10:31; see also 3 Ne. 28:35, "the justice of an offended God").

darkness: The Greek text pairs the demonstrative pronoun "this" with "darkness" (σκότος, *skotos*), not with "world" as in the KJV. The Apostle was pointing directly to "this darkness," the gloom that can and does arise in the lives of believers.[154] Whether this lurking darkness connects to "outer darkness," a locale for the wicked that Jesus warned about,[155] remains unknown (Matt. 8:12; 22:13; Alma 40:13; D&C 101:90–91; 133:73). Perhaps unsurprisingly, spiritual darkness possesses its own reservoir of power. Elsewhere, Paul wrote that "the Father . . . hath delivered us from the power [*exousia*] of darkness [*skotos*]" (Col. 1:13).[156] This viewpoint helps to explain the Messiah's need for "power" when "bringing . . . [his people] out of darkness unto light—yea, out of hidden darkness and out of captivity unto freedom" (2 Ne. 3:5; see also the Notes on 5:8, 11).

---

153. BDAG, 561; Thayer, *Lexicon,* 356.
154. BDAG, 932.
155. Louw-Nida, §1.23.
156. Conzelmann, *TDNT,* 7:442.

spiritual wickedness: Commentators have generally agreed that this expression stands as a summarizing element that pulls together the prior three, locating them in an elevated place above the earth ("principalities," "powers," and "cosmic rulers").[157] That high place is in "the air" (2:2). From this locale, the forces of "spiritual" (πνευματικός, *pneumatikos*) evil can throttle the essential revelation that brings unity of purpose among believers. That revelation initially led investigators to God himself, escorting them, as Paul prayed, to "the spirit of wisdom and revelation in the knowledge of him" (1:17). In tandem, Gentile investigators learned that the door to salvation had been opened to them "as it is now revealed unto his holy apostles and prophets by the Spirit" (3:5;[158] see also the Notes on 1:17; 3:5).

in high places: On four earlier occasions, we have encountered this Greek phrase (ἐν τοῖς ἐπουρανίοις, *en tois epouraniois*), translated in the KJV as "in (the) heavenly places" (1:3, 20; 2:6; 3:10). In all these cases, this celestial region links to Christ and his work, except this last one. Obviously, the phrase in 6:12 pertains to a realm of evil. This territory differs markedly from the area "far above all heavens" where Christ ascended after his Resurrection (4:10). Instead, we are to think of a lower region through which Jesus passed both on his way into this world (see John 1:14) and into the world of departed spirits (see 4:9).[159] For, when coming into this world, Jesus shined "in darkness; and the darkness comprehended it not" (John 1:5). The verb translated "comprehended" is the past tense of καταλαμβάνω (*katalambanō*), whose basic sense in this passage is "to seize" or "to arrest."[160] Hence, it appears that during his descent into this world Christ was set upon by powers above the earth that tried to interrupt his arrival as the infant Jesus (see D&C 6:21; 39:2–3; 45:7–8; the Notes on 1:3, 20; 2:6; 3:10; and the Analysis of 1:15–23).

6:13 *take:* The verb ἀναλαμβάνω (*analambanō*), here in the imperative, presents the military sense "to take up [weapons]."[161] A soldier's hefting of weapons after strapping on body armor was the last step before actually forming a fighting unit with fellow soldiers.[162] Hence, the image is one of full readiness just before the battle is to begin. The plural imperative refers

---

157. Lincoln, *Ephesians,* 444–45; Fowl, *Ephesians,* 204; Muddiman, *Ephesians,* 289; Winger, *Ephesians,* 705; Merkle, *Guide,* 213.

158. Kleinknecht, Baumgärtel, Bieder, Sjöberg, and Schweizer, *TDNT,* 6:444.

159. Winger, *Ephesians,* 706.

160. BDAG, 520.2.b; Louw-Nida, §37.19.

161. Delling, *TDNT,* 4:8; BDAG, 66.2.

162. Barth, *Ephesians,* 2:765.

to a military unit, not to a single soldier. Thus, the Christian community as a whole was to engage in the struggle. Implicit is the support that one believer offers to another, whether combating the onrushing apostasy or facing nagging temptations (see the Note on 6:16).

The verb *analambanō* also presents links to other nearby verbs that themselves tie to sacred deeds or holy rituals, for it is devotees who undertake these actions. Those sacred acts do not come as gifts from the divine world as in the case of "grace" or "love." The first is *enduō* with the meanings "to put on" or "to clothe oneself."[163] Appearing in 6:11 ("put on") and 6:14 ("having on"), *enduō* pushes forward the idea of wearing God's clothing, particularly his military gear. We encounter God putting on such items in Isaiah's book: "He put on [*enduō*] righteousness as a breastplate, and placed the helmet of salvation on his head" (LXX Isa. 59:17). The next verb is δέχομαι (*dechomai*), which occurs at 6:17 and features the ideas "to receive" and "to take."[164] In this case, a believer takes in hand and puts on "the helmet of salvation," as God did according to LXX Isaiah 59:17. Hence, we find *analambanō* and its associated verbs opening a view of God's clothing, particularly the clothing that he wears when confronting his enemies, "the rulers of the darkness of this world" as Paul expressed it (6:12; see also the Notes on 4:22, 24; 5:20; 6:11, 14, 16–17; Analysis of 6:10–20; and appendix 1).

whole armour: The noun πανοπλία (*panoplia*) has already appeared in 6:11. In its broad sense, it has to do with not only the pieces that soldiers put on as protection, such as breastplates and helmets, but also with their offensive weapons, such as swords and spears. Paul clearly has in mind all the gear that military men of his day carried and wore. The fact that the equipment came from God means that he is both the quartermaster and the commander in chief. His soldiers are to possess the best equipment and the most up-to-date guidance (see 2 Ne. 1:23, "put on the armor of righteousness"; and the Note on 6:11).[165]

that: The conjunction ἵνα (*hina*) introduces a "purpose clause" and might be rendered "so that." Such statements of purpose present "the goals which God has set for human action," not just the goals that humans have set.[166] Implied is the need for humans to assist God in reaching his goals. As a modern negative example, the actions of some church members in

---

163. BDAG, 333.2.a.

164. BDAG, 221.1; see Lincoln, *Ephesians,* 452.

165. Oepke and Kuhn, *TDNT,* 5:300–302; BDAG, 754; Thayer, *Lexicon,* 476.

166. Stauffer, *TDNT,* 3:332–33.

Missouri frustrated God's plans in 1831 to establish a Zion people in that state.[167] We listen to his complaint: "I, the Lord, am not well pleased with the inhabitants of Zion, for there are idlers among them; and their children are also growing up in wickedness; they also seek not earnestly the riches of eternity, but their eyes are full of greediness. These things ought not to be, and must be done away from among them" (D&C 68:31–32). A positive example also appears in modern scripture. When the Lord will "call upon the weak things of the world . . . to thresh the nations by the power of my Spirit," he affirmed that "their arm shall be my arm, and I will be their shield and their buckler; and I will gird up their loins, and they shall fight manfully for me; and their enemies shall be under their feet" (D&C 35:13–14).

be able: As in 6:11, this verb δύναμαι (*dynamai*), here in the second person plural, acts as a helping verb but does not lose its force as a term of power (see the Note on 6:11).

to withstand: The infinitive of ἀνθίστημι (*anthistēmi*) offers the sense "to resist [power]" (NR).[168] The thought is of meeting force with force, although in Galatians 2:11 it presents the meaning of resisting in a face-to-face encounter ("I withstood him"; see also Acts 13:8).[169] With a completely different tone from resisting evil as it descends onto us from invisible places, as in this verse, 6:13, we encounter Jesus' words when evil comes at us from other people: "I say unto you, That ye resist [*anthistēmi*] not evil: but whosoever shall smite thee on thy right cheek, turn to him the other also" (Matt. 5:39). This situation has nothing to do with taking the field of battle under God's banner to resist "spiritual wickedness in high places" (6:12).[170]

the evil day: This noun and its adjective (τῇ ἡμέρᾳ τῇ πονηρᾷ, *tē hēmera tē ponēra*), here in the singular, touch on a specific era. In the context, that day, that age, turned readers to a bleak moment in the future.[171] Two possibilities come to mind. The first bears on a threatening apostasy, the event that Paul wrote about in his second letter to his Thessalonian converts. There, while discussing the timing of Jesus' Second Coming, he pled, "Let no one deceive you by any means, because that day [of Christ's return] will not come until the apostasy comes first" (2 Thes. 2:3, Wayment). On a later occasion, when speaking to his friends from Ephesus about the future

---

167. Alexander L. Baugh, "Missouri," in Garr, Cannon, and Cowan, *Encyclopedia of Latter-day Saint History,* 769–71.

168. BDAG, 80.2; Louw-Nida, §39.18.

169. Louw-Nida, §39.1.

170. Grundmann, *TDNT,* 7:652–53.

171. Harder, *TDNT,* 6:554.

of their branch, Luke recorded Paul as saying, "I know this, that after my departing shall grievous wolves enter in among you, not sparing the flock" (Acts 20:29). Hence, Paul did not expect the church to survive (see 2 Cor. 1:8; 2 Tim. 1:15; and 1 John 2:18–19; 4:1–3). Similarly, Jesus' parable of the "tares" envisioned the tares mixed in with the wheat and not separated out until the end, "the harvest," a bleak prospect for the future of the wheat field or the church (Matt. 13:24–30).[172]

The other possibility has to do with the last great struggle with the devil and his minions.[173] Chapter 12 of the book of Revelation paints a picture of "a great red dragon" whose "tail drew the third part of the stars of heaven, and did cast them to the earth." There, they awaited the birth of a "child" to "a woman clothed with the sun" (Rev. 12:1, 3–4). After the "man child . . . was caught up unto God, and to his throne[,] . . . the woman fled into . . . a place prepared of God," where she waited out a "war in heaven" (Rev. 12:5–7). In that war, "Michael and his angels fought against the dragon; and the dragon fought and his angels." At the end of the struggle, "the great dragon was cast out, that old serpent, called the Devil, and Satan, which deceiveth the whole world" (Rev. 12:7, 9). Modern scripture adds a bit more color for the future. We learn "Michael, . . . even the archangel, shall gather together his armies, even the hosts of heaven." On the other side, "the devil shall gather together his armies; even the hosts of hell, and shall come up to battle against Michael and his armies." In the end, "the devil and his armies shall be cast away into their own place, that they shall not have power over the saints any more at all" (D&C 88:112–14). Hallelujah! (See the Notes on 1:10; 4:30; 5:16.)

day: Frequently, the term for "day" (ἡμέρα, *hēmera*) directs readers to a time of crisis, a time of high anxiety. This meaning surely applies to the line "the days are evil" in 5:16. A sense of reckoning arises in references to "the day of judgment." For instance, Jesus emphatically warned that "every idle word that men shall speak, they shall give account thereof in the day [*hēmera*] of judgment" (Matt. 12:36; compare Mark 6:11). A reckoning also occurs in Jesus' words about a servant who treats fellow servants badly, with "the lord of that servant [showing up] . . . in a day [*hēmera*] when he

---

172. Nibley, "Passing of the Primitive Church," in *When the Lights Went Out,* 4; John W. Welch, "Modern Revelation: A Guide to Research about the Apostasy," in *Early Christians in Disarray: Contemporary LDS Perspectives on the Christian Apostasy,* ed. Noel B. Reynolds (Provo, Utah: FARMS, 2005), 112–30.

173. Muddiman, *Ephesians,* 290.

looketh not for him" (Matt. 24:50; see also Luke 12:46).[174] In contrast, this last day, the day of Christ's unexpected return, also bears joy for the faithful. As Paul reminded his Corinthian associates, "We are your rejoicing, even as ye also are ours in the day [*hēmera*] of the Lord Jesus" (2 Cor. 1:14). We read the Apostle's further words to his friends in Philippi: "He which hath begun a good work in you will perform it until the day [*hēmera*] of Jesus Christ" (Philip. 1:6; see also Philip. 1:10; 2:16; and the Notes on 4:30; 5:16).

having done all: The participle of κατεργάζομαι (*katergazomai*) carries the meanings "to achieve" and "to accomplish."[175] It is preceded by the intensive form of "all" (ἅπας, *hapas*), which lays stress on a steady, maximal effort.[176] Whether these words refer "to full preparation for the battle or to the overcoming of all opposition is an open question."[177] That is, do these words in 6:13 pertain to completed preparations for the looming struggle, or do they center on a conflict already underway? Whichever the case, plainly believers needed to engage themselves fully for things to go their way. Slackers were not welcome.

to stand: We last met the verb ἵστημι (*histēmi*) at 6:11, where it carried the meaning "to resist." While that sense hovers close by, here in 6:13 one grasps the additional sense of standing courageously, without flinching, in the face of a strong force, even if it means sustaining wounds or being nicked by "the fiery darts of the wicked" (6:16). Modern scripture holds up one person, a military leader called Moroni, who stood against evil in its military and spiritual forms. He was said to be "a man that did not delight in bloodshed; a man whose soul did joy in the liberty and the freedom of his country." More than this, "he was a man who was firm in the faith of Christ, and he had sworn with an oath to defend his people . . . even to the loss of his blood." Moreover, "if all men had been, and were, and ever would be, like unto Moroni, behold, the very powers of hell would have been shaken forever; yea, the devil would never have power over the hearts of the children of men" (Alma 48:11, 13, 17; see also the Notes on 5:14; 6:11, 14).

6:14 Stand: The form of the verb ἵστημι (*histēmi*), an imperative, is from the same root as the last verb in 6:13. One almost hears Paul hitting a big, loud drum with a hammer to emphasize the need for a person to stand, now arrayed in God's armor, now wearing God's garment. And standing

---

174. Harder, *TDNT,* 6:554.
175. BDAG, 531.1.
176. BDAG, 98.2.
177. Georg Bertram, *TDNT,* 3:635.

against evil remains the primary thrust.[178] But when paired with other verbs of movement or action in this letter—"to sit" and "to walk"—the verb "to stand" draws a reader's attention to the high possibility of holy acts, of sacred moments reposing nearby. As an example, at the instant of his calling, Paul was obliged to "rise, and stand upon [his] feet" when the Resurrected Jesus gave him his charge (Acts 26:16). The same act was demanded of Ezekiel when God appeared to him: "Son of man, stand upon thy feet, and I will speak unto thee. And the spirit entered into me when he spake unto me, and set me upon my feet, that I heard him" (Ezek. 2:1–2). To each, Paul and Ezekiel, flowed divine knowledge, heavenly instruction while they stood before Deity. It was a moment of furnishing them with a celestial strength and understanding that they would need in order to fulfill their respective callings.

The verb's connection to ceremonial acts inside the Jerusalem temple becomes visible in Jesus' story about the Pharisee and Publican who came to the temple the same day. Inside the temple walls, "the Pharisee stood [*histēmi*] and prayed." "The Publican" also stood. As Jesus narrated the scene, this man, "standing [*histēmi*] afar off, would not lift up so much as his eyes unto heaven, but smote upon his breast, saying, God be merciful to me a sinner" (Luke 18:11, 13). We glimpse a further demonstration of the link between praying and standing in Epaphras, one of Paul's companions, "who is one of you, a servant of Christ [who is] . . . always laboring fervently for you in prayers, that ye may stand [*histēmi*] perfect and complete in all the will of God" (Col. 4:12).[179] Hence, the act of standing, the reception of divine instruction, and the effort to pray sincerely for others link together seamlessly (see the Notes on 2:10; 4:13, 20, 22, 24; 5:2, 8, 14; 6:11, 13; and appendix 1).

loins girt: Paul now leads readers to the pieces of armor that he will feature, pointing to armor that is defensive (see Alma 48:14).[180] The noun "loins" (plural of ὀσφῦς, *osphys*) directs our gaze to the waist or middle part of the body.[181] The accompanying verb περιζώννυμι (*perizōnnumi*), a participle, means to put a belt around oneself, to gird oneself.[182] The expression "loins girt" is drawn directly from LXX Isaiah 11:5, where a reader discovers

---

178. Lincoln, *Ephesians,* 446–47.
179. Grundmann, *TDNT,* 7:652–53 and nn. 40 and 42.
180. Best, *Ephesians,* 597.
181. BDAG, 730.1; Thayer, *Lexicon,* 457–58.
182. BDAG, 801.2.c.

that the Messiah "shall have his *loins girt* with righteousness, and his sides clothed with the truth" (emphasis added; see also 1 Pet. 1:13, "gird up the loins of your mind, be sober").[183] Such "robing with new garments" can express "the gift of new being" or new life (see 4:24, "put on the new man . . . after [the pattern of] God"; 1 Cor. 15:53–54; and 2 Cor. 5:1–4).[184]

The soldier's girdle consisted of a wide leather belt that he wore underneath the breastplate. It held in place a leather apron that hung in front of the soldier's legs for protection. The Roman legionary wore a second girdle outside of his armor that was studded by metal pieces and had attached to it metal strips that hung down in front of the midsection of the body and the thighs, adding another layer of protection. This second belt seems to be what Paul had in mind.[185]

According to the Old Testament, God dispensed such girdles: "It is God that girdeth me with strength," and "thou hast girded me with strength unto the battle" (Ps. 18:32, 39). The Lord also girds his people with joy, as the Psalmist sang: "Thou hast put off my sackcloth, and girded me with gladness" (Ps. 30:11). Even nature received a divine girding: "The pastures in the wild are rich with blessing and the hills wreathed in happiness" (Ps. 65:12 NEB). With a different tone, the Lord declared in metaphorical terms to Jeremiah that "just as a girdle is bound close to a man's waist, so I bound all Israel and all Judah to myself, . . . but they did not listen" (Jer. 13:11 NEB).[186] Returning to the image of a soldier whom God arms, in modern scripture the Lord promised to the faithful "who are unlearned and despised [that] . . . their arm shall be my arm, . . . and I will gird up their loins, . . . and their enemies shall be under their feet; and I will let fall the sword in their behalf" (D&C 35:13–14).

truth: The noun "truth" (ἀλήθεια, *alētheia*) lacks a definite article, turning it into a divine reality that, like a material object, a "believer can put on like the protective apron of the soldier."[187] This reality makes up the nature of God and consists of "truth [that] is knowledge of things as they are, and as they were, and as they are to come" (D&C 93:24), knowledge that comes concretely from a divine, revelatory source. According to Paul, the dismissive treatment of God's truth draws down severe consequences,

---

183. Heinrich Seesemann, *TDNT*, 5:496–97.

184. Ulrich Wilckens, *TDNT*, 7:691.

185. Oepke and Kuhn, *TDNT*, 5:303; Barth, *Ephesians*, 2:767; contra Lincoln, *Ephesians*, 447; Best, *Ephesians*, 598; and Fowl, *Ephesians*, 205.

186. Oepke and Kuhn, *TDNT*, 5:305.

187. Oepke and Kuhn, *TDNT*, 5:308.

even among unsuspecting Gentiles. As he wrote to his Roman readers, "The wrath of God is revealed from heaven against all ungodliness and unrighteousness of men, who hold the truth [*alētheia*] in unrighteousness." And why is God's wrath kindled against those "who hold the truth in unrighteousness"? It is simply "because that which may be known of God is manifest in them; for God hath shewed it unto them." Said more clearly, "the invisible things of him from the creation of the world are clearly seen [in nature], ... even his eternal power and Godhead; so that they are without excuse" (Rom. 1:18–20).

The trampling of God's truth brought the Apostle to write that "we are sure that the judgment of God is according to truth [*alētheia*] against them which commit such things." Why? Because "there is no respect of persons with God" (Rom. 2:2, 11). To the ancient prophet Hosea, the Lord stated that he had "a controversy with the inhabitants of the land, because there is no truth, nor mercy, nor knowledge of God in the land" (Hosea 4:1). In this case, the lack of "truth" and "knowledge of God" can be traced directly to the lack of revelation, to the lack of God's reality or real presence among his people. In Paul's letter to the Romans, the matter pivoted on both a general unwillingness to see God's hand in creation and a widespread, resisting malaise in responding to his creative and redemptive acts (see the Notes on 4:21; 5:9).[188]

having on: The verb ἐνδύω (*enduō*), with the meaning here of the middle participle "to put on for oneself" or "to wear,"[189] has appeared twice before, in 4:24 and 6:11. In its participle form, it completes the sense of the imperative "stand" with the thought "stand ... having [now] clothed yourselves."[190] The notion of putting on garments from God not only touches on wearing God's clothing or armor but also relates to putting on Christ at baptism: "As many of you as have been baptized into Christ have put on [*enduō*] Christ" (Gal. 3:27; see also Rom. 13:14),[191] recalling the language of the sacrament prayer, "to take upon them the name of thy Son" (Moro. 4:3; D&C 20:77; see D&C 109:22). Such robes, whether literal or metaphorical, recall dressing in garments "washed ... white in the blood of the Lamb." The people who wore clothing made white, like those in Paul's mind who faced an enormous challenge according to Ephesians, "came out

188. Quell, Kittel, and Bultman, *TDNT*, 1:235, 243; Oepke and Kuhn, *TDNT*, 5:308.
189. BDAG, 333.2.
190. Winger, *Ephesians*, 709, 711.
191. Wilckens, *TDNT*, 7:688; Winger, *Ephesians*, 711–12.

of great tribulation" (Rev. 7:14;[192] see 1 Ne. 12:10–11; Alma 5:21, 24, 27; and Ether 13:10; see also the Note on 5:26). There is more.

As we discovered in the Note on 6:11, the verb *enduō* travels with two other important, nearby verbs. They are ἀναλαμβάνω (*analambanō*, "to take up [weapons]"), which occurs at 6:13 and 6:16,[193] and δέχομαι (*dechomai*, "to receive" or "to take"), which appears at 6:17.[194] In each instance, the verb sends readers to a worshiper's actions undertaken with God's implements of war—that is, with his warrior clothing, as we see in LXX Isaiah 59:17 ("he put on [*enduō*] righteousness as a breastplate"). On Jesus' part, at the end of a full night of instructing a mixed group of disciples, he drew the attention of his followers to the inner, spiritual strength that comes from being "clothed [*enduō*] with power from on high" (Luke 24:49, Wayment). The strength inherent in taking (*analambanō*) "unto you the whole armour of God [and] . . . the shield of faith" is immediately apparent (6:13, 16). And the individual's acts of taking up such items and putting them on all direct us to ceremonial deeds, to actions made sacred by their connection to God, as do the activities of receiving or taking (*dechomai*) upon oneself "the helmet of salvation, and the sword of the Spirit" (6:17). This whole set of verses, 6:11–17, is filled with allusions, direct and indirect, to sacred ceremonies, to divinely sculpted actions that imitate God (see the Notes on 4:22, 24; 5:20; 6:11, 13, 16–17; the Analysis of 6:10–20; and appendix 1).

breastplate of righteousness: The noun "breastplate" (θώραξ, *thōrax*) brings up various styles of this piece of armor. A breastplate might consist of double-thick leather pads with metal studs, a metal piece that covered the chest and midsection of the body, or of chain mail. Depending on its lightness and strength, "the two qualities required in good armor," a quality breastplate can withstand and protect a soldier from a spear thrust and even an arrow shot from twenty paces.[195] Besides drawing in references to real armor, Paul placed a spiritual overlay because this armor is to resist evil.

Warding off evil comes about because of righteousness (δικαιοσύνη, *dikaiosynē*). In seeking a breastplate of righteousness, believers were following God: "He put on righteousness as a breastplate" (Isa. 59:17). Even though the terms differ, Paul's language elsewhere rings the same bell. We read, "Since we belong to the day, let us be self-controlled, putting on faith

192. Wilckens, *TDNT*, 7:691.
193. Delling, *TDNT*, 4:8; BDAG, 66.2.
194. BDAG, 221.1; see Lincoln, *Ephesians*, 452.
195. Oepke and Kuhn, *TDNT*, 5:308–9, quotation on 308.

and love as a breastplate" (1 Thes. 5:8 NIV). The thought of being "self-controlled" rests on the verb νήφω (*nēphō*), which can mean "to be sober" but is better rendered "to be self-controlled" or "to be well-balanced."[196] In this Thessalonian passage, Paul's "emphasis is not that faith and love encompass believers like protective armor." Rather, church members "should make ready for the final conflict *by putting on their [own] armor*" (emphasis added).[197] Hence, at the base of enjoying protection by means of a divine breastplate lie good works, righteous actions that protect.

In this passage, 6:14, the righteousness that protects "against temptation" consists of "armor which God gives." Thinking of righteousness as a gift, we are now talking about "the righteousness of God through faith in Jesus Christ for all who believe." Why do believers need this righteousness that comes from God and allows them to stand before him without guilt? It is because "all have sinned and fall short of the glory of God" (Rom. 3:22–23 RSV).[198] Thus, their need for the gift is ever with them (see the Notes on 4:24; 5:9).

6:15 *your feet:* The noun for "foot" (πούς, *pous*)[199] can pertain to the whole person, not just to the foot itself. Readers detect this sense emerging in Isaiah's song: "How beautiful upon the mountains are the feet of him that bringeth good tidings, that publisheth peace" (Isa. 52:7). This meaning lies beneath Paul's quotation of the same passage (see Rom. 10:15) and Zacharias's prophetic words about his newborn son, "to guide our feet into the way of peace" (Luke 1:79). John the Baptist's words about the Coming One point to the same feature of the feet representing the whole person: "There cometh one mightier than I after me, the latchet of whose shoes I am not worthy to stoop down and unloose" (Mark 1:7). Obviously, the Baptist felt that he was not worthy even to touch Jesus, including his foot coverings, which were the most dirt-stained part of his clothing. What do these observations have to do with what Paul has written in our verse? Simply, the soldier's feet direct readers to the thought that this person is wholly engaged in the struggle to overcome evil, no matter the cost. Moreover, the engaged believer will join God in his effort to "crush Satan under your feet" (Rom. 16:20 NIV).[200]

---

196. BDAG, 672; Thayer, *Lexicon*, 425.
197. Oepke and Kuhn, *TDNT*, 5:310.
198. Oepke and Kuhn, *TDNT*, 5:310.
199. Thayer, *Lexicon*, 534.
200. Konrad Weiss, *TDNT*, 6:628–29; Oepke and Kuhn, *TDNT*, 5:311; BDAG, 858.1.a.

shod: The verb ὑποδέω (*hypodeō*) occurs three times in the New Testament, each in an event laced with holiness. In this verse, in a middle-voice participle, it bears the meaning "to bind beneath" or "to put on [shoes]."[201] The first occurrence of the verb that sits in a brief list of items that newly called members of the Twelve were to take on their first missionary journey, a task associated with sacredness, tells us that they were allowed to "be shod [*hypodeō*] with sandals," taking one pair, not two. In another scene, unusual because of the presence of an angel, the angel approached Peter, who was being kept in a Jerusalem prison during Passover, and, after releasing his chains, instructed him, "Gird thyself, and bind [*hypodeō*] on thy sandals." They walked out of the prison together. After the angel's departure, Peter said to himself, "Now I know of a surety, that the Lord hath sent his angel, and hath delivered me out of the hand of Herod" (Acts 12:8, 11). Thus, a simple act of putting on sandals has made the story of Peter's divinely driven deliverance real and believable. In our verse, 6:15, a touch of paradox permeated Paul's words when he talked about resisting "the wiles of the devil" as if in combat (6:11) and doing so with "the gospel of peace." But this latter notion underlies much of the message in Ephesians. For we read that Christ "is our peace, who hath made both [Jew and Gentile] one, and hath . . . abolished in his flesh the enmity [between these peoples] . . . to make in himself of twain one new man, so making peace . . . that he might reconcile both unto God in one body by the cross." In a word, it was Christ who "came and preached peace to you which were afar off" (2:14–17). Thus, peace is to overcome and to quiet the jangling of the struggle with wickedness.[202]

preparation: The noun ἑτοιμασία (*hetoimasia*) occurs only here in the New Testament, and it features the basic sense of "readiness" (NR) or "preparedness."[203] That is, a person is in a state of being ready. Inside the New Testament, this notion expressed itself with different goals. It began with John the Baptist, who came in accord with the spirit of Isaiah 40:3: "The voice of him that crieth in the wilderness, Prepare ye the way of the Lord" (see Matt. 3:3 and Mark 1:3). Even in the angel's promise about John's impact on his people before his birth, his father, Zacharias, heard the divine words "to make ready a people prepared for the Lord" (Luke 1:17). But the story does not end here. Readiness is also to come into play in the believer's

---

201. BDAG, 1037; Louw-Nida, §49.17.
202. Oepke and Kuhn, *TDNT,* 5:311–12.
203. BDAG, 401; Louw-Nida, §77.1; Thayer, *Lexicon,* 255.2.

testimony about the gospel: "Be ready always to give an answer to every man [or woman] that asketh you a reason of the hope that is in you" (1 Pet. 3:15). More than this, a church member is to exhibit a readiness to undertake good works. For each is to become "an instrument for noble purposes, made holy, useful to the Master and prepared to do any good work" (2 Tim. 2:21 NIV; see also Titus 3:1). Further, a devotee is to be ever in readiness for Christ's return. It was Jesus who said, "Be ye also ready: for in such an hour as ye think not the Son of man cometh" (Matt. 24:44; see also Matt. 25:1–13 and Luke 12:40).[204]

gospel of peace: Peace (εἰρήνη, *eirēnē*) remains the ultimate object of salvation at the end-time. As the father of John the Baptist prophesied about his infant son, John's mission was "to guide our feet into the way of peace" (Luke 1:79). This walk in the path of peace does not confine itself to this life. For, as the heavenly choir sang at Jesus' birth, peace connects intimately with God and his place in "the highest." We listen to the following words: "Glory to God in the highest, and on earth peace, good will toward men" (Luke 2:14). Peace is the state that God, from his lofty residence, imparts to those on earth who will receive it. And as Jesus reminded his eleven disciples, it links hard and fast to the next world: "Peace I leave with you, my peace I give unto you: *not as the world giveth, give I unto you*" (John 14:27, emphasis added). In this light, *eirēnē* pertains to the "inner peace of soul" that can be enjoyed in this life, but experienced more fully in the next world, even though bouts of tribulation may be experienced in the here and now (John 16:33; see the Notes on 2:14–15, 17; 4:3).[205]

gospel: The "gospel" (εὐαγγέλιον, *euangelion*) in Paul's hands poses an interesting study. In two important passages, he set out its pieces, which summarized the essence of Jesus' ministry. In Romans 1:1–4, he told readers that "the gospel of God" had been "promised afore by his prophets in the holy scriptures." Then, in a clear reference to Jesus' birth, he wrote that God's "Son Jesus Christ our Lord . . . was made of the seed of David according to the flesh," a firm pointer to Mary. One majestic event "declared [him] to be the Son of God with power . . . by the resurrection from the dead." In this passage then, the emphasis reposes on the birth and Resurrection of Christ. In the second brief description, his masterful chapter on the Resurrection that he composed for his Corinthian readers, he wrote that "the gospel which I preached unto you [is the one] . . . by which also ye are

---

204. Walter Grundmann, *TDNT,* 2:706.
205. Von Rad and Foerster, *TDNT,* 2:412–13, quotation on 413.

saved." Next, he wrote a succinct summary of that gospel message, "how that Christ died for our sins according to the scriptures; and that he was buried, and that he rose again the third day according to the scriptures: and that he was seen of Cephas, then of the twelve" (1 Cor. 15:1–5). In the Corinthians verses, therefore, the stress lies on Christ's death, Resurrection, and post-Resurrection appearances. Two other items push forward for notice. The initial one centers on Christ as judge. In Romans, we read about "the day when God will judge people's secrets through Jesus Christ, as my gospel declares" (Rom. 2:16 NIV). The next relates to God's power to strengthen believers in their lives of faith beyond their own abilities. Paul's words are germane: "Glory to him who is able to give you the strength to live according to the Good News I preach" (Rom. 16:25, Jerusalem Bible;[206] see the Notes on 2:17; 6:19).

6:16 *taking*: The verb ἀναλαμβάνω (*analambanō*) is the same as in 6:13, though here it is a participle that links back to the main verb of 6:14, creating the sense "stand . . . having taken up the shield of faith."[207] As in 6:13, *analambanō* presents the military meaning "to take up [weapons]."[208] This verb also describes Jesus' ascension into heaven. In Luke's account, we read not only that "he was taken up [*analambanō*]" but also that "this same Jesus . . . is taken up [*analambanō*] from you into heaven" (the passive voice in Acts 1:2, 11; see also Mark 16:19 and 1 Tim. 3:16). The connector between these passages and 6:16 is about "transition" from one state to another.[209] In the Resurrected Jesus' case, he was transitioning from this world to the place of his permanent residence in heaven. In the case of a Christian soldier armed with God's weapons and clothed with his armor, he was making the transition from a peaceful, quiet believer to one who, for the sake of family and other church members, must take up spiritual arms for a major confrontation with evil (see the Note on 6:13).

206. Friedrich, *TDNT*, 2:730; see also Bednar, "In the Strength of the Lord," 121–28; Rasmus, "Enabling Power of the Atonement," 18–21; Eising, *TDOT*, 4:349, 353–55; Grundmann, *TDNT*, 2:313–16; Oepke, *TDNT*, 2:542–43; and Braun, *TDNT*, 6:464, who has discussed Elisabeth and Mary (see Luke 1:25, 49).

207. Merkle, *Guide*, 216, italics removed, renders the participle and its governing verb "stand . . . by taking up," which does not do justice to the past tense of the participle. A soldier did not stand ready for battle and then take up his armor. He strapped on his armor and then stood, ready for the conflict.

208. Delling, *TDNT*, 4:8; BDAG, 66.2.

209. Delling, *TDNT*, 4:8.

In a different vein, as was apparent in the Note on 6:13, *analambanō* not only relates to the notion of donning God's military clothing but also has forged attachments to the verbs ἐδνύω (*enduō*) and δέχομαι (*dechomai*). *Enduō* first shows up in 4:24 with the meaning "to put on," and then in 6:11 ("put on") and 6:14 ("having on"). *Dechomai* appears in 6:17 with the sense "to receive" or "to take."[210] Within the cluster of these three verbs sit references to holy actions whereby a believer comes to wear God's spiritually combative garments—"the whole armour of God" and "the shield of faith"—and joins him in the struggle "against the rulers of the darkness of this world, [and] against spiritual wickedness in high places" (6:12, 13, 16). An important emphasis rests on the worshiper's actions of putting on sacred clothing and taking up God's instruments in a ceremonial fashion. God does not put these items on the person (see the Notes on 4:22, 24; 5:20; 6:11, 13–14, 17; the Analysis of 6:10–20; and appendix 1).

shield: The term θυρεός (*thyreos*), appearing only here in the New Testament, features a figurative sense because of its connection to faith.[211] That said, plainly Paul had real shields in mind. In his era, Roman soldiers typically carried long or tower shields, which were made of up to "seven layers of oxhide" and measured four feet tall and two and a half feet wide. With strengthening wooden struts and metal studs to hold it together, the weight of the shield could exceed thirty pounds.[212] To this point, with the mention of "the breastplate" (6:14) and "the shield," it is apparent that the equipment was defensive. Why? Because Paul has described no offensive weapons or armor, nor will he except for "the sword" in 6:17. Furthermore, he has touched on nothing that protects a soldier's back. Thus, he had in mind those who would hold their ranks while facing forward against the onslaught of "the rulers of the darkness of this world" (6:12).[213]

In earlier scripture, God himself was said to be the shield of his people, a far more effective defense than a protective barrier hanging on a soldier's arm. We hear his words to Abraham, "Fear not, Abram: I am thy shield" (Gen. 15:1). Again, in the Psalmist's words of thanks and praise, "The Lord is my rock, my fortress and my deliverer, . . . my shield and the horn of my salvation" (Ps. 18:2 NIV). Similarly, "our soul waiteth for the Lord: he is our help and our shield"

---

210. BDAG, 221.1; 333.2.a; see Lincoln, *Ephesians,* 452.
211. Oepke and Kuhn, *TDNT,* 5:313.
212. Oepke and Kuhn, *TDNT,* 5:313.
213. Best, *Ephesians,* 597, 600.

(Ps. 33:20).[214] Perhaps significantly, modern scripture paints an equivalent picture. The Lord promised, "I will be their shield and their buckler; and I will gird up their loins, and they shall fight manfully for me" (D&C 35:14).

faith: How does faith or "believing" (πίστις, *pistis*) fit into Paul's portrait of a mighty struggle against evil? Surely, when paired with a shield, it represents more than a mental grasp of the facts of who Jesus was and is, though it includes such knowledge. Faith has to be more dynamic than that.[215] In the first place, faith or "trust" in divine things comes as a gift from God. For in his wisdom and generosity, he has "dealt to every man the measure of faith" (Rom. 12:3). More specifically, this faith, this trust in God, has brought to each Saint "gifts differing according to the grace that is given to us, whether prophecy, . . . or ministry, . . . or . . . teaching; or . . . exhortation" (Rom. 12:6–8).[216] In another place, we read that "through faith [the ancients] subdued kingdoms, wrought righteousness, obtained promises [from God], stopped the mouths of lions, quenched the violence of fire, escaped the edge of the sword, [and] . . . turned to flight the armies of the aliens" (Heb. 11:32–34).[217] More than these, faith links closely with unity (see 4:5, 13) and, with God's help, is capable of expansion (see 2 Cor. 10:15, "when your faith is increased"; and the Notes on 4:5, 13).[218]

be able: Here, the verb δύναμαι (*dynamai*), which appears in 6:11 and 6:13, occurs again. At base, it signals the power or capability to do something.[219] With heavy shields in the context, the term nods toward the arm strength of soldiers who have to heft such protective devices for long periods during combat (see the Note on 6:11).

quench: The verb σβέννυμι (*sbennumi*) means "to extinguish" or "to put out."[220] The question arises about how a shield, made of skins and wood, can extinguish a "fiery dart" or flaming arrow that strikes it and sticks. The answer is that soldiers would soak their shields in water before battling an opposing army known to shoot flaming projectiles, even though their shields became heavier because of the absorbed water.[221]

---

214. Best, *Ephesians,* 600; Lincoln, *Ephesians,* 449; Muddiman, *Ephesians,* 292.
215. Fowl, *Ephesians,* 207.
216. Gerhard Kittel, *TDNT,* 1:347–48; Bultmann and Weiser, *TDNT,* 6:212.
217. Winger, *Ephesians,* 716.
218. Bultmann and Weiser, *TDNT,* 6:212–13 and n. 286.
219. BDAG, 261–62; Louw-Nida, §74.5; Thayer, *Lexicon,* 158.
220. BDAG, 917.a; Louw-Nida, §14.70.
221. Barth, *Ephesians,* 2:773 and n. 84; Lincoln, *Ephesians,* 450; Best, *Ephesians,* 601; Muddiman, *Ephesians,* 292; Winger, *Ephesians,* 716.

fiery darts: The noun βέλος (*belos*) is found only here in the New Testament and exhibits the meanings of an "arrow" shot from a bow or a "dart" "hurled by hand."[222] From these meanings, one observes that the enemy is fighting from a distance, not in hand-to-hand combat, though the Christian has to be prepared for a close-up struggle ("wrestle," 6:12). To make the arrows or darts more lethal, their tips were dipped in a flammable pitch and lit before being shot or thrown. If shooting from a bow, the archer did not draw the string too taut so that the flame did not go out while the arrow was in flight. If hit with such an arrow or dart, the soldier suffered a severe burn that was slow to heal.[223] The fact that these devices carry deadly fire to opponents signals their menacing, lethal character.[224] Satan and his army are not at play.

The verb translated "fiery" is a participle of πυρόω (*pyroō*) and features the sense "to burn."[225] In our verse, those who hurl the burning projectiles at the faithful intend to take them down from their lofty spiritual perches. Such an outcome will leave the formerly steadfast believers at the mercy of the Final Judgment. We encounter this situation in Jesus' appeals that his followers not allow their hands or their feet or their eyes to create trouble for them (see Mark 9:43–47). Jesus then rounded off his warning by uttering the words "hell fire," the place "where their worm dieth not, and the fire [πῦρ, *pyr*, the noun related to *pyroō*] is not quenched" (Mark 9:48, quoting Isa. 66:24). Judgment stands front and center in Paul's words about "when the Lord Jesus shall be revealed from heaven with his mighty angels, in flaming fire [*pyr*] taking vengeance on them that know not God, and that obey not the gospel of our Lord Jesus Christ" (2 Thes. 1:7–8; see also Rom. 12:20 and 1 Cor. 3:13, 15).[226]

the wicked: The adjective πονηρός (*ponēros*), which can serve as a noun, occurs here for the third time in Ephesians (see 5:16; 6:13). Its basic sense is "wicked" or "evil."[227] In this case, because the term appears in the singular and has the definite article, the proper sense is "the evil one" (NR)—that is, the devil or Satan—just as we find in Jesus' explanation of the parable of the sower and what happens to some who hear the word of God: "Then cometh the wicked one [*ponēros*], and catcheth away that which was sown

---

222. Friedrich Hauck, *TDNT,* 1:608; BDAG, 174; Louw-Nida, §6.36.
223. Oepke and Kuhn, *TDNT,* 5:301, 314, and n. 10.
224. Hauck, *TDNT,* 1:608–9.
225. BDAG, 899.1; Thayer, *Lexicon,* 558.a.
226. Friedrich Lang, *TDNT,* 6:944.
227. BDAG, 851.1.a.α; Louw-Nida, §88.110.

in his heart" (Matt. 13:19).[228] Satan possesses a myriad of ways to tempt and try those who seek to remain steadfast before God. Paul sets the devil's power at the feet of the "lack of self-control" (1 Cor. 7:5 NIV)—that is, giving "place to the devil" (4:27; see also Rom. 16:17). As an expression, the "wiles of the devil" (6:11) run almost endlessly toward the horizon,[229] from fornication (see 5:3 and 1 Cor. 7:2) to refusing to forgive one another (see 2 Cor. 2:5–11), from accepting false teachers and apostles to receiving Satan as "an angel of light" (see 2 Cor. 11:12–14), from allowing our anger to run free (see 4:26–27) to becoming captive to pride (see 1 Tim. 3:6), and from pushing our noses into other people's business (see 1 Tim. 5:13, 15) to turning away from our submissiveness to God and our vigilance (see James 4:7 and 1 Pet. 5:8).[230] Unfortunately for those who slip and slide down Satan's slope, they become captive to their "father the devil, and the lusts of your father ye will do" (John 8:44; see also the Notes on 2:2; 4:27).

6:17 *take*: The verb δέχομαι (*dechomai*), with the basic meanings "to receive" or "to take,"[231] differs from the verb *analambanō* in 6:13 and 6:16, a term with clear military associations. In our verse, *dechomai* sits in a participle form and ties back to "stand" in 6:14 with the sense "stand . . . having received the helmet."[232] The meat of the matter continues to focus on God's gifts to those who are willing to wear his clothing or armor.[233]

Reception of "the helmet of salvation, and the sword of the Spirit" exhibits attachments to other acts of receiving or taking. At the beginning of their investigation of the gospel, converts "received [*dechomai*] it [the gospel message] not as the word of men, but as it is in truth, the word of God" (1 Thes. 2:13). That act of reception placed the investigator on a rising, spiritual trajectory unmatched by any worldly attainment. Frightfully, for those who turned their backs to the gospel, "they received [*dechomai*] not the love of truth [as a divine gift], that they might be saved" (2 Thes. 2:10). In their cases, such people remained as "the natural man [who] receiveth [*dechomai*] not the things of the spirit of God: for they are foolishness unto him" (1 Cor. 2:14).

---

228. Günther Harder, *TDNT*, 6:549 and n. 22; 6:558–59; Werner Foerster and Knut Schäferdick, *TDNT*, 7:161; BDAG, 851.1.b.

229. Foerster and Schäferdick, *TDNT*, 7:161.

230. Gerhard von Rad and Werner Foerster, *TDNT*, 2:80.

231. BDAG, 221.1.

232. Merkle, *Guide*, 217.

233. Oepke and Kuhn, *TDNT*, 5:301 nn. 27–28; Barth, *Ephesians*, 2:775 n. 106; Lincoln, *Ephesians*, 450.

In Jesus' teachings, even receiving a child elevates a follower to an everlastingly exalted place with the Father. We hear Jesus' words: "Whosoever shall receive [*dechomai*] this child in my name receiveth [*dechomai*] me: and whosoever shall receive [*dechomai*] me receiveth [*dechomai*] him that sent me" (Luke 9:48; see also Matt. 10:40–42 and Mark 9:36–37). The path to the side of the Father leads through baptism, but this ordinance is surely not the end-all. As Paul has written in this letter, more is required. And that involves becoming "imitators of God" (5:1 NR). In the act of imitating God, believers are to "put on" (*enduō*) his garments or his armor for the unavoidable conflicts ahead (see 6:11, 14, "having on"). In this process, they are to "take up" (*analambanō*) the weapons that will effectively defeat the opponents of righteousness (6:13, 16). Such deeds send readers into the world of sacred ceremony, where a person is the one who dons and wears holy clothing. God is not the one who dresses the worshipers. The participants dress themselves in sacred garments to prepare for the ceremony (see the Notes on 4:22, 24; 5:20; 6:11, 13–14, 16; the Analysis of 6:10–20; and appendix 1).

the helmet of salvation: This expression surely ties back to LXX Isaiah 59:17, where it is said that the Lord "put on righteousness as a breastplate, and placed *the helmet of salvation* on his head" (emphasis added; see also 6:14, "breastplate of righteousness"). In the world of real armor, the helmet formed the most crucial defensive item and was usually made of bronze with attached pieces for the cheeks and back of the neck and an inner lining of sponge or felt.[234] In a figurative sense, the helmet (περικεφαλαία, *perikephalaia*) represents a "helmet of victory," as it does in LXX Isaiah 59:17, where Jehovah strapped it on before donning "the garment of vengeance" to vanquish his enemies.[235] Again, metaphorically the helmet becomes a crown to be worn in the next life. This is the thrust of the celestial words spoken to the Saints in Smyrna: "Be thou faithful unto death, and I will give thee a crown of life" (Rev. 2:10).[236] This passage directs readers to the main question: How much are they willing to sacrifice in God's cause?

In the Isaiah verse cited above, Jehovah had clad himself with armor to aid and to offer salvation to his people. In a real sense, his followers, who will receive his garments or his armor, especially including his protective helmet, will stand side by side with him in the effort not only to thwart the

---

234. Barth, *Ephesians,* 2:775; Lincoln, *Ephesians,* 450.

235. Foerster and Fohrer, *TDNT,* 7:1023.

236. Muddiman, *Ephesians,* 293; see also Barth, *Ephesians,* 2:775.

enemies of righteousness but also to edify "the body of Christ . . . unto the measure of the stature of the fulness of Christ" (4:12–13). The meaning is essentially the same in another passage from Paul's hand: "Let us, who are of the day, be sober, putting on the breastplate of *faith* and *love*; [and] for an helmet, the *hope* of salvation" (1 Thes. 5:8, emphasis added). Besides the subtle emphasis in this latter passage on faith, hope, and charity, which are featured at length in 1 Corinthians 13, the main force of the Apostle's words focuses on what is coming—namely, salvation.[237]

salvation: The adjective σωτήριος (*sōtērios*) here functions as a noun with the meanings "saving" and " delivering."[238] Furthermore, this term has surely migrated from LXX Isaiah 59:17, where it appears and is not the usual term for salvation in the New Testament, occurring a mere four other times (see Luke 2:30; 3:6; Acts 28:28; and Titus 2:11). The customary word is σωτηρία (*sōtēria*, see 1:13), which is featured far more frequently.[239] Both terms link to the noun for "savior" (σωτήρ, *sōtēr*).

In two cases, the term *sōtērios* appears in passages that quote or almost quote a verse from the Septuagint rendition of the Old Testament. For example, at Luke 3:6, we read that "all flesh shall see the salvation [*sōtērios*] of God." In LXX Psalm 97:3 (Ps. 98:3 KJV), we come upon "all the ends of the earth have seen the salvation [*sōtērios*] of our God" (see LXX Isa. 52:10, where *sōtēria* occurs). Further, in the last testimony of Paul that Luke recorded, the Apostle came close to quoting LXX Psalm 97:2 when he uttered the words, "Be it known therefore unto you, that the salvation [*sōtērios*] of God is sent unto the Gentiles." The passage in the Old Testament reads, "The Lord has made known his salvation [*sōtērios*], he has revealed his righteousness in the sight of the nations" (LXX Ps. 97:2 [Ps. 98:2 KJV]), understanding "the nations" to refer to the Gentiles (see the Note on 1:13).

sword: The noun μάχαιρα (*machaira*) refers to a short sword or dagger.[240] This is not the long sword. Thus, Christians could expect to find themselves face-to-face with the enemy (see "wrestle" in 6:12) even though their opponents tried to fight at a distance (see "fiery darts" in 6:16). But believers possessed a distinct advantage because God in his mercy had prepared places for them out of "his great love wherewith he loved us" (2:4), seating them "together in heavenly places in Christ Jesus" (2:6).[241] Because they

---

237. Oepke and Kuhn, *TDNT*, 5:315.
238. BDAG, 986; Thayer, *Lexicon*, 612; Merkle, *Guide*, 217.
239. BDAG, 986.2.
240. BDAG, 622.1; Louw-Nida, §6.33.
241. Lincoln, *Ephesians*, 450–51; Winger, *Ephesians*, 720.

lived with the assurance that God protects them, as illustrated by the Lord donning his armor in Isaiah 59:17, devotees could confidently surge into the spiritual battle. For their sword really was "the word of God."[242] This expression brings up the lines recorded elsewhere that "the word of God is quick and powerful, and sharper than any two-edged sword, . . . and is a discerner of the thoughts and intents of the heart" (Heb. 4:12). Thus, "against it there is no defence" for evildoers (see Rev. 1:16; 2:12, 16; 19:15; and D&C 6:2; 11:2; 12:2; 14:2; 33:1).[243]

Spirit: A reader notices that the Spirit does not make up the sword. Rather, the sword itself consists of "the word of God." Here, the Spirit is the possessor of the sword and conveys or gives it to the combatant. And how is that done? One means is through scripture, which is itself a source of revelation. This is the fundamental sense of the lines "the sword of the Spirit, which is the word of God" (see the Notes on 1:17; 3:5).[244]

the word of God: The term for "word" (ῥῆμα, *rhēma*) occurs also at 5:26. In that setting, it has to do with something spoken orally, such as the sacramental prayer.[245] These kinds of spoken words carry divine powers that "sanctify and cleanse" those who receive the Eucharist or sacrament (5:26). In our verse, 6:17, the sense of *rhēma* changes. Here, it pertains to scripture and the revelation that comes from its words. In brief, this short expression "refers either wholly or in part to the OT [Old Testament] word."[246] To be sure, in general, "the word of God" can refer either to the Old Testament or to "the early Christian message" with the notion added to both possibilities that Jesus himself is the embodiment of God's word. For he came both as a fulfillment of the Old Testament and as the subject and essence of what Christian missionaries preached (see Heb. 1:1–2). Christ was not only "the end of the law" or its fulfillment (Rom. 10:4) but also arrived as God's "wisdom, and righteousness, and sanctification, and redemption" (1 Cor. 1:30). He is "the One who incorporates [the Word] in His person" (see the Note on 5:26).[247]

---

242. Wilhelm Michaelis, *TDNT,* 4:526 and n. 21; Lincoln, *Ephesians,* 451.

243. Bruce, *Ephesians,* 131.

244. Kleinknecht, Baumgärtel, Bieder, Sjöberg, and Schweizer, *TDNT,* 6:444; Barth, *Ephesians,* 2:776–77; Larkin, *Handbook,* 162; Merkle, *Guide,* 218.

245. BDAG, 905.1; Louw-Nida, §§33.9, 98; Thayer, *Lexicon,* 562.1.c.β.

246. Kleinknecht, Baumgärtel, Bieder, Sjöberg, and Schweizer, *TDNT,* 6:444. The quotation is from Debrunner, Kleinknecht, Procksch, Kittel, Quell, and Schrenk, *TDNT,* 4:116.

247. Debrunner, Kleinknecht, Procksch, Kittel, Quell, and Schrenk, *TDNT,* 4:113, 126.

6:18 *Praying:* This verse may hold the most important place among those that came before it. Why? Because readers have arrived at the spiritual underpinnings that allowed believers to survive the onslaught of evil. Not surprisingly, prayer stands at the heart of this kind of effort. Underscoring this observation, a reader notices that the verb translated "to pray" (προσεύχομαι, *proseuchomai*),[248] here a participle, is joined by three nouns in this verse that concentrate on "prayer"—προςευχή (*proseuchē*) once and δέησις (*deēsis*) twice. They also are surrounded by four instances of "all" or "every" (πᾶς, *pas*), each of which intensifies the need for effective praying.

Notably, *proseuchomai* and its noun *proseuchē* frame a general term for prayer (see Philip. 4:6 and Col. 4:2 for the noun),[249] including petitionary appeals, such as the prayers uttered by Jesus as he suffered in Gethsemane, where "his sweat was as it were great drops of blood falling down to the ground" (Luke 22:44; see also Mosiah 3:7, "blood cometh from every pore"; and D&C 19:18, "to bleed at every pore").[250] As Luke reported, when Jesus and his disciples arrived at "the place," he told them to "pray [*proseuchomai*] that ye enter not into temptation" (Luke 22:40; see also Matt. 26:41; Mark 14:38; and Luke 22:46). Concerning Jesus' entreaties, Luke wrote that Jesus "kneeled down, and prayed [*proseuchomai*]," asking his Father that he "remove this cup from me." Finally, in his unfathomable "agony he prayed [*proseuchomai*] more earnestly" (Luke 22:41–42, 44). These passages from Luke 22 accentuate the intensity that Paul was asking from his readers when they would supplicate God for his aid.[251] They were to approach him desperate for his help as they faced a well-equipped foe (see Col. 4:12, "laboring fervently for you in prayers [plural of *proseuchē*]").

---

248. BDAG, 879; Thayer, *Lexicon*, 545–46.

249. Johannes Hermann and Heinrich Greeven, *TDNT*, 2:807; Best, *Ephesians*, 605; Winger, *Ephesians*, 756.

250. The verses Luke 22:43–44 do not appear in the earliest manuscripts of Luke's Gospel. They were purposely added by a later scribe because the intense suffering of Jesus, underlined by his bleeding, was known among Christians, as demonstrated by its appearance in the writings of a number of early Christian authors. Metzger, *Textual Commentary*, 151. For a discussion of the evidence that Jesus' experience noted in Luke 22:43–44 was real, see Brown, *Testimony of Luke*, 1022–24, 1027–28. For an argument that these verses were first omitted and then restored to Luke's record, see Lincoln H. Blumell, "Luke 22:43–44: An Anti-Docetic Interpolation or an Apologetic Omission?," *TC: A Journal of Biblical Textual Criticism* 19 (2014): 1–35.

251. Best, *Ephesians*, 604; Fowl, *Ephesians*, 209.

always: The prepositional phrase translated "always" (ἐν παντὶ καιρῷ, *en panti kairō*) bears the literal sense "at all times" (NR), or "always," and projects, perhaps oddly, a limited time period over which events occur rather than a long, historical era.[252] Importantly, this concept frames a subtle pointer to the unfolding, soon-to-be rampant apostasy that would render the church impotent within a couple of generations. Incidentally, the appearance of *panti* in this phrase, when combined in this verse with the other three occurrences of the adjective *pas* ("all" or "every") and the single instances of the verb *proseuchomai,* the noun *proseuchē,* and the word for Spirit (πνεῦμα, *pneuma*), runs readers into a surprising alliteration pattern based on a long series of "p" sounds throughout the verse. The point? To make Paul's words about praying all the more memorable.

prayer: The Apostle has joined the noun προσευχή (*proseuchē,* "prayer")[253] with its verb, *proseuchomai* ("to pray"), adding a layer of emphasis to the need to engage in earnest prayer in order to overcome evil. Its strong petitionary sense presents itself in the account of the Eleven and others seeking the will of God when replacing the disgraced and deceased Judas. Of them, Luke wrote, "All these with one accord devoted themselves to prayer [*proseuchē*],[254] together with the women and Mary . . . and with his brothers" (Acts 1:14 RSV).

supplication: The meaning of the noun δέησις (*deēsis*) hardly differs from its companion *proseuchē* in this passage except that it conveys more of a sense of urgency.[255] Perhaps the distinction rests on *deēsis* focusing on the subject of the prayer. For instance, without saying directly what the subject of Zacharias's prayers had been, but plainly disclosing it, the angel Gabriel said to the humble priest, "Fear not, Zacharias: for thy prayer [*deēsis*] is heard; and thy wife Elisabeth shall bear thee a son" (Luke 1:13). We find a similar situation in an angel's message to Cornelius, the Roman centurion in Caesarea, this time with *proseuchē:* "Cornelius, thy prayer [*proseuchē*] is heard, and thine alms are had in remembrance in the sight of God" (Acts 10:31).[256] Hence, the difference between the two nouns comes down to the

---

252. Delling, *TDNT,* 3:461; BDAG, 497.1.a; Merkle, *Guide,* 219.

253. BDAG, 878.1; Louw-Nida, §33.178.

254. The KJV reads "prayer [*proseuchē*] and supplication [*deēsis*]" in this passage. But the second noun in this rendition was added by a later scribe, as the very few manuscripts that preserve *deēsis* illustrate. Aland and others, *Novum Testamentum Graece,* 28th ed., 321.

255. BDAG, 213; Louw-Nida, §33.171; Thayer, *Lexicon,* 126.2.

256. Hermann and Greeven, *TDNT,* 2:807.

width of a human hair. That said, with this noun, Paul has hit the drum ever harder about the need for focused, urgent prayer.[257]

in the Spirit: As the vision of Nephi informed him, the Spirit can be heard and seen (see 1 Ne. 11:2, 12). Thus, there is a spatial quality or a bodily character to him. In a word, he looks like a man. Yet the Spirit can dwell in us. From the Old Testament, we read that "Joshua the son of Nun, [was] a man in whom is the spirit" (Num. 27:18). Jesus' words to his Eleven on the eve of his death illustrate this idea: "The Spirit of truth; whom the world cannot receive, because it *seeth him not,* . . . but ye know him; for he dwelleth with you, and *shall be in you*" (John 14:17, emphasis added). From Paul's hand, we possess the following: "Ye are . . . in the Spirit, if so be that the Spirit of God dwell in you" (Rom. 8:9). A more famous passage lends credence: "Know ye not that ye are the temple of God, and that the Spirit of God dwelleth in you?" (1 Cor. 3:16; see also 1 Cor. 6:19, "your body is the temple of the Holy Ghost").[258]

These passages escort readers to our phrase "in the Spirit" (ἐν πνεύματι, *en pneumati*). When we turn to Jesus' words, we hear his voice during the last week of his life as he taught in the Jerusalem temple: "How did David, while in the Spirit [*en pneumati*], call him 'Lord'" (Matt. 22:43, Wayment). Plainly, in Jesus' language, the phrase "in the Spirit" is about inspiration from the Holy Ghost. In like manner, at the beginning of his stunning revelation, John wrote, "I was in the Spirit [*en pneumati*] on the Lord's day" (Rev. 1:10). Once again, the phrase pertains to a divine revelatory experience. From Paul, we learn that "no one who speaks with the Spirit [*en pneumati*] of God says, 'Jesus is cursed'" (1 Cor. 12:3, Wayment).[259] The overall sense of these instances centers on being inspired by the Spirit of God. In this light, the phrase in verse 6:18 sends readers to the observation that prayer in its highest form is inspired by God's Spirit and guides the worshiper in what to pray for. As an example, when the twelve disciples in the New World were praying to Christ in his presence, "they did not multiply many words, for it was given unto them what they should pray" (3 Ne. 19:24). Modern scripture cements this thought: "He [or she] that asketh *in the Spirit* asketh according to the will of God" (D&C 46:30, emphasis added; see also Hel. 10:5). That is to say, prayer "in the Spirit" connects worshipers directly to God's will and "the power of revelation."[260]

---

257. Bruce, *Ephesians,* 132.
258. Oepke, *TDNT,* 2:540.
259. Oepke, *TDNT,* 2:540.
260. Kleinknecht, Baumgärtel, Bieder, Sjöberg, and Schweizer, *TDNT,* 6:444.

watching: The verb ἀγρυπνέω (*agrypneō*) takes readers to the meaning "to care for" with the extended sense "to be alertly concerned about."[261] In another passage, *agrypneō* is tied to praying, particularly having to do with being vigilant at the prospect of Jesus' Second Coming. From Jesus' words spoken atop the Mount of Olives, we read, "Watch [*agrypneō*] ye therefore, and pray always, that ye may be accounted worthy to escape all these things . . . and to stand before the Son of man" (Luke 21:36). In this light, the watchfulness that Paul was encouraging his readers to undertake focused on the end-time.[262] The opposite of watching, of course, is sleepiness in its figurative sense. In this vein, Paul wrote "that now it is high time to awake out of sleep: for now is our salvation nearer than when we [first] believed" (Rom. 13:11; see also Matt. 25:5). The antidote to a spiritual sleep is to be alert and watchful, something that Paul himself pursued (see 2 Cor. 6:5; 11:27).[263]

all: We meet the third occurrence of πᾶς (*pas*) in this verse, this time the feminine form πάσῃ (*pasē*), which is in agreement with the following feminine noun. The "p" sound at its beginning fits within and adds to the alliteration that runs through these lines. Because it lacks a definite article, its sense is "total" or "full" so that the line could be understood as "with complete perseverance" (see the Note on 4:2).[264]

perseverance: In the only appearance of this noun (προσκαρτέρησις, *proskarterēsis*) in the New Testament, it carries the meaning of "perseverance" or "persistence."[265] This rather rare term occurs elsewhere only on two inscriptions dated to later than AD 80 that were found at the ancient site of Panticapaeum on the northeastern shore of the Black Sea in modern Crimea. The word bears the sense of praying continuously and persistently for a good outcome in "our spiritual warfare."[266]

supplication: We again come across the second word for "prayer" that we met earlier in this verse (*deēsis*). Thayer has suggested the more intensive translations of "a seeking" or "an entreaty" for this noun.[267]

for all saints: The noun "saints" is the plural of ἅγιος (*hagios*), a term that means "holy" in its adjectival form and "holy one" as a noun. The plural word refers generally to church members (see 1:1). Readers have already

---

261. BDAG, 16.2; see also Louw-Nida, §35.41; and Thayer, *Lexicon*, 9.

262. Oepke, *TDNT*, 2:338–39.

263. Horst Balz, *TDNT*, 8:554–55.

264. Reicke and Bertram, *TDNT*, 5:888.

265. BDAG, 881; Louw-Nida, §68.68.

266. Walter Grundmann, *TDNT*, 3:619–20, quotation on 620.

267. Thayer, *Lexicon*, 126.2.

encountered it fourteen times in this letter.[268] The adjective "all" (the plural πάντων, *pantōn*) is the fourth and last instance of a form of πᾶς (*pas*) in this verse and preserves the last of the "p" sounds. Surprisingly, the preposition in our phrase presents the more interesting case. The usual preposition that means "for" or "on behalf of" is ὑπέρ (*hyper*).[269] But in our case, the term is περί (*peri*), which usually means "about" or "concerning."[270] In certain constructions, however, it is interchangeable with *hyper* and likewise presents the meanings "for" or "on behalf of." Our verse, 6:18, preserves such a construction. In Jesus' ministry, we encounter other examples. For instance, when Jesus walked from the Capernaum synagogue to Peter's home and found Peter's mother-in-law afflicted "with a great fever," Peter and others "besought him for [*peri*] her" (Luke 4:38). In Jesus' instructions to his disciples at the Last Supper, he said to Peter, "I have prayed for [*peri*] thee, that thy faith fail not" (Luke 22:32). In one of Jesus' grand teachings, he required of his hearers that they "bless them that curse you, and pray for [*peri*] them which despitefully use you" (Luke 6:28).[271]

The thought of praying for others, including for those who wish believers ill luck and even seek to injure them in some fashion, directs church members' attention to the world of departed spirits. How so? To respond, it is well known that a practice among Jews of praying for the dead was in place at least two hundred years before Paul's day. We learn of it in the book of 2 Maccabees, a text preserved in the Old Testament Apocrypha along with more than a dozen other documents that modern Roman Catholics accept into their scriptural collection and that early Christians also accepted as part of their scripture.

According to this text, after a battle against the Idumeans and following a Sabbath, the commanding general of the Jewish forces, Judas Maccabee, and his soldiers went to the field of battle to gather up the dead in order to return their bodies to their families for burial. When Judas's men discovered that the fallen warriors were all wearing amulets of the sort forbidden by the Mosaic law (see Deut. 7:25–26), he took up a collection of money among the survivors to pay for a "sin offering" to be made at the Jerusalem temple. The author of the account then wrote that "if he [Judas] had not been expecting the fallen to rise again, it would have been foolish and

---

268. See 1:1, 4, 13, 15, 18; 2:19, 21; 3:5, 8, 18; 4:12, 30; 5:3, 27.

269. BDAG, 1030.A.1.a.α.

270. BDAG, 797.1.

271. Ernst Harald Riesenfeld, *TDNT*, 6:54–55.

superfluous to pray for [*hyper*] the dead." Judas's intent was to bring upon the deceased "the wonderful reward reserved for those who die a godly death" and a deliverance "from their sin" (2 Macc. 12:43–45 NEB). Thus, it is plain that both offering sacrifice and praying for the dead were intended to help their situation in the next world. We find a strong hint about this state of affairs in Jesus' words to Peter and his fellow apostles: "Whatsoever thou shalt bind on earth shall be bound in heaven: and whatsoever thou shalt loose on earth shall be loosed in heaven" (Matt. 16:19; see also Matt. 18:18). One can almost hear the combined language of the two prepositions *peri* and *hyper* in the words "for and on behalf of," pointing to vicarious acts on behalf of the dead (see the Notes on 3:8, 10, 19; 4:5, 9; 5:8; 6:10; and the Analysis of 3:1–13; 4:1–16).[272]

6:19 *And for me:* Paul stepped to the microphone, so to speak, and asked for church members to beg heaven's aid for him as well as for "all saints" (6:18). Although no verb "to pray" occurs here, its unwritten presence is clearly implied.[273] The conjunction "and" (καί, *kai*) bears an emphatic sense of "especially" so that a reader understood the expression "and especially for me."[274] The preposition translated "for" is ὑπέρ (*hyper*), the term that usually expresses the sense "for" or "on behalf of." The combination of *kai* and *hyper* marks the Apostle's request as "a special case."[275] It also becomes apparent that this kind of language would not be employed by a person writing in Paul's name while he was alive. Nor does it make sense to argue that a pseudonymous author would picture the Apostle begging for believers' prayers if he were already dead.[276] The untenable character of such a view goes beyond words to express (see the Notes on 3:8; 4:3, 21; 6:3; and the Analysis of 3:1–13).

The aspect that captures our attention in verse 6:19 is the unexpected lack of a request for Paul's companions, a regular dimension of his other letters when he made requests like this one. The briefest example reposes in his first letter to his Thessalonian converts. There, he wrote simply, "Brethren, pray for us" (1 Thes. 5:25). Elsewhere, he spelled out the needs of himself and his companions. For instance, we possess these words from him:

---

272. Riesenfeld, *TDNT,* 8:512–13; see also Oepke, *TDNT,* 1:542.

273. Lincoln, *Ephesians,* 453; Fowl, *Ephesians,* 209.

274. Barth, *Ephesians,* 2:779; Lincoln, *Ephesians,* 453; Larkin, *Handbook,* 164; Merkle, *Guide,* 219.

275. Riesenfeld, *TDNT,* 6:54–55; Riesenfeld, *TDNT,* 8:514 and n. 36; BDAG, 1030.A.1.a.α; Barth, *Ephesians,* 2:779, is the source of the quoted words.

276. Muddiman, *Ephesians,* 295; contra Lincoln, *Ephesians,* 453; Best, *Ephesians,* 606.

"Brethren, pray for us, that the word of the Lord may have free course, and . . . that we may be delivered from unreasonable and wicked men" (2 Thes. 3:1–2). Again, "Pray for us, too, that God may open a door for our message" (Col. 4:3 NIV; see also 2 Cor. 1:11). That said, we discover at least one instance of Paul asking for prayers for himself, with added details of why he requested the divine help: "I urge you, brothers, by our Lord Jesus Christ and by the love of the Spirit, to join me in my struggle by praying to God for me. Pray that I may be rescued from the unbelievers in Judea . . . so that by God's will I may come to you with joy" (Rom. 15:30–32 NIV).[277] The Apostle had surely grasped the power of prayer in his own ministry and that of his fellow missionaries.

that: The conjunction ἵνα (*hina*) introduces the content and purpose of the prayer that Paul seeks on his behalf—that God will give him "utterance . . . to make known the mystery of the gospel."[278]

utterance: The noun that sits under this English term is λόγος (*logos*), the customary term for "word" and related meanings. Within this verse, the core clearly centers on the gospel message that Paul will preach as it is "given"; this verb is a passive subjunctive form of δίδωμι (*didōmi*), which points to "God as the giver."[279] In this instance, *logos* has to do with the spoken word and not with the written, and its subject is called here "the mystery of the gospel." Jesus had promised to the Twelve that in daunting circumstances, like Paul's imprisonment, they would be given the words to say by "the Spirit of your Father which speaketh in you" (Matt. 10:20;[280] see also Luke 21:12–15). The granting of such utterance comes as a result of prayer.

open my mouth: Opening the mouth to disclose gospel truths ranged far from the activity of opening the mouth in "corrupt communication" (4:29). It was through the mouths of God's servants that his word was spread: "[God] spake by the mouth of his holy prophets" (Luke 1:70). It was through Christ's mouth that the people in the Nazareth synagogue heard his "gracious words" (Luke 4:22). It was through the mouth of God's servant Philip that the gospel was preached to the Ethiopian eunuch: "Philip opened his mouth . . . and preached unto him Jesus" (see Acts 8:35). It was through Christ's mouth, speaking words to Paul, that the Apostle received

---

277. Lincoln, *Ephesians*, 453; Merkle, *Guide*, 220.

278. Winger, *Ephesians*, 759; Merkle, *Guide*, 220.

279. Larkin, *Handbook*, 165; Merkle, *Guide*, 220; Best, *Ephesians*, 607; Winger, *Ephesians*, 759.

280. Winger, *Ephesians*, 759–60.

his calling to preach to the Gentiles (see Acts 26:13–18). One operating principle behind all such examples consists of the purity of the speaker. But purity among humans is not a given. Hence, they need the intervention of heaven to speak God's words. One suspects that this notion lies behind Paul's words in this verse, 6:19, though not directly expressed (see the Note on 4:29).[281]

boldly: Every person who on one occasion or another has needed to speak up on an important matter in a hostile setting knows what Paul was driving at. It is actually a short prepositional phrase that stands behind "boldly" in this passage. The phrase ἐν παρρησίᾳ (*en parrēsia*) presents the sense "in boldness" or "in fearlessness."[282] Another meaning closely related to boldness attaches to the noun παρρησία (*parrēsia*) and its verb, παρρησιάζομαι (*parrēsiazomai*), the latter of which shows up in 6:20, where it refers to openness.[283] In his second letter to the Corinthian Saints, the Apostle wrote that "since we have such a hope [of glory], we are very bold [*parrēsia*]" (2 Cor. 3:12 RSV). The underlying sense becomes clear as Paul went on. For he next discussed the veil that Moses wore when his face glowed brightly with God's glory after descending the holy mount (see Ex. 34:29–33). At the end, Paul concluded, "We all, with unveiled face, behold-ing the glory of the Lord, are being changed into his likeness from one degree of glory to another" (2 Cor. 3:18 RSV). What is the point? It is that with an unveiled gaze—that is, a gaze open toward heavenly things—we can behold "the glory of the Lord." It is a person's openness to celestial realities that makes all the difference. That openness can then be turned toward fellow human beings, creating a confidence that one enjoys both in God's presence and in the presence of others (see the Notes on 3:12; 6:20).[284]

make known: The verb γνωρίζω (*gnōrizō*) has previously occurred four times in this letter and will appear once more (see 1:9; 3:3, 5, 10; 6:21). The term presents the basic sense of "to make known" or "to reveal."[285] Its tie to sacred ceremony appears in the Old Testament when, on the occasion of the holy ark's arrival in Jerusalem, King David sang a psalm that began with these words: "Give thanks unto the Lord, call upon his name, *make known his deeds* among the people" (1 Chr. 16:8, emphasis added). Adding a link to

---

281. Konrad Weiss, *TDNT,* 7:696–97, 699–700; see also Georg Bertram, *TDNT,* 3:38–39.
282. BDAG, 781.3.a; Louw-Nida, §25.158.
283. BDAG, 781.2; Thayer, *Lexicon,* 491.1.
284. Schlier, *TDNT,* 5:883.
285. BDAG, 203.1; Thayer, *Lexicon,* 119.1.

heavenly gears, it was Jesus who, according to John's Gospel, disclosed the secrets of his Father: "All things that I have heard of my Father I have made known [*gnōrizō*] unto you" (John 15:15; see also John 17:26). In a different vein, prayer—an act of worship—intimately connects to this verb. As Paul reminded his friends in Philippi, "In everything by prayer and supplication with thanksgiving let your requests be made known [passive of *gnōrizō*] unto God" (Philip. 4:6).[286] Thus, the verb *gnōrizō* ties to sacred knowledge, what Paul will next call "the mystery of the gospel," as well as to secular information as we shall see in 6:21 (see the Notes on 1:9; 3:3, 5, 10; 6:21).

mystery: The noun μυστήριον (*mystērion*) has regularly appeared in Ephesians, normally touching on God's revelation that the Gentiles were to be brought within the gospel net (see 1:9; 3:3, 4, 9; 5:32). In the context of 6:19, the ground beneath *mystērion* has shifted, revealing a promising vein to explore. For Paul has drawn attention to himself as the one who has and will deliver the *mystērion* to others. In effect, he was the bearer of the revelation of this mystery along with the other apostles (see 3:3–5). In its main part, *mystērion* had to do with bringing Gentiles into the gospel fold. But God's mystery did not end there. The final consummation also formed an important element in this mystery. The Apostle was the bearer of news about this distant event. Though he could not say when it would occur, he could bear witness that it surely would happen, with Christ descending noisily "from heaven with a shout, and with the voice of the archangel, and with the trump of God" (1 Thes. 4:16). Furthermore, with his efforts and the efforts of other church leaders, the church itself would become involved in imparting "the manifold wisdom of God" to "the principalities and powers in heavenly places," a stunning component in God's *mystērion* (3:10;[287] see the Note thereon). Hence, God's mystery filled a broad and rich pattern in early Christian teaching (see the Notes on 1:9; 3:4, 9; 5:32).

gospel: Occurring for the fourth time (see 1:13; 3:6; 6:15), the noun εὐαγγέλιον (*euangelion*) is the object of Paul's unrelenting activity, of his unstoppable preaching. To this moment in time, all evangelizing was oral. No written texts of the Christian message were in circulation except Paul's letters, and the few recipients were scattered across the Roman world. As we noticed in the review of *euangelion* in 6:15, this term possessed a clear content that focused on the birth, death, Resurrection, and subsequent appearances of Christ (see Rom. 1:1–4 and 1 Cor. 15:1–8). But there is more to the

---

286. Bultmann, *TDNT,* 1:718.
287. Bornkamm, *TDNT,* 4:821–22.

story. The content and character of the gospel differs from other traditions that emphasized both the superiority of the teacher and the message that he bore to students, which often rested on "a fixed esoteric doctrine" that was not to be shared with outsiders.[288] In contrast, the gospel is a living faith, a trust that centers on eternal truths that in their turn rest on the actions and teachings of the man Jesus, who became, through his death, his descent into the spirit world, and his Resurrection, the heavenly Christ. Moreover, *euangelion* does not fit the tidy orbit of Paul alone in some manner. The gospel is one, not fragmented among the different apostles.[289]

More than this and more to the point, the gospel carries a power that brings believers to salvation. As Paul had written elsewhere, "The gospel of Christ . . . is the power of God unto salvation" (Rom. 1:16). Because the stakes were so enormous for potential converts, Paul and his companions relied on divine guidance to send them where God wanted them to preach. The Apostle hinted as much in his Corinthian correspondence: "As your faith continues to grow, our area of activity among you will greatly expand [beyond Corinth], so that we can preach the gospel in the regions beyond you" (2 Cor. 10:15–16 NIV; see also Acts 16:7–10). And because the *euangelion* is transmitted orally, Paul's "bonds" (6:20) would not restrict his ability to talk to others about his message.[290] Finally, the gospel carried a series of expectations for proper behavior and character development. Paul referred to this when he wrote about the gospel resting on "the command of the eternal God" with the goal "that all nations might believe and *obey* him" (Rom. 16:26, emphasis added; see also the Notes on 2:17; 6:15).[291]

6:20 *For which:* Again, we come upon the preposition ὑπέρ (*hyper*), as we did in 6:19. Here, the term exhibits the meaning "with reference to" or possibly "on account of." The sense of our verse then becomes clear: it was "in the interest of" propagating the gospel that Paul found himself "in bonds" while serving as "an ambassador" (see the Notes on 5:2, 25; 6:18–19).[292]

I am an ambassador: Lying below this expression rests a single verb, πρεσβεύω (*presbeuō*), whose personal noun is πρεσβύτερος (*presbyteros*), with the sense of presbyter or "old man" (see Philem. 1:9) or, as the KJV usually translates it in its Christian context, "elder." In its verb form, it means "to

288. Delling, *TDNT,* 4:12–13, quotation on 12.

289. Friedrich, *TDNT,* 2:733.

290. Friedrich, *TDNT,* 2:732–33; see Muddiman, *Ephesians,* 296.

291. Delling, *TDNT,* 4:12.

292. Riesenfeld, *TDNT,* 8:513–15; see also BDAG, 1031.A.2; 1031.A.3; and Louw-Nida, §90.24.

be an ambassador or envoy."[293] This verb occurs in only one other passage in the New Testament, where Paul explained exactly how he was God's representative: "We are ambassadors [*presbeuō*] for Christ, with God making his appeal through us" (2 Cor. 5:20, Wayment). In Paul's hands, the term recalled the picture of an ambassador, who represented the Roman emperor to a distant land and people, traveling at the risk of life and limb, with the unsubtle difference that the Apostle was an envoy for the grandest emperor of all, God himself.[294]

in bonds: The noun ἅλυσις (*halysis*) sits in the singular. It can refer to two very different but related things, imprisonment or a chain.[295] If we understand the meaning to be imprisonment, then Paul has brought readers inside a prison, like the one where he had once been held (see Acts 16:23–24). However, when held for long stretches of time, his usual fate was to be under house arrest (see Acts 24:23; 28:30). There is reason to believe that he was under house arrest in the light of his correspondence with Philemon, a longtime friend. In that letter, he mentioned that he was imprisoned, perhaps the same imprisonment that he was experiencing when he wrote Ephesians (see 3:1; 4:1; and Philem. 1:1, 9). He also wrote, "I beseech thee for my son Onesimus, whom I have begotten [in the gospel] in my bonds" (Philem. 1:10). Onesimus was a runaway slave who belonged to Philemon. After fleeing Asia, where Philemon resided, Onesimus had reached Rome, where Paul was evidently being held. Somehow, they had met and Paul had taught the gospel to the runaway. Could this have happened if Paul were stowed in a prison? If he were, how would a runaway slave even dare to approach a prison without any identification to show a jailer? Hence, they must have met in the city, where the Apostle dwelt "in his own hired house, and received all that came in unto him" (Acts 28:30). In this light, we must think of a chain that Paul wore, which allowed him a lot of mobility, likely linked to the wrist of a soldier who, handcuffed to Paul, would go where the Apostle wanted to go.[296]

If readers recognize the meaning of *halysis* to be a chain, the imagery becomes much more fluid and interesting. In the first place, ambassadors often wore a chain around their necks as a symbol that they represented

---

293. Günther Bornkamm, *TDNT,* 6:681–83; BDAG, 861; Thayer, *Lexicon,* 535.2, s.v. "πρεσβεύω."

294. Barth, *Ephesians,* 2:781–82; Lincoln, *Ephesians,* 454; Williams, *Paul's Metaphors,* 151–52.

295. BDAG, 48; Louw-Nida, §§6.16; 37.115.

296. Bruce, *Ephesians,* 133–34; Best, *Ephesians,* 609.

a dignified person of rank. Such a chain would have been made of the precious metal gold. In ironic contrast, Paul's chain was one that tethered him to a soldier who would be with him for four hours and then relieved.[297] The Apostle's chain of office linked him not to an earthly emperor whom he represented but to Christ, who had been crucified—that is, executed by a Roman official. But Christ had triumphantly risen from his tomb to become the resplendent co-emperor of the universe with his Father (see the Notes on 3:1; 4:1).[298]

speak boldly: The verb παρρησιάζομαι (*parrēsiazomai*), here in the subjunctive mood, sends readers to the meaning "to speak openly" or "to speak fearlessly."[299] One suspects that both senses were at play in believers' minds when they heard or read the words of the letter. As Paul had verbalized his need, he was to go forward in harmony with "a law of nonconcealment." And the core of full disclosure was to reside not just in his words but also in his body. To his friends in Philippi, the Apostle had written, "As I passionately hope, I shall have no cause to be ashamed, but shall speak so boldly that now as always the greatness of Christ will shine out clearly in my person, whether through my life or through my death" (Philip. 1:20 NEB). For him, the necessity to speak openly and honestly about the gospel was ever draped over his mind and his physical body.[300] And how might the soldiers handcuffed to Paul have fared? No doubt they all received an earful of gospel teachings (see the Notes on 3:12; 6:19).

ought: The simple, short, impersonal verb δεῖ (*dei*) connotes both workaday obligations and divine destinies that involved heavenly guidance. Its basic import comes to "it is necessary."[301] A few examples will illustrate its importance in Jesus' ministry and Atonement. At the beginning of the well-known story of Jesus and the Samaritan woman, we read that Jesus "must needs [*dei*] go through Samaria" (John 4:4). Thus, a divine necessity led Jesus to take his disciples upon the winding road to Samaria, whose inhabitants were not friendly to Jews, rather than to shepherd them along the more traveled road in the Jordan Valley. The same celestial push stands behind his words elsewhere: "I must [*dei*] preach the kingdom of God to

297. Bruce, *Ephesians*, 133–34.

298. Williams, *Paul's Metaphors*, 151–52.

299. BDAG, 782.1; Louw-Nida, §33.90; Thayer, *Lexicon*, 491.1.

300. Schlier, *TDNT*, 5:883.

301. BDAG, 214.1; Louw-Nida, §71.34; particularly Thayer, *Lexicon*, 126.e: "δεῖ seems to be more suggestive of moral obligation, denoting esp. that constraint which arises from divine appointment."

other cities also: for therefore am I sent" (Luke 4:43). When a resurrected being and walking to the town of Emmaus with two believers, he asked forcefully, "Ought [*dei*] not Christ to have suffered these things, and to enter into his glory?" (Luke 24:26).[302] Not unimportantly, this was the first time that Jesus had called himself by his title "the Christ," and he uttered it only after his Resurrection.[303]

Circling back to the necessity that drove Paul, the verb *dei* also exhibits a history in the New Testament of describing God's salvation that he offered to his children. In John's Gospel, we meet Jesus' nighttime words spoken to Nicodemus: "Ye must [*dei*] be born again" (John 3:7). We hear Peter's voice as he spoke to the Jerusalem Sanhedrin about Christ: "Neither is there salvation in any other [name]: for there is none other name under heaven given among men, whereby we must [*dei*] be saved" (Acts 4:12; see also Acts 16:30–31).[304] In this light, a divine necessity lay upon human hearers of the gospel message to respond positively and come to celestial salvation.

Analysis of 6:10–20

The verses that follow the imperative "become therefore imitators of God" (5:1 NR) spread out before readers the sweep of principles that bring them to imitate God, such as walking "in love" and behaving "circumspectly, not as fools, but as wise" and loving "their wives as their own bodies" (5:2, 15, 28). On the other hand, devotees' actions, choreographed and disciplined, stand front and center in 6:10–20, bringing them to don and wear God's celestial clothing and take up his armament.

An important question to resolve revolves around whether Paul was speaking literally or metaphorically when raising the topics of God's military clothing and weaponry. The short answer is both. As will be seen in the Notes above, the Apostle's itemizing matches exactly what is known about Roman military dress, armor, and weapons. On the other hand, Christians were to "put on the whole armour of God" as a spiritual dress and defense (6:11, 13). In a word, no flashing swords were ever apparent in their meetings. But the fact that they were engaged in a massive struggle "against the rulers of the darkness of this world" (6:12) and therefore needed God's protective clothing was never forgotten.

---

302. Walter Grundmann, *TDNT*, 2:22–24.
303. Brown, *Testimony of Luke*, 1122–23, 1128.
304. Grundmann, *TDNT*, 2:24.

Several commentators have drawn attention to the organizing dimensions of these verses, with some variation among these individuals. On the first level resides the command to "be strong in the Lord," which necessitated putting "on the whole armour of God" so that believers would "be able to withstand in the evil day," which was fast approaching (6:10–13). On the second level reposes the balancing of the implements of war. In effect, we come upon two pairs of three. In the initial pair, we meet loins, then breastplate, and finally feet (see 6:14–15). In the following three, we encounter shield, then helmet, and finally sword (see 6:16–17). The unifying element among the first three is that they were about protecting the soldier's body—the lower and middle areas of his body along with his exposed feet. One could add "the helmet" to this list of protections (6:17). The uniting dimension of the next three comes alive in the idea of defensive warfare fought at close quarters as the enemy attacked. To be sure, the shield was designed to turn aside flaming arrows shot from a distance, and one's helmet protected the head from arrows, thrown javelins, and other objects. But they were most helpful at turning aside blows delivered in hand-to-hand combat. And the short sword was designed for close-quarter fighting (see 6:16–17). On the third level, we encounter the key matter for Paul's readers: "Praying always with all prayer and supplication [for themselves and] . . . for all saints; and for me" (6:18–19).[305] Praying is not only welcome but essential. But this is only part of the story.

Another set of organizing strands runs through these verses. It consists of the three verbs "to put on" (6:11, 14, "having on"), "to take up [arms]" (6:13, 16), and "to take" (6:17). All of these have to do with believers' actions, not God's. To be sure, a person could argue that the protective clothing and armaments noted in 6:14–17 were provided by God. Or at the least he provided their pattern. But the doers who were putting "on the whole armour of God" were devotees, not God. Let us be clear that these people were dressing themselves in God's "whole armour," not in random pieces of equipment.[306] Let us also be clear that dressing in sacred garments and undertaking holy acts within boundaries that God had set match very precisely the sacred actions of ceremonial worship and activity. Yes, Paul had described the individual Christian's need to be prepared for a conflict that was approaching at high speed. But preparation to face "spiritual

---

305. Barth, *Ephesians*, 2:784; Lincoln, *Ephesians*, 430–32; Muddiman, *Ephesians*, 282, 285; Perkins, *Ephesians*, 141.

306. Houlden, *Paul's Letters from Prison*, 338.

wickedness in high places" and "the evil day" sounds like more than wrapping oneself in the blanket of baptism and hoping for the best. Rather, God needed to fortify his people against the conflict that would undo the church, against the fast-approaching apostasy. And sacred ordinances performed as part of holy rituals were one way to help believers survive severe spiritual challenges.

In summarizing these observations, the three verbs "to put on," "to take up," and "to take" open unexpected doors. We first meet "to put on" at 4:24 in the line "to put on the new person" (NR). Its double repetition in chapter 6 comes like a deep sounding drum, with a pounding, rolling rhythm and snare-drum-sounding trills: in 6:11 and 6:14, the focus crashes down on donning God's garments, specifically God's armor, something that he put on long ago when facing his adversaries. In those days, "he put on righteousness as a breastplate, and an helmet of salvation upon his head" (Isa. 59:17). God's actions then had become believers' actions now. Imitating the divine means holy acts, holy words, holy clothing (see 5:1 NR, "become therefore imitators of God"; the Notes on 4:22, 24; 5:20; 6:11, 13–14, 16; and appendix 1).

If we pivot to the virtues associated with the armaments, no organizing principle seems to emerge among such characteristics as "righteousness," "faith," and "salvation" (6:14, 16–17), with one possible exception. In positions of emphasis, the first in the list is "truth," which girds a person's "loins," and the last is "the Spirit," which forms the sword and arises from "the word of God" (6:14, 17). Truth, of course, can blossom from a number of sources. But God's truth ties directly to "the word of God"—that is, scripture, as we discovered in the Note on 6:17. For those who have experienced revelatory power when reading and studying scripture, it is an easy step to join scripture, which possesses the revealing power of "the Spirit," and God's "truth."[307]

Finally, from Paul's description of military clothing and equipment, the struggle that Christians must engage in was to remain defensive. Equipped with only a short sword for fighting, their task was to hold the line against an onrushing force that sought to unhinge them from their faith, a force that made its home beyond "the darkness of this world" and comprised "spiritual wickedness in high places" (6:12). The believers' task was to "stand" (6:14).[308]

---

307. Debrunner, Kleinknecht, Procksch, Kittel, Quell, and Schrenk, *TDNT,* 4:116; Kleinknecht, Baumgärtel, Bieder, Sjöberg, and Schweizer, *TDNT,* 6:444.

308. Lincoln, *Ephesians,* 460; Best, *Ephesians,* 610.

"That Ye Might Know Our Affairs" (6:21–24)

King James Translation

21 But that ye also may know my affairs, and how I do, Tychicus, a beloved brother and faithful minister in the Lord, shall make known to you all things: 22 Whom I have sent unto you for the same purpose, that ye might know our affairs, and that he might comfort your hearts. 23 Peace be to the brethren, and love with faith, from God the Father and the Lord Jesus Christ. 24 Grace be with all them that love our Lord Jesus Christ in sincerity. Amen.

New Rendition

21 So that you also may know about my circumstances and how I am doing, Tychicus, the beloved brother and faithful servant in the Lord, will make everything known to you. 22 I am sending him to you for this very purpose: that you may know how we are and that he may encourage your hearts.

23 Peace be to the brothers and sisters, and love with faith from God the Father and the Lord Jesus Christ. 24 Grace be with all who love our Lord Jesus Christ with an undying love.

Notes on 6:21–24

6:21 *that ye also may know:* One of the main reasons that commentators conclude that Paul was not the author of Ephesians grows out of this verse and those that follow. These last lines lack personal greetings to any church members in Ephesus or the adjoining region. Because the Apostle had spent a long two or three years in the city (see Acts 19:10; 20:31) and because presumably not a long time had passed since his departure, it is puzzling that he has omitted any greetings to old friends or salutations from his companions. These personal touches are items that we have come to expect from other letters (see Rom. 16:3–15; Philip. 4:21–22; Col. 4:10–15; and Philem. 1:23–24).[309] The number of possible reasons for this omission is large, though some appear more likely than others.[310] The simple fact is that we do not know why they are missing here and yet appear in letters that were likely composed about the same time (see Col. 4:10–15 and Philem. 1:23–24).

also: The conjunction καί (*kai*) has generated a lot of discussion. Does it stand closely with the plural pronoun "you" and carry the meaning "you too" as if it is pointing to the recipients of the letters to the Colossians and to Philemon, all of whom will soon learn more about Paul and his situation? Does it pertain to the composition of Colossians and hint that

---

309. Lincoln, *Ephesians*, 461–64.
310. Barth, *Ephesians*, 2:809–10.

Paul composed Ephesians and Colossians about the same time with both congregations receiving a similar letter? Does it have to do with Tychicus's journey to tell both the recipients of Ephesians and those of Colossians about the Apostle's circumstances as a prisoner? An answer is impossible to determine without a clearer grasp of the circumstances behind the composition of these three letters—Ephesians, Colossians, and Philemon.[311]

my affairs: The expression reads literally "the things concerning me" (τὰ κατ' ἐμέ, *ta kat' eme*). With these words begins a cluster of thirty-two words, running through 6:22, that occur in the identical order of words written in Colossians 4:7–8, with the exception of the words that appear next within this verse, "how I do" (τί πράσσω, *ti prassō*). These two Greek words, *ti prassō,* do not stand in the Colossians passage. Otherwise, the two sections in Ephesians and Colossians are exactly the same. The existence of the identical thirty-two words in the two letters, of course, has led to the conclusion that these words have been copied from one letter to the other and then has raised the question how this came about. One natural conclusion points to either Paul or his scribe writing out the two letters on the same occasion and simply copying these words into the second epistle because they fitted the Apostle's purpose. But not all scholars agree, and some see a plot afoot.

For those who seek to paint the author of Ephesians (and Colossians) as someone other than Paul, the treatment of these thirty-two words presents grand entertainment. At every turn, a commentator has to line up the pieces so that they point away from the Apostle and toward an unknown, presumed writer. Let us listen in on a discussion about the almost identical language in Ephesians 6:21–22 and Colossians 4:7–8, a series of words that is launched in each epistle just before the mention of Tychicus, who becomes a key: This "almost verbatim [language] . . . functions as part of the framework through which the writer [not Paul] presents his message as [if] a personal letter from Paul. By means of this device, the writer is able to avoid having to say anything more specific about Paul's situation and can instead simply point the readers to Tychicus. . . . This amounts to a thinly veiled self-recommendation on the part of the writer himself."[312] The conspiratorial character of such an imagined scene—that is, that a pseudonymous author supposedly undertook to hide both his identity and the fictitious nature of the letter by plopping the name Tychicus into his

---

311. Lincoln, *Ephesians,* 464–65; Best, *Ephesians,* 614–15; Winger, *Ephesians,* 763.
312. Lincoln, *Ephesians,* 465.

writing and not mentioning others of Paul's associates—simply leaves a person out of breath. One is left to wonder why commentators approach history as if it is a psychological exercise and assume that it is possible to get inside the heads of imposters and thus understand what really happened.[313] While deceivers exist in every society, why pin deception on a fictional, dishonest early Christian writer? (See the Notes on 3:8; 4:3, 21; 6:3; and the Analysis of 3:1–13; 6:1–9.)

how I do: The expression consists of two Greek words, τί πράσσω (*ti prassō*), whose insertion here forms the only difference between the identical thirty-two words that Ephesians 6:21–22 and Colossians 4:7–8 share. The verb is πράσσω (*prassō*) and carries the meanings of "accomplishing" and "doing."[314] This term remains rather colorless, not packing the heft of other verbs of doing and working. For example, Paul wrote κατεργάζομαι (*katergazomai*) to make a point about facing wickedness "and having done [*katergazomai*] all, to stand" (6:13). When he inserted ποιέω (*poieō*), he applied it to Christ's work. In one instance, the Apostle wrote that Christ, in uniting Jew and Gentile, "hath made [*poieō*] both one, and hath broken down the middle wall of partition between [them]" (2:14). In a second example, Christ created from these two parts "through himself the two into one new human, thus making [*poieō*] peace" (2:15 NR). Then, almost singing, Paul swung around to the majestic deeds of the Father: "To the one who is able, above all, to do [*poieō*] more abundantly whatever we ask or consider thoughtfully, according to the power acting in us—to him be the glory in the church and in Christ Jesus throughout all generations of time and forevermore, Amen" (3:20–21 NR). Hence, *prassō* was used for human actions, some of which were evil (see Rom. 1:32 [twice]; 2:1; 13:4; 2 Cor. 5:10; Gal. 5:21; etc.), and other verbs served Paul when he described activities undertaken by the Son and the Father.[315]

Tychicus: This man from Asia is known to be a longtime associate of Paul. He made Luke's list in Acts 20:4 as a companion of Paul when the Apostle began his final trip back to Jerusalem and to his arrest in the city. Whether Tychicus traveled all the way from Macedonia to Jerusalem with the Apostle, as chronicled in Acts 20–21, remains unknown. What is known is that he was the bearer of the letter to the Colossians and possibly to Philemon, bearing the charge to inform church members about Paul's

313. Muddiman, *Ephesians,* 296–98.
314. BDAG, 860.1.
315. Christian Maurer, *TDNT,* 6:635.

situation (see Col. 4:7). In effect, he was coming home to his province of Asia. He also served at Ephesus and on the isle of Crete in the city Nicopolis (2 Tim. 4:12; Titus 3:12).[316] Nothing more is known about him.

beloved brother: The sentiments "beloved brother and faithful minister" are high praise indeed. The adjective for "beloved" is ἀγαπητός (*agapētos*),[317] a relative of ἀγάπη (*agapē*), the noun for "love" or "charity," and the verb ἀγαπάω (*agapaō*), "to love." In its highest articulation, *agapētos* occurs in the expression "beloved [plural of *agapētos*] of God" (Rom. 1:7) and, in Jesus' case, "my beloved [*agapētos*] Son" (Matt. 3:17; 17:5; etc.).

Except for 6:23, this verse is the only one where "brother" (ἀδελφός, *adelphos*) appears in Ephesians. As we saw in an earlier verse, 6:10, the plural noun "brethren" was most likely added by a later scribe (see the Note on 6:10). The word *adelphos* appears more than 340 times in the New Testament, whereas its feminine counterpart, "sister" (ἀδελφή, *adelphē*), occurs a mere 24 times. But sisters or women are often implicitly present in the plural of *adelphos*.[318] For example, in Paul's plea "brethren, pray for us" (1 Thes. 5:25), he and his readers knew that his letter was not addressed only to his male converts in Thessalonica but to the women as well.

faithful minister: The adjective πιστός (*pistos*), with the strong meanings "trustworthy" and "dependable," is a term by which "Paul honors his co-workers" in the ministry.[319] The Apostle reckoned among his faithful "co-workers" not only Tychicus but also Timothy (see 1 Cor. 4:17), Epaphras, and Onesimus (see Col. 1:7; 4:9).[320]

The noun translated "minister" (διάκονος, *diakonos*) lies beneath the church office of "deacon." Its basic Christian sense relates to one who serves in the ministry of the church, whether man or woman, young or old (see Matt. 20:26).[321] The term exhibits some interesting connections. In Paul's case, he is both a minister to the church and a minister of Christ. To the Colossian Saints, he wrote, "I became a minister [to the church] according to the divine office which was given to me for you" (Col. 1:25 RSV). In his spat with certain teachers in Corinth, he asked, "Are they ministers of Christ? (I speak as a fool) I am more." How so? He went on: "In labors more abundant, in stripes above measure, in prisons more frequent" (2 Cor. 11:23;

---

316. Lincoln, *Ephesians*, 465.
317. BDAG, 7.2.
318. Louw-Nida, §11.23.
319. BDAG, 820.
320. BDAG, 820.1.a.
321. BDAG, 230.2; Thayer, *Lexicon*, 138.

see also 2 Cor. 6:3–5). Very obviously, serving as a minister brought with it deep challenges and trials for the Apostle. In this light, readers come to hold a high opinion of Paul's companion Epaphras, whom he called "our dear fellowservant, who is for you a faithful minister of Christ" (Col. 1:7;[322] see also the Note on 3:7).

in the Lord: Although this phrase brings the verse to a close in the Greek text, in English it occupies its current place for clarity. Mention of the Lord always elevates the level of discourse when a reader comes upon this title (κύριος, *kyrios*). Its inherent dignity as the designation for Israel's God cannot be matched. For instance, "every knee should bow . . . and . . . every tongue should confess that Jesus Christ is Lord" (Philip. 2:10–11). Why? Because God the Father "hath put all things under his feet, and gave him to be the head over all things to the church" (1:22;[323] see also the Notes on 4:1, 17; 5:22).

make known: Readers encountered this verb (γνωρίζω, *gnōrizō*) as recently as 6:19. In its basic senses, "to make known" and "to reveal,"[324] it pertains to both Tychicus's oral message that he was to deliver about Paul's activities and about "all things," likely doctrinal and behavioral matters that the Apostle wanted Tychicus to emphasize because they had been divinely impressed upon Paul.[325] This notion of divine inspiration reposes below his words to his Corinthian readers when, in leading up to his catalog of the Resurrected Christ's appearances, he wrote, "Brethren, I [now] declare [*gnōrizō*] unto you the gospel which I preached unto you" (1 Cor. 15:1). This declaration, which was really a reminder, about persons to whom the Risen Jesus had appeared is unparalleled in the New Testament, linking the verb *gnōrizō* to the most sublime of messages about Christ's Resurrection and about the witnesses of its reality (see 1 Cor. 15:3–8[326] and the Notes on 1:9; 3:3, 5, 10; 6:19).

6:22 *I have sent:* In general, the past tense of the verb πέμπω (*pempō*) refers to the simple act of sending (see Philip. 2:19, 23, 25; etc.) and here bears the sense "I am sending."[327] Its counterpart in the New Testament, the verb ἀποστέλλω (*apostellō*), stresses the commission or authorization

---

322. Hermann W. Beyer, *TDNT,* 2:89.
323. Quell and Foerster, *TDNT,* 3:1090.
324. BDAG, 203.1; Thayer, *Lexicon,* 119.1.
325. Bultmann, *TDNT,* 1:718.
326. Friedrich, *TDNT,* 2:730.
327. Merkle, *Guide,* 224.

that accompanies the one sent and bears the sense "to send forth."[328] Therefore, the latter verb, *apostellō,* links to Jesus sending forth the apostles (see Matt. 10:5, 16; Mark 3:14; etc.) and to God sending his Son (see Matt. 10:40; 15:24; Mark 9:37;[329] and the Notes on 1:1; 2:20; 3:5; 4:11).

for the same purpose: The preposition εἰς (*eis*) catches our initial attention. Here, with the accusative case, it exhibits "a final sense"; that is, its meaning is "for a goal" or "for a cause." As examples that have to do with Christ, Jesus said to Pilate, "Thou sayest that I am a king. To [*eis*] this end was I born, and for [*eis*] this cause came I into the world" (John 18:37). To Roman church members, Paul wrote about Christ's Atonement: "To [*eis*] this end Christ both died and rose . . . that he might be Lord both of the dead and living" (Rom. 14:9). Of the crusading Paul, then in Damascus, Christians nervously whispered, "Is not this he that destroyed them . . . in Jerusalem, and came hither for [*eis*] that intent, that he might bring them bound unto the chief priests?" (Acts 9:21; see also Acts 26:16, "for [*eis*] this purpose"; Rom. 9:17, "for [*eis*] this same purpose"; and 2 Cor. 2:9, "to [*eis*] this end"). In a passage well known to Latter-day Saints, we behold Peter's words about departed spirits: "For [*eis*] this cause was the gospel preached also to them that are dead" (1 Pet. 4:6; see also Rev. 11:18).[330]

that ye might know: The verb γινώσκω (*ginōskō*) appears in its secular, workaday sense of being informed rather than in its meaning of knowing religious truth (see 3:19, "to know the love of Christ"; 5:5).[331] The prior conjunction, "that" (ἵνα, *hina*), carries the everyday force "in order that," which we see in the jailer's words in Philippi when he tried to send Paul and Silas away without further ado: "The magistrates have sent an order that [*hina*] you may be released" (Acts 16:36, Wayment; see also Acts 9:21, "that [*hina*] he might bring them"; and the Notes on 3:19; 5:5).[332]

our affairs: The expression means literally "the things concerning us" (τὰ περὶ ἡμῶν, *ta peri hēmōn*). In light of Paul's consistent emphasis on himself throughout the letter, as if he were by himself, the surprise sits in the plural "us."[333] The question is, Whom did he have in mind? Surely Tychicus was with him. Were there more? If, in fact, this letter reached

---

328. BDAG, 794–95.1; 121.1.c.
329. Rengstorf, *TDNT,* 1:398, 404.
330. Oepke, *TDNT,* 2:429.
331. Louw-Nida, §27.2; BDAG, 200.3.a.
332. Stauffer, *TDNT,* 3:327 n. 37.
333. See 1:1; 3:1–4, 7–8, 13–14; 4:1.

Asia with Colossians in the hands of Tychicus, then we can appeal to Colossians to learn of others even though the names do not appear in Ephesians. In that letter, Paul mentioned several. The number incorporates Onesimus, the runaway slave and subject of Paul's letter to Philemon. Luke is probably the best known of the Apostle's companions (see Col. 4:9, 14). Besides appearing twice in Colossians, Epaphras's name also occurs at Philemon 1:23 as a "fellowprisoner in Christ Jesus" (see Col. 1:7; 4:12). For the rest, he wrote about a man whom he called "Aristarchus my fellowprisoner," a person identified elsewhere in the New Testament (see Acts 19:29; 20:4; 27:2; and Philem. 1:24), along with Marcus,[334] a nephew of Barnabas who himself served as a longtime associate with Paul and was noted frequently, especially in the book of Acts (Col. 4:10). One of his Jewish associates, Jesus Justus, is mentioned, perhaps the same person who resided in Corinth (see Acts 18:7), as does a man named Demas, apparently known from other passages (see Col. 4:7–14; Philem. 1:24; and 2 Tim. 4:10).

comfort: As we saw in 4:1, the verb παρακαλέω (*parakaleō*) can bear the meanings "to entreat" and "to beseech."[335] But it also can center on encouragement, where the verb serves up the meaning "to comfort" or "to encourage."[336] The force of the term here sends us to the senses of consoling and encouraging, concepts that stand next to each other in meaning. The assurance of God's comfort arose strikingly in Isaiah's emotionally reassuring words spoken to the Holy City: "Comfort ye, comfort ye my people, saith your God. Speak ye comfortably to Jerusalem, and cry unto her, that her warfare is accomplished, that her iniquity is pardoned" (Isa. 40:1–2). Paul picked up this scriptural thread of comfort and cited it as a source of instruction, even revelation, and encouragement. We read, "Whatever was written in former days was written for our instruction, that by steadfastness and by the encouragement of the scriptures we might have hope" (Rom. 15:4 RSV). In accord with Isaiah's promise, God himself is to be a source of consolation. On this topic, Paul wrote to his converts in Thessalonica about "God, even our Father, which hath loved us, and hath given us everlasting consolation and good hope through grace" (2 Thes. 2:16; see also Heb. 12:5, "word of encouragement," NIV; and the Note on 4:1).[337]

---

334. Marcus may be the same person known in the KJV as Mark and noticed at Acts 15:37 and, possibly, at 2 Tim. 4:11.

335. Schmitz and Stählin, *TDNT,* 5:775; BDAG, 765.3; Thayer, *Lexicon,* 482.II.2.

336. BDAG, 765.4; Louw-Nida, §25.150; Thayer, *Lexicon,* 483.II.3 and II.4.

337. Schmitz and Stählin, *TDNT,* 5:797.

6:23 *Peace:* Unlike four of the occurrences of εἰρήνη (*eirēnē*) in this letter (see 2:14, 15, 17; 4:3), the appearance of this noun here comes closest to the meaning that we find at 1:2: "Grace be to you, and peace, from God our Father, and from the Lord Jesus Christ." On the surface, we meet a greeting, essentially a wish that people will experience well-being in their lives. It embodies what we hear in the modern Hebrew greeting *shalom* (see the Notes on 2:14–15, 17; 4:3; 6:15, 24).[338]

the brethren: The masculine plural noun "brothers" (ἀδελφοί, *adelphoi*) regularly embraces women as well.[339] As we discovered in the Note on 6:10, the earlier occurrence of this term in the KJV translation of the letter was a late addition to certain manuscripts and is not authentic. In our verse, 6:23, Paul has extended his greeting and warm wishes to "the brethren," who he knew did not consist only of the male members of the branches that this letter would reach and thereafter be read aloud to during church services (see "brothers and sisters" NR; Col. 4:16; 1 Thes. 5:27; and Rev. 1:3).

love with faith: The noun for "love" (ἀγάπη, *agapē*) appears for the tenth time in this letter.[340] Here, it is paired with "faith" (πίστις, *pistis*), which occurs in seven other passages in Ephesians.[341] Paul, of course, wrote about a "living and dynamic" faith, not about the stone-cold concept. For he brought forward the growth of faith as an engine that enlivens and expands both the persons who have received it and those who associate with them: "When your faith is increased, . . . we shall be enlarged by you" (2 Cor. 10:15). In this sense, *pistis* bears the sense of "confidence" or "trust."[342] In its turn, love bridges the gap between Christ and humans, specifically the individuals who make up his church. But *agapē* is more than a bridge. For it enriches "all them that love our Lord Jesus Christ" (6:24). Moreover, it prospers and perfumes the relationship that began with Christ reaching out to the investigator and the investigator reaching back through faith and prayer. It is this love "that surpasses [earthly] knowledge" (3:19 NR; see also the Notes on 2:4, 8; 3:19; 4:5; 5:2, 25; 6:16).[343]

with: In this instance, the preposition μετά (*meta*) carries the fragrances of its Septuagint antecedents. For example, we read, "For a little while I left thee: but with [*meta*] great mercy will I have compassion upon thee" (LXX Isa. 54:7; see also LXX Isa. 29:6). Here, the sense "with" hearkens back to

---

338. Hans Windisch, *TDNT*, 1:500.

339. BDAG, 18.1; Louw-Nida, §11.23.

340. See 1:4, 15; 2:4; 3:17, 19; 4:2, 15, 16; 5:2.

341. See 1:15; 2:8; 3:12, 17; 4:5, 13; 6:16.

342. Bultmann and Weiser, *TDNT*, 6:212–13, quotation on 212.

343. Grundmann, Hesse, de Jonge, and van der Woude, *TDNT*, 9:558.

the meaning "by means of." In this light, the expression "love with faith" could be better understood as "love with the aid of faith" or "love together with faith."[344]

God the Father: As in other greetings, this expression appears without any definite article, which, in English, literally yields "God Father," a combination that is almost always accompanied by the personal pronoun "our," reading "God our Father" (see 1:2; Rom. 1:7; 1 Cor. 1:3; 2 Cor. 1:2; and Philip. 1:2). In addition, the words "God our Father" usually connect to the name "the Lord Jesus Christ." The effect turns the whole, "God our Father and the Lord Jesus Christ," into a rhythmic recalling of the church's divine leaders with a "loftiness of effect." Because church members read Paul's letters or portions of them when gathered (see Col. 4:16 and 1 Thes. 5:27), the regularity with which they recited this pair of names, with some slight variation (see 1 Thes. 1:1), came to enrich their lives of worship and devotion, anchoring them ever more deeply to the Father and to the Son. After all, the joining of these two, whether in praise (see 2 Cor. 11:31; Gal. 1:3–5; and Philip. 2:11) or for some other purpose, meant the conjoining of creation and redemption.[345]

6:24 *Grace:* The meaning of "grace" (χάρις, *charis*) in this passage differs from its appearance in the greeting at the letter's opening (see 1:2). There, it stood equivalent to a warm "hello" in Greek and was combined with the Greek equivalent of a second "hello" ("peace," εἰρήνη, *eirēnē*), which in Hebrew or Aramaic is *shalom*. In our verse, there is an implied strong wish like "may it be." The sense then becomes "may grace be with all them that love our Lord."[346] Hence, Paul was effectively uttering a prayer that God would continue to pour down his saving grace (see 2:8, "by grace are ye saved") onto the heads of those who "love our Lord Jesus Christ," the one through whom that *charis* has come to believers (see 2:7).

with: Unlike the occurrence of "with" (μετά, *meta*) in the prior verse, here the preposition exhibits its most potent personal meaning that stretches all the way to God. For within the noun "grace" reposes God himself, the giver of *charis*. Said another way, "God Himself is present in His gift [of grace]; in His gift He gives Himself." The simplest expression of this thought arises in the salutation "Grace be with you" (Col. 4:18), almost as if Paul wrote, "God be with you" (see 1 Tim. 6:21; 2 Tim. 4:22; Titus 3:15; and Heb. 13:25).[347]

---

344. Grundmann, *TDNT,* 7:772 and n. 36; Louw-Nida, §89.78.
345. Schrenk and Quell, *TDNT,* 5:1007, 1019, quotation on 1007.
346. Larkin, *Handbook,* 170; Merkle, *Guide,* 225.
347. Grundmann, *TDNT,* 7:778.

love: Those who love (the verb is ἀγαπάω, *agapaō*) as God loves do so because of their faith that springs into action (see Gal. 5:6, "faith that *worketh* by love," emphasis added). And what sort of action might that be? It centers on "service rendered to fellow-citizens in the new people of God." Such love makes "the welfare of the brotherhood [and sisterhood] the guiding principle of conduct."[348] It is this love that motivates those who serve in the church: "For the work of the ministry, for the edifying of the body of Christ" (4:12; see also the Notes on 2:4; 3:19; 5:25).

in sincerity: The noun ἀφθαρσία (*aphtharsia*) represents "the state of not being subject to decay."[349] We meet this term elsewhere: "The resurrection of the dead . . . is sown in corruption; it is raised in incorruption [*aphtharsia*]" (1 Cor. 15:42; see also 1 Cor. 15:50). Why then was the phrase ἐν ἀφθαρσίᾳ (*en aphtharsia*) translated "in sincerity" in the KJV? The idea of "sincerity" links to the related sense of "purity" as being a state in the next life.[350] A very different meaning arises out of the thought that a person's incorruptible state will characterize eternity and thus pertains to a nature that is unceasingly everlasting. In this light, the line would read, "Those who love our Lord Jesus Christ unceasingly."[351] At its heart, *aphtharsia* does not lose its fundamental mooring to the idea of incorruption, which, in Paul's eyes, focuses on the eternities.[352] Hence, a better rendition of the phrase "in sincerity" (KJV) would be "unceasingly" (NR).

Amen: This noun forms the ending of early Christian prayers and, more broadly, stands as an "acclamation in Christian worship." In Ephesians, the term ἀμήν (*amēn*) brought Paul's long doctrinal discussion to a close at 3:21, paving the way for his instructive part of the letter (chapters 4–6;[353] see the Note on 3:21).

Analysis of 6:21–24

The ending of a letter should be a simple matter to deal with, but not in the case of Ephesians. Three items popped up that needed treatment in the Notes. First, a reader notices that the letter incorporates no greetings to old

---

348. Quell and Stauffer, *TDNT,* 1:50–51, quotations on 51.
349. BDAG, 155.
350. Thayer, *Lexicon,* 88.
351. Louw-Nida, §68.57.
352. Günther Harder, *TDNT,* 9:104–5.
353. Schlier, *TDNT,* 1:335–38, quotation on 336.

friends and associates in Ephesus and, except for Tychicus, no references to any of Paul's companions who were with him at the time. This circumstance has caused commentators to wonder whether virtually all of Paul's former associates in Ephesus had died in the interim between his residence in the city and the composition of the letter. But surely some were still alive and yet were not mentioned by the Apostle. It is difficult to explain why this was so. A second possibility is that he was in a rush to finish the letter so that he could send both this letter and Colossians in the custody of Tychicus, his "beloved brother" (6:21). Hence, he omitted mentioning friends who were otherwise noted in Colossians 4:7–14. A third notion holds that Paul was not the author of this letter, nor of Colossians, and that the omission of people's names who had lived in and around Ephesus was the way the unknown author kept from revealing that he knew none of the old church members. If he had guessed at names, he would thereby have disclosed that the letter was not really from the Apostle. Needless to say, the second option seems to be the best.

The next issue that jumps out of the final verses of the letter sends readers to the thirty-two words that are identical between Ephesians 6:21–22 and Colossians 4:7–8. For some, these words frame a big puzzle, particularly if that person is trying to demonstrate that Paul was the author of neither epistle. For such commentators, the mention of Tychicus is crucial. For one modern scholar, there existed a "Pauline school," which remains unattested from antiquity. Within this hypothesized school, two or more budding authors had taken up the task of writing Ephesians and Colossians falsely in Paul's name. Among them, "they may have discussed together how they should end their letters and decided to introduce the name of Tychicus as messenger who would provide further information about Paul [to the fictional recipients], thus creating a standard way of expressing such sentiments."[354] All of this is without a shred of evidence. Much simpler is the view that sees Paul simply borrowing language from one letter to insert into another that he was writing at the same time, both to be carried by Tychicus. After all, this man was known as a companion of the Apostle and was acquainted with Christians in Asia, where his home was (see Acts 20:4; see also Col. 4:7; 2 Tim. 4:12; and Titus 3:12).

In the last two verses, 6:23–24, the chained Paul vaulted his readers into the skies. In this dimension of these lines, readers found themselves staring at the glowing vista of heaven. The Apostle had gently laid upon them

---

354. Best, *Ephesians,* 613.

a future filled with peace—eternal peace—that arose not only out of the love that they felt and expressed in actions to fellow believers but also out of the faith, the rock-solid confidence that the next life would bring eternal treasures to them, including everlasting family connections. Paul rounded off his letter with the prepositional phrase *en aphtharsia,* rendered as "in sincerity" by the KJV translators. Truth be told, the phrase presents the sense "unceasingly" because of *aphtharsia*'s meaning of "incorruption," an unceasingly blessed state (see 1 Cor. 15:42, 50).

Appendix 1:
Evidences for Sacred Ceremonies[1]

Paul famously wrote that when he preached the gospel, "I determined not to know anything among you, save Jesus Christ, and him crucified" (1 Cor. 2:2). We all know that he was being modest and that he had a lot to say about topics such as faith, repentance, baptism, the gift of the Holy Ghost, grace, and the kingdom of God. These were the basics. But he surely taught more than these. What is revealing to readers is that in a very brief teaching period, a mere three weeks in the Greek city of Thessalonica, he set out in clear fashion a number of other principles and doctrines that go beyond the basics. His three weeks of missionary preaching there came to a sudden halt when he had to flee for his safety and the safety of his companions (see Acts 17:1–10). The principles and doctrines that he taught to investigators in that city included topics as diverse as Christ's Second Coming (see 1 Thes. 2:19; 3:13; compare 2 Thes. 2:1–5), the enduring presence of persecution in believers' lives (see 1 Thes. 3:3–4), and the divine punishment that awaits those who persecute the Saints (see 1 Thes. 2:16; compare 2 Thes. 1:8–9). But there is more. Precisely, we find references interwoven into the Epistle to the Ephesians where we come upon pointers to sacred ceremonies. Such references go way beyond gospel basics and tell us that members of the early Christian church practiced holy rituals that enriched and gave further meaning to their spiritual lives. Let us take a look.

---

1. This study is to be published in a shortened form as "Sitting, Walking, Standing, and the Tantalizing Links to Sacred Ceremonies in the Epistle to the Ephesians," in *Steadfast in Defense of Faith: Essays in Honor of Daniel C. Peterson,* forthcoming.

To Sit

In Ephesians, the combination of the six verbs "to sit," "to walk," "to stand," "to put on," "to take up [weapons]," and "to take," has drawn scant attention. Importantly, they lead us to a promising reservoir of ritual links within that letter.[2] If we focus on the first verb, "to sit," we find Christ seated "at [God's] own right hand in the heavenly places" (1:20). In their turn, faithful believers will be seated "together in [the same] heavenly places in Christ Jesus" (2:6). In each of these passages, 1:20 and 2:6, the verb καθίζω (*kathizō*) means "to be seated,"[3] with God as the one who does the seating, thus pointing to a formal act or ceremony. As Andrew T. Lincoln has written, though he acknowledged no ritual actions, church members' "participation in Christ's victory . . . is expressed most strikingly in the assertion that they have been seated with Christ in the heavenly realms."[4] In this connection, scholars have detected a liturgical framework in Ephesians, including but not limited to an opening *berakah* or Jewish-like recitation of blessings (see 1:3–14),[5] prayers by the Apostle (see 1:15–23; 3:14–21), his kneeling position while praying (see 3:14), and other features that send us to fragments of hymns and oral recitations, perhaps even leading us to a baptismal service (see 4:5).[6] But is that the whole story? A close review offers a glimpse of distinct celebrations and holy actions woven into the letter, actions that require a physical body to carry them out.

The elements of a pattern, detected in scattered places, suggest activities that underlie clues of sacred celebrations or religious ceremonies.[7] After all, a perusal of the letter reveals a good many aspects associated with ancient forms of worship. Appropriately, it begins with a celebration of creation (see 1:3–4; see also 3:9, "from the beginning of the world . . . created all

---

2. For "to sit," see the Note on 2:6; for "to walk," see the Notes on 2:10; 4:20, 22, 24; 5:2, 8; for "to stand," see the Notes on 5:14; 6:11, 13–14; for "to put on," see the Notes on 4:24; 6:11, 14; for "to take up [weapons]," see the Notes on 6:13, 16; for "to take" or "to receive," see the Note on 6:17.

3. BDAG, 491; Thayer, *Lexicon*, 313–14.

4. Lincoln, *Ephesians*, 460.

5. Barth, *Ephesians*, 1:97; Lincoln, *Ephesians*, 10–11; Winger, *Ephesians*, 53.

6. See Barth, *Ephesians*, 1:6–10; Lincoln, *Ephesians*, xxxvi–xxxvii; Best, *Ephesians*, 61, 71–72; Muddiman, *Ephesians*, 14, for reviews and critique.

7. Philip Abbott, the translator of *The Epistle to the Ephesians: A New Rendition* (Provo, Utah: BYU Studies 2019), drew my attention to this possibility in a long note on the verbs "to sit," "to walk," and "to stand" at the end of his manuscript.

things"),[8] a common facet of temple activities (see Ps. 24:1–3). This is followed by a brief note about being "sealed with that holy Spirit of promise" (1:13). These arise out of chapter one alone. This is not all.

Before Christ was seated next to the Father, he was "raised . . . from the dead" (1:20), and then God "raised us up together" with Christ (2:6). Thus, the faithful will enjoy being raised from the dead, a concrete action, in bodily form as was the Savior. Such action, of course, hints strongly at a baptismal service, wherein "we are buried with [Christ] by baptism into death [and raised] . . . in the likeness of . . . his resurrection" (Rom. 6:4–5; see also Col. 2:12). To take the matter further, we find reference to Christ's "feet," which God has lifted and placed over "all things" (1:22; see also D&C 78:16). In each case, we get a quick look at physical movement, at intentional motion. These activities are all more than metaphorical or spiritual. They are real and direct us to holy acts.

Moreover, we meet mention of Christ's body. Of course, most of the references to Christ's body have to do with the church (see 1:23; 4:12, 16 [twice]; 5:23, 30). But at least once, the term "body" has to do with Christ's crucified body, the body that has reconciled "both [Jew and Gentile] unto God . . . by the cross" (2:16). This reference leads us to Jesus' physical remains that were placed into a tomb, not specifically to a spiritual gathering of believers into a church. As if to add gravity to this point, Paul declares, "Jesus Christ himself [is] the chief corner stone" that "fitly framed" grows into "an holy temple," all with the solid feel of chiseled stones and mortar (2:20–21). Paired with these stands a reference to real human bodies when the Apostle insists that men ought "to love their wives as their own bodies" (5:28). Then, in a twist with more ties to real bodies, Paul went on to write that "no man ever yet hated his own flesh; but nourisheth and cherisheth it" (5:29). Why all this interest in physical bodies? In reply, each of these examples invites our gaze onto tangible, palpable bodies with which worshipers undertook sacred actions and uttered words of covenant and pledge.

References to physical activities continue. We have not reached the end. As we observed earlier, Paul wrote about kneeling, about bowing "my knees unto the Father" (3:14). In addition, we notice his words of prayer for the recipients of his letter (see 1:15–23; 3:14–21) and his plea that believers give "thanks always for all things unto God . . . in the name of our Lord Jesus Christ" (5:20). All these relate to worshipful acts, including singing "psalms and hymns and spiritual songs" (5:19). Moreover, we run across the

---

8. Barth, *Ephesians*, 1:104.

Apostle's reference to "the washing of water with a promise" (5:26 NR).[9] This washing was to cleanse the church, and it was to be done with a "living voice"[10] (see 5:26). Further, this combination of washing and living words strongly hints at reciting precise words that accompany an ordinance of sacred washing. After all, the church is no cleaner or more ready for salvation than its individual members (see Titus 3:5). In addition to these activities, we come upon the verb which means "to put on a garment" (see 6:11, 14). Although this verb (ἐνδύω, *enduō*) can bear metaphorical meanings, such as "put on [*enduō*] the new man" (4:24) and, in the passive, "clothed [*enduō*] with power from on high" (Luke 24:49 NIV), its primary meaning has to do with putting on clothes.[11] This idea is exactly what we encounter in putting "on the whole armour of God [and] . . . the breastplate of righteousness," each of which has a divinely mandated purpose (6:11, 14). That purpose was "to stand against the wiles of the devil [and] . . . against spiritual wickedness in high places [and] . . . to withstand in the evil day" (6:11–13). Thus, these armaments or garments were to provide both physical and spiritual protection from the evil one.

To Walk

We now arrive at the references to walking and standing. Let us take up the sacred walk first. Such a walk toward and within a place that is made sacred for special ritual acts and worship is as old as Adam and Eve. As one account discloses, they followed a pathway and walked to a spot just outside the Garden of Eden to worship and receive instruction. There they "called upon

---

9. According to Louw–Nida, §53.43, the Greek term λουτρόν (*loutron*) can refer to baptism as well as to sacred washing. These authors, apparently looking for an easy solution by appealing to baptism, seem to have turned away from the constant need for washing by priests at the temple and the required *mikvah* baths that every traveler from a distant place underwent before entering the city of Jerusalem. See Chaim Richman, *The Holy Temple of Jerusalem* (Jerusalem: Carta, 1997), 31, 71; Leen Ritmeyer, *The Quest: Revealing the Temple Mount in Jerusalem* (Jerusalem: Carta, 2006), 232 (sketch) and 375 for the locations of mikvah baths south and northwest of the temple's holy area where pilgrims arrived for cleansing. In the Septuagint, the noun has to do with the shepherd washing sheep in pools following the spring shearing to get rid of the winter dust and dirt, as I have personally witnessed at the site of ancient Pella in the Jordan Valley. See LXX Song. 4:2; 6:6.

10. Thayer, *Lexicon*, 562.

11. BDAG, 333–34; Louw–Nida, §49.1.

the name of the Lord, and they heard the voice of the Lord from the [sacred path] way [where they had walked] toward the Garden of Eden, speaking unto them" (Moses 5:4).[12] Presumably, they either stood, bowed, or prostrated themselves on this path, which must have led to the garden on the east side (see Gen. 3:24 and Moses 4:31, "at the east of the garden of Eden [was] . . . the way [path] of the tree of life"). This kind of sacred path leading to a place of ceremonial worship is strongly implied, for example, in a song of the Psalmist: "Who shall ascend into the hill of the Lord?"—the hill being the place of the temple and the ascent following the pathway that led up to it (Ps. 24:3). At this juncture, when we turn back to Ephesians, we learn that, of the eight occurrences in the letter of the verb "to walk" (περιπατέω, *peripateō*), four do not overtly lead us to ceremony (see 2:2; 4:1, 17 [twice]) but the other four do (see 2:10; 5:2, 8, 15).

As a resident of Jerusalem for a number of years, Paul surely knew about walks linked to sacred acts. For example, during the Feast of Tabernacles, he had certainly witnessed one priest's daily walk down the hill to the Pool of Siloam to fill a golden jar with water and to carry it back up to the altar of sacrifice.[13] In a second instance, Paul had observed and probably participated in the crowded procession of six thousand men and boys who packed the small Court of the Israelites, just inside the Nicanor Gate, on the afternoon before Passover. Each adult male carried a lamb, which was considered to be a holy sacrifice (see Ex. 12:27; 34:25; and Num. 9:7, 13) and was to be slaughtered for the feast. When it was his turn, each man walked quickly to the slaughtering place and, after the lamb was dead, flayed the skin off the carcass. Then, washing the skin and carcass, the man carried them back to the still-packed Court of the Israelites before all the gathered men swarmed out through the gate at a fast walk to find a place to roast the lamb at one of the public ovens in the city. Later, the man would give the skin as payment to the landlord of the building where the meal was to take place.[14] In a third case, the Apostle knew the rule that travelers arriving from a distance of more than seventeen miles from Jerusalem (the distance to the town Modiin) must go to a *mikvah* bath and immerse themselves in the cleansing waters, rinsing

---

12. Draper, Brown, and Rhodes, *Pearl of Great Price,* 57–58.

13. Edersheim, *Temple,* 278.

14. *Mishnah Pesahim,* 5:6, 9, in Danby, *Mishnah,* 142–43; Edersheim, *Temple,* 215; Richman, *Holy Temple,* 75, 78–79; Jeremias, *Jerusalem in the Time of Jesus,* 82, 101–2; Leen and Kathleen Ritmeyer, *The Ritual of the Temple* (Jerusalem: Carta, 2002), the illustrations on 18, 38.

off their uncleanness before entering the city.[15] With ease, we could cite a dozen more examples, but these will suffice to underscore that Paul was well acquainted with walking with a holy purpose. The same can be said about temple-related activities in Ephesus.

Among the regular features of life in the city of Ephesus were the sacred processions of priests from the nearby majestic Temple of Artemis, known by her Roman name, Diana, in the New Testament (see Acts 19:27). Approximately every two weeks, a priestly procession wound its way from the temple east of the city through the southeastern city gate while carrying thirty-one silver and gold statues. Joined there by some 250 city leaders, the marchers passed among the city offices next to the upper market area. The religious officials and their now expanded entourage then descended the long street running to the west, walking down through the most expensive residential and business properties in the city. Finally, they turned north and walked along the eastern edge of the lower commercial part of Ephesus, where Paul doubtless plied his tentmaker skills among silversmith shops. The procession usually paused in the great theater, except when it went to the stadium to draw attention to and leave a blessing on physical contests hosted by the city. From the theater, the long line exited the northern city gate and the priestly group returned to the holy precinct of the temple, placing the silver and gold statues in their sacred places. The round trip covered about seven kilometers and required at least ninety minutes of walking time.[16] Of course, all of the Christian converts both in Ephesus and in surrounding towns knew of this regular celebration undertaken by walking. In a word, local pagan ritual was a regular feature in the lives of all citizens.

The richness of ritual in the Ephesian sphere was not limited to the regular processions from the temple of Artemis. Every year at the end of April and beginning of May came the grand celebration dedicated to the birthday of the goddess Artemis, including sacrifices, the burning of incense, banqueting, and dancing. Though not as fully developed as these festivities would become in the second century AD, these activities were well known and drew attendees from far and wide long before Paul came to Ephesus. In a word, Ephesus hosted the festival that attracted people to the city

---

15. *Mishnah Pesahim,* 9.1–2, in Danby, *Mishnah,* 148 and n. 6; Hayes, "Purity and Impurity, Ritual," in Berenbaum and Skolnik, *Encyclopaedia Judaica,* 16:752–53.

16. Guy MacLean Rogers, *The Sacred Identity of Ephesos: Foundation Myths of a Roman City* (London: Routledge, 1991), 83–86, 91, 98, 100–103, 110; Lilian Portefaix, "Ancient Ephesus: Processions as Media of Religious and Secular Propaganda," *Scripta Instituti Donneriani Aboensis* 15 (1993): 199.

from all over Asia Minor and beyond. Celebrations of the sacred were certainly not new to Paul's converts and even included prayers for the Roman Senate.[17] These circumstances do not mean that the earliest Christians of the city and surrounding areas borrowed or were influenced by Roman religious ceremonies. Rather, they were simply comfortable when introduced to Christian worship practices, beginning with baptism.

When we turn back to Ephesians, we notice that God had set before believers "good works . . . that we should walk in them" (2:10). A person may urge that this is a metaphorical walk. But the actual performance of good works requires physical exertion of one sort or another. Musing or praying about them will not complete the task. The other three references bear a similar sense. In 5:2, Paul asked his readers to "walk in love." Although we might read this as living with love in our hearts, we observe that the Apostle immediately turned to a very concrete example of love—namely, that of Christ giving "himself for us [as] an offering and a sacrifice to God" (5:2; see also 5:8, 15; and Rev. 3:4, "they shall walk with me in white").

TO STAND

Let us now examine the matter of standing, for it also has a place within sacred spaces. In a famous passage from the Old Testament, we find that "Abraham stood yet before the Lord" after the messengers had left Abraham's tent to descend to Sodom (Gen. 18:22). Obviously, the presence of the Lord among these messengers made the place holy where Abraham had stood with him because, in an act that reverentially acknowledged the power and judgment of the Lord, Abraham returned to that same spot a day later to gaze at the smoke rising from Sodom and Gomorrah (see Gen. 19:27–28). In another well-known account, we hear God's voice to Moses, saying, "Put off thy shoes from off thy feet, for the place whereon thou standest is holy ground" (Ex. 3:5; see also Josh. 5:15 and Acts 7:33). Here, standing worshipfully constituted the proper act at a holy site.[18]

---

17. Guy MacLean Rogers, *The Mysteries of Artemis of Ephesos: Cult Polis, and Change in the Graeco-Roman World* (New Haven, Conn.: Yale University Press, 2012), 3–14, 171–73; Rogers, *Sacred Identity of Ephesos*, 91.

18. In the New Testament, standing in a holy place appears chiefly in Revelation. See Rev. 5:6; 7:9, 11; 8:3; 20:12. Otherwise, all the references are to modern scripture. See JS–M 1:12 (an adjustment to Matt. 24:15); D&C 45:32; 87:8; 101:22, 64; 115:7; 124:39, 46.

As we might expect, on certain occasions, those who officiated in the religious life of the ancient Israelites also stood. In one passage, we read that "the Lord separated the tribe of Levi . . . to stand before the Lord to minister unto him, and to bless [his people] in his name" (Deut. 10:8; also Deut. 18:5; etc.). That was not all. The whole "congregation"—which consisted of the priests, who were to be present at the consecration of the altar, and "the elders of Israel," who represented all of the people (Lev. 9:1, 5)—"drew near" to the tabernacle "and stood before the Lord" (Lev. 9:5). Thus, the entire gathering, not just the priests, "stood" together at the holy place in front of the sanctuary where they would witness the consecration of the altar. That ceremony ended when "a fire [came] out from before the Lord, and consumed upon the altar the burnt offering and the fat" which had been placed thereon as a consecrating sacrifice (Lev. 9:24).[19] As is apparent, both officials and laity, standing near the altar, were witnesses and participants in this sacred ceremony.

Recalling the regular processions that passed through Ephesus, a person can imagine people in the city standing and watching while the priests and their associates walked by. At one point during the procession, in the theater, the priests and their entourage came to a stop for important meetings.[20] This standing was not lost on the onlookers, whether they themselves or the priests were standing. The quiet lack of movement was as much a part of the sacred march as the walking activity itself. Besides, during the procession, "such a throng of participants, bearing conspicuous silver and gold statues through the narrow streets of Ephesos, must have impeded, if not altogether halted traffic within the city at procession time."[21]

When we return to the New Testament and to Paul, we discover that he distinguished at least two levels of understanding, one that he called milk and one that he called meat. In a reference to his earlier stay among the Corinthian Saints, he prefaced his distinction by writing an uncomplimentary observation about them: "I could not address you [in those bygone days] as spiritual but as worldly—mere infants in Christ." What was the outcome? "I gave you milk, not solid food, for you were not yet ready for it. Indeed, you are still not ready" (1 Cor. 3:1–2 NIV). This difference between simpler and richer spiritual perceptions shows up in a more quoted passage in Hebrews. In a discussion of people slipping into disbelief

---

19. Milgrom, *Leviticus 1–16*, 571–72, 575.
20. Rogers, *Sacred Identity of Ephesos*, 102.
21. Rogers, *Sacred Identity of Ephesos*, 86.

from belief, we read, "You have gone back to needing milk, and not solid food. Truly, anyone who is still living on milk cannot digest the doctrine of righteousness because he is still a baby" (Heb. 5:12–13, Jerusalem Bible). There is more. We learn that "grown men can take solid food; their perceptions are trained by long use to discriminate between good and evil" (Heb. 5:14 NEB). Plainly, we encounter different levels of understanding sacred instruction. And our grasp of the higher level does not rest on light and breezy principles but on "perceptions [that] are trained by long use to discriminate." In other words, long spiritual experience counts both in church meetings and in other sacred settings.

At this point, we pivot back to Ephesians. All the references to standing appear in chapter 6, and all of the verbs are a form of "to stand" (ἵστημι, *histēmi*), either imperative or infinitive. At first, Paul asked his readers to don "the whole armour of God, that ye may be able to stand." Although one might think of this as a metaphorical requirement because this armor helps believers "stand against the wiles of the devil" (6:11), it need not be so. Why not? Because the actions—and we stress the word *actions*—needed to push back against the devil's influences involve such things as kneeling to pray, physically walking away from a temptation to do something wrong, or planning an activity that will keep devotees far from evil. Such acts require effort. The next occurrences of the armor of God make this idea even more secure. Within a few lines, the Apostle wrote a similar message—to wit, that we put on "the whole armour of God, that ye may be able to withstand the evil day." The "evil day," of course, is not some construct of a person's imagination. It will be real. And how did Paul sign off on his request? He wrote that "having done all, [we are] to stand" (6:13). The doing is also an activity of movement or effort.[22] In the last instance, the Apostle commanded his readers, "Stand therefore," with their special clothing on.[23] That is to say, they were to stand "having [their] loins girt about with truth, and having on the breastplate of righteousness" (6:14). To insist that all these are metaphorical in character is to blind the eye to their reference to real military gear—cut, scraped, trimmed, sewn, pounded into shape, and polished.[24]

Naturally, if the above discussion helpfully discloses threads of ritual acts running throughout the letter, we must ask where they came from. Why should we presume that Paul would write about them? In part, the

---

22. BDAG, 531, s.v. κατεργάζομαι; Louw–Nida, §§42.17; 90.47.
23. Wilckens, *TDNT*, 7:688, 690–91.
24. Oepke, *TDNT*, 5:307.

questions come to the matter of the breadth and depth of Paul's preaching. Was it totally fixed on "Jesus Christ, and him crucified" (1 Cor. 2:2), as he affirmed to church members in Corinth? As a matter of fact, as we have seen, his preaching was much broader than faith, repentance, the grace of the Holy Spirit, the kingdom, and proper behavior. For in that same epistle, 1 Corinthians, while discussing the Resurrection, he brought forward the subject of "celestial bodies, and bodies terrestrial" (1 Cor. 15:40). Where did he learn this doctrine? Moreover, he adopted the language of clothing oneself with a new, heavenly garment when he observed that "this corruptible [body] must put on [*enduō*] incorruption, and this mortal must put on [*enduō*] immortality." Further, writing of that distant day, Paul said, "This corruptible shall have put on [*enduō*] incorruption, and this mortal shall have put on [*enduō*] immortality" (1 Cor. 15:53–54).[25] Where did he discover this sort of teaching about the Resurrection? During his days as a Pharisee student? (see Philip. 3:5). Possibly the basics because Pharisees believed in a resurrection. Even if it is difficult to answer these questions, we can quickly turn to like instances that raise such questions anew since he touched on a broad set of teachings that he taught to new investigators. Among the most promising sources that reveal these teachings, as far as Paul allows us to see them, are his two Thessalonian letters. There, he made abundant references to teachings about various gospel subjects that he had taught during a mere three weeks among investigators in the city of Thessalonica. For as we know, he was forced to leave town after a mere three Sabbaths, fleeing at night for his own safety and that of his companions (see Acts 17:1–10).

THE TRADITION

Perhaps the easiest teachings for investigators to understand are "the traditions" or "the tradition" (2 Thes. 2:15; 3:6; the singular is παράδοσις, *parado-sis*).[26] This noun encloses Paul's teachings about "our gospel . . . which ye have been taught, whether by word or our epistle" (2 Thes. 2:14–15). It is important to grasp that the term *paradosis* indicates "what is transmitted, not [the] transmission [process]."[27] A part of this tradition that circulated among early Christians certainly included what we read in Paul's report

---

25. Wilckens, *TDNT*, 7:691.
26. BDAG, 763; Louw–Nida, §33.239.
27. Büchsel, *TDNT*, 2:172.

about the Last Supper and Jesus' institution of the sacrament. He attributed this information to Jesus himself: "I have received of the Lord that which also I delivered [παραδίδωμι, *paradidōmi*, the verb related to *paradosis*] unto you" (1 Cor. 11:23; see 1 Cor. 11:23–26). This episode, as well as the one about the early witnesses of the Resurrection (see 1 Cor. 15:3–7), derived from what some have called "the Jerusalem tradition," with the Eleven and other disciples as its witnesses.[28] During his ministry, Paul had met some of these Jerusalem people, as is recorded (see Acts 15:1–4 and Gal. 1:18–19; 2:1–2). This "Jerusalem tradition" was one of the sources for his teaching and surely included what the Eleven had learned from the Resurrected Jesus about "the things pertaining to the kingdom of God" during the "forty days" after the Resurrection (Acts 1:3).[29]

Another possible source of information, more directly linked to Christ, consisted of Paul's time in Arabia, where he retreated after his baptism in Damascus, presumably to harmonize his spiritual goals with and to grow closer to the Exalted Lord (see Gal. 1:17). Besides this interlude, and perhaps linked with it, the Apostle wrote about "a man in Christ," doubtlessly a reference to himself, whom he had known "above fourteen years ago" and who was "caught up to the third heaven [where he] . . . heard unspeakable words" (2 Cor. 12:2, 4). To be sure, Paul must have undergone other intense spiritual experiences, but we lack any record. Of these two, it is possible, though highly unlikely, that he learned doctrines by this mode of revelation and then taught them. Why is it unlikely? Because he stressed that it was "not lawful for a man to utter" what he had learned in his vision of the third heaven (2 Cor. 12:4). This divine prohibition dampens the idea that he was appealing to this vision, or even to his experience in the desert of Arabia, when he taught investigators. Concerning the Apostle's teachings of this sort, Richard D. Draper and Michael D. Rhodes have observed that "though it is possible that Paul received his knowledge directly through revelation, it is more likely that the Spirit had, at some point, confirmed the accuracy and correctness of the tradition as it had come down to him."[30] But that is not the end of the story. For when we turn to Paul's letters to the Thessalonian Saints, we soon learn that he taught a good many more subjects than the first principles and ordinances during his three short weeks

---

28. Büchsel, *TDNT*, 2:173.

29. Hugh Nibley, "The Forty-day Mission of Christ—the Forgotten Heritage," in *When the Lights Went Out*, 33–54, argued that virtually the entire teaching tradition growing out of the "forty days" that Jesus spent with the Eleven (see Acts 1:3) was suppressed by the mainline church and reappeared in a plethora of early Christian apocryphal sources.

30. Draper and Rhodes, *Paul's First Epistle to the Corinthians*, 557.

with them. This observation opens the door to the possibility of special teaching in the pages of Ephesians.

As a template, we discover that the Apostle attributed all to Christ—that is to say, the "commandments [which] we gave you by the Lord Jesus" (1 Thes. 4:2; see also 1 Thes. 4:15, "by the word of the Lord"). Although these particular commandments dealt with "how ye ought to walk and to please God" (1 Thes. 4:1; see also 1 Thes. 4:11–12), the observation holds that all tied back to Christ (see 2 Thes. 3:10–12 and the Note on 4:28). The question is, What besides good behavior did Paul teach during those three weeks? Near the top of the list stands Paul's prophecy about the persecutions that he, his companions, and their converts would surely suffer because of embracing Jesus Christ and his gospel. He wanted his hearers to know beforehand "that no man [or woman] should be moved by these afflictions: for yourselves know that we [Paul and his companions] are appointed thereunto. For verily, when we were with you, we told you before that we [all] should suffer tribulation" (1 Thes. 3:3–4). Did matters turn out as Paul had prophesied? Yes, exactly. Because persecution happened "even as it came to pass, and ye know" (1 Thes. 3:4). Further, "we ourselves glory in you [Thessalonian Saints] . . . for your patience and faith in all your persecutions and tribulations" (2 Thes. 1:4). But remarkably, in Paul's understanding, these afflictions did not carry a negative consequence. Far from it. For such experiences were "a manifest token of the righteous judgment of God, that ye may be counted worthy of the kingdom of God" (2 Thes. 1:5).

Paul's mention of "the righteous judgment of God" directs us to another principle, that of wicked persecutors filling their futures with God's punishment. In 1 Thessalonians, the Apostle had Jewish persecutors in mind because they had led the charge against him and his companions not only in Thessalonica but also in Berea, a town forty-five miles to the west (see Acts 17:5, 13). Writing about these braying and snorting individuals, he reported that they tried to stop him from speaking "to the Gentiles that they might be saved" but instead began "to fill up their sins . . . for the wrath [which is to] come upon them to the uttermost" (1 Thes. 2:16; see also 2 Thes. 1:6, 8–9). Not surprisingly, this principle of God—allowing persons to fill up their sins so that his punishment will be just—has been reiterated in the modern era (see Alma 14:11; 60:13; and D&C 103:3).

One of the major themes in these two letters concerns Christ's Second Coming, an event that Paul had treated at length during his stay in Thessalonica, as its frequent appearance in his first letter illustrates (see 1 Thes. 2:19; 3:13; 4:15–17; 5:23). Because a misunderstanding had arisen among church members about this event's nearness in time, Paul brought their attention back to it in his second letter. He begged that they not "be troubled . . . that the day of Christ is at hand" (2 Thes. 2:2). Rather, before that day, "there [shall] come a falling away first, and that man of sin be revealed, the son of perdition" (2 Thes. 2:3). Plainly, trouble lurked, for the term translated "a falling away" should be rendered "*the* falling away" or "*the* rebellion" (ἡ ἀποστασία, *hē apostasia,* emphasis added).[31] Further, time was to elapse and then a certain personality, "that man of sin," would be exposed. This teaching that the end-time was coming, including Jesus' return, was certainly tied to Christ's teaching of the Twelve on the Mount of Olives (see D&C 45:16–59) and to his "forty days" of instruction with the Eleven. For after spending those six weeks with the Risen Jesus, the Eleven asked him moments before his ascension, "Wilt thou at this time restore again the kingdom to Israel?" (Acts 1:6). Like Paul, the Resurrected Jesus insisted that the time was not yet: "It is not for you to know the times or the seasons, which the Father hath put in his own power" (Acts 1:7).

As we can see from this review, all such teaching about the Second Coming came from Jesus, though some individuals had misunderstood (see D&C 45:16–59). What Paul evidently added was the identity of those who will join the Savior at his Second Coming and some of what will happen in that grand moment. Among Jesus' teachings that Paul repeated was the fact that "all the tribes of the earth" will mourn when "they shall see the Son of man coming in the clouds . . . with a great sound of a trumpet" (Matt. 24:30–31). Of course, Paul alluded to this end-time scene when he wrote that "in the twinkling of an eye, at the last trump . . . the dead shall be raised incorruptible, and we shall be changed" (1 Cor. 15:52). This is not all. For when writing to the Thessalonians, the Apostle invoked "the word of the Lord" as his authority and then declared that "the Lord himself shall descend from heaven with a shout . . . and with the trump of God: and the dead in Christ shall rise first." Plainly, the dead will be the first to join the descending Savior. Only then, "we which are alive and remain shall be caught up together with them in the clouds, to meet the Lord in the air" (1 Thes. 4:15–17). Thus, from the sources of his information, Paul set out the order of those called up to meet the descending Christ at his Second Coming—first, "the dead in Christ" and "then we which are alive."[32] Besides all this, he characterized this "day of the Lord" as coming unexpectedly like "a thief in the night" (1 Thes. 5:2, 4), a teaching that Peter also shared with his readers from his

---

31. Louw–Nida, §39.34.

32. D&C 88:96–97 appears to reverse this order, saying that those "who are alive, shall . . . be caught up to meet [Christ]," and then "they who have slept in their graves shall come forth."

own store of knowledge (see 2 Pet. 3:10). The aggregate of these observations goes way beyond faith, repentance, baptism, the kingdom of God, and grace through the Holy Spirit.

Conclusion

What do these observations have to do with Ephesians and the visible ceremonial threads that weave themselves throughout this letter? The answer is, a lot. What we see especially in 1 Corinthians and the Thessalonian correspondence are a number of pieces from a deep pool of gospel truths and information that formed a part of Paul's preaching package. It is instructive and impressive that he was able to squeeze that message into the short three weeks that he spent in Thessalonica, taking up items as diverse as a prophecy about coming sufferings for new converts, the bleak future for those who persecute believers, and expected events linked to Christ's return. For all of these teachings, he invoked the authority of "the Lord Jesus" and "the word of the Lord," plainly tying them to his highest authority and most reliable source (1 Thes. 4:2, 15).

In summary, in Ephesians, we first discover a celebration of creation (see 1:3–4), and at the end, we encounter Paul's plea to stand arrayed in armaments and garments that offer protection "against the wiles of the devil" (6:11). The visible threads that tie to sacred actions and events come surprisingly thick and fast. And we need not think that these allusions bespeak a late date for the letter when the church had begun to settle on the form of its liturgical celebrations, such as baptism and the Eucharist or the sacrament. The pieces that have become evident from our review direct us to a much broader set of holy ceremonies than baptism and the sacrament. Instead, they link to sacred actions like that noted by Paul when he wrote about vicarious baptisms for the dead: "Else what shall they do which are baptized for the dead, if the dead rise not at all?" (1 Cor. 15:29), connecting this ordinance with the preaching of the gospel to departed spirits (see Rom. 14:9; 1 Pet. 3:18–20; 4:6; Rev. 11:18; and the Notes on 1:4, 6; 2:6, 11, 18, 20–21; 4:5, 12; for links to ceremonies, see the Notes on 2:10; 4:1, 13, 20, 22, 24; 5:2, 8, 14; 6:11, 13–14, 17; and the introduction, section XI).[33]

---

33. Draper and Rhodes, *Paul's First Epistle to the Corinthians,* 780, 785, 788–93.

Appendix 2:
Terrestrial and Celestial Inheritance
(Ephesians 1:14, 18; 5:5)

ABRAHAM

A meaningful life was measured in antiquity by one's inheritance, almost always from one's father. The size of the inheritance was based on the answer to several relevant questions. Am I the oldest in the family, or do I fit somewhere else? Does my father own a big farm or a small one? Does he have a lot of sheep and cattle? How much of his property, especially his land, will be coming my way? Can I stand to live around my brothers, especially my oldest brother?

All biblical stories of inheritance begin with Abraham. We hear the Lord's almost shouted directive: "Get thee out of thy country, and from thy kindred, and from thy father's house, unto a land that I will shew thee" (Gen. 12:1; see also Abr. 2:3). The keyword is "land." Land became one of the underpinning elements of the Abrahamic covenant in addition to posterity and priesthood (see Gen. 15:5–7; 17:1–8; 22:15–17; 26:1–5; 28:1–4; 35:9–12; and Abr. 2:6, 9–11). The future aspect of this covenant was that "in thee [Abraham] shall all the nations of the earth be blessed" (Gen. 12:3; 18:18; see also Gen. 22:18; 26:4).[1]

Importantly, as we have come to expect, Abraham obediently left his home in Ur of the Chaldees, taking his wife Sarah and his nephew, Lot. Years later, after the near sacrifice of Isaac, Abraham acquired his first piece of land, the field that included the cave of Machpelah, where he buried Sarah. He acquired

---

1. Noel B. Reynolds, in "Understanding the Abrahamic Covenant through the Book of Mormon," *BYU Studies Quarterly* 57:3 (2018), 39–74, especially 52–66, has recently set out the unusual perspective found in the Book of Mormon on God's covenant with Abraham.

it by purchase, not by inheritance nor by taking it away from another person by force. Rather, he measured out four hundred shekels of silver by weight to buy it (see Gen. 23:2–20). As significant as anything else in the account is the fact that the modest-sized property included what became the family burial plot, eventually welcoming Abraham, Isaac, and Jacob, as well as Rebekah and Leah, into its deep, dark interior (see Gen. 25:8–10; 35:27–29; 49:29–32; 50:12–13). This point about burial would become one of the substantial foundations for the resistance in Israelite law to one clan acquiring property from another clan. Family burial plots sat within family properties, and those properties had been received by sacred lot in the days of Joshua before the Lord at the sanctuary (see Josh. 14:1–5; 24:30, 32–33; Judg. 2:9; 1 Sam. 25:1; and 1 Kgs. 2:34).[2] The fact that the Lord guided the casting of lots for dividing the land conferred a sacred character on the whole countryside, including especially the plots of ground that fell to families (see Josh. 18:1–10; 19:51).[3] After all, every inch belonged to Jehovah, and the former Hebrew slaves effectively were now his tenants (see Lev. 25:23; Deut. 4:20; 9:26, 29; 1 Sam. 10:1; etc.).[4] But the story does not end here.

The Lord had been in the mix all along. Beginning with Abraham, continuing through the Joseph stories in the latter half of the book of Genesis, and ending with the Moses and Joshua narratives, the Lord had been in charge of the covenant with them, even when his people were away from the land of Canaan.[5] In this way, he chose to make his covenant with the descendants of Abraham, effectively making them his children.[6] We run into language like "Is not [Jehovah] your father, who created you, who made you and established you?" (Deut. 32:6 RSV). Again, "Thus saith the Lord, Israel is my son, even my firstborn" (Ex. 4:22). Further, "O Lord, thou art our father; we are the clay, and thou our potter; and we all are the work of thy hand" (Isa. 64:8; see also Hosea 11:1). In a different vein, the Lord himself effectively became the inheritance or the lot of the children of Israel. We read words like "The Lord is the portion of mine inheritance and of my cup . . . yea, I have a goodly heritage" (Ps. 16:5–6; see also Isa. 34:17).[7]

---

2. W. Dommershausen, *TDOT,* 2:452; Edouard Lipiński, *TDOT,* 9:325, 327; Herrmann, *TDNT,* 3:774–75.

3. Foerster, *TDNT,* 3:759; Herrmann, *TDNT,* 3:771–72, 774–75.

4. Lipiński, *TDOT,* 9:328, 331, 333.

5. Herrmann, *TDNT,* 3:769–70.

6. Lipiński, *TDOT,* 9:328.

7. Hans Heinrich Schmid, *TLOT,* 1:311; Foerster, *TDNT,* 3:762.

When we reach the New Testament era, we run headlong into two parables of Jesus that bring us into the world of ancient inheritance laws. The first has to do with the prodigal son. From this parable and from other ancient sources, we learn that it was possible for a child, a male child, to take the part of the inheritance that was due to him before the death of his father. We read, "The younger [son] . . . said to his father, Father, give me the portion of goods that falleth to me. And he divided unto [the two sons] his living," or his property (Luke 15:12).[8]

The second has to do with the wicked husbandmen who had leased a vineyard from an absentee landlord (see Mark 12:1–9). This parable is more important for our purposes because of how it was to be interpreted. When the landlord sent a representative to collect the rent, the husbandmen "beat him, and sent him away empty" (Mark 12:3). Sadly, the renters mistreated a series of agents sent by the landlord, beating some and even killing more than one. These men were not just angling to hold onto the produce from the vineyard but to take over the property itself through hostile actions, actions not unknown in earlier days.[9] They, of course, misjudged the owner on two counts. They did not know that he would extend kindness to try to bring them into conformity with the original agreement by initially sending a series of representatives and finally his son, the heir. Further, they did not know how ruthlessly forceful he would become after they abused and then killed the heir, judging that, after the heir's death, "the inheritance shall be ours" (Mark 12:7).

In reality, the point of Jesus' story about the renters tipped the world of inheritance on its side. Instead of husbandmen attempting to seize property that belonged to another, the parable really had to do with "the kingdom of God," which, as Matthew quoted Jesus, "shall be taken from you [husbandmen], and given to a nation bringing forth the fruits thereof" (Matt. 21:43). Hence, although Jesus' sketch rested on the matter of ancient heirship, his message carried a spiritual aim that bore upon those who at first enjoyed access to God's kingdom but, because of their treatment of his agents, patently in acts of hostility and apostasy, lost their access to an inheritance therein.[10] Jesus had effectively lifted the question of inheritance from the terrestrial world into the celestial.

---

8. Lipiński, *TDOT,* 9:321–22.

9. Lipiński, *TDOT,* 9:320–21; Foerster, *TDNT,* 3:759, 779.

10. Foerster, *TDNT,* 3:781–82.

In fact, certain passages in the Old Testament come very close to this sort of concept. For example, the last verse in the book of Daniel reads, "But go your way till the end; and you shall rest, and shall stand in your allotted place at the end of the days" (Dan. 12:13 RSV). In an intriguing shift, the Septuagint reading of the last expression brings the "allotted place" or inheritance into the heavenly world: "You shall rest, and shall stand in your glory [δόξαν, *doxan*] at the end of days" (LXX Dan. 12:13).[11] Psalm 16 presents the following: "Lord, you have assigned me my portion and my cup; you have made my lot secure." How secure? The Psalmist then sings, "The boundary lines [of my lot] have fallen for me in pleasant places; surely I have a delightful inheritance" (Ps. 16:5–6 NIV). All this was done by the Lord, setting the person's inheritance on a celestial footing (see Isa. 34:17; see also Acts 26:18 and Col. 1:12).[12]

The pseudepigrapha continue this trajectory toward an inheritance that will be located in heaven, particularly the document known as *1 Enoch,* which was evidently composed in the second century before the common era.[13] It breathes the air of the Old Testament and stands close to the New Testament in many of its ideas.[14] Initially we read, "From [the Lord of the Spirits], the lot of eternal life has been given to me" (*1 En.* 37:4).[15] Then, we come upon the following: "And I saw a dwelling place underneath the wings of the Lord of the Spirits; . . . and my soul desired that dwelling place. Already my portion is there; for thus has it been reserved for me before the Lord of the Spirits" (*1 En.* 39:7–8).[16] The final passage runs thus: "He [the Son of Man] has revealed the wisdom of the Lord of the Spirits to the righteous and the holy ones, for he has preserved *the lot of the righteous* . . . they will be saved in his name and it is his good pleasure that they have

---

11. Dommershausen, *TDOT,* 2:455.

12. Schmid, *TLOT,* 1:311; Foerster, *TDNT,* 3:761, 763–64.

13. Ephraim Isaac, "1 (Ethiopic Apocalypse of) Enoch," in *The Old Testament Pseudepigrapha,* ed. James H. Charlesworth, 2 vols. (Garden City, New York: Doubleday, 1983, 1985), 1:6–7; George W. E. Nickelsburg, *1 Enoch 1: A Commentary on the Book of 1 Enoch, Chapters 1–36,* Hermeneia—a Critical and Historical Commentary on the Bible (Minneapolis: Fortress Press, 2001), 81–108, 118–19.

14. Isaac, "1 (Ethiopic Apocalypse of) Enoch," 1:9–10; Nickelsburg, *1 Enoch 1,* 28–30, 68–70, 82–87.

15. See the comments in George W. E. Nickelsburg and James C. VanderKam, *1 Enoch 2: A Commentary on the Book of 1 Enoch, Chapters 37–82,* Hermeneia—a Critical and Historical Commentary on the Bible (Minneapolis: Fortress Press, 2012), 91–92.

16. Nickelsburg and VanderKam, *1 Enoch 2,* 124.

[eternal] life" (*1 En.* 48:7, emphasis added).[17] In the light of these passages, it becomes clear that a certain spiritual refinement had occurred in how the ancients saw a person's inheritance. That is, one's real inheritance lies in the heavens and not on the earth. A piece of ground paired with a flock of sheep and goats does not constitute a person's most important inheritance; rather, that choice heritage consists of a place by God's side.

NEW TESTAMENT

This is exactly where the New Testament stands on the matter of inheritance. How much its authors took their clues from the Old Testament and pseudepigraphic literature remains a matter for study. But we have to observe that the book of Jude quoted directly from the book of *1 Enoch* (see Jude 1:14–15 and *1 En.* 1:9). And the Epistle to the Hebrews cited an old story about Isaiah's death (see Heb. 11:37, "they were sawn asunder"). Moreover, the appearance of a number of pseudepigraphic pieces among the Dead Sea Scrolls brings us to notice that their influence reached into the world of ideas out of which the New Testament was born.

First, we pick up that, in the New Testament, "inheritance [rests] on the ground of a filial relationship to God."[18] This concept is not new, of course. We have already run across language that made the ancient Israelites the sons and daughters of God. In his dedicatory prayer for the temple, Solomon came close to this idea when he petitioned the Lord to "hear thou in heaven, and forgive the sin of thy servants, and of thy people Israel" (1 Kgs. 8:36). In its context, the expression "thy people Israel" bears a sense of intimacy and close relationship. Other expressions go beyond this. As early as the Exodus saga, Moses was commanded to say to Pharaoh, "Thus saith the Lord, Israel is my son, even my firstborn" (Ex. 4:22). Such language is mirrored in the song of Moses, which he intoned "in the ears of the congregation of Israel," singing, "Is not he thy father that hath bought thee? hath he not made thee, and established thee?" (Deut. 31:30; 32:6). From Jeremiah's record, we hear the Lord utter the words, "I am a father to Israel, and Ephraim is my firstborn" (Jer. 31:9). Then, from Hosea's pen, we discover

---

17. Nickelsburg and VanderKam, *1 Enoch 2*, 173–74; Foerster, *TDNT*, 3:761–62.
18. Foerster, *TDNT*, 3:783.

that "when Israel was a child, then I [the Lord] loved him, and called my son out of Egypt" (Hosea 11:1).[19]

In all of these cases, the relationship of father to son is reflected in the Lord's relationship with Israel, but only after the Lord brought the Hebrew slaves out of Egypt. Moreover, the relationship is not one of the Lord to an individual. That kind of link arose in the days of Israel's kings. In response to King David's offer to build a temple in Jerusalem, through Nathan the prophet the Lord told David that his successor would erect a temple. In addition, underscoring the special relationship with the temple's builder, the Lord affirmed that "I will be his father, and he shall be my son" (2 Sam. 7:14; see also 1 Chr. 17:13; 22:10). On a later occasion, David shared this message with his chosen leaders, repeating the words of the Lord about his son Solomon: "Solomon thy son, he shall build my house and my courts: for I have chosen him to be my son, and I will be his father" (1 Chr. 28:6; see also Ps. 2:6–7).[20] We note that in each of these passages, the Lord established the relationship of father; it was not by King Solomon's choice.

Three further elements are added to the father-son relationship in a later passage in Psalm 89. They consist of the presence of a covenant, a universal dominion over all the nations of the earth, and an everlasting salvation. We listen as the Psalmist, quoting the Lord, sings the words, "He [the king] shall cry unto me [the Lord], Thou art my father, my God, and the rock of my salvation. Also I will make him my firstborn, higher than the kings of the earth. My mercy will I keep for him for evermore, and my covenant shall stand fast with him" (Ps. 89:26–28; see also Ps. 2:8).[21]

All of these concepts lie behind language that we find in the New Testament. What is distinctive in the New Testament is the insistence on adoption in preference to natural, physical descent from Abraham. Such a concept was at home in certain ancient societies—although not in the Old Testament laws on inheritance—where we come upon the adoption of a foreigner as an heir.[22] According to Jesus' teachings, "many shall come from the east and west, and shall sit down with Abraham, and Isaac, and Jacob, in the kingdom of heaven. But the children of the kingdom shall be cast out into outer darkness" (Matt. 8:11–12; see also Luke 13:28–29). This prospect is dreary indeed for those who claim Abraham as their founding

---

19. Lipiński, *TDOT,* 9:328.

20. Lipiński, *TDOT,* 9:329–30.

21. Lipiński, *TDOT,* 9:330.

22. Lipiński, *TDOT,* 9:323.

ancestor.[23] As a matter of fact, John the Baptist had sent up a bright warning flare much earlier when he declared to his hearers that they should "think not to say within yourselves, We have Abraham to our father: for I say unto you, that God is able of these stones to raise up children unto Abraham" (Matt. 3:9).

We hasten to add that such children of Abraham become sons and daughters by adoption through faith, just as Abraham became God's chosen one because of his faith (see Gen. 15:6). These principles of adoption and faith, accompanied by God's Spirit, undergird much of the Apostle Paul's teaching. For example, we do not read far into his majestic letter to the Romans before we run into these words: "If the Spirit of him that raised up Jesus from the dead dwell in you, he that raised up Christ from the dead shall also quicken your mortal bodies by his Spirit." And what will be the result? Simply stated, "as many as are led by the Spirit of God, they are the sons of God." Indeed, "ye have received the Spirit of adoption, whereby we cry, Abba, Father." Moreover, "the Spirit itself beareth witness with our spirit, that we are the children of God," that is to say, the true heirs through adoption (Rom. 8:11, 14–16). And what does this adoption consist of? It consists of "the redemption of our body" (Rom. 8:23). But this is not the whole story. For "if [we are] children, then [we are] heirs, heirs of God, and *joint heirs* with Christ" (Rom. 8:17, emphasis added).

Turning back to Abraham, we encounter more of Paul's teachings. Knowing that a literal descent from Abraham counts for little, what does? And how do we know it? Paul answered by asking, "What saith the scripture?" Citing the language of Genesis in the Septuagint, he then answered that "Abraham believed God, and it was counted unto him for righteousness" (Rom. 4:3, quoting LXX Gen. 15:6). That is, being an heir of God does not depend on being a descendant but on merit, on something that we do.[24] What might that be? The key is that someone else is involved. That person is Christ.

In his struggle against those who were teaching another gospel to church members in Galatia, Paul made it abundantly clear that heirship does not come through the Mosaic law. Neither does it come from physical descent through Abraham nor, for Gentiles, by accepting the law as the path to heaven. Rather, "as Abraham believed God, and it was counted to him for righteousness," so "they which are of faith, the same are the children of

---

23. Foerster, *TDNT,* 3:782.
24. Foerster, *TDNT,* 3:782.

Abraham," not those who embrace the Mosaic law. Additionally, as if to make the point more forcefully, Paul wrote that "they which be of faith are blessed with faithful Abraham" (Gal. 3:6–7, 9). There is more.

In discussing heavenly inheritances, Paul seized on the singular term "seed" or offspring that appears in the Lord's repeated promises to Abraham in the book of Genesis. For instance, after Abraham reached the territory of Shechem on his way from Ur of the Chaldees, the Lord appeared to him and promised that "unto thy seed will I give this land" (Gen. 12:7). Again, after the near sacrifice of Isaac, the Lord uttered words that are repeated throughout scripture: "In thy seed shall all the nations of the earth be blessed" (Gen. 22:18; see also 1 Ne. 15:18; 22:9; 3 Ne. 20:25, 27; and D&C 124:58). To be sure, this "seed" or offspring represented the unborn generations who would make up Abraham's family (see Gen. 13:15; 15:5; 17:7–8; 22:17; 24:7; and Acts 7:5). But for Paul, who sought to make a point about Christ's role in securing our everlasting inheritances, the singular noun pointed to Christ. Paul therefore turned his considerable skills to say, "Now the promises were made to Abraham and to his offspring." Fair enough so far. Then came his main point: "It does not say, 'And to off-springs,' referring to many; but, referring to one, 'And to your offspring,' which is Christ" (Gal. 3:16 RSV).[25]

How does this work? First, we must understand that "if the [eternal] inheritance be of the law [of Moses], it is no more of promise: but God gave it to Abraham by promise" (Gal. 3:18). This promise to Abraham predated the law by "four hundred and thirty years" (Gal. 3:17). When it finally came, "the law was our schoolmaster to bring us unto Christ, that we might be justified by faith" (Gal. 3:24). Specifically, as if warming to a crescendo, Paul wrote that "ye are all the children of God *by faith* in Christ Jesus. . . . There is neither Jew nor Greek, there is neither bond nor free . . . And *if ye be Christ's, then are ye Abraham's seed, and heirs according to the promise*" (Gal. 3:26, 28–29, emphasis added). Significantly, as Paul taught here, this condition of being heirs was to extend to both Jews and Gentiles, with no barriers between them (see Eph. 2:11–22). Hallelujah!

We must quickly add that, just as it is possible to become an heir of God through faith, so it is possible to lose that heirship and its associated eternal blessings. The Old Testament sets the bar and hints at the serious consequences of such a loss. The classic case involved Reuben, Jacob's oldest son, who, because of incest (see Gen. 35:22), lost his right of primogeniture

---

25. Foerster, *TDNT*, 3:783–85.

(see Gen. 49:3–4 and 1 Chr. 5:1–2) and, astonishingly, his right to inherit two-thirds of his father's estate, not just a mere double portion.[26] When we move this loss into the heavenly realm, it is the pseudepigrapha that introduce us to the frightening results.[27] In the book of *2 Enoch,* also known as the Slavonic Enoch because of the language that preserves it, we learn about "a very frightful place ... [where] every kind of torture and torment ... and darkness and gloom [persists]." Enoch's angelic guides, who took him to view this place, informed him that it was "prepared for those who practice godless uncleanness on the earth, ... and who ... steal souls secretly ... [and] who do not acknowledge their Creator, but bow down to idols, ... bowing down to vile things made by hands." For these people, "this [dreadful] place has been prepared as an eternal reward" (*2 En.* 10:1–2, 4–6).[28] From the *Psalms of Solomon,* we hear that "the inheritance of sinners is destruction and darkness, and their lawless actions shall pursue them below into Hades" (*Pss. Sol.* 15:10; see also *Pss. Sol.* 14:9).[29]

Now, we turn to the language of the New Testament. Besides Paul, others spoke or wrote about the heavenly blessings that come to the faithful, from being "heirs of the kingdom" (James 2:5) to possessing "an inheritance incorruptible, and undefiled, and that fadeth not away, reserved in heaven for you" (1 Pet. 1:4).[30] That is only part of the story. This heirship is to be realized with one's spouse; that is, "*being heirs together* of the grace of life" (1 Pet. 3:7, emphasis added), not in some state of solitary loneliness.[31] Not incidentally, such a passage hints strongly at regularized steps or ordinances that swing this door wide open to coheirship with one's spouse. Moreover, heavenly heirship or inheritance always carries an implicit promise of ruling and reigning in the next life (see Matt. 25:21; Luke 19:17; Rom. 5:17; and Rev. 5:10; 20:4; 22:5; compare 1 Cor. 4:8).[32]

---

26. Lipiński, *TDOT,* 9:322–23; the Hebrew expression translated "double portion" in Deut. 21:17 means "two thirds"; see 2 Kgs. 2:9 and Zech. 13:8, where "two thirds" appears metaphorically.

27. Foerster, *TDNT,* 3:780–81.

28. Francis I. Andersen, "2 (Slavonic Apocalypse of) Enoch," in Charlesworth, *Old Testament Pseudepigrapha,* 1:119–20.

29. R. B. Wright, "Psalms of Solomon," in Charlesworth, *Old Testament Pseudepigrapha,* 2:664.

30. See Matt. 19:29; 25:34; Mark 10:17–21; Luke 10:25–28; 18:18–22; 1 Pet. 3:8–9; Rev. 21:7.

31. Thayer, *Lexicon,* 593.

32. Foerster, *TDNT,* 3:783.

In a different vein, when Paul wrote about the fate that awaits sinners, he did not fill in the blanks about the potentially gruesome suffering that such people may face. Without any elaboration, he wrote simply "that they which do [wicked] things shall not inherit the kingdom of God." Of course, he appended a list of what he called "the works of the flesh" before making this judgment, including "fornication, . . . witchcraft, . . . [and] murders" (Gal. 5:19–21). Elsewhere, he asked a straightforward question—"Know ye not that the unrighteous shall not inherit the kingdom of God?"—before appending a list of wrongdoers whose numbers, among others, are made up of "idolaters, . . . thieves, . . . [and] extortioners" (1 Cor. 6:9–10).

Other New Testament sources employ evocative language when touching on the eventual inheritance of the wicked, most of which speak of darkness in one way or another.[33] It is Jesus who declares that the defiant "children of the kingdom shall be cast into outer darkness," where one, sadly, will hear rather than see "weeping and gnashing of teeth" because of the darkness (Matt. 8:12; see also Matt. 22:13; 25:30). Other passages present images of darkness. In the book of Revelation, the kingdom of "the beast," after he is dethroned, is "full of darkness," where its inhabitants "[gnaw] their tongues for pain" and are full of "sores" (Rev. 16:10, 11). In the Second Epistle of Peter, we come upon the expression "the mist of darkness," which is to persist "for ever" (2 Pet. 2:17). The tiny letter of Jude speaks menacingly about "everlasting chains" and "the vengeance of eternal fire" coupled with "the blackness [gloom] of darkness for ever" (Jude 1:6–7, 13).

In its turn, the book of Revelation presents frightful details of that future existence and brings us into the world of liquid sulfur, often called brimstone in scripture. The usual expression is "fire and brimstone," which characterizes a lake where the wicked will spend a tortured eternity, not resting on the shore sipping cold lemonade but actually sitting in the heated liquid (see Rev. 21:8 and Ps. 11:6). With them will be prominent personalities, such as "the devil," who are to be "cast into the lake of fire and brimstone, where the beast and the false prophet are, and shall be tormented day and night for ever" (Rev. 20:10; see also Rev. 19:20). Others will join them, including "death and hell," who are from the unseen world and who will also be "cast into the lake of fire," a fate that represents "the second death" (Rev. 20:14). The most vivid torture facing the wicked is linked to "the beast" and his followers. They shall be forced to "drink of the wine of the wrath

---

33. Foerster, *TDNT,* 3:783, presents terms that characterize spiritual inheritance, though often without the term "inheritance."

of God," suffering torment "with fire and brimstone in the presence of the holy angels, and in the presence of the Lamb." Moreover, "the [hot] smoke of their torment ascendeth up for ever and ever: and they have no rest day nor night" (Rev. 14:10–11).

At this juncture, it is important to explore the opposite—what it is like to receive an inheritance inside the celestial world. We have already reviewed the principle of adoption, where the Father adopts us as his heavenly children and as "joint-heirs with Christ." Enjoying this status, we can address God as "Abba," the equivalent of "Dad," and "Father" (Rom. 8:15–16; see also Gal. 4:6–7). Plainly, adoption of believers comes as a result of their full embrace of the gospel message. The change in status from outsider to accepted one is immediate, and the accompanying blessings begin to flow in this life, with a crescendo in the life to come at the end-time.

This circumstance was anticipated in part by Old Testament passages that speak of inheritance not as land or animals but of ancient Israel as God's allotment. For example, we read that Israelites "are thy people and thine inheritance" (Deut. 9:29). Again, expressed more fully, "when the most High divided to the nations their inheritance, . . . he set the bounds of the people according to the number of the children of Israel. For the Lord's portion is his people; Jacob is the lot of his inheritance" (Deut. 32:8–9). That is not all.

God took "strangers" and "eunuchs" to himself as his own, indicating his interest both in individuals and in non-Israelites. We read that "the sons of the stranger, that join themselves to the Lord, to serve him, . . . them will I bring to my holy mountain, and make them joyful in my house of prayer: . . . an house of prayer *for all people*" (Isa. 56:6–7, emphasis added). Furthermore, "thus saith the Lord unto the eunuchs that keep my sabbaths, . . . and take hold of my covenant; . . . unto them will I give in mine house and within my walls a place and a name . . . an everlasting name, that shall not be cut off" (Isa. 56:4–5). Without subtlety, God pulls these people into the grand events of the end-time with an expression like "an everlasting name, that shall not be cut off." As we have already seen, the Septuagint reading of the last verse of the book of Daniel promised the prophet that "you shall rest, and *stand in your glory at the end of days*" (LXX Dan. 12:13, emphasis added).[34]

When we turn again to the New Testament, we come upon Paul's speech before King Agrippa, wherein the Apostle rehearsed the appearance of the Resurrected Jesus to him on the road to Damascus. Speaking about

---

34. Foerster, *TDNT,* 3:760–61; Dommershausen, *TDOT,* 2:455.

the Gentiles to Paul, the Risen Christ declared that "now I send thee" to them. What was his purpose? "To open their eyes, and to turn them from darkness to light, and from the power of Satan unto God, that they may receive forgiveness of sins, and inheritance among them which are sanctified by faith that is in me" (Acts 26:17–18). A heavenly sanctified inheritance, therefore, was available to all, especially to the Gentiles (see 3:6).[35]

What is more, believers go into heaven not as servants of God but as his sons and daughters because of Christ. Even Jews, who enjoyed the blessings of the law of Moses, needed to "receive the adoption of sons [and daughters]" before entering the next world. To them and to Gentiles, "God hath sent forth the Spirit of his [own] Son into your hearts" as a preparation. At the end, those who were children then are now to become "heir[s] of God through Christ" (Gal. 4:5–7). With this, the work of God to bring about "the immortality and eternal life of man" (Moses 1:39) stands complete.

---

35. Foerster, *TDNT,* 3:763, 785.

Selected Bibliography

Aharoni, Yohanan, Michael Avi-Yonah, Anson F. Rainey, and Ze'ev Safrai. *The Carta Bible Atlas.* 4th ed. Jerusalem: Carta, 2002.

Aland, Barbara, Kurt Aland, Johannes Karavidopoulos, Carlo M. Martini, and Bruce M. Metzger, eds. *Novum Testamentum Graece.* 28th ed. Stuttgart, Ger.: Deutsche Bibelgesellschaft, 2012.

Andersen, Francis I., and David Noel Freedman. *Amos: A New Translation with Introduction and Commentary.* Vol. 24A of the Anchor Bible. New York: Doubleday, 1989.

Anderson, Richard Lloyd. *Understanding Paul.* Salt Lake City: Deseret Book, 1983.

Arnold, Clinton E. *Ephesians: Power and Magic.* Cambridge: Cambridge University Press, 1989.

Atiya, Aziz S., ed. *The Coptic Encyclopedia.* 8 vols. New York: Macmillan, 1991.

Baker, Simon. *Ancient Rome: The Rise and Fall of An Empire.* London: BBC Books, 2006.

Barker, Margaret. *The Great High Priest: The Temple Roots of Christian Liturgy.* London: T&T Clark, 2003.

Barth, Marcus. *Ephesians: Introduction, Translation, and Commentary.* Vol. 34 of the Anchor Bible. 2 vols. New York: Doubleday, 1981.

Bauer, Walter. *A Greek-English Lexicon of the New Testament and Other Early Christian Literature.* Trans. William F. Arndt and F. Wilbur Gingrich. Chicago: University of Chicago Press, 1957.

———. *A Greek-English Lexicon of the New Testament and Other Early Christian Literature.* Ed. Frederick W. Danker. 3rd English ed. Chicago: University of Chicago Press, 2000. (Abbreviated as BDAG.)

———. *Orthodoxy and Heresy in Earliest Christianity.* Ed. Robert Kraft and Gerhard Krodel. Philadelphia: Fortress Press, 1971.

Beard, Mary. *SPQR: A History of Ancient Rome.* New York: Liveright Publishing, 2015.

Beare, Francis W. "The Epistle to the Ephesians." In *The Interpreter's Bible,* ed. George Arthur Buttrick, 10:597–749. 12 vols. New York: Abingdon Press, 1953.

Bednar, David A. "In the Strength of the Lord." In *Brigham Young University 2001–2002 Speeches,* 121–28. Provo, Utah; Brigham Young University, 2002.

Berenbaum, Michael, and Fred Skolnik, eds. *Encyclopaedia Judaica.* 2nd ed. 22 vols. Detroit: Macmillan Reference USA, 2007.

Best, Ernest. *A Critical and Exegetical Commentary on Ephesians.* Edinburgh: T&T Clark, 1998.

Bingham, Jean B. "United in Accomplishing God's Work." *Ensign* 50, no. 5 (May 2020): 60–63.

Blass, Friedrich, and Albert Debrunner. *A Greek Grammar of the New Testament and Other Early Christian Literature.* Trans. Robert W. Funk. Chicago: University of Chicago Press, 1961.

Blumell, Lincoln H. "Luke 22:43–44: An Anti-Docetic Interpolation or an Apologetic Omission?" *TC: A Journal of Biblical Textual Criticism* 19 (2014): 1–35.

Botterweck, G. Johannes, and Helmer Ringgren, eds. *Theological Dictionary of the Old Testament.* Trans. John T. Willis. 15 vols. Grand Rapids, Mich.: Eerdmans, 1974–2006. (Abbreviated as *TDOT.*)

Bright, John. *A History of Israel.* 3rd ed. Philadelphia: Westminster Press, 1981.

Brooks, Kent R. "Paul's Inspired Teachings on Marriage." In *Go Ye into All the World: Messages of the New Testament Apostles.* Ed. Ray L. Huntington, Jerome M. Perkins, Thomas A. Wayment, and Patty A. Smith. The 31st Annual Sidney B. Sperry Symposium. Salt Lake City: Deseret Book, 2002, 75–97.

Brown, Raymond E. *An Introduction to the New Testament.* The Anchor Bible Reference Library. New York: Doubleday, 1997.

Brown, S. Kent. "Fire and Speaking in Tongues: What We Can Learn about the Pentecost Festival in Acts." July 3, 2019. https://www.ldsliving.com/Fire-and-Speaking-in-Tongues-What-We-Can-Learn-About-the-Pentecost-Festival-in-Acts/s/91156.

———. "James the Just and the Question of Peter's Leadership in the Light of New Sources." In *Sidney B. Sperry Symposium Papers,* 10–16. Provo, Utah: BYU Press, 1973.

———. "Jesus' First Visit to the Temple." Publication pending.

———, and Richard Neitzel Holzapfel. *The Lost 500 Years: What Happened between the Old and New Testaments.* Salt Lake City: Deseret Book, 2006.

———. "Peter's Keys." In *The Ministry of Peter, the Chief Apostle,* ed. Frank F. Judd Jr., Eric D. Huntsman, and Shon D. Hopkin, 91–102. The 43rd Annual Brigham Young University Sidney B. Sperry Symposium. Provo, Utah: BYU Religious Studies Center; Salt Lake City, Utah: Deseret Book, 2004.

———. "The Nag Hammadi Library: A Mormon Perspective." In C. Wilfred Griggs, ed. *Apocryphal Writings and the Latter-day Saints,* 255–83. Provo, Utah: BYU Religious Studies Center, 1986.

———. "The Savior's Compassion." *Ensign* 41, no. 3 (March 2011): 53–55.

———. "The Seventy in Scripture." In *By Study and Also By Faith: Essays in Honor of Hugh W. Nibley,* ed. John M. Lundquist and Stephen D. Ricks, 1:25–45. 2 vols. Salt Lake City: Deseret Book; Provo, Utah: FARMS, 1990.

———. *The Testimony of Luke.* Brigham Young University New Testament Commentary. Provo, Utah: BYU Studies, 2015.

Bruce, Frederick Fyvie. *The Acts of the Apostles. The Greek Text with Introduction and Commentary.* Grand Rapids, Mich.: Eerdmans, 1979.

———. *The Epistle to the Ephesians: A Verse-by-Verse Exposition.* Basingstoke, Eng.: Pickering Paperbacks, 1983.

———. *The Epistle to the Hebrews.* The New International Commentary on the New Testament. Grand Rapids, Mich.: Eerdmans, 1964.

———. *New Testament History.* Garden City, N.Y.: Anchor Books, 1972.

———. *Paul: Apostle of the Heart Set Free.* Grand Rapids, Mich.: Eerdmans, Reprint 1996.

Buchanan, George Wesley. *To the Hebrews: A New Translation with Introduction and Commentary.* Vol. 36 of the Anchor Bible. Garden City, N.Y.: Doubleday, 1972.

Bultmann, Rudolf. *Theology of the New Testament.* 2 vols. in one. Trans. Kendrick Grobel. New York: Charles Scribner's Sons, 1951, 1955.

Caird, George Bradford. *Paul's Letters from Prison (Ephesians, Philippians, Colossians, Philemon).* Oxford: Oxford University Press, 1976.

Charlesworth, James H., ed. *Old Testament Pseudepigrapha.* 2 vols. Garden City, N.Y.: Doubleday, 1983, 1985.

Collins, Raymond F. *The Power of Images in Paul.* Collegeville, Minn.: Liturgical Press, 2008.

Cornell, Timothy, and John Matthews. *Atlas of the Roman World.* Oxford: Equinox (Oxford) Ltd. 1982.

Dahl, Larry E., and Charles D. Tate Jr., eds. *The Lectures on Faith in Historical Perspective.* Provo, Utah: BYU Religious Studies Center, 1990.

Danby, Herbert, trans. *The Mishnah: Translated from the Hebrew with Introduction and Brief Explanatory Notes.* Oxford: Oxford University Press, 1933.

Davies, Jamie. *The Apocalyptic Paul: Retrospect and Prospect.* Eugene, Oregon: Wipf and Stock Publishers, 2022.

Daube, David. *The Exodus Pattern in the Bible.* London: Faber and Faber, 1963.

Donelson, Lewis R. *Colossians, Ephesians, First and Second Timothy, and Titus.* Louisville: Westminster/John Knox, 1996.

Draper, Richard D., S. Kent Brown, and Michael D. Rhodes. *The Pearl of Great Price: A Verse-by-Verse Commentary.* Salt Lake City: Deseret Book, 2005.

Draper, Richard D., and Michael D. Rhodes. *Paul's First Epistle to the Corinthians.* Brigham Young University New Testament Commentary. Provo, Utah: BYU Studies, 2017.

———. *The Revelation of John the Apostle.* Brigham Young University New Testament Commentary. Provo, Utah: BYU Studies, 2016.

Dunn, James D. G., and John Rogerson, eds. *Eerdman's Commentary on the Bible.* Grand Rapids, Mich.: Eerdmans, 2003.

Eadie, John. *A Commentary on the Greek Text of the Epistle of Paul to the Ephesians.* 2nd ed. Grand Rapids, Mich.: Baker Book House, 1979.

Edersheim, Alfred. *The Temple: Its Ministry and Services as They Were at the Time of Jesus Christ.* Grand Rapids, Mich.: Eerdmans, 1983.

Edwards, Mark J. *Galatians, Ephesians, Philippians.* Vol. 8 of Ancient Christian Commentary on Scripture: New Testament, Downers Grove, Ill.: InterVarsity Press, 1999.

Ehat, Andrew F., and Lyndon W. Cook. *The Words of Joseph Smith: The Contemporary Accounts of the Nauvoo Discourses of the Prophet Joseph.* Provo, Utah: BYU Religious Studies Center, 1980.

Ellicott, Charles J. *A Critical and Grammatical Commentary on St. Paul's Epistle to the Ephesians.* Eugene, Ore.: Wipf and Stock, 1997.

Everitt, Anthony. *Augustus: The Life of Rome's First Emperor.* New York: Random House, 2006.

Falk, Ze'ev W. *Hebrew Law in Biblical Times.* 2nd ed. Provo, Utah: BYU Press; Winona Lake, Ind.: Eisenbrauns, 2001.

Farley, Lawrence R. *Prison Epistles: Philippians, Ephesians, Colossians, Philemon.* The Orthodox Bible Study Companion Series. Chesterton, Ind.: Ancient Faith Publishing, 2003.

Fiorenza, Elisabeth Schüssler. *Ephesians.* Vol. 50 of Word Commentary. Collegeville, Minn.: Liturgical Press, 2017.

The First Presidency and Council of the Twelve Apostles of The Church of Jesus Christ of Latter-day Saints. "The Family: A Proclamation to the World." *Ensign* 25, no. 11 (November 1995): 102.

Fitzmyer, Joseph A. *The Acts of the Apostles: A New Translation with Introduction and Commentary.* Vol. 31 of the Anchor Bible. New York: Doubleday, 1997.

———. *The Gospel according to Luke.* 2 vols. Vol. 28 of the Anchor Bible. New York: Doubleday, 1981, 1985.

Foulkes, Francis. *The Letter of Paul to the Ephesians: An Introduction and Commentary.* Tyndale New Testament Commentaries. Grand Rapids, Mich.: Eerdmans, 1989.

Fowl, Stephen E. *Ephesians: A Commentary.* Louisville, Ky.: Westminster/John Knox Press, 2012.

Fox, Robin Lane. *Pagans and Christians.* New York: Alfred A. Knopf, 1986.

Frend, William H. C. *The Rise of Christianity.* Philadelphia: Fortress Press, 1984.

Fronk, Camille. "Submit Yourselves . . . as unto the Lord." In *Go Ye into All the World: Messages of the New Testament Apostles,* ed. Ray L. Huntington, Jerome M. Perkins, Thomas A. Wayment, and Patty A. Smith, 98–113. The 31st Annual Sidney B. Sperry Symposium. Salt Lake City: Deseret Book, 2002.

Garr, Arnold K., Donald Q. Cannon, and Richard O. Cowan, eds. *Encyclopedia of Latter-day Saint History.* Salt Lake City: Deseret Book, 2000.

Gesenius, William. *Complete Hebrew-Chaldee Lexicon to the Old Testament.* Trans. Samuel P. Tregelles. Grand Rapids, Mich.: Baker Books, 1979.

Gnilka, Joachim. *Der Epheserbrief.* Freiburg im Breisgau: Herder, 1971.

Goodspeed, Edgar J. *The Key to Ephesians.* Chicago: University of Chicago Press, 1956.

———. *The Meaning of Ephesians.* Chicago: University of Chicago Press, 1933.

Hall, John F. *New Testament Witnesses of Christ: Peter, John, James, and Paul.* American Fork, Utah: Covenant Communications, 2002.

Hammond, N. G. L., and H. H. Scullard, eds. *The Oxford Classical Dictionary.* 2nd ed. Oxford: Oxford University Press, 1970. (Abbreviated as *OCD2.*)

Hardison, Amy Blake. "Unity and Atonement in Ephesians." In *Go Ye into All the World: Messages of the New Testament Apostles,* ed. Ray L. Huntington, Jerome M. Perkins, Thomas A. Wayment, and Patty A. Smith, 116–29. The 31st Annual Sidney B. Sperry Symposium. Salt Lake City: Deseret Book, 2002.

Harrison, James R. *Paul's Language of Grace in Its Greco-Roman Context.* Tübingen: Mohr Siebeck, 2003.

Harrison, Roland Kenneth. *An Introduction to the Old Testament.* Grand Rapids, Mich.: Eerdmans, 1969.

Hendricksen, William. *New Testament Commentary: Exposition of Ephesians.* Grand Rapids, Mich.: Baker Book House, 1967.

Hennecke, Edgar, and Wilhelm Schneemelcher, eds. *New Testament Apocrypha.* Trans. R. McL. Wilson et al. 2 vols. Philadelphia: Westminster Press, 1963, 1965. (Abbreviated as *NTA.*)

Houlden, James Leslie. *Paul's Letters from Prison: Philippians, Colossians, Philemon, and Ephesians.* Philadelphia: Westminster Press, 1977.

Hunter, Howard W. "Being a Righteous Husband and Father." *Ensign* 24, no. 11 (November 1994): 49–51.

Hymns of the Church of Jesus Christ of Latter-day Saints. Salt Lake City: The Church of Jesus Christ of Latter-day Saints, 1985.

Jenni, Ernst, and Claus Westermann, eds. *Theological Lexicon of the Old Testament.* Trans. Mark E. Biddle. 3 vols. Peabody, Mass.: Hendrickson Publishers, 1997. (Abbreviated *TLOT.*)

Jeremias, Joachim. *Jerusalem in the Time of Jesus.* Philadelphia: Fortress Press, 1969.
———. *The Parables of Jesus.* Rev. ed. New York: Charles Scribner's Sons, 1963.

Johnson, E. Elizabeth. "Ephesians." In *The Women's Bible Commentary,* ed. Carol A. Newsom and Sharon H. Ringe, 338–42. Louisville: Westminster/John Knox, 1992.

Johnson, Edna. *A Semantic and Structural Analysis of Ephesians.* Dallas: SIL International, 2008.

Joubert, Stephan. *Paul as Benefactor: Reciprocity, Strategy and Theological Reflection in Paul's Collection.* Tübingen: Mohr Siebeck, 2000.

Käsemann, Ernst. "Ephesians and Acts." In *Studies in Luke–Acts,* ed. Leander E. Keck and J. Louis Martyn, 288–97. London: S.P.C.K., 1968.

Kirby, John C. *Ephesians: Baptism and Pentecost: An Inquiry into the Structure and Purpose of the Epistle to the Ephesians.* London: S.P.C.K., 1968.

Kitchen, Martin. *Ephesians.* London: Routledge, 1994.

Kittel, Gerhard, and Gerhard Friedrich, eds. *Theological Dictionary of the New Testament.* 9 vols. Grand Rapids, Mich.: Eerdmans, 1964–74. (Abbreviated as *TDNT.*)

Kobelski, Paul J. "The Letter to the Ephesians." In *The New Jerome Biblical Commentary,* ed. Raymond E. Brown, Joseph Fitzmyer, and Roland Murphy, 883–90. Englewood Cliffs, N.J.: Prentice Hall, 1990.

Koester, Helmut. *Introduction to the New Testament: History and Literature of Early Christianity.* 2 vols. Berlin: Walter de Gruyter, 1982.

Kooten, Geurt Hendrik van. *Cosmic Christology in Paul and the Pauline School: Colossians and Ephesians in the Context of Graeco-Roman Cosmology, with a New Synopsis of the Greek Texts.* Tübingen: Mohr Siebeck, 2003.

Kuhn, Karl G. "The Epistle to the Ephesians in the Light of the Qumran Texts." In *Paul and Qumran,* ed. Jerome Murphy-O'Connor, 115–31. London: Geoffrey Chapman, 1968.

Lampe, Geoffrey W. H., ed. *A Patristic Greek Lexicon.* Oxford: Oxford University Press, 1961.

Larkin, William J. *Ephesians: A Handbook on the Greek Text*. Waco, Tex.: Baylor University Press, 2009.

Lawlor, Hugh Jackson, and John Ernest Leonard Oulton, trans.. *Eusebius, Bishop of Caesarea: The Ecclesiastical History and the Martyrs of Palestine*. 2 vols. London: SPCK, 1954.

Levine, Lee I. *The Ancient Synagogue: The First Thousand Years*. 2nd ed. New Haven, Conn.: Yale University Press, 2005.

Liddel, Henry George, and Robert Scott. *A Greek-English Lexicon*. Rev. ed. Henry Stuart Jones. Oxford: Oxford University Press, 1940. (Abbreviated as LSJ.)

Lincoln, Andrew T. *Ephesians*. Vol. 42 of the Word Biblical Commentary. Dallas: Word Books, Publisher, 1990.

Louw, Johannes P., and Eugene A. Nida. *Greek-English Lexicon of the New Testament Based on Semantic Domains*. 2 vols. 2nd ed. New York: United Bible Societies, 1989. (Abbreviated as Louw-Nida.)

Ludlow, Daniel H., ed. *Encyclopedia of Mormonism*, 4 vols. New York: Macmillan, 1992.

MacDonald, Margaret Y. "Citizens of Heaven and Earth: Asceticism and Social Integration in Colossians and Ephesians." In *Asceticism and the New Testament*, ed. Leif Vaage and Vincent L. Wimbush, 269–98. New York: Routledge, 1999.

———. *Colossians and Ephesians*. Ed. Daniel J. Harrington. Vol. 17 of Sacra Pagina. Collegeville, Minn.: Liturgical Press, 2008.

———. "Ephesians." In *The International Bible Commentary: A Catholic and Ecumenical Commentary for the Twenty-First Century*, ed. William R. Farmer et al., 1670–86. Collegeville: Liturgical Press, 1998.

Marshall, I. Howard. "Ephesians." In *Eerdmans Commentary on the Bible*, ed. James D. G. Dunn and John W. Rogerson, 1385–93. Grand Rapids, Mich.: Eerdmans, 2003.

———. *The Gospel of Luke*. The New International Greek Testament Commentary. Grand Rapids, Mich.: Eerdmans, 1978.

Maxwell, Neal A. "Becoming a Disciple." *Ensign* 26, no. 6 (June 1996): 12–19.

McConkie, Bruce R. *Doctrinal New Testament Commentary*. 3 vols. Salt Lake City: Bookcraft, 1965–73.

McConkie, Joseph Fielding, and Craig J. Ostler. *Revelations of the Restoration: A Commentary on the Doctrine and Covenants and Other Modern Revelations*. Salt Lake City: Deseret Book, 2000.

Meeks, Wayne A. "In One Body: The Unity of Humankind in Colossians and Ephesians." In *God's Christ and His People: Studies in Honour of Nils Alstrup Dahl*, ed. Wayne A. Meeks and Jacob Jervell, 209–21. Oslo: Universitetsforlaget, 1977.

Merkle, Benjamin L. *Exegetical Guide to the Greek New Testament: Ephesians*. Nashville: B&H Academic, 2016.

Metzger, Bruce M. *A Textual Commentary on the Greek New Testament, Second Edition: A Companion Volume to the United Bible Societies' Greek New Testament (Fourth Revised Edition)*. Stuttgart: Deutsche Bibelgesellschaft, 2016.

Miles, Carrie A. *Patriarchy or Gender Equality? The Letter to the Ephesians on Submission, Headship, and Slavery*. Stanford, Calif.: Dialogue Foundation, 2006.

Milgrom, Jacob. *Leviticus 1–16*. Vol. 3 of the Anchor Bible. New York: Doubleday, 1991.

———. *Leviticus 23–27*. Vol. 3B of the Anchor Bible. New York: Doubleday, 2001.

Millet, Robert L. *Grace Works.* Salt Lake City: Deseret, 2003.

Mitton, C. Leslie. *Ephesians.* New Century Bible Commentary. Grand Rapids, Mich.: Eerdmans, 1981.

Morenz, Siegfried. *Egyptian Religion.* Trans. Ann E. Keep. Ithaca, N.Y.: Cornell University Press, 1973.

Morris, Leon. *Expository Reflections on the Letter to the Ephesians.* Grand Rapids, Mich.: Baker Books, 1994.

Moule, Handley Carr Glyn. *Ephesian Studies.* London: Pickering and Inglis, 1975.

Muddiman, John. *The Epistle to the Ephesians.* Black's New Testament Commentaries. London: Continuum, 2001.

Murphy-O'Connor, Jerome. *Paul: A Critical Life.* Oxford: Oxford University Press, 1996.

Nelson, Russell M. "A Plea to My Sisters." *Ensign* 45, no. 11 (November 2015): 95–97.

Neufeld, Thomas R. *Put on the Armor of God: The Divine Warrior from Isaiah to Ephesians.* Sheffield: Sheffield Academic Press, 1997.

Neusner, Jacob. *Genesis Rabbah. The Judaic Commentary to the Book of Genesis, A New American Translation.* 3 vols. Atlanta: Scholars Press. 1985.

Nibley, Hugh. *Apostles and Bishops in Early Christianity.* Ed. John F. Hall and John W. Welch. Vol. 15 of the Collected Works of Hugh Nibley. Salt Lake City: Deseret Book; Provo, Utah: Foundation for Ancient Research and Mormon Studies, 2005.

———. "Before Adam." In *Old Testament and Related Studies.* Ed. John W. Welch, Gary P. Gillum, and Don E. Norton, 49–85. Vol. 1 of the Collected Works of Hugh Nibley. Salt Lake City: Deseret Book; Provo, Utah: Foundation for Ancient Research and Mormon Studies, 1986.

———. "Subduing the Earth." In *Nibley on the Timely and the Timeless: Classic Essays of Hugh W. Nibley,* 85–99. Vol. 1 of Religious Studies Monograph Series. Provo, Utah: BYU Religious Studies Center, 1978.

———. *When the Lights Went Out: Three Studies on the Ancient Apostasy.* Salt Lake City: Deseret Book, 1970.

Otten, Leaun G., and C. Max Caldwell. *Sacred Truths of the Doctrine and Covenants.* 2 vols. 2nd ed. Springville, Utah: LEMB, 1982, 1983.

Patzia, Arthur G. *Ephesians, Colossians, Philemon.* Peabody, Mass.: Hendrickson, 1984.

Perkins, Pheme. *Ephesians.* Abingdon New Testament Commentaries. Nashville: Abingdon Press, 1997.

Portefaix, Lilian. "Ancient Ephesus: Processions as Media of Religious and Secular Propaganda." *Scripta Instituti Donneriani Aboensis* 15 (January 1993): 195–210.

Quasten, Johannes. *Patrology.* 3 vols. Reprint. Utrecht: Spectrum Publishers, 1966. Vol. 4, Westminster, Md.: Christian Classics, 1978.

Rasmus, Carolyn J. "The Enabling Power of the Atonement." *Ensign* 43, no. 3 (March 2013): 18–21.

Rasmussen, Carl G. *Zondervan NIV Atlas of the Bible.* Grand Rapids, Mich.: Regency Reference Library, 1989.

Richardson, Matthew O. "Ephesians: Unfolding the Mysteries through Revelation." In *Go Ye into All the World: Messages of the New Testament Apostles,* ed. Ray L. Huntington, Jerome M. Perkins, Thomas A. Wayment, and Patty A. Smith, 130–44. The 31st Annual Sidney B. Sperry Symposium. Salt Lake City: Deseret Book, 2002.

Richman, Chaim. *The Holy Temple of Jerusalem*. Jerusalem: Carta, 1997.

Ritmeyer, Leen. *The Quest: Revealing the Temple Mount in Jerusalem*. Jerusalem: Carta, 2006.

Ritmeyer, Leen, and Kathleen Ritmeyer. *The Ritual of the Temple*. Jerusalem: Carta, 2002.

Roberts, Alexander, James Donaldson, and A. Cleveland Coxe, eds. *The Ante-Nicene Fathers: Translations of the Fathers down to A.D. 325*. 10 vols. Reprint. Grand Rapids, Mich.: Eerdmans, 1950. (Abbreviated as *ANF.*)

Robinson, James M., and Richard Smith, eds. *The Nag Hammadi Library in English*. 3d rev. ed. San Francisco: HarperCollins, 1990.

Robinson, Stephen E. *Believing Christ: The Parable of the Bicycle and Other Good News*. Salt Lake City: Deseret Book, 1992.

———, and H. Dean Garrett. *A Commentary on the Doctrine and Covenants*. 4 vols. Salt Lake City: Deseret Book, 2000–5.

Rogers, Guy MacLean. *The Sacred Identity of Ephesos: Foundation Myths of a Roman City*. London: Routledge, 1991.

———. *The Mysteries of Artemis of Ephesos: Cult Polis, and Change in the Graeco-Roman World*. New Haven, Conn.: Yale University Press, 2012.

Schmidt, Brent J. *Relational Grace: The Reciprocal and Binding Covenant of* Charis. Provo, Utah: BYU Studies, 2015.

Schnackenburg, Rudolf. *Ephesians: A Commentary*. Trans. Helen Heron. Edinburgh: T & T Clark, 1991.

Schoedel, William R. *The Apostolic Fathers: A New Translation and Commentary*. Ed. Robert M. Grant. Vol. 5, Polycarp, Martyrdom of Polycarp, Fragments of Papias. Camden, N.J.: Thomas Nelson and Sons, 1967.

———. *Ignatius of Antioch: A Commentary on the Letters of Ignatius of Antioch*. Ed. Helmut Koester. Hermeneia: A Critical and Historical Commentary on the Bible. Philadelphia: Fortress Press, 1985.

Schürer, Emil. *The History of the Jewish People in the Age of Jesus Christ*. Ed. Geza Vermes, Fergus Millar, and Matthew Black. Rev. ed. 3 vols. Edinburgh: T. & T. Clark, 1973–87.

Sherwin-White, Adrian Nicholas. *The Letters of Pliny: A Historical and Social Commentary*. Corrected ed. Oxford: Oxford University Press, 1985.

———. *Roman Society and Roman Law in the New Testament*. Sarum Lectures 1960–1961. Oxford: Clarendon Press, 1985.

Simpson, Edmond Kidley, and Frederick Fyvie Bruce. *Commentary on the Epistles to the Ephesians and the Colossians*. The New International Commentary on the New Testament. 3rd printing. Grand Rapids, Michigan: Wm. B. Eerdmans Publishing, 1965.

Smith, Joseph Fielding. *Answers to Gospel Questions*. 5 vols. Salt Lake City: Deseret Book, 1957–66.

Smith, Julie M. *The Gospel according to Mark*. Brigham Young University New Testament Commentary. Provo, Utah: BYU Studies, 2019.

Smyth, Herbert Weir. *Greek Grammar*. Rev. Gordon M. Messing. Cambridge, Mass.: Harvard University Press, 1956.

Snodgrass, Klyne R. "Jusification by Grace—to the Doers: An Analysis of the Place of Romans 2 in the Theology of Paul." *New Testament Studies* 32 (1986): 72–93.

Sperry, Sidney B. *Paul's Life and Letters.* Salt Lake City: Bookcraft, 1955.

Spicq, Ceslas. *Theological Lexicon of the New Testament.* 3 vols. Trans. James D. Ernest. Peabody, Mass.: Hendrickson Publishers, 1994. (Abbreviated as *TLNT.*)

Stamm, Raymond T. "The Epistle to the Galatians." In *The Interpreter's Bible,* ed. George Arthur Buttrick, 10:429–593. 12 vols. New York: Abingdom Press, 1953.

Stoeckhardt, George. *Ephesians.* Concordia Classic Commentary Series. Reprint. Trans. Martin S. Sommer. St. Louis: Concordia Publishing House, 1987.

Talbert, Charles H. *Ephesians and Colossians.* Paideia: Commentaries on the New Testament. Grand Rapids, Mich.: Baker Academic, 2007.

Talmage, James E. *Jesus the Christ.* 35th ed. Salt Lake City: Deseret Book, 1963.

Taylor, Walter F., and John H. P. Reumann. *Ephesians, Colossians.* Augsburg Commentary on the New Testament. Minneapolis: Augsburg, 1985.

Taylor, Willard H. *Galatians, Ephesians.* Beacon Bible Expositions. Kansas City, Mo.: Beacon Hill Press, 1981.

Thayer, Joseph H. *Thayer's Greek-English Lexicon of the New Testament.* Reprint of 4th ed. Peabody, Mass.: Hendrickson's Publishers, 2017.

Thielman, Frank. *Ephesians.* Baker Exegetical Commentary on the New Testament. Grand Rapids, Mich.: Baker Academic, 2010.

Thurston, Bonnie Bowman. *Reading Colossians, Ephesians, and 2 Thessalonians: A Literary and Theological Commentary.* Macon, Ga.: Smyth and Helwys, 2007.

Tischendorf, Constantin von. *Apocalypses apocryphae Mosis, Esdrae, Pauli, Johannis, item Mariae Dormitio: additis Evangeliorum et actuum Apocryphorum supplementis.* Leipzig: H. Mendelssohn, 1866.

Turner, Rodney. "Grace, Mysteries, and Exaltation." In *Studies in Scripture, Volume Six, Acts to Revelation,* ed. Robert L. Millet, 107–24. Salt Lake City: Deseret Book, 1987.

van Roon, A. *The Authenticity of Ephesians.* Vol. 39 of Supplements to Novum Testamentum. Leiden: E. J. Brill, 1974.

Walsh, Patrick Gerard, trans. *Pliny the Younger: Complete Letters.* Oxford: Oxford University Press, 2006.

Wayment, Thomas A. *The New Testament: A Translation for Latter-day Saints. A Study Bible.* Provo, Utah: BYU Religious Studies Center, 2019.

Welch, John W. "Modern Revelation: A Guide to Research about the Apostasy." In *Early Christians in Disarray: Contemporary LDS Perspectives on the Christian Apostasy,* ed. Noel B. Reynolds, 101–32. Provo, Utah: FARMS, 2005.

Wild, Robert A. "The Warrior and the Prisoner: Some Reflections on Ephesians 6:10–20." *Catholic Biblical Quarterly* 46 (1984): 284–98.

Williams, David J. *Paul's Metaphors: Their Context and Character.* Peabody, Mass.: Hendrickson Publishers, 1999.

Williamson, Peter S. *Ephesians.* Catholic Commentary on Sacred Scripture. Grand Rapids, Mich.: Baker Academic, 2009.

Winger, Thomas M. *Ephesians.* Concordia Commentary. St. Louis: Concordia Publishing House, 2015.

Scripture Index

This index is ordered by book under Old Testament, New Testament, Book of Mormon, Other Ancient Sources, Pearl of Great Price, and Doctrine and Covenants.

Subject Index

"ministry," 308
miracles, 491–92. *See also* healing(s)
miseō, 499
missionary work
  among Gentiles, 77, 197, 199–200, 201–2,
    209, 229, 503, 538, 631–32
  "I am an ambassador," 589–90
  inspiration in locations for, 589
  marriage and, 474
  and preaching gospel, 66–67
  in spirit world, 30, 213–14, 278–80, 281–82,
    291, 293–98, 308, 328–29, 560
moral exhortation, 262
moral impurity, 341
mōrologia, 412
Moroni, 564
Moses, 217–18. *See also* law of Moses
Mother in Heaven, 504, 510, 515, 525
mother(s), honoring, 522–23. *See also*
  parents
Mount Zion, 289
mouth, 371–72
  "open my," 586–87
Muddiman, John, 229, 230, 389, 547
music, 458–59, 528
"my affairs," 596–97
"my brethren," 551
mystērion, 17–18, 201, 217–18, 588
"mystery," 17–18, 201, 217–18, 510, 588
"mystery of Christ," 202, 203, 217–18
"mystery of his will," 56–57

N

name / named / naming, 233–34, 410
  "every name that is named," 97–98
  "is named," 236
  salvation and Jesus', 463
  of transgressions, 410
natural creation, 143–44, 146–47
nature, 123
neighbor, 362
  love for, 399, 451
Nelson, Russell M., 478
nēphō, 569
Nero, 3–4
New Jerusalem, 189
"new man," 356, 357–58, 360, 388
New World, Jesus visits, 322–23, 351–52
Nicholson, John, 245
nigh, 171–72
Noah, 147, 281–82, 405
noeō, 247–48
nokhri, 177
"not of works," 141–42
nouns, doubling and tripling of, 86
"nourisheth," 501
nous, 335–36. *See also* "mind"

nouthesia, 530
"now," 204, 220, 427
"now are ye light in the Lord," 425–28
nun, 15, 204, 220, 427. *See also* "now"
"nurture," 527–30

O

obedience
  blessings of, 140, 146, 246, 255
  of children, 435, 520–21, 524, 527
  of disciples, 531
  and God's approval, 435
  to masters, 533–34
  and righteousness, 432–33
  versus sacrifice, 541
"obey," 520–21
"obey your parents," 520
Oepke, Albrecht, 30, 279–80, 294, 343–44
"of Christ and of God," 418–19
"of his flesh, and of his bones," 503–4
"of our Lord Jesus Christ," 42, 233
"of the Lord," 530
"of them," 439
oikodomē, 308–9, 325, 372–73
oikonomia, 217
"old man," 353
Old Testament, 34, 475–76
  foundations in, 179
  God's titles in, 463
  hymns from, 459–60
  Lord of, 517–18
  love for neighbor in, 399
  Paul's bias against, 15
  prophets of, 183
  revelation in, 81
"on earth," 61
  "in heaven, and . . . on earth," 61
"one baptism," 280–83, 327
"one body," 276, 327
"one faith," 280, 327
"one flesh," 500, 508–9
"One God," 283
"One God and the Father of all," 283
"one hope," 277, 327
"One Lord," 278–80, 327
"one new man," 167
Onesimus, 19, 20, 590, 601
"one Spirit," 277, 327
onomazō, 236
"open my mouth," 586–87
opheilō, 497–98
ophthalmodoulia, 536
ordinances, 166–67
orgē, 380–82, 421–23. *See also* anger; "wrath"
"other Gentiles," 332, 336
"ought," 497–98, 591–92
oun, 261, 393, 448, 463–64